Secondary and Middle School Teaching Methods

Seventh Edition

Leonard H. Clark
Professor Emeritus,
Jersey City State College

Irving S. Starr
University of Hartford

Merrill, an imprint of
Prentice Hall
Upper Saddle River, New Jersey   Columbus, Ohio

W9-BMU-529

Library of Congress Cataloging-in- Publication Data
Clark Leonard H.
    Secondary and middle school teaching methods / Leonard Clark. -- 7th ed.
        p.   cm.
    Includes bibliographical references.
    ISBN 0-02-322871-7
    1. High school teaching. I. Starr, Irving S. II. Title.
  LB1737.A3C53   1996
  373.11'02—dc20   95-6915
                                                          CIP

Cover Art: Martin R. Jones/Unicorn Stock Photos
Editor: Deborah Stollenwerk
Developmental Editor: Linda Montgomery
Production Editor: Mary Irvin
Text Designer: STELLARViSIONS
Cover Design: Patti Ann C. Okuno-Levering
Production Manager: Diedra Schwartz
Electronic Text Management: Marilyn Wilson Phelps, Matthew Williams, Karen L. Bretz

© 1996 by Prentice-Hall, Inc.
Simon & Schuster Company / A Viacom Company
Upper Saddle River, New Jersey 07458

Earlier editions ©1991, 1986, 1981, 1976, 1967, 1959 by Macmillan Publishing Company.

Excerpts from IMPROVING MARKING & REPORTING PRACTICES IN ELEMENTARY & SECONDARY SCHOOLS, copyright 1947 and renewed 1975 by William L. Wrinkle, reprinted by permission of Holt, Rinehart and Winston, Inc., reprinted by permission of the publisher.

Printed in the United States of America
10 9 8 7 6 5 4 3

ISBN 0-02-322871-7

Prentice-Hall International (UK) Limited, London
Prentice-Hall of Australia Pty. Limited, Sydney
Prentice-Hall Canada Inc., Toronto
Prentice-Hall Hispanoamericana, S.A., Mexico
Prentice-Hall of India Private Limited, New Delhi
Prentice-Hall of Japan, Inc., Tokyo
Simon & Schuster Asia Pte. Ltd., Singapore
Editora Prentice-Hall do Brasil, Ltda., Rio de Janeiro

Preface

This is the seventh edition of this book. Since the publication of the first edition, many pedagogical innovations and experiments have been launched. We have attempted to incorporate the important changes into this revision. The purpose and treatment, however, except for minor reorganization to make the book more useful and cohesive, remain the same in this edition as in the first, because the basic pedagogical principles have not changed, despite innovations and experiments.

This book was written to help prospective teachers learn how to teach. It is designed as a college textbook for an introductory course in general methods of teaching in middle and secondary schools, although it might serve well as a reference work for preservice as well as inservice teachers. We have attempted to make the book as practical and useful as possible. To achieve this end, we have tried to write from a middle-of-the-road point of view, and to describe methods suitable for use in the types of schools in which students are likely to teach when they go to their first positions. For this same reason, we have attempted to write simply and clearly, to open each chapter with an outline and overview and to close with a summary. We have used numerous examples, pointed out important understandings by means of questions at appropriate places within the text itself, and kept quotations and references to scholarly works to a minimum.

To ensure that the student has the necessary background that one needs to choose and implement suitable teaching strategies and tactics, the first three chapters are devoted to basic background information about the schools, the learner, the learning process, and the teaching process. Nevertheless, in general, discussion of educational theory has been omitted except when it seemed necessary to explain the "why" of the methods advocated. The emphasis is, of necessity, on principles rather than recipes. There are no surefire recipes in teaching. Perhaps, however, this text will provide guidelines on what considerations need to be made to develop a personal teaching style.

In the development of this edition, we are grateful for thoughtful reviews provided by Dr. Kenneth M. Ahrendt, Oregon State University; Dr. Robert E. Anderson, Wichita State University; Dr. George Belden, North Georgia College; Dr. Lloyd P. Campbell, University of North Texas; Dr. Leigh Chiarelott, Bowling Green State University; Dr. Gary M. Crow, Louisiana State University; Dr. Robert H. Decker, University of Northern Iowa; Dr. Rosemarie Deering; Kansas State University; Dr. Fenwick

W. English, University of Cincinnati; Dr. Carol B. Furtwengler, Wichita State University; Dr. James M. Jennings, Hendrix College; Dr. J. Gary Knowles, University of Michigan; Dr. Kenneth Murray, University of Central Florida; Dr. Fran Reed, Olivet Nazarene University; and Dr. Mack Welford, Roanoke College. We are particularly grateful to Maria A. Clark, who not only typed the manuscript innumerable times for each of the editions, but also read the copy and made suggestions for improving the wording, and without whose help the book could never have been finished.

L.H.C.

Contents

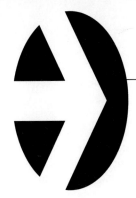

Chapter 1

Introduction to Teaching Methods

*What greater or better gift can
we offer the Republic than to
teach and instruct our youth?*
Cicero

■ **Overview**

■ **The Challenge**

■ **The Elements of Teaching Methods**

■ **Objectives**

■ **Subject Matter**

■ **Teaching Strategies and Tactics**

■ **A Pattern for Teaching**

▪▪▪ Overview

Teaching is exciting, rewarding work; like all other professions, however, it is demanding. The teaching profession requires its practitioners to clearly understand what should be done to bring about the most desirable learning in students, and to be highly proficient in the skills by which to carry out these tasks. These skills and understanding make up teaching method. They include a sound knowledge of the strategies and techniques available, an ability to select and use subject matter, a familiarity with the nature of the learner, and an understanding of learning theory and its application.

In this chapter, we take a quick look at the nature of the communications and management problems teachers face, as well as some of the factors that bear on the solutions. We hope that the discussion will make clear the absolute necessity of creating a positive climate and a feeling of cohesiveness in your classes; of having clear-cut objectives; and of selecting and using teaching strategies and techniques consonant with those objectives in view of the nature of the subject to be taught and the strategies and techniques available. Finally, we hope you will be convinced of the need for following the five-step process we see as basic to all effective teaching—diagnosis, preparation, guiding learning, evaluation, and follow up.

▪▪▪ The Challenge

An imaginary conversation (with apologies to Plato and Walter Savage Landor):

Scene: The Elysian fields
Time: The present
Characters: Socrates and a student reporter

What was your profession on earth, O Socrates?

I was a teacher.

Why did you follow that profession?

Because it was most satisfying and challenging to me. I was an ignorant man, yet, like a gadfly, I stung the minds of young men to action. I gave many of them new ideas and new knowledge. Some of them even learned to think.

Is that the teacher's job, Socrates?

A teacher's job is to help his pupils learn. If the pupils do not learn anything, the teacher has not taught anything.

When has a pupil learned something, Socrates?

A person has learned when he is able to do something he could not do, or he knows something he did not know, or he has an attitude, an ideal, or an appreciation he did not have before. I think your psychologists call it a change of behavior.

Must the learning always be something new, Socrates?

No, of course not. One learns when he changes an attitude, an ideal, or an appreciation, or in some way alters a skill or knowledge.

Is teaching difficult, Socrates?

Oh, yes. Teaching requires great skill and much knowledge. For instance, if one were to teach mathematics, or literature, or music, you would expect him to know considerable about these subjects, would you not?

Yes, Socrates.

And you would expect him to know what materials might best be used by his classes, and where this material might be obtained, would you not?

Yes, Socrates.

And you would expect him to know how people learn and those things that prevent learning so as to avoid them?

Yes, Socrates.

And you would expect him to know the best techniques and methods of teaching and when and how to use them most effectively, would you not?

Yes, Socrates.

And would you not expect him to understand thoroughly the nature of boys and girls and to know each of his pupils particularly well so that he could use the methods, techniques, and materials best suited to the pupils?

Of course, Socrates.

Do you not then agree with me that teaching is a profession that requires skill and much knowledge?

Yes, I do, Socrates. It is indeed fortunate that we have courses in teaching so that prospective teachers may learn the theory and practice of teaching.

That is true. In my day it was different. We were at a disadvantage.

Would you become a teacher again, Socrates?

Of course; it is a great profession. In no other has one more stimulating opportunities and pleasant associations. In no other has one a greater opportunity for service.

Yes, teaching is a great profession, full of stimulating, rewarding opportunities. But it is also very demanding, for teaching is not, as some critics seem to think, a simple matter of presenting one's message. Rather, it consists of complicated communications and management problems.

The Communications Problem

Even in the easiest classroom situation, the communications problem the teacher faces is complex.

THE RECEIVERS   There are many receivers—perhaps two dozen or more in a class—and each receiver presents a different challenge. Take the cases of two tenth-graders, Joe and Billy.*

Joe is slightly under middle height. In class he is very quiet. He never causes disciplinary disturbances. Neither does he do any work. In fact, one would hardly know he was in the class at all. He just sits there. When the teacher coaxes him to try, he says that he is "dumb and can't do it, so there's no use trying." But this is not true. Test scores show him to be well within the normal range. His other activities do not indicate lack of ability. He cannot read well, but he is one of the best soccer players in the school. On the field his playing is marked by its aggressiveness. The coach says that he is one of the "smartest" forwards he has seen on the soccer field in the last few years.

Joe has never been known to pick up a book voluntarily. It has been a long time since he has turned in an acceptable paper. He knows that his failures will make him ineligible for varsity athletics, but he sees no reason for working because he believes that he will fail anyway. If he does pass, he says that it is only because the teacher was "giving him a break." Seemingly, he has no interests other than athletics.

Difficult cases like Joe's challenge the ingenuity, the resources, and the skill of the teacher. The unskilled teacher might be overwhelmed by Joe's lack of enthusiasm and decide to give up. Not so the professional teacher, who knows that Joe must be taught—whether Joe wants to learn or not. The skilled teacher knows that he or she has the knowledge and the resources with which to undertake this task.

Joe poses a difficult problem; Billy, although very different from Joe, is another student in need of skillful teaching. Billy is an average tenth-grader with average intelligence. He is usually a happy person, and he gets along well with his teachers and his peers. Occasionally he has trouble with some of his schoolwork. All normal students

*The names are fictitious; the descriptions are not.

do, and Billy is normal, not brilliant. Although he is a willing worker and as cooperative as he can be, he finds many of his assignments too much for him. It will take plenty of skillful teaching for Billy to get the most out of his mathematics, for instance.

Joe and Billy are different, but not any more different than the other individuals in the class. When teaching such a variety of students, it is important to realize that the media and methods most effective for one student may not be the best for others.

THE MEDIA   In teaching, communication is complicated by the number of media used to present the teacher's messages. Among these media are the *spoken word* in the forms of lectures, informal talks, and discussions; the *written word* in books, magazines, pamphlets, and newspapers; *dramatic media* such as films and television; *pictorial* or *graphic media* such as illustrations, graphs, charts, and maps; *inquiry, questioning, and questing media,* such as in problem solving, and more. With such a variety of media available, deciding just which approach will be best in any given teaching situation becomes difficult. Unfortunately, some less sensitive teachers are unaware of this problem.

THE MESSAGES   Another complicating factor in teaching is the number of different messages that we must transmit to our pupils. Among them are information, concepts, intellectual skills, physical skills, habits, attitudes, appreciations, and ideals—all of which require different teaching strategies and techniques, and some of which may not be highly valued by the potential receivers.

THE GROUP DYNAMICS   Another factor contributing to communication problems is the dynamics of the student group. Each class soon develops its own dynamics, including leaders and followers, tensions and friendships, and even goals and aspirations that are not always compatible with those of the teacher.

THE COMPETITION   Yet another complicating factor in communication is outside competition. Not only do teachers have to compete with the inducements of television, computer games, and social activities for the attention and time of our students; we also have to compete with highly skilled media personalities who are selling messages that are often quite different from those we want our students to accept. Winning students' attention in a world filled with so many competing attractions is a real challenge.

THE COMPLEX LEARNING PROCESS   Communication in the classroom is made more difficult by the complexity of the learning process. Not everyone learns in the same way, nor does a particular individual learn in the same way all the time. Many a skillful teacher has found an approach that worked well with a tenth-grader such as Billy, yet got absolutely nowhere with his buddy, Joe; or has discovered that the plan used with such howling success in period four later bombed in period seven; or has noticed that the approach producing such impressive results on the civics assessment test seems to have no discernible effect on students' attitudes toward citizenship. To accommodate these differences, teachers must learn to teach in ways compatible with individual learning styles. Teachers must also adopt teaching strategies and techniques suitable both to their different teaching objectives and to the groups being taught.

The Management Problem

Teaching is more than just communicating a message to a class of students. For classes to be productive, they must run smoothly, be free of distractions, and operate efficiently for students to learn effectively. These goals call for skillful classroom management. Managing a classroom is not only a matter of managing learning activities, but also of managing everything that goes on in the classroom. Successful management creates a climate favorable to learning and provides the means of learning. Classroom management involves organizing the physical elements of the classroom, working with classroom logistics, organizing the materials and tools of instruction, being aware of classroom interpersonal relationships, and instructing itself. In addition to designing and carrying out effective teaching strategies and tactics, effective management includes building students' knowledge; creating and sustaining their enthusiasm; enriching their abilities to think and reason; helping them meet their need for belonging, self-esteem, and fulfillment; and developing wholesome interpersonal relationships among the students.

TIME ON TASK   One of the crucial elements in managing classes is managing time. What boys and girls do with their time makes a difference in learning! If they are actively engaged in real learning tasks (e.g., listening actively, forming questions, applying new knowledge to different situations, etc.), students will learn more than if they are not. One of the most important steps you can take to make teaching effective is to see to it that all your students are working at profitable learning activities. Too much time is wasted in too many classes. In all content areas, the most productive classes are those in which students actually work on academic learning tasks. These tasks must be well-organized; free from interruptions, misbehavior, time-killing dead spots, and other interferences; and focused on the teaching-learning objectives. The only exception to this principle of involving students in planned, organized activity may be in the area of creative learning, which seems to depend on insight, creative expression, and mulling things over rather than intense academic engagement. Too much pressure can interfere with thinking and creativity.(1)

Teaching as an Art Form

For many years, teachers and scholars have been trying to create a science of teaching, but teaching still is, and ought to be, more an art than a science. Not only does teaching require a large stock of skills, it also requires that teachers be able to put these skills together in new forms at the spur of the moment as new situations arise. All good teachers improvise; they must. Classes do not fall into set patterns. No one educational environment or approach serves all students equally well, just as no one environment or approach serves all educational goals equally well. To be effective, teaching must be adjusted to the nature of the task. Depending solely on tried-and-true formulas will surely backfire; good strategies become counterproductive when they are overused. The trick is to select old tactics and create new tactics that are right for the teaching-learning task and circumstances at hand.

Reflective Teaching

The heart of the art of teaching, then, is decision-making. *There is no best method of teaching, nor is there any method that will suit all occasions.* In almost every instance, to be the most successful, the teaching method you use should be tailored to the specific teaching-learning situation. In each one of these situations you, as teacher, must decide what objectives you should strive for, what content you should include (and exclude), what procedures you should use, how best to evaluate what you have accomplished, how to capitalize on what you have accomplished, and how to repair any errors and omissions in the students' learning. In doing so, consider such factors as the following:

- the goals, aims, and objectives of the curriculum
- the nature of the subject

- the strategies and techniques available
- the materials and equipment available
- the students
- how students learn
- the nature of the group
- your own skills and inclinations

Obviously, there are alternatives galore to choose from. The goal is to reflect on these choices and then select and use the strategies and tactics appropriate for obtaining the results you desire. Therefore, the more techniques you can handle well and the more you understand your subject matter and your students, the better your teaching will be.

Of course, many of these decisions should be made during the planning stage of your teaching, but most of them—perhaps as many as a thousand a day—must be made quickly during your actual teaching, at the spur of the moment, if you want to effectively adjust your procedures to meet the developing classroom situation.

Consequently, your teaching must be reflective. Each teaching episode calls for the teacher to decide what to do and how to do it. After the teaching has taken place, the teacher must consider how well the lesson went and how to carry out future instruction.

As you teach, you must make decisions about how to teach and how to make changes and adjustments in your teaching tactics. Then, after that teaching is finished, you need to consider how the teaching went and to plan for the next steps.

These decisions will be affected by the teacher's experience and his or her pedagogical knowledge. As Bellon, Bellon, and Blank point out, "reflection leads to action" and is a critical activity for all those who truly want to grow and develop.(2)

Stop and Reflect

Observe a class. What did the teacher have to do to teach the class? What preparations were necessary? What was done to keep the class moving smoothly and effectively? What follow-up would be necessary? How much of the give and take in the class had to be impromptu? Did the strategies, tactics, and techniques used seem to fit the nature of the learning? What decisions did the teacher have to make before and during the class?

List all the learning activities you can think of.

Individual Learning Activities
1. Flashcards   6.
2. Homework in class   7.
3. Board Work   8.
4. Computer Work   9.
5.   10.

Group Learning Activities
1.   6.
2.   7.
3.   8.
4.   9.
5.   10.

Some Definitions

TEACHING   The teacher's task is to bring about desirable learning in students. Some authorities say that as far as school classes are concerned, if the students have not learned anything, the teacher has not taught anything. This statement is perhaps too harsh, but it does introduce an important point: Since the goal of teaching is to bring about the desired learning in the students, the only way to tell whether your teaching has been successful is to determine whether or not the learners have actually learned what you intended them to learn. It follows then that to succeed at your job you must know (1) what the students ought to learn, and (2) how to bring about this learning. To carry out these requirements calls for considerable skill, artistry, and reflection.

Stop and Reflect

Discuss the phrase: "There is no teaching unless there is learning." Is this true or partially true? What implications does it have for the teacher?

Do you agree that it is the teacher's job to teach Joe whether Joe wishes to learn or not? Should the teacher's competence be judged on the basis of Joe's success or failure?

If the pupils do not learn well in your class, does that mean that you are a poor teacher?

TEACHING METHODS   *Teaching methods* are the means by which the teacher attempts to bring about the desired learning. Basically, method in teaching concerns the way teachers organize and use teaching techniques, subject matter, teaching tools, and teaching materials to meet teaching objectives. It consists of formulating the goals and objectives for teaching; selecting the subject matter and the teaching procedures that will best achieve those objectives; carrying out the procedures; evaluating the success of the learning activities; and following up on the successes and failures. Because teaching methods include selecting contents and instructional materials as well as actual teaching procedures, they determine to a large extent what students actually learn. For example, the understandings students gain about the political process from a political practicum or a community involvement project are likely to be much different from those derived from hearing recitations during a civics course. The *way* we teach a subject may be as much a part of the subject content as the information we include!

STRATEGIES, TACTICS, AND TECHNIQUES   Methods are made up of strategies, tactics, and techniques. A *strategy* is really a plan of attack. It outlines the approach you intend to take in order to achieve your objective. You may decide that in a certain lesson you will try to develop a concept by using Socratic questioning. That is your strategy. The means that you use to carry out the strategy, in this case asking specific questions and handling answers, are variously known as *tactics* or *techniques*. Technically, these words differ somewhat in meaning, but in this book we use them indiscriminately. The important things to remember are that

1. your strategies must be aimed at your objective and must be appropriate for achieving it, and
2. the tactics and techniques you use must be suitable to your strategy—otherwise your teaching will result in fiasco.

Another term you will encounter frequently is *learning activities,* or *teaching-learning activities.* By *learning activities* we mean the things students do, or are supposed to do, in their lessons and units. Reading a selection from a textbook is an activity, as is taking a test, or even listening to a lecture. Any learning activity that you incorporate into a lesson is part of your strategy. Learning activities are always specific for specific teaching-learning situations; they are never general.

TEACHING MODELS   Still another term you will find in the literature is *teaching model,* or *model of teaching.* In this sense the word *model* refers to a general strategy that teachers or theoreticians have concocted for various purposes. Weil and Joyce, for instance, list four families of models based on the way teachers "approach goals and means." These four general types are as follows:

- *Social interaction models,* which focus on "the individual's ability to relate to others, the improvement of democratic processes, and the improvement of society."
- *Information processing models,* which focus on "organizing data sensing problems, generating concepts and solutions to problems, and employing verbal and non-verbal systems."
- *Personal models,* which focus on "the processes by which individuals construct and organize their unique reality."
- *Behavior modification models,* which are built on operant conditioning reinforcement theory as a means to change student behavior and learning.(3)

Remember that these models are really strategies meant to bring about certain types of objectives or to use certain psychological or pedagogical principles.

The Elements of Teaching Methods

As we have seen, in any teaching-learning situation the teaching method you use should be based on the following basic elements: the objectives; the strategies and tactics; the subject matter content; the nature of the learners, both as individuals and as groups; and how the learners learn. Now let us consider these elements in greater detail.

Objectives

For every school program, curriculum, course, unit, or lesson, the planner should decide just what learning should result. These learning objectives are all-important. In planning courses, units, and lessons, learning objectives should be the basis for the content and the instructional approaches and teaching activities (that is, strategies and techniques) that are selected. Instruction can be effective only when the teaching methods and content are aimed directly at objectives.

Learning objectives and the behavior they describe fall into a number of categories. They may be very general curriculum or course objectives such as, "The student will be able to speak freely in idiomatic French," or they may be quite specific lesson objectives such as, "The students will be able to conjugate the verb *etre*," or they may fall somewhere in between. Still other categories of objectives include cognitive objectives (e.g., concerning knowledge, ideas, or thoughts), affective objectives (e.g., concerning ideals, attitudes, or feelings), or psychomotor objectives (as in physical skill development). In any case, the nature of your objectives determines, to a large extent, what kinds of instructional strategies, tactics, and techniques—and even content—will be most useful in any particular teaching situation. Teachers who try to teach without clear objectives do not know what they are doing.*

---

*We discuss objectives in greater detail in Chapter 5, "Planning for Teaching."

Subject Matter

THE IMPORTANCE OF CONTENT   Nothing we have stated minimizes the importance of content. Command of the subject matter is absolutely essential in secondary and middle school teaching. Teachers who are not knowledgeable and comfortable in their content are usually dull, boring, and ineffective.

The content of a certain subject area includes more than just information. As a rule, course information should primarily be a means for developing ideas, understandings, thoughts, attitudes, and skills. For instance, appreciation is essential content for literature courses, and objectivity for science courses. Intellectual skills such as critical thinking, problem solving, and writing are essential content for any course. In some cases, these skills and appreciations may be more important than the informational content; in fact, in some instances, the only real value of the informational subject matter in a course is as a medium by which to teach essential skills and attitudes. Knowing *how* can be as much a part of curriculum content as knowing *what*.

THE ROLE OF SUBJECT MATTER   When you select strategies and techniques, consider the subject matter to be taught. There seem to be three ways to think about subject matter. One is to consider it something valuable in and of itself. According to this position, one should learn the subject matter, whatever it is, not for any contingent value that may come from knowing it, but because to know it is good. The second position is to think of subject matter as having some utilitarian value. According to this position, one should learn the content, whatever it is, because one can use that particular knowledge for some practical purpose, such as earning a living or getting into college. The third position is to think of subject matter as a means of teaching process, methods, or structure. According to this way of thinking, it is not so much the content that has value; instead, it is the skills, attitudes, and generalizations we gain by learning the content. If the real object of learning history is to learn historical method or to think historically, then it does not matter particularly what history we learn as long as we learn it in such a way that we learn the method. In this view, content is only a vehicle to teach process.

Even though many teachers have never considered their own views about subject matter, all teachers, consciously or subconsciously, lean toward one of the three positions mentioned. Although they may not be aware of it, their inclinations determine to a large extent the content emphases in their courses as well as affecting the way they teach. *Your own philosophical orientation will be one of the determinants of the educational methods you use.*

Stop and Reflect

Which of the three ways of thinking about subject matter do you favor? Are you sure?
What approach to teaching do you think you ought to follow to teach properly and well?
What are your positions on each of the following:

1. *What is education?*
2. *What is the relationship of schools to society?*
3. *Why should children go to school?*
4. *How, why, and where do students learn?*
5. *How and in what way or ways do teachers teach most effectively?*
6. *What should be in the school curriculum and who should determine it?*
7. *Is teaching an art, skill, or profession?*
8. *Are schools now doing an acceptable job of educating American youth?*
9. *In what ways can schools be improved?*
10. *What is the reason for your decision to teach?*

THE STRUCTURE OF SUBJECT MATTER   Another consideration when selecting strategies and techniques is subject matter structure. In this context, *structure* is the interrelation or organization of a subject's parts. It includes the subject's scope and sequence, the vertical and horizontal organization, and the mode of investigation used to determine its truths. These all differ in some degree from subject to subject. These differences in structure have or should have considerable impact on the method used to teach various subjects. Poetry, for instance, should be taught as something to be savored and enjoyed rather than as facts to be learned.

THE REVISIONIST NATURE OF KNOWLEDGE   Every day knowledge changes faster and faster. Consequently, teaching facts alone can be dissatisfying when new discoveries prove the "facts" people have learned are facts no longer. Students need to know how to cope with new knowledge. Therefore, they need to become familiar with the structures of the disciplines being studied; they also must know the mechanisms by which knowledge in the disciplines is created. Above all, students need to master the intellectual skills and attitudes that will allow them to stay well-informed and well-educated, no matter what new knowledge appears. To meet these needs, you should adopt teaching strategies that encourage students to seek out rather than merely to accept knowledge.

THE FUTILITY OF COVERING A SUBJECT   When conveying ideas to students, it is important to find strategies that provide depth rather than superficiality. In the modern world, attempting to cover a subject fully is futile. One of the problems in schools today is that we have kept adding and adding new content to our curricula and courses to the extent that now we try to teach everything, but we have little time to teach anything well. Therefore we should limit ourselves to the content that seems the most desirable in view of our goals. Again, as with the revisionist nature of knowledge, the situation calls for an emphasis on the teaching of process and structure. What criteria to use when selecting subject matter depends somewhat on your philosophy. No matter what that may be, it is more important to select carefully than it is to try to include everything. Let your motto be: *Teach more effectively and thoroughly by concentrating on the most useful and ornamental and by eliminating the less important.*

In any event, the content and methods you choose for your classes should result in "authentic" achievement. That is to say, the resultant learning should be significant and meaningful in students' real lives; this is in contrast to so much of present-day school learning which is trivial and useless. According to Newmann and Wehlage, to qualify as authentic, school learning must result in discourse, products, and performances that have value or meaning in real life beyond success in school.(4)

Stop and Reflect

How can we teach so that what the students learn will not be soon out of date?

According to one educationist, a high school teacher who believes that it is necessary to cover the subject is incompetent. What then should the teacher be doing?

In what way is the teaching strategy you use likely to determine the nature of the subject matter students learn?

To what extent and in what ways does method determine content? And content, method? Think of some examples.

The basic problem of method is said to be selection. Do you agree? Explain.

Teaching Strategies and Tactics

As we discussed before, strategies and techniques that lead to one objective—for example, the learning of fact—will not necessarily lead to another objective—for example, learning to appreciate. *Remember that once you have decided on an objective, if you do not use strategies and techniques that will lead to that objective, you will never achieve your goal.*

As you select your learning activities, you will find many strategies and techniques from which to choose. Among them are those most suitable for the following:

- Building concepts
- Clarifying students' ideas
- Showing students how to do things
- Affecting or changing attitudes, ideals, and appreciations
- Giving security
- Motivating and set-inducing
- Evaluating or measuring
- Guiding or directing students' work
- Arousing, directing, or assuaging emotions
- Kindling critical and creative thinking[*]

Other examples include strategies and techniques you can use to

Direct
Request
Explain
Suggest
Praise
Point out possibilities and alternatives
Create problem situations
Show materials
Motivate students
Judge correctness
Praise or condemn student behavior
Reinforce a behavior or attitude
Point out suitable models for students to follow

CLARIFYING TACTICS   Some tactics help students view their ideas more clearly. Of course, no one can clarify understandings for anyone else. Neither can one person have insights for anyone else, nor do anyone else's thinking. Each person must do these things for him- or herself. It is possible, however, for you to help and guide a student to clearer understandings and insights. Clarifying tactics are the tactics you can use to accomplish this purpose. Some of them are described in the following paragraph. Note that almost all the operations described are based on questions and are examples of what Flanders calls indirect teaching.[**]

A typical clarifying tactic is to ask a student to define what she means in her own terms. Another is to ask her to illustrate or demonstrate her meanings. Yet another is to ask a student where she got her idea—what is its basis and is this basis a tenable one? Still another would be to throw back the student's idea to her, perhaps

---

[*]This list is, in part, based on Louis Raths' *What Is Teaching,* undated, mimeographed.
[**]See the following section.

rephrased, and to ask her whether that is what she meant. If it is what she meant, then another tactic would be to ask her to forecast the implications or logical consequences of this idea. In other words, if so, then what? Still another tactic is to ask the student to summarize what she means or to organize her meaning into a logical outline. Another is to question her basis for belief—is she dealing with fact or opinion, fact or feeling, fact or emotion? Questioning the student about what is causing his difficulty can help her solve the problem, and is still another example of a clarifying tactic.

SHOW-HOW TACTICS   Show-how tactics are mostly concerned with skills. They include such techniques as demonstrating a concept by using visual and audiovisual aids, and helping students to perform a task, perhaps by showing them alternate or better methods to use or by analyzing their present techniques to see where they are at fault. Telling students how to do something and taking them through the task step by step can also be included among show-how tactics, even though such tactics are often not so much "show-how" as "tell-how." Correcting faults in techniques or form during a practice session, as when a golf instructor tells the student to hold the club like this and not like that, is a show-how tactic.

SECURITY-GIVING TACTICS   Security-giving tactics are the operations that make it possible for students to feel free to learn. For many students, school is a challenging and frightening experience full of many strong pressures. You will need to help students gain the confidence they need to meet the pressures and to cope with the challenges. The tactics that provide these qualities are the ones by which you let students know that they are welcome in the class and that you respect their individualities and will support them in their efforts to learn, even when they make mistakes.

One of the most important aids to providing security is being consistent in your behavior and in the types of operations you use in teaching. Although you should use many different types of teaching activities, do not confuse variety with inconsistency. The teacher who is authoritarian one day and permissive the next, or who swings from using very conservative to very progressive procedures without adequately preparing the students for the change, adds not interest but insecurity, confusion, and chaos.

Stop and Reflect

Try to think of an example of a teaching strategy or technique that could be suitable in teaching each of the types of learning described here.

Perhaps you would like to arrange the various strategies and techniques into a set of categories of your own.

How can a teacher determine which strategy and technique to use in any specific situation?

What differences in strategy and techniques would be called for in teaching situations in which the main objective was (a) an appreciation, (b) a skill, (c) an attitude, and (d) information?

DIRECT AND INDIRECT APPROACHES   Some tactics influence students directly and some indirectly. In their analyses of verbal teaching tactics, Amidon and Flanders report four categories of teacher-talk operations that influence students indirectly.(5) These include accepting students' feelings, praising or encouraging them, accepting their ideas, and asking questions. In addition, two student-talk categories, student responses and student-initiated talk, also represent indirect teacher influence. Teacher-talk operations that Amidon and Flanders say influence students directly include lecturing, telling, giving facts or opinions, asking rhetorical questions, giving directions, scolding, and justifying class procedures. When so defined, indirect teaching seems to be more efficient than direct teaching.(6)

Rosenshine and others, in their studies of elementary school teaching, have defined direct teaching somewhat differently.(7) To them direct teaching is "academically focused, teacher-directed instruction using sequenced and structured materials." It combines large-group teaching with highly teacher-directed comments, questions, and goals. In direct teaching, there is little opportunity for students to choose activities or for individual work. Emphasis is on large-group instruction rather than on small-group instruction; single-answer, factual low-order questions rather than high-order questions; and controlled practice.

Rosenshine found this kind of teaching effective. It involves students in active work much of the time. There is little wasted motion. With indirect teaching, as he defines it, there is more likely to be dead time, fooling around, lost time because of not knowing what to do, and so on. Direct teaching, on the other hand, is likely to produce more time on task.

However, time on task and direct teaching may not always be the best routes to teacher effectiveness. The intensiveness of the contact between the student and the learning may be more important. Direct instruction seems to be effective for teaching basic skills, but not so effective for high-order skills and understandings. Indirect, less structured, more open methods seem to work better for concept development, creativity, and high-order thinking. Direct instruction seems to be more effective in mathematics instruction and indirect methods in teaching English. Low socioeconomic and young students seem to benefit more from direct teaching, whereas higher socioeconomic, older students do better in indirect classes. Cognitive learning style is also a factor.(8) Evidently, then, direct teaching styles should be more useful in middle schools and indirect teaching more useful in high schools.

INDIVIDUALIZED INSTRUCTION   For many years, teachers and theorists have advocated the use of individualized instruction to allow for the differences in students' talents, abilities, interests, goals, attitudes, values, and learning styles. Some of the techniques used for individualized instruction called for self-pacing programs, some for individualized learning activity packages, some for independent study within units, and some for mastery learning. A number of individualized instruction systems, in which students work through units at their own rates, have been developed. At the college level some of these systems seem to be spectacularly effective. Their success has not been so great at the middle school and high school levels, however. Although more mature high school students probably can benefit from doing much work independently, evidently most secondary and middle school students should do considerable amounts of their schoolwork in group situations. Seemingly they need "more stimulation, guidance, support, and constraint, than the individualized systems ordinarily provide."(9)

Stop and Reflect

Has the instruction you have received been direct or indirect, or both? Have teachers changed their style for various instructional purposes? How has the teaching style affected you personally? Do certain styles bother you? Do certain styles motivate you? Which does which and why?

How much has instruction been individualized in your classes? In what ways have your teachers individualized instruction? What advantages do you see in individualizing instruction? What disadvantages? Were your individual needs and tastes considered in your classes? If not, could they have been? What did teachers do to meet your needs?

▓ ▓ ▓   **A Pattern for Teaching**

In general, the procedure in most good teaching follows a five-step pattern:

1. Diagnosing the learning situation
2. Preparing the setting for learning
3. Guiding learning activities
4. Evaluating the students' learning
5. Following through

These steps are, or should be, the basis for all teaching strategies (see Figure 1.1). They hold for lessons, units, courses, or educational programs.

Diagnosing the Learning Situation

The first step in effective teaching is to diagnose the teaching-learning situation. You must find out the needs of the students so that you can plan experiences that will help them satisfy their needs. This entails knowing every class member as well as possible. The more you know about your students' abilities and aptitudes, strengths and weaknesses, likes and dislikes, aspirations and anxieties, competencies and deficiencies, and the like, the easier it will be to devise ways to help them learn the things they ought to learn. Use the tools of diagnosis to find whether students have already learned what you intend to teach; whether they are ready to move on; whether they ought to take more time to strengthen, reinforce, deepen, and clinch their learning; or whether you ought to go back and reteach something that has been missed. Such diagnosis will also give you important leads about students' personalities, interests, and nonacademic lives. You should also use diagnosis to judge what teaching approaches are best suited for the content to be studied.

Preparing the Setting for Learning

The job of a theatrical producer is to provide a setting in which the action of the play can take place. So it is with the teacher. As a teacher, you must provide a setting for learning that includes many things. First, the setting should include a pleasant physical environment that will invite students to learn, as well as including the materials for learning. The setting also should include an intellectual atmosphere that will cause young people to want to learn and an emotional atmosphere that will provide the security and support so important to learning. Set induction (that is, attempting to produce favorable mental sets or attitudes in the students) is an essential step in any teaching-learning situation.

▓ **FIGURE 1.1**
Complete Teaching-Learning Cycle

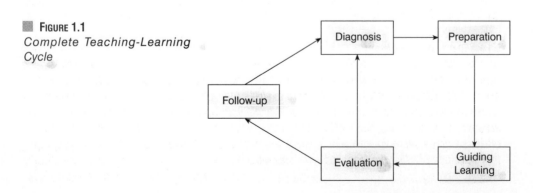

To this end some teachers present students with advance organizers, directional questions, or study guides to alert them to what is coming and to direct their energies in proper paths. In summary, it is important to remember that preparing for learning consists of deciding (1) what should be accomplished (that is, your objective) and (2) how to accomplish it (that is, your strategy) in view of what you have learned about your students in the diagnostic stage.

Guiding the Learning Activities

Once the stage has been set and your students are ready to work, you must guide their learning by carrying out the necessary strategies and tactics. This can be done in many ways. For example, you can explain to students what they are supposed to be doing and why; show them how to do things; or present new facts and concepts as well as explain old ones through such techniques as asking questions, giving vivid examples, and using audiovisual aids. You can also guide students by pointing out their errors. Show them where they have taken the wrong approach, where they have gone off on a tangent, or where their thinking has gone awry. Praising good work and encouraging successful and profitable lines of endeavor are also among the effective techniques to use in guiding learning.

Evaluating Students' Learning

Guiding students' learning is another continuous process of evaluation and reevaluation of the progress of learning. From the feedback that evaluation gives, you can tell what has been missed and so must be retaught, and what to emphasize in succeeding classes. Evaluation also tells students where they have hit or missed the mark. Evaluation is essential for diagnosis and necessary for good instruction. It gives the basis for determining what steps to take next. After a course gets rolling, the evaluation phase of one unit can often be used as the diagnostic phase of the next one.

Following Through

Much teaching is not truly effective because teachers often omit the final step of the pattern, which is the follow-through, or follow-up, step. Without it teaching all too often becomes a case of "so near and yet so far," for it is the follow-through that drives home and clinches the learning. Follow-through can take any of many forms. At times a simple summary will do. At other times you must repeat a point again and again or apply the learning in new practice situations. In every case, however, you should try to make the learning more thorough than in the original teaching-learning situation.

In many instances, this extra effort must consist of reteaching concepts that the evaluation tells you the students have not learned, because the follow-through step is not only an opportunity to clinch students' learning, but also a chance for correcting mistakes and filling in gaps. Thus, any good mathematics teacher who, upon checking the students' work, finds that they have not mastered one of the principles of the latest unit, should review the principle again to be sure students understand it before moving on to the new unit. The teacher's failure to clinch basic learnings is an all too frequent cause of students' failure at more advanced levels. Whatever is worth teaching is worth teaching well, and, if students miss learning the first time around, the follow-up gives them a chance to make up the loss. A little additional effort can make the difference between half-baked learning and real understanding.

Frequently, when an evaluation tells you that the objectives of a unit are pretty well mastered, your follow-up should be to move on to a new unit. Use the information you have learned about the students, as well as their learning in this unit, as the basis for building new learning in the next unit. Evaluation information can also serve as a signpost indicating the need for individual help and for gaps that need filling in as the new unit proceeds.

Stop and Reflect

Is the fact that a student has successfully passed the prerequisites to a course any guarantee of readiness for it? How might you tell if the student is ready?

Without continuous evaluation, teaching is seldom efficient. Why?

Recall the five steps in the general pattern of teaching. Can you think of any teaching-learning situation in which any of these steps should be omitted?

Evaluation usually shows that not all students have reached the same point. What implications does this have for guiding learning activities?

The Pattern's Fluidity

An interesting characteristic of this model for effective teaching is that it is not fixed. As we have seen, the evaluative phase in one unit may serve as the diagnostic phase of the next. The follow-up for one unit may be preparing and guiding the learning activities for the next one. A unit's evaluation activities and teaching activities frequently operate side by side. Still, even though the five steps of the teaching process may not always follow each other in strict order and may sometimes change places with each other, to be truly effective you must make use of all of them in all your teaching.

Furthermore, be sure that teaching objectives, subject matter content, teaching strategies and tactics, and evaluation match. The diagnosis should determine what is needed. Select the objectives to fulfill that need and build the teaching to meet the objectives. Your tests and other evaluations should determine whether the objectives have been met. The objectives, methods, and evaluation must all be aligned; that is, they must all call for, teach, and test the same thing.(10)

Stop and Reflect

Try to remember the three most successful teachers you have known in your middle and high school years. What characteristics made them successful in your opinion?

Prepare a questionnaire in which you have your students rate your teaching.

S U M M A R Y

The role of any teaching method is to bring about learning. Method includes both content and techniques, strategies and tactics. The key to method is to bring about the desired learning in students by selecting the proper strategies and tactics and consequently the proper content and techniques. This is complicated by the difficulty in communicating well with students, by the management problems in teaching, and by the abundance of alternative strategies and tactics that are possible.

This abundance of options along with the need to make spur-of-the-moment decisions makes teaching an art, not a science. Teachers must select or create the teaching objectives that are most suited to the needs of their students, and then must choose the content and the teaching strategies and tactics that will bring about these objectives.

Subject matter is not all the same, and so not all subjects should be taught in the same way. Rather, the teaching approach should vary according to the structure and methods of the disciplines concerned. No longer can teachers be content merely to teach students specific information and thus "cover the subject." The modern world contains too much information to cover and the facts are changing too swiftly. Modern teaching must concentrate on organization, method, process, structure, skills, and attitudes so that young people can cope with the new and different knowledge they will discover before they even get the previous knowledge well-digested. It is for these reasons that the teacher must teach more by covering less.

The strategies and tactics available for such teaching include clarifying operations, show-how operations, and security-giving operations. The approach to them may be direct or indirect, and they may be individualized. Which strategy or tactic is best depends on the circumstances. Sometimes it is better to teach directly; sometimes indirectly.

Whatever the teaching situation, good teaching requires that teachers follow a teaching model such as the following:

1. Diagnose the situation.
2. Prepare for the learning.
3. Guide the activities.
4. Evaluate the learning.
5. Follow up.

Effective teaching also requires that these elements all be aligned.

ADDITIONAL READING

Biehler, R. F., and J. Snowman. *Psychology Applied to Teaching,* 5th ed. Boston: Houghton Mifflin, 1986.

Blue, T. W. *The Teaching and Learning Process.* Washington, DC: National Education Association, 1986.

Borich, G. D. *Effective Teaching Methods.* Columbus, OH: Merrill, 1988, Ch. 1.

Crabtree, J. *Basic Principles of Effective Teaching.* Cincinnati, OH: Standard Publishing, 1982.

Fenstermacher, G. D., and J. F. Soltis. *Approaches to Teaching.* New York: Teachers College Press, 1986.

Gage, N. L., and D. C. Berliner. *Educational Psychology,* 3rd ed. Boston: Houghton Mifflin, 1984.

Gagne, R. M., and W. W. Wager. *Principles of Instructional Design,* 3rd ed. New York: Holt, Rinehart and Winston, 1988.

Glasser, W. *The Quality School.* New York: Harper and Row, 1990.

Good, T. L., and J. E. Brody. *Looking in Classrooms.* New York: Harper and Row, 1987.

Hill, D. J. *Humor in the Classroom: A Handbook for Teachers.* Springfield, IL: Charles C. Thomas, 1988.

Joyce, B. et al. *Flexibility in Teaching: An Excursion Into the Nature of Teaching and Training.* New York: Longman, 1980.

Joyce, B., and M. Weil. *Models of Teaching.* Englewood Cliffs, NJ: Prentice-Hall, 1990.

Levin, T., with R. Long. *Effective Instruction.* Alexandria, VA: Association for Supervision and Curriculum Development, 1981.

Levine, J. M. *Secondary Instruction: A Manual for Classroom Teaching.* Boston: Allyn and Bacon, 1989.

Peterson, P. L., and H. J. Walberg, eds. *Research on Teaching.* Berkeley, CA: McCutchan, 1979.

Reigeluth, C. M. *Instructional Theories in Action.* Hillside, NJ: Erlbaum, 1987.

Rubin, L. J. *Artistry in Teaching.* New York: Random House, 1985, Part 2.

Sparks, D., and G. M. Sparks. *Effective Teaching for Higher Achievement.* Alexandria, VA: Association for Supervision and Curriculum Development, 1984.

Troisi, N. F. *Effective Teaching and Student Achievement.* Reston, VA: National Association of Secondary School Principals, 1983.

Wragg, E. C., ed. "Teaching Skill." In *The Research Findings of the Teacher Education Project.* New York: Nichols, 1984.

NOTES

1. Renate Nummela Caine and Geoffrey Caine, *Teaching and the Human Brain* (Alexandria, VA: Association for Supervision and Curriculum Development, 1991), Ch. 6.

2. Jerry J. Bellon, Elner C. Bellon, and Mary Ann Blank, *Teaching from a Research Knowledge Base* (New York: Macmillan, 1992), 426–459, 473–474.

3. Marsha Weil and Bruce Joyce, *Information Processing Models of Teaching* (Englewood Cliffs, NJ: Prentice-Hall, 1978). *See also* Bruce Joyce and Marsha Weil, *Models of Teaching,* 2nd ed. (Englewood Cliffs, NJ: Prentice-Hall, 1986).

4. Fred M. Newmann and Gary G. Wehlage, "Five Standards of Authentic Instruction," *Educational Leadership* 50 (April 1993): 8–12.

5. Edmund J. Amidon and Ned A. Flanders, *The Role of the Teacher in the Classroom* (Minneapolis, MN: Amidon and Associates, 1963).

6. Allan C. Ornstein, "How Good Are Teachers in Effecting Student Outcome?" *NASSP Bulletin* 66 (December 1982):61–70.

7. *See,* for instance, Barak V. Rosenshine, "Content, Time, and Direct Instruction," in *Research on Teaching*, edited by Penelope L. Peterson and Herbert J. Walberg (Berkeley, CA: McCutchan, 1979).

8. Shirley A. McFaul, "An Examination of Direct Instruction," *Educational Leadership* 40 (April 1983): 67–69.

9. Robert L. Bargert, James A. Kulik, and Chen-Lin C. Kulik, "Individualized Systems of Instruction in Secondary Schools," *Review of Educational Research* 53 (Summer 1983): 143–158.

10. S. Alan Cohen, "Instructional Alignment: Searching for a Magic Bullet," *Educational Researcher* 16 (November 1987): 16–20.

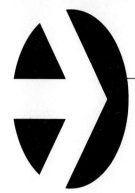

Chapter 2

Students and How They Learn

*If you become a teacher, by
the pupils you'll be taught.*
Oscar Hammerstein II ("The King and I")

■ **Overview**

■ **The Students**

■ **How Students Learn**

Overview

If the five-step teaching pattern discussed in the preceding chapter is going to work for you, you must adjust your teaching strategies to a reasonably accurate diagnosis of the teaching-learning situation. To arrive at such a diagnosis, you must understand the characteristics of middle and high school students in general, the ways students learn, and the particular traits of the individual students in your classes. In this chapter, we first look at some of the characteristics of adolescents. We then discuss how students learn, both as individuals and as group members, and some implications of learning theory for teaching.

The Students

Adolescence

Every student is unique. The set of characteristics that make up any person's physical, mental, emotional, and social being can never be duplicated exactly. Still, a number of generalizations are true enough of youth in general to be used as a tentative guide. Remember, however, that when you apply these generalizations to any individual, you must be prepared for variations from the norm.

Between the ages of 10 and 18—the range of the middle and high school years—boys and girls move from childhood to young adulthood. It is no wonder that the teenagers who are our middle and high school students are full of complexities and enigmas. The business of growing up is a complicated one. Adolescents are torn by many conflicts and many moments of indecision. At one moment, they may demand complete independence; at the next moment, they may need the reassurance and protection typical of much younger children.

As students enter early adolescence, they encounter personal, social, educational, and vocational problems that they are incapable of analyzing and logically solving on their own. Often their lives are stormy. Although most youngsters come through these trials relatively unscathed, if you understand the reasons behind an adolescent's behavior, you can better help him or her during this trying period. By getting to know and understand your students, you will be in a better position to help them solve their problems and to adapt your programs to make the most of the situation.

It is here that you, the teacher, must be aware of factors that contribute to many of the changes in behavior that are taking place. The early adolescent, now more descriptively called a *transescent,* is often confused by the mysteries of physiological changes, the development of secondary sex characteristics, and new social and emotional pressures. Thus, he or she needs strong support, not only from home but also from school. The rebellion of the middle adolescent is understandable, too, if you are aware of the conditions of life that help create their uncertainties, confusions, and concerns. Boston University's Professor William C. Kvaraceus was probably right when he said in his lectures that being a teenager is the most dangerous occupation in our society.

GROWING UP   Adolescence, as we have discussed, is a period of growing up. However, students do not grow up at the same speed. Some mature rapidly; some mature more slowly. For some girls, puberty comes as early as age 9; for others it comes as late as age 16. Similarly, for boys the onset of puberty may range from age 11 to age 18. You must be prepared to face classes of boys and girls whose appearances range from quite childish to very mature. Looks may be deceiving, though, because the various parts of a child's personality grow at different rates, too. Very mature-looking boys, for instance, may be quite childish in strength, interests, and personality. The maturation process is also not consistent. Students who act in a mature manner today may behave childishly tomorrow. Adolescence is a period of change accompanied by rapid, uneven growth.

These adolescent changes may cause many conflicts within the adolescent and in the adolescent's social relationships. Consequently, adolescents tend to be emotional, moody, and flighty—a combination of naïveté and sophistication. For them, schools are likely to be sources of frustration, failure, humiliation, and punishment as well as opportunities for experiencing social growth, feeling pleasure, learning new skills and knowledge, and gaining experience in the art of becoming an adult.(1)

MIDDLE SCHOOL STUDENTS Much of what we have just discussed applies to both transescents (that is, beginning adolescents and pubescents) and older adolescents. However, when you think about middle school students, keep several things in particular in mind. Transescence is a period of change from childhood to adolescence. Many middle school students are still children. Moreover, those students who are already adolescents are only beginning adolescents. They need much support as they start their journey toward independent adulthood. That is why they need a transitional program like that of the middle school before moving on to the complexities of the high school departmentalized program.

Intellectually, transescents are moving from a period of concrete knowledge to more formal abstract knowledge. During this latter period, they learn to work with the abstract, the theoretical, and the hypothetical. Middle school teaching should help them make this transition. Middle school students also continue, to some extent, the imaginative thinking of childhood. Middle school teachers should capitalize on these traits and encourage them. Too often, schools tend to kill imagination and creativity.

Socially, transescents are more vulnerable than at any other time in their lives. They are unsure because they are entering a new world. They are divorcing themselves slowly from their dependence on adults, so they turn to their peers for support and guidance. Sympathetic guidance from adults at this point is most critical because it is at this age that a person begins to form his or her values, life view, and mode of living.

Emotionally, transescents are just beginning to come to grips with the complexities of adult life. Sometimes their feelings can be overwhelming—even adults who have lived with varied emotions for many years sometimes find feelings difficult to handle. Middle school personnel would be wise to tone down adult-type social, sporting, and other activities until boys and girls have become more ready to cope with them. When children are forced to grow up too fast, growing up becomes more difficult. The same caution can be expressed about physical growth. Transescent growth is rapid, uneven, and sometimes deceptive. Middle school teachers should be very careful not to confront transescents with tasks for which they are not yet ready. For example, many a boy has suffered serious injury because he was urged to play football before his leg bones finished developing.

Educators should always remember that sixth-, seventh-, and eighth-graders are not high schoolers. They need time to grow up. If they can get off to a good start with positive self-images, they should do well both as youths and adults. Transescence is one of the most interesting and exciting times of life.

THE HIGH SCHOOL YEARS Boys and girls do not change overnight just because they graduate from middle school and enter high school. The transition is slow and uneven. For some students, the period of transescence lingers well into their high school years. In some instances, students gain adolescent or young adult characteristics and then slip back to more childish behavior. This should not be surprising, because we all may know senior citizens who have never attained fully adult status in all facets of their lives.

Many students find the transition from middle school to high school difficult because of the many adjustments they must make. In addition to the advent of sexual maturation with its attendant social and emotional demands, high school youth are faced by many role changes. For one, they are thrust into a new and different environment. As freshmen in a new school, they have little or no status in high school society. The school structure is much less intimate and personal than what they have been used to. Often they feel lost in the crowd; some never fully find themselves in this new environment.

Under the circumstances, it is not surprising to find that some high school youths are not happy in school. They feel incompetent, inferior, powerless, ignored, and rejected. They believe that they are not learning anything—at least not anything worth learning. They are bored. They have poor grades. They feel unwanted. Like everyone else, high school youths want to be respected, to be treated politely, to be treated fairly, to be understood, and to be listened to. When the school climate seems unfriendly, they see no point in attending school. Therefore, many of them (more than 1 in 10) drop out before finishing high school.(2)

Evidently, what high school students want from school is discipline and order, plus opportunities for social contacts with their peers. In their eyes the social functions are the best part of school. They want teachers to relate to them and to respect them. The best teachers, they say, are warm, understanding, humorous, yet authoritative. Good teachers, they think, know their stuff and conduct efficient, orderly classes.(3)

Stop and Reflect

What implications do the characteristics of adolescents have for you?

Observe a few classes in a high school and a middle school. Which group would you prefer to work with? In what ways do they seem different?

From what you have seen of adolescents, what sorts of things should you do in your classes to attract their interest and attention?

In what ways do you think you would teach transescents differently from older adolescents? Or would you?

DEVELOPMENTAL TASKS   Becoming an adult is not an easy task. It requires boys and girls to establish themselves as young men and young women in an adult world. To succeed in this process, they must take on new roles and cope with the problems that accompany them. In making this change to adulthood, young people must accomplish a number of developmental tasks such as learning what it is to be a young man or a young woman and to act accordingly. This process involves the completion of several steps such as:

Establishing one's self as an independent person.
Deciding upon a suitable vocation and preparing for it.

Middle and high school students both consciously and unconsciously strive to complete these tasks. To them, these goals are much more important than schoolwork.

COGNITIVE GROWTH   Boys' and girls' cognitive skills develop greatly during adolescence. As transescents, they are more ready to learn through verbal means than are younger students. Although they are no longer as dependent on demonstration, manipulation, nonverbal perception, and the like as they were in elementary grades, middle school transescents are almost completely dependent on concrete thought and haphazard trial-and-error thinking. It is not until their high school years that they become systematic thinkers. Then adolescents tend to become skilled in and fascinated by abstraction, theory, and higher meanings.

Preoccupation with abstractions and theories may lead to role confusion, as well as confusion about what might be, what ought to be, and what is. Consequently, adolescents tend to have high ideals and to judge the world by impossibly high standards. Such preoccupation may also lead to adolescent egocentrism marked by introspection, self-consciousness, overconcern with others' opinions, and overdependence on the practices, standards, and values of peer groups.

Because high school youths entering the formal operation stage of cognitive development may be inclined to be unrealistic, teachers should quiz them about their facts and ask them to back up their theories, hypotheses, and solutions to society's problems. A skillful teacher will require students to find out what the facts are, provide facts for them, face them with any incongruities in their positions, play the devil's advocate, require them to debate another person's belief as well as to argue against their own positions, and in other ways induce them to face reality and consider the various sides of issues.

Adolescents' growing ability to use formal thinking processes does not limit boys and girls to systematic thinking. Adolescents can and do think originally and creatively. Their imaginations are strong and free. They are capable of cognitive leaps—and dreams. Youth is a time for dreaming. As that old Lapland song reminded Mr. Longfellow

> *A boys' will is the wind's will*
> *And the thoughts of youth are long, long thoughts.(4)*

The high school years, then, are an age of cognitive growth. Even less promising young people can produce if given opportunities. They can learn whatever they need to learn if they are given enough time and proper instruction. However, schoolwork that is too difficult and unreasonable demands that are placed on students may cause them to become uninterested and give up.

ESTABLISHING INDEPENDENCE   Because part of becoming an adult is to become more and more independent from the supervision of parents, teachers, and other authority figures, adolescents try to establish this independence. In the process, they often become highly critical of adults and the adult world. To demonstrate their independence, adolescents tend to reject adult authority, opinions, and values. They often experiment with undesirable or unconventional behavior calculated to illustrate their independence, manliness or womanliness, and adulthood. Yet, in spite of their desire for asserting their independence, adolescents have a great need for security. They are greatly concerned about themselves—their bodies, social relations, future, image, status, and so on.

These concerns are liable to cause adolescents to become obsessively conformist. Even the "nonconformists" are really "conformists" who tend to be ruled by the standards of their adolescent community rather than by those of adults— although their long-range goals may be strongly influenced by their parents. Their need for support and security is also evident in the rapid and extreme swings in behavior exhibited by so many adolescents.

Obviously then, since adolescents seek both independence and security, middle and high school personnel should try to give them plenty of opportunities to try their own wings in a supportive atmosphere.

DESIRE FOR SELF-REALIZATION   Connected with the adolescent's desire for independence and adulthood is a desire for self-realization. Adolescents need to achieve, to feel important, and to be accepted by their peers and by adults. They do not want to be talked down to or to be treated like children. They need responsibility. They need the chance to be leaders sometimes. Therefore, you should give your students opportunities to shine, to show off a little, and to assume some real responsibility.

Because of their own desire for recognition and achievement, adolescents are likely to be sympathetic to the desires of others, particularly the disadvantaged and downtrodden who may be searching for civil rights, economic opportunity, freedom, and so forth. Adolescents tend to be "suckers for causes." They are also concerned about the meaning of life and self. Some of them at least are concerned with vocational choice; often they do not see much relevance or pertinence to their own lives in most of the content of the curriculum.

VALUES   Adolescents tend to see things in black and white and fail to take into account the perplexities and complexities of the real world. As they grow older and more experienced, they begin to see things in better perspective. They become aware of the varying values of rules and customs and see how the rules and customs apply in particular situations. They see the purpose of the rules and the need for rules. They understand that sometimes rules must be flexible and that the spirit of the law should override the letter of the law. As they become more understanding of the need and purpose of rules, they become desirous of participating in forming their own rules. In short, they gradually adopt what Piaget calls *the morals of cooperation.*

A WHOLE PERSON   Finally, each student is a whole person. Anything the student learns or does affects that individual as an entity. All activity has emotional, mental, and physical aspects. This applies to school learning as well as to other activities. Although students can be directed, in the process they interact with the environment. They are not wax tablets to be written on. Therefore, your teaching must give students opportunities to participate actively in their own learning. This type of teaching should involve the physical and emotional as well as the intellectual aspects of students' personalities in every lesson. In other words, you should make your teaching holistic.

Stop and Reflect

Consider the developmental tasks. In what ways did they affect your life in your middle and high school years? Were any of them particularly troublesome to you and your friends?

Look at some middle school textbooks. Do they seem to match the cognitive development of transescents? Similarly examine some high school textbooks. Do these books give students opportunities to stretch their minds?

Some Problems of Adolescence

Most adolescent problem behaviors consist of a syndrome of related behaviors adopted by students

1. to achieve blocked goals
2. to express opposition to adults and/or society
3. to cope with such problems as anxiety, fear, and frustration

4. to get approval from their peers
5. to demonstrate their worth(5)

It follows, then, that since the student often is engaged in more than one type of problem behavior, teachers should concentrate on preventing problems and reenforcing nonproblem behavior rather than trying to correct specific problems.

APATHY   A major problem among high school students is apathy. This is not as true among middle school students. In part, at least, student apathy is undoubtedly the result of curricula that seem to students irrelevant and meaningless and that fail to rival the excitement of social activities, television, and the like.

Another factor is that about two thirds of twelfth-graders and almost half of tenth-graders work. Their jobs take time that might otherwise be spent in schoolwork (including homework) and school activities. These working hours detract from whatever feelings of school as community the students may have. Furthermore, the world of work may seem more exciting, more real, and more important to students. As a result, they turn their backs on what they see as unrealistic, irrelevant, and boring curricula and classes.

Additionally, many high school students are apolitical and cynical. These feelings, along with attitudes and beliefs that striving and schooling for the future are futile, can result in a lack of interest in other aspects of life and cause students to view schools, at best, as a waste of time.(6)

Such feelings of apathy and rejection can be combatted by involving young people in civic community activities and by encouraging participation in school activities. Real opportunities for taking part in school governance and community affairs can often awaken students' interest.

DRUGS AND ALCOHOL   The use of drugs and alcohol creates all too many adolescent problems. Drug use inhibits short-term memory, creativity, energy, and motivation. It makes school seem unappealing and irrelevant. Teachers should refuse to teach students who are under the influence of drugs or alcohol, as well as make clear to these students that their presence while under the influence will not be tolerated. To this end, you should become well-acquainted with the symptoms of drug abuse. Any student exhibiting these symptoms should be referred to the proper school authorities at once.

FAMILY PROBLEMS   Family problems can lead to adolescent problems. Many of today's students are the products of broken homes, single-parent homes, and poorly supervised homes. The self-involvement of some parents has led to neglect and a lack of supervision, guidance, and care for their children. Boys and girls often are left in charge of their own supervision before they are ready for such responsibility. (Witness the number of elementary and middle school children who are on their own from the close of school until their parents come home in the evening.) Some children may come from homes where they are verbally and physically abused. The result is that many young people do not feel good about themselves. Boys and girls become less trusting, less happy with themselves and with society, and more apathetic. Schools and teachers can contribute to rebuilding feelings of worth in youths by giving them chances to be responsible.(7)

FINDING ONE'S ROLE   For adolescents, finding one's role in life may be an ordeal. They are continually faced with such problems as: How should I behave today? How can I be popular? Should I follow the crowd or do what I think is right? What should my goals for the future be? For some, solving such puzzles may lead to identity problems. Girls, for instance, may be torn between a desire to achieve and a longing for the traditional soft femininity that some hold as an ideal. (Some girls refuse to answer too many questions or appear to be "too smart" for fear the boys won't like them.) These identity problems and role confusion are magnified and made more dangerous by the threat of sexually transmitted diseases such as AIDS. The varied ethnic and racial backgrounds of the adolescents in our classrooms also complicate their search for role identification and self-understanding. Sometimes, the identity crises caused by these confusions may lead to withdrawal, negative identities, rebellious behavior, or depression. Role confusion is another indication of the necessity for our schools to be supportive.

Since large departmentalized high schools do not lend themselves to creating a supportive climate, teachers must try to make their classes as humane as possible. Students need to be recognized as people. Middle school block schedules are more helpful in this regard.

Stop and Reflect

What steps do you think you could take in your teaching to make schooling more relevant?

Are there ways in which you can involve students in their community? How can you make your courses part of the real world?

What position will you take about student use of drugs and alcohol?

What can you do to make your classes seem more humane?

Are the courses in your field irrelevant or useless in any respect? What could you do to make them seem relevant and useful?

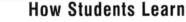

■ ■ ■ ■ How Students Learn

Causes for Not Learning

Why is it that so often students do not learn in our schools and classrooms? A major reason is that the classes are boring and seemingly irrelevant to students' needs. Although it is essential that subject matter be useful and appealing to the students, too much of what is taught in secondary schools has little bearing on the lives or needs of the students. Probably half of the high school curriculum could be dropped from the school program tomorrow without anyone's noticing its passing. It is not surprising that for many students their studies seem too futile and dead-end to be worth their exerting any real effort to learn them. If we wish students to make an effort to learn, we ought to provide something for them to learn that at least seems worth learning.

Another major cause of nonlearning is poor teaching. Teaching is often ineffective because it is inadequately planned or because it violates the laws of learning. Some courses are poorly organized and lack direction. Some classes are poorly motivated. In some courses, the work is too hard or too easy. Some teachers attempt to cover a subject rapidly instead of giving it time to sink in. Some teachers ignore the fact that students are individuals with varying backgrounds, talents, and interests, and attempt to teach everyone the same material at the same rate in the same way.

Poor teaching and poor courses undoubtedly cause many students to fail to learn, but they are not the only causes. Students are often handicapped by poor health, fatigue, physical or mental limitations, emotional difficulties, environmental factors, family attitudes, or peer pressures. If a student's parents and friends feel that studying a Shakespearean sonnet is a waste of time and money, it probably will not be easy to convince the student that he should devote much time to it. Or again, a young person may believe, as did the poet, in burning her candle at both ends.(8) Although this practice may give "a lovely light," it promotes fatigue that hinders learning, and too many interests also can distract students from the desired learnings.

This brings us to another major block in school learning: Few teachers and few faculties do much to make school learning seem important or attractive when compared to life's other activities. In fact, many things we teachers do seem to be designed to convince students that learning is undesirable and unpleasant. In what other endeavor would a person try to sell a product by using it as a punishment? Yet every day some teachers assign classwork as a punishment.

These, then, are some of the blocks to learning. They also can be causes of student misbehavior. If we teachers are to do the job required of us—helping students learn—we must overcome these blocks. Of course, we are not always in a position to do much to overcome them. But good teachers try, by using the best methods and materials they know, to help each of their students learn in spite of any obstacles. This is a key challenge of teaching.

Stop and Reflect

Evaluate the teaching to which you have been subjected. Did it stimulate interest in learning the subjects? Give examples of teaching that promoted learning and teaching that did not.

Learning Styles

The strategies and techniques we use in our teaching should be consistent with the best principles of learning. Let us now look at a few basic principles and draw some generalizations about teaching methods from them.

First, learning is an individual matter. It is the learner who does the learning—not the teacher. For this reason as well as others, teaching should be centered on the students. Each individual learns differently than others do. Some individuals learn quickly; some more slowly. Some are verbally oriented; some more physically oriented. Some are visually oriented; some are more aurally oriented. Some like to read; others do not. Some have well-developed skills; others have poorly developed ones. Some are active; some are passive. Some are interested in one thing; others in another. And so on and on.

Furthermore, students come to you bearing more than one intelligence. It was once believed that people had one general intelligence which could be measured by one instrument like the I.Q. test. However, experts have become convinced that we each have multiple intelligences, such as verbal, logic-mathematical, musical, visual, kinetic, personal, and social intelligences.(9) Consequently, it is necessary for teachers to

1. provide different learning environments and teaching strategies for different students, or
2. vary their teaching enough so that every student finds the learning situation compatible with his or her cognitive style at least part of the time, or
3. help boys and girls develop learning styles conducive to effective content learning and to the teaching styles used in the school.

The best teachers probably use all three options. In any case, it is imperative that students be taught how to learn if schooling is to be effective.

Stop and Reflect

Observe, if you can, differences in the way students learn. Do you and your friends have the same or different preferences for learning activities, approaches, situations, and methods of attacking learning? What are your own preferences in learning? Would you rather work alone or in a group? Do you like to have the radio on, or would you rather have complete silence while working? Does your thinking tend to be divergent or convergent, analytical or global, field-independent or field-dependent?

Learning How to Learn

One reason why students have different learning styles and abilities is that learning techniques are not entirely innate. Some of your students may have become very skillful in learning academic content, while others of equal potential may have not. Do not write off students because they do not do well in the schoolwork you have assigned. It may only be that they have *not learned how to learn academic material,* or it may be that their cognitive learning styles and your teaching style are too far apart. Perhaps by using different strategies and by redirecting your teaching, you can help these students to learn and to study effectively.

The methods and materials we use in our schools sometimes do not help students learn how to learn. For example, learning by rote memorization, listening to lectures, reciting facts, and the like do not help students cope with learning problems that require such intellectual skills as thinking, investigating, and problem solving. These strategies and techniques must be used in teaching, but you should also use strategies and techniques that help students build higher order intellectual skills. Learning how to learn transfers directly.

Learning and the Brain

To understand learning and learning styles, it is important to know something of how the brain works. Researchers have learned much about the structure and function of the brain. This knowledge has caused many educators and educationists to revise their views on teaching and learning. It is now believed that humans are aggressive, not passive, learners. The brain is always active; it never turns itself off. Even during sleep, the brain is working.

Learning occurs when the brain makes patterns from the stimuli it encounters. It recognizes these patterns by spotting similarities and differences—what does and what does not belong in the pattern. In this way, the brain creates meaning and constructs perceptions and thought. It does not absorb ideas from the outside ready-made; however, its activity is influenced by anticipation and intention.

Contrary to what has been sometimes thought, the brain seems to work from the top down, from the superordinate to the subordinate. In building patterns, the brain evidently first spots the big picture and then fills in the details. For this reason, logically piling up small segments of instruction seems an inefficient way of learning. Apparently, learning is not a particularly logical performance!

According to Renate and Geoffrey Caine, two essentials are necessary for the mind to be in an optimal state for learning.

1. A relaxed nervous system and a sense of safety and security that operates at mental, emotional, and physical levels.
2. Student self-motivation, which is critical to the expansion of knowledge at more than surface levels.(10)

In short, for effective learning to occur, the environment must be both nonthreatening and rich.(11)

For this rich, positive environment to be most effective for learning, students must *do* things. Sitting still and keeping quiet in the traditional setting is counterproductive. Learning situations should be active as well as supportive.(12)

THE TWO HEMISPHERES   Recently, much has been made of the differences between the left and right cerebral hemispheres of the brain. Verbal learning, logical thinking, and the like are supposedly lodged in the left hemisphere, and spatial, emotional, and affective aspects are lodged in the right. To some extent, this is true. However, to be most successful, teaching should be "whole brain". Although each hemisphere has its separate specialties, it is the *whole* brain that processes the information.(13)

Your classes, therefore, should combine intellectual, emotional, affective, and physical elements. In most schools and classes, left-hemispheric approaches too often dominate instruction. To make teaching more balanced, in addition to ordinary expository teaching, use hands-on experiences, diagrams, highly visible visual aids, and models. Also offer experiences that include attitudes, values, and the like. Such teaching allows one hemisphere to tie in its processes with those of the other. Strategies of this type that integrate and relate the processes of both hemispheres are called *holistic strategies.* Holistic teaching tends to build on the strong and build up the weak learning functions.(14)

PROBLEMS AND THE BRAIN   As John Dewey believed, people are apparently natural problem-solvers. They need problems to solve in order to develop intellectually. A brain without problems does not work up to capacity.(15) It follows then that to be what Hart calls "brain compatible," curricula and teaching should be problem-centered. Classroom activities should be free from threats, of course, but they should also be challenging, of real importance to learners, and to some extent student-directed, although carefully supervised and guided by the teacher. In ideal teaching, rote learning would be used only to achieve mastery after students have established the basic skills and knowledge, according to Hart.(16)

A key word in this description of problem-solving teaching is *challenging.* The brain was built to solve problems. It does so from the moment of birth and thrives on it throughout all the 70 years or more allotted to us. The human ability to cope with problems is amazing. Given the opportunity, most high school youth are good problem solvers who need opportunities to whet their talents on challenging problems.

Consequently, secondary school students should have opportunities to do high-level thinking. They need curricula that give them opportunities to think creatively—to make imaginative leaps—in order to develop intellectually and emotionally and to enrich the meaningfulness of their lives.(17)

Stop and Reflect

Observe your college teachers. Do the methods they use encourage the development of learning skills and thinking?

Are the methods they use in their classes oriented toward left-brain or right-brain learning, or a mix of the two?

Verbalism versus Knowing

One reason teachers sometimes pick inappropriate teaching strategies and techniques is that they have not thought through what it is they are trying to do and do not comprehend what the processes of understanding and knowing entail.

To understand something, one must have clear concepts. Many times we think we know something when actually we have only a vague notion. When we try to explain the meaning of a word and find that we cannot do it, we say, "I know what it means, but I just can't explain it." More often than not, the truth is that we have only a fuzzy idea of what the word means and do not really understand its definition clearly. If we do not know information explicitly enough to use the knowledge, we do not really know at all.

There are several types of knowing: We can know *about,* we can know *that,* and we can know *how.* Learning about something is not the same as learning it or learning how to do it. The boy who only reads about how to swim may drown when thrown into the water. Neither does one learning product guarantee another. The girl who learns the rules of grammar and can do all the exercises in her grammar workbook perfectly may not be able to write a clear, idiomatic sentence. Or again, a graduate student may find that studying technical French has not helped a bit when trying to order a dinner in Paris. Neither does studying American history necessarily produce good citizens. To learn something, we must study *it*—not about it or something like it. To learn to do something, we must study and practice how to do it.

An example of the confusion surrounding learning is the common error of mistaking memorization for understanding. We confuse the word with the deed, the name with the object. Children are often asked to learn words and phrases that mean nothing to them. It is quite possible for a student to repeat the fact: "In a right triangle, the square of the hypotenuse is equal to the sum of the squares of the opposite sides." Yet being able to recite this fact does not mean that the student has the slightest idea of the meaning of square, hypotenuse, opposite sides, or right triangle. Thousands of persons can glibly recite that a noun is the name of a person, place, or thing, and yet cannot pick a single noun out of a sentence. The cartoon of Miss Peach's class (Figure 2.1) illustrates how little some elementary school children understand the pledge of allegiance to the flag.

Parroting information this way is called *verbalism.* One of the banes of both the elementary and secondary school, it is an example of what can result when teachers use the wrong strategies and techniques. To really know something, we must know it well enough to use the knowledge.

THE NEED FOR BOTH VICARIOUS AND DIRECT LEARNING   In some instances, verbalism is the result of an overuse of vicarious learning. Much of our best learning

▓ **FIGURE 2.1**

Miss Peach's Pupils Recite the Pledge of Allegiance
Copyright 1957, *New York Herald Tribune,* Inc. Reproduced with permission.

comes through direct experience; for example, a child who gets burned learns to fear the fire. However, direct experience is not the only way to learn, and fortunately, it is not necessary to get burned. We can learn vicariously, through the experiences of others. Not everyone can go to see the pyramids, but anyone can learn about them from descriptions and pictures.

While direct experience usually results in more vivid learning, it is not always efficient. Sometimes it is quite inefficient, time-consuming, costly, and dangerous, as in the case of the burned child. "Learning the hard way," we call it. For this reason, we must rely on vicarious experience for much of our schoolwork. To do so is quite proper. It saves time, money, and effort. Used correctly, it can be quite effective. It is often the only type of experience possible. However, many teachers rely too much on vicarious learning. Everything else being equal, direct learning is usually more effective than vicarious learning.

THE NEED FOR REALISTIC LEARNING   Realistic learning situations help make learning meaningful to the student and thus help to avoid verbalism. Only meaningful material can be learned efficiently. First, if the learning is meaningless to the learner, it is useless. Second, meaningless material is much more difficult to learn than is meaningful material. To avoid mere verbalism and inefficient learning among students, see to it that all learning situations in your classes are meaningful. Eliminate meaningless material either by omitting it altogether or by preparing the students for it so that it will have meaning when they study it.

Building Understanding

One reason for the prevalence of verbalism in our schools is that it has become a general practice to teach (1) isolated facts or bits of information, (2) generalizations presented as isolated facts or bits of information, or (3) a combination of facts and generalizations stated as isolated facts or bits of information. This is not the way to build understanding. To build understanding effectively, you must give pupils opportunities to examine the information, to establish the relationships among the facts, and to draw conclusions.

In this process, because concept building is a matter of categorization, you must make sure that your students understand what is included in the concept and what is not. Research suggests that you should present pupils with distinct examples of both positive and negative instances of the concept. It also seems to help if students meet several positive cases at once, if the examples of positive instances are uniform, if positive instances are shown side by side with negative ones, if irrelevant attributes are kept to a minimum, and if students' attention is focused on the relevant attributes. Concept teaching is especially effective when you provide pupils a framework or scaffolding on which to build their concepts. For instance, definitions followed by examples seem to work well. Since it is also helpful to teach concepts in related groups, it usually pays to examine the structure of your subject matter before teaching it.

Mixed methods, as a rule, work best when teaching concepts. Learning through a variety of instances and examples seems to aid understanding and transfer. Thus, activities such as looking at and handling things and talking to oneself about their attributes while studying them tend to make concepts clearer. So does feedback. Students should learn why such and such is right and so and so is wrong.

All this takes time. Students need time to digest the various factors. If they are rushed through concept learning, they do not have time to assimilate the concepts properly. Therefore, the atmosphere of the class should not be too rushed or pressing. Neither should it be threatening. Although anxiety may aid in the learning of simple concepts, to learn complex concepts requires a supportive, anxiety-free climate.

Building Skills

Skills must be learned directly by actually performing the skills. One can, and probably must, learn a lot about a skill in other ways, but the only way to master a skill is to practice it. As Comenius pointed out in 1657,

What is to be done must be learned by practice. Artisans do not detain their apprentices with theories, but set them to do practical work at an early stage; thus they learn to forge by forging, to carve by carving, to paint by painting, and to dance by dancing. In schools, therefore, let the students learn to write by writing, to talk by talking, to sing by singing, and to reason by reasoning.(18)

All too often, teachers forget this obvious, long-known fact. And so they make the mistake of trying to teach students how to write by teaching them grammar, and how to reason by memorizing rules and facts.

Teaching Attitudes, Appreciations, and Ideals

To develop in your students an attitude, appreciation, or ideal, you must provide them with experiences that foster that attitude, appreciation, or ideal. You cannot develop critical attitudes suitable for scholarly study by requiring students to regurgitate the wisdom given out in your lectures. Neither can you teach the ideals of scientific investigation by drilling students on scientific facts. Nor can you instill a love of music by making students memorize the dates of composers' lives. Rather, you must try to provide an atmosphere conducive to the attitudes you seek, give the students many chances to emulate suitable models and to practice the learning desired, and then reinforce these attitudes, appreciations, and ideals at every opportunity. Exhortations and lectures seldom bring about the affective learning teachers desire.

Stop and Reflect

What sort of learning techniques does a student need to learn to cope with the learning tasks common in your field?

What implications do the findings in brain research have for you as a teacher?

What classroom activities could you use to harness the brain's proclivity for problem solving? List a half dozen specific problem-solving activities that call for a high level of creative thinking.

What type of problem-solving activity would seem best suited for middle school transescents?

Can you give examples of different types of knowing? What implications do these different ways of knowing have for the teacher?

Can you cite examples of verbalism from your own school experience?

Can you cite examples from your own school experience of methods that seemed to bring out the wrong learning?

Can you think of tactics in your own field of teaching you think would be effective for teaching such objectives as

1. A deep understanding?
2. An appreciation?
3. A change in attitude?
4. An intellectual skill?
5. A physical skill?
6. Memorization?

Readiness

Learning is usually developmental. That is to say, *new learning builds on previous learning.* Students need to understand simple multiplication before they can succeed with long division. A student who does not know the principles of solving simple equations will probably have a difficult time with quadratics. Learning should follow an orderly sequence, with new learning building on past learning.

Learning is not merely the accumulation of new concepts, skills, ideals, attitudes, and appreciations. Rather, it is the integration of these new learnings with the concepts, skills, ideals, attitudes, and appreciations already present. The new learning becomes interwoven into one's personality. The result is really a personality change. This takes time. Although many students learn many things rapidly, thorough learning is apt to be a relatively slow process.

Because learning is developmental, it follows that one learns better when one is ready to learn. The principle of "readiness" has confused both teachers and laypeople. Psychologically, it can have many ramifications, but for classroom purposes it can be defined quite simply: *Readiness* is a combination of maturity, ability, prior instruction, and motivation. Individuals are ready to learn something when they have matured enough to learn it efficiently; when they have acquired the skills, knowledge, and strengths prerequisite to learning it; and when they are sufficiently motivated. When students have reached such a state of readiness, the teacher's job is relatively easy; when they have not, the teacher's job is more difficult and sometimes absolutely impossible. No one would attempt to teach a toddler classic ballet; one must learn to walk before one can learn to run. Therefore, it is essential to pick strategies, techniques, and subject matter for which the students are ready. When students are not ready, you can try to make them ready by using suitable methods and approaches. Otherwise, all you can do is to wait for the child to grow older, stronger, and wiser.

Transfer and Retention

PLANNING FOR TRANSFER AND RETENTION　Courses are not very productive unless they bring about transfer and retention of learning. *Transfer,* in this context, means using the outcome of learning in another situation. Thus, when students use in a history class skills they originally learned in English, transfer has taken place. If such transfer does not take place, the learning is of little value.

As you might expect, students do not transfer and remember extrinsically motivated learning as well as intrinsically motivated learning. When people want to learn something because they want to learn it, they are more likely to use the learning in other situations and to remember it. This is another argument for using intrinsic motivation whenever feasible.

Unmeaningful material does not transfer well, either. Transfer is more likely to result when the application of the learning to other situations is pointed out. When that is not done, transfer may not take place because the learner does not make the necessary connections. Transfer also takes place when components common to the original learning situation are present in the situation in which the learning is to be used. In other words, the more the learning situation is like the application situation, the greater chance there is that the learning will transfer.

Another aid to transfer is thorough learning. One can transfer what one knows and understands thoroughly much more readily than something less well-known. Thorough knowledge also helps in retaining learning, but the best way to retain what is learned is to use it. What is not used is soon forgotten. People remember extremely vivid happenings well, and have learned some things so well that it seems they can never forget them. Still, in spite of exceptions, the rule holds. Even one's native tongue becomes rusty if one does not use it. The key to retention is renewal through frequent use.

Both transfer and retention are encouraged by mastering and using generalizations, for as a rule, generalizations can be remembered and used better than can detail. The best-remembered generalizations (and therefore the generalizations most available for use) are those the student derives for him- or herself from specifics. Predigested generalizations worked out by the teacher and handed to the student are liable not to make any impact at all, or will probably remain at the level of mere verbalism. When you must present generalizations to students, it is probably best to support a generalization with "forgettable details" to help make the generalization stick. Ordinarily, however, it is more effective to give the students the details and encourage them to draw their own generalizations, or to let them encounter details and applications that will make their generalizations clear. The more opportunities students have for applying principles, the clearer their generalizations become.

THE NEED FOR FEEDBACK   If any learning is to be successfully retained and transferred, it must be reinforced. Feedback that shows students their successes and failures is one way to provide this needed reinforcement. For instance, research indicates that immediate correction and feedback after quizzes promotes both learning and retention. Another type of reinforcement is strengthening a particular behavior by having students repeat it. Behavior that is not reinforced or renewed by practice, drill, or some other form of repetition soon drops out. Thus, in selecting your teaching strategies and techniques, make sure to provide for rewarding desirable behavior, for giving immediate feedback, and for encouraging frequent reuse and renewal of what the students have learned so that they will not forget.

Learning in Groups

Although students learn as individuals, teachers must teach these individuals in groups. Consequently, teachers should try to use strategies and techniques that will produce effective learning in classroom groups. To do so, it is necessary to understand something of the nature of groups and how they work.(19)

THE NECESSITY FOR A POSITIVE CLIMATE   Most authorities seem to agree that a positive climate is one of the conditions necessary for maximum school learning. In other words, they believe that classroom learning is enhanced when students exhibit the following characteristics:

1. They know and accept one another and are accepted by the teacher.
2. They work well together.
3. They understand the group goals.
4. They know and accept their own roles and responsibilities and how these work toward the group goals.
5. They take satisfaction in their roles.

In such classrooms, students develop the feelings of personal worth, belonging, and security that support learning.

OTHER GROUP CHARACTERISTICS   Not only is the social climate within a group important in determining the group's effectiveness, but so also are the characteristics of the group, such as the attraction of the members for one another, the group's leadership patterns, its norms, its communication patterns, and the amount and kind of cohesiveness within the group. Classes lacking in leadership, mutual attraction, suitable norms, student-centered communication patterns, and cohesiveness do not function well. Fortunately, it is within the power of a teacher who is aware of these characteristics and the processes that affect them to influence the characteristics of any class. A teacher's influence is limited, however. You should not expect to make great changes in group structure overnight; rather, you should expect to make progress slowly.

GROUP LEADERSHIP   People become group leaders because of what they do and how they do it, rather than because of who they are. This process involves both interpersonal relationships and leadership skills. Students are more likely to perform well for persons they like than for persons they dislike or for whom they have no feeling. Students also respond more readily to persons who have acquired skill in the functions of leadership. These functions include those that are task-oriented, such as the initiating and selling of ideas that get things done, and the social, emotional functions, such as the encouraging, harmonizing, and compromising that smooth over interpersonal relationships and maintain a congenial, productive atmosphere.

You cannot depend on your position of authority to make you the true leader of the class. Although students are influenced by coercion and the authority of a position, they respond more readily to the leadership of someone they accept as an acknowledged expert (someone with expert power) or someone they consider charismatic and with whom they identify (someone with referent power). Although teachers are leaders by virtue of their position, students who exert expert power or referent power are apt to be as influential—sometimes more influential—than the teachers.

Similarly, democratic leadership is much more likely to be productive than is authoritarian leadership. (Laissez-faire leadership in which the leader lets students do as they please is quite useless.) Although the authoritarian leader may get things done, the democratic leader usually gets better quality work in a much more positive climate. Authoritarianism tends to cause, or at least aggravate, hostility, high dependency, friction, and other negative qualities. The more students feel that they have some influence on the decisions that are being made, the better things are for the group. Consequently, it helps to involve students in decision making as much as possible. Chapter 5 describes cooperative group planning techniques suitable for this purpose.

Some students are natural leaders. Their feelings toward particular teachers and classes have great impact on the other students around them. Other students seem to have no influence at all. On the whole, the group is not much affected by teacher relationships with low-status students, but positive relationships with natural leaders can cause a ripple effect that carries over to the rest of the students. Consequently, you would do well to seek the cooperation of high-status students. If they are on your side, probably all the students will perform better. In the long run you will find it very advantageous to involve these high-status students in decision-making processes.

It is wise to try to spot the natural leaders as soon as you can. Although sociometric tools may be useful, probably the best technique for spotting high-status students is careful observation. If you set aside part of each day for observation, you should soon find who the leaders are. Put the students to work in small groups or in a laboratory-type study situation and watch to see whom the other students turn to for help, guidance, or ideas.

To encourage optimal performance, distribute leadership roles to as many students as possible. Try to arrange it so that everyone has influence and responsibility. Your goal is not to make leaders out of the low-status students, but to raise everyone's participation level in leadership roles. You can further this objective by providing students with many opportunities to lead in small ways. Small-group work, for instance, makes a natural setting for a large number of students to take part in leadership and decision-making roles. So does entrusting some planning and decision making to a class steering committee in which personnel change from time to time. Small successes in leadership and decision-making roles of this type may lead to success in larger roles in the future.

ATTRACTION AND THE GROUP PROCESS   To create an environment favorable to learning, you must demonstrate that you like the students, and you must also foster an atmosphere of mutual liking among the students. In short, you should try to make your class into a diffusely structured group.

Diffusely structured groups differ from centrally structured groups in that there is no in-group or out-group. In diffusely structured groups, most of the students like one another equally well. There is no group of high-status favorites. In fact, differences in status are pretty well obscured by a democratic atmosphere in which most pupils have a fairly high sense of self-esteem.

Centrally structured groups are classes in which the teacher asks all the questions and a small group of students do all the reciting and garner all the teacher's praise. In the centrally oriented group, differences in status stand out. Relatively few students make up the in-group; the rest of the class makes up an out-group, which feels neglected, unwanted, and disliked. Students are well aware of these differences in status and feel its effects. To the students who are not a part of the high-status in-group, the centrally structured class is a threatening, hateful place, and they do not learn well.

Usually students tend to live up to what is expected of them. In centrally structured groups, little is expected of all class members; the accepted few are the only ones expected to participate. Consequently, large numbers of students do not perform well, because they do not feel that they are expected to perform well. In diffusely structured groups, where self-esteem is spread more evenly around the group, students respond much better. Because self-esteem tends to foster good performance, and good performance reinforces self-esteem, diffusely structured groups provide the positive social climate that encourages learning. Therefore, it is beneficial to concentrate on building self-esteem, attractiveness, and good feeling in your classes. Opportunities for establishing relationships of mutual respect and liking are easier in diffusely structured groups than in centrally structured groups.

To develop the wide range of friendships and mutual liking that are basic to the diffusely structured class, you can use teaching techniques that force students to get to know one another and to associate with different students from time to time. Almost all student-centered teaching strategies help make the class structure more diffuse. Teacher-centered strategies do not. The more evenly you can spread responsibilities and leadership roles, the more diffuse the class structure will be. Therefore, you should find small-group and committee work productive, especially if the committee membership is changed occasionally. A group should never be allowed to form itself into a permanent committee. Other techniques that you can use include games in which students mix with one another, exercises in which students compile biographies of other students, or radio or TV interviews in which students interact with one another. Some teachers have had considerable success with role-playing activities in which students act out roles different from those they normally take in the class.

Stop and Reflect

Are your college classes centrally structured or diffusely structured? If there are some of both types, which type seems to be the more effective? What does the teacher do to create the atmosphere found in these classes?

Visit some middle or high school classes. Are they centrally structured or diffusely structured? How does the structure seem to affect the classroom atmosphere? How does it affect the effectiveness of the class?

NORMS AND GROUP BEHAVIOR   Norms are expectations common to most of the students in the group. In a large measure, they determine the behavior of the group members. Thus, if the students expect teachers to be dictators, as they often do, they will be suspicious of teachers who say that they want open class participation. Similarly, if students expect teachers to give them information, they may resist or rebel against teaching methods that require them to dig up information and think for themselves. Educational goals and curricula that do not harmonize with students' notions of what is valuable and relevant may backfire.

If the class social climate is to be positive, the group norms should allow for a wide range of behavior. When norms are flexible, allowing for differences in individual behavior, they create an atmosphere of tolerance, encouragement, and good feeling. Narrow, rigid norms cause an atmosphere of restraint, threat, and anxiety.

With luck, you can change group norms so as to make them more favorable. If, for instance, you continually encourage and support students who participate openly, students may come to accept open participation as the norm. You can also use group discussion to change group norms. Discussion allows students to examine a norm closely. It may turn out that the assumed norm does not really represent the true feelings of the group members. Adolescents, like adults, often have incorrect notions about what other people think and believe. Discussion also seems to bring out feelings of group solidarity so that the group members support the norm once the group has accepted it. For that reason, cooperative teacher-student planning is useful for fostering desirable norms. When students work together to make the rules or to plan the units they will study, they are more likely to incorporate these norms into their behavior.

COMMUNICATION WITHIN THE GROUP   To facilitate a positive social climate, communication—both verbal and nonverbal—should be free, open, and supportive. Although there must be plenty of interaction, dialogue, and feedback among teachers and students, basically the communication pattern should be student-centered. Optimum communication does not occur in a highly teacher-centered class (Figure 2.2).

▓ **FIGURE 2.2**
Patterns of Group Communication

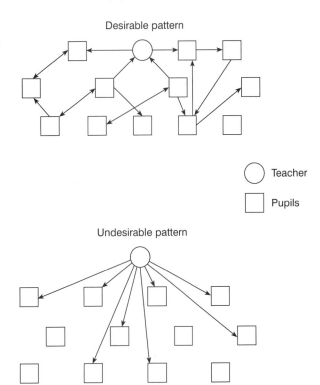

You can establish better communication in the classroom by teaching students such communication skills as

■ paraphrasing
■ behavior description
■ describing one's own feelings
■ checking perceptions
■ feedback

GROUP COHESIVENESS   Groups are most effective when they are cohesive—in other words, closely knit, purposeful, and well-organized. In a cohesive group, the students have high morale and positive feelings toward the group. Because the students know where they stand, what they are supposed to be doing, and are doing it, they produce. In short, a cohesive group works together.

You can build classroom cohesiveness by creating a diffusely structured classroom in which student participation and involvement are encouraged. Building self-esteem by supporting students and involving them in the decision-making process also helps establish cohesiveness, as does anything you can do to make students feel important and influential. Try to create cohesiveness by fostering an atmosphere of liking in which students have many opportunities to become involved with one another, by keeping classes student-centered, and by involving students in planning and evaluating their class activities. Diffused structure plus clear goals produce a cohesive group.

Stop and Reflect

Practice communication skills (because many teachers are less than proficient in using them). You can also use a combination of direct teaching and observation of class discussion. The techniques described in Chapter 8 are also useful as a guide for observing communication skills. Role-playing activities in which the spectator analyzes the communication process can also be used.

How do the characteristics of effective instructional groups differ from ineffective ones? In what ways can you as a teacher influence each of these group characteristics so as to make your teaching more effective?

Time on Task

According to J. B. Carroll's research, students can learn almost anything if they give it sufficient attention and work at it long enough.(20) Therefore, to be most effective, try to manage your classes so that students actually spend their time on the academic learning task—not on side trips.

Teaching Styles and Teacher Goals

One implication of all that we have discussed so far is that we must adjust our teaching methods to meet our goals. Direct expository teaching is effective for teaching young students the fundamentals, while indirect inductive styles, discussion, independent study, and the like are more successful for teaching the higher mental processes and academic skills to older, more sophisticated and talented students. Individualized study plans, which are most successful with college students, do not seem to work well with young middle school students.

SUMMARY

Adolescence is a time of growing up. During this period, youths attempt to complete certain developmental tasks, to become independent persons, and to realize their dreams and potentials. To many of them, school seems like a hindrance rather than a help toward achieving their most important, most personal goals. In their middle school years, they move from childhood to adolescence. This period, called transescence, is marked by the beginning of change from concrete thinking to abstract thinking, from childhood to sexual maturity, and from total dependence on adults to comparative independence and physical maturity. But adolescents are not grown-ups.

High school youth carry on the transition process toward more complete fulfillment. Although many high schoolers are unhappy in school, most of them give school fairly high marks. They appreciate its social functions most, and would be happier if teachers would treat them with more respect, run classes more efficiently, and demand higher standards. As they enter the formal operation stage of mental development, high schoolers need opportunities to think systematically and creatively.

Among the major problems of high school youth are apathy, drug and alcohol use, family problems, and role confusion. Usually, students who have problems are faced with a combination of problems. Therefore, adults wishing to help young people should concentrate on preventive approaches rather than on attempts to cure specific difficulties.

Schools are for learning. As often as not, nonlearning in school is the fault of the school and the system rather than the students. These problems would not be so great if teachers gave more attention to adapting methods to students' learning styles, to teaching them how to learn and how to study, and to using teaching approaches compatible with the working of the brain. It is particularly important that instruction be aimed at real learning—not mere verbalism. The methods used should be those best-suited to building clear, full concepts, thoroughly developed skills, and appropriate attitudes. Consequently, teachers must pay attention to student readiness and plan for transfer and retention of the knowledge to be learned. To do so, they must see to it that there is plenty of reinforcement of the important learnings and that sufficient time is spent on the important things to be learned.

Much teaching should be individualized, but almost all our common teaching methods involve working with groups. Consequently, teachers should understand the characteristics of groups, which include leadership, attraction, norms, communication, and cohesiveness. Teachers must also learn how to influence those group characteristics. Teaching is most effective when leadership is democratic and groups are diffusely structured.

ADDITIONAL READING

Applebee, A. *Writing in the Secondary School.* Urbana, IL: National Council of Teachers of English, 1981.

Bell-Gredler, M. E. *Learning and Instruction: Theory into Practice.* New York: Macmillan, 1986.

Blue, T. W. *The Teaching and Learning Process.* Washington, DC: National Education Association, 1986.

Borich, G. D. *Effective Teaching Methods,* 2nd ed. New York: Macmillan, 1992, Ch. 2.

Bugelski, B. R. *Some Practical Laws of Learning, Fastback 9.* Bloomington, IN: Phi Delta Kappa Educational Foundation, 1977.

Caine, R. N., and G. Caine. *Teaching and the Human Brain.* Alexandria, VA: Association for Supervision and Curriculum Development, 1991.

Cornett, Claudia E. *What You Should Know About Teaching and Learning Styles, Fastback 191.* Bloomington, IN: Phi Delta Kappa Educational Foundation, 1983.

Dembo, M. H. *Applying Educational Psychology in the Classroom,* 3rd ed. White Plains, NY: Longman, 1988.

Derry, S. A. "Putting Learning Strategies to Work," *Educational Leadership* 46 (December 1988/January 1989): 4–10.

Dunn, R., and S. A. Griggs. *Learning Style: Quiet Revolution in American Secondary Schools.* Reston, VA: National Association of Secondary School Principals, 1988.

Elkind, D. *All Grown Up and No Place to Go: Teenagers in Crisis.* New York: Addison Wesley, 1984.

Gage, N. L. *Educational Psychology,* 3rd ed. Boston: Houghton Mifflin, 1984, Ch. 20.

Gardner, Howard. *The Unschooled Mind: How Children Think and How Schools Should Teach.* New York: Basic Books, 1991.

Holden, P. E. *Classroom Tactics for Teachers of Young Teens.* Springfield, IL: Charles C. Thomas, 1989.

Ingersoll, G. M. *Adolescents,* 2nd ed. Englewood Cliffs, NJ: Prentice-Hall, 1988.

Jacobsen, D. A., P. D. Eggen, and D. P. Kauchak. *Methods for Teaching.* New York: Macmillan, 1993.

Johnson, E. W. *Teaching School,* rev. ed. Boston: National Association of Independent Schools, 1987.

Kauchak, D. P., and P. D. Eggen. *Learning and Teaching: Research-Based Methods.* Boston: Allyn and Bacon, 1989.

Keefe, James W., ed. *Profiling and Utilizing Learning Style.* Reston, VA: National Association of Secondary School Principals, 1988.

LeFrancois, G. R. *Psychology for Teaching,* 6th ed. Belmont, CA: Wadsworth, 1988.

Lipsitz, J., ed. *Barriers, A New Look at the Needs of Young Adolescents.* New York: Ford Foundation, 1979.

Newman, B. M., and P. R. Newman. *Adolescent Development.* Columbus, OH: Merrill, 1986.

Phillips, D. C., and J. F. Soltis. *Perspectives on Learning.* New York: Teachers College Press, 1985.

Slavin, R. E. *Educational Psychology. Theory and Practice,* 2nd ed. Englewood Cliffs, NJ: Prentice-Hall, 1988.

Sonnier, I. L., ed. *Methods and Techniques of Holistic Education.* Springfield, IL: Charles C. Thomas, 1985.

NOTES

1. Howard Gardner, *The Unschooled Mind* (New York: Basic Books, 1991), Ch. 1.
2. *Education USA* (October 11, 1993), 3.
3. Robert T. McNergney and Carol A. Currier, *Teacher Development* (New York: Macmillan, 1981), 35–45.
4. Henry W. Longfellow, *My Lost Youth.*
5. Richard Jessar, "Adolescent Problem Behavior and Developmental Transmission," *Education Digest* 48 (November 1982): 47–50. Condensed from *The Journal of School Health* 52 (May 1982): 295–300.
6. James Mackey and Deborah Appelman, "The Growth of Adolescent Apathy," *Educational Leadership* 40 (March 1983): 30–33.
7. Gerald Grant with John Briggs, "Today's Children Are Different," *Educational Leadership* 40 (March 1983): 4–9.
8. Edna St. Vincent Millay, *Figs from Thistles, First Fig.*
9. Howard Gardner, *Frames of Mind: The Theory of Multiple Intelligences* (New York: Basic Books, 1985). *See also* David G. Lazear, *Teaching for Multiple Intelligences, Fastback 342* (Bloomington, IN: Phi Delta Kappa Educational Foundation, 1992).

10. Renate Nummela Caine and Geoffrey Caine, *Teaching and the Human Brain* (Alexandria, VA: Association for Supervision and Curriculum Development, 1991), 131.

11. Leslie A. Hart, *Human Brain and Human Learning* (White Plains, NY: Longman, 1983).

12. Ibid.

13. James W. Keefe, *Learning Style Theory and Practice* (Reston, VA: National Association for Secondary School Principals, 1987), 30.

14. Isadore L. Sonnier and Joe Goldsmith, "The Pedagogy of Neural Education" in *Methods and Techniques of Holistic Education*, edited by Isadore L. Sonnier (Springfield, IL: Charles C. Thomas, 1985), 26–27.

15. Based on Ralph Tyler's comment in Jeri Ridings Nowakowski, "On Educational Evaluation: A Conversation with Ralph Tyler," *Educational Leadership* 40 (May 1983): 26.

16. Leslie A. Hart, *Human Brain and Human Learning*.

17. Based on John Barell, "Reflections on Critical Thinking in Secondary Schools," *Educational Leadership* 40 (March 1983): 45–49.

18. John Amos Comenius, *The Great Didactic*.

19. This section, "Learning in Groups," has been based largely on Richard A. Schmuck and Patricia A. Schmuck's excellent *Group Processes in the Classroom* (Dubuque, IA: Brown, 1971).

20. John B. Carroll, "A Model of School Learning," *Teachers College Record* 64 (1963): 723–732.

Chapter 3

Motivation

*The teacher who is attempting to teach
without inspiring the pupil with a desire
to learn is hammering on cold iron.*
Horace Mann

■ ■ ■   Overview

In this chapter we discuss motivation, which is the backbone of all student behavior. To have well-run classes in which students learn, teachers must see to it that students' motivation is favorable toward learning. Lack of motivation is responsible for problems in classroom management, discipline, and control, as well as for deficiencies in learning. To teach, teachers must present worthwhile concepts and provide valuable learning activities. To learn, students must do the work and engage in the learning activities. If teaching and learning are to occur, both students and teachers must be orderly, well-behaved, disciplined, and courteous. None of these conditions is likely to occur in your classroom if students are not well-motivated. Therefore, motivating students should be one of your highest priorities.

Many high school principals feel that student apathy and lack of motivation are about the most troublesome of all the problems they face.(1) Yet in spite of what the principals' report says, it is important to realize that the difficulty is not really so much a *lack* of motivation as it is an *incompatibility* between students' motivation and classroom learning and discipline. Your challenge is to somehow steer their motivation so that it will support your instructional goals.

Therefore, when you teach, it is important that you do your best to build up students' feelings of self-esteem and to try to capitalize on the motives that students already have. Make the learning seem worthwhile, and encourage students to establish suitable objectives. This can be done by putting particular care and thought into making assignments. If you can keep the class moving along in a lively fashion and provide a pleasant, supportive atmosphere in which you reinforce desirable behavior and furnish students with desirable models, the students' resultant motivation should make your teaching pleasurable. Although there is no royal road to student learning, there is no reason why it should be completely frustrating, either. Let us make learning attractive. Motivation is not only a key to learning; it is also a key to good discipline.

■ ■ ■   The Nature of Motivation

Learning results from interactions with the environment—both what individuals do to the environment, and their reactions to what the environment does to them.

As a teacher, your job is to get students to engage in activities that will result in the desired learnings. We call this process *motivation.* By definition, motivation is whatever it is that arouses people to do whatever it is they do.

The Complexity of Motivation

Influencing another person's motivation is not a simple task. First, every person is already a tangle of different and perhaps conflicting motives. Some of these motives are innate, such as the need for security, the avoidance of hunger, the dread of pain, the need for activity, the craving for stimulation, and the need for sex. Other motives are learned. Learned motives include a desire for certainty, the need to achieve, a craving for companionship, the desire to reduce anxiety, the need for independence or dependence, and many more. Innate motives are very powerful, since they comprise basic human needs. When innate motives are aroused, they are likely to take over; learned needs must usually stay on the back burner until the innate needs have been met. Learned motives themselves vary in intensity. Some may be very strong and some very weak; however, the strength of these motives may change, because circumstances can alter cases. Motives, both basic and otherwise, tend to compete with one another.

Second, when students walk into your classroom, each one brings along a hierarchy of motives that range from very strong to very weak. These hierarchies are personal; they differ from individual to individual. One girl's need to achieve may be much stronger than her need for peer approval, whereas her sister may be much more influenced by peer pressure than by a desire to achieve. The priorities within an individual's hierarchy of motives change with time and circumstances. At times everyone suppresses certain desires; at other times circumstances make certain motives almost uncontrollably powerful. Still, most motives retain their relative positions within one's hierarchy of motives even though circumstances modify motives and alter their importance.

Third, motives are affected by many factors. In classroom situations, for instance, student motivation depends not only on the power of the student's competing personal emotions but also on the impact of his or her attitudes toward the subject matter to be learned. Other factors include past experiences, the learner's interests, the difficulty of the learning task, the knowledge of results, the relationship of the activity to the reward for learning, the student's learning style, the teacher's teaching style, the classroom atmosphere, the student's attitude toward the content, and the student's previous experience with the subject.

Stop and Reflect

What is motivation? What are its implications for teaching?

"Learning takes place only through activity." What does this mean? What are the implications for teaching?

What causes people to do things? List the reasons why you have done the more important things you have done today.

Do you recall what your teachers did in your high school classes that made you wish to study and work in their courses? What did they do that caused you to dislike schoolwork in general and the assignments in their courses in particular? What types of teacher actions particularly bother students? What motivates them?

How to Motivate Students

How does one motivate students? Unfortunately, it is not easy. Techniques that work well in one situation may be useless in another. Incentives that create enthusiasm in some individuals in a class leave others completely indifferent. Often teachers depend too much on negative aversive punishment measures in their attempts to motivate and discipline. However, as a rule, the best motivational strategies are positive in nature. The following are some approaches that generally result in positive motivation.

Use both intrinsic and extrinsic motives.
Try to build up students' self-esteem.
Make classes interesting.
Demonstrate enthusiasm.
Add variety and playfulness.
Provide pleasant environments.

Give positive reinforcement.

State learning objectives at the beginning of learning; explain why these objectives are important to the students.

Plan for success.

Induce curiosity.

Correct students in a positive way.(2)

Cultivating Self-Esteem

Everyone wants to feel important and respected by friends and associates. No one wants to be a failure. For this reason, competent teachers give students plenty of opportunities to preen their feathers. Good teachers do their best to help even the least successful students find something of which to be proud.

Recognition of one's success by others is most enjoyable. When this recognition takes a tangible form, it is usually even more enjoyable. In addition, just the feeling of having succeeded, whether anyone praises you or not, can be motivating. See to it that students have many successes in their schoolwork. You can do so by differentiating the work to be done and assigning to your students tasks commensurate with their abilities. Repeated failure soon puts an end to the desire to try.

Figure 3.1 gives some indication of how self-esteem and praise lead to good motivation. You can see that good feelings of self-esteem lead to a higher level of aspiration, and that this in turn leads to an enhanced need for achievement, which leads to stronger efforts to reach the learning goal. You can promote these feelings by showing that you expect students to do well, by giving them positive feedback, and by using praise judiciously.

LEVELS OF ASPIRATION   As a rule, after students experience success, they raise their goals; after failure, they lower them. One's level of aspiration is generally a compromise between fear of failure and hope for success. Success-oriented students usually set themselves reasonable goals that they can reach, but students accustomed to failure tend to set either impossibly high goals—thus perpetuating their failure—or unnecessarily low ones—thus avoiding the stigma of defeat. Because of their fear of failure, low achievers are liable not to try; students who experience success, being more confident, are more likely to exert real effort.

Because these feelings of self-esteem are engendered by success, it is wise to "accentuate the positive." This approach is more profitable because negative motivation tends to inhibit and retard learning and may be accompanied by other

■ **FIGURE 3.1**
Self-Esteem, Praise, and Motivation

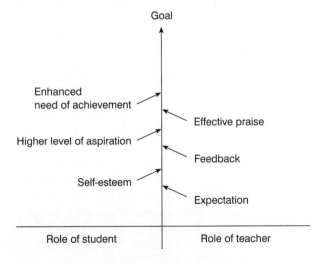

unwelcome side effects. Positive approaches build positive student attitudes and self-esteem. Reasonable objectives and assignments that are challenging, plus positive feedback, promote self-direction and self-confidence. Such feelings arouse in students the will to try to do well.

Of course, there will be times when even the highest achievers fail; this cannot be avoided. This, too, can be a beneficial experience if you treat failure positively. Students can learn from mistakes. Use student failures as a step toward success. If students correct their errors and learn to avoid mistakes, the failures will not have been in vain.

In middle and high school grades, to raise individual levels of aspiration may be difficult, but a positive empathetic class climate, plus plenty of experience with legitimate success, teacher encouragement, and social approval should help. When you encourage students to take over their own learning, students develop feelings of confidence in their own ability. This is especially true if you teach students to do things well, since doing well is a powerful ego booster.

GREAT EXPECTATIONS   When you show students that you confidently expect them to do well, you raise their aspiration levels and self-esteem. This is partly because if you have high expectations for your students, you will act more positively than do most other teachers. Because you expect much of your students, you will be inclined to give them more time to answer questions, to help by providing more clues, to utilize more extended questions, and to offer more praise and encouragement. In other words, you will tend to create a more motivating climate.

It is important, then, that you encourage students by arranging your classes so that students have experiences with success, encouragement, and support.

Providing a Favorable Climate

The school and classroom atmosphere can make the difference between an enthusiastic learner and a hater of a particular subject.(3) The ideal classroom climate seems to be one in which an active partnership exists between the teacher's enthusiasm for teaching the subjects and for the students. It includes five conditions, according to Riordan:

1. Communication is open and active, featuring dialogue rather than monologue.
2. High levels of attraction exist for the group as a whole and among its members.
3. Norms are supportive for getting work done, as well as for optimizing individual opportunities to be different.
4. Members share high amounts of potential and actual influence both with one another and with the leader.
5. The processes of working and developing together as a group are important in themselves and open to examination and change.(4)

Teachers who are punitive, righteous, and power-bent get negative results.(5) Harsh discipline raises resentment, and that resentment usually is transferred to the subject matter. Therefore, for the sake of good motivation, avoid harsh, restrictive disciplinary measures, unpleasant teaching methods, and anything else that may cause dislike and antagonism. Remember that you are trying to sell a valuable commodity. People who dislike you, your product, and your store will not buy from you. Punishment *can* motivate, but it should seldom be used for classroom motivation because it tends to create an atmosphere of surly, sullen repression in which students' work is usually halfhearted.

Since the object of teaching is learning, you need more efficient motivating devices than punishment. Still, students must learn that if they misbehave or neglect their work, they must suffer the consequences. Occasionally, you will have to use negative measures to make these points clear. Poor papers should be redone. Neglected responsibilities should lead to loss of privileges. Undone work should be made up—perhaps during after-school hours or detention periods, or even, on occasion, in another term during a repeated course. Such treatment should always be fair, just, reasonable, and preceded by fair warning.

The knowledge that a customer must be put in a receptive state of mind is almost axiomatic among salespeople. So it is with teaching. The goal is to get learning across to students. If the learning or the learner is disagreeable, it is counterproductive. Making your subject pleasant may seem to be sugarcoating it; however, remember that it is the learning that counts. *Any method or device, within reason, that you can use to expedite learning is legitimate.* If to expedite learning, you must sugarcoat the subject, do not spare the sugar.

A "PLEASANT HOUSE"   It is also axiomatic that boys and girls (and for that matter, men and women) work better in pleasant surroundings. A dark, dirty, repressive atmosphere holds back the average person. In a bright, cheerful atmosphere, students are more likely to become interested in their schoolwork and perform it conscientiously. Therefore, strive for a pleasant classroom.

While it may be that you can do little about the classroom's decor (although you can usually help it considerably), you *can* do something about the social setting. Social setting has much to do with motivation. For instance, in small schools there is generally a more personal social climate which seems to enhance motivation, probably because everyone is known.(6) Although teachers in larger schools cannot replicate all the virtues of a small school, they can take steps to make their classes warm and intimate by adding a personal touch.

The spirit of your students can also be enhanced by eliminating an overly serious attitude in the classroom. Learning is not necessarily solemn. People learn better in a happy frame of mind. Laughter, fun, humor, cooperation, pleasantness, and politeness all make the classroom a happy place. Vittorino da Feltre, the great Renaissance schoolmaster, called his school "The Pleasant House." As part of your motivational technique, strive to make your school a "pleasant house."

CREATURE COMFORTS   Finally, remember the "creature comforts." As we have seen, innate motives and basic needs are very powerful. Therefore, be aware and try to take care of students' physical needs. Students who are sleepy, thirsty, hungry, hot, tired, or craving physical activity do not learn academic material with optimum efficiency. They need breaks, physical activity, comfortable classroom conditions, relief from physical stress, and opportunities to socialize. In addition, they need an occasional change of pace. No one can keep going at top level continuously; therefore, try to provide opportunities for students to relax and to consolidate their learning. On the other hand, students cannot stand continuous low-activity levels, either. They work best when periods of strong stimulation are interspersed with periods of rest, relaxation, and rehabilitation.

Stop and Reflect

What does psychology tell us about the effect of praise, reproof, rewards, and punishment on learning? What are the implications for teaching?

Should emulation, competition, and rivalry be used to motivate classroom learning? What are the advantages and disadvantages of each?

Evaluate sarcasm, ridicule, and fear as motivating techniques.

What will you do to raise the level of aspiration in your classes?

Making Learning Seem Worthwhile

To make learning more purposeful to students, introduce learning tasks in ways that stimulate motivation, that is, note purposes, note intended outcomes and future uses, and stimulate curiosity. Show enthusiasm when you make introductions to material. Real enthusiasm is hard to resist; it soon rubs off on students—perhaps in spite of themselves. Enthusiasm alone will not inspire every member of the class, but it helps. If you do not like a subject, you really have no business teaching it.

IMMEDIATELY USEFUL LEARNING   Students are more likely to be motivated if they see that what is to be learned is useful *now.* Whenever possible, try to make students aware of the immediate value in their lessons. You can do so by centering classwork on everyday concerns of students, by including current issues in the school and community, by pointing out how the classroom learning may be used in other classes and activities, and by consciously attempting to tie the lessons to the present attitudes and interests of students. For example, in a mathematics class you can use graphs to illustrate problems being studied in the social studies class, or you can relate the study of percentages to the standings of the major league baseball teams. Such techniques are much more likely to succeed in setting students to work than are exhortations to "study because you will need to know it in college."

APPLYING THE LEARNING   Using what one has learned is one of the best ways to show that the learning is worthwhile. As Torrance asserts

Many children and young people not now motivated to learn in school will become excited about learning and will achieve in line with their potentialities, if given a chance to use what is learned, if given a chance to communicate what is learned, if we show an interest in what is learned rather than in grades, if learning tasks are not too easy or too difficult, if there is a chance to use their best abilities and preferred ways of learning, if we reward a variety of kinds of excellence, and if learning experiences are given purposefulness.(7)

Stop and Reflect

Select a course you probably will teach. Why should students study it?
Can you justify teaching your major fields?
Go through a textbook you might use in your teaching. How can you make this material seem worthwhile to a group of teenagers? Why is it worthwhile? In what ways can students immediately apply the subject matter learned in units of this text?

Utilizing Present Motives

INTRINSIC AND EXTRINSIC MOTIVATION   Ordinarily, learning proceeds best when it is intrinsically motivated, that is, when students learn what they learn because they want to learn it. An example of intrinsic motivation is learning to drive a car. Most young people learn to drive because knowing how to drive has intrinsic value to them.

When the things students should learn in their classes seem to have no intrinsic value to them, extrinsic motivation can be used. In this case, teachers try to provide students with a stimulus to learn even though students do not see value in the learning. An example of this type of motivation might be a student who learns geometric theorems because she wishes to earn an A in the course or because her parent has promised her a reward if she learns them. Here, the goal is not the learning itself but something that can be obtained through the learning. Such goals are called *incentives.* They are really ulterior motives for undertaking activities otherwise considered not worth doing. Ordinarily, it is preferable for students to do their schoolwork because of its intrinsic value to them.(8) When this proves impossible or impractical, it may be necessary to fall back on extrinsic motives to obtain the desired response. However, modern research tells us that in the long run, dependence on extrinsic rewards is more likely to kill motivation than to enhance it.(9)

HARNESSING STUDENT MOTIVES   As we have seen, every child comes to school with certain basic drives. These motives are often more powerful than any incentive you can invent. Be alert to these drives, and use them in your teaching whenever you can. If you cannot utilize them, at least strive to adapt your classwork so that it does not conflict directly with natural motivation. For instance, in a social studies class one morning, the juniors were all upset because they had had a most interesting and exciting speaker from Russia at a school assembly. However, because some faculty members dominated the discussion, the students had not had a chance to ask the speaker their questions. So, rather than go on with the prepared lesson, the teacher took time to discuss their questions, in this way easing their frustration and taking advantage of their interest.

Let us look now at some of the motives that you may be able to capitalize on.

STUDENT CURIOSITY   People are naturally curious. Watch children examine things. Listen to them asking questions: Why? Why? Why? This curiosity abides in adults also, and it is probably just as strong. Witness the crowds that gather whenever there is an accident. Even when people are not naturally curious about a certain thing, usually it is fairly easy to arouse their curiosity. One way of doing so is to puzzle them a little so that they ask themselves what will happen next, or what the result will be. Another is to make use of suspense. If you can capitalize on the curiosity of youth, your students will do their schoolwork more eagerly because they will want to find out. This is an important type of motivation.

ATTITUDES AND IDEALS   Among the motives students bring to school are their ideals and attitudes. Try to harness the attitudes of cooperativeness, neatness, diligence, fairness, courtesy, patriotism, and honesty, and utilize them in your teaching. Often students will willingly carry out group-project roles they do not particularly like because the teacher has appealed to their sense of cooperation. Undoubtedly, you can think of examples in your own school life in which you have performed downright distasteful tasks simply because an attitude or ideal told you that this was the thing to do under the circumstances. This type of experience frequently leads us to our most useful and valuable learning. Sometimes, in spite of our prejudice, the experience itself turns out to be extremely rewarding. Many older students find great enjoyment in academic activities they thought to be distasteful when they first encountered them. Adults have developed fulfilling careers stemming from academic tasks they once had to do against their will.

NEED FOR CERTAINTY   Among the learned motives is the need for certainty. Sometimes people like to be surprised, but most of the time they like to know what to expect. Students want to know: Where do we stand? What is expected? What is acceptable? What is the routine? By giving classes structure, teachers can meet this need for certainty. By building into the routine things such as daily classroom procedures, carefully presented assignments, clear directions, definite standards of behavior, precise delineation of requirements, well-organized orderly classes, and explicit feedback, your teaching will provide the structure necessary for students to understand where they stand and what they must do. Without this structure, both students and classes tend to drift. With it, the students (and the teacher) feel more secure.

NEED FOR SECURITY   Any threat to a young person's security makes learning more difficult. For this reason, you should avoid using fear as a classroom motivational device, even though fear is one of the most powerful of motives.

Frightened persons cannot think well. When intensely afraid, they may become completely disorganized. Constant worry, a milder form of fear, may lead to mental and emotional idiosyncrasies if not to actual illness. A little anxiety can be motivating, but too much anxiety is debilitating. Adolescents have fears and worries enough without teachers creating more. Fear as a motivator should be saved for such important things as life-and-death situations—for example, to prevent young people from driving too fast or to keep little children from crossing the street alone.(10)

Because of these reasons, overemphasis on tests and marks should be discouraged. Also to be avoided are class recitations in which students are shamed if they answer incorrectly. Ignorance is not a crime to be punished. Overharshness keeps students from trying their best and tends to make students who do try very rigid so that they cannot think their best. Students learn better in a more relaxed atmosphere. Your classes will become more profitable when you find good ways to reduce anxiety to reasonable levels.(11)

DESIRE FOR ADVENTURE AND ACTION   Paradoxically, the need for security is accompanied by a desire for action, adventure, and excitement. This desire causes young people to take chances that seem to belie their desire for security. Students often balance these needs by seeking adventure in groups and by soliciting the approval and admiration of their peers for their adventuresomeness. You would do well to feature, at least part of the time, activities and materials that have plenty of excitement and action. Use competitive games to give excitement to practice and drill lessons. Enrich English classes with adventure stories. Provide puzzles to spice up mathematics classes. Focus on the exploits of such men and women as George Washington, Lewis and Clark, Chief Joseph, Andrew Jackson, Peggy O'Neill Eaton, Sacajawea, Frederick Douglass, Amelia Earhart, and Martin Luther King, Jr., to give history courses excitement and adventure.

DESIRE TO PLAY AND HAVE FUN   Enjoying oneself is a prominent goal in every person's life. We all need to play and amuse ourselves—even hypochondriacs enjoy their poor health! This motive is closely akin to the need for action, adventure, and excitement. The usual class abounds with opportunities to use games—one example is to use pseudobaseball games in drill activities. One New Jersey high school teacher adds fun to tests by including silly questions such as, "In ten words or less, explain why this is the best course you ever heard of."

NEED FOR FRIENDSHIPS   One of the most powerful natural drives is the desire for friendship. Youths are gregarious. Any attempt to keep them quietly working by themselves in a crowded classroom for long periods of time is against the laws of nature. Capable teachers usually refrain from making quiet periods overly long and are not too harsh on students who feel the need for conversing with their friends. Youth's gregariousness and friendship can be of considerable help to the able teacher—especially in group situations and during group activities.

Friendships are exceedingly important for adolescents, but perhaps the most important of all are the friendships based on sexual interest that begin to form at this stage of life. Sex and the desire to establish one's own home are basic drives. Their power and importance should not be underestimated.

During transescence, the need for friendship creates strong peer pressures. As beginning adolescents start to free themselves from parental supervision, they turn to their peers for support and approval. Consequently, transescents tend to conform with the norms of their peer group, although in the long run they may hold to the standards taught them by their parents and other adults. Peer pressures continue to be powerful in adolescence and youth. As people get older and more sophisticated, their need to conform usually lessens.

Stop and Reflect

Perhaps you can think of examples of natural motives interfering with the normal course of learning. Have there been any instances in your college classes when the teaching has been hampered by the natural motivation of the students? What, if anything, did the instructor do? What might have been done?

What student attitudes and ideals would be desirable aids to classroom motivation? How might you use them? How might you develop them?

What could you do to encourage favorable student attitudes toward the subject you hope to teach?

UTILIZING AND BUILDING INTERESTS

THE IMPORTANCE OF INTEREST   Students undoubtedly learn more efficiently those things that interest them; therefore, you should try harnessing student interest as a means to effective teaching. This doctrine of interest does not imply that the whims of students should determine the curriculum. It does imply, however, that whenever possible, you should capitalize on student interests that are already established or, if suitable student interests are not established, you should try to create interest.

As we grow older, most of us find it increasingly difficult to know and understand the interests of young people. The goals of youth are not always the same as the goals of adults. Adults are sometimes shocked to find that the things they feel ought to be of the utmost intrinsic value to all people seem to be quite worthless from the perspective of young people. Even young adults find that what is intensely interesting and exciting to them at age 22 may not capture a single response in a group of 15-year-olds. For this reason, make a point to find out the interests, attitudes, ideals, and goals of your students. Once you know what your students think is important, you can adapt your motivational techniques accordingly.

Students who have strong college or vocational goals may persevere through lackluster lessons and courses, but most students who find their coursework drab and uninteresting will reject it. It may help if you talk over with students the possible benefits of studying the course or unit. In doing so, remember that exhortations to study are not nearly as productive as actually showing students how they can make use of the learning. If you can encourage students to relate the learning to their own interests, so much the better. Using student ideas may convince them that the subject has interest to them. An English teacher, for instance, who encouraged her students to develop their own ideas, found that their interest in literature increased greatly.

PARTICIPATING IN ONE'S OWN LEARNING   Increasing student involvement in learning through democratic participatory approaches may well stimulate student interest, as well as cause students to accept more responsibility and expend greater effort.

Learning may be its own reward, since it is always emotionally tinged and usually quite gratifying to the learner. As new vistas open up for students and they experience the excitement of new ideas and skills, as well as the sheer involvement of the learning process, they can get caught in the excitement of intellectual attainment. For many adults, the intellectual experience alone is enough to keep them working diligently all the rest of their lives. It is important that you give students opportunities to really participate in true learning experiences. When you do, you give them a chance to share the emotional experience that Keats had "On First Looking into Chapman's Homer."

> *Then felt I like some watcher of the skies*
> *When a new planet swims into his ken;*
> *Or like stout Cortez* when with eagle eyes*
> *He stared at the Pacific—and all his men*
> *Look'd at each other with a wild surmise—*
> *Silent, upon a peak in Darien.*

Such experiences make learning worthwhile; for the person who has a real chance to participate in his or her own learning, these experiences are rather frequent occurrences. Many scholars derive their greatest motivation from their involvement in the learning. Fresh ideas and fresh insights really make life exciting. In addition, these things help students realize that they are responsible for their own learning. The assumption of such responsibility is one of the strongest of motivating factors.

What people elect to do themselves usually interests them more than something imposed on them by someone else. At least, they are likely to think it is more interesting and are, therefore, more willing to start learning it. Consequently, students who plan their own activities may begin the activities more willingly than students who do not. If you allow students to pick what they will read, or to choose which of the activities they will do or in which order they will do them, or to discuss what is important to learn in the new unit or topic, then a favorable attitude in the students toward the work to be done is usually engendered. This favorable attitude also gives you a considerable advantage: If you can capitalize on this start, quite often the students' enthusiasm will carry over to the study of the rest of the topic or activity. Therefore, try to encourage student participation in the selection of topics and activities to capitalize on their motivational value. Involving students in such decision making is discussed in Chapter 5, "Planning for Teaching."

PROBLEMS AND PROBLEM SOLVING   You can often create interest by utilizing problems and problem-solving techniques. Problem solving is particularly useful in challenging the interests of young people. Humans have always loved to try to solve problems. Having a challenging problem to solve appeals to the natural drives of activity, success, and curiosity. Problems posed to students should not be too hard, neither should they be too easy. Although you should be ready to help and guide, beware of helping too much. Most people prefer to solve their problems themselves, free from kibitzing.

SOMETHING SUITABLE FOR EVERYONE   What we know about individual differences tells us that not all students are interested in the same things. This complicates the process of motivating a class of adolescents. We want our classes to seem worthwhile to the students so that the students will work at high levels, but what one student finds worthwhile, another may find a waste of time. What is the answer? Obvi-

---

*Keats was mixed up. It was really Balboa who stared at the Pacific. In former times, the Isthmus of Panama was known as the Isthmus of Darien.

ously, one way out is to provide enough types of activities and materials so that everyone finds something interesting and worthwhile. Try to arrange students' activities so that they have opportunities to pursue individual interests.

Stop and Reflect

It has been suggested that students could well participate in determining which short story or novel the class should read, or in deciding the order in which units should be learned, or in discussing what should be emphasized in a particular unit. Give specific examples of matters that students could decide in teacher-student planning in your own field.

Pick a unit from a middle or high school text for a course you might teach. What would you do to make this topic exciting? How could you involve the students in democratic participatory approaches in this area?

Getting Set

SET INDUCTION   When student interest in your subject is minimal or when you and the students are encountering something new, interest can often be stimulated by set induction activities. For instance, a student teacher in a junior high school general science class performed an experiment in which he attempted to demonstrate the power of air pressure by creating a vacuum in a large can. He first talked to the students, telling them what he intended to do, and then asked them what they thought would happen when he created the vacuum. Several theories were proposed, among them the theory that the pressure of the atmosphere would crush the can. "All right," he said, "let's see if the atmosphere can smash the can." He then heated some water in the can, filling it full of steam. Capping the steam-filled can he said, "O.K., now let's see what happens." An air of intense expectancy hung over the classroom as the eighth-graders stared at the can. Suddenly, one student yelled, "There it goes!" as the can slowly started to crumble. In a few minutes, the class was off on a lively discussion of what had made the can "smash." By using a simple experiment to harness the natural appeal of curiosity through suspense, the student teacher had aroused the class to productive activity.

This type of activity is often called *set induction*. A set is, psychologically speaking, a predisposition to respond or act, as in "on your mark, get set, go!" In most cases, starting off a new lesson or activity with an interesting, exciting opener will catch the students' attention so that they will get set for the new activity. Such techniques are useful for launching units, lessons, and all sorts of classroom activities, assignments, and learning tasks. Techniques that arouse students' interest, tickle their curiosity, point out relationships between the new learning and past learning, and establish the worth of the new endeavor are effective for this purpose. The introduction should set the proper mood, give the students adequate direction so that they can get on with the task, and orient them so that they will act and react properly as they proceed with the learning task.

SETTING DIRECTIONS   Both long-term and short-term goals are necessary to keep students moving in the way they should go. Long-term goals are necessary for giving overall direction, but short-term goals move us through daily tasks and keep us going forward. For this reason, if classes are to be worthwhile, you must have a definite goal for each lesson. Your students should know approximately what this goal is and why it is important, and thus adopt the goal for themselves.

As a matter of fact, students always participate in selecting their own objectives anyway. That is to say, they establish tasks. These tasks are in essence their objectives, even though they may be considerably different from what you had in mind. Your role is to provide situations in which the students will select, or accept, tasks that will help them toward the learning desired. You can do so through the use of directions, advance organizers, study guides, assignments, and learning packets. The most important of these is the assignment.

Stop and Reflect

Describe a set induction activity you might use to get students interested in a topic you expect to teach.

Assignments

Good assignments are absolutely essential for both motivating and guiding learning. It has often been said that students usually would be quite willing to do their schoolwork if they could only figure out what the teacher wanted them to do and how to do it. There is more than a kernel of truth in this statement. Most of us have been in classes in which we did not know what to do. This dilemma is all too common. If you find your students are not doing their assignments, but instead are saying, "I don't know," or "I didn't have a book," and the like, check your directions. Perhaps the fault lies in the assignment. If you hope to keep students working, you must be sure that the assignments are definite, the directions are clear, and the materials are available.

PURPOSES In the past, assignments have been almost synonymous with homework. In many classrooms, even today, the assignment consists of a hurried instruction at the end of the period—often drowned out by the clamor of the bell and the scuffling of feet eager to be on their way. Good assignments should be viewed in a different way: as a job to be done, whether at home or in class. It may be assigned by the teacher or arrived at through the cooperative effort of both teacher and students. No matter who prepares the assignment, it should serve the following purposes:

1. To set the direction of study and outline the scope of the task.
2. To motivate the students and prepare them for the task.
3. To help the learners establish the means for accomplishing the task, that is, establish possible methods and materials. If necessary, show them how.
4. To adapt the tasks to the needs of the various students.

The assignment is an essential factor in motivation and a basic part of any lesson. Let us look at these functions briefly.

TO SET THE DIRECTION AND THE SCOPE OF THE TASK It is almost impossible to do anything unless one knows what to do and how to do it. The purpose of the assignment is to make each student's task clear and definite. Some teachers merely tell students what is to be done; others develop the task cooperatively with the group. Whichever method you use, however, try to make sure that each student knows exactly what is expected.

To this end, the assignment must be clear and definite. It usually helps to give an assignment to students in writing. Short assignments may be written on the chalkboard. A wise practice is to reserve a specific spot on the chalkboard for assignments and always to write the daily assignment in that spot. Longer assignments should be duplicated. By writing out the directions for a specific assignment, the chances for students to forget what it is they were going to do is minimized. Also, setting the assignment down in writing helps to lessen chances for misunderstandings—both on the part of the students and the teacher—of what the task is.

TO PREPARE STUDENTS FOR THE JOB TO BE DONE   This preparation includes supplying the background material students need before starting the new task, and providing for adequate motivation. Since the assignment determines what is to be done, it is particularly important to communicate to students the reason(s) why they should do the assignment and why it is worth doing.

TO POINT OUT HOW TO DO IT   Although you should avoid spoonfeeding your students, you should also be sure they know how to go about carrying out the task. If the job is to study a reading section, for instance, point out the key words and make suggestions concerning concepts to look for. Try to make sure that your students know how to use the methods and materials available to them.

TO PROVIDE EVERY STUDENT WITH AN APPROPRIATE TASK   It is hard to prove that any subject is truly essential, except by relating it to the ways in which it meets the needs of young people. If this is true, any assignment that places the subject matter above the individual differences of your students is of doubtful validity.

THE MARKS OF A GOOD ASSIGNMENT   What, then, are the marks of a good assignment? The following list suggests some criteria for evaluating an assignment:

1. Is it worthwhile?
2. Does it seem worthwhile to the students? In other words, does it capitalize on their interests or create interest? Can students see a real reason for doing the assignment?
3. Is it clear?
4. Is it definite?
5. Does it provide for the differences in students—that is, their different aptitudes, abilities, and interests?
6. Is it reasonable as far as length and difficulty are concerned?
7. Does it show the students how to go about it? Does it suggest methods and materials that may be used profitably?
8. Does it provide the students with the background necessary for completing the assignment satisfactorily (e.g., vocabulary)?

Stop and Reflect

Use the list describing a good assignment to judge assignments given in your college courses.

Do your college assignments perform the functions assignments should perform? If they fail, in what ways do they fail?

A student teacher's assignment in his United States history class was, "Read pages 184–297 for tomorrow." In what way is this assignment deficient?

MAKING THE ASSIGNMENT   In order to make an assignment effective, take time to develop it sufficiently. Even a short assignment may require 10 minutes for its presentation. For longer assignments, using one or more entire periods is not unusual. To develop properly a long-term assignment or a unit assignment in less than a period is virtually impossible, particularly if the assignment is cooperatively developed by the teacher and class. Beware of giving an assignment at the last minute just as the bell is going to ring (or has started to ring). Students seldom take such assignments seriously. They cannot listen to instructions carefully in the last-minute rush. There is not time for them to digest the assignment, to ask questions, or to make notes, or for you to give the students direction, to clarify what is to be done, and to motivate the students.

It matters little whether the assignment is developed at the beginning, middle, or end of a period as long as you allow time enough to do the job properly and make sure that the assignment fits into that spot naturally. Therefore, give homework assignments at the propitious moment in the lesson when the lesson's content serves as a background for making the assignment.

TEACHING STUDY SKILLS IN THE ASSIGNMENT   Although teachers often neglect it, an assignment offers a golden opportunity for teaching study skills. It gives the teacher and the students an opportunity to discuss the materials and sources available, how to use the materials, the relative merits of various study techniques and procedures, and ways to carry out these techniques and procedures.

The reverse side of the assignment coin can also be used to improve study skills. After an assignment has been completed, students can learn about different kinds of study skills and their efficiency by discussing the methods different students used to study the assignment and the relative success of the various methods.

ORGANIZERS   An advance organizer can be used to motivate and give direction to student learning. In teaching, organizers appear as introductions to the unit or content to be learned, and are designed to give the learners a structure to build on as they learn—or, in the words of their inventor, to provide "an educational scaffolding for the stable incorporation and retention of the more detailed and differentiated material that follows."(12) Organizers may be either written or visual. For example, an organizer may consist of a short exposition that provides students the information they need to tackle the new learning (an expository organizer); or, an organizer may show students graphically the relationship of what they have already learned to what they are about to learn (a graphic organizer). In either case, organizers give principles on which students can hang the facts and concepts they will learn, and in general help them see the meaning and relationship of the new subject matter to be learned. In this way, organizers serve both to motivate and to give direction to the students' learning.

According to Richard E. Mayer, organizers usually have the following characteristics:

(1) Short set of verbal or visual information, (2) Presented prior to learning a larger body of to-be-learned information, (3) Containing no specific content from the to-be-learned information, (4) Providing a means of generating the logical relationships among the elements in the to-be-learned information, (5) Influencing the learner's encoding process. The manner in which an organizer influences encoding may serve either of two functions: to provide a new general organization as an assimilative context that would not have normally been present, or to activate a general organization from the learner's existing knowledge that would not have normally been used to assimilate the new material.(13)

Mayer goes on to say that "existing research seems to suggest that subject areas that might be most influenced by organizers are topics in mathematics and science."(14)

Organizers presented as diagrams, models, or illustrations are especially helpful for alerting students to the relationships and structure in the content they are about to study. For teaching reading within a content subject, Herber recommends the use of "graphic organizers" that give students a "structural overview" of what they are to read and study.(15) He also recommends that students develop graphic organizers of their own as postreading activities.

The following is an example of how to prepare such an organizer:

1. Prepare a list of words that seem to you to be the most important in your unit. Include both new and old words.
2. Arrange the words into a diagram that shows the relationships among the ideas to be taught in the unit. Add and delete words as necessary to make the diagram clear and accurate.
3. For the first class of the unit, put your diagram on the board. As you do so, explain the words and tell why you placed them in this pattern. Try to get as much class participation as you can. Be sure that you and the students discuss the reasons for the placement of all the words, and the relationships among the words and ideas they express.
4. At opportune moments in your teaching, refer to the diagram. Sketch portions of it on the board, project the diagram by the overhead projector, or give out copies of the diagram to the students so that they can study their arrangements as you discuss them. Have the students contribute to the discussion of the meanings of the words and the relationships of the concepts they represent.(16)

This type of organizer will presumably direct students toward the key concepts and the relationships to be studied and learned, as well as provide a scaffold upon which to build their learning.

Stop and Reflect

Make up an organizer for the reading in this section of the text.

STUDY GUIDES AND LEARNING PACKETS   Study guides and learning packets serve somewhat the same purpose. Basically, they are usually duplicated materials that outline for the students what they are to study; ask questions that will highlight important points to study; suggest problems that will initiate students' thinking; and provide exercises that will build up concepts, show relationships, and generally identify and pull together the ideas, skills, and attitudes that are the instructional goals.*

COMBATING BOREDOM   People must have stimulation. Lack of stimulation causes boredom—perhaps the greatest cause of discipline problems and nonlearning in our schools.

To combat boredom, try to add life to classes by introducing interesting, exciting materials and inventive teaching techniques. You can also address the problem of boredom by talking things over with students to make them aware of constructive activities they can use to make studying more interesting. In the course of conversations with individuals, you can bring up such questions as the following:

---

*See Chapter 8.

Question 1:   Are you *aware* of what you are doing?
Question 2:   What are the *consequences* of what you are doing?
Question 3:   Is what you are doing *useful* to you as a student?
Question 4:   If not, what *constructive plan* can you make for dealing with your boredom?(17)

Such questioning should not be inquisitorial; instead, it should come from the natural flow of the conversation. Aim it at helping students understand themselves and their options.

Keeping Classes Lively

Students are naturally active. They do not relish sitting still all day. Because they enjoy doing things, activities in which they can actively participate interest them. Moreover, once students are actively participating, their interest is much more easily kept at a high level. Witness the difference between a lecture and a workshop or laboratory. Quite often, the very people who anxiously wait for the bell during lecture classes do not know when to stop during a workshop or laboratory situation. To keep motivation high, use such activities to the optimum. Active, lively lessons may make even rather uninteresting subject matter seem fascinating.

Once a class is started, keep constantly alert to prevent dead spots from creeping into the lesson. Dull classes lead to "wool gathering," and students often will switch their attention and interests to other less desirable activities and goals. In every meeting of every class, students should feel that the class is going somewhere important. They should also feel a certain amount of pressure, however gentle, to exert themselves to go along too.

Providing Challenging, Not Discouraging, Work

One way to reduce boredom is to see that the work is challenging but not discouraging. Some adolescents do not do their schoolwork well because it does not challenge them. This is particularly true of gifted and talented students. Young people want to test themselves; they want to exceed the limits. They do not want "baby work." An industrial arts teacher, for instance, was having trouble with discipline. This was not surprising, since the class mostly consisted of discontented boys who were impatiently awaiting their sixteenth birthdays. The situation was aggravated by the teacher, however. In an attempt to make the instruction fit the needs of the boys, the teacher had devised a course in home mechanics. The activities consisted of such things as puttying windows, changing fuses, and the like. These activities were not interesting to the class and provided no challenge. When the teacher switched to assigning more challenging activities, his discipline problems abated considerably. On the other hand, work that is too difficult can be frustrating. When people see little hope of succeeding, they usually do not try very hard.(18)

VARYING THE STIMULUS   Although too much variety in method or activities may be confusing to some learners, effective teachers vary their strategies and tactics from time to time to keep motivation high. They liven up their classes with such interest-catching tactics as the use of vivid illustrations, audiovisual aids, and demonstrations. Even such a simple technique as moving around the classroom while teaching can help. Too much movement on the part of the teacher can be distracting, of course, but a moderate amount of changing teaching positions (e.g., the side, middle, or back of the room) can aid both control and motivation. Similarly, skilled teachers use head, body, arm, and hand movements effectively. They also take care to focus students' attention on important content by tactics such as using verbal emphasis, stressing key words, or incorporating gestures during teaching (e.g., pointing or pounding on the desk).

Changing the tempo of instruction is also a valuable technique. Pauses in lectures and discussions can be effective. Use them to call student attention to important points, to provide opportunities for ideas to sink in or gel, or to give students a chance to think. Shifting the sensory pattern (e.g., from oral stimuli to visual by changing from a lecture to an audiovisual aid) may give the class a lift. So may switching the interaction from teacher-group activities (e.g., lectures) to teacher-student activities (e.g., making a point with one student), or to student-student activities (e.g., small-group projects, interstudent explanations, and discussions).

Almost any type of activity change can relieve humdrum classes, but do not overdo it. Too much change may deprive students of the security gained from an accepted pattern or framework. This is particularly true for at-risk students.

PROVIDING FEEDBACK   Students need to know how they are progressing. Knowing one's own progress makes it possible to reform goals and take further strides ahead. The knowledge that a certain amount has been accomplished is often sufficient cause to go further—with renewed vigor. To make the most of this phenomenon, try to see that students understand and appreciate their own achievement. For this knowledge to be really effective, students need to know how they did almost immediately. If, for instance, you take a couple of weeks to read and evaluate papers, their motivational value may have pretty well evaporated by the time you hand back the papers. Feedback should also be quite specific. A simple mark on the paper does not really help students' motivation much. If your students are going to understand how they did, you must provide some analysis of each paper's strengths and weaknesses. A checklist or comments written in the margin can serve this purpose. Students can improve only if they understand where they hit and where they missed the mark.[*]

If you expect high performance, utilize class comments, group corrective comments, private conversations, and detailed written comments to make sure that students know what standards you expect them to be measured against, know in what areas they are doing well, and know what they can do to do better.(19) As always in teaching, accentuate the positive.

Effective teachers find positive reinforcement techniques useful in discussions and recitations. Reinforcement of this sort can increase student participation, which in turn causes students to become more involved with the material to be learned, and to pay better attention. Examples of positive reinforcers include the following:

1. Using verbal clues (e.g., "That's right," "Go ahead," "Yes," "O.K.")
2. Using facial expressions (e.g., smiles)
3. Using gestures (e.g., nods)
4. Using tangible rewards
5. Writing responses on the board

Negative reinforcers may also be used. Examples of negative reinforcers include:

1. Using words expressing disapproval (e.g., "No," "That's not right")
2. Using facial expressions (e.g., scowls, frowns)
3. Using negative gestures (e.g., shaking the head)
4. Using silence, moving away from students

PRAISE   The judicious use of praise can be a strong motivating force. Used indiscriminately, however, praise can lose its impact and can even backfire. Beware of using it too profusely, which tends to make it meaningless to students. To be effec-

_____
[*]See Chapter 14 for further explanation of this concept.

tive, praise should be sincere, deserved, and immediate. Praise that is unearned is soon recognized as empty flattery. Praise should also be specific. Tell students exactly what about their work is praiseworthy and why. Informing students of the frame of reference you use in making your judgment not only helps direct the students' efforts but also provides them with a goal at which to aim.

Stop and Reflect

What does psychology tell us about the effect of praise, reproof, rewards, and punishment on learning? What are the implications for teaching?

Should emulation, competition, and rivalry be used to motivate classroom learning? What are the advantages and disadvantages of each?

Evaluate the following as motivating techniques: sarcasm, ridicule, fear.

MARKS AND GRADES   The incentive most used in schools today is the school mark, or grade. That it should have become so important is most unfortunate because in many classes, the real learning and understanding tend to be lost in the race for the highest grade. When this happens, too much stress on the incentive defeats the purpose of education. When students and teachers place too much value on grades, one result is cheating. Another is the transient learning that often occurs from cramming for tests—knowledge that is "here today but gone tomorrow."(20)

Letter grades have equally failed as a motivating force for nonacademic, non-college-bound students. Our grading practices are very discouraging to them. Only in schools is it necessary to compete with everyone in the total population. Because students may feel that they will not do well and because they suspect that their marks will never really have much influence on their lives, many of these young people do not care about school marks. To them, good grades are unattainable and not very desirable. Even to the average student, grades are not a very sharp goad. Their only effect seems to be to arouse spasmodic bursts of effort to cram in as much knowledge as possible during certain periods of stress. So it is that the typical classroom reward structure is effective with only the top students.(21) As a rule, when the teacher promises good grades for hard work, 25 percent of the students will respond positively, 75 percent will not; if the teacher threatens poor grades for poor work, again about 25 percent will respond and 75 percent will not.(22)

Actually, it seems that marks, or grades, give the least incentive to those who need it the most—students who are at-risk or who demonstrate little ability. Rather than depending too much on grades for motivation, it is ordinarily more profitable to adjust the lessons and curriculum so that the learning appeals to students' intrinsic motives, and to use such techniques as computer-assisted instruction or continuous promotion as additional incentives.

Stop and Reflect

It has been stated that grades, prizes, and punishment are poor motivating devices for school use. Why do some authorities take this position? Do you agree? Defend your position.

What techniques might a teacher use to induce students to adopt goals that will lead to the learnings desired by the teacher? Consider such things as the following:

teacher talks and lectures	*demonstrations*
field trips	*suspense*

movies   *problem raising*
stories   *quizzes and tests*
dramatizations   *study guides*
organizers

REINFORCEMENT THEORY AND TECHNIQUES   Basic to reinforcement theory is the belief that people tend to behave in ways that produce some sort of reward that is valuable to them. That is to say, when a behavior results in a positive outcome, it is reinforced and so is more likely to be repeated. Therefore, in order to encourage students to engage in a certain action, reward them when they engage in that action. When you wish to discourage students from certain misbehavior, reward them when they engage in behavior incompatible with the misbehavior. In teaching, reinforcement theory tells us that the basic principle to follow is to give praise and attention to student behavior that facilitates learning, and to avoid giving rewards for behavior that hinders learning.

For instance, as Margaret Cohen suggests, teachers can facilitate motivation by using reinforcers that give students "information about their competence" or help them accomplish an "instructional activity"; these activities should "involve memorization, convergent thinking, applying formulas and using well learned skills".(23)

Earlier in the chapter we tried to show how to harness your students' attitudes and ideals. Fortunately, attitudes and ideals are acquired, or learned, characteristics; so it *is* possible to teach students new attitudes and ideals and to change old ones. Therefore, do your best to create and cultivate attitudes and ideals that foster learning. Reinforcement techniques useful for this purpose include contingency contracts based on Grandma's law, reinforcement menus, and modeling. While all these techniques are useful, they are also dangerous. Be on guard against using them to manipulate young people.

CONTINGENCY CONTRACTS   Contingency contracts are particularly effective at the secondary school level, according to Clarizio.(24) They are based on the common practice that L. E. Homme calls Grandma's law: "If first you do this, then you can do that (or have that)." Most of us probably remember this law in the form of "If you first eat your vegetables, then you can have some dessert." To be effective, the contingency contract must lead to an extremely desirable reward that the student cannot attain outside of the contract. These contracts are best worked out by the teacher and the students together before the term of the contract begins. Occasionally, teachers may set up the details of the contract unilaterally and get the students to agree to its terms, but this procedure is usually not very satisfactory. Sometimes students may work out the terms of the contract and present them to the teacher. Figure 3.2 is an example of a contingency contract.

REINFORCEMENT MENUS   A reinforcement menu is similar to the contingency contract. It consists of a list of highly desirable activities that students can do once they have completed a specific assignment. Ordinarily, these activities should be congruent with educational goals, but this is not always necessary. Activities that are pure fun or relief from class activities may sometimes be more effective. An example of a reinforcement menu appears in Figure 3.3.

MODELING   Much of what we learn we learn by imitating a model. It is imperative then to try to provide students with good models to copy. To be effective, these models should be highly esteemed by students. Models whom students do not

Between (<u>student's name</u>) and (<u>teacher's name</u>)

Student agrees to
1. Complete assigned homework—   5 points
   if well done and accurate   2 extra points
2. Hand in assignments on due date—   5 points
   if handed in before due date   2 extra points

Teacher agrees to
1. Check homework and give appropriate number of points to the student (as indicated above)
2. Not reprimand or comment when homework is not completed or handed in.
   (a) If two consecutive assignments are not handed in, 3 points are subtracted from accumulated total.
   (b) If three consecutive assignments are not completed and handed in, the contract is considered void.

Student can exchange his points for
(1) Free period time during class (5 points per 5 minutes).
(2) Access to the driving range (10 points per 15 minutes).
(3) Excuse from the weekly social studies (30 points each week).
(4) Being helper to shop teacher (10 points per 15 minutes).
(5) Credits for purchase of pocket book (5 points per credit—10 credits for free book).
(6) Being a student referee for a varsity game (30 points per game).
(7) Access to student lounge during free period (study hall) (30 points per period).

Signed _____
                                 STUDENT

Signed _____
                                  TEACHER

■ FIGURE 3.2
Educational Contract
Harvey F. Clarizio, *Toward Positive Classroom Discipline* (New York: Wiley, 1971), p. 15.

respect or identify with are usually of little value. Nevertheless, students will model themselves after the behavior of a person whom they do not regard especially highly if they know that they will be expected to demonstrate that they can reproduce that person's behavior and that they will be rewarded if they can do so.

A model may be almost anyone students admire and can identify with. Seek out models among the students' peer group and in the community. Admired personalities such as the stars of stage, screen, sports, and television, as well as other public figures in the news, are natural models that some young people imitate. You yourself may be a model. Teachers who are carefully organized, well-planned, enthusiastic, and knowledgeable may well influence students in scholarly ways.

Students also look to certain peers as role models. In this respect, there seems to be a "ripple effect" that causes students to learn from the experiences of others in their classes.(25) Thus, if students see a certain behavior in Student A, they are likely to adopt that same behavior themselves. Consequently, it is desirable to utilize methods by which students can learn from one another—that is, from each other's example and from the effects of their behavior on others.

Models are not always predictable, of course. They sometimes act in ways one would rather students did not imitate. It is often necessary to resort to symbolic models—films, tapes, stories, drama, simulations, role playing, and the like—in

1. Challenging teacher or another student to a game of chess.
2. Using the portable computer.
3. Doing extra credit problems and seeing how they can raise his grade.
4. Making up a geometry quiz and then giving it to the class.
5. Sitting at the teacher's desk while doing homework problems.
6. Preparing the bulletin board using a display of the student's choice.
7. Writing letters.
8. Playing chess.
9. Reading.
10. Playing charades.
11. Talking over the past or forthcoming athletic or social events.
12. Having a creative exhibit period (a grown-up version of show-and-tell).
13. Comparing a 1902 Sears-Roebuck catalogue with the current one, discussing changes in style, price, and the like, and trying to discover why the changes occurred.

Daily Specials

Monday.   Appear as guest lecturer in the other math classes.
Tuesday.   Do the special crossword puzzles involving geometry concepts learned.
Wednesday.   Time in which you can play a math game with another student.
Thursday.   Construction of special paper models using geometrical figures to complete.
Friday.   Do mystery problems involving mathematical solutions.

FIGURE 3.3
Reinforcement Menu for a High School Geometry Class
Harvey F. Clarizio, *Toward Positive Classroom Discipline* (New York: Wiley, 1971), p. 30.

which students can see the behavior to be imitated at the appropriate time and place and in the proper sequence.

Stop and Reflect

A certain teacher says that it is impossible to teach her students anything because of the no-failure policy of the school. The supervisor says that the teacher is merely excusing her inability to make her teaching interesting. React to these statements.

- *Prepare a list of motivational devices for possible use in a class you expect to teach.*
- *Show how you could use a contingency contract in a class you expect to teach. What would you use as point-getting devices? What would you use for rewards?*
- *What rewards could you include in a reinforcement menu?*

In a National Education Association poll, members reported using the following techniques to motivate learners:

- *One high school teacher writes personal notes to students about their extracurricular activities. If she learns that a student has done very well on a test, she immediately calls the parents to compliment them.*
- *A middle school teacher waits until a student has left the room and then tells the class how well the student has done.*
- *Another high school teacher uses flash cards, bingo games, and prizes when teaching her students vocabulary.*

- *A New Jersey middle school teacher guarantees a final C to every student who does all the homework and retakes and passes any test for which a D or F grade had been given.*
- *Another New Jersey teacher takes time for students to play getting-to-know-you games and to draw posters illustrating some aspect of their personalities so that she can get to know them better and can create positive attitudes toward learning.(26)*

What do you think of these techniques? Would you use them or not? What other sort of activities could you use to create a motivating atmosphere in your classes?

During a middle school social studies class model of a U.N. Assembly debate, a matter came up that, according to the U.N. rules, can be decided only by the Security Council vote. Pupils representing countries not in the Security Council protested because they felt that they should be allowed to vote. They argued that to forbid them the right to vote just because they represented countries that were not Security Council members was ridiculous.

How would you handle this situation?

SUMMARY

Motivation is too important in the teaching-learning process to be left to chance. It is the key both to good learning and to good discipline. Only students who are well-motivated learn well. When students fail to learn, chances are that the basic cause of the trouble has to do with motivation. As often as the fault lies with students, it also lies with the teacher and the school, because they have not taken the steps necessary to motivate students to work and study. Fortunately, all pupils can be motivated.

Since knowledge is a valuable commodity that teachers must sell to sometimes unwilling clients, it is important to find a way to motivate them to buy. If teachers can do so by positive means, the chances of successfully teaching students will be greatly enhanced. Unfortunately, positive motivation does not always come naturally. More frequently than not, teachers must work to convince reluctant students of the value of learning. Fortunately we have many tools and techniques at our command to help in this endeavor.

One of these tools is the assignment, which should make clear to the students what is to be done, why it should be done, how it should be done, and how doing it will pay off. Teachers should pay much more attention to giving their assignments than they usually do. Because students cannot study effectively unless their assignments are clear to them, teachers should be sure that the assignments do the following:

- Set the direction and scope of the task
- Prepare the students for the job to be done
- Point out how to do what is to be done
- Provide every student with an appropriate task

To carry out these goals, the teacher may need to go into great detail when making the assignment. It may be necessary to take time to teach study skills, to discuss objectives, to issue study guides and organizers, and to familiarize students with the materials to be used.

Another technique is to harness, as far as possible, students' natural motives, such as curiosity, attitudes and ideals, desire for success, self-esteem and security, love of fun, adventure and action, and need for friendship. Still another method is to point out the value of the subject matter to the students. The best way to do this is to really believe in the material's importance yourself. Remember that students are more likely to be moved by immediate rather than deferred values, and by intrinsic rather than extrinsic values. Because people respond differently to things, individual motivation may be fostered by making adequate provisions for individual differences. Grades have not proved to be adequate motivating devices for most students; teacher-student planning has been somewhat more successful.

New approaches in developing techniques and strategies that can be helpful in motivating students can be found in reinforcement theory. Basically, this theory holds that a teacher should reward students when they behave in desirable ways, but not when they behave in undesirable ways. Unfortunately, many of our present disciplinary procedures tend to reward unacceptable behavior. As we develop and use teaching methods that utilize reinforcement techniques properly, we should find our students becoming better motivated and better behaved. Among the techniques recommended are the judicious use of rewards and the use of contingency contracts, reinforcement menus, and modeling.

ADDITIONAL READING

Alderman, M. K., and M. W. Cohen. *Motivational Theory and Practice for Preservice Teachers.* Teacher Education Monograph No. 4. Washington, DC: ERIC Clearing House on Teacher Education, 1985.

Alschuler, A. F. *Developing Achievement Motivation in Adolescents: Education for Human Growth.* Englewood Cliffs, NJ: Prentice-Hall Educational Technology Publications, 1983.

Borich, G. D. *Effective Teaching Methods.* New York: Macmillan, 1992, Ch. 9.

Bragstad, B. J., and S. M. Stumpf. *Study Skills and Motivation: A Guidebook for Teaching,* 2nd ed. Boston, MA: Allyn and Bacon, 1987.

Brophy, J. "Synthesis of Research on Strategies for Motivating Students to Learn." *Educational Leadership* 45 (October 1987): 40–48.

Emmers, A. P. *After the Lesson Plan: Realities of High School Teaching.* New York: Teachers College Press, 1981, Part II.

Gage, N. L., and D. C. Berliner. *Educational Psychology,* 4th ed. Boston: Houghton Mifflin, 1988.

Glasser, W. *Control Theory in the Classroom.* New York: Harper and Row, 1986.

Grant, C. A., and C. E. Sleeter. *Turning On Learning.* New York: Macmillan, 1989.

Grossnickle, D. R. *Helping Students Develop Self-Motivation.* Reston, VA: National Association of Secondary School Principals, 1989.

Grossnickle, D. R., and W. Thiel. *Promoting Student Motivation in School and Classroom.* Reston, VA: The National Association of Secondary School Principals, 1988.

Johnson, S. O., and V. J. Johnson. *Motivating Minority Students: Strategies That Work.* Springfield, IL: Charles C. Thomas, 1988.

Pares, S. G., G. M. Olson, and H. W. Stevenson. *Learning and Motivation in the Classroom.* Hillsdale, NJ: Lawrence Erlbaum Associates, 1983.

Reilly, R. R., and E. L. Lewis. *Educational Psychology.* New York: Macmillan, 1983, Ch. 8.

Stipek, D. J. *Motivation to Learn: From Theory to Practice.* Englewood Cliffs, NJ: Prentice-Hall, 1988.

Wlodkowski, R. J. *Motivation and Teaching: A Practical Guide.* Washington, DC: National Education Association, 1984.

NOTES

1. David R. Byrne, Susan A. Hines, and Lloyd E. McCleary, *The Senior High School Principalship,* Vol. 1 (Reston, VA: National Association of Secondary School Principals, 1978). *See also* Vernon Smith and George H. Gallup, *What*

the People Think about Their Schools: Gallup's Findings, Fastback 94* (Bloomington, IN: Phi Delta Kappa Educational Foundation, 1977); and Gallup Polls on schools reported in the September *Phi Delta Kappan* annually.

2. Peggy Odell Gonder, "Getting Kids out of the Middle of the Middle-Ability Education," *Education Digest* 59 (September 1993): 23–26.

3. Jerry J. Bellon, Elner C. Bellon, and Mary Ann Blank, *Teaching from a Research Knowledge Base—A Development and Renewal Process,* 2nd ed. (New York: Macmillan, 1992), Ch. 5.

4. Richard J. Riordan, "Educational Climate: Discussion," in *Improving Educational Standards and Productivity* edited by Herbert J. Walberg (Berkeley, CA: McCutchan, 1982), 309.

5. Ibid., 310.

6. Willard Duckett, "Student Motivation: Finding the 'Missing Link'," *Practical Applications of Research* 5 (September 1982): 1–4.

7. E. P. Torrance, "Are There Open Tops to the Cages?: Using Educational Resources," in *Mental Health and Achievement*, edited by E. P. Torrance and R. S. Strom (New York: Wiley, 1965), 260. Quoted by Lita Linzer Schwartz, *Educational Psychology,* 2nd ed. (Boston: Holbrook Press, 1977), 111.

8. Paul Chance, "The Rewards of Learning," *Phi Delta Kappan* 74 (November 1992): 200–207. *See also* Raymond J. Wlodkowski, *Motivation and Teaching* (Washington, DC: National Education Association, 1984), Ch. 7.

9. Alfie Kohn, "Group Grade Grabbing versus Cooperative Learning," *Educational Leadership* 48 (February 1991): 83–87.

10. Renata Nummela Caine and Geoffrey Caine, *Teaching and the Human Brain* (Alexandria, VA: Association for Supervision and Curriculum Development, 1991).

11. Bellon, Bellon, and Blank, *Teaching from a Research Knowledge Base,* 94.

12. David P. Ausubel, *Educational Psychology: A Cognitive View* (New York: Holt, 1968), 148.

13. Richard E. Mayer, "Can Advance Organizers Influence Meaningful Learning?" *Review of Educational Research* 49 (Spring 1979): 382.

14. Ibid.

15. Herber, Harold L., and J. Nelson-Herber, *Teaching in Content Areas with Reading, Writing, and Reasoning* (Boston: Allyn and Bacon, 1992), Ch. 5.

16. Herber, *Teaching in Content Areas,* 147–149.

17. Joseph S. Karmos and Ann H. Karmos, "A Closer Look at Classroom Boredom," *Action in Teacher Education* 5 (Spring-Summer 1983): 51.

18. Margaret M. Clifford, "Students Need Challenge not Easy Success," *Educational Leadership* 48 (September 1990): 22–25.

19. Howard Kirschenbaum and James Bellanca, "Grades—Help or Hindrance," *The Practitioner* 9 (January 1983): 4–5.

20. Bellon, Bellon, Blank, *Teaching from a Research Knowledge Base,* 95.

21. James W. Michaels, "Classroom Reward Structure and Academic Performances," *Review of Educational Research* 47 (Winter 1977): 87–98.

22. Duckett, "Student Motivation," 1–4.

23. Margaret W. Cohen, "Extrinsic Reinforcers and Intrinsic Motivation" in *Motivation Theory and Practice for Preservice Teachers.*, edited by M. Kay Alderman and Margaret W. Cohen (Washington, DC: Clearing House on Teacher Education, 1985), 12–13.

24. Harvey F. Clarizio, *Toward Positive Classroom Discipline* (New York: Wiley, 1971), 41.

25. J. Kounin, *Discipline and Group Management in Classrooms* (New York: Holt, 1970).

26. Diane Dismuke, "NEA Members Say Positive Reinforcement Is Best Motivator," *NEA Today* (December 1987), 23.

Chapter 4

Classroom Management and Discipline

Take a firm attitude from the beginning—that's the secret of it.
James Hilton, *Good Bye Mr. Chips*

▧▧▧ Overview

Classroom management is the process of organizing and conducting a class so that it runs smoothly. When it is well done, it reduces wasted time and wasted motion. Because it aims the efforts of both teachers and students at the important goals and tasks of schooling, effective management enables students to spend their time on learning tasks rather than on nonessentials. Classroom management reduces problems of discipline and control. It ensures that students know what to do and have the time and materials with which to do it. Without it, classes are neither efficient nor effective.

Successful management is achieved by careful planning, attention to business, explicit instructions, and thorough follow-up. It is essential for establishing and maintaining classroom discipline, which should be democratic discipline instead of dictatorship. The law requires you to treat students as citizens, not subjects; however, you are expected to maintain reasonable control and order. In this endeavor, you should depend largely on preventive measures and good classroom management. Rules must be enforced. To enforce them, accentuate the positive whenever possible. Use punishment sparingly, but consistently. Negative approaches such as harsh punishment, nagging, and verbal abuse do more harm than good. Minor disturbances should be kept minor. More serious incidents and major offenses require more drastic action. Fortunately, in cases of emergency, help is available in the "office." In dealing with chronically disruptive students, your major responsibility is to teach—not to treat the students' mental, emotional, or social problems.

▧▧▧ Some Definitions

Classroom management and discipline are two of the most crucial elements in determining teaching success. When commonly used in informal discussion, these terms seem synonymous.(1) However, in more formal situations, classroom management includes the "provisions and procedures necessary to establish and maintain an environment in which teaching and learning can occur."(2) Discipline, on the other hand, refers to "the treatment of misbehavior in classrooms or schools."(3)

As shown in Figure 4.1, among the provisions and procedures involved in classroom management are such tasks as the following:

- Planning, organizing, coordinating, directing, controlling, communicating, and housekeeping.
- Manipulating time, space, personnel, materials, authority and responsibility, rewards and punishment.
- Resolving conflicts between school and society, between roles and personalities, between the group and individuals, between immediate and long-term goals, among personalities, and among roles.
- Maximizing students' time on task.

These tasks are influenced by such situational factors as

- Group size
- Age and background of students
- Solidarity of groups
- Organizational content
- Space, facilities, and resources

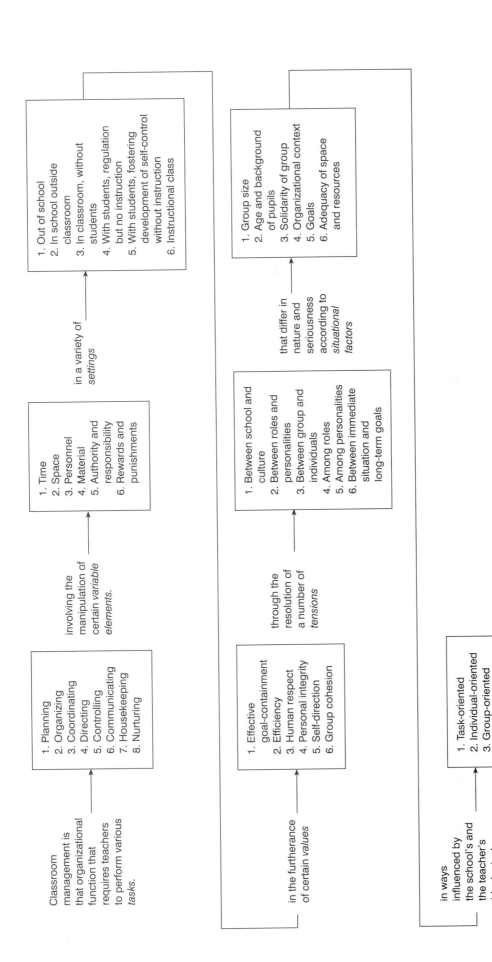

Classroom management is that organizational function that requires teachers to perform various *tasks*.

1. Planning
2. Organizing
3. Coordinating
4. Directing
5. Controlling
6. Communicating
7. Housekeeping
8. Nurturing

involving the manipulation of certain *variable elements*.

1. Time
2. Space
3. Personnel
4. Material
5. Authority and responsibility
6. Rewards and punishments

in a variety of *settings*

1. Out of school
2. In school outside classroom
3. In classroom, without students
4. With students, regulation but no instruction
5. With students, fostering development of self-control without instruction
6. Instructional class

in the furtherance of certain *values*

1. Effective goal-containment
2. Efficiency
3. Human respect
4. Personal integrity
5. Self-direction
6. Group cohesion

through the resolution of a number of *tensions*

1. Between school and culture
2. Between roles and personalities
3. Between group and individuals
4. Among roles
5. Among personalities
6. Between immediate situation and long-term goals

that differ in nature and seriousness according to *situational factors*

1. Group size
2. Age and background of pupils
3. Solidarity of group
4. Organizational context
5. Goals
6. Adequacy of space and resources

in ways influenced by the school's and the teacher's *ideological stances*.

1. Task-oriented
2. Individual-oriented
3. Group-oriented

■ **FIGURE 4.1**

A Conceptual Model of Classroom Management

Mauritz Johnson and Harry Brooks, "Conceptualizing Classroom Management," in *Classroom Management*, The Seventy-Eighth Yearbook of the National Society for the Study of Education, Part II, edited by Daniel L. Duke (Chicago: The University of Chicago Press, 1979), p. 41.

They are also affected by the ideological stances of both the school and the teacher; for example, are activities to be task-oriented, individual-oriented, or group-oriented?

Classroom management is both difficult and complicated, but when it is done well, it is worth the effort. It sets the tone for the class. It allows teaching strategies to move smoothly. It improves class morale, group cohesiveness, and student motivation. It directs student effort toward learning. When classes are well-managed, students work more thoroughly, make fewer mistakes, and, in general, become more productive. *Remember: The purpose of classroom management is to ensure that class time is concentrated on teaching and learning, not on side issues.*

Building the Classroom Climate

Today's notion of what constitutes a well-ordered class differs from that of the past. Totalitarian classrooms and martinet teachers are obsolete. In today's ideal classroom, teachers are expected to emphasize courtesy, cooperation, and self-control. In classes, teachers and students alike ideally practice the freedoms of democracy. The students are supposedly free from fear; after all, they are citizens of the class, not subjects of the teacher. As citizens, their job is to cooperate for the common good, to obey the laws of their classroom democracy, and to respect and obey proper authority.

Reasonable Control

There are a number of reasons why democracy in the classroom is favored over dictatorship. First, dictatorship does not seem to pay off in long-range educational results. Second, dictatorship is out of tune with the times and modern theories of government. Third, exercising absolute control is not within the legal role of the teacher. Boys and girls, young men and women, are United States citizens. They do not shed their rights (or their responsibilities) as citizens when they enter the school door. The Supreme Court has been quite adamant about this fact. In the words of Mr. Justice Fortas,

In our system, state-operated schools may not be enclaves of totalitarianism. School officials do not possess absolute authority over their students. Students in school as well as out of school are "persons" under our Constitution. They are possessed of fundamental rights which the State must respect, just as they themselves must respect their obligations to the State.(4)

The courts, however, strongly support teachers and the teaching profession in making reasonable attempts to enforce reasonable rules and to provide a reasonable climate for education in our schools. The key word in dealing with discipline and control from the legal, and probably any other, standpoint, is *reasonable.* If teachers make it a point to become familiar with the laws and regulations applying to their school district and to carry out their responsibilities in a reasonable fashion in view of these laws and regulations, the courts will support them even in this litigious age. Every school should have a statement of its rules and regulations printed in a student handbook, and all students should be required to read it. You should follow these rules faithfully.

Teacher Personality and Classroom Atmosphere

Classroom management is dependent on the students' respect, which can be won only by treating students "fairly and compassionately over a sustained period of time."(5) Teachers who rub students the wrong way, who do not like adolescents, who are more interested in the subject than in their students, who are inconsiderate, unhappy, and lack a sense of humor, are not likely to command the respect or cooperation of their students. Students are much more likely to cooperate with teachers who show themselves to be empathetic, warm, and genuine.(6) You should be friendly, cheerful, fair, consistent, interested, honest, interesting, and helpful. If you can create a feeling of rapport with your students, you will probably have little difficulty with discipline.

For this reason, get to know your students as individuals as soon as possible. Most particularly, from the very first learn each student's name and use it in class. This practice is not only good for the students' egos, but also serves to notify the students that their behavior will not be anonymous. In addition, if you know something of the students' backgrounds and interests, you can use this knowledge to cement friendly relations and to direct their interests in desirable directions.

As the chapter on motivation points out, teachers' attitudes, whether positive or negative, tend to spread to the class. Tense teachers usually convey their tenseness to their students, and teachers who expect misbehavior usually get it. By acting on the assumption that everything is going to be all right, and by concentrating on the main job—that is, teaching—you may eliminate a good share of the potential difficulties. In securing and maintaining good classroom relationships, a businesslike, matter-of-fact bearing can be very persuasive.

Nevertheless, even in the best-regulated classes and schools, students do misbehave. When this happens, try to take it in stride. Keep a tight rein on your own emotions, even though this is not always an easy thing to do.

ACHIEVING THE PROPER PERSPECTIVE   One of the best techniques for keeping on an even keel is not to take yourself too seriously. Teachers are human, too. They do not know everything, and they do make mistakes. What is more, students know it. No amount of dissembling can keep this truth from them. The sooner you realize this and relax, the better off you will be.

Many young teachers seem to think that every incident of student misbehavior is a personal insult. This is not so. You should not be upset by students' misconduct any more than you should be upset by students' lack of knowledge. This is the way young people are; your job is to help them achieve the highest goals they can. If you view student misdemeanors as personal insults, you may soon find that they have become just that.

Try to combine a sense of humor with a sense of proportion. When you get to the point where you can laugh at your own failings, you will be well on the way to developing a pleasant classroom atmosphere and good classroom control. Laughing with students clears the atmosphere. It is always easier to learn in a pleasant atmosphere than it is in a repressive one, and after all, student learning is what you are after. You need a sense of perspective, too. Try to put first things first. You are not a police officer; you are a teacher. Your primary job is not to enforce rules but to draw out learning. Try not to let little things upset you.

CREATING A FRIENDLY ATMOSPHERE   A well-managed classroom is a friendly place. By your actions, rather than by your words, let students know that you would like to be a friend. This does not mean that you should attempt to be a buddy. Familiarity may breed contempt. Since no one can be a best friend to everyone, it is best not to try, especially since teachers must avoid setting some students up as favorites. Besides, adolescents prefer that adults act their age.

SETTING A GOOD EXAMPLE   Perhaps the best summary of what we have been discussing so far is that you should set a good example. If your behavior is truly considerate, patient, pleasant, and sympathetic, and shows that you care for the students as individuals and are truly trying to teach them well, then the class will probably respond favorably to your teaching. But what sort of behavior can you expect of your students if you run a sloppy, unpleasant class? Without self-discipline, teachers make little progress.

Diffusely Structuring the Class

In your planning, try to take advantage of the nature of the group. Try to use student leadership potentials to build a positive social climate, to establish suitable group norms, to construct student-centered communications patterns, and to foster group cohesiveness. You can usually further your goals by creating diffusely structured classrooms in which you encourage the students' participation and involvement and exhibit your democratic leadership. These strategies are discussed in Chapter 2.

Stop and Reflect

What is your philosophy of classroom management? What sort of atmosphere do you hope to have in your classes? How do you hope to achieve this atmosphere?

 Organizing for Classroom Management

Planning

"Our teacher is funny," a small boy reported to his mother. "She wants you to keep at work all the time whether you have anything to do or not." This anecdote, which appeared in the February 4, 1892 issue of the *Journal of Education,* is as true today as it was a hundred years ago. "Down time" in the classroom when students have nothing to do can ruin many classes. If you plan carefully, you can eliminate most of these empty spots. In your planning, you must be sure that everyone has plenty of worthwhile work to do. Avoid teaching in which you do all the work and the students just sit and vegetate, as can occur if the beginning teacher gives in to the tendency to overuse the lecture. Be sure that the learning activities proceed in a logical sequence.

Not only should the students have plenty of worthwhile activities to do, but also you should be sure that the students know how to carry out the activities. A little instruction in how to study, or how to use the tools of learning, or how to carry out the assignments may pay off by producing more profitable classes.

Another essential of good planning is to provide plenty of good materials for students to work with. To eliminate mischief-breeding periods of waiting, make sure that the materials needed for the lesson are on hand and that you have included procedures for rapid delivery and collection of materials.

Arranging the Setting

If you can arrange the classroom so that it is attractive and easy for the students to work in, your classes are likely to progress more easily than they will in a dull, drab, old-fashioned classroom. In fact, many modern methods and techniques do not work as well in traditional formal classroom setups as they do in more relaxed environments.

Most modern schools are equipped with movable chairs rather than fixed furniture. This being so, arrange the class according to the classwork the students are to do. For watching a movie, or even for listening to a lecture, variations in the ordinary row setup may be desirable; for committee work, small circles of chairs may be best; for a discussion, a circle or some segment of a circle may be suitable. Move the chairs to suit the activity—after all, presumably that is why the school board bought movable furniture.

Some teachers like to seat students in alphabetical order or with taller students in the back. In the traditional class, these practices may make the routine easier, but when using flexible methods, such plans are pointless. Allowing the students to select their own seats is probably as good a plan as any. However, for at least the first few days, require students to keep the same seats so that you can make a seating chart to help you learn their names. Some examples of possible class arrangements are shown in Figure 4.2.

Stop and Reflect

Some teachers recommend breaking up close companions, cliques, and troublemakers by seating them so that they cannot talk to each other easily. Others say this is a useless procedure and creates more harm than good. What is your opinion on this problem?

Setting Up Routines

Middle and high school classes usually make better progress if the more usual tasks are fit into a routine. Routines make it possible for students to know what to do without being told over and over again. For instance, there should be no question about whether to write on both sides of a paper, or whether to give one's oral report from

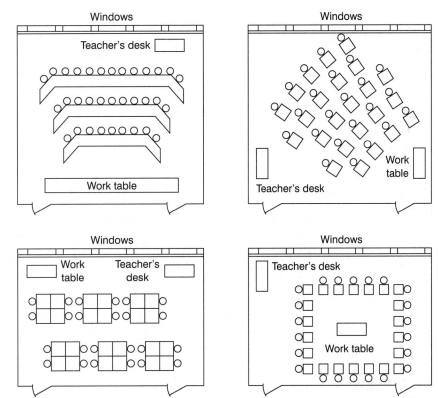

■ **Figure 4.2**
Diagrams of Possible Room Arrangements

one's desk or from the front of the room, if the routine is to *always* write on only one side of a sheet and *always* to give oral reports from the front of the classroom.

Time is critical in any class, so working housekeeping activities into the routine is an effective way to save time. The more time you can save for active instruction the better. However, too much routinizing can lead to boredom and loss of interest. A good rule is to make routine as many of the administrative and managerial aspects of the classroom as possible, but to leave the instructional activities free from unnecessary routinizing.

Routine can be incorporated into such administrative matters as attendance, tardy slips, and excuses. In handling these, you must, of course, carry out the school's regulations. However, to save time and interruptions, all this work should be completed before the class starts. Attendance might be taken by some quick method such as noting the unfilled chairs. To do this quickly, it is usually a good practice to have students start off at the beginning of the class in assigned stations, even though they move to other work stations later. The traditional means of taking attendance—calling the roll—is a time-wasting procedure.[*]

To start your classes with a minimum of confusion, work routine procedures into the issuing of equipment and materials. Issuing papers and books can often be delegated to students. Before the class starts, materials to be used during the period should be ready for instant distribution. A good way to minimize confusion is to list on the board those things that will be needed during the various periods. Thus, students can equip themselves with the necessary materials without asking a single question. A similar routine can be set up for putting things away at the end of the period. In some classes, you can routinize the collection and distribution of student papers. One method is to have students pass the papers to, or from, the ends of rows or the head of the table. However, in a classroom laboratory, a better way is to circulate unobtrusively about the class to collect or distribute the papers without interrupting the students' work.

Never become a slave to routine, but if certain tasks must be done again and again, a properly used routine can make the class more efficient and pleasant.

Stop and Reflect

If you were to begin teaching next week, how would you plan to learn the students' names speedily? What sort of lesson would you use to get the course off to a good start? What procedures would you use to make passing out and collecting papers, taking attendance, and so on, speedy and smooth? What about such details as sharpening pencils, using reference works, and the like?

Establishing Rules

One of the maxims of our country's forefathers was that the government that governs least governs best. To some extent, this maxim applies to the classroom. Every class needs some rules; however, no class needs many rules. Too many rules confuse students. A few definite rules that make sense to students and teachers alike will prove to be more successful. If you have more than 10 or 12 rules, you probably have too many. A few general principles such as "You must not interfere with the learning of others by being loud and rude" may work just as well.

Rules should not be too rigid. Rigid sets of rules tend to encourage rule breaking. Furthermore, you become trapped into enforcing rules you do not wish to

---

[*]Roll call is useful, however, as a means for learning who the students are.

enforce. Keeping to a few general rules or principles of conduct will give you room to maneuver. These rules should not only give students considerable freedom, but also should let them know exactly what the limits are.(7)

A rule can be considered a good one when it clearly spells out what it is that students must do, seems reasonable, and can be enforced. Such rules are usually more effective when they are stated as standard operating procedures, spelling out what is expected rather than what is forbidden. Emphasis on the positive is almost always more fruitful than negative statements or threats.

The following are some sample classroom standards for a ninth-grade class:

1. Have books, paper, and pencil ready. Begin work immediately.
2. Participate and help in class planning.
3. Maintain an atmosphere that helps everyone to study.
4. Contribute to the class and help fellow students.
5. Always do your own assignments—never "crib" from others.
6. Get all work in on time and in acceptable form.
7. Help keep the room clean, neat, and orderly.
8. Keep an individual progress record and try to keep improving it.
9. Never bring gum, toys, animals (except on assignment), or other distracting materials into the classroom.
10. Take pride in clean speech, appropriate dress, and courteous manners.
11. Protect desks, books, and other school supplies and equipment.(8)

When establishing classroom rules, use a method that will develop positive behavior in the students. One way to do this is to have the students participate in developing their own standards of behavior. For instance, one teacher had great success with the following technique. For many years at the beginning of the term, he addressed his class in the following manner: "We are going to have to spend the rest of the year here together. In order to keep out of each other's hair we need some rules. Let's talk the situation over and see if we can figure out what rules we want to have in this class." Then the class set to work to discuss why they needed rules and what kind of rules they needed. Finally, they drew up a set of rules that a committee put into final form for class adoption. During the discussion, the teacher presided and made suggestions. Most of his comments were questions such as, "Is that what you really want to do? Do you need that? Aren't you being a little strict?" The resulting rules were usually a workable code that the students could follow quite well. Interestingly, the teacher's greatest difficulty was to keep the rules from becoming unworkably strict and detailed. Sometimes, after a few weeks, the teacher had to suggest that the rules be reviewed and revised.

A procedure of this type tends to take the onus of rule making and enforcement off the teacher. Arbitrary imposition of rules on students is an invitation to rebellion, but students tend to abide by their own rules quite willingly.

The technique just described worked for this social studies teacher for more than 20 years, but it may be unsuitable for other teachers in different situations. Teachers must suit their methods to their classes and their own personalities. The important thing is to develop for each class standards of conduct the students will accept as reasonable and worthwhile. Extra time spent on this important task at the beginning of the year can result in much greater class progress throughout the rest of the year.

Stop and Reflect

What rules or standards for behavior are appropriate for a high school class? A middle school class? Prepare a list of rules you think would be suitable for a class you might teach at the high school level. Prepare a similar list for a middle school class.

Should a set of rules for classroom behavior be provided? (Some texts say yes; some say no.) If so, who should make it and how should it be enforced? Be prepared to defend your position.

Do you agree with the practice of having students develop their own rules for behavior? How would you go about developing such rules?

Lay out the strategies you think you should use to set up an excellent, orderly, supportive learning environment in your classes.

■ ■ ■ Managing the Class

Getting Off to a Good Start

Because classroom management sets the tone for the class, you should give careful attention to its details from the very first day of school. You need not only to plan carefully your management strategies, but also you should be fairly strict and keep student movement at a minimum during the beginning of a course. After patterns of suitable classroom behavior have been established, it may be profitable to loosen the reins. To make sure that early lessons move effectively and create the type of atmosphere they wish, some teachers arm themselves with alternate plans in case their first plans fail. In any case, your lessons should always start the moment the period begins. Neophytes, who often are a little unsure of themselves, are sometimes tempted to give themselves a little respite by stalling a minute or two at the opening of the class. To do so is dangerous; the class that has time to fool around before the lesson begins may never find time to get down to business before the period ends.

Keeping the Class Moving

To keep the class moving smoothly, to avoid dead spots, and to evade confusion, you should become adept at what Kounin calls "movement management," that is, the technique of guiding the class smoothly through its activities and from one activity to another.(9) To attain smooth movement, be careful to avoid interrupting the progress of the class yourself.

- Be sure that students are ready to hear you before you make an announcement, give directions, or make statements. Particularly avoid interrupting students with your instructions or statements when they are busy doing something else. Otherwise, you may interrupt the progress of ongoing work, or your remarks may fall on deaf ears.
- Finish one activity before you start on the next. Do not leave students dangling.
- Do not let yourself start another topic or activity before finishing something you set out to accomplish; otherwise, you might find that you must jump back to the unfinished previous one, which is an ineffective use of time.
- Avoid letting yourself be distracted by irrelevant happenings or thoughts. Do not interrupt yourself to harp on inconsequential matters not pertinent to the activity at hand.
- When you have said what you have to say, quit. Do not hold up progress by talking about a subject more than necessary.
- Avoid going into too much detail. Do not break things down into a million steps when only a few are needed. If you need to communicate with a group, then call them all up at once, not one by one.

Other techniques that you should develop to manage classes well include the ability to keep an eye on the entire class at once, thus making the class aware that you are alert. Kounin calls this technique "withitness." Others used to call it "having eyes in the back of your head." In any case, this technique calls for keeping tabs on the entire class and resisting the tendency of so many beginning teachers to concentrate their attention on just a few members of the class.

Another technique allied to "withitness" is "overlapping," or the ability to do two things at once. For example, listening to one student at his or her desk while keeping tabs on the progress of another group in a different part of the room is a use of this technique. Such procedures help keep students on their toes. To accomplish your tasks, refrain from getting overinvolved with any one student or group, look around the room frequently, and avoid staying in only one spot of the room. Other techniques that keep students alert are calling out students' names after asking the class questions, calling on students randomly, involving everyone in the lesson, and frequently checking on student progress and activity.(10) Keeping up a high level of classroom management requires continual monitoring.

Allow for students' predispositions, however. Any class procedure that violates the natural inclinations of boys and girls creates a situation that can lead to misconduct. Adolescents are naturally gregarious, social creatures. A class that is all keyed up cannot easily settle down to a placid routine. By adjusting the material and tempo of the instruction to the predispositions and mood of the class, the predispositions of students can be an aid to learning rather than a threat to peace. Switching from a lecture or recitation to a discussion, snap quiz, or written assignment when a class is restless is an effective example of this principle. This is the reason some teachers make a point to plan unusually interesting, sprightly lessons or activities for Friday afternoons.

Above all, try to keep the class highly motivated. Provide students with tasks that appeal to them or that they know will pay off in a gratifying way. Avoid letting your classes fall into the same routine day after day.

Stop and Reflect

On Friday afternoon students may be feeling the need to release tension before the school day is over. What other periods are likely to be stressful? Think out and note down activities you think might relieve such occasions and make for invigorating classes.

In a Vermont intermediate school, it has become the practice to show movies every Friday afternoon to relieve classroom tedium. What do you think of this practice?

Some Specific Suggestions

BEFORE THE SCHOOL YEAR STARTS   Managing a classroom starts well before the first day of school. As soon as you receive your teaching assignment, become as familiar as you can with your school, your students, and your classes.(11)

1. *Climate.*   What is the overall climate in the school?
2. *Policies and routines.*   What are the standard operating procedures and routines for reporting attendance, requisitioning equipment and supplies, and the like? Who is responsible for what? To whom do you report what? What are the school policies? To find out, consult the school handbook and talk to other teachers, your department head, the assistant principal, and other school personnel.

3. *The students.*   Find out as much as you can about your students. At what levels are they? What prior experience have they had? If feasible, look through their permanent record folders for clues about their hearing, eyesight, interests, outside activities, and so on.

4. *The classroom.*   What facilities are at your disposal? What can you do to make the environment optimally attractive and efficient? If you are to share facilities, what arrangements can you make with the other teachers for the organization and use of common facilities and equipment?

5. *The courses.*   Become familiar with the courses you are to teach. What is the level of each course? What is its place in the curriculum? What are its course goals and instructional objectives? Is there a syllabus or guide? What resources (e.g., texts, supplementary readings, instructional aids, materials of instruction, equipment, and supplies) are available?

6. *You.*   Clarify to yourself what you believe about teaching and how it should be carried out. What are your overall teaching goals? That is, what do you really want boys and girls to get out of your courses? What type of class climate do you wish in your classes? What do you consider appropriate behavior? How loose or how tight do you want to run your classes? To what extent do you think your classes should be teacher-centered or student-centered? What steps must you take to run the type of classes that you want?

Once you have gathered this information about the school, the students, your courses, and yourself, you must make some decisions. You must decide on how you will organize your class. What rules, routines, and procedures will govern the conduct of the class? What incentives, penalties, rewards, and punishments will you use? As soon as you have made these decisions, you should write down what the rules, procedures, and routines will be. Before the beginning of the first class, post the rules where all can see them. Routines and procedures such as passing out materials, checking work, turning in papers, and checking attendance may be explained later as the occasion arises.

The most important decisions you will make have to do with the conduct of your courses. Block out a course outline for each of them. Set up your course objectives. Prepare your first lessons. It is very important that you appear well-prepared and well-organized in the first days of the courses. The impression you make on your students in the first days can make the difference between a successful and an unsuccessful year.

Make sure your classroom is well-organized, and try to make it as attractive as possible. Set up work and seating arrangements, bulletin boards, display areas, and so on. Decorate the room. Obtain your supplies, equipment, and materials of instruction. Check them for adequacy: Are they enough? Are they in good condition? Do they work? Organize and store them so that they are readily available and usable. Be sure that all the forms, gradebooks, passes, tardy slips, paper, and the like are readily available and ready for use, and that any pertinent notices, rules, regulations, pictures, and so on have been posted.

ON THE FIRST DAY   Your first class should be impressive. It should demonstrate to the students that you are in charge, well-organized, and well-prepared.

Begin by starting the class at the bell. Introduce yourself, and take care of the necessary administrative tasks. Then briefly introduce the course. Tell the class what the course is about and what you hope to accomplish. Explain the rules and what you expect of your students. Actually begin teaching with some short, easy, academic activity. About a half minute before the end of the period, stop for a short cleanup session. Then, when you are ready, dismiss the class. Remember! *You dis-*

miss the class; the bell does not. The students should understand this from the very first day.

Sometime during the first class, present and explain the rules (which you have already written out and posted). Be sure the students understand them and understand the reasons for them. After the class has progressed a few weeks, you may wish to have the students review the rules and to participate in their adjustment, but the time for such student participation is not during the first class. Rather, on the first day teach the rules just as though they are subject matter to be learned. The success of your teaching depends in a large part on students' understanding and compliance with the rules.(12)

It might be helpful to prepare a seating plan during the first period. One method is to write the students' names on slips of paper before the period starts, or in a pinch let the students write their names on the slips. When they have chosen their seats (do not assign seats at the middle or high school level), call the roll and insert the name slips in the appropriate slots of a pocket-type seating chart (see Figure 4.3). Then, as soon as you possibly can, associate the names of the students with their faces. When the students know that you know who they are, it is much easier to establish rapport with them.

Begin the course with a lively, worthwhile lesson. At this point, students are often in a mood to learn. They have hopes that the new course and new teacher may have something worthwhile for them. So your first lesson should be one of your best. If you can possibly do so, use an interesting experiment, a demonstration, an exciting story, an intriguing problem, or something equally appealing. Some teachers devote the first day to a discussion of what students hope to learn in the course. Others introduce an interesting problem. Then, while their students search for the solution, the teacher performs any necessary administrative duties. Another possibility is to conduct a review in the form of a game or a television quiz program.

	Kiesman Walter		Costa Beverly	
Jones William	Regan Pauline	Martin John	Bassett Charlotte	Reynolds Barbara
Edgerton Ronald	McNeill Margaret	Williams Henry	Beyer George	Parsons Russell
Eastman Louise	Hill Caroline	Graves James	Faust Paul	MacArthur Carole
Wasserman Joseph	Swanson Kathleen	King Andrew	Bonham Robert	Bell Albert
Donahue Donald	Werbach Walter	Meehan Nancy	Armstrong Susan	Perry Lloyd

Room No. _____2_____   Period _____3rd_____

Teacher _____H Lewis_____   Subject ___General Math___

■ **FIGURE 4.3**
A Sample Seating Chart

Stop and Reflect

If you were going to teach next September, what would you need to review and study? What could you do in the summer to make your work easier in the fall?

Plan a first day for a course you may teach. What introductory activities would you try? How might you work in administrative tasks? What would you do to motivate the students?

THE SECOND DAY AND THEREAFTER   Ordinarily you should start introducing your classroom routines and procedures on the second day of the course. It is usually best to introduce these as they come up. (For example, if now is the time for students to pass in their papers, now is the time to explain the routine for handing in papers.) Take time to explain things thoroughly, but do not overdo it. Explanations that slow down class progress may be as bad as no explanation at all. In any case, you should plan the explanation and how you intend to present it as carefully as you would plan the introduction of important academic course content. Write out instructions for complicated standard procedures, and pass them out or post them so that students will have the instructions for reference. The point, of course, is to have your students learn the routines and procedures so that they will carry them out automatically as the class gets rolling along. For that reason, review the procedures and routines from time to time until they become second nature to the class.

Use the content activities as a medium for setting standards. Ordinarily, it is best if learning activities planned for the first few weeks are short, relatively easy, whole-class activities at which all your students can succeed. (Individualization, small-group activities, and the like can come later.) Use these whole-group activities to show the students what you expect of them, what the work procedures will be, and what you consider acceptable—in addition to showing them that the course will be interesting, worthwhile, and important. These early activities demonstrate to students that you expect them to be productive and do well. The activities should also give students needed opportunities to firm up their understanding of the rules and how they work.

To inculcate desirable habits, understandings, knowledge, and attitudes from the very first, you must monitor, monitor, and monitor! First, make sure that the students understand each assignment and have the tools necessary for completing it. Routinizing the procedure for giving assignments is very helpful. So is clarifying your standards for marking and grading. Then, check the students' work to be sure they really do understand what they are supposed to be doing and that they have the basic understandings necessary for doing it. At this stage, provide feedback so that the students will know what they are doing correctly and what incorrectly. If students are acting inappropriately, correct them. Make sure they know why what they are doing wrong is wrong, and what they should do to make it right.

To carry out this monitoring, move around the classroom to see what students are doing. Learn to scan the class frequently for signs of misunderstanding, confusion, and other difficulties. Check the students' work often. If you can catch and correct mistakes, wrong procedures, misunderstandings, inappropriate behaviors, and misbehaviors before they develop into major problems, you will do much to smooth out the students' rocky road to learning. In this connection, it is essential to curb any misbehavior before it gets out of hand. Do not overreact, however. If you take misbehavior in stride, it probably will not become a big thing.

In sum, your teaching should be clear, logical, and smooth. Your lesson objectives should be set forth clearly. It can be helpful to list them on the chalkboard. The use of an advance organizer, a study guide, study questions, or a unit outline can help students focus on the understandings or skills to be learned. Make your presentation clear and logical. Usually, it helps to follow an outline. Presenting the outline on a transparency or a chalkboard ordinarily makes the presentation easier for students to follow. You can also make the presentation easier to follow by concentrating on one thought at a time. Finish each thought and reinforce it before you move on to the next. To avoid confusion, be sure to let students know when you stop presenting one idea and start on the next one. Assure clarity of expression by using complete sentences, a vocabulary level appropriate to your students' sophistication, and uncomplicated sentence structure. Use plenty of examples to make things clear, repeat major points, be specific, speak directly to the students, and keep the content and examples as concrete and precise as feasible. In short, each lesson should be a smooth, orderly, direct sequence to the learnings that are your instructional objectives.(13) You should always be in charge, and the students should always be aware of their tasks and be working to complete them.

Stop and Reflect

What is good discipline? How can you identify a well-ordered classroom? Observe a class. How much freedom should there be in a classroom?

Disciplinary Techniques

Preventive Discipline

Seldom is any misbehavior the result of a single motive. Rather, it is the result of the confluence of many factors triggered by some immediate happenstance. According to Feldhusen:

> . . . it is clear that the causes of disciplinary problems, violence, and delinquency in high schools are multifarious. They include weakened home and family structure, the heavy dose of crime and violence modeled by TV, school experiences that precipitate a failure-frustration-aggression sequence, and school and societal conditions that make it easy and rewarding for youth to engage in violence and crime as an effective mechanism for adaptation or coping.(14)

In addition, much student restlessness in class may be related to a simple need to work off energy. It might also be caused by the problems inherent in finding and adjusting to adolescents' new roles in society, aggravated by poor curricula and methods of teaching. What you can do to alleviate the problems caused by society and the advent of adolescence is minimal, but you can and should take steps to prevent your teaching and your classes from being the cause of discipline problems. You can do so by focusing on preventive discipline in your planning and teaching.

First, try to make sure that you yourself are not part of the problem. Some teachers act as though they want to create misbehavior by playing the role of martinet, bully, inefficient incompetent, or bore. They come to class late or start class late. They waste time. (Did you ever think of how much time students spend just waiting?) Problem teachers have sloppy work habits, and their class organization is careless as well. They abuse their students by using sarcasm, calling students names, making fun of them and their mistakes, giving them injudicious tongue lashings, and generally treating them like dirt. Other teachers are unconsciously discourteous, brusque, and unsympathetic. They are unfair and inconsistent in their demands. Some act as though they dislike students. It is difficult to get cooperation from people who feel you dislike them.

Second, try to make sure that your classes are not part of the problem. Often the curriculum and teaching methods can cause problems. Lesson planning is the key to good teaching, yet many teachers never seem to plan well. Their classes never seem to go anywhere because they have no real objective. There are no provisions for motivating the students. There is no variety; every day the classes repeat the same monotonous grind. Boring classes are always invitations to misbehave. Sometimes the classes contain dead spots in which students have nothing to do. The assignments are vague; students are not sure what they are supposed to do and how they are supposed to do it. Such assignments are frustrating. Also frustrating are lessons that are too hard or too easy, too fast or too slow.

Third, teach students how to behave. Discipline must be taught; it does not come naturally. Teaching discipline is "the most basic of the basics."(15) The steps in this process are

1. Establish your own self-discipline.
2. See to it that students know what is expected of them and why.
3. See to it that the students live up to these expectations. (In the realm of school behavior, as in other areas, practice tends to make perfect.)

As you can see, these steps are simply those of good classroom management.

Stop and Reflect

Think back over the classes you have attended in which there have been disciplinary incidents. What seemed to be the cause? What were the causes of disciplinary incidents involving you or your friends when you were in secondary school?

Why do students misbehave? List all the possible causes for misbehavior that you can name. How might knowledge of the causes of misbehavior influence the teacher's action?

Many (some say most) behavior problems are teacher-created. Can you think of some examples? How can the teacher avoid creating such situations?

Enforcing Rules

Classroom rules must be enforced. The students should have no doubt that these rules are operative and that breaking them will not be permitted. They should also know that living up to them pays off in some worthwhile reward. Laxity in enforcing rules makes the rules worthless. The students lose respect for them and resent subsequent attempts to enforce them. By consistently enforcing the rules, you quickly establish what behavior you will accept and what you will not tolerate. Although it is possible to be too rigid, one characteristic of teachers whose classes are well-controlled is that they consistently enforce class rules. Students like to know where they stand. The teacher whose rules are all-important today and then are forgotten tomorrow is lowered in students' respect. Also, since getting away with mischief is sometimes possible, students will be tempted to try their luck.

Because of this connection, firmness pays off; remember that your actions can cause a "ripple effect." The way you handle one case of misbehavior has considerable effect on other students who see or hear of the incident. If students find that you are consistently firm in handling a few cases initially, they will assume that you are strict and will act accordingly. The ripple effect is particularly strong when high-status students are involved. Consequently, you should work hard to control these

consistency
fairness

students. If you bring the high-status students into line, the other students will follow along. Obviously the ripple effect can make a great difference in your relationship with students. If students find you to be fair, just, pleasant, and empathetic in your dealings with others, they will tend to respond to you in the same way.

Along with consistency goes fairness. Treat all students alike. If you have favorites or treat some students preferentially, you will create behavior problems. This, of course, does not mean that you should never make an exception to a rule. As long as students have different personalities, they must be treated differently from one another. For instance, the punishment that one student might find devastating, another might actually enjoy. In this case, the punishment must suit the offender. Nevertheless, the enforcement of rules must be done consistently, even if the means of enforcement may vary. Exceptions should be made only for extraordinarily good reasons. It helps considerably if the reasons and their merits are evident to the class as a whole. Otherwise, students may accuse the teacher of favoritism and unfairness.

AVOIDING POOR ENFORCEMENT TECHNIQUES   When working to enforce rules, especially guard against nagging, because it disturbs the lesson and may cause additional student misbehavior. At times, it is better to disregard minor infractions than ceaselessly to attempt to correct the students. Criticizing or scolding a student too much will result only in arousing the support and sympathy of the other students. Besides, it slows down the lesson.

Instead of scolding, try the basic technique of Teacher Effectiveness Training:

Start describing BEHAVIOR instead of judging, evaluating, or making inferences about it. Want to transform your classes Monday morning? Then stop telling students what is going on in terms of assumptions you have made ABOUT their behavior. Start telling them what you see, what you hear . . . without blame, judgment or evaluation. A student who is late to class is not irresponsible, he or she is LATE TO CLASS. Get it? A kid can deal with being late to class. Irresponsibility is tough. Besides that, you have ABSOLUTELY NO IDEA WHETHER THE KID IS IRRESPONSIBLE OR NOT. The only thing you know is that here is a kid coming in after the class has begun.

When you get used to doing that, you are well on your way to being ready to take the next step, defining conflicts (continuing unacceptable student behavior) not as fights to be won or lost, but as problems to be solved.

The key to doing this is to define the conflict in terms of unmet needs. If a kid is behaving in an unacceptable way, some need of yours as the teacher must be unmet. You have a right to get your teacher (read human) needs met. But that unacceptable behavior! What is that about? Well, it is about the kid's way of getting some need of his or hers met. Once you get it that there is no such thing as "good" or "bad" behavior, just behavior, then you can begin to find all sorts of ways to see that both you *and* the kid get your respective needs met. This way you both win. Therefore, there is no need for either you or the kid to form coping mechanisms to handle each other.(16)

Nagging often results when teachers insist on unnecessarily high standards of student behavior and when their classes are poorly organized. If you find it necessary to keep admonishing a student, check to see whether the student has something worthwhile and appropriate to do. Sometimes a good remedy is to direct a question to the student whose mind seems to be wandering, or to start the restless student off on a new activity. Often just a reproving glance, a gesture, or moving in the direction of a student who is showing signs of misbehaving will bring the potential culprit back in line before anything really untoward has had a chance to happen. Such techniques can distract students from mischief. The teacher who keeps alert can often head off cases of misbehavior before they start. This is what Kounin means by "withitness."

Besides nagging, there are other poor methods of enforcing rules that can lead to misconduct. Harsh punishment, for example, often brings about resentment and revolt. In spite of the number of people who believe that force is the supreme disciplinary agent, harshness has never been really successful. According to Quintilian, the great Roman teacher, harsh punishment did not work in ancient Rome.(17) It still doesn't, according to modern researchers. In fact, as we pointed out earlier, harsh punishment may make students hate their studies and can cause them to rebel or to stop trying. Besides, it may lead to more trouble because of the resentment it builds up. A good teacher can do better without it.

When enforcing rules, try to avoid making big scenes out of insignificant acts. To do so is utterly pointless. Most little things can be brushed off lightly. Often a look or a pleasant word will suffice. Teachers who make major issues of minor transgressions soon find that the transgressions do not remain minor. It is better to save your fire for something important. You should also avoid threats and ultimatums. These tend to create scenes; and if a student does misbehave, your course of action is likely to be stalled, since you must carry out your threats if you are to keep the students' respect.

PUNISHMENT   Sooner or later, no matter how sensible the rules and how careful the planning, some student will commit an offense for which he or she must be punished. The Mikado probably meant well when he sang

My object all sublime
I shall achieve in time—
To let the punishment fit the crime—
The punishment fit the crime;
And make each prisoner pent
Unwillingly represent
A source of innocent merriment,
Of innocent merriment!(18)

But his scheme would not have worked well. Punishment should never be used as a source of "innocent merriment." Rather, it should be appropriate and, whenever possible, constructive. For example, if a student smashes a window willfully or carelessly, that student should clean up the mess and make proper restitution for it. In general, if your punishment is the logical result of misconduct, students are likely to accept it without resentment and may learn not to offend in the same way again. Any punishment is more likely to be effective when students see its reasonableness.

Use punishment sparingly; its overuse creates the repressive atmosphere you should avoid. Furthermore, overusing punishment takes the force out of it. Sometimes it causes lying, cheating, truancy, and rebellious behavior. Punishment should be held as a reserve for specific important offenses; it should never be used as a general disciplinary measure. If you commit your reserves too soon, or too often, or on too wide a front, you will find yourself with nothing to fall back on in real crisis.

When you do use punishment, it should be swift, sure, and impressive. Never punish on impulse; think twice before you act, but act at once. Should you become emotional, however, it is wise to calm down before prescribing the punishment, since punishing students in anger can be disastrous. To ascertain, without the shadow of a doubt, who the guilty party is and then select a punishment appropriate for both the offense and the offender requires self-control and levelheadedness on the teacher's part.

To make punishment most effective, combine it with positive measures. It is important for students to know just what behaviors are expected of them. Positive reinforcement techniques, modeling, and direct instruction in how to behave will give point to the punishment, and will bring out the desired behavior when punishment alone will not.

CORPORAL PUNISHMENT   Some teachers, clergy members, and newspaper editors trace all the ills of modern civilization back to the schools, claiming that because teachers no longer "beat out the tune with a hickory stick," students can no longer be controlled. That anyone should have so much faith in corporal punishment is astonishing in view of its centuries-long history of little success.

Under no circumstances should you ever use corporal punishment except in a formal situation with suitable witnesses according to the laws of your state and school district. Otherwise, you may lay yourself open to accusations and legal difficulties. If such drastic measures as corporal punishment are to be used, discretion tells us to turn the matter over to the principal. *Never, ever use it yourself!*

DETENTION   Detention, or staying after school, is one of the most frequently used punishments. There are two kinds of detention. One is the sort common in large schools in which the students must report to a detention hall. The other is a do-it-yourself arrangement whereby each teacher looks after his or her own detainees. In spite of its widespread use, detention is not very effective. Detention periods are a waste of time unless they are used constructively. Their force as a deterrent is not strong enough to warrant keeping a student sitting in a chair doing nothing. When you use detention, it is better to combine it with a conference or some educationally valuable activity.

VERBAL PUNISHMENT   The reprimand is probably the most common and most poorly used kind of punishment. Like many other measures, its effect soon dissipates when it is overused. Then it becomes mere nagging, the futility of which we have already discussed. Loud, frequent reprimands are ineffective; they only add to the turmoil. Calm, firm reprimands are much more effective. As a rule, reprimands should be given in private. Public reprimands tend to reinforce misbehavior. The class may sympathize with the student being reprimanded or make him a folk hero. However, a quiet, calm, firm reprimand describing the fault, if given when needed by a teacher who is fair and gives plenty of honest praise for what the student does well, will be effective and have no deleterious side effects. From time to time, however, a whole class may need to be told the hard facts of life. Whenever such explanations are in order, they should be businesslike and matter-of-fact. It is not a time for emotionalism.

Sarcasm and ridicule are two other common types of verbal punishments. Although in faculty lounges one is likely to be regaled with stories of the Mr. Chips type who ruled his classes with a tongue of acid and so endeared himself to the hearts of generations of students, on the whole, such weapons should not be used. They hurt people's feelings, cause resentment, destroy students' self-esteem, and in general break down the classroom atmosphere. Avoid them.

ISOLATION   Separating students to break up seating arrangements that permit cliques and too much opportunity for social visiting is a common practice. This procedure has much to recommend it as long as you do not create a situation in which the students who formerly whispered to each other now shout and pass notes. Another similar plan is to change the seat of a chronic offender so that he or she is isolated from the rest of the class, such as positioning him or her all alone in the back of the room. Other teachers like to put students who misbehave up front in the first row next to the teacher's desk or podium. Placing the student up front may be objectionable for two reasons: (1) It places the student where he or she is assured of an audience if the student wants to show off, and (2) it seems to assume that the teacher will work entirely from the desk at the front of the room, a practice not generally recommended. In the case of an extraordinarily bad incident, you can send the student out of the classroom. Do this sparingly—only when faced with a major problem with which, for one reason or another, you cannot cope at the time.

ASSIGNING EXTRA WORK   At one time, the most common method of punishing secondary school students was to assign them a number of lines of Latin verse to translate. Today the assignment of extra work continues to be a common punishment, but really it is an irrational practice. Associating schoolwork with punishment creates a prejudice against learning in the minds of the students. If you want to create dislike for the subject you teach, this is one way to do it. However, there should be no objection to making students redo sloppy work—in fact, if you accept papers that have been carelessly prepared, you are encouraging poor work habits. Likewise, there should be no objection to keeping students busy doing class assignments during detention periods.

DEPRIVATION OF PRIVILEGES   One of the few punishments that seems to be both effective and acceptable to experts in pedagogy is to take away privileges from students who misbehave. In general, this practice is a good one. Unfortunately, many students do not have many privileges to lose, and often the loss of these privileges would not greatly concern them. For students in schools located in low-income areas and for chronic offenders, such deprivation may carry no weight at all. The best way to capitalize on this type of punishment is by combining it with a system in which you reward good behavior by granting the students desirable privileges.

DEDUCTING FROM ACADEMIC MARKS   Punishing students by lowering their grades in the course is a tempting technique that you should avoid. Academic marks, if they are to have any validity at all, must be based on students' achievement. To lower course marks because of misbehavior is unfair to the students, their parents, and prospective employers or college admission officers. Under no circumstances should such punishments be tolerated.

Stop and Reflect

Why should you avoid use of the following?

- *Sarcasm*
- *Threats*
- *Nagging*
- *Yelling*
- *Constant vocal correction*
- *Arguments with students*
- *Corporal punishment*

Are any of these listed techniques ever permissible? If so, when? Justify your reply. What techniques do you propose to use to enforce your rules?

POSITIVE APPROACHES   After reading such a devastating description of the punishments at your disposal, you may be somewhat discouraged. Is there nothing that can be done to maintain control in the classroom? Yes, of course there is. The answer, however, lies almost entirely in preventive approaches and positive corrective measures.

Using positive measures is not only productive but also is relatively easy if you establish the rules and standards, rewards, and penalties in advance. Think of rule enforcement as a way of teaching students to behave properly rather than as retribution for academic crimes. In the long run, it is more effective to focus attention on rewards rather than on penalties. Try to recognize every individual who does something well. Display students' good work or congratulate them on their successes, for instance. Take care to spread rewards and praise to all the deserving—not just to the brightest. Every student does something worth recognizing at one time or another.

Dealing with Minor Disturbances

On occasion minor disciplinary problems will arise. They are often not really anyone's fault, but instead are usually the result of herding together human beings in schools and classes. Often, if a particular behavior is not outrageous or dangerous, it may be wise to simply ignore it. Usually, however, you must take some action. If students are noisy, merely asking for quiet and moving on to the next item may be all that is necessary. If a student is distracting other students' attention, simply standing next to him may quiet him down. Finding other work for troublemakers to get them out of the public view may solve the problem. Many disciplinary situations may be avoided before incidents happen if you talk out problems with the students concerned and have the class help you draw up rules for procedures and standards of behavior that they accept as fair and reasonable.

Sending Students to the Office

Sometimes misbehavior is such that help is needed from a school administrator. Usually it is better to handle disciplinary problems yourself, because principals and vice-principals are not in a good position to deal with routine cases. They are handicapped by not knowing exactly what has happened, and their special disciplinary powers are best suited for dealing with major offenses. Sometimes their sympathies may lie with the student. Furthermore, sending a student to the office may be taken as a sign of weakness and can lower your prestige among your students. Doubtless there will be crises when you must cast students into outer darkness, but keep these occasions to a minimum. If you handle your own discipline problems, you will usually rise in your students' esteem and in that of your principal's as well.

In spite of these warnings, do not hesitate to send a misbehaving student to the office for correction when it is necessary—for example, when correcting a student in class would disrupt or interfere with the progress of the class lesson, or when the offense is beyond the scope of your power and authority. In no case should the misbehavior of one student be allowed to break up a class.

When sending students out of class, be sure to inform them exactly where they are to go and what they are supposed to do; also inform the official to whom the students report. He or she should know why a student is coming, either by a note or by the intercommunications system.

Dealing with Major Offenses

At times you will need to deal with a major offense. These types of infractions might include carrying weapons, stealing, using drugs, committing arson, vandalizing school property, defying authority, and leaving the room without authorization. Your major responsibility in such cases is to try to stop the behavior and see to it that it does not occur again. This is not always possible, of course. If the case is really serious, report it to the principal immediately. Administrative personnel have greater resources at their disposal than you do, and are ultimately responsible for major problems. Furthermore, it helps officials if they know of these problems before they are confronted by irate parents, concerned central administrative personnel, or the police. If an incident merits calling in the police, it is the principal's job to do so.

Helping Students with Problems

Every school has difficult students who for some reason or other do not seem able to adapt to the school program. This inability to adjust to a school situation may be caused by problems at home, the social environment in the community, or personality defects. Frequently, such students seek distraction from their problems in undesirable ways.

Teachers are usually well-aware of obstreperous students; however, students who are quiet and withdrawn can be concealing a behavior problem that is just as serious. Such students often develop severe emotional problems. These students need to be helped; treat them with sympathy and understanding. In most cases, such students can be referred to guidance counselors for help. In the meantime, try to find out as much as possible about these students and treat them accordingly.

Direct Instruction

In some school systems, the most difficult students are removed from regular classes to attend alternative schools or to serve in-house suspensions. In most systems, however, you will be expected to resolve the situation on your own. When you must do the job yourself, focus on attempting to improve the overt behavior of the student rather than trying to find and correct the underlying causes. After all, your job is to teach; you cannot allow one student, even a student with problems, to upset the entire class. Besides, you are not trained to treat mental or emotional problems. Even if you could identify the underlying problems, you are not in a position to do anything about them, and even if you were, the behavior might continue to exist even after the causes have been treated. (Problem behaviors often continue after the student returns from the specialist.) So there is little you can do except to deal directly with the behavior. Fortunately, direct instruction that involves the motivational and disciplinary techniques at your command can, and frequently does, change misbehavior to acceptable behavior. There is no excuse for allowing students to continue to misbehave just because they have problems.

Stop and Reflect

Critique the following discipline rules:

1. *Watch carefully for the first small signs of trouble and squelch them at once with no exceptions.*
2. *Hold your group to very high standards at first. You can relax these standards later if the situation warrants it.*
3. *Be a real friend to the students.*
4. *Employ self-government only if you are sure the class is ready for it.*
5. *Be fair.*
6. *Be consistent.*

Critique the following practice reported by a national wire service:

The Boston School Committee recently directed that the following commandments be read bi-weekly to students in grades 7 through 12.

1. *Don't let your parents down; they've brought you up.*
2. *Be smart, obey. You'll give orders yourself some day.*
3. *Stop and think before you drink.*
4. *Ditch dirty thoughts fast or they'll ditch you.*

5. *Show-off driving is juvenile. Don't act your age.*
6. *Pick the right friends to be picked for a friend.*
7. *Choose a date fit for a mate.*
8. *Don't go steady unless you're ready.*
9. *Love God and neighbor.*
10. *Live carefully. The soul you save may be your own.*

What can you do about the student whose behavior problems arise from home experiences? From emotional difficulties? From social problems?

Think back to your high school days. Try to picture the teacher who had the most trouble with discipline and the teacher who had the least difficulty. What was it about those teachers that made the difference in their relations with students?

■■■ Student Rights

The U.S. Constitution, state constitutions, laws, and legal decisions have given students certain rights. Make it a point to become familiar with these rights and to conduct yourself so that these student rights will not be violated. Not to do so is illegal and leaves you open to unpleasant consequences.

Perhaps the first right of students is the right to an education. This right guarantees that the schools must be open to every child; no boy and girl may be excluded (e.g., suspended or expelled) except for sufficient cause established by suitable due process. This right implies that without exception the schooling provided all boys and girls must be of high quality. Schools may not discriminate against any student or group of students, or favor one type of student over another. When students have been the victims of discrimination, they have the right to special treatment to counteract and alleviate their mistreatment.

The U.S. Constitution gives all students the right to be left alone except for good and sufficient reasons. Therefore, except for reasons of misbehavior, or other actions prejudicial to the welfare of the school, the class, the other students, or the student himself, teachers and administrators must respect students' privacy and their right to be free of harassment.

All students have the right to religious freedom. They may not be bothered because of any religious belief or nonbelief they hold. They may not be forced to take part in any religious exercise or be embarrassed because of nonparticipation in religious activities. Students may not be subjected to semi- or quasi-religious teaching. All teaching of values, morals, and ethics must be free from any religious bias. Neither may students be required to recite prayers, pledges of allegiance, creeds, or similar statements that conflict with their beliefs.

The constitutional rights of free speech, expression of ideas, and the press extend to students also. These rights, however, do not include the use of obscenity or practices that may be injurious to others. Neither may they be used in a manner, time, or place that would interfere with normal educational activities and school decorum. Publications may be censored by school officials only if they are subsidized by the school.

Punishment of students is also limited and regulated by law. Students have the right to know what the rules and regulations are. Therefore, school and class rules and regulations should be published so that students will know what is permitted and what is not. When students do transgress, punishment may not be arbitrary or capricious; rather, it should follow the course of due process. The rules must be enforced fairly. Persons enforcing school rules and regulations must be careful to avoid cruel punishments and to follow reasonable procedures for establishing guilt. Students have the right to be presumed innocent until they are proven guilty. They also have the right to remain silent; certainly this is true in legal cases and presumably is true in schools, for no one is obligated to convict himself. Likewise, searches and seizures should be conducted only under controlled conditions, since everyone has the right to be secure from improper searches and seizures. Last, all accused have the right to defend themselves. They have the right not to be branded for past misbehavior or mistakes. School officials must ensure that permanent records do not include ill-based, deleterious information. To protect students from incorrect prejudicial entries, parents have the right to review their children's records when they think it advisable.

Stop and Reflect

A Problem in Discipline

At Lloyd Road Intermediate School, two boys got into a fistfight in their science classroom just as their science class was about to begin. It seems that the two boys were the Norwegian representatives in the model U. N. Assembly being conducted in the social studies–English block. They were arguing in the hall between classes about how Norway should vote on a resolution before the assembly that was to be voted on the following morning. When they got to the science class, their argument culminated in blows.

If you were the science teacher, what would you do?

As the social studies teacher, what would you do?

Building Self-Discipline

A major goal of effective classroom management is student self-discipline. Self-discipline is a necessity for success in one's studies as well as in later life; however, it does not come naturally. It must be learned, and learning it takes time. Consciously try to help your students develop self-discipline, but in doing so, expect to proceed slowly. Help students learn the importance of accepting responsibility for working diligently, for being dependable, and for carrying out what they have agreed to do. This can be done by running well-organized, efficient classes in which students learn what appropriate behavior is and that behaving appropriately is rewarded. Depend on the reasonableness and workability of your standards rather than on authority alone. Without preaching, show students how many people make their lives more satisfying by following good codes. Also, let the students know how teachers and other people feel about proper conduct. You may be able to help students realize that these standards will make life better for them and thus induce them to adopt suitable patterns of behavior voluntarily.

SUMMARY

Classroom management refers to the process of organizing and carrying out classes so that learning occurs smoothly and efficiently. Its major purpose is to focus classes on learning. The attainment of this purpose depends on establishing a suitable classroom climate. For this reason, strive to treat students fairly, reasonably, and pleasantly. It will help if you do not take yourself too seriously, and if you try by your own actions to exemplify the type of behavior you expect of students. Creating a diffusely structured class will facilitate the type of classroom climate you need.

To organize classroom management requires careful planning. You must arrange a physical setting for learning, set up suitable routines, and establish a few carefully chosen rules. Managing the class is largely dependent on getting off to a good start and then keeping the class moving smoothly. To do this, you need to develop skill in movement management and "withitness." Perhaps most important is checking on both your own and the students' work and behavior. Specifically you should concentrate on being well-prepared before the first day of school starts. On the first day, conduct an interesting, well-organized class to set the tone for the course. After that, take care to keep things rolling smoothly. Introduce routines and procedures as necessary. Take care of details. Be sure students understand what is expected of them. And, finally, monitor, monitor, monitor! If in the process you can teach the students to discipline themselves, your classroom management will prosper. Developing self-discipline is a slow process but one that is essential for good learning.

The following rules that combine principles of motivation and classroom management should help any teacher to achieve and maintain good classroom control.

PREVENTIVE MEASURES
SET A GOOD EXAMPLE.
> Don't take yourself too seriously.
> Develop a sense of humor.
> Do as you would be done by.
> Be friendly, but not too friendly.
> Control your own temper.
> Let sleeping dogs lie (i.e., do not go looking for trouble).
> Expect good conduct.
> Remember, you are an authority figure. Act that way.

STAND ON YOUR OWN FEET; ASSUME THE RESPONSIBILITY FOR YOUR OWN CLASSROOM CONTROL.
> Take a personal interest in your students.
> Be businesslike.
> Assume everything will be all right.
> Act like an adult.

DEVELOP GOOD RELATIONSHIPS WITH STUDENTS.
> Promote a democratic atmosphere.
> Respect students' feelings and try to build their self-esteem.
> Do not demean the students either by your rules or by your enforcement of them.
> Avoid laissez-faire techniques. Students need to know where they stand.
> Create a friendly atmosphere.

GET OFF TO A GOOD START.
> Start with an impressive lesson on the first day.
> Start each class at the sound of the bell.
> Be strict at first.
> Learn students' names as quickly as you can.
> Prepare a seating plan.
> Pay attention to classroom management.
> Be sure the materials and equipment are ready.

Demand quiet before you speak.

Adapt your techniques to the situation and the mood of the class.

Use all means of support available.

Set up routines for the more usual tasks such as passing out papers, taking attendance, and so on.

PLAN CLASSES WELL.

Eliminate lags and dead spots.

Provide for individual differences.

Vary classroom activities.

Make classes interesting.

Make classes seem worthwhile.

Help students feel important.

Adjust teaching to students; avoid creating student failure and frustration.

Be sure your classes are relevant.

Be sure everyone has plenty of worthwhile things to do.

SET UP A FEW RULES.

Be sure the rules are reasonable and not too strict.

Do not make the rules too rigid; leave yourself room to maneuver.

Be sure everyone understands the rules.

Let students help make the rules.

TRY TO DEVELOP SELF-DISCIPLINE.

CORRECTIVE MEASURES

ENFORCE THE RULES FIRMLY, FAIRLY, AND CONSISTENTLY.

Don't make mountains out of molehills.

Avoid scenes.

Avoid ultimatums.

Avoid threats.

Do not nag.

Take it easy; don't get excited.

Utilize the ripple effect.

Be reasonable.

Do not scold; try describing behavior instead.

Avoid harsh punishment.

UTILIZE POSITIVE APPROACHES TO CORRECT AND REDIRECT BEHAVIOR.

Try to redirect behavior via positive reinforcement and socialization techniques.

PUNISHMENT SHOULD BE RARE BUT, WHEN NECESSARY, SWIFT AND CERTAIN.

Never use sarcasm, ridicule, or harsh or humiliating punishments.

Never embarrass students.

Do not use corporal punishment—ever! If it must be used, let one of your superiors do it.

Don't punish the entire class for the faults of a few.

Be sure that your punishments are reasonable.

Use soft reprimands; avoid shouting, scolding, and roughness.

Utilize isolation techniques with care.

Never assign schoolwork as a punishment.

Never give poor academic marks as punishment.

UTILIZE THE HELP OF SPECIALISTS WHEN NECESSARY.
Refer serious cases of student problems to the guidance staff.
Refer really serious disciplinary cases to the principal or the assistant in charge of discipline.
Handle your own discipline problems. Call in the principal or assistant principal only in extraordinary circumstances.

REMEMBER AND RESPECT STUDENTS' RIGHTS AS UNITED STATES CITIZENS.

ADDITIONAL READING

Baron, E. B. *Discipline Strategies for Teachers, Fastback 344.* Bloomington, IN: Phi Delta Kappa Educational Foundation, 1992.

Blendiger, J., L. Cornelius, V. McGrath, and L. Rose. *Win Win Discipline.* Bloomington, IN: Phi Delta Kappa Educational Foundation, 1993.

Cangelosi, J. S. *Classroom Management Strategies: Gaining and Maintaining Students' Cooperation.* New York: Longman, 1988.

Carter, M. *A Model for Effective Discipline, Fastback 250.* Bloomington, IN: Phi Delta Kappa Educational Foundation, 1987.

Charles, C. M. *Building Classroom Discipline: From Models to Practice,* 3rd ed. White Plains, NY: Longman, 1989.

Doyle, W. "Classroom Organization and Management" in *Handbook of Research in Teaching,* 3rd ed., edited by M. C. Wittrock. New York: Macmillan, 1986, 392–431.

Duke, D. L., ed. *Classroom Management, The Seventy-eighth Yearbook of the National Society for the Study of Education,* Part II. Chicago: University of Chicago Press, 1979.

Duke, D. L., and A. M. Mickel. *Teacher's Guide to Classroom Management.* New York: Random House, 1984.

Emmers, E. T. et al. *Classroom Management for Secondary Teachers,* 3rd ed. Englewood Cliffs, NJ: Prentice-Hall, 1989.

Englander, M. E. *Strategies for Classroom Discipline.* New York: Praeger, 1986.

Evertson, C. M. et al. *Effective Classroom Management and Instruction: An Exploration of Models.* Washington, DC: National Institute of Education, 1988 (ERIC).

Gathercoal, F. *Judicious Discipline.* Ann Arbor, MI: Prakken, 1987.

Glasser, W. *Control Theory in the Classroom.* New York: Harper and Row, 1986.

Good, T. L., and J. E. Brophy. *Looking in Classrooms,* 4th ed. New York: Harper and Row, 1987.

Grossnickle, D., and F. Sesko. *Promoting Effective Discipline in School and Classroom.* Reston, VA: National Association of Secondary School Principals, 1985.

Harvey, K. *Classroom Management.* Glenview, IL: Scott Foresman, 1985.

Hoppenstedt, E. M. *A Teacher's Guide to Classroom Management.* Springfield, IL: Charles C. Thomas, 1991.

Johnson, E. W. *Teaching School,* rev. ed. Boston, MA: National Association of Independent Schools, 1987, Ch. 1–4, 12, 15.

Johnson, S. O., and V. J. Johnson. *Better Discipline: A Practical Approach,* 2nd ed. Springfield, IL: Charles C. Thomas, 1990.

Jones, F. *Positive Classroom Discipline.* New York: McGraw-Hill, 1987.

Kerr, M. M., and C. M. Nelson. *Strategies for Managing Problems in the Classroom.* Columbus, OH: Merrill, 1983.

Laslett, R., and C. Smith. *Effective Classroom Management.* New York: Nichols, 1984.

Lemlech, J. K. *Classroom Management: Methods and Techniques for Elementary and Secondary Teachers,* 2nd ed. White Plains, NY: Longman, 1988.

McCarthy, M. M., and N. H. Cambrow. *Public School Law: Teachers' and Students' Rights.* Boston: Allyn and Bacon, 1981.

Madsen, C. H., Jr., and C. K. Madsen. *Teaching Discipline: A Positive Approach.* Raleigh, NC: Contemporary Publishing Co. of Raleigh, 1983.

Mann, L. *Discipline and Behavioral Management.* Aspen, CO: Aspen Publications, 1983.

Moles, O. C. *Student Discipline Strategies: Research and Practice.* Albany, NY: State University of New York Press, 1990.

Sanford, J. P., and E. T. Emmer. *Understanding Classroom Management: An Observation Guide.* Englewood Cliffs, NJ: Prentice-Hall, 1988.

Seeman, H. *Preventing Classroom Discipline Problems.* Lancaster, PA: Technomic, 1988.

Seltzer, L., and J. Banthin. *Teachers Have Rights Too: What Educators Should Know About School Law.* Boulder, CO: Social Science Educational Consortium, 1981.

Sevich, K. J. *Disruptive Behavior in the Classroom,* rev. ed. Washington, DC: National Education Association, 1987.

Steere, B. F. *Becoming an Effective Manager: A Resource for Teachers.* Albany, NY: State University of New York Press, 1988.

Strother, D. B., ed. *Effective Classroom Management.* Bloomington, IN: Phi Delta Kappa, Center of Evaluation, Development, and Research, 1984.

Sweck, K. J. *Disruptive Student Behavior in the Classroom.* Washington, DC: National Education Association, 1985.

Taylor, B. W. *Classroom Discipline.* Dayton, OH: Southern Hills Press, 1987.

Wayson, W. W. et al. *Handbook for Developing Schools with Good Discipline.* Phi Delta Kappa Commission on Discipline. Bloomington, IN: Phi Delta Kappa, 1982.

Weber, W. A. et al. *Classroom Management: Reviews of the Teacher Education and Research Literature.* Princeton, NJ: Educational Testing Service, 1983.

Wolfgang, C. H., and C. D. Glickman. *Solving Discipline Problems: Strategies for Classroom Teachers,* 2nd ed. Needham Heights, MA: Allyn and Bacon, Longwood Division, 1987.

NOTES

1. Jerry L. Bellon, Elner C. Bellon, and Mary Ann Blank, *Teaching from a Research Knowledge Base* (New York: Macmillan, 1992), 124.

2. Daniel R. Duke, "Editor's Preface" in *Classroom Management,* The Seventy-eighth Yearbook of the Study of Education, Part II, edited by Daniel L. Duke. (Chicago: University of Chicago Press, 1979), p. xii.

3. Walter Doyle, "Classroom Organization and Management" in *Handbook of Research in Teaching,* 3rd ed., edited by M. C. Wittrock (New York: Macmillan, 1986), 394.

4. *Tinker v. Des Moines Independent Community School District* 309 U.S. 508–9 (1969).

5. William G. Spady, "Authority, Conflict, and Teacher Effectiveness," *Educational Researcher* 2 (January 1973): 4–10.

6. Duane Brown, *Changing Student Behavior: A New Approach to Discipline* (Dubuque, IA: Brown, 1971), 12.

7. Elizabeth M. Reis, "Effective Teacher Techniques: Implications for Better Discipline," *The Clearing House* 61 (April 1988): 356.

8. Emery Stoops and Joyce King Stoops, *Discipline or Disaster, Fastback 8* (Bloomington, IN: Phi Delta Kappa Educational Foundation, 1972), 36.

9. Jacob S. Kounin, *Discipline and Group Management in the Classroom* (New York: Holt, 1970), 102–108.

10. Ibid.

11. Carolyn M. Evertson and Arlene H. Harris, "What We Know About Managing Classrooms," *Educational Leadership* 49 (April 1992): 74–77.
12. Edmund T. Emmer et al., *Organizing and Managing the Junior High Classroom* (Austin, TX: The Research and Development Center for Teacher Education, University of Texas, n.d.), 75–84.
13. Kounin, *Discipline and Group Management,* 111–112.
14. John Feldhusen, "Problem of Student Behavior in Secondary Schools" in *Classroom Management,* The Seventy-Eighth Yearbook of the National Society for the Study of Education, Part II, edited by Daniel L. Duke (Chicago: University of Chicago Press, 1979), 229.
15. William W. Wayson et al., *Phi Delta Kappa Commission on Discipline: Handbook for Developing Schools with Good Discipline* (Bloomington, IN: Phi Delta Kappa, 1982).
16. Noel Burch, "What You Already Know About Discipline," *NJEA Review* 52 (October 1978): 22. Reprinted with permission from the October 1978 (Vol. 52, p. 22) *NJEA Review,* copyright New Jersey Education Association.
17. Marcus Fabius Quintilianus, *Institutes of Oratory,* Book 1.
18. W. S. Gilbert and Arthur Sullivan, *The Mikado,* Act II.

Planning for Teaching

Overview

There is no substitute for good planning. Planning is necessary to create a pleasant classroom atmosphere as well as to create a purposeful teaching-learning activity that is free from dead spots and wasted motion—in short, good planning promotes worthwhile learning. No one can teach well for long without planning well.

The first step in planning and teaching must be diagnosis. In this context, *diagnosis* means sizing up the situation so as to understand it fully and to find clues for deciding what to do. It provides the teacher with the following information:

1. The level of learning students have reached.
2. The areas in which students are weak and strong.
3. The students' aptitudes, aspirations, backgrounds, problems, and needs.

Although these data are only approximations, they make it possible to understand the teaching-learning situation; thus, diagnosis provides a basis for successful planning.

Planning consists of deciding 1) what needs to be accomplished, 2) how to accomplish it, and 3) how to tell what has been accomplished. It requires the teacher to consider for each plan the following questions:

What is to be accomplished?
How is it to be done?
Who is to do what?
When, and in what order, shall things be done?
Where shall they be done?
Why do we want to accomplish this, and why do we plan to do it this way?
How will we know how well we have succeeded?

Therefore, the task you, the teacher, face in planning is to set up, on the basis of your diagnosis, the following:

1. The teaching objectives.
2. Specific teaching-learning activities designed to attain these objectives.
3. A plan for evaluating the success of the teaching and the progress of the students toward reaching the objectives.

Diagnosis

Diagnosis is really a continuous process of evaluation and assessment. To establish a firm basis for your teaching, as early as possible make a general diagnosis of the status of each student's learning and any associated traits; continue with similar diagnoses as the course goes on. The evaluation phase of each succeeding unit should become, in effect, the diagnosis phase for the next one. (The planning and teaching of the next unit thus becomes the follow-up phase of the preceding one.) In any course, or sequence, there is an initial diagnosis at the beginning and continuing diagnosis and reassessment as the course, or sequence, proceeds. The process for both initial and continuing diagnosis should conform to a pattern something like the following:

1. Assess the situation.
2. Determine if there are any difficulties or any strengths.

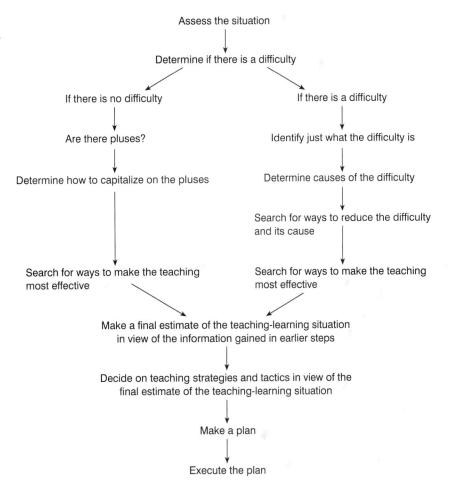

3. If there is a difficulty:
   a. Identify just what the difficulty is.
   b. Having pinpointed the difficulty, determine just what the cause of the difficulty is.
   c. Search for factors in the situation that would help you make your teaching more effective and, if there is a difficulty, eliminate the difficulty and its cause.
4. Make a final estimate of the situation in view of the information obtained in the earlier steps.
5. Make decisions on the basis of the final estimate of the situation (see Figure 5.1).

▓ ▓ ▓ ▓ Initial Diagnosis

Initial diagnosis provides a basis for placing students in appropriate curricula, tracks, courses, and units. Of course, most of the decisions about placing students in courses and curricula will have been made before the students arrive at your classroom. Sometimes, however, initial diagnosis will point out a need for reassigning students. For example, perhaps the student who did so well on the achievement test should be allowed to drop this course and take a more advanced one.

Frequently, students are placed in courses, sections, and units on the basis of their grades in previous ones. Such procedures are dangerous. A single grade may hide more information than it shows. In general, grades give you little basis for judging what is best for the students in a new situation. Furthermore, grades tend to be self-fulfilling. Students who have not done well in last year's course tend not to do well in this year's course even though they have plenty of aptitude and ability. You would be wise to make as careful an analysis as you can of all your students. In modular courses, your analysis should determine where each student should be placed in the sequence of units. In other courses, careful diagnosis can be used as the basis for providing for individual differences in students, remedial work, review, and selection of their instructional strategies.

For the initial diagnosis, you might give a test to ascertain each student's position in relation to the goals and demands of the course. Norm-referenced, standardized tests may be useful for giving a general picture of how students stand. Students who score much below average on standardized achievement tests may not have all the prerequisites for the course; students who score very much above average may already know everything that the course has to offer. Some commercial tests give charts that describe what students' weaknesses may be and suggest possible remedies. Usually, however, these tests are not sensitive enough to give you anything more than a general indication that a difficulty exists. To pinpoint the difficulty and its magnitude, you will most likely have to use other kinds of diagnostic techniques.

Teacher-made instruments may be just as satisfactory (perhaps more so) as standardized tests for finding each student's initial position in relation to the goals of the course. In many courses, an objective paper-and-pencil test can be a good device to show where each student stands, while in other courses another type of test may be more desirable. Paper-and-pencil tests are usually not the best device for measuring skills, attitudes, appreciations, and ideals. To get at these learnings, you may find more benefit in portfolios that contain examples and evaluations of the student's past work.

In addition, more general information such as the following may help to give you a clearer picture of each student and might also suggest steps that you can take to make learning more thorough and efficient.

1. Vital statistics
   a. Name, grade, course, and so on
   b. Health record—mental and physical (any challenges?)
   c. Any standard test results (reading grade level, aptitude and ability, and so on)
   d. Attendance record
2. Home situation
   a. Family background
   b. Intrafamily relationships
   c. Social contacts with community (club memberships and so on)
   d. Religious attitudes and affiliations
   e. Economic status
3. Social outlook
   a. Friends
   b. Social activities, such as use of spare time, school extracurricular activities
   c. Group acceptance
4. Personal qualities
   a. Ethical standards and attitudes
   b. Talents and capabilities

    c. Goals and ambitions (immediate and future)
    d. Interests and hobbies (in or out of school)
    e. Antisocial traits causing discipline problems

A careful examination of the students' cumulative records is usually well worth the effort.

Continuing Diagnosis

After the initial diagnosis, continue to evaluate, revising your assessment as new evidence comes up. Try to take stock at the end of each unit. One way to do this is to give your students a formative unit test to see where they stand in relation to the goals of the unit. For this purpose, a criterion-referenced mastery test would be most in order. In addition, consider the information you have gleaned from observing your students and analyzing their oral and written work during the unit. Pre-assessment tests before a unit begins may also give you essential information, particularly if your course is modularized. Sometimes, however, the posttest for one unit can and should serve as the pretest for the next one.[*] In any case, you should perform some sort of preassessment before each and every unit.

▓ ▓ ▓ The Tools of Diagnosis

Accurate diagnosis depends on a sufficient supply of accurate information. Among the tools useful for gleaning diagnostic information are the following:

1. Records
   a. Cumulative record folder (Permanent Record Card)
   b. Test results (vocational, aptitude, ability, intelligence, achievement, and so on)
   c. Anecdotal records
   d. Physical examinations (dental, visual, auditory, and so on)
   e. Portfolios of past work
2. Indirect contacts
   a. Home visits
   b. Reliable members of community (Boy Scout leaders, priests or ministers, police, and so on)
   c. Contacts with parents
   d. Guidance nurse or guidance counselor
   e. Other dependable teachers
3. Direct contacts
   a. Personal observations during informal discussions, conferences, special help periods, and nonschool activities
   b. Conclusions drawn from autobiographies, questionnaires, sociograms and other sociometric devices, and portfolios of past work
   c. Diagnostic, formative, and summative evaluation—tests and quizzes, written and oral classwork, homework
   d. Portfolios of classwork
   e. Checklists, analyses of papers, rating scales

[*]For information on building diagnostic, formative, preassessment, and post-assessment mastery tests, see Chapter 14.

■ ■ ■   The Objectives

General and Specific Objectives

Your diagnosis of the teaching-learning situation should point out the objectives your teaching should strive for. Some learning products are extremely broad and general; others are narrow and specific. For instance, the central purpose of education in the United States, according to the Educational Policies Commission, is to teach students to think independently.(1) Nothing could be much broader than that. In contrast, an objective for a science lesson might be for students to commit to memory the chemical formula $NaSO_4$, which is a very narrow goal.

As Figure 5.2 shows, the aims of teaching-learning objectives may fall at any level between the broad and narrow extremes. In other words, although there are general objectives and specific objectives, some objectives are more general or more specific than others. In theory, and in the best practice, specific objectives are subordinate to and contain the basic ingredients of the more general objectives (as shown in Figure 5.3).* In general, the broadest objectives are those for all education, followed by (in descending order) those for specific schools, those for specific curricula in schools, those for specific units, and finally, the least broad, those for specific lessons and exercises. If lessons, courses, and curricula are well-built, the specific objectives of the lessons contribute directly to the more general objectives of the course, which in turn are the ingredients that make up the more general objectives of the curriculum. Similarly, each unit, course, and lesson may contain a number of specific objectives that combine to form a more general objective. For instance, the teacher may set the learning of the formula $NaSO_4$ as a beginning step toward the more general, although still rather specific, objective of learning the properties of sulfuric acid. (See Figure 5.4.)

Overt and Covert Objectives

Learning sometimes results in overt (i.e., observable) behavior. A pupil who learns to conjugate the Latin verb *amare* in the present tense learns to say or write:

Amo	I love
Amas	You love
Amat	He, she, it loves
Amamus	We love
Amatis	You love
Amant	They love

■ **FIGURE 5.2**
General to Specific Objective Continuum

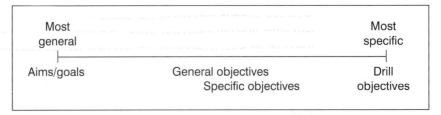

Most general		Most specific
Aims/goals	General objectives Specific objectives	Drill objectives

*Writers on educational topics have developed a nomenclature that differentiates between the kinds of general and specific objectives. Unfortunately, there is little agreement about the terminology. The terms *educational goals, educational aims,* and *educational objectives* are often used to denote the broad general goals of education in the United States or in a school system or school. The term *general objective* is most often used to describe the major goals of a unit or course. The terms *specific objectives* or *instructional objectives* are used to describe subsidiary objectives that combine to make up general objectives. They are usually used to denote specific learnings to be taught in units or lessons.

In general, these definitions hold true, but in the literature the words are sometimes used indiscriminately and are even intermixed. It is wise, therefore, to check an author's definition to be sure that you are speaking the same language.

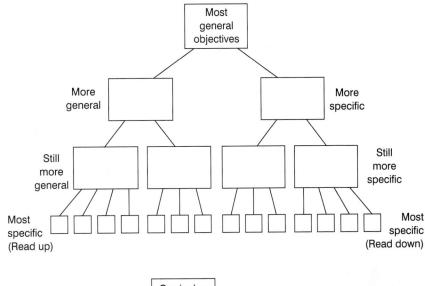

■ FIGURE 5.3

Pyramid of General and Specific Objectives. Note that the pyramid extends from the very specific to the very general and the specific objectives at each level make up the components of the general objective in the next level above it.

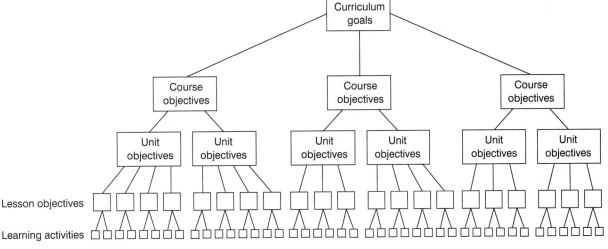

■ FIGURE 5.4

Lesson, Unit, Course, Curriculum Pyramid

Similarly, if the learning goal for a student was to translate the simple Latin sentence *Nauta puellam amat* (the sailor loves the girl), from the student's ability to tell what the sentence means and his or her ability to distinguish it from the sentence *Puella nautam amat* (the girl loves the sailor), the teacher can tell when the student has reached the goal. In such a situation, the learning can be substantiated by the behavior.

Many objectives are covert, however, which means that the learning products are not easily or directly observable. *Understandings, appreciations, attitudes,* and *ideals* are all covert objectives. For example, if the object of instruction is to help students appreciate the beauty of a Van Gogh painting, it is hard to tell whether that objective has really been achieved. The observable behavior of the student may or may not give a true indication of his or her appreciation. Students may be able to recite the right words and simulate the proper actions without having any real feeling, appreciation, or understanding.

The Cognitive, Affective, and Psychomotor Domains

According to a committee of college and university examiners headed by Benjamin Bloom, objectives fall into three domains:

1. *The cognitive domain.* "Objectives which emphasize remembering or reproducing something which has presumably been learned, as well as objectives which involve the solving of some intellective task for which the individual has to determine the essential problem and then reorder given material or combine it with ideas, methods, or procedures previously learned. Cognitive objectives vary from simple recall of material learned to highly original and creative ways of combining and synthesizing new ideas and materials."(2)
2. *The affective domain.* "Objectives which emphasize a feeling tone, an emotion, or a degree of acceptance or rejection."(3) Interests, attitudes, ideals, appreciations, and values are included in the affective domain.
3. *The psychomotor domain.* "Objectives which emphasize some muscular or motor skill, some manipulation of materials and objectives or some act which requires a neuromuscular co-ordination."(4)

Objectives in these domains have been arranged into hierarchies or taxonomies. In the following paragraphs, we try to explain the significance of these hierarchies.

A HIERARCHY OF COGNITIVE DOMAIN OBJECTIVES   When inventing their taxonomies of educational objectives, Bloom and his associates classified educational goals in the cognitive domain into categories according to their complexity—from simple remembering, believed to be the least complex form of the cognitive processes, to evaluation, supposedly the highest type of thinking. The classifications they arrive at are as follows:

1. Knowledge (1.0)   In Bloom's taxonomy, to "know" something is simply being able to master information well enough to remember it. In this sense, knowing something does not imply understanding what is remembered. Among the subcategories included in this general category are remembering specific information; remembering generalizations, principles, and theories; and remembering the ways and means of dealing with specifics.

2. Comprehension (2.0)   Comprehension refers to low-level understanding. At this level, the learner understands a concept well enough to be able to translate it into different words, to interpret the meaning of the information or notion, and to extrapolate the implications or consequences that may follow from it.

3. Application (3.0)   Application refers to a somewhat higher level of understanding than that which occurs in the comprehension stage. At the application level, the learner can apply abstract knowledge and use it in real life.

4. Analysis (4.0)   At this level, thinking begins to be a much higher mental process. Here the learner breaks down complex ideas, principles, theories, and information into their component parts to see relationships—for example, cause and effect, or subordinate and coordinate elements—and thus derives a more complete, clearer understanding. Analysis includes analysis of elements, analysis of relationships, and analysis of organizational principles.

5. Synthesis (5.0)   At the synthesis level the learner puts together things so as to make new wholes. This is the basic process of creativity; for example, synthesis is the process one uses in writing a poem, evolving a theory, or inventing a new machine. It requires very complex mental processes.

6. Evaluation (6.0)   In Bloom's taxonomy, evaluation is at the top of the cognitive ladder. It consists of placing considered objective judgment on something, and is thought to be the highest of all mental processes.(5)

Whether these categories really progress from the least complex to the most complex in all instances is doubtful. However, it is certain that synthesis and evaluation are considerably more complex processes than remembering is. By attaining objectives in these categories, then, students can develop higher cognitive powers. Although it is necessary to be sure that students do acquire knowledge and remember it, unless you aim at least some of your teaching at application, analysis, synthesis, and evaluation, you will not help students develop their cognitive powers fully. To make teaching most effective, you must include objectives from all levels.

A HIERARCHY OF AFFECTIVE DOMAIN OBJECTIVES To create a taxonomy of objectives in the affective domain, Krathwohl, Bloom, and Masia arranged the affective domain into categories according to the degree of internalization they represent. By internalization, the researchers mean the degree to which one has assimilated an affective behavior into one's personality. As set forth in the taxonomy, this behavior ranges from the lowest level of simply being aware of the affective stimulus without reacting to it in any way, to, at the highest level, total acceptance of the affective stimuli and incorporation of them into one's personality as determiners of one's overall pattern of behavior. In the following paragraphs we try to give you a notion of the main orientation of each category and some idea of the range of subcategories it includes.

1. Receiving (1.0) The lowest category, receiving, ranges from 1.1, which is a simple state of awareness of the affective stimulus without any reaction or feeling about it pro or con, through 1.2, a feeling of tolerance toward the stimulus, to finally 1.3, a moving toward a preference for this affective stimulus. At the lowest levels, the behavior is really not affective at all because the person has no feeling about the stimulus one way or another. At the highest of the three levels, however, the person seems to begin to have feelings favoring the stimulus.

2. Responding (2.0) At this second level in the taxonomy, the person responds to the stimulus. In the first responding level (2.1), the person starts to take an interest in the stimulus; then at the next level (2.2), the person begins to respond to the stimulus favorably and voluntarily; and finally, at the highest level (2.3), the person comes to enjoy it.

3. Valuing (3.0) In valuing, the third category of this taxonomy, the person becomes committed to the affective behavior. At the lowest level (3.1), the person starts off with a sort of tentative belief in the value of the affective behavior, but at higher levels (3.2) this belief becomes strengthened to the point that the person prefers it, and in the last level (3.3), he or she becomes committed to it.

4. Organizing (4.0) After committing to a particular value, the person organizes personal values into a value system. Finding that more than one value may apply to a situation and that sometimes values conflict, the person finds it necessary, first (4.1), to gain a better understanding of the values; then, in the next level (4.2), the person organizes the values into a system of dominant and subordinate values, or values the individual holds precious and values less highly prized.

5. Becoming characterized by a value or value complex (5.0) At the highest level of the taxonomy (5.1), the values already internalized become so much a part of the person that they form a hierarchical cluster of attitudes that rules the individual's general behavior and determines personal opinions. Finally, in the next level (5.2), by shaping the person's attitudes, ideas, and behaviors, this generalized set of values becomes an integral portion of the person's general character and the person's philosophy of life.(6)

These categories and levels of affective behavior are not as precise as these descriptions make them seem. As you might expect of behavior that develops over a period of time and in which the higher levels develop out of the lower levels, the signs of the higher levels of behavior can be found at the lower levels and elements of lower level behavior continue to persist at the higher levels. Also, the common subdivisions of affective behavior—attitudes, appreciations, adjustment, interests, and values—overlap the various categories. Figure 5.5 shows the degree of overlap among categories and subdivisions of the affective behavior.

It is somewhat unusual for teachers consciously to aim their teaching at categories in the affective domain, notwithstanding pious statements about teaching appreciation, interest, values, and attitudes. Nevertheless, it seems self-evident that teachers should attempt to achieve goals on the higher side of the affective domain taxonomy. No doubt these objectives are difficult to achieve, but because they represent a high degree of internalization, achieving them is essential if there are to be real changes in students' affective behavior.

A HIERARCHY OF PSYCHOMOTOR DOMAIN OBJECTIVES   It may well be that a taxonomy of objectives for the psychomotor domain is really superfluous, since in skill development the goal is the degree of proficiency desired, and the enabling objectives are, on the whole, simply steps from unskillful to most skillful. However, the following hierarchy may be helpful for forming educational objectives.

1. Familiarization   The first level in this set of objectives is familiarization. At this level, learners find out what the skill is all about. They may read about what to do

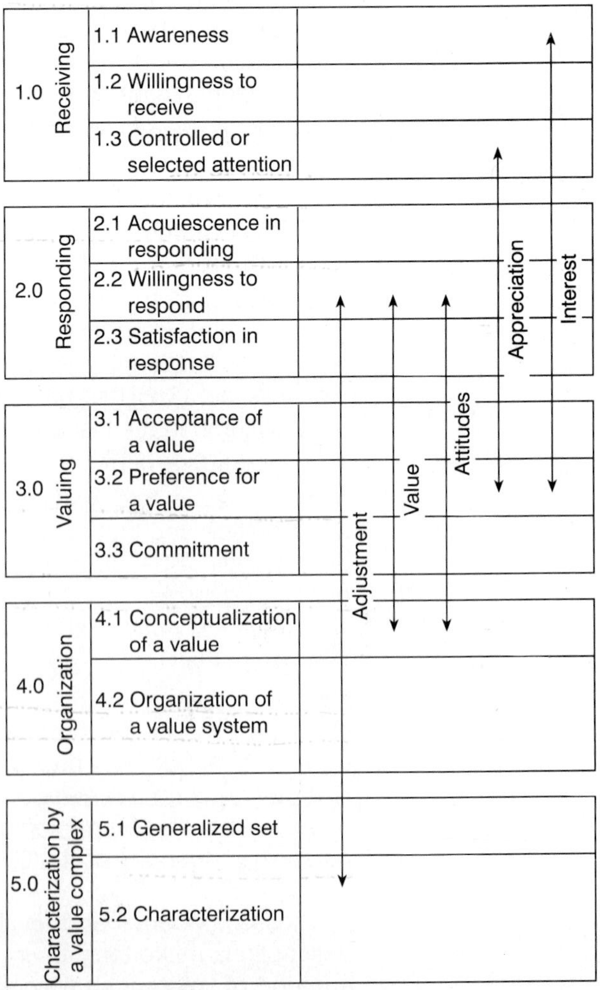

[handwritten margin note:]
Psychomotor Domain
1. Familiarization
2. Fundamentals
3. Development
4. Adjusting/Adapting
5. Perfection/Maintenance

■ **FIGURE 5.5**

Objectives in the Affective Domain

David R. Krathwohl, Benjamin S. Bloom, and Bertram B. Masia, *Taxonomy of Educational Objectives. Handbook II: Affective Domain* (New York: McKay, 1964), p. 37.

and how to do it, they may see someone demonstrate it, they may handle the tools or equipment, or they may actually practice the motions. All these activities give them knowledge about the skill, but do not give mastery of the skill itself.

2. Fundamentals   The second level is to develop fundamental skills. At this level, learners may learn such basics as how to hold the ball, grasp the racquet, locate the keys on the computer keyboard, swing the club, or put a spin on the ball so that it goes into the court instead of over the fence. The learners practice these basic skills while trying to avoid imperfections in style and technique that they would have to unlearn at a later stage.

3. Development   The third level is to develop the skill through guided practice. The goal is to eliminate errors, master techniques, and perhaps develop speed. At this level, the learner's performance at first requires continuous conscious thought and guidance, but as the skill develops, the behavior becomes automatic until finally the learner can perform the acts smoothly and skillfully without conscious thought, and habit takes over.

4. Adjusting and Adapting   When the skill has reached the level of habituation, it still is subject to adjustment to suit the situation and to allow the learner to become more proficient. The pianist adapts his technique to play loud or soft dynamics, fast or slow rhythms, and legato or staccato styles depending on the particular piece of music. The tennis player learns to lob, chop, and drive, and to adjust these strokes to her position in the court, the speed and direction of the approaching ball, and so on. In a fast-paced soccer match, the player who decides to try to head the ball forward, or to the right, or to the left, must first learn to adjust his actions to the situation and his objective automatically.

5. Perfection and Maintenance   The last stage is that of perfecting and maintaining the skill. As we all know, skills that are not maintained will soon become creaky even though not forgotten. Skillful performers must continue to practice if they wish to maintain their skill. If they wish to become better, they must work at their performance, varying their techniques a little here or there in a continual search for improvement, just as does the world-famous concert pianist who practices five hours a day to keep up his skills, maintain his dexterity, and perfect his renditions.(7)

IMPLICATIONS OF THE TAXONOMIES FOR TEACHING   There are at least two principal implications of these teaching taxonomies for the teacher. One is that learners must learn to flap their wings before they can fly. In other words, before someone can judge something, he or she must know it; before a person can create a values system, he or she must have values; before a pianist can play Beethoven at a Carnegie Hall recital, he or she must learn to play the scales.

The other implication is that teachers should be trying to lead students to higher levels than teachers usually do. Teachers should encourage and help students to evaluate carefully and objectively; to integrate an exemplary set of values into their characters; to develop at least some of their skills to high levels of proficiency, and to perfect and maintain these skills at the high level. Of course, no one can reach the highest levels in everything. There is not enough time or ability in all creation. Yet everyone should have a chance to reach the highest level in something.

Stop and Reflect

Consider a course you might teach. What overall objectives would you like to achieve in such a course? Would you want to achieve general affective and psychomotor objectives as well as cognitive ones?

List several general cognitive objectives and then list specific unit objectives that would help you attain the general objectives. List objectives at each level of Bloom's taxonomy that are suitable for a unit in your subject.

Examine the general objectives of a school. List specific objectives suitable to a course you might teach that would contribute to the school's various general objectives.

What are some of the affective and psychomotor objectives in your subject area?

Setting Up the Objectives

From our previous discussion, it follows then that the first step in lesson, course, or unit planning is to set up objectives. You must decide what you hope the students will learn as a result of your teaching. These learning products may include the following:

1. What the learner will know (concepts)
2. What the learner will be able to do (skills)
3. What the learner will feel (attitudes, appreciations, or ideals)

Select the desirable learning products for your students on the basis of your diagnosis of such considerations as the following:

- The nature and structure of the subject
- The needs of the students
- The readiness of the students
- The interests, abilities, attitudes, and other characteristics of the students
- The larger educational goals and general objectives
- Your own philosophy, inclinations, and capabilities
- Community expectations
- The feasibility of the objectives—for example, the facilities, equipment, supplies, and time available
- Other elements of the curriculum

Do this diagnosis before you proceed further in your planning. Remember, *much teaching fails because teachers do not really understand what they are trying to accomplish.*

WRITING THE OBJECTIVES   When planning your instruction, it is ordinarily best to write your objectives. Doing so

- ensures that you have acquired the learning yourself. (If you cannot describe the learning, you probably never learned it thoroughly.)
- gives you a definite goal for which to aim.
- gives you a standard by which to evaluate student achievement.
- helps to eliminate fuzzy thinking about the learning and thus helps to avoid soft pedagogy—that is, pedagogy that results in no learning or little learning.

DESCRIPTIVE OR BEHAVIORAL OBJECTIVES   You may choose to write your objectives in either a descriptive form or a behavioral form. In writing a descriptive objective, all you do is describe the learning product desired, as in the following examples.

DESCRIPTIVE COGNITIVE DOMAIN OBJECTIVES

A theme in music, or musical sentence, expresses a musical idea or feeling.

No modern society has invented more than a small fraction of its present culture—all owe tremendous debt to cultural inventors of other places and other times.

The works of the Romantic poets illustrate the eloquent beauty of lyrical language and point out universal feelings and emotions.

DESCRIPTIVE AFFECTIVE DOMAIN OBJECTIVES

No nation can depend entirely on itself.

Cooperation is more desirable than warfare.

One should respect the rights and feelings of others.

The study of international politics can be exciting.

DESCRIPTIVE PSYCHOMOTOR DOMAIN OBJECTIVES

The ability to write the vowel-inside curve, as in *ail e* and *ray ɔ* (short-hand).

The ability to play a single paradiddle—both open and closed—on the drums.

The ability to run the 100-yard dash in 12 seconds flat.

Behavioral objectives are somewhat more complicated. Their essential element is a description of what the student will be able to do as a result of the learning. You may write behavioral objectives in terms of covert (i.e., not observable) or overt behavior. The following is an example of a covert objective: "Upon completion of the unit the student will understand the forces that caused the United States and the British Empire, now called the Commonwealth, to develop a real friendship." In this objective, the key word is "understand," an action that is not readily observable. An overt behavioral objective is illustrated by this example: "Upon completion of the unit, the student will be able to explain in his or her own words the significance of at least three of the principal reasons why the United States and the British Empire, now called the Commonwealth, developed a real friendship." In this objective, the key action is "to explain," which is readily observable.

As a rule, use covert behavioral objectives only for broad, general objectives or course goals. In such objectives, the verbs that delineate the behavior are words such as *know, understand, appreciate, feel, enjoy,* and *comprehend,* as in the following examples: "At the completion of the unit, the students will know the basic properties of simple geometric figures." "At the completion of the unit, the students will appreciate the beauties of Shakespearian poetry."

Often, however, general objectives of both the cognitive and affective domains are more useful when expressed as overt behavior, as the following example from the affective domain illustrates: "At the completion of the course, students will read Shakespearian poetry for recreation." Always write general objectives in the psychomotor domain in terms of overt behavior.

In all the domains, specific behavioral objectives should be in terms of observable behavior. In other words, at the level of specific behavioral objectives, the objectives should be what Tyler calls performance objectives, that is, objectives that describe the performance of the students.(8) For example, "At the end of the lesson, each student will be able to describe, step by step and without error, the procedure for constructing a map profile." In this example, the overt behavior is "describing." You can easily observe and evaluate it.

Specific behavioral objectives of this kind are valuable because they give you specific targets at which to aim your teaching and specific behavior to use as criteria for evaluating teaching and learning. In writing these objectives, always use action verbs such as *identify, describe, list, explain, display, define, demonstrate, execute, state, tell, construct, organize, select, write, present, interpret, locate, compare, pronounce, perform, draw,* and so forth. The following are examples of specific behavioral objectives: "At the completion of the lesson, the students will be able to draw a trapezoid." "At the completion of the lesson, the students will be able to identify a *non sequitur.*"

SIMPLE OR CRITERION-REFERENCED BEHAVIORAL OBJECTIVES   Behavioral objectives may be either simple or criterion-referenced. Simple behavioral objectives tell only what the learner will do at the end of the instruction, as in the preceding examples. Criterion-referenced behavioral objectives go one step further and specify the level of performance the student will have to achieve to meet the objectives. For example, the previous objective—"At the end of the lesson each student will be able to describe, step by step and without error, the procedure for constructing a map profile"—is criterion-referenced. It sets errorless performance as the criterion for achievement of the objective.

Thus, as we have seen, simple behavioral objectives consist of three elements:

1. an introductory phase
2. who
3. does what

On the other hand, criterion-referenced behavioral objectives, when written out completely, contain four or five elements:

1. the introductory phase
2. who (i.e., the learner)
3. does what (i.e., the behavior required)
4. how well (i.e., the level of performance required or the "criterion of acceptable performance")

and when desirable,

5. under what conditions (i.e., the givens and/or restrictions or limitations that govern an acceptable performance)(9)

The following are examples of both simple and criterion-referenced objectives and analyses of their elements.

Example 1   In the simple behavioral objective "The student can cite three evidences of the friendship of the United States and Great Britain in the first half of the twentieth century," the elements are

1. at the conclusion of the unit (understood)
2. the student (who)
3. can cite three evidences of the friendship of the United States and Great Britain in the first half of the twentieth century (does what)

The action verb in this instance is *cite.*

Example 2   Similarly, in the simple behavioral objective "The student can demonstrate how the Hague Court, the World Court, and the United Nations were evidences of the role of the English-speaking nations as a force for keeping the peace," the elements are

1. at the conclusion of the unit (understood)
2. the student (who)
3. can demonstrate how The Hague Court, the World Court, and the United Nations were evidences of the role of the English-speaking nations as a force for keeping the peace (does what)

In this objective the action verb is *demonstrate.*

Example 3   When describing an objective in the affective domain, it is usually helpful to include a notation telling what affect is being described. Thus, in the objective "The student shows enjoyment of classical music by purchasing and playing classical records," the elements are

1. at the end of the instruction (understood)
2. the student (who)
3. shows enjoyment (the affect)
4. by purchasing and playing classical records (does what)

The action verb is *purchase.*

Stop and Reflect

Following are examples of simple behavioral objectives in the affective and psychomotor domains. Point out the elements in each:

- *As a result of the instruction in scientific thinking, the students demonstrate the scientific attitude by searching out and examining evidence before making decisions.*
- *At the completion of the unit, the student will be able to play a closed paradiddle on the drums.*

Write several simple behavioral objectives for a unit in a course you might teach.

Example 4   In this criterion-referenced behavioral objective in the cognitive domain, "Given examples of the type X^5/X^3, students will be able to solve the examples by subtracting the exponents in at least nine out of ten cases," the elements are

1. at the completion of instruction (understood)
2. the students (who)
3. will be able to solve the examples by subtracting exponents (does what)
4. in at least nine of ten cases (how well)
5. Given examples of the type X^5/X^3 (under what conditions)

The action verb in this objective is *solve.*

Example 5   In another example of a criterion-referenced objective in the cognitive domain, "The student will be able to pick out proper and common nouns from a page of a textbook with 90 percent accuracy," the elements are

1. at the completion of instruction (understood)
2. the student (who)
3. will be able to pick out proper and common nouns (does what)

4. with 90 percent accuracy (how well)
5. from a page of a textbook (under what conditions)

The action verb here is *pick.*

Example 6   In the following example of a criterion-referenced objective from the psychomotor domain, "The student will be able to run the 100-yard dash in 12 seconds," the elements are

1. at the completion of training (understood)
2. the student (who)
3. will run the 100-yard dash (does what)
4. in 12 seconds (how well)
5. (under what conditions, not stated)

Here the action verb is *run.*

Criterion-referenced objectives must always be overt. They are best suited for use as specific objectives in the cognitive and psychomotor domains. Because of the difficulties in judging affective behavior, we do not recommend their use for the affective domain in ordinary classroom instruction.

Because criterion-referenced specific behavioral objectives are more precise than are simple specific behavioral objectives, they usually provide (1) better targets for the instructor, and (2) more definite standards by which to judge the success of the teaching and learning than other types of objectives do.

Stop and Reflect

Point out the elements in the following criterion-referenced objective:

Given a quadratic equation in one unknown, the student will solve the equation in eight out of ten instances.

TIPS FOR WRITING COGNITIVE BEHAVIORAL OBJECTIVES   Although behavioral objectives are not difficult to prepare, there are some cautions you should bear in mind to make your objectives effective.

1. *Express behavioral objectives as statements that begin "At the completion of the lesson (or unit, or course), the student. . . . "*   For purposes of brevity, some or all of the beginning portion of the behavioral objective may be omitted so that the behavioral objective as written begins with a verb—for example, "Types at the rate of 40 words per minute without making more than one error per minute." When an objective is written this way, it is understood that the beginning words "At the completion of the instruction, the student" have been omitted; the objective in full would read "At the completion of the instruction, the student will type at the rate of 40 words per minute without making more than one error per minute."

2. *Be sure each behavioral objective describes potential student behavior.*   Sometimes the behavioral objectives teachers write are not behavioral objectives at all. Behavioral objectives must describe the student behavior expected. For example, the objective "To discuss the picaresque novel" is not a

behavioral objective because it does not describe the students' end behavior. Rather, it describes the learning procedure. Similarly, the phrase "the picaresque novel" is not a behavioral objective because it merely names a topic and describes no behavior at all. "In this class I will demonstrate the cause-and-effect principle" is also not a behavioral objective because it describes teacher behavior rather than student behavior. We repeat, *if it does not describe the students' terminal behavior, it is not a behavioral objective at all.* The following, however, is an example of a behavioral objective because it tells us what the student will be able to do, (i.e., identify the best painting): "From a group of three paintings, the student will be able to identify the one painting that most closely adheres to the principles of quality set forth in the course."

3. *Be sure that each behavioral objective includes one and only one learning product.*   The objective "At the end of the unit the students will understand the principles underlying the problem-solving methods and apply them rigorously in their daily work" is not really satisfactory, because it calls for two different learning products requiring different types of evidence. A student may understand the principles, but because of an attitude or lack of skillfulness, may not use them.

4. *When you write criterion-referenced objectives, be sure that the criteria you list are really indexes of the learning you seek.*   Objectives such as the following beg the question because they do not provide any honest criteria by which to judge the student's achievement: "When you finish this packet, you will be able to answer with reasonable accuracy questions on ions, isotopes, and static electricity."

5. *Beware of trivia.*   To write objectives that measure the higher mental levels is difficult, particularly when we limit ourselves to overt behavior. Consequently, the behavioral objectives listed for many courses, units, and lessons largely concern memory work, simple skills, isolated facts, and other low-level learning. This is unfortunate. Even though writing objectives that sample the higher mental processes may become frustrating, do not give up trying. They are the important objectives that make education worthwhile. The following is an example of an objective at synthesis level: "Given an unknown, the student will be able to construct a reasonable procedure for determining the chemical consistency of the unknown."

Student Objectives

So far we have discussed only the teacher's objectives: the objectives set forth by the teacher for the students to accomplish. These objectives will be futile unless the students adopt them, or compatible objectives, as their own. It is the student's objectives that cause him or her to act. It is excellent policy to inform students early in the lesson, unit, or course just what it is they are supposed to gain from the instruction and to convince them that the learning is worthwhile. If the students think your objectives are desirable and adopt them as their own, the learning process is well on its way. If they do not, you must resort to some other motivational scheme, or you will fail.

One technique that has good motivational effect is to ask students to choose their own objectives from among alternative objectives. Another is to encourage students to set up objectives as part of a teacher-student planning activity. Knowledge of the goals and feedback concerning one's progress is among the best motivators of student learning. More often than not, if students know what it is they are supposed to learn, they usually will try to learn it. When teachers state their specific objectives as learning products, students are quite likely to accept them as legitimate objectives and work to achieve them.

Stop and Reflect
Exercise A

Critique the following objectives, showing why they do not qualify as behavioral objectives. Rewrite each of them as a viable specific objective suitable for a single lesson.

1. *My goal in this lesson plan is to teach a geography course. I will attempt to show regions of Anglo-America as to its original occupants—the American Indians. I will attempt to show how these people in their specific regions developed specific cultures in relation to their surroundings.*
2. *Aim: To review the four major parts of speech.*
3. *Purpose: To reaffirm the definition, recognition, and the use of the parts of speech.*
4. *What are the effects of a volunteer army on military security?*

Exercise B

The following set of objectives was designed for a unit on "Organizing for an Emergency." Evaluate them. Do you find them clear? Would they be better stated as descriptive objectives than as behavioral objectives? Why or why not? Do the specific objectives sufficiently support the general objective? Would they be more useful if criterion-referenced? Why or why not? How could you criterion-reference them? What steps would you take to ensure that the students set for themselves objectives consonant with the stated teaching objectives?

GENERAL OBJECTIVES

Through a simulated disaster situation, the students will develop a change in attitude and behavior leading to planned and rational action in any community disaster.

SPECIFIC OBJECTIVES

When presented with the simulated disaster situation, the students will demonstrate ability to make decisions.

The students will be able to interpret through discussion the decisions they made and how they affected them, their families, and their community.

The students will be able to compare their experiences in the simulation to the responsibilities and decisions of citizens in their community.

The students will be able to define the responsibility of civil defense to their community.

■ ■ ■ ■ The Learning Activities

Selecting the Learning Activities

MATCHING ACTIVITIES TO INSTRUCTIONAL NEEDS   Once you have selected and described your objective, it is time to decide what learning activities you will use and the way you will organize and conduct these activities. When planning the learning activities, you should be guided by several considerations.

1. There are many different methods or techniques that may help students meet your objectives. Bruce Joyce and Marsha Weil have identified more than 80 "models of teaching," each of which is slightly different from the other models and is useful for a slightly different purpose.(10) Presumably the learning resulting from each of these models will be somewhat different from that resulting from any of the others, since teaching strategies do make a difference in what students learn and

in how well they learn it. In fact, as we have indicated earlier, the way a person learns may have as much impact on his or her final understanding, attitude, or skill as the subject content itself. So to a certain extent, teaching strategies are, for practical purposes, a part of the content. For example, if you use a teaching method that encourages creative thought, chances are that your teaching will kindle not only a fuller understanding but also a greater inclination to think creatively than would another method. Therefore, take care to choose the type of learning activity that fits your objectives.

This is not to say that only one specific method can achieve your objective, or that one method is necessarily the best for your purpose. No learning activity guarantees the attainment of any particular objective; most learning activities can be used for several types of objectives. Neither can you depend on any method to stand long alone. Always try to support it by other strategies and techniques that will combine their impact to produce the learnings you desire. Even with these disclaimers in mind, however, some strategies are likely to be much more useful than others for your purposes.

For instance, if your goal is to teach information or basic skills, try direct telling and showing, mastery learning procedures, questions directed toward specific contents or skills, constant checking, and immediate feedback. These strategies are usually most effective if the content is offered in small incremental steps. No matter what the method or technique chosen, you should always point out what is to be learned and why.

If your goal is to develop social attitudes, try case studies, guided questions, laboratory procedures, action learning, independent investigation, group investigation, and problem solving or other strategies that feature inquiry, practice of social analyses, and observation of oneself and other people.

If your goal is self-development, try nondirective, nonthreatening, student-centered activities concerning "practical problems, social problems, ethical and philosophical problems, personal issues and research problems, moral dilemmas, and moral problems."(11) Group discussion seems to be an effective technique for executing such strategies.

If your goal is to develop information and problem-solving skills, try inquiry, problem solving, advance organizers, and inductive questioning, and follow inductive techniques and the methods of the discipline.(12)

Your first concern is to pick an approach that will bring about your most desired objectives without interfering with other desirable learning. However, that problem is not as bothersome as it may seem because most learning activities can be used for more than one type of objective. If you concentrate on selecting methods that will further your principal objective, you will probably also attain your secondary goals.

2. Learning activities, as we have seen, can carry out different roles in the teaching process. Some are excellent for motivating; some for clarifying; some for skill development; some for clinching the learning (closure), and so on. Try to pick learning activities that will maximize the effects you are seeking.

At the beginning of a unit or lesson, for instance, try to use an activity that will catch the students' attention and attract their interest. Telling a simple anecdote may do the trick; so may facing them with a problem situation, or leading a lively discussion on a relevant issue. Using an advance organizer, or describing what the unit or lesson will cover and why, and what will be expected of the students, may help them set their directions. Involving the students in planning and conducting activities can spark student interest and stimulate their willing effort and cooperation.

In the development portion of your class, you can act as a manager of instruction, or as a coach, or as an inquiry trainer. You can help students develop concepts and intellectual skills by such operations as problem solving, using Socratic discussion, practicing logical decision making, drawing inferences, and determining facts. Or you can fill in students' background and widen their horizons by the skillful use of lectures, demonstrations, audiovisual media, careful questioning, and other clarifying operations. To develop skills, you can use show-how activities and practice. Reviewing, practicing, reinforcing activities, role playing, discussing points and issues, and testing may serve to drive home the desired knowledge and skills and to tie the learning together. Security-giving operations are particularly necessary for promoting a supportive classroom climate.*

Adapt the methods you use to the classroom situation. When it seems desirable, change your technique to add to the class structure; at other times it may be better to make the class looser. More often than not, decisions of this sort must be made according to your feel for the situation. Your choice of techniques does not have to follow any rigid pattern.

3. Individual students react differently to various methods. As Bruce Joyce points out, the students are really part of the method, for it is they who do the learning. What they do, their attitudes, their abilities, and so on, determine what is learned. The method influences the outcome in any learning situation, but it does not determine it. Therefore, the learning activities you select should be compatible with the students' abilities, style of learning, and background.(13)

Students who have not learned the prerequisites for an activity should not be expected to attempt the activity until they have gained the necessary background, knowledge, or skill. On the other hand, students who have excellent background knowledge and skills should not be sentenced to relearn things they already know or can do. Similarly, students should not be forced to partake of a steady diet of activities that are incompatible with their learning styles. Students who are not very flexible need structured activities, whereas flexible students are more productive in less structured classes. Similarly, sociable students fit into social group activities more readily than do less sociable students, and creative youngsters react more favorably to methods calling for divergent thinking and originality than do less creative types. The most reasonable way to match students' capabilities and attitudes is to individualize your teaching in some fashion, or use a variety of activities so that all students have compatible learning experiences at least part of the time.

4. Insofar as is feasible, the learning activities you choose should be appealing to the students. Although philosophers tell us there is no royal road to learning and much of school learning consists of hard work that students must buckle down and do, you will get a lot more mileage out of your plans if they contain learning activities that are appealing to the students. Teachers who push hard at mastery teaching, for instance, find that after a while students get sick of striving; it pays to introduce a change of pace at times. There is always a place for exciting content in every course. Films, dramas, simulations, discussions, games, real problems, field trips, and the like can add interest and student involvement to classes. Although you do not want your classes to become slack, an occasional relaxed class may make your total effort more effective.

5. Consider also your own abilities, aptitudes, and preferences. We all have methods and techniques with which we are more comfortable. Ordinarily, we are more effective when we use them. Too many teachers, however, have only a small repertory. If you limit yourself to only a few approaches, you soon become dull, repetitive, and ineffective. You need to have a number of methods and techniques at your fingertips to cope with different teaching goals and learners, to create the climate you wish, and to give variety and depth to your teaching.

*See Chapter 1.

6. Bear in mind such practical factors as the time and space available, supplies and equipment needed, expense, and health and safety.

7. Subject matter is an integral part of the learning activity. Without subject matter, there can be no learning. When appropriate, use learning activities that include high-level cognitive, affective, and psychomotor subject matter rather than merely simple information and low-level skills. Be sure that the subject matter contributes to the objective. Remember that subject matter content is a means to an end and is not an end in itself; the goal is to attain your teaching objectives.

8. The teaching strategies and techniques that make up your learning activities must be suited to the subject matter to be taught.

9. Each of the learning activities you use should be aimed at at least one of your teaching objectives, and every teaching objective should have at least one learning activity aimed at it. In short, activities and objectives should be aligned.

10. Finally, once you select them, you must arrange the learning activities into a sequence or an organization for learning. This organization is the body of the course, unit, or lesson.

EVALUATION ACTIVITIES   Plan for evaluating the students' progress and the success of your course, unit, or lesson before you begin to teach it. Some experts who espouse competency-based education say that you should do so before planning your learning activities. This does not mean that every lesson plan should have a section entitled "Evaluation." It does mean, however, that you should consider how you are going to assess student learning for each one of your objectives, determine the procedures you will use, decide how to weigh the various elements in your evaluation, and build the instruments before you start to teach. Make sure your evaluation is well-aligned with your objectives and learning activities.

Implications

At this point, you should note several implications of the preceding sections.

1. Any teaching-learning activity that is not aimed at one or more of your objectives is useless and should be discarded.
2. Any teaching-learning activity that is not of a kind suitable for bringing about the learning desired is useless and should be discarded.
3. Any evaluation plan that does not fully assess the attainment of your objectives is incomplete and should be discarded, rebuilt, or supplemented.
4. Any evaluation item that does not assess the attainment of one or more of your teaching objectives is useless and should be discarded.

Stop and Reflect
Make up two or three instructional objectives for a lesson you might teach. Give a half dozen learning activities you might use to achieve each of these objectives.

Team Planning

School district curricula, programs of study, and course syllabi are generally planned by committees of teachers and supervisory or administrative personnel, or by central district office staffs. We shall not concern ourselves with this sort of planning. Instead, this section focuses on the planning that actually happens in classes. Usually this type of planning is the work of individual teachers who sit down by themselves and figure out what it is they want to do and how they want to do it. Presumably, this is as it ought to be if it is not overdone. Sometimes, however, courses, units, and even individual lessons are carried out as team projects.

Team planning may be part of a formal team teaching arrangement or simply an informal ad hoc arrangement among colleagues. For example, a social studies teacher and an English teacher, finding that by chance they share the same group of students, may decide to collaborate on assignments. A more formal arrangement is involved if the social studies, science, and English teachers agree to cooperate on assigning and reading major research papers.

Another more formal type of team-planning arrangement in a middle school involves multidisciplinary teams that share the same students in their classes. The members of the team meet regularly to coordinate the planning in the various courses. In such planning, the team members may agree to share assignments, or agree not to give long, difficult homework assignments or tests on the same day, or they may discuss the strengths and weaknesses of various students and work out special assignments and activities for them.

Still another type of team planning is the formal teaching team of the so-called Trump Plan, in which different teachers play different roles, some conducting large groups, some small groups, and so on. Teams of this sort require careful planning. To allow sufficient time for such planning, team-planning sessions may be incorporated into the daily schedule.

Except that it is done cooperatively by the team, team planning is not so different from other planning. The problems of what, how, when, and where bear the same importance in cooperative efforts as in individual planning. The real difference is that the planning is complicated by the need to merge the varying notions and inclinations of several teachers into one unified, workable whole. Bringing about such harmony requires team members who are well-versed in group process; members must also pay careful attention to details so that each member knows what to do and how and when to do it. It also requires an infinite amount of following through and checking to ensure that the plans are properly executed.

Team planning does not necessarily imply teaching teams of any sort. Teachers who teach the same or similar courses may collaborate on the planing of course sequences and course content. Such planning can be instrumental in making a harmonious, well-articulated curriculum.

■ ■ ■ ■ Teacher-Pupil Planning

In a social studies classroom, a group of junior high school students were conducting a lesson. This lesson consisted of a series of committee reports on research projects just completed; following was a class discussion of the implications and significance of each of the reports. The lesson was capably directed by a competent young lady.

The young lady was a ninth-grader. The lesson, the culmination of several weeks' work, had been organized and conducted by the students who elected her as leader. Three or four weeks before, the students had selected their topic from a short list of alternatives suggested by the teacher, who had developed the list from topics naturally following their previous unit. In a group discussion, the students had decided the various facets of the topic they thought ought to be the most important to investigate. Then they formed committees to look into the various aspects of the topic and to report to the group what they had learned. But before letting the committees start their work, the class as a whole had to develop a set of standards to guide them in their research and to use in evaluating their success. Now they had come to the last step.

Almost every activity in this unit had been planned by the students themselves under the supervision of the teacher. At no time had the teacher dictated to them just what they must or must not do. Neither had she ever left them without support or guidance. She was always there to remind them of the essentials, to suggest alternatives, to point out untapped resources, to correct errors, to question unwise decisions. This sort of teaching is teacher-pupil planning at its best. To do it well requires great skill, much forbearance, and the careful training of one's students.

As you can see, cooperative teacher-pupil planning is an excellent method for involving students in the learning process. It is particularly effective in long-term planning (for example, unit planning) and in planning individual projects. Furthermore, involving students in planning can aid motivation. No one knows what students find interesting and important better than the students themselves. In addition, once the group has planned an activity, if the planning has been really successful, it becomes a group concern. Students who fail to do their part not only face the displeasure of the teacher but let the group down. Most important of all, teacher-pupil planning *offers students a laboratory in thinking, in making choices, in planning, and in learning to work with others—in short, in democratic citizenship!*

In spite of its many virtues, teacher-pupil planning is not suited to every course and every teacher. To ask students to plan the topics in a course whose sequence is largely determined by the nature of the subject matter, as in mathematics, may be pointless. Besides, the students may not have enough information about the subject at hand to know what can be learned, what its potential values are, or how to proceed. To plan well, one needs information.

In addition, cooperative teacher-pupil planning is not student planning. It does not relieve you of your responsibilities and role as mentor. You must guide and limit; seldom, if ever, should you turn the students completely free. The amount of freedom the students should have depends on many things, such as their maturity, their ability level, the subject, and their previous experience in cooperative planning. Students who have not learned how to plan will be overwhelmed if suddenly allowed to direct themselves. You either should explain to them potential directions they can take, or direct them to activities that will give them the knowledge they need, even if you must assume the major role in the planning and make most or even all the decisions.

Teacher-pupil planning should not be used in the same way with all students or in all subjects. Neither is teacher-pupil planning suited to all teachers. It requires teachers who do not need to be the center of the picture, who are not afraid of making errors, who can command respect without demanding it, who are relatively sure of their control, and who are not afraid to subordinate themselves to the group.

Teachers are sometimes tempted to use teacher-pupil planning as a device for tricking students into doing what they have already planned for them to do. Such planning is not teacher-pupil planning; it is fakery. Do not do it. In all things, be honest with your students. If you plan for them to choose within limits, prescribe the limits in advance. If you do not, go along with the students' decisions even though they be poor ones. To allow the students to plan and then to veto or revoke the plan is dishonest and destroys the students' faith in your integrity. So do attempts to manipulate students' decisions. If you are not ready to accept students' decisions, you are not ready for teacher-pupil planning.

Introducing Teacher-Pupil Planning to a Class

The natural way to start on the road to teacher-pupil planning is to encourage students to plan their own individual activities. Once their objectives are firmly fixed and they know what activities they may choose from, or what activities may help them learn what they want to learn, then individual students can do much of their own planning without your doing much more than approving their plans. Of course, you will usually need to suggest a few changes of plan, recommend sources of materials and references, and guide the students as they work. Using this procedure will relieve you of much of the detail, so that you can spend more time working with individuals. In addition, the students learn how to do their own planning. It is unfortunate that many students have been deprived of this type of learning by overzealous teachers.

After starting by planning their own individual activities, students can move up to planning small group activities. Again, you must expect the students to make mistakes; be ready to help them. The use of guide sheets can be quite helpful for students who are attempting to plan their own individual or group activities.

As they develop more maturity and skill in working as groups, the students can proceed to the more difficult task of planning class activities. Later, when they have become more sophisticated, they can move on to such difficult tasks as planning what to include in a topic, and finally, what topics to include in a course. With inexperienced students, do not expect great success initially. The secret of success is to give them small responsibilities at first and gradually to increase these responsibilities as they show they are ready.

This principle of moving from a small beginning shows up in other techniques recommended for introducing teacher-pupil planning. One of these is to present alternative plans and to allow the students to select the plans they prefer. Thus, in a general mathematics class that is studying how to prepare a budget, you might ask them whether they would prefer to make up a personal budget or to set up an organizational budget. In a music class, you might ask the group to choose between preparing "The Soldiers' Chorus" or "When the Foeman Bares His Steel." In an English class, the students might decide whether to study the short story or the drama next. Similarly students, as individuals or as a class, might choose their own goals from a list of behavioral objectives.

Another way to involve your students in the teacher-pupil planning process is to propose a plan of action and then ask for their suggestions and approval. In business education, for example, you might ask the students if they would like to go to a bank and see how it operates. If they agree that this idea has possibilities, then they can discuss ways and means of making the visit and things to see when they get there.

Discussion Techniques in Teacher-Pupil Planning

As groups become skillful in using teacher-pupil planning techniques, they can do much of their planning in group discussion. *Discussion techniques are especially useful in deciding what to include in a topic.* For example, if you were about to begin the study of insects, you might ask, "What do you think we should learn about insects?" During the discussion the students may propose such things as the following:

- What do insects eat?
- How do they reproduce?
- What are insects, anyway?
- How do you make an insect board to display insects?

Undoubtedly, you will have to suggest some things yourself. For instance, somewhere in the discussion you can ask: "Don't you think we ought to know something about the insect's life cycle?" Perhaps the students will not know what a life cycle is. Once they learn about life cycles, they probably will want to include this information. If they do not, perhaps you should indicate the importance of the life cycle and point out the necessity for including it in the study.

Discussion techniques can also be used to plan learning activities. For example, as the class decides what it wants to study, you or the student leader should ask, "How do we go about it?" Thus, through class discussion, committees can be formed, readings can be suggested, dramatic roles can be cast, and field trips can be projected. Sometimes the class may ask a student or group to investigate and report on the feasibility of a project. Included in these plans should also be plans for evaluating what has been learned.

The same group discussion techniques can be used by a relatively mature group to select a topic for study. A good way to launch such discussion is to ask the students to suggest possible plans for consideration. Perhaps you might ask the students to skim a chapter or a book to find topics they would like to learn more about. Their curiosity may be piqued by a movie, a story, a teacher talk, or a discussion of some current event.

If discussion techniques are used in teacher-pupil planning, someone should keep a record of the decisions as they are made. If this record is kept on the chalkboard where everyone can see it, it makes the planning easier. As soon as the group has finished its planning, the final plan should be reduced to writing and given to the students, or posted on the bulletin board or the chalkboard, so that the students will have it for ready reference.

In making group decisions, straw votes are usually helpful. The aim of this technique is not to put the question to a formal vote, but rather to seek an expression of opinion. This allows easy elimination of unpopular alternatives and avoids foundering on difficult decisions. When the straw vote shows a split decision, further discussion may bring the students to agreement. If no agreement is reached, the students will usually be willing to compromise, as in "first your topic, then ours." If necessary, you can resort to a formal vote, but doing so may defeat the purpose of teacher-pupil planning and is liable to split the group.

Teacher-pupil planning is usually more satisfactory when the group has some criteria on which to base its decisions. These criteria can be arrived at jointly or by the teacher with class approval. During the planning session, the teacher often may have to remind the class of the criteria: "Is this the sort of thing you really wanted to do? Is this really pertinent to our problem?" By so doing, teachers can usually improve the quality of group decisions without seeming to impose their own wills on the students.(14)

Stop and Reflect

What are the advantages of teacher-pupil planning? What are its dangers? When and where would you use it? How would you set about using it?

Is teacher-pupil planning really better suited to certain subjects and courses than to others? Explain your answer.

How would you introduce teacher-pupil planning to a high school class that had never had experience in planning?

■ ■ ■   Resources for the Planner

Many resources are available to help you in your planning. Among them are textbooks, commercially developed courses and curriculum materials, curriculum guides and syllabi issued by local school authorities, curriculum bulletins from state and federal school agencies, and resource units. In some districts, curriculum guides specify in great detail what should be taught and how. Often these materials are meant to provide suggestions only. When this is true, how closely you should follow the text or the school curriculum guide is up to you. Until you feel at ease with teaching and the course, however, it is wise to follow these suggestions rather closely.

You may find considerable help from the curriculum guides published by other school districts. Curriculum bulletins published by state departments of education and teachers' professional organizations are also helpful. So are such professional journals as *The English Journal, The Mathematics Teacher,* and *Social Education.* Many of these list suggestions that can be particularly helpful for specific lessons.

Resource units can be especially valuable when you are planning units and lessons. They usually include such helpful information as the following:

- An overview
- A list of desired outcomes divided according to understandings, attitudes, and skills
- An outline of content
- A list of activities divided according to initiatory activities, developmental activities, and culminating activities
- An annotated bibliography
- An annotated list of films
- An annotated list of filmstrips

Teachers who use sources such as these usually find it easier to prepare good lessons than when they go on unassisted.

If they are not available in your school, look for curriculum guides, resource units, bulletins, textbooks, and other materials in teacher centers maintained by local county and state education agencies and colleges. In addition, ERIC Clearing Houses have multitudes of inexpensive resources available. Finally, you should always remember that other teachers and supervisors have hoards of information collected over the years. Teachers should share their ideas; most would be flattered if asked to do so.

SUMMARY

Diagnosis provides a basis for planning instruction that fulfills the needs of students. The process of diagnosis is a continuing one in which the teacher first attempts to find the facts of the case, then from time to time rechecks to see if these facts still hold true, and, as the occasion demands, makes decisions about appropriate instructional approaches and content. Among the resources teachers can use in diagnosis are the cumulative record, diagnostic tests, observation techniques, analysis of the students' classwork, conversations, and conferences, all of which may provide clues from which to devise plans for teaching.

The basic ingredients of a good teaching plan map out (1) what you plan for students to learn, and (2) how you plan to bring about this learning. In addition, the planning must provide for evaluation; without evaluation the two basic ingredients will not work. Good planning must be based on adequate diagnosis. Also helpful as a basis of planning are such instructional and curricular aids as textbooks, curricular programs, curriculum guides and bulletins, and resource units. Teachers do well to consult these resources carefully before they commit themselves to any particular plan.

Determining your objectives is perhaps the most crucial part of planning for teaching. Many teachers neglect this aspect of planning, and as a result, their teaching is pointless and ineffective.

Objectives may range from low-level to high-level learning in any of the cognitive, affective, or psychological domains. They may also range from very specific to extremely general. In any case, because they are potential learning products, you should state them as learning products—clear, precise descriptions of the skills, understandings, and/or attitudes you are seeking to develop, or of behaviors by which you can judge the presence or absence of the skills, understandings, or attitudes desired.

One of the more useful kinds of instructional objectives is the behavioral objective. Behavioral objectives may be either overt or covert, simple or criterion-referenced. Criterion-referenced behavioral objectives consist of five elements: *introductory phase*; *who* (i.e., the learner); *does what* (i.e., the performance required); *how well* (i.e., the level of performance); and *under what conditions* (i.e., the givens and/or restrictions or limitations that govern an acceptable performance). When you write behavioral objectives, be sure of the following:

1. That each general behavioral objective is written in general terms as a statement describing the behavior sought, covert or overt, using words such as *understands, comprehends, knows, or appreciates.*
2. That each behavioral objective, general or specific, describes student performance rather than teacher performance.
3. That each behavioral objective, general or specific, describes the terminal behavior of the student rather than subject matter, learning process, or teaching procedure.
4. That each behavioral objective is stated at the proper level of generality.
5. That each general behavioral objective is defined by a sampling of specific behavioral objectives, which in turn describe terminal behaviors that will show when the objective has been reached.
6. That there is a sufficient sampling of relevant specific behavioral objectives to demonstrate that each of the more general objectives has been achieved.
7. That the behavioral objectives include the complex high-level cognitive and affective goals that are so frequently omitted because they are so difficult to write.
8. That each specific behavioral objective includes only one learning product rather than a combination of learning products.

The learning activities in the plan should always be aimed at learning objectives. Therefore, take care to pick the types of activities that will further your goals. Also consider the abilities, interests, and learning styles of the students, the classroom situation, the materials available, the subject matter to be taught, and your own abilities and inclinations. No one method will meet all the requirements, so be prepared to use a variety of methods as the occasions demand.

Although the responsibility always rests on your shoulders, the students can often cooperate with you in planning. If such planning is to be successful, students must to taught to plan. Usually, you and the students should start by designing class activities together. For a class to decide what it hopes to learn from a topic and what the topics of a course should be, the class requires a considerable amount of sophistication. With inexperienced students, do not expect great success initially. The secret is to give them small responsibilities at first and then increase the responsibilities as the students show they are ready.

ADDITIONAL READING

Bellon, J. J., E. C. Bellon, and M. A. Blank. *Teaching From a Research Knowledge Base.* New York: Macmillan, 1992, Unit 1.

Biehler, R. F., and J. Snowman. *Psychology Applied to Teaching,* 7th ed. Boston: Houghton-Mifflin, 1994.

Bloom, B. S., G. F. Madaus, and J. T. Hastings. *Evaluation to Improve Learning.* New York: McGraw-Hill, 1981.

Borich, G. D. *Effective Teaching Methods.* New York: Macmillan, Chapters 3 & 4.

Brandt, R. S., ed. *Content of the Curriculum: 1988 Yearbook*. Alexandria, VA: Association for Supervision and Curriculum Development, 1988.

Clark, C. M., and P. Peterson. "Teachers' Thought Processes," in *Handbook of Research on Teaching,* 3rd ed., edited by M. C. Wittrock. New York: Macmillan, 1986.

Eggen, P. D., and D. R. Kauchak. *Strategies for Teachers; Teaching Content and Thinking Skills.* Englewood Cliffs, NJ: Prentice-Hall, 1988.

Emmers, A. P. *After the Lesson Plan: Realities of High School Teaching.* New York: Teachers College Press, 1981.

Gronlund, N. E. *Measurement and Evaluation in Teaching,* 5th ed. New York: Macmillan, 1985.

Gronlund, N. E. *Stating Objectives for Classroom Instruction,* 3rd ed. New York: Macmillan, 1985.

Henson, K. T. *Strategies and Methods for Teaching in Secondary and Middle School.* White Plains, NY: Longman, 1988.

Jacobsen, D., P. Eggen, and D. Kauchak. *Methods for Teaching,* 4th ed. New York: Macmillan, Chapters 2–4.

Kim, E. C., and R. D. Kellough. *A Resource Guide for Secondary School Teaching,* 4th ed. New York: Macmillan, 1987, Part II.

Lorber, M. A., and W. D. Pierce. *Objectives, Methods and Evaluation for Secondary Teaching.* Englewood Cliffs, NJ: Prentice-Hall, 1983.

Mager, R. F. *Preparing Instructional Objectives,* 2nd ed. Belmont, CA: David S. Lake, 1984.

Orlich, D. C. et al. *Teaching Strategies: A Guide to Better Instruction,* 2nd ed. Lexington, MA: D. C. Heath, 1985, Ch. 5.

Rosenshine, B., and R. Stevens. "Teaching Functions" in *Handbook of Research on Teaching,* 3rd ed., edited by M. C. Wittrock. New York: Macmillan, 1986.

TenBrink, T. D. "Writing Instructional Objectives" in *Classroom Teaching Skills*, edited by J. M. Cooper. Lexington, MA: D. C. Heath, 1986.

NOTES

1. Educational Policies Commission, *The Central Purpose of American Education* (Washington, DC: National Education Association, 1961).
2. David R. Krathwohl, Benjamin S. Bloom, and Bertram B. Masia, *Taxonomy of Educational Objectives, Handbook II: Affective Domain* (New York: McKay, 1964), 6–7.
3. Ibid.
4. Ibid.
5. Ibid.
6. Ibid.

7. This taxonomy was developed in a Jersey City State College graduate class. For a more formal taxonomy of the psychomotor domain, *see* Anita J. Harrow, *A Taxonomy of the Psychomotor Domain* (New York: McKay, 1972).

8. R. Tyler, *Basic Principles of Curriculum and Instruction* (Chicago: University of Chicago Press, 1975).

9. Robert F. Mager, *Preparing Instructional Objectives* (Palo Alto, CA: Fearon, 1962), 43.

10. Bruce Joyce and Marsha Weil, *Models for Teaching* (Englewood Cliffs, NJ: Prentice-Hall, 1972). *See also* the introduction to their *Personal Models of Teaching, Information Processing Models of Teaching, or Social Models of Teaching* (Englewood Cliffs, NJ: Prentice-Hall, 1978). (The same introduction is repeated in each of these books.) *See also* Bruce R. Joyce, *Selecting Learning Experiences: Linking Theory and Practice* (Alexandria, VA: Association for Supervision and Curriculum Development, 1978), and Bruce R. Joyce, Clark C. Brown, and Lucy Rich, eds., *Flexibility in Teaching* (White Plains, NY: Longman, 1981).

11. C. R. Rogers, *Freedom to Learn* (Columbus, OH: Merrill, 1969), 162. Cited by Doris T. Gow and Tommye W. Casey, "Selecting Learning Activities," in *Fundamental Curriculum Decisions, ASCD Yearbook 1983*, edited by Fenwick W. English (Alexandria, VA: Association for Supervision and Curriculum Development, 1983).

12. Based on Gow and Casey, "Selecting Learning Activities," Chapter 9.

13. Joyce, *Selecting Learning Experiences.*

14. Johnson, W. W., and R. Johnson, *Learning Together and Alone* (Englewood Cliffs, NJ: Prentice-Hall, 1991); Robert E. Slavin, *Cooperative Learning: Theory, Research, and Practice* (Englewood Cliffs, NJ: Prentice-Hall, 1988).

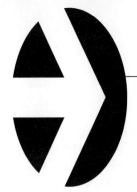

Chapter 6

Course, Unit, and Lesson Planning

- Overview
- Course Planning
- Unit Planning
- Lesson Planning

◼◼◼ Overview

This chapter focuses on how to apply the general principles of planning to the planning of courses, units, and lessons. By the end of the chapter, you will have the basic information you need to write course, lesson, and unit plans. In each case, it is a simple matter of setting objectives, selecting the content and learning activities, planning the sequence and timing, providing the materials for instruction, and deciding how to evaluate your success. This process is theoretically simple, but it is complex and difficult to execute.

Courses are divided into units. A *unit* is a planned sequence of learning activities or lessons that cover a period of several weeks and that center on some major concept, theme, or topic. A unit may consist of a series of mainly expository, content-oriented lessons; or of semi-individualized, laboratory-oriented, experience-centered unit assignments; or any of a variety of combinations or variations of either of these extremes. Learning activity packets, learning modules, and learning contracts are all examples of variations on the unit idea.

Lessons are the atoms that make up units, courses, and curricula. They usually last for a single period, although sometimes they may be continued for several days. Their success determines the effectiveness of the unit, course, or curriculum; therefore, the daily lesson plan is a key element in successful teaching.

Ordinarily, teachers are best served by carefully thought-out, written lesson plans. In this chapter, we examine in some detail how to write lesson plans according to one format. We also present several alternative formats. The type of plan you adopt is not so important as long as it is clear, logical, and easy to follow. We also present several sample lesson plans. It is hoped that when you finish this chapter, you will better understand why careful lesson plans are needed and what the essential elements of lesson planning are.

◼◼◼ Course Planning

In some school systems, the central authority provides curriculum guides and course outlines that set forth the course and the content the course is expected to cover. Such curriculum guides or course outlines can be of great help in building a sequence of topics or units for the course. This sequence should consist of broad topics that you expect to accomplish in two to four weeks of class time. It is not advisable to map out the course in great detail day by day, because at this stage no one can forecast just how the course will develop. Save your detailed planning for your unit and lesson plans. At this time, also consider what general approach you will take for the various topics, as well as decide what major assignments such as research papers and projects will be included. You need to consider these items because they will to some extent affect the time allotments of the various topics; also, you need to schedule them if you want them to be integral parts of the course.

Some courses of study or curriculum guides outline in great detail suggested topics, sequences, and time allotments. Other courses of study and curriculum guides, although they do not list the topics to be studied, do suggest what content should be covered. If your school system provides curriculum guides and courses of study of either type, make use of them. Not to do so may introduce confusion into a carefully planned school program. At times, however, courses of study contain suggestions only and allow for considerable variation. Even when courses are rigidly laid out, teachers find they must vary them to suit the interests, needs, and abilities of the students. You can do so by such procedures as changing the course sequence, modifying the time spent on various topics, determining which topics should receive most emphasis, and by varying the methods of teaching.

Textbook and Course Planning

If your school system does not provide a curriculum guide, syllabus, or course of study, the most common method of selecting the content of a course is to follow a basic textbook. The chief merit of this plan is that it gives the beginning teacher an organized outline of the subject content to follow. However, the teacher should recognize that not all chapters are of equal importance, and the text sequence is not always the best for every class. Slavishly following a textbook may cut you off from taking advantage of opportunities for creativity, from making use of new ideas, from using a flexible approach, and from employing a variety of methods. It often leads to merely covering the subject rather than engaging students in significant learning.

Three Steps in Course Planning

Whatever you use as a basis for planning, the procedure for planning a course is relatively simple. You may enlist the aid of your students in carrying out the procedure, or you may do it all yourself. In either case, the responsibility for all the decisions made is yours. The procedure consists of the following steps:

1. Decide what it is that the students are to learn from the course. These are the course objectives, which should determine the nature of all later procedures. This step may require considerable evaluation and diagnosis before you can complete it.
2. Decide what course content will bring about the desired objectives. Course content consists of two parts: (a) the subject matter of the course (i.e., the sequence of topics), and (b) the approach or strategy to be used in teaching the topics.
3. Decide the amount of time to be spent on the various topics in the sequence. This step is essential to ensure that the various portions of the course receive the attention they deserve. Neglect of this step is one cause of the all too common practice of proceeding slowly in the beginning of the course and then rushing through the last weeks of the course because of lack of time.

The Course Calendar

Once you have decided on the topics to be discussed, map out a calendar for the course year. As you pick topics and arrange them in order, estimate the amount of time to be spent on each topic. Again, the decisions should be approximate—in weeks and fractions of weeks rather than in days. You should, however, base the course calendar on the days available in the school year. In making this estimate, remember to allow for assemblies, examinations, storms, and other contingencies that cause class periods to be canceled. Ten days is a reasonable allowance for missed periods. If at the end of the year you find that this allowance is too great, you can use the extra time for review or for a special topic at the end of the term.

Continuous-Progress Modulated Courses

Planning individualized modulated curricula or courses is similar to planning ordinary courses. About the only difference is that you must divide the course into modules (i.e., units) and provide the students with instructional or learning-activity packets.

As a rule, students work through the modules according to the sequence set up by the instructor. However, in many courses in which sequence is not essential, it may be better if you build the modules so that the students can choose their own sequence of units on the basis of their interests and abilities rather than having to follow a set sequence of modules.

The planning and conducting of continuous-progress curricula are discussed in Chapter 10, "Providing for Individual Differences."

Stop and Reflect

Of what value are textbooks, curriculum guides, and courses of study in the planning of a course? How should each of them be used? How rigidly should they be followed?

Examine a text for a course you might teach. What would you stress? What, if anything, would you omit?

Study a course guide for a course you might teach. Compare it with a text. In what ways would the course guide help you with your planning?

One author says that one should not follow a text in planning a course. Do you agree? Why, or why not?

Unit Planning

Planning an Ordinary Unit

An ordinary unit is simply a sequence of daily lesson plans that present a topic, a chapter, or a portion of a course. To plan such a unit, simply devise a sequence of daily plans that will present the contents and objectives of the topic, chapter, or section of the course outline. Planning an ordinary unit is a relatively simple matter. In general, it can be reduced to the following steps:

1. *Select the topic.*   Presumably the topic will be one suggested by the course outline or the textbook outline. In any case it should do the following:

- Center on some major understanding, problem, issue, or theme.
- Fit the course objectives and further the course plan.
- Be relevant to students' lives and to the society in which they live.
- Be manageable—not too difficult, too big, or too demanding of time and resources.
- Be suitable to students' abilities and interests.

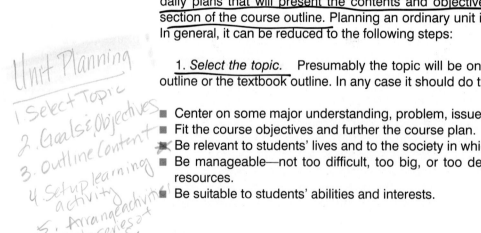

Stop and Reflect

How can a teacher determine whether a particular topic is worth the time and effort?

It has been stated that the basic criteria for judging a topic are the nature of the student and the nature of the society in which the student lives. Is this a valid statement? Why, or why not?

Where might you turn to find suggestions for suitable topics?

2. *Prepare the goals or objectives.*   Again, these may be set forth in the local course outline, curriculum guide, resource unit, or curriculum bulletin. If not, you may wish to consult curriculum materials published by other schools. Or, after studying the textbook or from drawing on your own experience, you may wish to decide yourself what you want the students to get out of the unit. In any case, you should decide and note down what your general objectives will be. These should correspond to the course outline. Then you can decide what learnings are necessary to meet these objectives. These learnings will be your specific objectives and, to some extent, your content. The point is to pick objectives that are worthwhile and that contribute to the achievement of course and unit goals. Then write the objectives in the form of descriptive or behavioral objectives. If these have been spelled out in the course outline, so much the better. If the district has set them up as performance objectives (criterion-referenced behavioral objectives), it is usually imperative that you use these objectives as your specific objectives.

3. *Outline the content if it seems desirable to do so.*   If the specific objectives delineate the unit content sufficiently, a content outline may be superfluous. Otherwise, preparing an outline can help to clarify the subject matter to be covered and can help you give organization to your unit. Again, if an outline of the unit content is provided in the district's curriculum guide, bulletin, or course outline, you should adopt (rarely adapt) the suggested outline. The following content outline is an example of a unit on American Education. This course was taught in a junior high school ninth-grade block-of-time core course in a Bergen County, New Jersey, school district.

Course: Ninth-Grade Block

Unit: American Education
Outline of Content

1. Why do we have public schools?
   a. History of public education in America
   b. Comparison of education in the United States with other countries, both free and total-itarian
   c. Value of private and parochial schools in American life
   d. Purposes of the public schools:
      (1) Health
      (2) Command of fundamental processes
      (3) Worthy home membership
      (4) Vocational preparation
      (5) Civic education
      (6) Worthy use of leisure time
      (7) Ethical and moral character
   e. Achievements of our public schools in America
      (1) Americanization of 30,000,000 immigrants in the past (assimilation)
      (2) Helped unite American people (promoted nationalism)
      (3) Promotion of ethical and moral values, tolerance, respect for groups, etcetera
      (4) Promoted equality of opportunity for all
      (5) Provided leaders and skilled workers to promote the miracle of American economic production
      (6) Promoted loyalty to America
2. What is our local school organization like?
   a. Levels of schools:
      (1) Elementary
      (2) Junior High
      (3) Senior High
      (4) Possible local college

    b. Purposes of various levels:
       (1) Elementary
          (a) Development of basic skills
          (b) Social competencies
          (c) Good citizenship
          (d) Security through the self-contained classroom
       (2) Junior High
          (a) Continuation of basic skills
          (b) Beginning of departmentalization in some areas
          (c) The core (block-of-time) program of integration of subject matter
          (d) The junior high as a transition between elementary and senior high
          (e) The junior high designed for early adolescents and their problems
          (f) Improved guidance services
          (g) More school services
       (3) Senior High
          (a) Continuation of basic skills
          (b) More departmentalization
          (c) More emphasis on vocational training or college preparation
          (d) Special courses such as typing, driver training
3. What do we need to carry out our school program?
    a. Personnel: What are the functions of the following?
      (1) Board of Education
      (2) Superintendent
      (3) Assistant Superintendent
      (4) Principal
      (5) Vice-Principal
      (6) Teachers
      (7) Counselors
      (8) Psychologist
      (9) Nurse
      (10) Librarian
      (11) Custodians
      (12) Matron
      (13) Maintenance workers
      (14) Cafeteria workers
      (15) Curriculum coordinator
      (16) Secretaries
      (17) Lay committees
      (18) P.T.A.
    b. School Plant
       (1) School buildings old and new
       (2) Functional design of our building
    c. School Materials. Summary of books, supplies, equipment and furnishings we use, and the cost of each
4. What is the cost of public education and how do we pay for it?
    a. Cost
       (1) of buildings
       (2) of current expenses
    b. Sources of funds
       (1) Local
       (2) State
       (3) Federal
    c. The school budget
       (1) What it is
       (2) How it is made up
       (3) What this year's budget looks like
       (4) Analysis of items

5. Our program at Thomas Jefferson J.H.S.
   a. Basic subjects offered
   b. Extra-class activities
   c. Special things our school offers, such as foreign language, advanced curriculum, and block-of-time programs

4. *Set up the learning activities.* At this point, it may not be necessary to plan each activity in detail, so long as the activities are specific enough to be organized into a plan. In setting these up, consider what activities you wish to use to introduce the unit (introductory activities); what activities will help to develop the unit (developmental activities); and what activities can be used to clinch the learning, assess the success of the teaching and learning, and generally bring things to a satisfactory conclusion (culminating activities).

5. *Arrange the activities into a series of lessons and then set up a schedule or calendar for the lessons.* You can list the lessons in a calendar format—for example:

FIRST WEEK
   Monday: Introductory lecture, discussion
   Tuesday: Movie; American Revolution
and so on. Or you can use the layout sheets of a lesson plan book.

6. *Plan the unit's logistics (i.e., the gathering and preparation of the materials of instruction).* This step includes the preparation of study guides, bibliographies, lists of materials, photocopies, and the like, plus the collection of audiovisual materials, reading materials, supplies and equipment for group and individual projects, and so forth. Also prepare for your own guidance lists of materials, equipment, audiovisual aids, and readings pertaining to the unit, indicating the materials and equipment that you will need and the references you must read to be properly prepared.

7. *Plan and prepare the tests and other evaluative exercises.*

Stop and Reflect
Pick a topic from a text for a course you might teach. Outline what you would include in a unit on that topic.

- *What introductory activities might you use?*
- *What developmental activities might you use?*
- *What culminating activities might you use?*

Arrange these activities into a sequence of lessons.

Planning Laboratory Units

MR. JONES'S UNIT The unit on American Education that appears in the previous section is simply a series of lesson plans focused on a certain topic or central idea. When developing such a unit plan, the author must first schedule tentative plans for each day and then provide for additional optional activities such as projects, writing assignments, and the like.

An alternate method of unit planning is illustrated by Mr. Jones's unit on minority groups. Mr. Jones, a teacher at Quinbost High School, always tries to make his course interesting and challenging so that it will stimulate and motivate students. To this end, he decided that to induce in students a proper set for the beginning of this unit, he would play the devil's advocate: On the day he was to begin the unit, he came to the classroom seemingly in an angry mood, tossed his books on the desk, and glared at the class. He then began a tirade on a particular minority group, telling the class about something a member of this group had done to him the day before, and concluded by saying that all members of that particular group were alike.

Immediately his class began to challenge him, disagreeing and telling him that he was unfair to generalize from one incident and that he shouldn't talk like that. Seizing on this reaction, Mr. Jones then asked the class whether they had ever expressed such feelings toward any group. As the animated discussion continued, the class members began to see what Mr. Jones was doing. Almost as one body, they suggested discussing minority groups as a class topic.

The stage had been set! The teacher had fired their interest and their desire to study the topic was evident.* Mr. Jones then set the class to talking about what subject matter they felt should be discussed and what outcomes there should be. This led to general teacher-pupil planning. Soon students were choosing committees and projects on which to work. Then, with the aid of study guides and their committee and project assignments, individual students completed tentative plans for their role in the unit.

The study guide they used consisted of three parts. The first part noted questions and problems everyone was to find answers for and suggested where the students might look to find these answers. The second part listed a number of readings and activities that the students might find interesting. All students were expected to do some of these, but no one had to do any particular one. In none of these optional activities or the required problems and questions were the students held to any prescribed reading or procedure. All they were asked to do was carry out the activity, solve the problem, or find the information; they had free choice of ways and means. The third part of the study guide was a bibliography.

Once the teacher and students had finished the planning, they began to work. Except for two periods that Mr. Jones used for motion pictures, the next two weeks were devoted to laboratory work. The committees met; the researchers researched; the pupils carried out their plans.

Then the committees began to report. Some of the groups presented panels. One did a play. Another conducted a question-and-answer game. In all these activities, students tried to bring out what they had learned. In between these reports, Mr. Jones and the students discussed the implications of the findings and other points they thought pertinent and important.

The unit ended with all the students writing down their ideas concerning the treatment of minority groups. This writing session was followed by a short objective test that was based on the teacher's objectives, which were shown in the questions of the study guide.

Thus, after a little over three weeks, the unit was finished.

Stop and Reflect

What do you think of Mr. Jones's method of set induction? Do you see any dangers in using such an approach?

What advantages does this type of unit have over a unit made up of a series of lesson plans? What disadvantages?

---

*You will recognize this tactic of Mr. Jones's as a form of set induction.

PLANNING A CLASSROOM LABORATORY UNIT   Mr. Jones's unit was carried out as a classroom laboratory. Planning a classroom laboratory unit is similar to planning an ordinary unit except for the embellishments discussed in the following paragraphs.

After setting up the unit objectives and deciding on the unit learning activities, prepare a unit assignment that includes both required and optional activities.

THE BASIC ACTIVITIES   Prepare the basic required activities so that all your students may have experiences suitable to their own levels. At least some of the activities should be appealing to nonacademically minded students. Sometimes teachers reserve all the interesting projectlike activities for optional activities or for extra credit work after the required work has been finished; this is poor practice. Those same students who need stimulation most may never have a chance to do anything stimulating.

The students should be able to reach all the teacher's specific objectives by way of the basic activities. To be sure that the activities really do contribute to all these learnings, note just what learning product or products each activity is supposed to produce. This practice will help to ensure that each activity does contribute to some objective and that all the objectives are provided for.

THE OPTIONAL ACTIVITIES   Optional related activities are activities that students may do if they wish. They should be truly optional; students' marks should not depend on completing any of them. Although no student should be required to do any of these activities, you can make an effort to interest particular students in whichever of these activities might be especially beneficial to them. Allow students to drop optional activities that prove to be distasteful if it seems desirable. In a sense, the optional activities are projects. Encourage students to suggest other activities not yet included in the unit assignment. Often student-suggested activities are the best of all.

PHASES IN THE LABORATORY UNIT   As in other units, the activities in the unit assignment should be arranged into introductory, developmental, and culminating phases. In addition to introducing the unit, engaging students' interest, and showing the relationship of this unit to other units, the introductory phase should be used by students to plan their individual assignments, especially if, as in Mr. Jones's unit, students are to do individual or small-group work. A good procedure is to distribute study guides and let the students, under guidance, prepare their own plans. A sample form for a student plan is shown in Figure 6.1. The students should not be held too closely to their plans; instead, students should be permitted to change and amplify them throughout later phases of the unit.

FIGURE 6.1
A Sample Work Plan

NAME _____   CLASS _____

UNIT _____   DATE _____

Activities I plan to do.

Committees I plan to work with.

Materials I plan to read.

Things I plan to make.

Stop and Reflect

Select a unit for a course you hope to teach. What specifically might you do to challenge and motivate the students during the introductory phase of the unit?

What are the merits of using a pretest as an introductory activity? Under what circumstances would you recommend using a pretest?

The following are two examples of interest-catching introductory activities. Read and critique them.

1. *Example One: Demonstration   To get things moving quickly, one chemistry teacher makes a practice of starting his unit on oxidation with a bang. As he starts his introductory talk, he casually mixes together the ingredients for a demonstration that, he says, is yet to come. Suddenly an explosion nearly knocks the students off their seats. Questions and discussion are the natural outcome: What happened? Why? And so on.*

2. *Example Two: Laboratory Procedure   For this activity, the directions are as follows:*

   - *After pairing off with another student, select five substances with characteristic odors, such as onion, orange, fish, mint, and peanut. Place each substance in a small corked bottle.*
   - *Blindfold your partner and ask him to hold his nose so he cannot smell the substances. Let him taste each substance separately and describe it to you. Record each description carefully. Make two trials.*
   - *Keep your partner blindfolded, but do not have him hold his nose. This time let him smell each substance before tasting and describing it. Make two trials.*
   - *Compare the descriptions (with and without smell) of the taste of each substance as your partner gives them to you. How do they differ? Can you draw any conclusions about a person's relative ability to taste and smell? Do you think a cold in the nose makes any difference in the enjoyment of food? If so, why?*

   In your opinion, are these good examples of interest-catching introductory activities? Why, or why not? If not suitable as is, how might you adapt them?

In the developmental phase, the student jumps off from the theoretical springboard set up in the introductory phase to accomplish the nitty-gritty of the learning process. In this phase, for instance, the teacher might involve the students in a series of lessons—teacher talks, discussions, investigative assignments, small-group work, composition writing, reading, oral reports, evaluation and research, as well as optional activities—or the teacher might decide to use a laboratory class approach as Mr. Jones did in his unit on minority groups. Although this approach may be somewhat difficult to organize and control, the use of the laboratory class and unit assignment has the advantage of making it easier to organize teaching techniques and teaching devices to facilitate individualization of instruction, motivation, student planning, and student responsibility for their own learning. It also places teaching emphasis on the higher levels of cognitive and affective learning.

In the laboratory unit assignment, the students should find a wide selection of both required and optional activities from which they may choose. Usually, these activities are best presented to the students in a duplicated study guide. This gives students a basis for planning their own activities and allows them to begin new activities without waiting for other members of the class. It also frees you to work with individuals and small groups who need help, guidance, and counseling.

Logically, the laboratory unit assignment approach should culminate in sharing the interesting things learned during the laboratory experience. Ordinarily, the students should do the programming themselves, but you must guide them carefully to ensure variety and sparkle. Some devices that you may use are the following:

1. panels
2. oral talks
3. dramatizations
4. writing for publication
5. debate
6. group discussions
7. meetings of the class
8. exhibits
9. demonstrations
10. preparing an anthology of student work
11. presenting and defending a position
12. recordings and tapes
13. audiovisual materials
14. moving pictures
15. British style debate
16. mock trials
17. student-conducted summaries
18. teacher-conducted summaries

A laboratory unit assignment type of unit plan can succeed only if it is kept flexible. It does not always roll forward relentlessly. Not everyone spends Monday and Tuesday working on individual projects and Wednesday and Thursday sharing what they have learned with one another, although sometimes this makes an excellent plan. Instead, progress in the unit's developmental phase may vary from student to student. For some it speeds; for others it dawdles. For many students it starts, stops, turns back, and then starts again. If one group has finished the preparation of a dramatization and is ready to present it to the class long before any other group is ready to share the experience, a good unit plan must be flexible enough to allow this group to present its dramatization then and there. Later, the students may go on to some other activities. Thus, the unit will have passed from the laboratory activities to the sharing of experiences and back again.

In units that emphasize individualization, various students may be working on each of the phases at the same time. Furthermore, the developmental activities may be interspersed with evaluative activities from time to time. In a good unit, the process of evaluation is continuous. Both laboratory and sharing of experience activities give you excellent opportunities to assess students' progress and needs. The unit assignment laboratory class approach is especially adaptable for student self-evaluation.

Stop and Reflect

How can you provide for individual differences if you prepare a unit assignment in advance? Should optional related activities be done only by the brilliant students who finish early? Would it be good practice to suggest a number of activities and then insist that every student freely select and do at least one of these activities whether interested in any of them or not?

It is sometimes said that the unit assignment should consist largely of a series of problems. Do you agree? What would the advantages be? The limitations?

At what point and how much should the students plan the unit assignment or their part in it?

STUDY AND ACTIVITY GUIDES   After selecting the basic required and optional activities, prepare a study guide that contains instructions for carrying out basic activities and assignments, problems to be solved, suggestions for optional activities, and so on.

Some theorists decry the use of study guides on the basis that study guides may limit the creativity and originality of the student. To some extent this may be true, but good study guides have advantages that seem to outweigh the disadvantages. For example:

1. They give the students a *source* to which they can refer if they forget the assignment.
2. They give the students a *picture* of possible activities so that they can pick the activities they wish to do and the order in which they wish to do them.
3. They give the students a *definite assignment* so that they can go ahead to new activities on their own without waiting for a new assignment from the teacher.
4. They give *definite instructions* that help to eliminate misunderstandings about assignments and many excuses for incomplete or unattempted assignments.

The following is an example of a study and activity guide developed for a unit on race relations. This unit was the focus of a twelfth-grade class called Problems of Democracy.

GENERAL STUDY AND ACTIVITY GUIDE
1. What are the various groups that make up the population of the United States? (2:42–45)*
2. Make a classification of the different groups and give numbers. (14:521–527)
3. What is the composition of our population in Middletown?
4. What are the various sects (religious) in the United States? (1:101)
5. Give the names and numbers of the ten largest. (1:101)
6. How many of these religions are represented in Middletown? In Middletown High School?
7. How have these various groups affected the growth and development of the United States? Name the contributions of these groups. (14:512–517, 521—524)
8. What are some of the problems of harmonious relationships between different races and groups? (14:498–502)
9. When is a group regarded as a minority? (6:582)
10. How does prejudice destroy harmony between groups? (6:586–587)
11. What is prejudice? (26:Ch. 1)
12. How do we get our prejudices? (26:16; 22:29–33)
13. What are the principal races in the world? (6:84–89)
14. What is the meaning of discrimination? (6:89)
15. Give one example of political, social, and economic discrimination from your own experience.
16. How can we improve on the existing efforts to destroy prejudice and discrimination?
17. What is the work of the Commonwealth Fair Employment Practices Commission?
18. What can you do to prevent discrimination?
19. Name four types of groups often regarded as minorities. (6:582–606)
20. What is the dominant group in America? (6:582–606)
21. What constitutes the differences between groups? (6:606)
22. Name the effects of prejudice on the person who practices it. (27)
23. Discuss the relationship of prejudice to democracy. (27)
24. Is there such a thing as "racial superiority"? Explain your answer. (6:84–95)

*These numbers refer to readings that the student may consult to find the answers to a particular problem. These have been omitted from this sample study activity guide to save space.

25. Make a full report in writing on social adjustment involving the immigrant.
26. Read the Roll of Honor in your neighborhood for World War II. Copy ten names at random and try to determine their ancestry.

The study guide should also include a list of any materials needed by the students as well as a bibliography. The bibliography should consist largely of materials at the reading level of the students. However, there should be readings difficult enough to challenge gifted students, as well as readings suitable for poor readers. References in the text may be keyed into this bibliography by a system similar to that illustrated in the sample study and activity guide.

Lists of materials required for specific activities should be part of the description of the activity. If including the list makes the description of the activity too long, the detailed description may be filed on 4 × 6 or 5 × 8 cards or placed on the bulletin board, thus keeping the size of the study guide reasonable.

SPECIAL STUDY AND ACTIVITY GUIDES   Optional activities should usually be described by title and perhaps by a brief notice in the study and activity guide or on a bulletin board. This serves to make the students aware of optional activities that may interest them. Detailed instructions for such activities can be kept on 5 × 8 or 4 × 6 file cards. Then if a student spots a likely optional activity in the general activity and study guide, the student can go to the file, examine the card, and if the activity seems worthwhile, proceed to carry it out with the teacher's permission. This means that several cards must be available for each activity. If this is not feasible, the student can copy the instructions.

Another type of special study guide is that which is prepared to help students get more out of such activities as field trips and audiovisual materials. Such special activity and study guides are used to point out the things that students should observe and the things they should investigate in such activities.

The following is an example of a special guide for an optional activity in Mr. Jones's unit on Race Relations.

SPECIAL ACTIVITY GUIDE: REPORT ON AMERICANIZATION WORK IN MIDDLETOWN
1. Interview Mr. Rand in Room 310. Mr. Rand is head of the evening school in Middletown. Ask him questions along this line and take notes on his answers.
   a. What is the work of the Americanization classes?
   b. Who teaches these classes? What are their qualifications?
   c. What people are eligible for these classes?
   d. Why are the classes necessary?
   e. What subjects are taught and why?
   f. When a person completes the course what happens?
   g. How long does this course last?
   h. Who pays for it?
   i. What is the attitude of the people in the class toward America?
   j. How many people in Middletown have completed the course in the last 10 years?
   k. Where do these people come from?
2. Write the answers in the form of a report and submit it to the teacher for approval. Indicate whether you would be willing to give the report to some other class if called on to do so.

THE DAILY LESSON PLAN IN THE UNIT ASSIGNMENT   The unit plan does not eliminate daily planning. Before each class, think through what is to be done that day and jot down the agenda for the day. This plan will include such things as announcements, programs of activities, reminders to work with certain students or groups, notes for teacher talks, and the like. When the major part of the planning has been taken care of by the unit assignment, the daily plan may be quite sketchy and informal. At times, it may be as simple and brief as "continue laboratory session"; at other times, it may be simply a list of the committee and individual reports or activities to be presented that period. Sometimes, however, it will be necessary to work out detailed lesson plans for carrying out what the unit plan outlines.

Stop and Reflect

What part of the unit assignment should be placed on cards or on the bulletin board? Why?

What is the use of a study guide? Some authorities do not approve of using study guides. Do you?

What is the use of a special study guide?

Should all students begin at the beginning of a unit assignment and proceed with the suggested activities in order? Why, or why not? If not, how should they proceed?

Learning Activity Packets

Learning modules (sometimes called instructional learning packets, learning activity packets, instructional modules, instructional packets, or learning packets) are really a variation of the unit plan. They are especially useful for individualizing instruction. The procedure for planning and building a learning module is basically the same as that for any other unit. The differences lie in the provisions for individualization and continuous progress.

I. The general objective is written as an overview that includes not only a description of the terminal behavior expected but also includes reasons for studying the module and acquiring this learning.

II. The specific objectives are written as behavioral objectives, either simple or criterion-referenced, that tell the students what they are supposed to know, do, or feel at the end of the module. Usually these should be written in the second person.

III. The activities are so designed that students can work on their own without having to depend on the teacher for direction. The idea behind the learning module approach is for the learner to be largely self-directing and the teacher to be a guide rather than a master.

IV. The evaluation plan should include some sort of self-correcting pretest that will show students where their strengths and deficiencies lie. In individualized programs, there should be some means for capable students to "test out" of a module by demonstrating that they have achieved its objectives. Teacher-administered pretest schemes can be used for this purpose. Self-correcting progress tests are also useful for helping students evaluate their own work as they progress through the module. In addition, a posttesting device should be used to measure the students' final progress. Probably this should be some sort of teacher-corrected, criterion-referenced posttest or performance instrument.

V. The instruction is centered on the study guide or learning packet, the document that students will use to guide themselves through the module. Since it is the basis of individual study and self-guidance, it should be prepared very carefully. In it students will find:

A. The topic.

    B. The rationale, including the general objectives and reasons why the learning is worthwhile.

    C. The specific objectives—stated as specific behavioral objectives—addressed to the student (e.g., "At the end of this module you should be able to locate the principal oceanic streams on the globe"). Sometimes provisions are made for students to check off each of these behavioral objectives upon mastering the behavior called for.

    D. Directions for the student to follow while completing the module. These directions should include:

        1. General directions: agenda, time limits (if any), and options.

        2. Specific directions, such as the directions and explanations for specific activities. For example,

            a. Problems to be solved: What the problem is, what the background of the problem is, and what requirements must be met to solve the problem successfully.

            b. Reading: Purpose of the reading, what information is to be learned, what is to be done with the information, questions on the reading, and exact citations.

            c. Information to be learned: Possible sources of the information.

        3. Where to go for materials and information.

    E. The bibliography.

    F. The instructional materials that you have prepared for the module. (These may be included with the study guide or distributed separately.)

    G. The self-correcting and other testing and evaluating materials. These should include both pretest and posttest material and perhaps intermediate progress tests. These may be included with the study guide or distributed separately. Note, however, that mastery tests should be administered separately, supervised and corrected by the teacher. Progress tests, on the other hand, are more useful when they are self-correcting.

An example of a learning activity packet may be found at the end of this chapter.

The Contract Plan

The contract plan is a variation of the unit plan, in which the student agrees to do a certain amount of work during a specific time period.

In preparing contracts, you can follow a procedure something like the following:

1. Set up objectives and activities whereby students may achieve the objectives.
2. Decide which activities will be required.
3. Decide which activities will be optional.
4. Provide the objectives and activities to the student, in writing, for study.
5. Let the student decide how he or she will meet the requirements and what optional work he or she will do.
6. On the basis of the decision, have the student make out a contract in writing. Each contract may be different from every other contract.

An example of a contract is shown in Figure 6.2.

Another type of contract calls for setting up certain requirements for the various grade levels. An example is shown in Figure 6.3.

FIGURE 6.2
A Sample Contract

CONTRACT

John Jones   To be completed by May 1.

During the period of April 10 to May 1, I will

1. Read Chapters X–XII of book A.
2. Do problems and exercises # 1, 2, 4, 7, 8, 9, 11 of the study guide.
3. Participate on the map committee with Mike Smith, John Walsh, and Ted Burke.
4. Prepare a report on the topography of the area.
5. X X X X
   (Remaining activities omitted to save space)

Signed   _____
                              Student
Approved _____
                              Teacher

FIGURE 6.3
A Sample Contract

To pass with a D you must complete activities 1–12 and pass the posttest.

To receive a C you must complete activities 1–12, receive at least a C on the posttest, and do two (2) of the optional activities satisfactorily.

To receive a grade of B, you must complete activities 1–12, receive at least a grade of B on the posttest, and satisfactorily complete at least four of the optional activities very well.

To receive a grade of A you must complete activities 1–12, do four of the optional activities excellently, complete at least one major optional activity very well, and receive at least a B+ on the posttest.

What is your opinion on contracts? Would you be more motivated if you had one?

Lesson Planning

Every lesson should be planned. Sometimes the daily lesson plan should be minimal. For instance, you may be carrying on a unit in a laboratory fashion. In such a case, the procedure may be simply to help and guide students' endeavors as they do their laboratory work. Other unstructured classes include certain kinds of problem-solving and discussion classes. Nevertheless, no teacher can face a class for long without having carefully thought out what the students are to learn from the lesson and how they are to learn it. You need to know what the lesson's objectives are, what the content is, what the procedures will be, and how they will be executed. Perhaps it is not always necessary that the plan be carefully written out; experienced teachers may know the content well enough and be so skilled in the strategies and tactics that much of their teaching can be both intuitive and successful. Some teachers are convinced that the best classes are unstructured; they believe that students experience true learning best in such an atmosphere.

Whether or not they are right is doubtful, but, right or wrong, as a beginner you will do well to avoid such approaches. They are too likely to end in mere drifting and, all too often, sheer chaos—another waste of time and taxpayers' money. You will be wise to learn to plan and conduct a tight, closely structured, well-knit lesson before you venture off into the unmapped unknown of unstructured classes.

Even the most experienced teachers must give careful thought to their lesson plans if they are to be successful for long. Careful planning ensures familiarity with the content. It helps give you the confidence that comes from knowing what you are doing, and it shows the students that you are prepared. It gives the lesson structure, organization, and sequence and helps ensure optimum time on task.

Preparing the Lesson Plan

No matter what approach you take to lesson planning, the general principles of planning apply. In planning your lessons, be sure that

- The lesson objectives contribute directly to your unit and course objectives.
- The lesson objectives are clear in your own mind.
- Each lesson objective is a learning product or terminal behavior so definite and specific that you can aim directly at it.
- Your lesson is feasible. To try to teach something that is too difficult or cannot be completed is pointless. Avoid attempting to cover too broad a range of material. *It is better to do a little well than a lot badly.*
- The teacher-learning activities will yield the objectives you desire and are aimed at those objectives.
- You are prepared to carry out the activities you have selected, that is, you know what to do and how to do it, and have the materials to do it with.
- You have provided for a suitable introduction and a culminating clinching activity.
- You have allotted a suitable amount of time for each activity.

The Lesson Plan Format

In writing up a lesson plan, you can follow a number of formats. Which format you use is not particularly important; use the one that seems easiest and most comfortable to you. We prefer an outline based on the following six elements, but you may find some other format more congenial. Examples of other formats can be found later in this chapter.

The six elements of our preferred format are the following:

1. The objective
2. The subject matter or content
3. The procedure (teaching strategies and tactics and learning activities)
4. The materials of instruction
5. Special notes
6. The new assignment

Let us now look at these elements.

THE OBJECTIVE   As we have seen, the lesson objective should describe precisely what is to be learned in the lesson. This objective may be in the form of behavioral or descriptive objectives as long as it points out clearly what the students are expected to learn. At this level, the objective should be quite specific and aimed at furthering a more general unit or topical objective.

THE SUBJECT MATTER   Indicate the subject content of the lesson. Often it is helpful to outline the content as a separate part of the plan. In other circumstances, it may be more suitable to write out the content outline on a separate sheet of paper (for use in a lecture, for instance). Sometimes it is best to incorporate it into the procedure.

THE STEP-BY-STEP PROCEDURE   In sufficient detail so that you can follow them easily, list the activities by which you hope to attain your objectives. List the key questions, exercises, and other learning activities in the order you plan to use them. Include introductory set-inducing motivational activities to get the lesson started, developmental activities to keep the lesson going, and culminating, clinching activities to bring the lesson to a conclusion. Also include evaluation activities as needed or desired.

Figure 6.4 shows a sample lesson plan written by Harry Lewis, a teacher with 40 years of classroom experience, and the author of successful secondary school mathematics texts. Notice how meticulously Dr. Lewis has mapped out the activities in this plan for a lesson demonstrating the discovery approach in mathematics.

INTRODUCTORY ACTIVITIES (GETTING SET)   Introductory activities set the stage for the developmental activities to follow. You may use these activities to tie the new lesson to past lessons and to make sure the students have sufficient understanding on which to build the new learning. Review and recapitulation exercises may be useful for these purposes. You may also use introductory activities to set forth the direction and objectives of the new lesson and for other motivational purposes. For instance, you might plan a set-induction tactic that will induce in the students a favorable attitude or mental set toward the lesson. It is difficult to teach when you do not have students' attention, and set-induction activities are intended to be attention-grabbers. You might also incorporate activities that point out the worth of what is to be learned. Although exhortations on the part of the teacher do not usually aid much in creating student interest and energy, attempts to point out the usefulness or relevancy of the work may bear fruit. More effective in capturing student interest are high-energy activities, interesting content, student planning and decision making, and other techniques that draw students' attention and convince them that the learning is worthwhile. If such attention-catching activities come early in the lesson, they may catch and hold otherwise apathetic students through to the end. Items 1a, b, c, and d of Dr. Lewis's plan (Figure 6.4) are introductory activities.

DEVELOPMENTAL ACTIVITIES   When building your lesson procedure, do not make the mistake of skimping on the planning for the development activities. It is not enough to write in the plan book: "Lecture on the amoeba—fifteen minutes." Plan for what will be in that lecture. It is not enough to state that there will be a discussion on the civil rights law; plan the direction the discussion will take, the main points it will bring out, and the questions you will use. It is not enough to resolve that you will have students work some problems at the chalkboard; plan which problems and work out the answers ahead of time. Therefore:

- If you plan to use questions, decide what questions you will ask; note the wording and the answers you expect to the most important ones.
- If you plan to use demonstrations or films, gather the necessary materials and equipment beforehand and check them carefully to be sure that everything is in working order.
- If you plan to use an experiment or demonstration, try it first to make sure the apparatus works, the technique is sound, and the expected result occurs. Nothing is flatter than a demonstration that does not work.
- If you plan to use a problem or exercise, check to see that it is solvable by first solving it yourself.

■ FIGURE 6.4 (PP. 147–149)
An Illustrative Lesson Plan

► *Plane geometry*

Objective: The student will be able to prove:

1. A ray to be the bisector of an angle.
2. A point to be the midpoint of a line segment.
3. A line to be the bisector of a line segment.
4. Similar conclusions that are an outgrowth of the congruence of triangles.

Text: Geometry—A Contemporary Course, pages 222–224.

Procedure:

1. Ask the following questions to point up the information that the students already have that is a prerequisite for understanding the topic that is to be developed in this lesson.

   a. *Teacher:* "I wonder if one of you would summarize the nature of the material we have been exploring over the past few days?" [*Ans.:* "We have been proving line segments congruent, and we have been proving angles congruent."]*

   b. *Teacher:* "Just what have we been using as a basis to conclude that a pair of angles are congruent?" [*Ans.:* "We have been showing that these angles are corresponding parts of congruent triangles."]

   c. *Teacher:* "Why are we in a position to say that two angles will be congruent if they are corresponding parts of congruent triangles?" [*Ans.:* "The reverse of the definition of congruent polygons permits us to draw this conclusion."]

   d. *Teacher:* "Hence, in general then, if we are asked to prove that a pair of line segments are congruent or a pair of angles are congruent, what will probably be our method of attack?" [*Ans.:* "We will find a pair of triangles that contain these parts as corresponding parts and then try to prove those triangles to be congruent."]

2. *Teacher:* "I would like to explore something with you today that is just a bit different from what we have been doing over the past few days. For instance, consider this situation in which we are asked to prove that *AD* is the bisection of ∠ *BAC*." With the aid of a straightedge draw the accompanying figure and write the following Given Data and Conclusion.

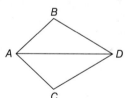

Given: $\overrightarrow{DA}$ bisects ∠BDC
$DB \cong DC$
Conclusion: $\overrightarrow{AD}$ bisects ∠BAC

---

* Because this is a demonstration lesson, Dr. Lewis has, he says, included student answers to illustrate the type of answers he would expect. Ordinarily, he would leave them out, but perhaps a beginning teacher should include them to be sure to know what the students' answers should be. It is quite embarrassing when you cannot remember the answers to your own questions or how to solve your own problems. In any case you should provide yourself with good notes, because it is almost impossible to remember everything in the hurly-burly of an active class. It is better to plan too carefully than not to plan carefully enough. Notice also that the lesson procedure begins with initiatory activities, continues with developmental activities, and ends with culminating activities.

■ **Figure 6.4** *continued*

a. *Teacher:* "In searching for the proof to a problem such as this, what should be the *very first thing* we must examine?" [*Ans.:* "The conclusion."]

b. *Teacher:* "From what standpoint do we examine the conclusion?" [*Ans.:* "We mentally try to come up with all the ways we have for proving a ray to be the bisector of an angle."]

c. *Teacher:* "Well, how many ways do we have at our disposal for proving a ray to be the bisector of an angle?" [*Ans.:* "Just one, the reverse of the definition of the bisector of an angle."]

d. *Teacher:* "What does this imply we will have to prove before we can show that a ray is the bisector of an angle?" [*Ans.:* "That the ray forms two congruent angles with the sides of the angle."]

e. *Teacher:* "Then, in terms of the letters in our diagram, exactly what will have to be shown to be true before we can conclude that $\overrightarrow{AD}$ is the bisector of $\angle BAC$?" [*Ans.:* "That $\angle BAD$ is congruent to $\angle CAD$."]

f. *Teacher:* "Just what would you suggest we do in order to prove that these two angles are congruent?" [*Ans.:* "Try to prove that $\triangle BAD$ is congruent to $\triangle CAD$."]

g. (Now attempt to reverse the direction of the thinking of the students.) "Assuming that the two triangles can be shown to be congruent, what will follow?" [*Ans.:* "$\angle BAD$ will be congruent to $\angle CAD$."]

h. *Teacher:* "And on this information, what conclusion will we be able to draw?" [*Ans.:* "That $\overrightarrow{AD}$ is the bisector of $\angle BAC$."]

i. *Teacher:* "In view of our analysis, basically, what does the proof of this problem depend upon?" [*Ans.:* "Proving two triangles to be congruent."] *Teacher:* "And this we have done many times over during the past few weeks!"

j. *Teacher:* "Incidentally, why is it that we do not merely prove the triangles to be congruent and then simply say that $\overrightarrow{AD}$ is the bisector of $\angle BAC$ as a consequence of this?" [*Ans.:* "The information that triangles are congruent merely leads to pairs of congruent angles or pairs of congruent line segments and nothing else. The fact that triangles are congruent does not immediately imply that a ray is the bisector of an angle."]

3. Ask one of the brighter students in the class to go to the board and give a formal proof of the problem.

4. At the completion of the proof ask the following questions, calling on only the average or below average students in the class for the answers.

a. "In developing her proof, Dorothy stated that $\overline{DB}$ is congruent to $\overline{DC}$. How did she know this?"

b. "I notice that she has marked the diagram in such a way as to imply that $\angle BDA$ is congruent to $\angle CDA$. What enables her to do this?"

c. "What remaining parts of the two triangles did she have to prove congruent before she could conclude that the two triangles were congruent? What theorem, postulate, or definition permitted her to conclude that $\overline{AD}$ is a congruent to $\overline{AD}$? Is the statement you have just given a definition, a postulate, or a theorem?"

d. "Why did Dorothy want to prove these two triangles to be congruent?"

e. "Now that the triangles are congruent, what will follow?"

f. "And where does the fact that $\angle BAD$ is congruent to $\angle CAD$ lead us?"

5. *Teacher:* "There are other situations that are very much the same as the one we have just examined. As an illustration, consider the situation here (at this point make a freehand drawing of the figure). Suppose that we are called upon to prove that *B* is the midpoint of $\overline{AC}$, how would you suggest proceeding?" [*Ans.:* "Prove that $\overline{AB}$ is congruent to $\overline{CB}$."]

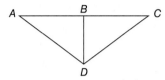

a. *Teacher:* "What would you probably have to do in order to arrive at this conclusion?" [*Ans.:* "We would probably have to prove △ *DBC* congruent to △ *DBA*."]

b. *Teacher:* "Hence, here again, what seems to be our method of attack?" [*Ans.:* "Prove a pair of triangles to be congruent. This leads to a pair of line segments being congruent and, in turn, this leads to a point as the midpoint of a line segment."]

c. *Teacher:* "Let's consider that the conclusion we are asked to reach is that $\overleftrightarrow{DB}$ is the bisector of $\overline{AC}$ rather than that *B* is the midpoint of $\overline{AC}$. In what way will the attack just outlined have to be altered?" [*Ans.:* "It would not have to be altered at all."] *Teacher:* "Justify that." [*Ans.:* "Well, to prove a point to be the midpoint of a line segment we have to prove two line segments to be congruent and to prove a line to be the bisector of a line segment we have to do the same."] *Teacher:* "Is there any part of the write-up of the proof that will have to be altered?" [*Ans.:* "Yes, the last 'Reason.' Rather than being the reverse of the definition of the midpoint of a line segment, it will be the reverse of the definition of the bisector of a line segment,"]

6. *Teacher:* "Let's all of us open our texts to page 223 and examine exercise 1."

a. Now call upon only the average or below average members of the class to answer the following questions:

(1) What is the first thing you will examine in Exercise 1, [John]?* In order to prove that $\overrightarrow{DB}$ bisects ∠ *ADC*, what will you have to show to be true, [Mary]? How would you suggest that ∠ *ABD* is congruent to ∠ *CDB*, [James]? What ways do we have for proving triangles congruent, [Bill]? Let's look at the Given Data for a moment. Which of the two ways of proving triangles will probably be applied in this situation, [Eleanor]? What makes you think that this is so? Once the triangles are proved to be congruent, what will follow, [Henry]? What reason would you write for that conclusion, [Paul]? What follows from the fact that those are congruent, [Judith]? And, finally, why can this conclusion be drawn, [Ann]?

b. Exercise 3 is examined in exactly the same manner as Exercise 1 has been.

Homework: If at all possible, this should be begun in class. Pages 223 and 224: Exercises 1, 2, 3, 7, and 9.

---

* Ordinarily one would not include the names of specific students in one's plan. The names here are merely to show that here one calls on students.

In other words, lay out your developmental activities in detail. Items 2 through 5 of Dr. Lewis's plan (Figure 6.4) are developmental activities.

CULMINATING ACTIVITIES (CLOSURE)   Every objective needs to be driven home. Many teachers fail—when they fail—because they neglect to make the little extra effort needed to clinch the learning that meets their objectives. Again, how to do the closure step depends upon the situation. In many lessons, the clincher may be a summary at the end of the session. In others it may be a review or drill. In still others it may be a student summation to the question: "What was the main point that we were trying to get at in this discussion, John?" It may even be a short quiz. Even though lessons must sometimes carry over to the next class, it is axiomatic that any lesson plan that does not make provision for a clincher is not a complete plan. This culmination is what we mean by following through. Part 6 of Dr. Lewis's plan (Figure 6.4) gives examples of culminating activities.

Stop and Reflect

Go over Dr. Lewis's mathematics lesson carefully. How does he try to launch the lesson? What does he do to create interest? What does he do to get students thinking? What does he do to allow for differences in student ability? What does he do to tie together and clinch the learning in the lessons? How does he prepare students for the homework assignment?

THE PROBLEM OF TIME   When listing the activities in the lesson plan procedure, estimate how much time the class will spend on each activity. Beginning teachers find this estimate so difficult to make that they often ask for ways to determine just how long to allow for each activity. Unfortunately, no one can provide this kind of specific help, because there is really no way to tell how your individual students will react to any particular event. An activity that can be done in 5 minutes in one class may take 15 minutes in another. All this notwithstanding, we shall attempt to provide a few rules of thumb to use as guides:

1. The first of these rules is, at first, to make your procedure longer than you will possibly need. By doing so, you may prevent the embarrassment of running dry with the period only half over. Beginning teachers tend to talk fast and move through activities swiftly, mostly because of the tenseness they feel in the newness of the classroom situation. This tendency wears off with experience. New teachers are often troubled because they do not have enough material; experienced teachers are more likely to be troubled because they do not have enough time.

2. The second rule of thumb is to provide a few minutes at the beginning of the period for taking attendance and making announcements, and five or more minutes at the end of the period for clinching the lesson. At some point, you also need to provide time enough to make an adequate homework assignment. It is this need to provide for classroom and teaching details that accounts for the astonishing fact that a 40-minute video may be too long for a 50-minute period.

3. A third rule is to mark in your procedure, by an asterisk or by underlining (some teachers use red ink), the activities that really must be covered during the period in case time starts to run out. This procedure can save you from such situations as hearing the bell ring before you have shown students how to do their homework assignment.

4. A fourth rule is to give students time to learn. Don't rush. Points have to be made and remade. The fact that one of your gifted students grasps the answer in a flash should not be taken as a sign that everyone else does. Take time to be sure by asking others about the same point in different ways. People learn concepts clearly by turning them over and over in their minds. Give the students a chance to do that. Introduce your points and follow them up.

5. Finally, if you do run out of material, don't panic. Use the time for a review of what has gone on before, or for a chance to let the students start their homework under supervision. For a while at least, you would be wise to have some extra activities planned for just such a contingency.

These rules of thumb are based on the principle that a lesson should be completed in a single period. There are several reasons for advocating this, the primary one being that lessons seem to be more effective when the period can be finished with a clinching experience. Lesson closure of this type at the end of the period seems to fix the learning in the students' minds and to lead to a good jumping-off place for the next day's lesson. Without such closure, it is more difficult to generate another introductory activity that will get students' attention in the next day's class, although a quick review of what had been done the day before and a quick résumé of what is to come now may suffice.

These generalizations probably hold true for all expository teaching. Longer expository lessons should undoubtedly be divided into shorter daily plans. However, other types of lessons (e.g., research, inquiry, problem-solving, group work, and so on) may be more fruitful if they continue for several periods. In such lessons, the work naturally flows on from one period to the next. Although you may need to stop the lesson from time to time to sum up, reorient, and regroup, the clinching may better be saved for the culmination of several days' work.

THE MATERIALS OF INSTRUCTION   Lessons will not go well unless you have arranged for suitable instructional materials. Find out what materials and equipment are available before you firm up your lesson plan. This may mean arranging for audiovisual machines and software, running off photocopies, assembling auxiliary readings, procuring maps or charts, setting up displays, gathering materials for laboratory work or seatwork, and so on. Lesson planning also includes making decisions about the classroom environment and preparing the classroom for the lesson (e.g., rearranging the chairs for a discussion). Notes in your lesson plan concerning these matters will help remind you to make provisions for details when preparing for your classroom activities and will serve as reminders of things that you need to take care of for the lesson later in the week.

THE SPECIAL NOTES   The special notes section of the lesson plan provides room for reminders of anything that might be forgotten. Here you usually include matters that are out of the ordinary. Announcements, special work for individuals, and reminders to speak to particular students about their assignments are examples of the type of thing that may be included here.

THE NEW ASSIGNMENT   In this section, you note preparations to communicate to students for the new assignment. It may be only a brief note about tonight's homework and preparation for tomorrow, or it may be a detailed explication of what is to be done. The point is to set forth the assignment in sufficient detail so that you can present it clearly. Unless the assignment is presented well, you cannot be sure that the students understand exactly what they are to do and how they are to do it. Making assignments is discussed in some detail in Chapter 3.

Stop and Reflect

Prepare several lesson plans for a course you hope to teach. Evaluate the plans according to the following criteria:

- *Are your objectives clear?*
- *Are your objectives reasonable?*
- *Will your learning activities lead to the objectives?*
- *Do the lessons have a beginning, middle, and end (i.e., introductory, developmental, and culminating activities)?*
- *Are the learning activities worth doing?*
- *Assuming a 50-minute period, have you allowed enough time?*

Observe a lesson in a middle or high school. Does the lesson seem well-planned? Does it have a beginning, a middle, and an end? Does it seem well-organized? Does it make its point?

Using Plan Books

School officials often provide teachers with plan books to use to plan their lessons. These are valuable for planning the long-term sequence for the school year; however, some of the commercial plan books do not allow enough space to enter an entire plan. They are merely layout sheets for indicating the general nature of the work projected for various days and periods. Because this is the case, you may want to prepare your daily plans on sheets of composition paper or in a notebook kept for that purpose.

Even though you keep more detailed plans elsewhere, you still need to keep skeleton plans in your plan book for at least a week ahead. Here you should record the lessons to be studied, the assignments, and a word about the approach. Keeping these plans up to date is important because they may be used by supervisors as an index for estimating the adequacy of the course; they also can serve as a basis for teaching the class if a substitute has to take over. Plan books are particularly important for substitutes. Without the basic layout of a weekly plan, a substitute has nothing to build the teaching on and will be completely at a loss, and so will your class. A sample layout sheet is shown in Figure 6.5.

Following the Plan

On the whole, you would do well to follow your plan fairly closely, for it is about the only way you can be sure to do what you have intended to do. Otherwise, in an active classroom situation you can easily get sidetracked and lose sight of your objectives. Nevertheless, do not let your plan handcuff you. At least two types of situations may require you to leave your plan: (1) when the lesson planned is going so badly that something must be done to save it, and (2) when something happens before or during the class to indicate that the students would benefit more from a different approach.

As a rule, it is foolish to stick to a lesson plan that is obviously not succeeding. Although it should be seldom that such a contretemps occurs, it is always wise to have an alternate approach ready to use in case of emergency.

Often a change of pace is needed to cut off an incipient behavior problem. Students who are growing restless during a lecture or recitation may be ripe for a discussion or a problem-solving activity. Sometimes a written assignment can be quite effective for channeling energies that seem about to break the bonds of propriety. At other times, you can see by the looks on students' faces that what you are trying

Period Subject Grade	Subject ______ Week Beginning ____19__		**LESSON PLAN**	Teacher's Name ______ Home Room ______	
	Monday	Tuesday	Wednesday	Thursday	Friday

FIGURE 6.5
A Lesson Plan Layout Sheet

to teach is not getting through to them. In such cases, a few well-directed questions may pinpoint the difficulty so that you can reorient yourself and start off with a different approach, or perhaps even switch to a different, more elementary lesson.

At times, students raise questions during the lesson that warrant immediate follow-up. Sometimes a point or problem is worth pursuing in detail. In such circumstances, perhaps you should discard your lesson plan completely and devote the class's attention to this new point. More often, however, students' questions warrant only a short diversion from the planned procedure.

Sometimes events of importance may occur within or outside the class that make your plan obsolete. In the case of an event of national importance or of great importance to the school or community, it may be desirable to interrupt the class to talk about the event, even though it has no apparent relationship to the course or subject you are teaching. In the case of an exciting school event, it is wise to let students talk about it for a few minutes at the beginning of class to let them blow off steam, then request that they settle down to work.

No one can tell you when to stick to your plan and when to depart from it. What you do must be decided on the basis of what seems best at the time. The criteria on which to base your decision, though, are simple:

1. What will benefit the students most?
2. What will advance the cause of learning most?
3. How relevant and significant to the course is the change?

Remember that, after all, the lesson plan is only a means to an end. If something better comes along, feel free to use it.

On the other hand, do not change plans capriciously. Usually, if you are inspired by a "better" idea while in the midst of a lesson, it is wise to resist it and stick to your original plan. Good inspirations are hard to find; chances are that your original plan will serve you better than any spur-of-the-moment idea. Only rarely does it pay to be daring and completely discard your plans.

Stop and Reflect

One day a supervisor visited a beginning teacher who was having difficulty. This young person had taken on a job that was almost too much for him. He was teaching material difficult for him and was having a considerable amount of trouble keeping up with the class. When the supervisor asked him for his plans, he replied, "I am so busy I have not been able to make any lesson plans yet." What would your answer be to this beginning teacher?

Alternative Lesson Plan Formats

Although we prefer the lesson plan format just described, you may prefer another format, or your school system may prescribe a different format. Of course, if your school system prescribes a specific format, you must follow the mandated format although you may find it necessary to supplement the prescribed format with additional details for your own use.

Format 1

This lesson plan format (Figure 6.6) is prescribed by a suburban school district. In addition to the identifying data at the top of the plan, it provides spaces for the lesson objectives, content, procedure, instructional material, and evaluation. In this lesson plan format, the evaluation section is for planning test items, classroom questions, and exercises to be used for evaluating student progress.

Format 2

The alternative lesson plan format shown in Figure 6.7 is also used by a city school district. Basically, it is similar to Format 1, except that a section for assignments has been added and provisions have been made for notes concerning the content. The identifying data at the beginning of the plan are quite specific, because these plans may be inspected by supervisors from time to time.

Format 3

This lesson plan format, shown in Figure 6.8, follows an outline advocated by William Meisner.(1) In addition to the identifying data, this outline provides a place for the general objective of the unit of which this lesson is to be a part and the specific objective for the lesson. These objectives may be stated descriptively or behaviorally. The plan format also provides sections for content and procedure. Included in these are places for describing the lesson introduction, the content of the lesson development, the instructional methods and activities, key points, and the conclusion. It ends with an evaluation section that should be used after the lesson to indicate how successful the plan was and how it could be improved if it is ever used again.

Lesson Topic   *suburban school.*   Date

Unit   Grade

1. Lesson objective

2. Content

3. Procedure

4. Instructional Materials

5. Evaluation

■ **FIGURE 6.6**
Alternative Lesson Plan Format 1

Many experienced teachers keep a file of lesson plans with notes about the success of the plans. In that case a plan format such as Meisner's is helpful. Other teachers find this not to be helpful, because they never really repeat their lesson plans.

Formats 4 and 5

Formats 4 and 5 differ from the other formats in that they present the procedure in two columns. Format 4 (Figure 6.9 on page 158) lists the content in one column and, on the same line in a second column, lists the key questions to be asked about the various items. Format 5 (Figure 6.10 on page 159) lists the objectives in one column and in the opposite column lists the specific learning activities to be used to teach those objectives. These formats have the advantage of tying the methods to be used to the content or objectives they are supposed to teach.

city school district

Teacher:	Course Topic:	Date:

Unit:

Objectives:

Content	Notes

Procedures

Evaluation and Questions

Assignment

Materials of Instruction

FIGURE 6.7
Alternative Lesson Plan Format 2

■ **FIGURE 6.8**
Alternative Lesson Plan Format 3

This is more detailed.

 1. Name of course and grade level
 2. Name of unit
 3. Topic to be considered within the unit
 4. General objective for the lesson (may be the same for the entire unit)
 5. Specific objective for the lesson (daily)
 6. Content to be included
    a. New material to be included
    b. Questions for discussion
 7. Introduction
    Review of preceding lesson
    Old vocabulary
    New vocabulary
    Old concepts
 8. Key points or point
 9. Conclusion
10. Method or methods to be used
11. Materials of instruction
12. Assignment
13. Evaluation

Format 6

Format 6 (Figure 6.11 on page 160) is adapted from the format used in a large metropolitan school district. It provides for the listing of the understandings, skills, and attitudes that the lesson will focus on, as well as reminders and student assignments for the next day or so. Then, in a three-column format, it shows the time sequence, the content, and the teaching methods, techniques, and instructional materials. This format is designed to supply the class with a detailed organization and to promote smooth classroom management.

■ ■ ■ ■ **A Sample Learning Activity Packet***

Instructions for Use of This Packet

This packet is divided into several sections. Each section is designed to aid you in acquiring specific information and skills. The following suggestions will aid you in using this packet.

1. Take time to explore the *whole* packet.
2. Read the rationale and the primary and secondary ideas for this packet. If you've read these you'll know the WHY and the WHAT you'll be studying.
3. There are goals or objectives in each packet you'll use. For each goal there are activities to aid you in achieving the goal. Familiarize yourself with goals and activities.
4. Your assignments while using these packets are given DIRECTLY THROUGH THE ACTIVITIES, so READ CAREFULLY. (continued on p. 160)

---

*By Dennis Caulk, Washington Irving Junior High School, Colorado Springs, Colorado. Reprinted by permission of the author.

Tying method to content

Unit	Course	Date

Lesson Topic

Objective

Introduction

Content	Key Questions

Summary

Materials

Assignment

■ FIGURE 6.9
Alternative Lesson Plan Format 4

Ties method to content

Lesson   Course   Date

Objectives   Activities

1.
$$\begin{cases} 1. \\ 2. \\ 3. \\ 4. \end{cases}$$

2.
$$\begin{cases} 5. \\ 6. \\ 7. \\ 8. \end{cases}$$

3.   9.

Materials of Instruction Needed

Assignment

■ **FIGURE 6.10**
Alternative Lesson Plan Format 5

large metro district

School _____

Class _____ Grade _____   Date _____ Day _____

Period(s) or Mod(s) _____   Room(s) _____   Week Ending _____

Daily Lesson Plan

Day's Aims & Objectives *Major Misunderstandings:*	Routines (General Housekeeping Reminders)
Skills to be Developed:	Student Assignment(s) (For one or more days)
Attitudes:	

Chronological Time Sequence (Minute by minute or number of minutes to be used in each part of outline)	*Outline of Content to Focus Upon in Order to Achieve Aims & Objectives.* Content should be arranged so as to begin with *Initiatory Activities:* interest getters, previews, or previous unit work; move to *Developmental Activities* (those which expand understanding of what is known); and end with *Culminating Activities* which can include summary, review, and evaluation.	*Teaching Methods Techniques* (and needed materials). Student involvement is prime consideration for choice of method.
	(continue on additional paper if needed)	

■ **FIGURE 6.11**
Alternative Lesson Plan Format 6

(continued from p. 157)

5. All assignments resulting from activities completed in reaching the goals or objectives will be recorded by YOU in your personal folder.
6. Remember that you *do not* have to complete all activities. If and when you feel you've fulfilled the goal or objective, go on to another.
7. Most of the materials you'll use in working on these packets will be found in the library, the resource center, the audiovisual bank, teacher-led discussions, and

your textbook. Be sure you keep your notes from these sources as they will help you later.

8. There are corresponding *Annexes* in the back of the packets to aid you in your study. These annexes include the following: lists of films, tapes, records, and so on; outlines of information and other material. When working with audiovisual materials you select what you need and use them. If what you are looking for is not listed, ask your teacher to help you.

9. At times in the packet you will finish activities and be expected to report to a certain teacher for a small-group lecture over certain important topics. If the teacher leading the discussion has only two or three people in a group, he will have you sign up and then call on you to come into the discussion later. In the meantime you may go on with another activity.

10. There are self-assessments at the end of each objective. If you can answer the questions and fulfill the goals, you are ready to take the unit test. If you can't answer the self-assessment questions, review the activities until you can do so.

11. When you have finished the self-assessment and have satisfied yourself that you can answer all questions, report to your teacher for the UNIT TEST. This unit test will evaluate the objectives of the unit as well as the content knowledge you should have acquired while doing the activities.

12. If you have a grade of 76 percent or better you may go on to the next packet. If, however, you have a grade of 75 percent or below you *must* complete the recycling activities in the packet before going on.

13. You may move as rapidly as you like through this packet. Remember you only cheat yourself if you don't fulfill the goals as they are set up.

14. If you are having any problems with this packet, report to one of the teachers for help. This way, they will aid you early, and straighten out the problem.

15. DO NOT WRITE IN THIS PACKET!

Packet 1　Colonial America and the French and Indian War

RATIONALE　The chance to earn a living brought many people to the English colonies. In the northern area, New England, people worked at lumbering and fishing. They were also sailors, shippers, and merchants.

Most people in the middle colonies were farmers. They raised wheat and other grains. Because their agriculture produced chiefly grain for flour-making, these middle colonies were called the "bread colonies."

The people in the southern colonies also engaged in agriculture. Southern farms grew rice, tobacco, indigo, and hemp. Southern farmers often used slaves from Africa to raise their crops.

The chance to earn a living was not the only reason settlers came to the English colonies. Many people came to America because they wanted religious freedom. They wanted to worship God in their own way. In most parts of Europe, they could not. They had to belong to a national church.

Quakers, Catholics, Puritans, and Jews were among the people who came to America for religious reasons. Catholics found refuge in Maryland. Puritans founded Massachusetts. The Quakers first settled Pennsylvania. The idea of free worship came early to America.

Political rights of Englishmen also brought settlers. England allowed the colonists a considerable amount of self-rule, and this also made people want to live in the English colonies.

English colonists had helped fight for their liberties. They fought alongside British soldiers in the wars against France. In 1763, the French lost their lands in

North America to England. After that, the colonists did not have to fear attack by the French, or Indian raids from Canada.

Defeating the French had cost England a great deal of money. England needed money for her empty treasury and decided to collect taxes from her colonies. England had placed taxes on the colonists before but, until 1763, she had not tried very hard to collect them. When England did try to seriously collect these taxes, it led to trouble with the colonists.

PRIMARY IDEA   The people who came to America to set up colonies did so mainly to have a better way of life.

SECONDARY IDEAS

1. Early colonization in the New World was carried out by the English, French, and Dutch.
2. Three distinct sections developed in the thirteen colonies. They were the northern or New England colonies, the Middle colonies, and the Southern colonies.
3. Because of geographical conditions each section (New England, Middle, and Southern) had different patterns of living.
4. French settlement in the New World was not based primarily on religion as had been true of English settlement.
5. Rivalry between France and England in Europe led to wars which extended to North America.
6. France was defeated in the French and Indian War and her territorial claims were lost.
7. French influence is still present in North America.

OBJECTIVE A   You will be able to write a paragraph for at least three (3) of the four reasons explaining why the English came to settle colonies in the New World between 1607 and 1733.

ACTIVITY 1   Read section 1 of Chapter 4, page 81, in *This Is America's Story,* or Chapter 4, page 37, in *Adventures in American History.* Also see the filmstrip *England Prepares to Colonize.* Take notes on your reading and viewing.

ACTIVITY 2   Make a list of four (4) causes for English colonization in America. Could you write a paragraph summary of each cause?

ACTIVITY 3   Make a chart showing the thirteen English Colonies. Use these headings for your chart: *Name of Colony; Date Founded; Who* (leader or group) *Founded It;* and *Reasons for Founding.* Now research and fill in the chart.

ACTIVITY 4   With the information you've gathered from activities 2 and 3, write four (4) paragraphs. Each paragraph will describe a reason for English colonization.

ACTIVITY 5   Imagine you have been hired by the Pilgrims, Lord Baltimore, or William Penn to make posters to attract settlers to one of the three colonies. Before you make your poster, decide what point or points you want to emphasize, then illustrate these in your poster.

SELF-ASSESSMENT   At this point, can you write four (4) paragraphs explaining the four main reasons for English colonization, 1607–1733? If not, see your teacher.

OBJECTIVE B   You will be able to construct an outline or a chart which will give the order of settlement of the New England, the Middle, and the Southern colonies between 1607 and 1733.

ACTIVITY 1   Read and take notes on sections 2, 3, 4, and 5 in Chapter 4 of *This Is America's Story,* or review Chapter 4 in *Adventures in American History.* You may group with three (3) other students to go over these notes.

ACTIVITY 2   Make a chart or outline pointing out how the New England, Middle, and Southern colonies were founded. Make sure you get the names under the right heading or sections of colonies. Hint! Activity 3 for Objective A may help you in doing this activity.

ACTIVITY 3   Write entries in an imaginary diary kept by a boy or girl who went to the New World with (a) the Jamestown settlers in 1607, (b) the Pilgrims in 1620, (c) the Puritans in 1630.

ACTIVITY 4   Find pictures showing costumes worn by French, English, Spanish, and Dutch colonists. Show these to the class or prepare a bulletin board display.

Take your chart or outline to a teacher and, using it, explain how the three colonial areas were founded.

OBJECTIVE C   You will be able to fill in the names of the thirteen colonies on a blank map.

ACTIVITY 1   Review the activities you've completed for the previous two objectives.

ACTIVITY 2   Study the map on page 87 in *This Is America's Story,* or page 50 in *Adventures in American History.* Be sure you can spell correctly the name of each colony.

ACTIVITY 3   With a blank outline map of the eastern coast of America fill in the names of the colonies. Your teacher will give you the map.

ACTIVITY 4 (OPTIONAL)   Include on your map for Activity 3 the major topographical features (major rivers, mountain ranges, and so on) of the eastern America colonial area.
    Now—Put your name on your map and post it on the bulletin board.

SELF-ASSESSMENT   If you were given a blank map of the thirteen colonies, could you fill in the names of the colonies in their right locations?

OBJECTIVE D
You will be able to write a paper explaining how people lived in the New England, Middle, and Southern colonies.

ACTIVITY 1   Read Chapter 5 in *This Is America's Story,* or Chapter 5 in *Adventures in American History.* Also take the time to view those filmstrips in the *English Colonies Series* (see Annex) that interest you. Take notes!

ACTIVITY 2   Using your notes from Activity 1 write a paper of a page or more describing what it was like living in America during the Colonial Period. You should include the following in your paper:

    a. the geography of each section
    b. the ways of making a living
    c. the class structure
    d. the educational opportunities
    e. religion
    f. recreational opportunities
    g. types of homes
    h. anything else you would like to add

ACTIVITY 3 (OPTIONAL)   Trace the development of freedom of worship in colonial America. Note the established churches, and list as many other denominations or faiths you can find.

ACTIVITY 4 (OPTIONAL)   Compare the educational opportunities in the New England, Middle, and Southern colonies.

ACTIVITY 5 (OPTIONAL)   Write a paper showing comparisons between the life of indentured servants and of slaves in colonial America.

SELF-ASSESSMENT   Could you now write a one to two page report describing the different ways people lived in the New England, Middle, and Southern colonies? If not, go to a teacher for further assistance.

OBJECTIVE E   You will be able to trace the settlement of the French in the New World and point out in writing or orally how French colonization differed from that of the English.

ACTIVITY 1   Read and take notes on Section 1 of Chapter 6 in *This is America's Story* or parts 2 through 4 (pages 29–36) in *Adventures in American History.*

ACTIVITY 2   Make a list of the developments that occurred as the French settled in the New World.

ACTIVITY 3   With your list from Activity 2 write a comparison between British and French colonization in the New World.

ACTIVITY 4   Write or prepare orally a report describing how the French and British went about colonization in different ways.

ACTIVITY 5 (OPTIONAL)   Read Longfellow's "Evangeline" (in your literature book), which deals with the troubles faced by the Acadians. Draw conclusions from your reading and then write a paper naming any similar groups of displaced persons in the world today.

SELF-ASSESSMENT   Can you trace the settlement of the French in the New World and explain how it differed from English settlement? Can you do this in a one page written paper or a one to two minute oral report?

OBJECTIVE F
You will be able to write a paper or give an oral report on the French and Indian War, including the causes of the War, the main events, and the results.

ACTIVITY 1   Read Sections 2 and 3 in Chapter 6 of *This is America's Story* or part 5, page 36 in *Adventures in American History.* Also see the film *French and Indian War: Seven Years War in America.* Be sure you take notes—you'll need them later on.

ACTIVITY 2   Make a list of: (a) three (3) reasons why the British and French went to war; (b) three (3) advantages the French had and three (3) the British had in the war; (c) five (5) of the main events of the war, and (d) all of the results you can find that came from the war.

ACTIVITY 3   From the lists you made in Activity 2, write a two page summary or prepare a five minute oral report demonstrating your knowledge of the French and Indian War. At this point, turn in your summary, or make an appointment with your teacher for presenting your oral report.

ACTIVITY 4 (OPTIONAL)   By working with two other students, answer the following questions in a panel discussion:

1. What geographical area in North America was the prize which the French and the British wished to hold? Why did both have such ambitions? What were the results of that struggle between the two countries? Name the states that lie within the area today. In what way is it still a prize?
2. How did geography aid the French in protecting Quebec? How did the British overcome this French advantage?
3. Canada today may be called a country of two cultures. What are they and why is this true?
4. Name the large area of land in North America that Spain gained after the French and Indian War. With what other possessions on the continent was it joined?
5. Why was England so eager to gain control of Florida? When?

When you are ready to present your panel discussion, contact one of the teachers.

SELF-ASSESSMENT   Can you write a two page paper or give a five minute oral report covering the causes, events, and results of the French and Indian War?

SELF-ASSESSMENT   If you can answer the following questions at this time, you should report to your teacher for the Unit Test. If, however, you cannot answer the questions, review the activities of this packet until you can.

1. Given four (4) reasons for English colonization can you write a paragraph describing each?
2. Can you construct an outline or a chart showing how the New England, the Middle, and the Southern colonies were founded?
3. If you were given a blank map of the thirteen colonies could you fill in the names of the colonies in their right locations?
4. Can you write a one to two page report describing the different ways people lived in the New England, Middle, and Southern colonies?
5. Can you trace the settlement of the French in the New World and explain how it differed from English settlement? Can you do this in a one page written paper or a one to two minute oral report?
6. Can you write a two page paper or give a five minute oral report covering the causes, events, and results of the French and Indian War?

Annex A

Listed here are materials to aid you in the study of this packet. Take advantage of these resources as they will benefit you greatly. These materials are stored in the Audio Visual Resource Bank and are available to you when you need them.

1. *The Beginnings of the American Nation* 209 Filmstrip

2. *Colonial America* 0410 Filmstrip
3. *Earning a Living in the Colonies* 0431 Filmstrip
4. *Eighteenth Century Life in Williamsburg, Virginia* 981 Film (44 min.)
5. English Colonies Series—Filmstrips
   a. *England Prepares to Colonize:*   1528–0239
   b. *Virginia Colony:*   0261–0246
   c. *Other Southern Colonies:*   0244–0263
   d. *Colony of Massachusetts:*   0267–0237
   e. *Other New England Colonies:*   0243–0264
   f. *New York Colony:*   0241–0268
   g. *Colonies of Pennsylvania and New Jersey:*   0236–0269
   h. *England Conquers New France:*   0238–0266
   i. *Occupations and Amusements of the Colonists:*   0242
   j. *Social and Cultural Life of the Colonists:*   0262–0245
6. *French and Indian War: Seven Years War in America:*   1321–1059 Film (16 min.)
7. *Landing of Pilgrims*   T–179   T–100 Tape (15 min.)
8. *French Colonization*   1166 Filmstrip

Be sure you check with the *Social Studies Bibliography* for additional resources.

Enrichment reading from your literature book:

1. Bradford and Winslow's "So Goodly a Land."
2. Hawthorne's "The Pine Tree Shillings."

Annex B (Content Outline)

THE FRENCH COLONIES
I.   Obstacles to French colonization in North America
     A.   Feeling that North America was not as valuable as the West Indies
     B.   Troubles in recruiting colonists
II. Government and society in the French colonies
     A.   Royal governor
     B.   No self-government
III. French treatment of Indians
     A.   Indians were treated well
     B.   Indians were allies and a source of furs
     C.   Algonquins and Hurons
IV. Slow growth of French colonies
     A.   Mistakes in policy and lack of interest
     B.   French kings were not as interested in granting New World lands to individuals and to small groups of settlers as were the English kings

THE FOUNDING OF THE ENGLISH COLONIES
I.   Rivalry between England and Spain
     A.   Sir Francis Drake and defeat of the Spanish Armada (1588)
     B.   Expanding English trade throughout the world
     C.   Growing English interest in colonization
II. Motives and Methods of English colonization
     A.   English colonies were founded by private enterprise rather than by government
     B.   The English allowed religious dissenters to settle in their colonies

    C. The English also allowed settlements to be established for reasons of social necessity (Georgia) and because of western movement from more settled colonies (New Hampshire)

    D. English colonies enjoyed a great deal of local self-government

III. Making a living in the English colonies

    A. New England colonies

       1. Thin soil, harsh climate, and few natural resources

       2. Lumbering develops (ship building)

       3. Fishing industry grows

       4. Trade (shipping)

    B. The Middle or "Bread" colonies

       1. Rich soil and navigable rivers

       2. Farming

         a. grains

         b. livestock

       3. Some fur trading was done

       4. Trade (shipping)

    C. Southern colonies

       1. Plantation system used in agriculture—tide water area

       2. Farming

         a. rice

         b. indigo

         c. tobacco

         d. livestock

       3. Forests

         a. lumber

         b. turpentine

IV. Colonial Society

    A. Upper class—superior position by law and custom

       1. Merchants

       2. Clergymen

       3. Large land owners

    B. Mobile society—you can move up the ladder, and up the river

    C. Indentured servants

       1. Passage given for a promised number of years of service

       2. Wages were higher in America than in England—workers were scarce

V. Effects of the Frontier

    A. Leveled the social class barrier

    B. Land was abundant and usually free

    C. Women became more self-reliant

VI. Widespread prosperity

    A. Hardly any paupers or beggars

    B. Crime was seen very little

    C. Most people were busy all the time (no idle rich)

    D. Extra energies spent in improving colonial life (for example: Ben Franklin, Thomas Jefferson)

SUMMARY

The responsibility for planning is the teacher's. You must plan your own courses and units, although you may have curriculum guides, courses of study, resource units, textbooks, and other materials to draw from. When planning courses, you can find these devices greatly helpful. In some school systems, you may be expected to follow a particular resource exactly. Often, however, such tools are intended to be suggestive rather than prescriptive. In either case, select subject matter that has contingent value, clear, reasonable objectives, and content and procedures that will build these objectives. To lay out the course, set up a sequence of broad topics or units and suggest a timetable for the completion of the topics. Care should be taken not to overload the course, because attempting to cover too much may result in not doing anything well. Many teachers use the textbook as the course outline. This is good practice, but do not become a slave to the text. Often you will find that you must adapt the text or a suggested course outline to meet the exigencies of the teaching situation.

Prepare continuous modulated courses just as you would any other course, except that in addition to laying out the topics or units, you must prepare learning activity or instructional packets for the students as well. In such courses, allow the course timetable to vary from student to student. When a student finishes one packet satisfactorily, he or she can then go on to another one.

In planning an ordinary unit, your goal in effect is to assemble a group of lessons around a particular topic. Basically, the procedure consists of the following:

1. Selecting teaching objectives.
2. Building a series of lessons by which to reach these objectives.
3. Arranging the lessons into a sequence consisting of
   a. Introductory lessons
   b. Developmental lessons
   c. Culminating lessons (including unit tests)

Variations on the unit plan include classroom laboratory units, learning activity packets, and contracts.

The following is an outline of the type of classroom laboratory unit plan suggested in this chapter:

1. An overview that describes the nature and scope of the unit.
2. The teacher's specific objectives that are the understandings, skills, attitudes, ideals, and appreciations he or she hopes the students will gain from the unit.
3. The unit assignment that includes activities in which the class will participate during the teaching of the unit. The activities are of two types: (1) the basic activities to be done by all students to some extent during some period of time, and (2) the optional related activities.
4. The study and activity guide that contains the instructions for carrying out the core activities to be done individually and in small groups.
5. The special study and activity guides that contain the instructions for carrying out the optional activities.
6. A list of materials and readings the students may use in their study.
7. A short bibliography and list of materials for the use of the teacher alone.
8. Testing or other devices to be used in evaluating the success of the unit. These devices should test adequately each of the learning products described in 1 and 2 of this outline.

As in the ordinary unit, introduce the unit assignment with introductory activities that will catch the students' interest and help you to get to know the students. Following the introductory phase comes individual and small-group work, interspersed by class activities and opportunities for the students to share their experiences and learning. Finally, the unit of work ends in some sort of culminating exercise.

Learning activity packets or modules are really special types of units. The procedure for planning them is essentially the same as for other units. In carrying out the modules and packets, you will find that they are most successful when you use the laboratory approach.

Contracts are simply units in which the student agrees to do certain things. A contract may or may not specify the grade the student can expect for satisfactorily completing the work contracted for.

Every lesson needs a plan. The essentials of a daily lesson plan are the objectives, the subject matter, the activities, the list of materials needed, the assignment, and any special notes. These essentials tell the teacher what to do and how to do it. The format you use for a lesson plan is not so important, as long as the plan is clear and easy to follow. Sometimes daily lesson plans used in conjunction with units need not be very detailed. The important thing is to know what you wish to teach in the lesson and to provide activities that lead to these goals. One test of a lesson plan is to ask how each activity in the procedure will help to bring about the desired goal. Once you have decided on a plan of action, keep to that plan unless there seem to be very important reasons for changing course.

ADDITIONAL READING

Bellon, J. J., E. C. Bellon, and M. A. Blank. *Teaching from a Research Knowledge Base.* Englewood Cliffs, NJ: Merrill/Prentice Hall, 1992, Unit One.

Borich, G. D. *Effective Teaching Methods,* 2nd ed. Englewood Cliffs, NJ: Merrill/Prentice Hall, 1992.

Briggs, L., ed. *Instructional Design: Principles and Applications.* Englewood Cliffs, NJ: Educational Technology Publications, 1977.

Callahan, J. F., L. H. Clark, and R. D. Kellough. *Teaching in the Middle and Secondary Schools,* 4th ed. New York: Macmillan, 1992, "Part II: Planning for Instruction."

Dunkin, M. J. "Lesson Formats" in *International Encyclopedia of Teaching and Teacher Education*, edited by M. J. Dunkin. New York: Pergamon, 1987.

Eggen, P. D., and D. P. Kauchak. *Strategies for Teachers: Teaching Content and Thinking Skills,* 2nd ed. Englewood Cliffs, NJ: Prentice-Hall, 1988.

Henak, R. M. *Lesson Planning for Meaningful Variety*. Washington, DC: National Education Association, 1980.

Henson, K. T. *Methods and Strategies for Teaching in Secondary and Middle Schools.* White Plains, NY: Longman, 1988.

Hoover, K. H. *The Professional Teacher's Handbook*, 2nd ed. Boston: Allyn and Bacon, 1976.

Hunter, M. "Knowing, Teaching, and Supervising" in *Using What We Know About Teaching*, edited by P. L. Hosford. Alexandria, VA: Association for Supervision and Curriculum Development, 1984, Ch. 8.

Jacobsen, D. P. Eggen, and D. Kauchak. *Methods for Teaching*, 3rd ed. Englewood Cliffs, NJ: Merrill/Prentice Hall, 1989, Unit One.

Johnson, D. W., and P. T. Johnson. *Learning Together and Alone*. Boston: Allyn and Bacon, 1991.

Levine, J. M. *Secondary Instruction*. Boston: Allyn and Bacon, 1989, Ch. 3.

Romiszowski, A. J. *Producing Instructional Systems: Planning for Individualized and Group Learning Activities*. NY: Nichols, 1984.

NOTES

1. William Meisner, "Lesson Planning," in *Teaching in Middle and Secondary Schools,* 3rd ed., edited by Joseph F. Callahan and Leonard Clark (New York: Macmillan, 1988), 101–125.

Chapter 7

Direct Expository Approaches

Eschew surplusage.
Mark Twain

- Overview
- Student-Teacher Interaction
- Direct Teaching
- Teacher Talks and Lectures
- Demonstrations
- Questions
- Recitations
- Practice and Review

Overview

In this chapter we discuss some of the more formal and traditional teaching approaches: lecture and teacher talks, recitation, questioning, practice, and review. These methods are basically associated with the direct teaching of the lower cognitive objectives and skills. And while these are all strategies with which you have had much experience, perhaps there is more to them than meets the eye. As you read the chapter, think about how you would use these techniques in your teaching and student teaching. For what purposes would you use formal lectures? Formal talks? Of what advantage are open-text recitation techniques?

Think, too, about your questioning procedures. Most teachers use many questions but limit themselves almost entirely to memory questions. What advantages do you find in each of the various kinds of questions? How can you use questions to make students think and to help them understand? How can you use questions to probe without nagging? As you study, try to form questions that will do more than just check knowledge. Similarly, try to think of ways in which you can introduce into your courses the repetition necessary for implanting knowledge and skills deeply enough to ensure recall and transfer without boring the students unnecessarily.

Student-Teacher Interaction

Before we begin our study of the various teaching methods or strategies, let us first consider the matter of student-teacher interaction in the classroom. In the United States, most teaching is done by teachers who tell things to students.

This of course is to be expected, since teachers must tell students things. Teaching is not telling, but telling is an important ingredient in teaching. No teacher can get along without it.

Still, teachers should guard against talking too much and overdominating classroom activities. Without an optimum amount of student-student and teacher-student interaction, classes tend to become stifling. Although in any particular lesson the objectives and design of the lesson plan, plus other factors in the specific situation, determine what types and amounts of interaction are desirable, certain criteria apply to most lessons in general:

- Students should be actively participating at least half the time. (If you find yourself talking more than half the time, check your procedures.)
- As far as possible, every student should participate in some way. (Classes that are dominated by only a few students are hardly satisfactory.)
- A good share of the class time should be given to thoughtful, creative activity rather than to mere recitation of information by either teacher or students.

Direct Teaching

At the lower academic levels and when teaching highly structured basic subject matter, successful teaching is largely a result of direct teacher-centered instruction, according to Rosenshine and Stevens.(1) In such teaching, they tell us, teachers follow a model something like the following:

1. *Review of pertinent previous learning.*   This review includes previously taught concepts, processes, and skills, and the reteaching of any elements in which the students' grasp appears weak.

2. *Teacher presentation of the new material.*   Presentation of new material usually should include a short statement of the learning objectives of the lesson, its relationship to previous lessons, and a careful explanation and demonstration of the concepts, processes, and skills to be learned. Although the presentation should be given in some detail with plenty of illustrations, demonstrations, and stress on important points, it should not be overlong. Ordinarily it would be more effective to interrupt the teacher talk from time to time to ask questions designed to make sure the pupils understand.

3. *Guided practice.*   Once it seems that the pupils do understand, it is time to guide them while they practice the new material.

4. *Feedback and correction.*   During guided practice, you must monitor the practice session carefully. If a student's first response is wrong, try to help him or her find a correct response. To this end, prompts and clues can be useful. In any case, ensure that the student learns the correct answer even if you have to reteach the concept.

5. *Independent practice.*   When students have practiced, under guidance, enough to achieve a success rate of 80 percent or so, it is time for independent practice or seatwork. This type of practice, which you should supervise as carefully as feasible, should be carried on to provide enough overlearning to ensure that students will remember and can transfer the learning to new situations. A safe rule of thumb is that if the students can respond correctly about 90 percent of the time, they are ready.

6. *Weekly and monthly review.*   After students complete their independent practice and seatwork, do not drop the matter. Rather, schedule weekly and monthly reviews and occasional tests. If the students miss material in the reviews and tests, it should be retaught.

The more mature and sophisticated your students are, the more time you can spend on the presentation phases of the model and the less time you need for guided practice. Thus, in the senior high school, you can include more material in your presentations (lectures and teacher talks) and replace much of the guided practice with the covert rehearsal, restating, and reviewing activities of independent practice. In the middle school, however, you should expect to follow the model fairly closely.

The techniques suggested in the model are most useful for teaching facts that students need for further learning, and for teaching processes and skills such as mathematical computation, algebraic equations, geometry, map reading, business correspondence, bookkeeping, and auto mechanics. These same techniques, however, are not so useful in less well-structured areas such as problem solving, composition, literature, evaluating ideas, or criticism.(2)

Now let us look in more detail at some of these techniques.

Teacher Talks and Lectures

There are three basic types of "telling" activities: (1) short teacher talks in which the teacher presents or explains certain concepts, objectives, or procedures; (2) formal lectures in which the teacher presents content in a relatively long discourse; and

(3) teacher comments and reactions that are made while other activities progress. Several guiding principles underline the effective use of all three methods.

1. They should be clear.
2. They should be motivating.
3. They should be supported by audiovisual media, demonstrations, illustrations, and the like.
4. They should involve student activity—for example, student comment and reaction, questions and discussions, and demonstrations.
5. They should be well-organized.
6. They should tie in with previous and future lessons.
7. They should be couched in natural and easily understood language.

In the following sections, we shall concentrate on teacher talks and lectures generally, because they have much in common. Teacher comments will be discussed later in the chapter.

Making It Clear

Undoubtedly the most important need for any teacher talk or lecture is that it be clear. Beginning teachers and student teachers are inclined to talk over the heads of their students, because concepts and words familiar to college seniors and recent graduates may be foreign to sixth-graders, and even to high school students. Although you should avoid talking down to your students, be careful to talk to them in language they understand.

The language you use should be good English, of course. Some teachers attempt to reach the students' level by introducing slang and street language into their talks. This is usually a poor policy. Slang and overinformality are more likely to muddy a lecture than clarify it. Furthermore, whether you like it or not, you are a model whenever you speak. If your influence on the students is to be good, your language must be the kind that you wish the students to imitate.

The use of illustrations and figures of speech often makes lectures clearer and livelier, but their injudicious use can at times defeat your purpose. Particularly treacherous in this respect is the metaphor, which can truly be a two-edged sword. With middle school students particularly, you should call things by their proper names and leave flights of poetic fancy for other situations. If you must use fanciful figures of speech, at least take steps to make sure that the students understand what you really mean. Not doing so may make the entire lecture meaningless.

Illustrations, audiovisual aids, and demonstrations in lectures can also help to clarify and emphasize desired concepts. Frequently, visual representations can give meaning to what would otherwise remain just a mass of words. Even when the lecture, talk, or explanation is clear and interesting without them, visual aids can reinforce the learning by allowing students to experience a concept by using another sense. Teachers who depend solely on their voices to present ideas are being unfair to themselves and to their students. Especially since, as Dunn and Dunn's research points out, most people are not primarily auditory learners but rather visual or tactual/kinesthetic learners.(3)

Speech mannerisms can reduce the clarity and effectiveness of a teacher's presentation dramatically. Four detractors that you should particularly avoid are "vagueness terms," "mazes," "inconsistencies," and "uh".(4)

AVOIDING "VAGUENESS TERMS"   The presentation of your ideas, concepts, and facts should be explicit—free from "iffiness" and unnecessary, impertinent comments. Avoid such "vagueness terms" as *might, maybe, sometimes,* or *probably,* as in the following example.

The mathematics lesson might enable you to understand a little more about some things we call number patterns.(5)

Instead, speak straight out without elaboration:

This mathematics lesson will enable you to understand number patterns.

(There are, of course, situations in which the subject matter is such that you must be somewhat misty and indefinite in order to be accurate.)

AVOIDING MAZES   To be clear you should also avoid "mazes"—that is, false starts or halts in speech, redundant words, and tangles of words, as in the following:

The mathematics lesson will *enable . . . help* you understand *number uh . . . number* patterns. Before we get to the *main idea* of the, *the main idea of the lesson,* you need to review *four con . . . four prerequisite concepts.*

AVOIDING DISCONTINUITY   Be sure to give your talk an easy, straightforward flow without digression, interruptions, irrelevant comments, or out-of-sequence references.

AVOIDING "UHS"   Saying "uh" while seeking your next word, or adding such irrelevancies as "you know" or "you know what I mean," interrupts the flow of your presentation and turns off the listener.(6)

To aid in promoting clarity and in helping students understand your teacher talks and lectures, make it plain to students just how the learning to be pursued relates to past and future learning and to all-around goals. In this way, you can create unity and make the course flow forward smoothly. In "choppy" courses, pupils cannot see the relationships of the lessons and units and so remain ignorant of where they are going.

Making It Interesting

Lectures should attract students' interest and attention. One way to arouse attention and interest is to open the lecture with a challenging question, a problem, or a perplexing fact. If at the beginning of the lecture you can puzzle the students a little, they may be anxious to listen in order to solve the puzzlement. It will also help if you show the students what it is you intend to do and your reason for doing it. If you can establish a purpose that relates directly to the students' purposes and concerns, so much the better. You should point out how the information in the lecture relates to past and future content and to what students already know and like. Real and rhetorical questions, the use of humor, and, above all, lots of illustrations and examples, will help maintain interest and make points clear. Demonstrations, pictures, exhibits, projects, and other instructional aids all spice up a lecture and hold students' attention when their minds begin to wander.

Not Too Much Too Fast

Although teacher talks and lectures are excellent media by which to present information to students, guard against moving too quickly and presenting too much information at a time. The human brain is not capable of retaining new knowledge in overlarge doses. Therefore, when presenting new material, it is best to progress in relatively small steps and to follow them up with practice, elaboration, rehearsing, and summarizing. By such activities, you can help students process the new information so that it will be retained in their long-term memories. Otherwise, the new knowledge will stay in their short-term memories and soon will be forgotten. Consequently, interrupt lengthy talks and lectures to take time for such activities as student summaries and to give students opportunities to draw relationships between the new work and past learning. Remember, if you wish the learning to stick, and to be usable, it needs to be overlearned.

The Formal Lecture

In the formal lecture, the teacher presents the lesson by what amounts to making a speech. There is a minimum amount of give and take in this type of teaching. This one-way formula partly results from the history of teaching, particularly as it was done in medieval universities. In those days, the professor was the only person who had access to the text, so he read it to the students with appropriate commentary.*

Lately, and largely because of a reaction against its long years of misuse and overuse, it has been fashionable in some circles to downgrade the lecture, but the lecture has been used with success in the past, is being used with success at the present, and no doubt will be used with success in the future. As a matter of fact, most teachers find lectures almost indispensable for certain purposes. For example, lectures are valuable for

- introducing activities or units
- motivating students
- summing up
- explaining difficult points
- bridging gaps between units or topics
- establishing a general point of view
- pointing out a different point of view
- providing information otherwise not readily available
- providing additional information
- proposing theories

Moreover, as long as the lecture remains the predominant form of teaching in our colleges, it is appropriate for collegebound students to have considerable exposure to lectures in the last stages of their high school careers. The lectures presented to students should be accompanied by instruction in how to profit from lectures, with emphasis placed on the art of taking notes.

In spite of its values, however, the formal lecture is ordinarily a rather ineffective method for teaching middle and secondary school students. That is why it is good to insert breaks for questions, for student reactions, and short discussions. Unless the students do something with the information presented in a lecture, their learning and retention may be rather thin, since the lecture format gives little opportunity for reinforcement to take place or for the lecturer to assess the students' progress in learning.

One reason that many secondary school lectures are not more stimulating is that good lectures require more preparation than most teachers have time to put into them. Very seldom can a teacher present a lecture effectively on the spur of the moment. If you want to have a high degree of effectiveness in your lectures, then, you must plan them meticulously. Not only must you plan what you wish to say, you also must plan how you intend to say it.

---

*The word *lecture* is derived from the Latin *legere (lectus)*, which means "to read." In England some college instructors are called readers.

Stop and Reflect

Why is the lecture considered to be a poor technique for use in middle schools? In secondary schools?

You have been assigned a ninth-grade general science class. This class consists largely of at-risk learners and has a reputation of being hard to handle. The students are restless and not much interested. How much would you plan to incorporate lectures when teaching such a group? What might you be able to do to hold the attention of such a group when you do lecture?

PRESENTING THE LECTURE   If they are to be effective, lectures must be both clear and persuasive. With this goal in mind, the teacher planning a classroom lecture must guard against attempting too much. Because of its one-way format, it is very easy for the teacher who lectures to present ideas quickly and then move on to new ones before the students have processed the first ones. Neither secondary school students nor adults are likely to learn much from ideas skimmed over lightly.

Expert lecturers claim that the way to put your points across in a lecture is to

First, tell them what you are going to tell them.
Then, tell them.
Finally, tell them what you have told them.

This formula translates into

1. Present an overview.
2. Develop the new content.
3. Restate to clinch learning.

This formula is a good one and, over the years, has served the best lecturers well.

To carry out this procedure, state clearly what each point is and support it with illustrations, examples, and other details which, in themselves, may not be important, but which do tend to make the point stand out. Then, after all this has been done, come back to your point again and restate it clearly, which helps drive it home and clinch it as firmly as possible in a final summation. As a rule, this type of procedure will carry your ideas across to your audience, whereas attempting to cover many points may only confuse the listeners.

As you develop your points, try to adjust your ideas and their sequence to your audience. In general, the content should move from the concrete to the abstract and back again to the concrete so as not to leave things hanging in midair. Try to be sure the lecture develops logically enough so that students have the background necessary for understanding new material. The content should be original, however. There is no excuse for lectures that parrot the textbook. The major idea of lecturing is to give students new, fresh ideas or information that is not otherwise readily available.

As you lecture, try to help the students learn from the lectures. To do so, help students learn to take good notes. For this purpose, an outline of the lecture on the chalkboard or overhead projector can be most helpful. The common practice of providing a skeleton outline for the students to fill in as the lecture goes on has much to recommend it. So does the even more common practice among good teachers of stopping to point out to the students that what has just been explained, or is about to be explained, should be put in their notes. Once students have become skilled in note-taking these practices should no longer be necessary, although in the secondary and middle grades they are probably always helpful.

Informal Teacher Talks

Much, if not most, of the average teacher's instruction is done through informal talks to the class or to small groups. These talks differ from lectures in that they are usually short, sometimes extemporaneous, discourses that arise out of the needs of the moment. They often stem from class discussion or students' questions and ordinarily make up the presentation portion of direct teaching lessons. Because these talks are short, you do not need to prepare for them quite as diligently as you do for lectures. However, most of what we have said about preparing and delivering lectures applies equally well to the shorter teacher talks. In fact, except for their length and complexity, lectures and teacher talks that form the presentation portions of direct teaching lessons are essentially the same.

All of the previous comments about clarity of language are applicable to short informal teacher talks. So too are the suggestions for utilizing aids to make the instruction clearer and more effective. The greatest danger is that the teacher will talk too much. When teachers talk, all too often students stop thinking. Oftentimes teachers must explain, but *try to turn many of your teacher talks into student activity by asking questions, posing problems, seeking comments, and entertaining questions.* Also, beware of the danger of thinking that students have learned something just because you have told it to them. Whenever it is possible to do so, students will misunderstand, misinterpret, or miss altogether what the teacher tells them. Therefore, make it a habit to follow up your explanations and other short talks with questions designed to check the students' understanding. If you limit your talking to a minimum and intersperse it with questions (both student and teacher questions), Socratic episodes, and discussion, your talks will probably be more effective.

Stop and Reflect

For what purposes would you plan to use lectures in your secondary school teaching?

What kinds of lectures are there? How can they be used?

How does one plan a lecture or informal talk? Consider objectives, outline, illustrations, motivations, length, aids, clarity, and interest.

How does one tell whether a lecture or talk has been successful?

Listen to an excellent lecturer's classes. What does this lecturer do that makes his or her lectures excellent?

Listen to a lecturer whose lectures are not very good. What makes these lectures less than excellent?

Listen for vagueness terms in your college lectures. How do they detract from the lecture?

Demonstrations

Just telling others how to do something does not necessarily make it clear to them exactly how to do it; nor does this process always explain what happens in certain processes. In these instances, seeing is believing. To get understandings and skills across, you must depend on what Raths called "show-how tactics"—audiovisual media, film, television, pictures, computer simulations, and demonstrations.(8) Done well, demonstrations can be particularly effective, and they are in most cases relatively easy techniques to use.

When using demonstrations and other show-how techniques, you must first set the stage. This step includes not only preparing any necessary props, but also explaining what you are going to do and why, as well as pointing out what students should look for as they watch the demonstration. Then, you must make sure that everyone can see. Beware, for instance, of showing a reaction in a test tube to a class of 30 students. We have all sat through classroom demonstrations during which we could not see what was happening. Be sure also that the demonstration is in the proper perspective. (Remember, for instance, that when you are facing the class, your right is the students' left. This can be very confusing unless you are facing away from the class.)

Once you are ready to start, proceed slowly so that the students can follow the procedures. A good strategy, particularly if the procedure is complex, is to demonstrate a few steps at a time, then stop to clinch the learning. A better way to ensure that the students see and understand the whole process is to run through the whole procedure, and then do it again a few steps at a time, explaining each step as you go along.

You will ordinarily have to repeat the demonstration, or portions of it, several times before the students understand what they see. After students have begun to practice, additional demonstrations may be more meaningful and helpful. To make the learning firm, follow demonstrations by practice sessions and confirming exercises and activities. A summary of what was to be learned and the procedures demonstrated should clinch the lesson.

Questions

Use of Questions

Throughout the course of educational history, questioning has been one of the most common teaching techniques. It continues to be so in spite of modern changes in educational theory and technology, for it is a fine tool. Use the questioning technique to

1. Find out something you did not know.
2. Find out whether someone knows something.
3. Develop students' ability to think.
4. Motivate student learning.
5. Provide drill or practice.
6. Help students organize materials.
7. Help students interpret materials.
8. Emphasize important points.
9. Show relationships, such as cause and effect.
10. Discover student interests.
11. Develop appreciation.
12. Provide review.
13. Give practice in expression.
14. Reveal mental processes.
15. Show agreement or disagreement.
16. Establish rapport with students.
17. Diagnose.
18. Evaluate.
19. Obtain the attention of wandering minds.

Stop and Reflect

Can you think of a question to illustrate each one of the purposes for using questions? After you have formed the questions, test them against the criteria in the following section. How well did you do?

Attend a class in a school or college classroom. Observe the teacher's use of questions. What techniques were used? Were they successful? Why, or why not?

The Right Question

Questions may be categorized in many ways; they may be broad or they may be narrow. *Narrow questions* usually prompt students to recall facts or specific correct answers. *Broad questions,* on the other hand, call for more complicated answers. They seldom can be answered by a single word. Rather, they require the answerer to think and develop original responses. By so doing, these questions broaden the learning situation and stimulate interaction and original thinking among the pupils.

Questions may also be categorized as cognitive memory questions, convergent questions, divergent questions, or evaluative questions. *Cognitive memory questions* are ones that require simple recall of information. Thinking is not needed to answer them, only memory. *Convergent questions* are thought questions that call for single correct answers. *Divergent questions* are open-ended thought questions that stimulate thinking and imagination, but have no correct answer. *Evaluative questions* call for students to pass judgment on some action.(9)

As these categories of questions illustrate, different types of questions elicit different responses. You should be careful to ask questions that will further the instructional goals you want to achieve. The appropriate questions should sometimes be of the cognitive memory type; at other times, they should be convergent thought questions, or divergent thought questions, or evaluative questions. Skillful teachers can aim their questions to bring out whichever category of Bloom's Taxonomy of Cognitive Goals they wish, as Table 7.1 shows.

Stop and Reflect

Which of the sample questions in Table 7.1 are cognitive memory? convergent? divergent? evaluative?

Prepare sample questions for each of the Bloom categories.

Prepare a question that would fit each of the purposes listed at the beginning of this section of the chapter.

Prepare an example of

1. *a cognitive memory question*
2. *a convergent question*
3. *a divergent question*
4. *an evaluative question*

Four Basic Criteria

For questions to be effective, try to ask them so that they measure up to four basic criteria. (Although in this context we are dealing only with oral classroom questions, these criteria, plus a few additional rules, also apply to written test and examination questions.) These four criteria are:

Sample Question	Goal Category	Sample Question	Goal Category
1. Knowledge		*4. Analysis*	
What is the principle ingredient in the air we breathe?	1.1 Knowledge of specifics	Which part of the argument we have just read is fact and which is opinion?	4.1 Analysis of elements
What steps would you have to take to become a licensed operator? What is the correct form for presenting a motion before a meeting?	1.2 Knowledge of ways and means of dealing with specifics	What propaganda devices can you find in this automobile advertisement? Does the conclusion that Senator X made logically follow from the facts he presented?	4.2 Analysis of relationships
What is the basic principle behind the operations of a free market?	1.3 Knowledge of universals and abstractions in a field	In this poem what devices has the author used to build up the characters of the principal antagonists?	4.3 Analysis of organizational principles
2. Comprehension		*5. Synthesis*	
In your own words, what does "laissez-faire" economy mean? What does it mean to say that to the victor belong the spoils?	2.1 Translation	Describe the procedure you used and the results you observed in your experiment.	5.1 Production of a unique communication
In what ways are the Democratic and Republican positions on support for the military budget similar?	2.2 Interpretation	How would you go about determining the composition of this unknown chemical?	5.2 Production of a plan or a proposed set of operations
If the use of electrical energy continues to increase at the present rate, what will be the demand for electrical energy in A.D. 2000?	2.3 Extrapolation	You have heard the description of the situation. What might be the causes of this situation?	5.3 Derivation of a set of abstract relations
3. Application		*6. Evaluation*	
If you measure the pressure in your barometer at the foot of a mountain and then measure it again at the summit of the mountain, what difference in the reading would you expect?	3. Application	In what way is the argument presented illogical?	6.1 Judgment in terms of internal evidence
If one of two sailing vessels leaving New York at the same time en route to London took a route following the Gulf Stream and one kept consistently south of the Gulf Stream, which would you expect to reach London first, everything else being equal?		Does the theory that organically grown foods are more healthful than other foods conform to what we know of the chemical composition of these foods? Explain.	6.2 Judgment in terms of external criticism

See Francis P. Hunkins, *Questioning Strategies and Techniques* (Boston: Allyn & Bacon, 1972) for other illustrations of various types of questions. *See also* Gary D. Borich, *Effective Teaching Methods,* 2nd ed. (Englewood Cliffs: NJ: Merrill/Prentice Hall, 1992), pp. 260ff.

1. *A successful question asks something definite in simple, clear, straightforward English that the students can understand.*   Be careful to avoid ambiguity, confusing construction, double questions, parenthetical remarks, and other verbiage that might cause students to lose the point of the question.

Try to word the question so that it makes a definite point consistent with the goal of the lesson. As a rule, vague generalities are usually not valuable in furthering the learning that the lesson is trying to promote. This criterion does not rule out general questions, however. Often questions calling for general answers are needed to open up the students' thinking, but these questions, too, should be worded so that students can perceive what you are driving at. Vague, poorly thought-out questions tend to evoke fuzzy irrelevancies rather than to advance good thinking about the topic at hand.

2. *A good question is challenging and thought-provoking.*   A main purpose of questioning is to stimulate learning. A good question challenges students to think. Questions that can be answered by merely repeating some fact from a book can never be as stimulating as are thought questions. In fact, these fact-fishing questions may not be stimulating at all, although often they are necessary.

3. *A good question is adapted to the age, abilities, and interests of the students to whom it is addressed.*   There is no great benefit in embarrassing or frustrating students by asking them questions they cannot answer. Neither is there much point in allowing gifted youths to slide along on easy questions that do not stretch their intellects. Moreover, you can harness the interests of various students by asking them questions that appeal to their special interests. For instance, the 4–H club member who raises stock could contribute greatly to a social studies unit on the country's resources, or to a general science unit on conservation. He may even be able to make a considerable contribution to the line from Thomas Gray's "Elegy Written in a Country Churchyard": "The lowing herd winds slowly o'er the lea."

4. *A good question is also appropriate to its purpose.*   You must be able to use all the types of questions—cognitive memory, convergent, divergent, and evaluative—when the occasion calls for them. Sometimes your questions should be closed-ended and sometimes open-ended.

When facts are needed, closed-ended, cognitive-memory, fact questions are needed. At other times, you ought to ask questions that will converge students' thinking on a certain point. Sometimes you should ask wide-ranging questions that open up students' imagination. A good question is one that serves its methodological purposes, and the effective teacher is one who knows how and when to use all types of questions.

Stop and Reflect

It has been said that a question should be couched in language considerably easier than the students' reading level. Why? Why not?

Of what value is a question that can be answered with one word?

Suppose that one of your purposes is to stimulate the students' thinking. How can this be done by questioning? Just how would you word the question? Prepare some examples and try them out.

Techniques of Good Questioning

PLANNING YOUR QUESTIONS   It is evident that questioning requires skill and preparation. Usually good questioners carefully brief themselves on the subject under discussion and prepare key questions in advance. Although some teachers seem to be able to ask well-worded questions on the spur of the moment, to do so is quite unusual. If you prepare your key questions in advance, you will be more successful. Write them out; they will probably be clearer and better worded if you do.

In preparing key questions, consider the following:

1. The teaching objectives.
2. What you want the questions to do. (Well-prepared key questions should give the lesson structure and direction.)
3. The kinds of questions that will best do the job.
4. The desirability of using questions that are in the affective domain.
5. The range of objectives covered by your questions. (Unless you plan your questions in advance, is it too easy to become involved in minutiae and irrelevancies rather than in significant learning. That is why it is wise to write key questions into your lesson plans.)
6. The intellectual development of the learners. (Questions that are too difficult or too abstract will lead only to frustration—not learning.)

ASKING THE QUESTIONS   The notion of the teacher as a grand inquisitor attempting to catch the recalcitrant student should be foreign to the modern classroom. Questioning should be thought of as a technique by which to teach—not just to see how much the student knows. Inquisitions are out of place in the classroom.

Many of your questions should be quite informal as you try to help individuals and groups with their various assignments. You may frequently address questions to the entire class, of course, but often they should be addressed to an individual student or a small group. As a matter of fact, in a lively class, the students may ask most of the questions.

You should ask your questions in a pleasant, friendly, easy, conversational manner. If you can maintain an atmosphere of easy informality without sacrificing decorum, so much the better. Always ask your questions in a fashion that indicates that you expect a reasonable answer. If the student does not know the answer, or cannot contribute at the moment, do not tease him about it. Just let him say "I don't know" and move on. Exhortations to think will not bring back a forgotten lesson.

When using questions in a whole-class situation, you should usually first ask the question, wait for the class to think about it, and then ask someone for an answer. In this way, everyone has a chance to consider the question before anyone tries to answer it. *Remember, there is little use in asking thought questions if you don't give the pupils time to think about them.*

This technique of asking and waiting has another merit in its favor: When you ask the question first, no one knows which individual will be asked. This helps to keep the students alert. When you call on a student before asking the question, other members of the class may heave a sign of relief and not bother to listen to the question.

As usual, there are exceptions to the rule. When you call on an inattentive student, it is sometimes better to call out the name first and then the question. In this way you may recapture the student's attention and bring the wanderer back to work. Similarly, it is often best to name an at-risk or shy student first to allow him or her to anticipate what is coming and so be able to prepare for the ordeal.

Another technique that may help keep a class attentive is to refrain from repeating questions. If, for some legitimate reason, a student does not understand or hear, then to repeat the question is only fair. But when the cause is inattention, move on to someone else. This rule also applies to repeating answers. Repeating answers merely wastes time and encourages inattention. If you want to reinforce the learning, it is better to come back to the matter in some other way than to repeat answers. Of course, as with other techniques, it is the teacher's responsibility to decide what is best for his or her particular class and to adjust the teaching accordingly.

Distributing the questions around the class also helps keep students alert. However, you should not resort to any mechanical system for doing this. Students soon catch on to these devices. The old system, for instance, of going around the class in alphabetical order, or row by row, is sure death to student attention. Rather, encourage volunteers, pause after asking questions, give students time to think, and call on nonvolunteers frequently (especially those who probably can answer correctly).(10)

The best way to direct student attention to questions is to ask really interesting, thought-provoking questions. Leading questions, questions that give away answers, one-word-answer questions, and the like have the seeds of boredom in them. Avoid overusing them, because they have killed many a potentially good class.

WAIT TIME   Most teachers do not allow students much time for thought. One study reported that the average amount of time teachers allowed students to answer a question was only one second. If a student had not answered by then, the teacher either "repeated or rephrased the question, asked another question, or called on another student."(11)

Giving students more time to think about their answers may increase both student learning and class participation. Waiting several seconds for an answer has several benefits. According to Rowe, teachers who increased their wait time to from three to five seconds achieved the following results:

1. increased length of student responses;
2. increased number of unsolicited appropriate responses;
3. decreased number of failures to respond;
4. increased student confidence in responding;
5. increased speculative thinking;
6. decreased teacher-centered teaching, increased student-student interaction;
7. increased student-provided evidence preceding or following inference statements;
8. increased number of student questions;
9. increased contributions of at-risk students; and
10. increased variety of student structuring, soliciting, and reacting moves.

Rowe also found that teachers developed greater response flexibility, changed the number and kind of questions they used, and tended to wait longer for responses from more capable students.(12)

Other research indicates that the optimum wait time may be three seconds. However, the research also suggests that you should vary post-question wait time according to the difficulty and cognitive levels of the questions. As a rule, cognitive questions require longer wait times.(13) Perhaps learning to count to five before closing off answers to unanswered questions will result in more effective teaching. If you do use this technique, be sure to tell the students that you plan to give them more time to think up answers; then launch the technique gradually.(14)

HANDLING STUDENT ANSWERS   To create an atmosphere of friendly cooperation, one in which the students feel free to do their best even if their best is none too good, you should accept every sincere response appreciatively. Immature thinking and lack of knowledge are not serious faults. If students were mature and knew all the answers, schools would be unnecessary. Allow students to make mistakes without fear of embarrassment, but do not encourage them to do careless work.

For example, when a student does not answer to the best of his ability, follow up with other questions that will shake him out of his complacency. Such an approach will usually make your point. Insist on an answer to every question you ask, even if the answer is "I don't know." The practice of evaluating students' answers, grade book in hand—so common in the standard recitation—has little to recommend it, although some students seem to be motivated by it.

Along with expecting students to present well-thought-out answers, you should insist that students make themselves understood. An unclear answer is not a good answer. If a student fails to make a valid point, ask for more detail. Every answer should form a complete thought unit, although not necessarily a complete sentence. If you throw students' incomplete thoughts back to them to complete, the students will soon learn to answer more clearly. Do not let yourself get bogged down on grammar, however. Instead, emphasize ideas. Avoid sacrificing thinking to the niceties of academic English, even though you should still strive to develop your students' skill in correct, effective English expression.

Although you should listen appreciatively to all sincere answers, approve only the good ones. When an answer is not satisfactory, you must tell the student why it is incorrect and how to improve it. Recognize any portion of an answer that is correct, of course, but correct any part of an answer that is incorrect. You can do this by pointing out the error yourself or by throwing the question open for discussion. In either case, in order to maintain a positive classroom atmosphere, correcting in this way should be done tactfully. Avoid pumping!

You can sometimes use an incorrect answer as the basis for a discussion or investigation that may crystallize a difficult concept. Skillful teachers often use incorrect answers as springboards for other questions, as in the Socratic technique. Such capitalization on mistakes can be achieved by asking other students to comment on the previously given answer or by asking additional questions that will yield a correct or more thorough understanding. These are often called *probing questions.* Probing questions are explained more extensively later in this chapter.

If a question is answered well, express approval. You do not need to be effusive about it; in fact, too much praise may be distracting. For most answers a friendly "yes" or "OK" or "That's right" is quite sufficient. If an answer to a question is partly correct, recognize the correct portion and then go after the rest of it. Use clues, rephrasing, probing, or prompting as the situation suggests to bring forth the complete correct response. Give more emphasis to those questions designed to bring out major points by using such questions as a basis for further discussion.

At times, the best response to a student's answer may be to use nonquestioning techniques such as declarative statements, reflective statements, state-of-the-mind remarks, invitations to elaborate, or just plain silence.

When a question brings forth no response other than blank stares from the entire class, the chances are that you have skipped some steps. You can usually get the desired response by breaking the question down into component parts or by backtracking a bit and asking questions that will provide background for the baffling original question. At other times, the whole difficulty may be in the wording of the question. When such is the case, restating the question may clear up the problem.

Stop and Reflect

What are the faults of the questioning techniques of teachers you have observed? How can you avoid these faults? What good points did you observe?

Prepare a list of principles to observe in questioning. Check yourself by these principles in a classroom situation. How well did you do?

THE USE OF THOUGHT QUESTIONS   If you aspire to high-order teaching, you will want to use thought-provoking questions. Although thought questions are not really difficult to use, to use them well requires a little extra skill and preparation. It is easy to fall into the trap of asking only cut-and-dried questions about what the book says. Therefore, to avoid this temptation toward easy but uninspiring practice, use thought questions until it becomes second nature. Learn to use open-ended, divergent, or evaluative questions at every opportune moment. Challenge students to consider what they have said or believe. Build on their contributions. Ask them to comment on one another's answers—not in a carping or criticizing manner but in the spirit of sharing ideas, opinions, and thinking. "Do you agree with John on that, Mary?" "Do you feel this argument would hold in such and such a case, John?" If you ask questions of this sort, obviously you cannot limit yourself to questions with pat answers. Ask at least some questions whose answers are not in the text. Remember, the best thought questions may have *no correct* answers. It is thinking that you are trying to promote, not set conclusions. Try to insist on valid logical reasoning. Make the students show their evidence, point out why the evidence supports their position, and defend their reasoning.

Before you go too far in this way, make sure that students have the basic facts they need to think with. Use techniques like the following to give them a base for informed thinking.

1. Ask fact questions first and then follow up with thought questions. Sometimes, however, it is wise to ask a thought question first and then follow up with fact questions that will test the thought. In either case, the bulk of your questions usually must be low-order to build a basis for higher-order questions, but overall the type of questions you ask should depend largely on the subject matter and your objectives.
2. Use some sort of springboard presentation, oral or written, to present the necessary background information before you spring your thought-provoking, follow-up questions.*
3. Use good summary questions to ensure that all students have the necessary background to lead to your thought questions.
4. Incorporate necessary facts in the question itself.
5. Give students fact sheets that they can consult as they try to think through suitable answers to your challenging questions.
6. Similarly, let students consult their texts before and during the questioning.
7. Give students the facts before you ask the question. Put the facts on the chalkboard, use an overhead projector, simply tell students the facts, or let students use their texts.

At times students resent being asked high-level questions; they may much prefer the low-level questions they have become used to in daily recitations over the past years. But if higher-level learning is to occur, students must develop positive attitudes toward higher-level questions. Perhaps you can develop more positive attitudes by encouraging a more congenial climate and by using non-question alternatives. It is usually helpful to make a gradual change from an emphasis on low-order questions to a greater emphasis on high-order cognitive questions. Expect to use more low-order questions than high-order questions in most classes to lay groundwork for later higher-order questions, and to ensure that pupils learn the necessary facts and procedures, that is, the basics.

---

*A *springboard* is any type of presentation that you can use to launch a discussion or inquiry lesson. Springboards are discussed more fully in Chapter 9.

Incorporating real "perplexity questions" into your lessons may make the transition to high-level questioning more acceptable. *Perplexity questions* are real questions that the questioners do not know the answers to, although they would like to. Dillon suggests the following technique to encourage the use of student perplexity questions:

1. Have all the students make up four questions for which they know the answers.
2. In addition, have them make up another question on a matter that perplexes them.
3. Let them ask questions of each other, reserving the ones that perplex them until the teacher is quite sure the students understand the basic subject matter fairly well.(15)

Encourage the students to bring up real, relevant questions whenever they feel perplexed by the lesson or subject matter.

Finally, encourage students to share each other's thinking by questioning other students. Your goal should be to establish a friendly, courteous give-and-take in which the students examine the issues and debate the evidence without acrimony so that individuals may make their own decisions as rationally as they can. Good use of thought questions leads to true discussion, rather than question-answer inquisitorial teaching.

PROBING QUESTIONS AND CLARIFYING RESPONSES   Many thought-provoking questions are *probing questions,* or questions by which the teacher hopes to dig more deeply into the matter at hand, thus giving students a clearer and more correct understanding. A *clarifying response* is a probing question by which the teacher hopes to persuade a student to reconsider and think through a statement, belief, or value. The idea is to challenge students to look at their own behaviors or ideas and to clarify them in their own minds by thinking out implications and ramifications. The clarifying response is especially useful for helping students clarify their values and beliefs.

The technique for the clarifying response is a simple one. Once a student has expressed an opinion or belief, you ask such questions as, "How did you arrive at such a belief? Is that belief based on solid evidence or hearsay? Give an example of what you mean. Should everyone believe that? What would be the result if they did? What are the implications of that belief?" Ask any question at all that will cause a student to self-examine a belief or value. You can ask the pupil to summarize, to compare, to provide supporting data, to point out alternatives, to identify the assumptions that underlie the pupil's statements, and in other ways to build on the ideas that have been expressed. Encourage students to extend their thinking to new areas, to generate hypotheses, to interpret data, to apply principles to new situations, to make predictions, and to make judgments. Because the whole idea is to help students clarify their own thinking, do not force students to come to set conclusions. Sometimes the best type of clarifying response is merely to repeat the student's response, or to say "You mean you believe . . . " without further comment.

Use probing questions in the cognitive domain to dig out facts, follow up statements, and in general clarify students' understanding. For instance, if a person states that it is essential in a nation for everyone to speak the same language, you might ask about Switzerland. You might ask students to explain meanings, to think of implications, to develop reasons why such and such is so. Often probing questions can be raised to move the class from lower-level to higher-level thinking. When you receive an answer that needs to be followed up by probing questions, it is sometimes best to move to another student for the follow-up question; at other times you may prefer to ask the same student a few follow-up questions. Beware, however, of becoming involved in a dyadic conversation that leaves out the rest of the class. Again, the overall goal is to develop critical-thinking skills, not just to formulate a "right" answer.

Above all, try to avoid responses that inhibit thought—for example, questions that bring about closure, or answers that limit the student to a single response, or questions that undermine a student's confidence. Particularly beware of heckling responses that put down a student's ideas, and of responses that reject the student's answers hurtfully.(16)

When a student cannot answer your question, or answers it inappropriately, try using prompting questions to rescue the situation. *Prompting questions* are simple questions that the student *can* answer or that provide clues leading to the proper response. Research indicates that prompting of this sort, or otherwise helping the student, results in higher student achievement than does simply correcting the student or moving on to another student with the question.(17)

Stop and Reflect

Pick a chapter from a textbook or topic for a course you might teach. Develop a number of thought-provoking questions that call for high-order thinking. Try to think of thought-provoking follow-ups that you might use to bring out the conclusions you are seeking. Try the questions and the follow-up tactics on some of your colleagues.

Prepare a series of thought-provoking questions of both the divergent and convergent type to use with a specific open-text recitation lesson.

Handling Student Questions

Encourage students to ask questions. If they leave class with inquiring minds, you will have accomplished much. But how do you encourage student questions? By welcoming them! If you encourage a free, permissive atmosphere in which students know that they and their opinions will be respected, you can expect student questions to increase, especially if the material studied is interesting and important to them. If, before you plan the lesson, you will only ask yourself what your students may want to know, you can increase the chances of your material's being interesting and important.

Not all student questions are as important as others. Some questions are so important that if the class is interested it would be wise to depart from your agenda and consider the question in detail, even if it is not exactly pertinent. Other questions are not as important and can be answered very briefly. Some questions are trivial and have no place in the class at all. If the student asking the trivial or irrelevant question is sincere, answer the question, but briefly. Without being hurtful, explain that class time is scarce, that class goals are important, and that there is little time for the trivial. In case the student is not satisfied by a brief answer in class, arrange to go into the matter more deeply in private sometime later when the discussion will not interrupt the progress of the class. Be sure to follow up your promise and discuss the question with the student at your earliest opportunity.

At times it is best to turn a question over to some other member of the class or to the class as a whole for discussion. In fact, there is no reason why students should not ask each other questions directly as long as they are pertinent to the discussion and asked courteously. In "good" classes, this practice is often encouraged.

You will occasionally be asked questions you cannot answer. In that case, promptly admit your inability. Perhaps another member of the class does know the answer. If not, you can either find out yourself or ask someone to find out for you. If the latter choice is made, be sure to look up the answer too. Thus, you can check to be sure that the student reports back correctly.

Recitations

Several decades ago V. T. Thayer wrote a well-known book entitled *The Passing of the Recitation.* That title was somewhat premature. Today the recitation still remains a common teaching strategy.

The method in this strategy is simple. Teachers assign students content to study in their textbooks and then orally quiz the students on what they have learned in this textbook assignment. Although this technique is not very satisfactory for achieving high-level learning, it does have the advantage of teaching basic information. It reinforces the knowledge that students have already acquired and gives them immediate feedback concerning the accuracy of their answers. The recitation process also gives students the opportunity to learn from the replies of other students. In addition, the fact that students will be questioned on what they have studied often is a motivating factor. Many a student has read the homework text assignment solely because he is afraid he may be called on to recite in the next class.

Still, the ordinary recitation yields little besides the rote learning of information. It does not encourage true understanding of the information learned, to say nothing of encouraging students to apply knowledge, to solve problems, or to think. In fact, recitation actually discourages the development of listening and discussion skills. Instead, it tends to create an unfriendly, inquisitorial class atmosphere that is really antisocial and works against the development of class cohesiveness and cooperativeness. It would be difficult to find a more antiintellectual, antisocial pedagogical method than the recitation as it is ordinarily used. This does not need to be so, however. This technique might work better if one took advantage of the direct teaching questioning techniques described earlier.

To increase full understanding, as soon as the students seem to understand the basic information, try to build the recitation around thought questions. Key thought-provoking questions should be carefully planned in advance, to make sure the purpose, sequence, and wording are most effective. The answering procedure should emphasize thinking as well as remembering, utilizing discussions, and Socratic questioning. That is why the open-text recitation is likely to be more advantageous than the ordinary recitation, particularly at the secondary school level.

Open-Text Recitation

The open-text recitation differs from the ordinary recitation in that it is really a discussion; during this recitation, students can refer to their books and other materials as the discussion progresses. It can be used effectively as part of either controlled or open discussions.

Open-text recitation has many merits. It frees students from the rote memorization of facts. It shows students that facts are not so much ends in themselves as they are a means for understanding and for thinking. On the other hand, by stressing the use of facts and the necessity for factual accuracy, the open-text recitation strategy emphasizes the need for factual information and for getting the facts straight. This strategy also helps students master the intellectual skills needed to locate and check facts, and to determine which facts are important and which are immaterial to the discussion. All in all, the open-text method is an effective and efficient strategy.

Briefly, the procedure for conducting an open-text recitation is as follows:

1. Assign a reading and study activity or some other information-gathering activity.
2. In the assignment, include suggestions and questions that will cause students to read the text in an inquiring manner, to think, and to draw inferences from what they read or study (or otherwise gain information).
3. During the class, use Socratic or open-ended, thought-provoking questioning. If possible, encourage various interpretations, inferences, and conclusions from various students. Encourage students to react to and challenge each other's ideas. During the discussion allow students to consult their books, notes, or other material to justify their views and substantiate their opinions. In this type of recitation, it is not remembering the facts that matters; it is using the facts in the higher mental processes.
4. Sum up (or have a student sum up). No final conclusion or agreement is necessary. At times it may be better if no common conclusions are made.

Stop and Reflect

V. T. Thayer, in his The Passing of the Recitation, advocated the elimination of the recitation from the teacher's arsenal of teaching strategies. Do you agree that the recitation should be eliminated? What would you do to make a recitation more than a meaningless repetition of inconsequential details? Develop a plan for conducting an open-text recitation that would further the higher mental processes and result in clear concepts and full understandings.

Practice and Review

Sometimes one can learn something quite thoroughly as the result of one powerful, vivid experience. Such impressive experiences are rare in the classroom, however. More often, learning must be renewed through drill, practice, or review.

The differences in these words are largely differences of connotation. *Drill* ordinarily connotes an emphasis on unthinking, meaningless repetition, whereas *practice* seems to connote more purposeful, varied repetition. *Review* implies a second look at what has been learned before. By implication, review is often thought of as less intense than drill or practice. For our purposes in this book, there seems to be little merit in drawing distinctions between drill and practice. We use the word *practice* to denote repetition of both sorts.

The Value of Repetition

Repetition is necessary in school learning for several purposes. One of them is to help students retain what already has been learned. To be sure that students do not forget, learning must be renewed often, much more frequently than is necessary for immediate recall. This extra renewal is called *overlearning*. Overlearning is essential in memorizing, in making behavior automatic, and in creating desirable habits. One major purpose of practice is to provide the overlearning necessary for retention.

Another reason for practice is to develop skill. Great concert pianists practice their selections again and again to improve their renditions. As they practice, they may try to play more accurately or with more feeling; they may experiment with the tempo or they may vary their technique in other ways. No matter what changes they make, they always hope to improve their playing. So it is with learning any skill. No one can repeat anything exactly. Because during practice the learner varies his or her behavior, practice makes it possible to improve.

Practice can also increase understanding. As students repeat and renew the learning, the concepts become much clearer to them. Just as actors find that with numerous repetitions of a role they discover new insights into the character they are portraying, so students can acquire new understanding by restudying a topic. Clarification, however, can be done only if the repetition is meaningful, purposeful, and varied. New skills and new concepts seldom result from dull, dry, aimless repetition.

Practice and Drill

MAKING PRACTICE MEANINGFUL   In one sense, people do not learn through drill or practice. Practice merely consolidates, clarifies, and emphasizes what has already been learned. (However, this, too, is learning in a sense.) Therefore, before practice sessions start, students should already understand what they are doing and how to do it. Repeating meaningless words or actions is a waste of time. When the students *know* what copper sulphate is, or *understand* the meaning of a particular verb, this is the time to overlearn $CuSO_4$ = copper sulphate, or to conjugate the verb.

Repetition is usually more meaningful in context. Students often find it difficult to understand concepts when the material to be learned is isolated from its context. Therefore, practice should occur in as real a setting as possible. For instance, practicing foreign words in sentences and in conversation is more effective than is practicing them in isolated lists.

Practicing in wholes rather than in parts also makes practice more meaningful. When practicing something very difficult or involved, it is sometimes necessary to practice the difficult parts separately, but, in general, it is best to practice the whole thing. Then, because no part is learned at the expense of the others, the learning becomes a unit. For example, when practicing the crawl stroke in swimming, a student may need to concentrate on her kick or her breathing separately, but she must also practice the entire stroke if she wishes to swim well. Or when memorizing a literary passage, a student can usually learn most efficiently by using the whole or part-whole method. If the selection to be memorized is short, it is best to memorize the whole thing at once, but if the selection is long, it is easier to memorize if it is divided into meaningful divisions, each of which can be learned separately. For example, a student might learn a sonnet as a whole but a longer poem stanza by stanza.

For similar reasons, practice seems to be most successful when it is spread over many types of activities in many classes. Making practice part of regular classwork rather than relegating it to special practice sessions tends to make practice and the skills or knowledge to be practiced more meaningful. This procedure also tends to give to the practice its proper proportion and emphasis. When you use special practice sessions as a means of teaching particular skills or knowledge, you will tend to treat the practice itself as the end of the instruction. Such a distortion of the teaching-learning process can lead to confusion.

GUIDED PRACTICE   Although students should do a large share of practice activities independently, initial practice should always be teacher-guided. Introduce guided practice only after you have explained and demonstrated what the students are to do, why they are to do it, and how they are to do it. Guided practice consists of a large number of questions or of overt practice materials. As the students tackle these questions and exercises, monitor them meticulously to check for understanding. If any student makes an error, correct it at once. At first, use prompts or guides to get the students on track; then reduce the guides gradually and eventually eliminate them altogether. Provide corrective help where necessary and reteach if needed. Be sure to accompany your monitoring with process feedback (i.e., pointing out the correct way of doing it) and explanation. You will ordinarily find it necessary to repeat the explanations and demonstrations. Be sure that everyone participates, that a large proportion of the responses are correct, and that everyone keeps up the practice until their success rate is at least 80 percent.

In reacting to student responses, follow these guidelines:

1. If the student is correct and sure, say "That's right," and proceed.
2. If the student response is correct but hesitant, follow up with a confirmatory expression (e.g., "Yes, that is right because . . . ").
3. If the student answers incorrectly because of carelessness, correct the response and move on.
4. If the student responds inappropriately because of lack of knowledge, skill, or understanding, use prompts to help or reteach. Prompts are usually most effective if you use them quickly, but on many occasions you will need to reteach. You can reteach individuals while other members of the class are busy with seatwork. *In any case, see to it that the errors are all corrected as quickly as possible.* Not correcting errors immediately only creates problems in the future.(18)

MOTIVATING PRACTICE SESSIONS   Because of its very nature, practice needs to be well motivated and should occur under some pressure. The pressure should not be onerous, but it should be heavy enough to be felt so that the student will strive to improve. Lackadaisical practice is wasteful practice.

The hunger to learn is probably the most desirable motive, but it is not always present in students. Sometimes you need to use devices designed to make practice more attractive. The use of games, either individual or competitive, often serves the purpose admirably. Occasionally, someone objects to using competitive games in the classroom. However, if you take care to make the games fun for all and to eliminate petty glory-seeking by individual students, such games have a place. Individual games that can be used include such things as anagrams, authors, crossword puzzles, and other puzzles of all sorts. These can be played as a "solitaire" setup, but some of them can be competitive as well. Group games such as charades, or "baseball" and "basketball" games in which questions take the place of "base hits" and "baskets," are also effective. In fact, almost every parlor game can be adapted for classroom use.

In utilizing such games, be careful to include only the pertinent and important. Be particularly wary of quiz games made up of student-developed questions. Students too often search for the trivial and the obscure. Games that feature such questions help very little and should be avoided. Also avoid games that eliminate those players who make errors. The old-fashioned spelling bee is not very useful because the people who need the practice most are eliminated first.

USING THE PRINCIPLE OF SPACED LEARNING   Partly because of motivation factors, learning is usually more efficient over a period of time with rather frequent breaks than when it is concentrated in long, continuous practice sessions. This phenomenon, known as the *principle of spaced learning,* operates because of several reasons. One of them is that a person can keep motivation and effort at a high level for only a short time before tiring. Short practice periods interspersed with rest periods make it easier for learners to perform at or near top level, thus giving them maximum benefit from the practice. Also, the shortness of the practice sessions, plus the opportunities for rest, prevent the pupils from developing incorrect habits by practicing when overtired. Another reason for spacing practice sessions is that the intervals of rest between practice give the learners a chance to forget their mistakes before they go on to the next practice session. Because after each rest period the students concentrate anew on learning correctly, spaced learning tends to reinforce correct learning and to cause mistakes to drop out.

As the learning becomes more firmly entrenched, the practice periods should become shorter and the intervals longer because less time is needed to renew the learning. This also helps to keep the practice from becoming too monotonous.

ELIMINATING UNNECESSARY DRUDGERY   Practice can be dreadfully boring, as we all know. To keep it from becoming so, eliminate as much unnecessary work as possible. If the exercise is to punctuate a paragraph, asking students to copy the entire paragraph is pointless. Indicating the words preceding the punctuation should be enough. It is better still to photocopy the paragraph and allow students to add the correct punctuation directly to the copied sheet.

Because of the boredom factor, do not use practice or drill unnecessarily. Teachers need to bear down on some things but not on others. If you emphasize drill too much, you run the risk of making the class unnecessarily boring. *Reserve hard practice for important learning that needs to be habitualized or retained a long time.* Concentrate practice on whatever is most important. Also, because memorizing is at best a dreary pastime, you should not demand that students memorize things that they need not remember. There are quite enough things a person should know by heart without loading students up with unnecessary memorizing. (By this, however, we do not mean to imply that students should never have an opportunity to learn a poem by heart for the pure pleasure of knowing it.)

WHEN DRILL IS NEEDED   In spite of the warnings in the previous sections, you cannot expect to eliminate all rote learning from your teaching. Some facts and abilities simply must be developed by direct attack and repetition. Among these are such things as idiomatic expressions, conjugations, chemical formulas, and mathematical facts. Historical dates provide an excellent example of such facts. Most dates in history can be taught by always associating the event with the date during the discussion. Other techniques, such as making time lines and time charts, are also available and valuable. However, to have a skeleton on which to hang historical events, students must learn key dates. These key dates must be taught directly once the students have learned their significance. To ensure that students learn them and retain them, a few minutes at the beginning or end of the period might well be given to practicing key dates several times a week.

INDEPENDENT PRACTICE   When students have a good understanding and some skill (when they are about 80 percent effective, according to Rosenshine and Stevens), they should begin independent practice that directly follows and builds on the guided practice.(19) Do not start independent practice until you are reasonably sure that the students are ready, and even then expect to help with the first examples. To ensure that the independent practice sessions progress smoothly, before you begin, set up routines and explain them to the pupils, so that the pupils will know how to proceed when working alone.

Seatwork provides a good medium for independent practice and application. Before assigning seatwork, be sure to introduce it carefully and go over some practice examples before the students start on their own. Seatwork yields the best results when the students work on common worksheets or exercises cooperatively in small groups or pairs and coach one another or explain the material to one another. As with any other type of practice activity, you must monitor seatwork carefully to spot student error and misunderstanding. If there is evidence of a lack of understanding, you will have to reteach. Following are some research-based suggestions for improving student engagement during seatwork:

1. Give clear instruction—explanations, questions, and feedback—and sufficient practice before the students begin their seatwork. Having to provide lengthy explanations during seatwork is troublesome for the teacher and for the student.
2. Circulate during seatwork, actively explaining, observing, asking questions, and giving feedback.
3. Have short contacts with individual students (i.e., 30 seconds or less).
4. For difficult material in whole-class instruction, have a number of segments of instruction and seatwork during a single period.
5. Arrange seats to facilitate monitoring the students (e.g., face both small groups and independently working students).
6. Establish a routine to use during seatwork activity that prescribes what students will do, how they will get help, and what they will do when they have completed the exercises.(20)

Individualizing Practice

If practice is to be really valuable to students, it should be individualized. However, to find a practice exercise that is valuable and important to every teenager in your class is virtually impossible. Almost invariably some of the students will have mastered the skill to the point where it would be better for them to move on to something else. On the other hand, other students probably do not understand the concept well enough to truly benefit from the practice at all. So, except for such things as marching drill and similar mass group exercises, use group practice sparingly. Instead, practice should be tailor-made for each student.

To individualize practice is easier than it sounds. Since practice ordinarily consists of experiences designed to strengthen learning that has already been acquired, you can leave much of the teaching to the students themselves. By providing self-administered and self-correcting materials and arranging situations in which pairs and small groups can work together correcting and helping one another, you can make it possible for each student to be largely self-directing.

For this reason, diagnosis, particularly self-diagnosis, is an important aid to effective practice. When students recognize their weaknesses, they are more likely to see the necessity for practice. Then, if their practice is rewarded by visible progress, they are more likely to redouble their efforts. Nothing is as encouraging as success.

An example of such a practice technique was used in a ninth-grade grammar class. In this class the teacher supplied the students with a multitude of exercises designed to give practice in each of the areas studied in grammar. (The exercises were mostly composed of old cut-up grammar tests.) Before studying each grammatical topic, the students took a pretest. If they scored very high in the pretest, they could skip that topic and go on to another; if they did not, they practiced the exercises for that topic until they thought they had mastered the material. As they finished each exercise, they corrected their own work, sometimes consulting a teacher or a neighbor about why such and such was so. When they thought they were ready, they tried another mastery test. When they had demonstrated by the test scores that they had mastered the topic, they were allowed to move on to the next one. The teacher administered the tests and was available to help and guide the students with their practice. The result was a busy class in which individual students worked on the exercises that most concerned them.[*]

Stop and Reflect

How might you adapt a spelling bee to give everyone plenty of practice?
How can you avoid the poor attitudes that often accompany drill?
Why is it recommended that practice should be under some pressure?
Make up some self-correcting, individualized practice material for a topic you might teach.

Review

Review differs somewhat from practice and drill. It does not require drill techniques; what it does require is reteaching. Instead of drill activities, use such activities as the following:

1. Summarize what has been taught.
2. Have students summarize or outline the essentials that have been taught.
3. Reteach the lesson in a different context.
4. Have students build questions to ask each other about content to be reviewed.
5. Utilize quiz games such as Jeopardy.
6. Dramatize, role play, or simulate the content to be reviewed.
7. Build open-ended discussion around the main points of the content to be reviewed.
8. Use broad questioning techniques to get students to think about and apply the information in the lesson.
9. Do problems based on the content to be reviewed.
10. Allow students to build questions for a test on the subject.
11. Use the content to be reviewed in practical situations or apply it to other situations.
12. Build time lines, charts, tables, diagrams, and so on that bring out the relationships and important points in the content to be reviewed.

Conduct reviews frequently. Some teachers make it a habit to end each class with a review of the main concepts taught that day; others start each class with a review of what has gone before. Almost all do some reviewing at the end of each unit and term. Do not limit reviews to the end of the unit or lesson, however. Use them any time that loose ends need to be tied together or students' thoughts need to be regrouped or reorganized. By reviewing, you can drive points home, make learning stick, bind ideas together, and clarify relationships among past, present, and future learning.

SUMMARY

Active student involvement in the learning process is essential for effective teaching. In American schools, the students' role is liable to be completely passive too much

---

[*]You will recognize this as another variation on the continuous progress approach.

of the time. Consequently, you should concentrate on using teaching techniques that cause active student participation in the lessons.

To focus on active student learning, several educational researchers have recommended the adoption of direct teaching techniques. In the model they recommend, the teacher presents the content to be learned in talks or demonstrations which make good use of student questions, comments, and discussion. This presentation is followed by guided and then independent practice, and a final summing up. The techniques in this type of teaching are much more suited for teaching skills and low-level cognitive learning than they are for teaching higher-level cognitive subject content.

Although the use of the lecture has been severely criticized, it has a place in today's schools; however, it should not be your mainstay. Short, informal teacher talks are much more effective for most purposes. If you desire quality learning of the higher cognitive and affective sort, other teaching methods involving group process, inquiry, problem solving, and the higher mental processes are often more useful. However, at times, the lecture is the only appropriate method. In such situations, follow the rules laid down by our best speechmakers: Make it short, lively, and to the point. Tell students what you are going to tell them, tell them, and then tell them what you told them.

To give students clear understanding of processes and skills and how to perform them, you must use show-how techniques, including audiovisual media presentations and, especially, demonstrations. Carefully prepare and present demonstrations, and follow them up with summarizing and clinching activities.

Questioning is one of the oldest and most dependable tactics. Its uses are legion and range from checking memory and understanding to bringing about higher learning. Unfortunately, of the four categories of questions suggested by Gallagher and Aschner, most teachers are content to concentrate on memory questions and neglect convergent, divergent, and evaluative questions. Yet it is quite possible, after a little practice, to phrase questions that cover each category in the Bloom taxonomy.

Good questions are clear, simple, straightforward, challenging, thought-provoking, adapted to the students to whom they are addressed, and suitable for the purpose for which they are being used. If your questions are to meet these criteria, you probably will have to write out your key questions in advance. To get the most out of your questioning, ask questions of individuals rather than the whole class. Usually the best technique is to ask the question first and then call on a specific person to answer it, to refrain from repeating questions, and to distribute the questions evenly and randomly among the class members.

Handle student answers courteously. Support all honest attempts to answer, even when the students do not come up with the right answer, but do not allow pupil misunderstanding and error to go uncorrected. Encourage students to ask questions. The best classes are full of student questions and comments. Clarifying responses are most useful for starting students' thought processes.

As commonly practiced in our schools, recitation is obsolete. Teachers who care about learning should replace it with methods that encourage understanding and the use of the higher mental processes. Thought-provoking questioning and open book recitations are examples of the types of methods that might be used instead.

Practice makes perfect. Secondary school classes should allow plenty of opportunity for the repetition and review necessary to drive learning home. To be most effective, practice should be meaningful, varied, and as free from boredom as possible. To eliminate drudgery and to make practice efficient, individualize practice exercises and activities as much as possible after carefully diagnosing the needs of the individual students.

ADDITIONAL READING

Broadwell, M. M. *The Lecture Method of Education.* Englewood Cliffs, NJ: Educational Technology Publications, 1980.

Brookfield, S. D. *The Skillful Teacher.* San Francisco: Jossey-Bass, 1990.

Brown, G., and R. Edmondson. "Asking Questions." In *Classroom Teaching Skills,* edited by E. Wragg. New York: Nichols, 1984.

Costa, A. L. *The Enabling Behavior.* Orangevale, CA: Search Models Unlimited, 1989.

Dillon, J. T. *Questioning and Teaching—A Manual of Practice.* New York: Teachers College Press, 1988.

Dillon, J. T. *Teaching and the Art of Questioning, Fastback 194.* Bloomington, IN: Phi Delta Kappa Educational Foundation, 1983.

Friedman, P. G. *Listening Processes: Attention, Understanding, Evaluation.* Washington, DC: National Education Association, 1983.

Henson, K. T. *Methods and Strategies of Teaching in Secondary and Middle Schools.* New York: Longman, 1988.

Hunkins, F. P. *Involving Students in Questioning.* Boston: Allyn and Bacon, 1976.

Hyman, Ronald T. *Strategic Questioning.* Englewood Cliffs, NJ: Prentice-Hall, 1979.

Kowalski, T., R. Weaver, and K. Henson. *Case Studies on Teaching.* New York: Longman, 1990.

McLeish, J. "The Lecture Method." Chap. 8 in *The Psychology of Teaching Methods, The Seventy-fifth Yearbook of the Society for the Study of Education,* edited by N. L. Gage. Chicago: University of Chicago Press, 1976.

Orlich, D. C. et al. *Teaching Strategies: A Guide to Better Instruction,* 2nd ed. Lexington, MA: Heath, 1985, Part IV, Ch. 6.

Rosenshine, B., and R. Stevens. "Teaching Functions" in *Handbook of Research on Teaching,* 3rd ed., edited by M. C. Wittrock. New York: Macmillan, 1986.

Sudman, S., and N. M. Bradburn. *Asking Questions.* San Francisco: Jossey-Bass, 1982.

Wilen, W. W. *Questioning Skills for Teachers,* 2nd ed. Washington, DC: National Education Association, 1987.

Winfield, I. *Learning to Teach Practical Skills,* 2nd ed. New York: Nichols, 1988.

NOTES

1. Barak Rosenshine and Robert Stevens, "Teaching Functions" in *Handbook of Research on Teaching,* 3rd ed., edited by Melvin C. Wittrock (New York: Macmillan, 1986), 377.

2. Ibid., 379.

3. Rita Dunn and Kenneth Dunn, *Teaching Students Through Their Individual Learning Styles* (Reston, VA: Reston Publishing, 1978).

4. Jere Brophy and Thomas L. Good, "Teacher Behavior and Student Achievement," in *Handbook of Research on Teaching,* 3rd ed., edited by Melvin C. Wittrock (New York: Macmillan, 1986), 355.

5. Ibid.

6. Ibid.

7. D. Sparks and G. M. Sparks, *Effective Teaching for Higher Achievement* (Alexandria, VA: Association for Supervision and Curriculum Development, 1984). Jerry L. Bellon, Elner C. Bellon, and Mary Ann Blank, *Teaching from a Research Knowledge Base* (Englewood Cliffs, NJ: Merrill/Prentice Hall, 1992), 242–244.

8. Louis Raths, *What Is Teaching?*, undated, mimeographed. *See also* Louis E. Raths, Selma Wasserman, Arthur Jonas, and Arnold Rothstein, *Teaching for*

Thinking, 2nd ed. (New York: Teachers College, Columbia University Press, 1986).

9. James J. Gallagher and Mary Jane Ascher, "A Preliminary Report of Analyses of Classroom Interaction," *The Merrill Palmer Quarterly of Behavior and Development* 9 (July 1963): 183–194. Gary D. Borich, *Effective Teaching Methods,* 2nd ed. (Englewood Cliffs, NJ: Merrill/Prentice Hall, 1992), 253ff.

10. Brophy and Good, "Teacher Behavior and Student Achievement," 362–363.

11. M. B. Rowe, "Wait-Time and Reward as Instructional Variables," *Journal of Research on Science Teaching* 11 (1974): 81–94. Cited by William W. Wilen, *Questioning Skills for Teachers* (Washington, DC: National Education Association, 1982), 18.

12. Ibid.

13. Brophy and Good, "Teacher Behavior and Student Achievement," 359–360, 363.

14. L. B. Gambrell, "Think-Time: Implications for Reading Instruction," *Reading Teacher* 34 (November, 1980): 143–146.

15. J. T. Dillon, *Teaching and the Art of Questioning, Fastback 194* (Bloomington, IN: Phi Delta Kappa Educational Foundation, 1983), 13–17.

16. Louis E. Raths, Selma Wasserman, Arthur Jonas, and Arnold Rothstein, *Teaching for Thinking* (New York: Teachers College, Columbia University Press, 1986), 170–173.

17. Paul D. Eggen and Donald P. Kauchak, *Strategies for Teachers: Teaching Content and Thinking Skills,* 2nd ed. (Englewood Cliffs, NJ: Prentice-Hall, 1988), 120.

18. Rosenshine and Stevens, "Teaching Functions," 379–386.

19. Ibid.

20. Ibid., 388.

Chapter 8

Group and Discussion Methods

- **Overview**
- **Discussion**
- **Panels and Debates**
- **Speech**
- **Small Groups, Cooperative Learning Teams, and Committees**

Overview

In this and Chapter 9, we consider indirect methods of teaching. These methods are most effective when teaching loosely structured subject matter and when trying to develop higher-level cognitive learning. This chapter is devoted to discussion and small-group or committee approaches.

Open communication and a supportive atmosphere are essential for good discussion. The success of discussions also depends on the teacher's skillful use of questions and his or her careful staging of the classroom situation to promote a free flow of ideas and thinking. This preparation is one reason why it is necessary for you to plan carefully for discussion lessons. Well done, such lessons pay off by arousing interest, molding attitudes, and encouraging thinking. In this chapter, we point out techniques for making your discussions work. We also show ways to conduct the more formal types of discussions, which may be used very effectively to involve students in high-level consideration of controversial and multisided matters. Finally, we examine small-group and committee approaches—strategies that, although difficult to conduct well, have many uses. Effective teaching of small groups requires attention to detail and constant supervision; at the same time, it permits students the freedom to carry out their own initiatives.

Discussion

Characteristics of a Good Discussion

A discussion is not just a bull session or a rap session. Rather, it is a purposeful conversation that proceeds toward some goal with a minimum of rambling and bickering. For a discussion to be successful, the participants need sufficient background to know what they are talking about and to base their arguments on fact. Moreover, the topic must be discussable. For example, the equation $a^2 + b^2 = c^2$ is a fact and so is not subject to discussion, although perhaps you might discuss its implications.

A discussion is a conversation, not a monologue or a series of questions. In a really effective discussion, everyone should participate, although it is not always necessary for each person to talk. People can participate in different ways, sometimes by only sitting and listening. In general, however, you can assume that during a discussion, the more people who participate actively, the better. In other words, *discussion* is not a synonym for *lecture* or *recitation.*

A really successful discussion is not only purposeful; it also achieves its purpose. If it is at all possible, a discussion should lead to some sort of conclusion. Certainly, even if no conclusion is reached, an effective exchange should always culminate in a summing up. Sometimes the summing up may have to include a minority report.

Although discussions should be purposeful and conclusive, true discussions are not vehicles for expressing the teacher's point of view or devices by which to win support for a particular position (although discussions *can* be very effective when used to convert people to a particular view). In a true discussion, all the members of the group think for themselves, and all have a chance to express an opinion, no matter how unpopular the position may be. At best a discussion is informal, but it is always serious. Humor, of course, is welcome, but frivolity is not. Although the group members remain courteous at all times, there is no formal hierarchy of membership. The discussion chairperson is merely a moderator who supervises rather than directs the conversation. The flow of conversation should travel around the

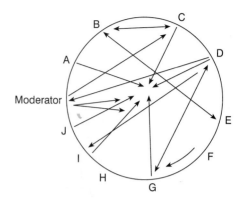

■ **FIGURE 8.1**

Satisfactory Patterns of Discussion Flow. The moderator's questions have elicited general responses and exchanges among students. (Arrows to the center indicate a statement or question addressed to the entire group rather than to an individual.)

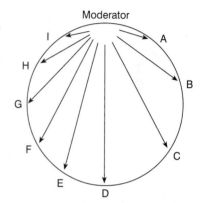

■ **FIGURE 8.2**

Unsatisfactory Pattern of Flow of Discussion. All conversation emanates from the leader or moderator.

group almost at random (Figure 8.1). Discussions that consist of questions asked by the leader and then answered by the students without considerable side interchange are not really discussions at all (Figure 8.2).

Advantages of True Discussions

Teachers who handle true discussions well find them to be effective. For instance, when comparing the discussion to the lecture, while the lecture has the edge as far as conveying information, the discussion seems to help students develop better skills in thinking as well as clearer understandings, and is more likely to effect changes in attitude. The discussion process—including, as it does, defending, applying, modifying, explaining, and reworking one's ideas—gives students the opportunity to develop concepts with deep personal meaning. Concepts developed in this way are more likely to stick with students than are concepts developed by more static strategies. In addition, this process is more effective in shaping attitudes, ideals, and appreciations than are the expository teaching strategies. Discussions are also a useful medium for training students in communications skills and for building positive social attitudes and a sense of belonging. The major contribution of discussions, however, is the opportunity they give students to practice thinking—to look at their own ideas, to formulate and apply principles, and to accept immediate feedback from their peers. The discussion is an excellent tool by which to develop creative thinking.

Stop and Reflect

What is a discussion? How does it differ from a recitation?

What values do discussions have? For what purposes are they best suited? What sorts of things can best be learned through discussion?
What makes a good discussion?

Conducting Discussions

THE ROLE OF THE LEADER   Active, purposeful leadership can make the difference between successful and unsuccessful discussion. Effective discussion leaders see to it that the discussion starts smoothly; they introduce the topic succinctly but clearly so that everyone understands what is to be discussed and what the purpose of the discussion is, and then they pose provocative opening questions or statements. Competent leaders keep the discussion moving by encouraging all participants to take part and by tactfully bottling up any monologists. They also try to keep the discussion from wandering off into unproductive byways by clearing up errors of fact or judgment and by recalling the group to the question at hand when the conversation digresses. Good leaders summarize from time to time and help the group members evaluate their progress so as to be sure that everyone understands what has been said and so that no one is left behind. Sometimes leaders suggest next steps and guide the conversation into new or different paths, as well as cut off unproductive side issues and overlong prolongation of the argument. They keep track of the time to be sure that the group can accomplish its task in the time allotted. Finally, when all has been said and done, effective leaders try to tie together all the ideas, conclusions, and generalizations in a final summary.

In spite of the importance of the leadership role, discussion leaders should be careful not to dominate discussions, for a true discussion is an opportunity for all participants to share ideas. Effective leaders try to see that the ideas of all participants are treated with respect and to keep the participants' discussion open so that the truth—or at least notions about truth—may come out. At the same time, leaders should not turn the discussion over to the group and let its members do as they please. Laissez-faire leadership seldom leads to profitable discussions. Rather, good leaders seek to create an atmosphere in which participants feel free to speak and think freely without fear of embarrassment, but in which all the energies of the group are kept pointed toward the goal.

An ideal discussion leader has such qualities as the following:

- An evident interest in the topic at hand
- A sense of humor
- A sense of seriousness
- The ability to suppress his or her own opinions
- A nonjudgmental attitude and bearing
- An accepting and encouraging manner

Although it may seem that this list calls for paragons, many teachers have trained students to be excellent discussion leaders. Figure 8.3 is an observation form that Schmuck and Schmuck suggest secondary school students use to rank student discussion leaders.

THE ROLE OF THE RECORDER   Designating someone to act as a recorder or secretary can be helpful in most group discussions. The job of the recorder is to keep a record of the important points and decisions made during the discussion. From time to time, at the request of the leader, the recorder may help clarify the course of the discussion, resolve conflicts and confusion, and put wandering discussions back on track by summarizing what has been said.

Task Functions	Time				
	1	2	3	4	5
1. Initiating: proposing tasks or goals; defining a group problem; suggesting a procedure for solving a problem; suggesting other ideas for consideration.					
2. Information or opinion seeking: requesting facts on the problem; seeking relevant information; asking for suggestions and ideas.					
3. Information or opinion giving: offering facts; providing relevant information; stating a belief; giving suggestions or ideas.					
4. Clarifying or elaborating: interpreting or reflecting ideas or suggestions; clearing up confusion; indicating alternatives and issues before the group; giving examples.					
5. Summarizing: pulling related ideas together; restating suggestions after the group has discussed them.					
6. Consensus teaching: sending up "trial balloons" to see if group is nearing a conclusion; checking with group to see how much agreement has been reached.					
Social Emotional Functions					
7. Encouraging: being friendly, warm and responsive to others; accepting others and their contributions; listening; showing regard for others by giving them an opportunity or recognition.					
8. Expressing group feelings: sensing feeling, mood, relationships within the group; sharing his own feelings with other members.					
9. Harmonizing: attempting to reconcile disagreements; reducing tension through "pouring oil on troubled waters"; getting people to explore their differences					
10. Compromising: offering to compromise his own position, ideas, or status; admitting error; disciplining himself to help maintain the group.					
11. Gatekeeping: seeing that others have a chance to speak; keeping the discussion a group discussion rather than a 1-, 2-, or 3-way conversation.					
12. Setting standards: expressing standards that will help group to achieve; applying standards in evaluating group functioning and production.					

FIGURE 8.3

Observation Sheet for Goal-Directed Leadership (Secondary)

Richard A. Schmuck and Patricia A. Schmuck, *Group Processes in the Classroom* (Dubuque, IA: Brown, 1971), p. 48.

The recorder's main task is to keep a record of the discussion. Because this task is a difficult one for many young people, you should take special pains to help the student recorder. In classroom discussions, verbatim transcripts of the discussion are not usually desirable. Instead, the group needs to have an account of the major positions taken and the conclusions reached.

One method that will help ensure good recording by beginners is to have the recorder keep the record on the chalkboard. This technique makes it possible for all the participants to see the notes and also permits the teacher to coach the recorder if the need arises. Similarly, an overhead projector can be used, which provides the added advantage of being able to save the notes for future reference or for reprojecting. In any case, help the recorder keep good notes, and also keep notes yourself to supplement any lapses the student recorder may make.

THE ROLE OF THE PARTICIPANTS   The ability to speak and listen well as participants in group discussions is a rather difficult skill that relatively few adults have truly mastered. When speaking, participants should try to be clear and precise. Although it is difficult to do so during a lively discussion, they should try to organize what they say before they say it so that they can make points more easily. In this respect, they should learn that their presentations will be more successful if they speak clearly and simply without affectation. A simply worded direct argument in which points are made one by one in a simple linear order is usually much more likely to be understood than are more complicated approaches.

One danger of placing too great an emphasis on the way students present their opinions is that they may forget to listen to the discussion. Many persons, even participants in television debates and panels, are guilty of being so busy thinking about what they want to say that they never listen to the other participants or to the questions asked of them. To train students to listen, some teachers ask each participant to repeat the germ of the last speaker's comments before adding his or her own.

THE ROLE OF THE TEACHER   In discussions, as in other methods, your role as teacher is to prepare, execute, and follow-up. However, during the actual discussion, your role should be *subdued.* The bulk of the discussion should be the students' own. Even so, you will probably find that conducting a discussion is hard work.

Before the discussion begins, you, the teacher, must see to it that everyone is properly prepared. During the class's first experiences with real discussion, you will have to act as moderator or chairperson. At all times, you will need to act as supervisor and observer. In these roles, you must do the following:

- Make sure that the problem to be discussed is properly defined and delimited.
- Furnish information when it is required.
- Set guidelines.
- See to it that gross errors do not remain unchallenged.
- Post questions that reflect the content and feeling of the comments made.
- Relate the comments to one another and to the central topic.
- Keep the discussion moving on the right track.
- Provide a follow-up.

When you act as moderator, you must do all these jobs yourself. When a student is moderator, you will have to do most of these tasks by indirection. Sometimes a hint to the moderator or recorder will suffice. Sometimes you may have to stop the discussion and restart it. However, the more unobtrusively you can do the job, the better.

Most important, during the discussion you should assume the role of a consultant who is always available as a resource person or advisor for whatever contingency might arise. In discussions, perhaps more than in other strategies, the teacher must act as the servant rather than the master of the group.

PREPARING FOR A DISCUSSION   Students often think of a discussion as an "easy class," but discussions are really quite difficult to carry out. Both teachers and students must be well-prepared for discussion classes if they are to be successful. During the period of preparation, you can make sure that students understand exactly what the point at issue is to be and what their roles in the discussion are. Early in the year, you may find it desirable to do some direct teaching concerning the how and why of carrying on discussions.

STARTING THE DISCUSSION   Not only must you, the teacher, be well-briefed on the topic to be discussed, but also you need a plan for conducting the discussion. In the plan, include provisions for getting the discussion started and questions for possible use. Also be prepared with possible conclusions.

Starting a discussion may be something of a strain. It may take a little persuasion or some special introductory activity. Before starting, try to arrange the group in a homey, informal fashion. As a general rule, the more pleasant the atmosphere, the better chance the discussion has of being successful. If possible, seat the students so that they can see each other. A circle is usually the best seating arrangement for a discussion, although any other arrangement that brings the participants face-to-face will do.

Be sure the students understand the subject they are to discuss, the procedure they will use in discussing it, and how long they have to conduct the discussion. Sometimes the introductory portion of the discussion needs to be devoted to clarifying the issues. Presenting the topic to be discussed in the form of a problem sometimes makes the clarifying and launching of the discussion easier.

To get a discussion off to a good start, make use of some activity that will develop interest among the participants. People need an opportunity to think and react before they can discuss anything sensibly. Consequently, it helps to have the discussion develop out of some other activity. Buzz sessions—groups of four to six people who discuss the question for four to six minutes—sometimes help to get the discussion under way. Another common device is to start the discussion with a short introductory talk or to have someone pose some challenging questions (prepared in advance) to the group. A test, quiz, or pretest can sometimes be used to stimulate a brisk discussion.

In any case, provide an opening statement of some sort to orient the group and establish the ground rules for the discussion. Other ways to stimulate discussion include the following:

- introducing a specific case or problem
- role playing
- films or filmstrips
- exhibits
- pictures
- visitors
- news items
- tape recordings
- demonstrations
- staged incidents
- provacative questions, especially questions emphasizing *how, why,* and *what if.*

Whatever tactic is used to get the discussion going, it should be only long enough to arouse interest and to point out the direction the conversation should follow. The discussion immediately should pursue this opener. Waiting for the next day may be too late; once the mood has been lost, it may be impossible to reestablish it.

No matter how dramatic or exciting an initiatory activity may seem, you must be prepared for the students' response to be negative or for the participants to start off in directions you never dreamed of. Have a few spare tricks up your sleeve "just in case." Teachers must be prepared for such contingencies in order to save both their own and student-led discussions.

Stop and Reflect

What can the leader do to start a discussion when the group seems reluctant to participate? Can you suggest at least five approaches that may help the discussion get started?

How would you arrange the physical setting to encourage discussion? Suppose you wished to use the chalkboard in connection with the discussion. Would that change your plans?

GUIDING THE DISCUSSION   Once the discussion is started, you must keep it moving briskly in the right direction. Skillful questioning as well as outlining the most important points on the chalkboard will help maintain the tempo and hold the group to the topic. So will being sure that all the students know and accept the problem under discussion. Should the group digress, you can redirect the focus by restating the question. Allow the group to pursue a digression if it seems to have promise, however. Occasionally groups that have become lost and cannot agree can be helped by a minute of silent consideration of the problem, an impromptu buzz session, or role playing.

SKILLFUL QUESTIONING   One key to successfully guiding the discussion is the skillful use of questions. The leader's role is to draw students out and to keep the conversation moving in the direction it should go. To draw students out, ask open-ended, broad, thought-provoking questions. Divergent questions are much more likely to be successful than are convergent ones; evaluative questions are likely to be most valuable of all. You should usually present questions in such a way that anyone who wishes can respond. Sometimes, however—in order to involve a new participant, to start things moving, to reengage someone's wandering attention, or perhaps even to forestall still another comment by a monopolizer, for instance—it may be better to address your questions to specific individuals.

To involve more students, bounce the questions around. Asking students to comment on other students' answers can be effective. Questions such as "Do you agree with Mary, Susie?", "What would you do in such a situation?", and "If you had a choice, which would you prefer?" tend to keep the conversation going and tend to free students' ideas. When leading a discussion, you should seldom answer questions or express an opinion except when asked a direct question demanding a factual answer. Even then, it is better to ask if anyone else can provide the information requested.

ALTERNATIVE NONQUESTIONS   All too often, teachers' questions stifle discussion. By their very nature, the questions tend to turn the discussion into a two-way exchange between the teacher and a student. To stimulate discussion and to encourage wide participation, make optimum use of what Dillon calls alternative nonquestioning techniques.(1) Let us look at a few of these.

Sometimes the teacher's best technique is to keep silent. Teachers usually talk too much. Often when the discussion falters for a bit, if the teacher keeps quiet, the students will pick up the thread and start making a new pattern with it. Because nature abhors vacuums and people abhor empty silence, you can almost always depend on someone's saying something just to fill in the void. Moments of silence also give students a chance to consider what has been said, and to reformulate their thoughts and arguments. Remember Rowe's suggestion in Chapter 7 that a teacher count up to five before picking up on an unanswered question. This practice works just as well, if not better, in discussion situations.

When a discussion bogs down because students are unsure of facts or unclear on a particular point, a simple declarative sentence may clear the air and start things moving again. In many situations, trying to clear up misconceptions and misunderstandings by using questioning procedures becomes too inquisitorial. A short explanatory sentence may clarify the point without putting any onus on anyone. It also provides a basis for further comment by the students. Questions call for answers, but declarative sentences may provide a point of departure or a foundation for further thought. Remember, however, to make the statements short. A discussion is no place for a speech from the podium.

A student's statement can open up discussion and lead to clearer explanations. Merely asking students to explain what they mean is likely to be fruitless. Instead, restating what you understood a student to say may be more profitable. Statements like, "If I understand you, you believe that . . . ," "I take it you think that . . . ," and "So you maintain that . . . " encourage students to clarify their positions, develop their meaning in more detail, and, in general, to participate more fully. This technique is particularly useful when it seems that the students' ideas are not well-formed.

If you do not understand what a student means, it is important to let the student know. In such cases you can say something like, "I am sorry, but I do not understand what you are getting at," or "I am not sure I understand what you mean." Another type of approach is to say, "I wonder if what you say applies to such-and-such situation," or "I wonder if that [what you described] would really make a difference."

Invitations to elaborate on an expressed idea may be more effective than are probing questions asked during discussions. Invitations to elaborate seem to work best when presented obliquely: "That sounds like a great idea; would you like to tell us more about it?" "That's interesting, I'd like to hear more of your feelings about it." If the student takes up your invitation to expand, it will not only help the discussion, it may make the speaker's thought clearer to himself and to the rest of the class. Class members are usually more attentive when other students express their ideas and feelings than when speakers merely respond to questions.

Encourage students to ask questions. If confused students ask questions, perhaps the confusion can be cleared up. Probably the best way to encourage student questions is to answer them. Avoid answering questions with counterquestions, however. Particularly encourage student-student exchanges. Students are more willing to ask questions of other students than of teachers. They are also more willing to give detailed, full answers to other students' questions than to their teachers.(2)

CREATING A SUPPORTIVE ATMOSPHERE   Strive for a supportive atmosphere, accepting all contributions graciously even when they are not very helpful. To this end, refrain from expressing your approval or disapproval of participants' comments. Try to ensure that all are heard with equal respect.

On the other hand, you must not let error pass unchallenged. Always challenge inconsistencies, faulty logic, and superficialities. By using skillful questions, you can get the students to see their own ideas and those of their colleagues more clearly. To help them clarify their thinking, ask them to explain why they said what they said and believe what they believe. In this way, in combination with other skillful questions, you can get the students to look beyond their statements and see the causes and consequences of their beliefs. Dare them to prove their statements and cite their authorities. When confusion is rife, try to clarify the situation by asking such questions as

■ Just what does that term mean?
■ Exactly what is the issue facing us?

KEEPING ON TRACK   One of the most difficult problems you must face when leading a discussion is that of keeping the discussion on the right track. Usually you can bring the group back into focus by asking a question that deals directly with the topic at hand. Other times you may have to point out, "I think that we are forgetting the point of our discussion." Sometimes you may have to stop to reorient the group.

From time to time, draw the threads of the discussion together by summarizing or by asking the recorder to summarize. This gives the group a chance to stop and look at its progress, to see how it stands, and perhaps to decide in which direction to proceed. To bring out these values, you may include any or all of the following:

1. A résumé of the major points made so far.
2. A review of the facts and evidence presented.
3. A synopsis of what has been accomplished and what remains to be finished.
4. A restatement of any conclusions that have been made.
5. An analysis of the course or conduct of the discussion up to this point.

Whatever the gist of the summary, it should be brief, well-organized, and to the point. Too many or too long summaries may break up the thread of the discussion and so do more harm than good. Also harmful are summaries that do not represent the thinking of all the group. The final summary at the end of the discussion should pull together all the important ideas and conclusions. To be sure that all points of view are presented fairly, it is often advantageous to elicit the aid of other participants when developing the summary. Note these ideas and conclusions on the chalkboard to emphasize their importance and to clarify their meaning.

Although a good summary is essential for ending a discussion, it should not end the consideration of the topic. A suitable follow-up activity that drives home the importance of the things learned, or that leads into the next activity, can increase the value of almost any discussion.

Stop and Reflect
What can be done about discussions that seem to get nowhere?
What can you do with students who monopolize the discussion?

EVALUATING THE DISCUSSION   The value of discussion will ordinarily increase as the students learn how to carry on discussions and gain experience. Good discussion techniques must be learned and practiced. Frequently, self-evaluations will help to improve discussion skills. When students take stock of themselves and their discussion skills from time to time, progress in those skills can be expected. Having group members complete a form as simple as the following can be of considerable value:

1. Did the group discussion do what it set out to do?
2. In what way did we fall short?

3. Did we get off the topic?
4. Did everyone participate?
5. Did anyone monopolize the conversation?

Students' self-evaluation of their discussions can often be enhanced by letting them listen to taped recordings of their discussions. For evaluating a taped discussion, using a list of criteria similar to that just mentioned, or the one prepared by the ASCD (Association for Supervision and Curriculum Development), can be of great help (Figure 8.4). In spite of its obvious value, a tape recording of group dis-

---

Each Group Member and the Discussion Leader in Particular

Helps decide on specific problems and ways of working as a group

_____ Contributes ideas and suggestions related to the problem

_____ Listens to what other members say and seeks helpful ideas and insights

_____ Requests clarification when needed

_____ Observes the group process and makes suggestions

_____ Assumes various roles as needed

_____ Helps group get acquainted

_____ Helps group establish ground rules

_____ Reports results of preconference planning for work of group

_____ Helps group proceed with planning and deciding

_____ Calls on group to clarify, analyze, and summarize problems and suggested solutions

_____ Draws out the "timid soul" and keeps the dominant person from monopolizing

_____ Knows particular contributions which different persons can make

_____ Assists the recorder

_____ Summarizes the thinking of the group as needed.

The Recorder

_____ Consults with the group concerning the kind of record that is developing as the discussion moves forward

_____ Keeps a record of the main problems, issues, ideas, facts, and decisions as they appear in discussion

_____ Summarizes the group discussion upon request

_____ Requests clarification when his or her notes are unclear

_____ Prepares resolutions and other final reports with other designated members of the group

_____ Attends any scheduled clearinghouse or inter-group sharing committee sessions

_____ Prepares final group report and is responsible for getting it to proper clearinghouse.

Each Group Member

Pays attention to the way the group:

_____ States its goals clearly

_____ Permits participation to be easily and widely spread

_____ Keeps its discussion clear

_____ Assumes leadership responsibility

_____ Uses its resources

_____ Progresses toward its goals

_____ Revises its goals as necessary

_____ Participates in evaluation of the group process

_____ Reports to the group if asked regarding observations on the group process.

Group Members as Resource Persons

Every member of a discussion group is responsible for:

_____ Supplying information or other material to the group when requested, or when the discussion seems to call for it

_____ Citing his own experience freely when it is relevant

_____ Assisting the leader in moving toward the achievement of group goals.

■ **FIGURE 8.4**

The ASCD Checklist

Association for Supervision and Curriculum Development, *1954 Convention Program* (Washington, DC: The Association, a department of the National Education Association, 1954), pp. 54–55. Adapted by the 1954 Committee on Conference Orientation and Evaluation from material prepared for the 1950 Convention Program by J. Cecil Parker, University of California, Berkeley.

cussions can present problems. To record a large group discussion with an ordinary school tape recorder can be very difficult. For recording, the group needs to be seated in a circle with each person as close to a microphone as possible. More than one microphone will probably be needed. In small groups, the microphone can be passed from speaker to speaker, but in most class discussions this technique is too cumbersome to be practicable. Another danger is the temptation to play the recording too long or too often. Running through a tape recording may be advantageous for training in group discussion, but overdone it can become a pernicious timewaster. Rerun only parts of the tape to illustrate good or poor portions of the discussion, or to reinforce the report of what happened.

Sometimes, in order to evaluate the group's discussion, ask one of the members to act as an observer. The observer's job is to watch the group as the discussion progresses and to evaluate and report on their performance. When evaluating, the observer may use as a guide such criteria as those in the preceding list.

The comments of the observer on the progress of the discussion and on the participation of the group members are both effective means of making overtalkative or noncooperative persons aware of their faults. Frequently the students will respond more positively to criticism from one of their peers acting as observer than from the teacher.

A flow chart such as the one in Figure 8.5 can be of great help in evaluating the discussion. Yet another way of recording the progress of a group discussion is for

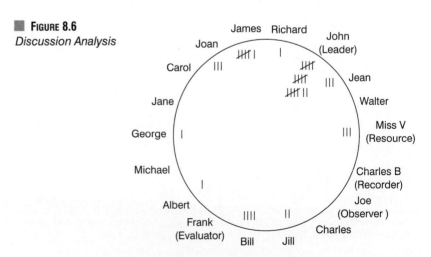

FIGURE 8.5
A Flow Chart

FIGURE 8.6
Discussion Analysis

the evaluator to place a tally alongside a speaker's name each time he or she speaks (see Figure 8.6).

Two of the most effective evaluation techniques are discussions *about* the discussion in which pupils examine their own techniques, and free reaction sheets in which pupils anonymously and briefly state their reactions, favorable or unfavorable, and tell why they feel as they do. Simple rating forms such as the one illustrated as Figure 8.7 are also useful. The evaluations may be more honest if reaction sheets or rating forms are turned in to a student committee charged with assessing the success of the activity rather than handed in to the teacher.

Stop and Reflect

Make a simple rating scale with which to evaluate a group discussion.

What does the flow chart (Figure 8.5) tell you about the participating group?

Would flow charts be helpful in high school classes? How would you use them?

Examine the ASCD criteria for discussion groups. How can they be used in a secondary school class?

How can student leaders, recorders, and resource persons be used in secondary school classes?

Discussion and Thinking

Group discussion can be used as a thinking tool. Our democracy is based on the premise that problems can be thought out and solved through the group process. Evidently, properly used, group discussion is a method that frees creative power in ways no other method can.(3) When a group freely discusses a problem that is real to its members, their combined thinking utilizes many skills, insights, and backgrounds. For the discussion to be a thinking process, however, the topic must seem important to those participating, and the discussion must be both free and, at the same time, disciplined and orderly. Think of what a high school group could do with topics such as the following (which happen to be the first two topics of several included in an article on using discussion in English classes) in an open, supportive discussion.

◼ FIGURE 8.7
Discussion Rating Form

This discussion was:

| | Excellent | Indifferent | Bad |

What I liked best was:

What I liked least was:

Suggestions:

1. Discuss objects or areas of human relations in which inventors, customs, or public policy has been highly uncreative, inflexible, or unadaptable. Have students suggest alterations for the betterment of the individual or society.
2. Have students throw a critical, yet creative eye on their own school to identify problems in school life which are not being adequately recognized or met; e.g., evaluate effectiveness of student government, cocurricular program, assemblies; discuss overall needs in the school's program which could be improved for benefit of incoming freshmen.(4)

The procedures in a discussion designed to encourage problem solving are just the same as in any other discussion—after all, group discussions should be exercises in group thinking. Seldom does the thinking of the group proceed toward the solution of the problem in strictly logical fashion; however, the discussion should generally follow the steps of the usual pattern of problem solving. According to these steps, the group members

1. become aware of the problem,
2. define the problem in group discussion,
3. gather and discuss data pertinent to the problem,
4. make hypotheses on the basis of data discovered and straw reviews and summaries, and
5. test the hypotheses to arrive at final conclusions.

The great value of discussion in problem solving is that it opens up the process to so many ideas. Narrow, stereotypic thinking is difficult to maintain when one is bombarded by the differing values, biases, levels of insight, standards, conclusions, and beliefs of others. Free discussion brings these differences out in the open. It thus not only forces discussants to put their own values and beliefs on the line for examination, but also forces them to consider beliefs and values that are new and different.

Stop and Reflect

Think up topics that are excellent for discussion in the subject you teach.

Use the self-evaluation form shown in Figure 8.8 to analyze the performance of a discussion leader in one of your college classes or of your own performance in a student-teaching class.

Panels and Debates

Panels, symposia, debates, and jury trials combine audience activities with the give-and-take of the discussion. They are useful in large-class activities when more informal whole-class or small-group discussions would not be feasible. Activities of this sort mentioned in the literature include the following:

- *The round table*   A quite informal group, usually five or fewer participants, who sit around a table and converse among themselves and with the audience.
- *The panel*   A fairly informal setting in which four to six participants with a chairperson discuss a topic among themselves, followed by a give-and-take with the class. Each participant makes an opening statement, but there are no speeches.

■ **Figure 8.8**
Self-Evaluation Form for Discussion Leaders

---

1. a. Did I have a legitimate objective?
   b. Were the objectives suitable for the discussion technique?
   c. Did I get good participation?
   d. Did I encourage participation, or did I tend to cut people off?
   e. Did I keep from letting people dominate?
   f. Did I encourage the shy, timid, and others?
   g. Were my questions open-ended?
   h. Did I keep the group to the subject?
   i. Did I domineer or dominate?
   j. In what did I best succeed?
   k. In what was I least successful?
   l. Did I solicit evocative questions and tentative solutions?
   m. Did I summarize conclusions or positions so as to follow through and tie the discussion together?

2. a. Identify the techniques you used that seemed to make the discussion effective.
   b. Identify the techniques that seemed to detract from the effectiveness of the discussion.

- *The forum*   A type of panel approach in which the panel interacts with the audience.
- *The symposium*   A more formal setting in which the participants present speeches representing differing positions, then allow questions from the floor.
- *The debate*   A very formal approach consisting of set speeches by participants of two opposing teams and a rebuttal made by each participant.
- *The British debate*   A somewhat less formal approach in which principal presentations are given by spokespersons of each side. The floor is then opened, alternately for each side, for comments and questions.
- *The jury trial*   An approach in which the class simulates a courtroom.

The procedures for conducting all these techniques are pretty much the same. As a matter of fact, many people use the terms so loosely that one can never be quite sure exactly what a *panel,* for instance, means in any given conversation. Truly the techniques are so similar that distinctions may be superfluous. In any event, any of these techniques is likely to be more interesting if it involves questions and input from members of the class other than the panelists. It is good policy to schedule either a time for general discussion or a question-and-answer period no matter what the type of presentation.

When to Use Panels and Debates

As we have said, panels, debates, and trials are useful for spicing up and personalizing large classes. These techniques need not be limited to large classes alone, however. Panels and symposia make excellent springboards for discussion in any group. Teachers also use them as

1. Culminating activities.
2. Methods of presenting committee reports:
   a. Each member of the committee becomes a panelist, or
   b. Representatives of various committees who have studied different areas or taken different positions make up the panelists.

3. A way to get differing points of view on the floor. This technique is particularly useful when discussing controversial issues. Students representing differing points of view make up the panels and present their arguments.
4. A way to present the findings of student research.
5. A way to give classes a change of pace.

Conducting Panels, Symposia, Round Tables, and Forums

All discussions work best when the students discuss matters really important to them. For this reason, if for no other, when setting up a panel it is wise to involve students in the selection of the topics to be discussed.

Most student panelists will need your help as they prepare for the discussion. Have them do at least part of their preparation in class during a supervised study period so that you can oversee the development of their presentations. A day or so before the panel is to meet, it is a good policy to require the panelists to present their presentation plans for your approval. The procedures for preparing for panels, symposia, debates, and so on are much the same as they would be for any other committee project, report, or research study.

Before the panel or symposium begins, carefully brief the students on the procedures to be followed. If there are to be initial presentations, arrange the order of presentation and set time limits. The students can usually best arrange these details by themselves in an informal planning meeting under your guidance. There need be no rehearsal, although when the discussion format requires set speeches, students should be encouraged to rehearse their speeches.

As we have said, after the formal portion of the discussion has ended, there should be an open discussion or a question-and-answer period in which everyone may participate, followed by the chairperson's summary of important points. In addition, you will usually find it advisable to follow-up and tie up loose ends. If lack of time is a factor, the summary and follow-up can become review activities for another day.

To encourage students other than the panelists to benefit from formal discussions, you may take such steps as the following:

■ Require students to take notes on the formal presentations and discussion.
■ Ask students to summarize the major points and different positions. (Summaries may be oral, written, or even quizzes.)
■ Ask students to evaluate the logic and accuracy of the arguments of the panelists. (Students should not criticize the panelists' rhetorical skill, however.)

Just as in more informal discussions, the chairperson can make a great difference in the success of a panel. At first, you should chair the discussion yourself, but once students have developed some skill with the medium, they can take over that role. Among the duties the chairperson performs are the following:

1. *Make the introduction.*   Announce the topic, map out the procedure to be followed, and prepare the audience by setting the mood, filling in necessary background, and explaining the purpose.
2. *Control the conduct of the panel.* Introduce the participants. Stop them when their time is up. Moderate give-and-take within the panel. Sum up when necessary. Redirect the flow of discussion if it bogs down.
3. *Moderate the question, answer, and discussion period with the audience.*   To encourage audience participation, it is sometimes wise to have some questions planted. Students can be assigned to make up ques-

tions as homework. (If you do assign questions as homework, collect them whether they were asked during the discussion or not.) In this role, the chairperson must solicit questions, accept and refer questions in such a way as to encourage more participation, and again sum up and redirect discussion as necessary.

4. *Close the discussion.*   Sum up. Tie up loose ends. Thank the panelists and audience participants.

Conducting Debate

Debate is the most formal of the discussion procedures. It requires that there be (1) a formal question to be debated (e.g., *Resolved:* That all television broadcasting stations be owned and operated by the federal government), (2) two teams of debaters, one to argue for the resolution, one to argue against it, and (3) a formal procedure for debating the issue.

DEBATE PROCEDURE
1. Each of the two teams consists of two or three debaters.
2. A moderator introduces the topic and the speakers. After the formal debate has ended, the moderator may conduct an open discussion in which members of the audience express their views and perhaps ask questions.
3. A timekeeper times the speeches, warns the speakers when their time is growing short, and stops them when their time has run out. Ordinarily, the timekeeper stands to mark the beginning of the warning period, and then calls the time when the time has run out.
4. Each team member makes a formal presentation that is to be no longer than a fixed number of minutes (decided well in advance of the debate).
5. Each team member makes a rebuttal to counter the arguments of the other team. Again the time is limited to a prearranged number of minutes.
6. The order of presentations and rebuttals runs as follows:
   First speaker pro
   First speaker con
   Second speaker pro
   Second speaker con
   First rebuttal pro
   First rebuttal con
   Second rebuttal pro
   Second rebuttal con
7. After the formal debate has ended, the moderator can open a general discussion.
8. If you wish, you may select student or faculty judges to decide, on the basis of a check sheet, which side argued more skillfully.

ADVANTAGES AND DISADVANTAGES   The use of the formal debate is advantageous because it

1. Provides an opportunity for study in depth.
2. Can arouse interest.
3. Shows two sides of an issue.
4. Brings controversy into sharper focus.

On the other hand, the formal debate has several serious drawbacks. It

1. Emphasizes dichotomous (black or white) thinking.

2. Involves too few students.
3. Tends to emphasize fluency in debate and winning rather than attempting to get at the truth of the matter.

Conducting British-Style Debate

The British-style debate* is more useful for most classes than is the ordinary formal debate because it opens up the discussion to more participants. The procedure for conducting the British-style debate is simple.

1. Select a question or proposition to be debated.
2. Divide the class into two teams, one for the proposition, and the other against it.
3. Select two principal speakers for each team.
4. Have the principal speaker for each team present her or his argument in a five-minute talk.
5. Have the second speaker for each team present her or his argument in a three-minute talk.
6. Throw the question open to comments, questions, and answers from the other team members. To be fair, alternate between members of the pro and con teams.
7. Let one member of each team summarize its case. Often the summarizer is the first speaker, but if a third principal speaker does the summarizing, it makes for better class participation.
8. Follow up with general discussion.

The Jury Trial Technique

Another debate technique that is excellent because it can involve a large number of the class in active participation is the jury trial. In this technique, the class simulates courtroom procedures to discuss an issue or problem. Although the procedure seems to be a simple one, it requires careful preparation if it is to go smoothly.

1. Select an issue or problem to debate. It adds interest if one student acts as a defendant.
2. Select lawyers, researchers, and witnesses for both sides. These groups can be as large as you wish, but if they are too large, they become cumbersome. You can act as judge, or better yet, some responsible student can be named for that position. Another student should be selected court stenographer, or recorder, to keep a record of what transpires. All members of the class who are not lawyers, researchers, witnesses, or court officials are the jury. (If you want to do it up brown, you can select someone to be clerk of the court, bailiff, and so on, to give the courtroom verisimilitude.)
3. All students should research the problem. The lawyers and witnesses should get the facts from their own research and from that of other class members.
4. Conduct the trial.
   a. The lawyers open up with their arguments.
   b. Witnesses present their evidence.
   c. Lawyers question and cross-examine.
   d. Lawyers from each side sum up. Each should point out how the evidence favors his or her side.

*So named because of its similarity to procedures used in the British parliament.

e. The judge sums up and points out errors in the arguments, fallacies, misstatements of fact, and so on.

f. The class, acting as the jury, votes on which side won the argument.

Stop and Reflect

Think of other techniques you might use to get the nonpanelists to prepare for the panel.

What would you do to ensure that the nonpanelist members pay attention and participate in the lesson?

Which type of panel or debate do you prefer? Which seems to be most effective? Why? When would you use formal debate techniques? British debate techniques? Jury trials?

Think of several topics in your subject field that lend themselves to the jury trial technique. How would you conduct jury trials for these topics?

Speech

Although most classroom time is spent in talking, teachers do relatively little to help students learn to speak correctly and effectively. Because speech is the principal means of communication in classes of all subjects, all teachers must accept the responsibility for teaching students to speak well. Students need lots of chances to talk under supervision. Oral activities, such as discussing, telling stories, reporting, chairing groups, and participating in dramatizations can and should be part of every course. When conducting these oral activities, encourage students to use colorful, correct, effective language. To accomplish this purpose, work on oral vocabulary building just as you work on written vocabulary building, since the techniques used for building written vocabularies can be used equally well for building oral vocabularies. You should also work to eliminate lazy speech habits such as the overuse of slang and the meaningless repetition of phrases such as "you know," "I mean," and so on.

Being overcritical and trivial when correcting the mistakes students make in speaking will not help you teach students to speak effectively. You will be much more likely to succeed if you set a good example and give students clear rules to follow. As far as you reasonably can, be a model of an effective speaker of good English. However, you do not have to carry the whole load yourself. Tapes, recordings, and videos can be used to provide examples of good speaking. Tape recordings of the students' speaking are also effective. They show students their strengths and weaknesses as well as adding a motivating factor to learning to speak well. Sometimes just hearing and seeing oneself on a videotape is enough to encourage phenomenal efforts to learn to speak more effectively—particularly after having had an opportunity to compare one's speech with that of an admired expert speaker.

Oral reading is another helpful technique to use for teaching students to speak well. Choral speaking, reciting or reading poetry, speech making, and dramatization are also useful. They should probably be used more frequently than they are.

When you use such techniques, aim them at improving speech skills and subject-matter goals. The content of the exercises is important, but in your concern for content, do not lose sight of the importance of learning to speak well. Oral reading in class may be quite helpful in this regard.

Oral Reading

Oral reading has many uses. For one, it is an excellent diagnostic tool as we have already seen. For another, it makes it possible for students to learn from one another. It gives the nonreaders a means for learning the content and entering into a discussion; it helps them strengthen their reading skills as they silently follow along in the text while another student or the teacher reads orally. Further, it has a motivation factor. Some students, even those who cannot read well, love to read aloud to the class. Sometimes reading orally or listening to someone else read orally is more interesting and meaningful than reading silently—especially when the selection to be read is dramatic or poetic. People seldom fully appreciate dramatic works or lyric poetry until they've heard them read aloud well—even if they are reading to themselves. Probably, therefore, there should be frequent oral reading in English classes—when teachers or students illustrate a point, bring out the effect, savor the flavor, point up the meaning, or just read for fun—and additional oral reading in other classes. Often, a selection gains much meaning when it is read well orally.

Read to your students from time to time, both to give pleasure and to facilitate learning. By reading to your students, you can create interest, give meaning to difficult passages, foster appreciation, and provide a model for their reading. Practice reading orally until you are adept. In the early normal schools and teachers' colleges, prospective teachers studied public speaking, elocution, and oral reading as essential tools of the profession. You would do well to emulate the practice. Read selected important portions of your text to students as they follow along. Bring in documents, incidents, dramatic pieces, pertinent anecdotes, relevant humor, and read them to students. Don't be afraid to ham it up if necessary. True, you weren't hired to be an entertainer, but a little entertainment does not hurt at appropriate moments.

Stop and Reflect

It is recommended that there be daily oral reading in English classes. Should there be oral reading in other classes such as science, mathematics, industrial arts, and business education? If so, for what purpose? How would you organize it? If not, why not?

Do you agree that oral reading should be used as a means for building clear concepts? Why or why not? If you do, how would you conduct oral reading for this purpose?

Small Groups, Cooperative Learning Teams, and Committees

Teachers quite often divide classes into small groups. Among the various types of small groups commonly found are work groups or committees, student teams, discussion groups, buzz groups, ability groups, and interest groups. As often as not, a specific small group is a combination of two or more of these types. A committee, for instance, may also be an interest or ability group. Small groups are used frequently because they are useful for many purposes, such as the following:

1. Small groups allow for individual instruction and help provide for the many differences in pupils by allowing them to participate in different roles and on different committees.
2. Small-group work promotes effective learning.

   a. They seem to be more successful in problem solving than individuals are.
   b. Their techniques tend to develop critical discrimination.
   c. They provide a wide range of information.
   d. They provide opportunities for depth study and wide coverage.
   e. They provide opportunities to develop research and study skills.
3. Small groups provide pupils with opportunities to learn social skills and to develop good social attitudes as a result of the give-and-take.
4. Small groups can help develop leadership ability.
5. Small groups can help develop self-reliance and self-direction.
6. Small groups add variety and interest to classes.
   a. They make it possible to match method with purpose.
   b. They give a change of pace.
   c. They provide release from the tedium of the ordinary class and give pupils an opportunity to work off their energy through active participation.(5)

Launching Small-Group Work

When students are not familiar with small-group work and lack the social skills necessary to make group work successful, begin working with them slowly. Perhaps the best method is to start off by forming small transitory committees to perform definite tasks (e.g., the bulletin board committee, the lab cleanup committee, the committee in charge of handing out materials for students to work with). The use of buzz groups is another approach often used by teachers to introduce small-group techniques to their students.

Buzz Groups

Buzz groups are small groups of about a half dozen students who discuss a topic freely and informally for about six minutes. Because of these characteristics—six people meeting for six minutes—buzz groups are sometimes called 6 × 6 groups.* Buzz groups are transitory groups called together for a specific immediate purpose. As soon as its mission is accomplished, the group is dissolved.

Buzz groups are extremely useful because they can prevent classes from centering on the teacher or on a small group of dominant (or even domineering) students. They are often used to do the following:

[handwritten note in margin: Buzz Groups are good to launch these ideas]

- Launch large group discussions.
- Reformulate the objectives and background ideas of a discussion that has broken down.
- Decide what to do next.
- Brainstorm.
- Set up rules.
- Exchange ideas and experiences.
- Formulate questions and problems for investigation.
- Formulate questions and problems as a basis for group discussion, to put to guest speakers or panelists, and so on.
- Bring out and speak frankly about controversies and differences.
- Draw out students.
- Share learning gleaned from such experiences as homework, plays, films, and so on.
- Provide a forum for students to express quick reactions to issues.

---

*The term *6 × 6* comes from the army jargon for a six-wheeled vehicle with six-wheel drive. In a buzz group, all the wheels should be drive wheels.

CONDUCTING BUZZ GROUPS   Buzz groups are relatively easy to organize and run. They do have to be planned, however, or they may blow up. Impromptu buzz groups organized on the spur of the moment to solve some classroom exigency (e.g., a disastrous discussion) may work well in experienced classes, but wise teachers keep impromptu buzz groups to a minimum.

Selecting the members of a buzz group is usually done by some simple informal and somewhat arbitrary means. Among the methods used successfully are the following:

1. By the seating plan (e.g., the first four persons in this row, the six students sitting in the first three seats of rows 1 and 2).
2. By the alphabet.
3. By counting off (1, 2, 3, 4, 5, 6; 1, 2, 3, 4, 5, 6).
4. By lottery (e.g., all who draw number 1 from a group of numbered cards are in group one).
5. By virtue of the teacher's knowledge of the students' talents, interests, background, and so on. (There may be times when you will wish to make special provisions based on these characteristics, but usually buzz groups work for such short periods of time that it seems hardly worth the effort.)

Each buzz group should have at least three, but no more than six, members.

To prepare students for the buzz group, take care that the mission for the group is clear and simple. Then make sure that everyone understands the mission and knows what to do. Time limits should be set explicitly. It is better that the time limits be too short than too long—six minutes is usually about right. If the students need more time, you can extend the limit. Each group needs a leader and a recorder or secretary. The choice of leader and secretary is not crucial because of the shortness of the buzz group's life.

FOLLOWING UP THE BUZZ SESSION   At the end of the buzz session, the group may report its conclusions. When group reports are expected, make sure that the students know just what the reporting procedure will be before they start working. A common method of reporting is for each group to appoint a representative to a panel that discusses the suggestions of the buzz groups. When this is done, a recorder may keep an account of the major suggestions on the chalkboard or overhead projector. It is sometimes better to omit the group reports and let the class move from buzz group sessions to a whole-class discussion without any intermediate steps.

The Fishbowl Technique

The fishbowl technique is useful for developing skills in participation and for making group decisions. To conduct the fishbowl technique, use the following procedure:

1. Confront the class with a problem, issue, or conflict that requires a solution or decision.
2. Divide the class into subgroups and arrange the groups around a circle.
3. For each group, select or have them select a representative who will argue the group's position.
4. Give the group members five or six minutes to discuss and to take a position on the problem, issue, or conflict under consideration.
5. Have the representatives of the various groups meet in the center of the circle and argue the case in accordance with their instructions. No one else can talk, but group members may pass instructions to their representatives by written notes.

6. Allow any representative or group to call a recess for group-representative consultation, if it seems necessary.
7. End the fishbowl after a set period of time or when the discussants have reached a decision or resolved the conflict.
8. Follow up the discussion with a critique.(6)

Student Teams

Small student teams are particularly effective since they are a medium for cooperative learning. Cooperative learning is an excellent motivation stimulator, because when students work together toward a common objective, they tend to encourage each other and to reinforce each other's effort. Cooperative learning also tends to produce more and better ideas, to increase retention, and to aid in problem solving. These results are an outcome of three concepts always present in student team cooperative learning: team rewards, individual accountability, and equal opportunities for success.(7)

STUDENT TEAMS—ACHIEVEMENT DIVISIONS   The approach that uses student teams, called achievement division, is best used for teaching well-defined objectives of a low cognitive level. Basically, it follows the direct teaching model described in Chapter 7. Here the teacher presents the lesson to the students, who then divide into pairs to work together on exercises and practice. Within the pairs, the students compare their answers to questions, discuss differences, point out discrepancies and errors, and generally help each other. In this way they not only strengthen their learning, they also motivate each other to do well in order to share in the team reward.(8)

THE JIGSAW APPROACH   The jigsaw approach is really a sort of game in which the students are formed into groups of six or so, and the content to be studied is also formed into an equal number of segments. Then each group member is assigned one of the content segments on which to become expert. The experts in each content segment from each of the groups meet together to discuss their content segments and thus further build up their expertise. Finally, the experts report back to their groups to inform them of what they have learned.

In a slightly different version of the jigsaw technique, all the students read or study the same content material. Then each student is assigned a content area in which he or she is to become an expert. The experts from each group meet together to bone up on their content assignments. After their consultations, they return to their original groups to pass on what they have learned.

GROUP INVESTIGATION   In the group investigation technique, the topic under study is divided into subtopics. Each of these subtopics becomes the province of a subgroup, which divides the subtopic into individual tasks. After the individuals complete their investigations or other tasks, the group combines the individual findings into a group report which is presented to the entire class. This is the technique underlying the procedures of many working committees.

The Working Committee

THE VALUE OF COMMITTEES   Working committees have specific tasks to perform. Although committee groups are not supposed to be ability groups, you should at once recognize that committees do help provide for individual differences in ability and interest. For example, let us suppose a class is studying family life. The class might form one committee to investigate the family life of animals, another to survey adolescent-parent relationships, still another to investigate family life in a polyg-amous society. In such an assignment, students might be able to work on the topic that seems the most interesting to them. Within the committee, students should be allocated different tasks depending on the committee's needs and the students' interest and abilities. Thus, using committees makes it possible for students to assume various degrees of responsibility and to tackle tasks of varying difficulty, as well as to study things interesting to them.

In addition to providing for differences in individuals, teaching via committees has several other values. It allows more students to participate actively than do the class recitation techniques, thus helping students develop skills of leadership, communication, socialization, cooperation, and thinking. Skillfully used, commit-tees can be instrumental in teaching students how to search out, evaluate, and report on scholarly information. Furthermore, by its very nature committee member-ship should help students accept and carry out roles that will be theirs in adult life, for one skill, as important as it is rare in adult life, is that of organizing and carrying out effective committee work. Teaching through committees also makes it possible to combine in-depth teaching with wide coverage. Each committee can delve deeply into its own area and then share its findings with the rest of the class.

SELECTING THE COMMITTEE   Ideally, a committee should consist of four to seven members. Whenever a classroom committee grows to include eight or more mem-bers, it should probably be broken into smaller committees or subcommittees. Committee members can be chosen in many ways. Sometimes you should choose the committee members yourself to suit your own purposes. As a general rule, however, it is probably wise to honor student preferences whenever possible.

In every class, students tend to form natural groups and follow natural leaders. As a rule, it is advantageous to make use of these natural groups and natural lead-ers when forming committees. In this respect the use of sociograms can be particu-larly helpful.

Whereas forming committees according to natural group lines may be advanta-geous, several other requirements must also be considered. Among them are the nature of the committee's task and the interests of the students. One reason for having student committees is to allow students to work at tasks that seem impor-tant to them. You should see to it, insofar as possible, that each student works on the committee in which he or she is most interested. Furthermore, each committee calls for members with different abilities. In choosing committee members, provi-sion should be made for these various abilities.

Whenever possible, committees should be made up of volunteers. This is not always feasible, of course, but you may be able to approach this ideal more closely if all students make two or three choices in writing rather than volunteering orally. Making choices in writing allows the more timid to volunteer without embarrass-ment. Even so, you or a student steering committee working under your guidance will have to make some committee assignments. In either case, take care to see that the membership of each committee meets the criteria noted earlier.

No matter how the group members are selected, keep a record of the committee memberships and committee assignments. Such a record will give you insight into the relationships among the students in your class. Also, it will give you the infor-mation you need to be sure that all students have opportunities to participate to the fullest and to be sure that no one is neglected.

DETERMINING THE COMMITTEE PROCEDURES   Every committee should have a spe-cific mission to perform, and the committee members should have a clear under-standing of what their mission is before they start to work. This task may be assigned to the committee or be the result of group planning. In either case, the work of each committee should further the plan worked out for the entire class.

It is usually more satisfactory to use cooperative group planning than teacher assignments when establishing committee goals and tasks. Even when the task is teacher-assigned, the committee will have to talk over the assignment and map out a plan for attacking it. In general, committee planning follows a procedure something like the following:

1. One of the first things to be done is to appoint or elect a chairperson to lead the committee and a recorder to keep a record of what is done.
2. Next the students discuss their mission and its objectives. In their discussion they consider such questions as "What might we do? What must we do? Exactly what will we do? How will we do it?" and "How do we report what we have done?"
3. Then they work out in detail the subordinate problems and tasks and prepare an outline of how they intend to proceed. In this discussion they must find out what they will need to work with and what is available.
4. Finally, they divide the tasks among the committee members and make provisions for sharing the results of their individual endeavors. For instance, the committee may ask one student to be responsible for securing certain material and another to be responsible for looking up a specific item of information. In the laying out of the work tasks, a form similar to that shown in Figure 8.9 can be most useful.

As soon as this planning is finished, the students work together to complete their task. If this procedure is to succeed, the students must have a clear understanding of the procedures they can use as well as the mission they are supposed to accomplish. Frequently, the students will find that their original plan was not realistic. You, the teacher, should stay alert to detect problems as they may develop. On some occasions, it will be necessary to stop and start over. Open-ended questioning may cut off deficiencies in planning before the problems develop. However, even if you see faults in the proposals early in the planning, be careful not to interfere too quickly. Too much interference may stop the students from thinking for themselves. It is usually better to let students find their own solutions without undue interference or too pointed suggestions. After all, people learn from mistakes, it is

■ FIGURE 8.9
Committee Assignment Form

Committee Work

Form for Assignment of Committee Members

Unit _____

Committee _____

Pupil _____ Job _____

1. _____

2. _____

3. _____

4. _____

said; however, you should certainly do everything in your power to keep the committee from ending in abject failure.

HELPING STUDENT COMMITTEES   Committees usually require a great deal of teacher guidance. Inexperienced students will need much help in determining how they should go about completing their work. They need help in determining their goals, the procedures for fulfilling these goals, and ways of reporting the fruits of their labor to the total group. In advising them, act as a consultant, not as a dictator. Point out alternatives open to them and the dangers inherent in some lines of approach to the problem. Since young people, like adults, are likely to take the line of least resistance and stick to the tried and true, you should take special care to make students aware of different approaches to committee work.

TIPS FOR COMMITTEE WORK   Among the procedures that you may find helpful in carrying out committee work are the following:

1. Teach students how to work in committees before they start working on their own.
2. Discuss committee work and committee procedures with the entire class before they break into committees.
3. Be sure that the committees set up a reasonable time schedule.
4. Check on all groups frequently. Make sure that everyone has a job to do, knows what the job is and how to do it, and is doing it.
5. Check to be sure everyone is certain what the objective is.
6. Help groups as necessary. Use provocative questioning rather than direct suggestions. Point out alternatives. Let students make their own decisions.
7. Provide access to necessary materials. Help students find what they need. A little coaching in library skills may go a long way here.
8. Keep a log of what goes on. In it include committee assignments, committee members, tasks assigned, tasks completed, leadership responsibilities, and the like.
9. Keep a schedule of jobs showing when they are due for completion.
10. Ask for progress reports.
11. If a committee gets stuck, (a) recommend that the members reconsider their objective (perhaps they should change it); (b) get them to consider the strategies and tactics they have used (maybe there are others that might be better); and (c) use Socratic questioning with them to get them to see what they are doing wrong. If possible, let them find out for themselves, but if necessary, tell them what to do.
12. If a group's discipline breaks down, (a) find out what the trouble is; (b) work with students who need help; (c) try role playing; and (d) talk over the problem with the group.
13. If a student causes trouble, (a) talk things over with him or her; (b) try to clarify the student's objectives, tasks, and strategies; (c) let him or her try a new role or a new group; (d) try role playing; and (e) if all else fails, take direct disciplinary action.
14. If a student is shy, (a) encourage him or her all you can; (b) do not push; (c) help the student avoid getting into embarrassing situations; (d) make frequent evaluations and checks; and (e) see to it that his or her contributions are recognized.

Stop and Reflect

Observe your college classes. Do they ever include small-group work? Do you see instances when they might be improved by the use of buzz groups and committee work?

Pick a topic for a course you might teach. What types of committee work or what committee assignments would you suggest for this topic?

How self-directing do you think committees should be?

You find that a committee does not seem to be producing. What would you do to find and correct the trouble?

THE COMMITTEE REPORT   After the committee has accomplished its work, it should report to the class in one way or another. An oral report to the class is a common practice. Unfortunately, oral reports can become deadly, particularly if the class must listen to several of them, one following the other. To relieve the class from boredom, try to space the reports between other activities and see to it that committees report in other ways as well, such as dramatic presentations, panels, tape recordings, written reports, and the like.

EVALUATION OF COMMITTEE WORK   Students can evaluate the effectiveness of committee work as well as anyone else. Self-rating scales, such as those described in the section on evaluating discussions, are excellent. So are discussions in which the students analyze their performance and list the things that they did well and did not do well. More formal reports, such as those shown in Figure 8.10 and Figure 8.11, are also effective. Grambs, Carr, and Fitch recommend the form shown in Figure 8.11.

THE TEACHER'S ROLE   Obviously, then, your role in small-group committee work is very sensitive. You must encourage the students to work on their own initiative, but at the same time see to it that their work is productive. At all times, your students must understand that you are in charge of the class no matter how much freedom you allow them. You must oversee and approve student plans and procedures, as well as be sure that the committee work is properly scheduled and coordinated with other class activities. In this respect, you should note that it is poor practice to

FIGURE 8.10
An Evaluation Form

Group Project Evaluation

1. Did you think the group project succeeded? Why? Why not?

2. Did everyone on the committee carry his or her load?

3. Were the members of the group interested in the project?

4. Which group member do you think contributed most?

5. Was the planning adequate?

6. If you were to do this over again, what would you do differently?

7. What exactly was your contribution?

8. How do you rank your contribution?
   Excellent _____   Average _____   Poor _____

■ FIGURE 8.11

Group Evaluation Form

Jean Grambs, John C. Carr, and Robert M. Fitch, *Modern Methods in Secondary Education* (New York: Holt, Rinehart and Winston, 1970), p. 202.

	Effort	Leadership	Quality of Work	Cooperation
Joe				
Jane				
etc.				
etc.				
etc.				
etc.				
etc.				

try to do all your instruction by means of small groups and committees. It is seldom desirable to give more than two or three consecutive days to small-group or committee work. Rather, such work should be intermixed with other whole-class and individual activities of various sorts.

You must also be sure that students have suitable materials readily available for their use. At times, this duty will require you to make arrangements with the library. At other times, it will mean that you must collect materials yourself. Occasionally, it will mean that you must steer the committee in some other direction because there is no way to provide them with the materials they need. A good procedure may be to require students to establish the availability of resources themselves before committing themselves to any particular problem or course of action. Obviously, teaching by committees requires you to have great knowledge of the content to be covered and the resources available in the area. For this reason, a good resource unit or curriculum guide can be of tremendous assistance.

FOLLOWING UP COMMITTEE WORK   Teaching by small groups and committees requires follow-up. Student reports may do much to tie things together, but by their very nature they tend to leave learning fragmented. Your follow-up is needed to fill in gaps, smooth out rough spots, tie up loose ends, show relationships, and drive home important concepts. Without adequate follow-up, the learning of the committee members may stop dead in a frustrating *cul de sac*. All too often, teachers' neglect of the follow-up step brings the students up to the door of understanding and leaves them standing there at the threshold, so near to and yet so far from real learning.

Special-Interest Groups

When you divide the class into small, special-interest groups, the procedures are similar to those used for conducting committee work:

1. First make the assignment clear to the students and ensure that they have the things they need to work with. If feasible, the group may plan its own procedures. Specialized study guides or learning packets may be extremely useful at this point.
2. If it is a group venture (for example, a group project), see to it that students know what their individual roles are and that all the necessary jobs are cov-

ered. You may have to appoint students to do certain missions. Check to be sure they know how to do what they are supposed to do.

3. Then see to it that they get to work. As the students go about their tasks, supervise them, checking to be sure that they are profiting from their tasks, guiding and helping as seems necessary, and even teaching directly when it seems desirable.

4. After the group has finished its work, check up on the students' results, evaluating, correcting, reteaching, and generally following up as necessary.

Stop and Reflect

Do you see any advantage to using the formal report forms for evaluating committee work? What advantage?

Too often committees are made up of one or two persons who do all the work and other committee members who let them. How would you proceed to see to it that committee members all chip in to do their share of the committee work? How would you see to it that committees do not waste their time in unproductive activity and goofing off?

Some Caveats

In spite of the many advantages of using small-group work, sometimes small groups fail. There is often a pedagogical reason for such failures. Perhaps the most common one is that the teacher has inadequately prepared the group. The goal of the groups and the role of the workers may not be sufficiently defined. It is most important to establish what is to be done and the procedure to be followed before the group begins. Also make sure that the students know how to do what they are supposed to do and have the materials they need to do it with.

Failure sometimes results from the assignment; the task assigned to the group may not be the kind of job that can be done by a group. Perhaps it is too complicated, perhaps too simple, or perhaps it is something that should be done by individual study or projects.

Failures are sometimes caused by inappropriate groups in which the students do not get along with each other or in which the members are not capable of performing the tasks required. Consequently, you need to be careful when selecting group members.

Sometimes students have simply not learned to work together as a group. The young people who come to our classes may or may not have learned to work in groups when they were in earlier grades. It may be necessary to work with these students before they will be prepared to carry out small-group assignments successfully.

Lack of student motivation can make any approach fail. You should do everything you can to make small-group activities enticing. In every case, group work should center as much as possible on student concerns and ideas. Students work best when a project is their own, so involve them with the planning. The more relevant a project is to the students' lives and concerns, the more likely they are to work on it.

Stop and Reflect

Observe classes that have been divided into small groups.
Are the students clear about what they should be doing?

Are all participating?
Is someone in charge?
Does the group process seem to be productive and efficient?

SUMMARY

Because of the characteristics of classroom groups, some of the most effective teaching is group teaching, that is, teaching by and through groups and group methods. By using committee work and discussion, teachers can quite often increase their teaching efficiency. This type of teaching is frequently effective in changing attitudes, ideals, and appreciation. It is particularly useful in raising learning above the verbalizing level. Thus, group methods often lead to thorough, permanent learning. Although teaching by group methods takes considerable time and effort, the results are usually worth it.

A discussion is not a monologue, a question-and-answer period, or a bull session. Rather, it is a controlled conversation in which participants pool their thoughts on a topic or problem in a purposeful, orderly way. The discussion leader's task is to lead the group into fruitful dialogue without dominating the participants or allowing them to meander. In this task, the aid of a good recorder is extremely desirable. Observers can help the group learn how to discuss matters more effectively. Formal discussion techniques are often not as useful as informal discussions, but techniques such as the British debate and the jury system can be used, often with telling results, for getting students to examine, to think about, and to analyze critical issues and problems.

Discussions, committee work, reports, and the like call for expertise in speech. To raise standards in this area, students need to be taught. One of the methods useful for this purpose is oral reading. Of course this activity will be of no avail unless the students are taught how to do it well.

Teaching via student teams and committees has become quite popular. It is an effective means of providing for individual differences and laboratory experiences as well as involving students in active learning. Well done, teaching via committees helps to build a classroom climate that is supportive of learning. The membership of student committees may be determined in several ways, but when feasible, you should take advantage of natural student leadership and groups. Although student committee members should do the bulk of their own planning and research, you must always be ready in the background with necessary help and guidance. Sharing the results of the committee work with the rest of the class can be a particular problem. You should place considerable stress on lively, original reporting and serious, careful class follow-up of committee work.

ADDITIONAL READING

Adams, D. M., and M. E. Hamm. *Cooperative Learning: Critical Thinking and Collaboration Across the Curriculum.* Springfield, IL: Charles C. Thomas, 1990.

Cohen, E. G. *Designing Group Work.* New York: Teachers College Press, 1987.

Dillon, J. T. *Questioning and Discussion: A Multidisciplinary Study.* Norwood, NJ: Abley Publishing, 1988.

Dishon, D., and P. W. O'Leary. *A Guidebook for Cooperative Learning: A Technique for Creating More Effective Schools.* Holmes Beach, FL: Learning Publications, 1984.

Fox, W. M. *Effective Group Problem Solving.* San Francisco: Jossey-Bass, 1987.

Gall, M. D., and J. P. Gall. "The Discussion Method." In *The Psychology of Teaching Methods. The Seventy-fifth Yearbook of the National Society for the Study of Education, Part I*, edited by N. L. Gage. Chicago, IL: University of Chicago Press, 1976.

Hilke, E. V. *Cooperative Learning, Fastback 299.* Bloomington, IN: Phi Delta Kappa Educational Foundation, 1990.

Johnson, D. W. et al. *Circles of Learning: Cooperation in the Classroom.* Alexandria, VA: Association for Supervision and Curriculum Development, 1984.

Johnson, D. W., and R. T. Johnson. *Cooperation and Competition: Theory and Research.* Edina, MN: Interaction Book Co., 1990.

Johnson, D. W., and R. T. Johnson. *Learning Together and Alone,* 3rd ed. Boston: Allyn and Bacon, 1991.

Johnson, D. W., and R. T. Johnson, eds. *Structuring Cooperative Learning: Lesson Plans for Teachers.* Minneapolis, MN: Interaction Book Co., 1984.

Kagan, S. *Cooperative Learning Resources for Teachers.* Riverside, CA: University of California, 1989.

Kohn, A. "Group Grade Grubbing versus Cooperative Learning." *Educational Leadership* 48 (February 1991): 83–87.

Schmuck, R. A., and P. A. Schmuck. *Group Processes in the Classroom,* 5th ed. Dubuque, IA: Brown, 1988.

Sharon, S. *Cooperative Learning: Theory and Research.* New York: Praeger, 1990.

Sharon, S., and H. Shachar. *Language and Learning in the Cooperative Classroom.* New York: Springer-Verlag, 1988.

Slavin, R. *Cooperative Learning: Student Teams,* 2nd ed. Washington, DC: National Education Association, 1987.

Slavin, R. *Cooperative Learning: Theory, Research and Practice.* Englewood Cliffs, NJ: Prentice-Hall, 1990.

Slavin, R. "Small Group Methods" in *International Encyclopedia of Teaching and Teacher Education*, edited by M. J. Dankin. New York: Pergamon, 1987.

Wasserman, S. *Asking the Right Questions, Fastback 343.* Bloomington, IN: Phi Delta Kappa Educational Foundation, 1992.

Weil, M., and B. Joyce. *Social Models of Teaching: Expanding Your Teaching Repertoire.* Englewood Cliffs, NJ: Prentice-Hall, 1978.

N O T E S

1. J.T. Dillon, *Teaching and the Art of Questioning* (Bloomington, IN: Phi Delta Kappa Educational Foundation, 1983).
2. Ibid.
3. William H. Burton, Roland B. Kimball, and Richard L. Wing, *Education for Effective Thinking* (New York: Appleton, 1960), 327.
4. Gladys Veidemanis, "A Curriculum View of Classroom Discussion," *English Journal* 51 (January 1962): 21–25.
5. Leonard H. Clark, *Teaching Social Studies in Secondary Schools: A Handbook* (New York: Macmillan, 1973), 95.
6. Joseph F. Callahan and Leonard H. Clark, *Teaching in the Middle and Secondary Schools,* 3rd ed. (New York: Macmillan, 1988), 223.
7. Robert E. Slavin, *Cooperative Learning: Student Teams* (Washington, DC: National Education Association, 1987).
8. Ibid.

Chapter 9

Thinking and Inquiring

Stuffed only with facts.
Anatole France

▪▪▪ Overview

The ability to think is a basic requirement for students' success in inquiry learning. Unfortunately, skill in thinking is not the easiest skill to attain. Therefore, if your students are to be successful thinkers and learners, you must take time to teach them directly how to perform the various thinking skills. In doing so, you must carefully explain and model what the thinker must do to carry out the thinking skill well, and then provide a lot of well-monitored practice. This practice can be individualized or carried on as a cooperative group venture in which students examine their thinking processes via self-talk analysis of their actions. Once the students have caught on, then they should practice using their thinking skills in heuristic activities.

One of the oldest principles of teaching is that learners must do their own learning and develop their own understandings, skills, and attitudes; therefore, the teacher's job is not so much to impart knowledge as to help and guide the students as they discover the meanings, practice the skills, and undergo the experiences that will shape their learning. This notion is the basis for the discovery, or inquiry, approach to teaching. In this heuristic approach, teachers try to actively involve students in the learning process. Among the techniques teachers may use to encourage discovery or inquiry learning are skillful questioning, discussions, problem solving, springboards, and case studies—to name only a few. These strategies and techniques are attractive because they have high motivating value and help students to develop intellectual skills, including skill in thinking rationally, seeing relationships, understanding processes, and building values and attitudes. As a rule, inquiry or discovery strategies can be depended upon to build firm concepts and deep understandings.

This approach does not preclude the teacher's presentation of information to students. For students to rediscover and re-create all knowledge would be most inefficient. The principal point in discovery teaching is, rather, to provide many instances for students to draw inferences from data by using logical thinking, inductive or deductive, as the case may be. The more realistic and down-to-earth the inquiry learning, the better, which is why community-involvement activities, simulation, role-playing activities, and real problems are so effective.

In this chapter, we investigate a number of heuristic methods for learning and developing thinking skills via inquiry and discovery.

▪▪▪ Teaching Thinking Skills

Undoubtedly the most important goal for American education is to teach students to think clearly and well, for as Louis Raths has stated, in a democracy like ours, people "cannot be both stupid and free."(1) For this reason, in recent years scholars have concocted numerous schemes for teaching students how to think.* Many of these schemes are set apart from the regular classroom curriculum, and to use them, teachers must obtain special training. Other methods, more general and less esoteric, are available for use in regular classes during the progress of ordinary courses. They include the direct teaching of the various thinking skills and the use of inquiry and problem-solving type approaches involving the use of these skills. We discuss some of these methods in this chapter.

---

*For example CoRT (Cognitive Research Trust), the Thinking Skills Program, the Learning to Learn Thinking Improvement Program, the Instrumental Enrichment Program, and the Strategic Reasoning Program.

According to John Barell, thinking is the process of searching for and creating meaning.(2) It involves creating symbols, metaphors, analyses, and so forth, and establishing relationships between the "world of the particular and the ideas and concepts that give them stature." In short, thinking is a search for meaning, and it is the type of experimenting one undergoes when one does not know precisely what to do.(3)

Any action you take to give meaning to things or to determine what you ought to do is a thinking operation. Among these operations are the following:

Summarizing
Comparing
Classifying
Interpreting
Criticizing
Developing valid inferences
Identifying assumptions
Imagining
Collecting, organizing, analyzing, and applying data
Hypothesizing
Decision making
Testing data
Designing projects
Applying rules of logic
Generalizing(4)

Students' Thinking Faults

To a degree, using these operations comes naturally. After all, all of us can think a little. Nevertheless, skill in the use of these applications seldom rubs off from casual encounters. Rather, these skills have to be carefully taught—another instance of practice, under guidance, making perfect. Over the years, students have not only not learned to be skillful thinkers, but have also picked up a number of faults that reduce the effectiveness of their thinking, such as

1. Impulsiveness
2. Overdependence on the teacher
3. Inability to concentrate
4. Rigidity and inflexibility
5. Dogmatic assertive behavior
6. Extreme lack of confidence
7. Missing the meaning
8. Resistance to thinking(5)

Fortunately, research evidence indicates that plenty of practice in thinking skills, provided in well-conducted classes, can, over a period of time, reduce these faults considerably if the practice is accompanied by exposure to various types of thinking operations, judicious use of rewards, and thoughtful teacher guidance.(6)

Teaching Thinking Directly

Although we see that practice in thinking skills does tend to improve students' effectiveness, practice is not enough. As in the development of any other skill, thinking skills are best initially taught according to the direct teaching model described in Chapter 7. According to this model, to teach a thinking skill well, the skill must be properly introduced and then the students must be given guided practice, followed by independent practice and teaching for transfer. In carrying out this model, if the thinking skills are to become really usable, the pupils must not only practice until the skills become considerably overlearned, but also they must practice the skills in a variety of contexts to facilitate transfer. For example, Beyer recommends the following procedure for introducing a new thinking skill:

1. The teacher introduces the skill . . . by writing the label on the board, developing synonyms and a definition for the skill, and helping students recall similar examples of where they may have performed the skill or seen someone do it earlier.
2. The teacher then describes how an expert executes the skill, instead of asking students to practice it. A teacher who chooses this strategy to introduce making an analogy would at this point explain step-by-step how the skill is executed, . . .
3. The teacher next demonstrates the skill with whatever contributions students care to volunteer, highlighting important operational cues as the demonstration proceeds.
4. After discussing reasons for executing the skill procedures and any relevant knowledge, the teacher then has students apply what they have seen, heard, and discussed to executing the skill themselves.
5. To conclude this introductory lesson the teacher guides students in reflecting on and discussing the extent to which they followed the steps modeled for them, what they did mentally to execute the skill, any modifications they thought they were making in the modeled procedure, and what they learned about the skill.(7)

During a lesson of this sort, you must concentrate on the thinking techniques, not the course content. The course subject matter should be postponed until the next lesson.

When teaching these techniques, give the students specific instruction in the various cognitive processes—for example, what to do when making comparisons, how to check to see if data are accurate, and how to go about making decisions. For instance:

1. *Decision making*   Point out that to make decisions you must get the necessary data, categorize them pro and con, weigh the evidence resulting from your analysis, and then make your decision.
2. *Generalization*   Show pupils that generalizations are really abstractions formed by the process of synthesizing bits of information and experience, then making a hypothesis, and, if possible, verifying it.
3. *Comparing and contrasting*   First define the skill; then present the objects or ideas to be compared. Next, have the students note the similarities and the differences; then note which of these similarities and differences are important. Finally, sum up the significant similarities and differences.
4. *Creative thinking*   To develop creative thinking, use such techniques as brainstorming, encouraging students who come forth with new or different ideas, and elaborating on ideas.
5. *Criticism*   Ask students to read or examine an article. Have them set standards and then determine what seems good and what not. Note: Criticism does not mean finding fault, but judging worth.
6. *Hypothesizing*   Present problem material to the class with plenty of information. Let students propose possible solutions based on the information available, and then, if possible, have them test the solution's validity.
7. *Interpreting*   Present students with information and let them draw conclusions from it. For example, some teachers ask students to draw conclusions from articles from which the author's conclusions have been removed. Later, the teacher gives the students the author's conclusions and compares them with those of the students.

8. *Assumptions*   Present students with material that presents conclusions. Ask them to determine on what assumptions the conclusions were based. In mathematics, for instance, ask them, "If you believe this answer to be true, what else do you have to believe?"(8)

9. *Analysis*   First, determine what you wish to find out. Then, break down the material being investigated into elements, and search the material piece by piece so as to establish the relationships among the elements. Now, identify the organizing principles underlying the relationship of the various elements to the whole. Finally, summarize what the elements and their relationships are and their significance.

10. *Logical analysis*   Point out that people seldom think logically. Human thinking powers are far too unsystematic and disorderly for that. Rather, logical thinking is a key for *post hoc* analysis of the validity of arguments, ideas, positions, or what have you. So give your students opportunities to apply the rules of logic to your course content. Let them look for such violations as the assumption that because B follows A, A causes B; statistical fallacies; argument from anecdote; argument from insufficient evidence; and false analogies in newspapers, advertisements, other students' writing, and even in the course's reading material. Those explanations should all be part of your initial presentation of the skill, but you will find that your students will need additional help and clarification as the practice sessions go on and as they try to apply these skills in your courses.

Instead of marking and grading papers, you may want to use a code like the following suggested by Raths and his colleagues to indicate possible logical flaws in students' writing.

X   All or none. Do you really mean always? Is this an overstatement?

E—O   Either—Or. Do you really mean one of two ways? Must it be one or the other?

Q   Qualifying words or phrases. Do you want to qualify, or say it straight out?

I—T   If—Then. Does the "then" really follow the "if"?

An   Analogy. Is this a true analogy?(9)

This type of feedback should be introduced very slowly. The idea of the system is to induce students to examine the logic of what they say and to judge whether they are saying what they really want to say.

After the students become really familiar with these codes, they can use them to examine student papers, published articles, newspaper stories, and even the course texts.

In your initial presentation, and in subsequent reviews and explanations of the procedures, in addition to explaining the skills to the students it usually helps for you to model the skills. In modeling, run through an example of the skill step by step, explaining your thoughts as you go along so that the students can see clearly what is entailed in the skill. Another tactic to make the presentation clear is to provide graphic organizers that visually portray the elements in the thinking process being described. These organizers might include such graphics as Venn diagrams, story maps, criteria grids, and flow charts.(10)

Scaffolds

Barak Rosenshine recommends the use of scaffolds when teaching higher level cognitive strategies. Scaffolds, according to his definition, are "forms of support provided by the teacher (or another student) to help students bridge the gap between their current abilities and their intended goal."(11) They consist of concrete prompts, i.e. "scaffolds specific to the strategy being taught yet general enough to allow application to a variety of different contexts which may be used as a basis for thinking."(12) Often teachers may place these prompts on cue cards to help students find their way in developing the particular skill. Then, having presented the cues, the teacher may model the learning procedure. Another procedure is for the teacher to think aloud as he or she goes through the learning process. This amounts to describing what one is doing and what one should do next, for example,

"Now what does that mean?"
"How can I use this idea?"
"What is the use (value) of this approach?" etc.

As the students progress toward learning the cognitive strategy, the teacher reduces the prompts until the students are on their own and begin to use the strategy independently.

MONITORING THE PRACTICE   After the initial presentation of the workings of the teaching skill comes the time for the students to practice—first under guidance and then independently. Carefully monitor these practice sessions to help individual students stay on the right track so that they do not become badly lost. In addition to monitoring, take advantage of the potentials found in cooperative learning teams and in student self-tutoring. It may seem odd to you, but many people have found it helpful to talk themselves through the thinking process. As they work at the processes, they tell themselves, "Now I am going to do this because . . . ," or "Perhaps it would be better to do this . . . ," or "Evidently that fits over here," and so on. It may be even more helpful if students work in pairs or groups of three or four. In a pair or small group, the thinker explains at each step what he or she is doing and why, while the other student (or students) acts as coach, monitoring the thinker's thinking processes and correcting and helping whenever it seems desirable. Cooperative learning teams in which four students work together to solve problems and share each others' learning have worked well in mathematics.(13)

In any case, encourage students to think about their thinking. In your monitoring, ask students to explain their reasoning, the thought processes they used or are using, why they did what they did, why they are doing what they are doing, what data they need, and what plans they have for the next steps. Alert them to the dangers of vagueness and help them to define correctly the terms they are using. Require them to be specific, accurate, and precise in their language, comparisons, and descriptions. Help them use linguistic clues in their reading to identify the relationships among ideas presented in sentences and paragraphs and to form a basis for making inferences.

Avoid giving students solutions to their problems. Finding solutions is their job. You have no need to be the font of all wisdom; instead, let students figure things out from the data you have given them, or you helped them find, or they have found on their own.

THE ROLE OF CONTENT   Although teaching thinking skills is of high importance, we must remember that thinking is not only process; it also involves facts. Obviously, skill in thinking is not of much use to anyone unless he or she has sufficient dependable information on which to base the thinking. Therefore, it is the way teachers work with the content of instruction that affects the way students learn to think effectively.

Consequently, in your teaching you must use activities by which students learn information as well as activities that advance their skill in thinking. You cannot teach thinking skills if you limit yourself to textbook teaching alone. If students spend most of their time on textbooks and workbook exercises that call for single correct answers, they will never learn higher-level cognitive skills. Teaching for thinking requires additional hard work, creative instruction, and hours of practice.(14) "It cannot be overemphasized that the teaching of thinking does not take place by working directly with the mental processes. It is the way that teachers work with content of instruction that affects the way students learn to think effectively."(15)

A Hospitable Atmosphere   If such thinking skill techniques are to prove successful in the long run, we must take care to create in our classes an atmosphere in which students feel free to "take risks, to experiment with alternative behaviors, to make mistakes without being chastised, and to learn from failures."(16) To do so allows students to speak up. When students speak out, listen to what they say. Encourage them to express their own ideas. Give them opportunities to observe, react, compare and contrast, examine, classify and interpret data and assumptions, suggest hypotheses, and to take on real problems. Do not be upset if students make mistakes in these endeavors. If they are wrong, let their errors become the basis for reconsideration and the building of new understandings. Use facilitative feedback to help them improve their skills and understanding. Give them plenty of time to think, to find right answers, and to gain confidence. Avoid harsh, punitive feedback, heckling, or impossible assignments. In short, let students know that thinking can be difficult work but very rewarding, and show them how to make it pay off. Be sure that they understand that it is they who must do the learning; learning is a student-centered responsibility.

Using the Skills   Once you have introduced the various thinking skills, it is time to use them in indirect heuristic teaching strategies. In these strategies (also called *inductive teaching* or *discovery teaching*) "students are led with little teacher support to discover abstract principles from concrete instances and make connections among seemingly disconnected events."(17) Heuristic methods are methods by which the teacher induces the students to learn for themselves. These methods minimize teaching by telling and maximize learning by doing. Heuristic learning includes such strategies as discovery learning, controlled discussion, problem solving, simulation, sociodrama, dyadic role playing, inductive teaching, and even, at times, deductive reasoning. Any method by which students figure things out for themselves is heuristic teaching. It includes the methods most often recommended for achieving the highest cognitive objectives.

Inquiry Teaching

When teaching by heuristic inquiry or discovery strategies, assume the role of guide rather than dictator. As a guide to student learning, try to raise problem issues and questions that will pique the students' interest and call for further investigation. Encourage the students to pursue these matters and guide them in their investigations, helping them to clarify the issues, the facts, and their own thinking as well as to draw reasonable conclusions. Then carry the students a step or two further by inducing them to test their conclusions and generalizations and apply them to other situations.

A major aim of inquiry teaching is to stimulate independent resourceful thinking. To that end, use such tactics as the following:

■ Checking the students' data-gathering techniques.
■ Asking thought questions.
■ Asking for interpretations, explanations, and hypotheses.
■ Questioning the interpretations, explanations, and hypotheses that the students arrive at.
■ Asking students to draw conclusions from their data and information.
■ Asking students to apply their principles and conclusions to other situations.
■ Asking students to check their thinking and their logic.
■ Confronting students with problems, contradictions, fallacies, implications, value assumptions, value conflicts, and other factors that may call for reassessment of their thinking and positions.

In carrying out these tactics, it is extremely important to keep the climate supportive. Students must be encouraged to think, even though sometimes the conclusions they draw may be somewhat bizarre. To encourage thinking try to:

■ Accentuate the positive.
■ Encourage students by showing approval and by providing clues.
■ Accept for examination all legitimate hypotheses and means by which students attempt to arrive at truth.
■ Encourage the exchange and discussion of ideas.
■ Create an open atmosphere in which students feel free to contribute and to analyze the various ideas, interpretations, and logical processes.

Try to foster an atmosphere of earnest thinking, free debate, open discussion, and, above all, freedom so that students can try to think things out without fear of reprisal for errors in reasoning.

As said before, this teaching method can be very effective. However, when teaching middle school students, you should remember that few students can really understand abstract learning until they are 12 or 13 years old, and many are not ready for this type of learning until they are older.

Inductive Lesson

As presented by Eggen and Kauchak, the inductive lesson model is a structured example of inquiry teaching. These lessons consist of the following four phases:

1. *Open-ended questioning*   In this phase, you present the students with an example of the concept or generalization to be used. Then you ask questions concerning students' observation of the example. These questions are open-ended; that is, they do not require any specific correct answer so that almost any answer can be accepted. Since almost any answer is acceptable, student answers to open-ended questions are seldom wrong, a fact that tends to increase student motivation markedly.

2. *The convergent phase*   Narrow the questions so that the students' responses will bring out the basic characteristics or relationships of the concept or generalization. In this process, use prompting questions and repetition questions—that is, questions which give students clues or prompts to the answers and that ask students to recall what has already been stated in the class.

3. *Closure*   During closure, students draw conclusions and state them formally. In the case of a concept, their conclusions would be stated as a formal definition; in

the case of a generalization, it would be a statement describing the relationships that make up the generalization.

4. *Application*   The final step in this inductive lesson model is for students to apply their learning by classifying examples or making up examples of their own. After this application phase comes homework or exercises by which to reinforce and clinch the learning.(18)

Stop and Reflect
Develop a lesson plan for an inductive lesson in a course you might teach.

The Socratic Method

In the fifth century B.C., Socrates, the great Athenian teacher, used the art of questioning so successfully that to this day we still speak of the Socratic method. Socrates's strategy was to ask his pupils a series of leading questions that gradually snarled them up to the point where they had to look carefully at their own ideas and to think rigorously for themselves. In several ways his technique foreshadowed the most progressive teaching of the most ardent progressivists. Socratic discussions were informal dialogues taking place in a natural, easy, pleasant environment. The motivation of the students was natural and spontaneous although sometimes Socrates had to go to considerable lengths to ignite his students' intrinsic interest. In his dialogues, Socrates tried to aid students in developing ideas. He did not impose his own notions on the students. Rather, he encouraged the students to develop their own conclusions and to draw their own inferences. Of course, Socrates usually had preconceived notions about what the final learning should be and carefully aimed his questions so that the students would arrive at the conclusions desired. Still, his questions were open-ended. The students were free to go wherever the facts led them.

Many teachers have tried to adapt the Socratic method to the modern secondary school. In some cases, it has proved to be quite successful. However, it must be remembered that Socrates used this method in the context of a one-to-one relationship between the student and the teacher. Some teachers have adapted it for ordinary class use by asking questions first of one student and then of another, moving about the class slowly. This technique may work well, but it is difficult because the essence of the Socratic technique is to build question on question in a logical fashion so that each question leads the student a step further toward the understanding sought. When you spread the questions around the classroom, you may find it difficult to build up the desired sequence and to keep all the students with the argument. Sometimes you may be able to make use of the Socratic method by directing all the questions at one student—at least for several minutes—while the other students look on. This is the way Socrates did it. When the topic is interesting enough, this technique can be quite successful and even exciting, but in the long run the Socratic technique works best in small-group sessions, seminars, and tutorial sessions with individual students.

To conduct a class by the Socratic technique, (1) pose a problem to the class, and (2) ask the students a series of probing questions that will cause them to examine critically the problem and their solution to the problem. The main thrust of the questioning and the key questions must be planned in advance so that the questioning will proceed logically. To think of good probing questions on the spur of the moment is too difficult.

Controlled or Guided Discussion

The controlled or guided discussion is a variation of the Socratic discussion frequently advocated by proponents of discovery or inquiry teaching. It consists simply of (1) providing the students with information by means of lecture, reading, film, or some other expository device, and (2) by the use of probing questions, as in the Socratic method, guiding the students to derive principles and to draw generalizations from the material presented. This method differs from a true discussion in that it is teacher-centered with the teacher doing most of the questioning, and differs from true inquiry in that the principles and generalizations to be arrived at by the students have been decided by the teacher in advance. The controlled discussion is not ordinarily an open-ended method of teaching, although there is no reason why it should not be.

Springboard Techniques

A *springboard* is any type of presentation that can be used as a jumping-off point for a discussion, research project, or inquiry activity. Springboards serve both as sources of information and as motivating devices. They give the students something to work on and some reason for working on it. One use of the springboard can be seen in the controlled discussion technique that was explained earlier in this chapter. Movies, still pictures, playlets, role playing, models, textbook selections, and anecdotes are only a few examples of what can be used as springboards. Anything that lends itself to such questions as Why? So what? How can this be true? or If this is so, then what? can be used as a springboard. Usually the teacher must follow up the springboard with questions that will bring out ideas, relationships, or conclusions to be discovered, analyzed, or evaluated. A really effective springboard is so stimulating that the students are eager to investigate without further prompting. Parables, contrived incidents, and value sheets are examples of springboards.

The method of the parable used in Biblical times is really a kind of controlled discussion. To employ this approach, relate an incident or story and then use it as a springboard, asking probing questions until your students see, from their own thinking, the principle you wish to get across. As used by the great teachers of yore, the point of the parable often was definite and obvious. The parable can be used to introduce open-ended debate and discussion as well, however.

Contrived incidents are simply exciting incidents realistically staged by the teacher to get students to react and think. To all appearances, the incidents are real until the teacher and players let the class in on the secret. For example, a couple of students might come into the class and start a loud argument with each other about a controversial issue. On a signal they would stop the argument and the teacher would launch a discussion on the merits and demerits of the proposition under discussion. Role-playing techniques may be used in the same way.

Value sheets consist of a presentation of an issue, a situation, or an incident followed by a series of questions that focus on the values raised by the presentation. The presentation may be in the form of a short statement or anecdote written on the value sheet itself, or can be presented by some other springboard technique such as role playing, tape recording, videotape, or story. The purpose of the technique is for the students to study the presentation and then answer the value sheet questions in writing. Since these questions deal with the values aroused by the springboard incident or statement, they have no right answers—they require only the personal opinions of individual students. You can then use one of the following procedures as a follow-up:

1. Have a class discussion based on the questions and answers in the value sheet.
2. Have a small-group discussion based on the value sheets.
3. Read certain selections from the value sheets without commenting or identifying the writer.
4. Have the students turn all the value sheets over to a committee that will analyze them and present to the group the various positions taken by the students in the class.

Reaction sheets are the same as value sheets except that the questions asked may cover a wider range. They may have to do with beliefs, attitudes, logic, reasoning, morals, judgment—in fact, any type of question that will get the students thinking. They may be followed up in any of the ways that value sheets are, or they may be made the basis for vigorous intellectual inquiry.

Stop and Reflect

Read Meno by Plato. Here Socrates describes his theory of teaching and illustrates his techniques. What do you see as the virtues of Socrates's basic strategy? Do you see faults?

Basically, a controlled discussion is an attempt to adapt the Socratic technique to large groups. Build a plan for conducting a controlled-discussion lesson for a course you might teach.

How open-ended do you think a controlled discussion ought to be? For what purposes are controlled discussions best suited? For which open discussions?

What sort of activities could you use for springboards in your courses? Give some specific examples. The controlled discussion is one type of activity you can initiate by a springboard. Can you think of examples of other types of activities? Give specific examples.

What is the difference between the use of a springboard and set induction?

The Problem-Solving Approach

Perhaps problem solving should not be called a teaching technique; rather, it is a general strategy in which the teacher can use many different techniques and tactics. Many theorists feel it to be the most effective of all teaching strategies. It has been used successfully with both individuals and groups. For example, solving problems through group activity has been used extensively in teaching and in business and government.

Whether a problem is solved by an individual or by a group, the general technique is about the same. Perhaps this explains in part the popularity of problem solving. It seems to be the natural way to learn.

Problem solving is a sophisticated form of trial-and-error learning. It provides people a chance to learn from their successes and failures. Furthermore, because it provides students with an opportunity to become really involved in their learning, problem solving may lead to real understanding in a way that memorization and drill seldom can. A brief review of the steps of this technique shows how actively the student participates in learning through problem solving:

1. The learner becomes aware of the problem.

2. The learner defines and delimits the problem.
3. The learner gathers evidence that may help solve the problem.
4. The learner forms a hypothesis of what the solution to the problem is.
5. The learner tests the hypothesis.
6. The learner successfully solves the problem, or repeat steps 3, 4, and 5, or 4 and 5, until the problem is solved, or gives up.[*]

SELECTING THE PROBLEM   Although problem solving is a natural way to learn, as a general rule, students do not naturally become expert in the techniques of problem solving. This is particularly true when the class attempts to solve problems by group techniques.

Students need help in finding suitable problems. Sometimes you may find it necessary to suggest problems or to suggest areas in which students may seek problems. When suggesting a problem to a group, it may be better to propose the problem directly, or you may prefer to set the stage in such a way that the problem will suggest itself to the students.

For instance, in a social studies class the teacher introduced a problem by telling the class about the number of people in the country who do not vote. She cited figures showing how light the voting was in the local municipal election. This led to a discussion of why citizens do not exercise their franchise. From this discussion the students developed two problems: What causes the apathy of our citizens? What can be done to get people to vote in city elections? In another class, the teacher launched a group problem by asking the following question: How does a plant get its food? After a short discussion, the group set out to find the answer to the problem.

No matter what source students are given in which to find their problem, they will probably need guidance in selecting a suitable problem, for, left alone, even the most experienced adolescent, or group of adolescents, may flounder. Sometimes they can find no problems at all; sometimes they select problems not suitable to the course; sometimes they select problems whose solution requires materials and equipment beyond the school's resources; sometimes they select problems too big and unyielding, and blithely set out to solve in a weekend problems their elders have struggled with for centuries. In view of these considerations, you and your students should cooperatively test the problems to be selected against such criteria as: Is this problem pertinent? Is the necessary material available? Can it be completed in the time allotted?

Stop and Reflect

Prepare a complete list of questions you feel should be considered when testing to determine whether a problem should be selected or not.

Prepare a list of eight or ten problems that young people might attempt to solve while studying a topic in your field of major interest. Where might you advise students to search for suitable problems in the context of such a topic?

"To be worthwhile, problems should be real and have real solutions." Explain. Do you agree? How are such problems created and carried through to a conclusion?

Why is it often claimed that all secondary school learning should be of the problem-solving variety? Do you agree? Why, or why not?

DEFINING THE PROBLEM   Once the problem has been selected, it is important to help the students clarify and define it by means of questions and suggestions. The

---

[*]Based on the analysis of the thought process by John Dewey.

important thing is to get the problem sharply defined so that the students know exactly what they want to find out. Beginning teachers sometimes neglect this step. When they do, students find it difficult to know exactly what they are expected to do, which is, of course, a handicap in solving any problem.

Let us suppose that the problem selected is: Why does an airplane fly? The problem is quickly and easily defined, for it is obvious to all that we are to find out what it is that keeps an airplane up in the air. Yet, even with such an easily defined problem, you may have to make it clear to some students that this problem does not refer to helicopters or to rockets.

SEARCHING FOR CLUES   Once the students have defined their problem, they should start to look for clues to the solution, which involves amassing data on which to base a hypothesis. Here you can be of great help to your students. You can point out areas in which to look for clues; you can provide the necessary materials, or see to it that they are available; you can provide references; and you can acquaint the students with the tools by which they can gather data.

Even when solving group problems, gathering evidence may best be done by individuals or small groups. After a period of individual searching for information, the group can meet to pool the data gained and to attempt to find a solution to the problem.

For instance, if the problem were to prepare a menu suitable for a week's camping trip for a group of teenagers, individual students might gather the information necessary for solving this problem. Once they have in their possession information concerning what the components of a healthful, well-balanced diet are, what foods make up these components, and any other pertinent data, they might attempt to build suitable menus individually. The final menu could be made during a class discussion in which the individual suggestions are evaluated and combined.

An excellent way to handle such discussions is to have an individual or group present to the class a solution to the problem, and then let the class review the proposal and suggest improvements. In the menu problem, for example, before concluding that the problem has been solved, the students should test the menu to be sure it meets the criteria for a healthful, well-balanced camp menu.

SOLVING THE PROBLEM   Preparing the menu in the foregoing example was a case of setting up and testing a hypothesis. Each individual menu prepared was a hypothetical solution to the problem. These solutions were tested by the students until they found one that met the requirements of a healthful, well-balanced diet. When they found such a menu, the problem was solved.

At this stage of solving a problem, young people often need assistance. Many students find it difficult to think of tentative solutions. To help them, Hart suggests that you do the following:

1. Focus on the type of answer they are looking for—"how will they know when we have solved the problem?" Doing so often helps them to define the problem and approach needed for finding a solution.
2. Consider a variety of approaches so as not to be saddled with a possibly unproductive one too early.
3. Examine and evaluate all available data carefully.
4. When a problem is complex, study each of its aspects thoroughly, then leave it to gestate for a while.(19)

Although you should be careful not to solve the problem for your students, you can help them in these processes by pointing out relationships, by asking pointed questions, and by using other similar techniques.

Similarly, you can help the students test their proposed solutions. Unless students first establish appropriate criteria by which to judge the worth of a solution, they may think they have a problem solved when they really have not. Consequently, you should help them set up criteria that will assist them in evaluating whether or not the problem has actually been solved and that will help them check their solutions against the criteria. Without this aid, students often arrive at very poor solutions to their problems.

Stop and Reflect

Select a problem that a student might attempt in one of your classes. Where might the student look for clues? What materials should be available to the student? What tools of research might be needed to gather the necessary data? What skills would the student need? How could you prepare yourself to help a student gather the data for this problem?

The Case-Study Method

Case studies are special components of the problem-solving technique in which the students study individual cases representative of a type of institution, issue, problem situation, or the like in order to draw conclusions about the type as a whole. Case studies are useful because they not only give students insights into knotty problems, they also give them opportunities for study in depth. The latter result is particularly important since at present, much secondary school learning is superficial.

The procedures for conducting case studies are relatively simple, but their execution is difficult. Briefly, the steps in the procedure are as follows:

1. Select a topic to study.
2. Provide the pupils with the necessary means for studying. They should have materials that allow them to explore the problem in depth. Some of the newer texts and curriculum programs on the market provide such materials. Frequently, you and your students will have to gather them for yourselves. Common materials will include reading matter to study, but films, pictures, tapes, laboratory experiments, and the like may be more useful. For many social studies and science topics, fieldwork is the best resource. For instance, in one middle school, the students closely studied the flora and fauna of a small patch of the Jersey swamp which made up part of their science laboratory to see if they could establish certain ecological relationships.
3. The students then study the case. Before they begin their investigations, introduce them to the problem or issue at hand, point out the goals and questions to consider, and establish the ground rules. This orientation can sometimes be done through group-planning techniques. As students proceed with their investigations, they will find study guides very helpful. Some of the newer books and curriculum programs have developed useful study guides. If such are available, you should use them; otherwise, develop guides of your own.
4. Follow up the study with a discussion in which the students share their findings and conclusions. Role playing, panels, symposia, and similar methods of presentation are often effective at this stage. Any technique that helps students examine their own thinking and conclusions will do.

Stop and Reflect

What advantage do you see to using the case-study approach? What technique would you use to generalize knowledge learned in a case study? Is it better to spend time studying a case in detail so as to build full concepts, or is it better to teach these concepts quickly by expository approaches?

The Project

A DEFINITION   A *project* is a natural, lifelike learning activity involving investigation and problem solving by an individual or small group. Ideally, it should consist of a task in which a student sets out to attain some definite goal of real personal value. Projects frequently involve the use and manipulation of physical materials and result in tangible products.

A classic example of such a project is the agriculture project; here students conduct farming enterprises such as raising an animal or a crop. Building and selling a house or installing a solar- or wind-powered energy system by vocational education students are other examples of practical projects of the classic type. A less ambitious project in an academic class might be making a scrapbook anthology for an English class or an illustrated history of the life of the honeybee for a science class.

SELECTING THE PROJECT   Ideally, students should plan, execute, and evaluate the entire project themselves, but your role is important. You must help and guide the students. One of the more important ways you can guide them is in selecting a suitable project. Perhaps you could provide a list of possible projects from which students can choose, or you might suggest readings in which the students can find project ideas. Occasionally, you may be able to stimulate ideas for projects through a class discussion or a teacher talk about what others have done, or by a demonstration of former projects. An interesting device is to have members of previous classes act as consultants and tell the class about some of the projects completed in past years. Of course, students sometimes formulate projects completely on their own; then you need only to approve their plans.

In any case, you should make it a practice to approve a project before a student attempts it, since selecting projects requires sound judgment. The following criteria may help in selecting useful projects:

1. *The project should consist of real learning activities.*   Unless one is careful, projects sometimes turn out to be mere busywork. For example, one such unproductive project was a notebook for an English class that consisted of bibliographies of authors copied from the appendix of the English textbook. Guard against this danger by continually asking yourself, "What learning will result from this project?"
2. *The project should be pertinent to the course.*   Because of their very nature, projects often include materials and activities that spread across many subjects. Consequently, there is a constant danger that the project may get out of the field completely.
3. *The learning to be gained from a project should be worth the time spent on it.*   Not only must you consider the length of time a project will take to be completed, but also you must decide whether the learning might be gained more economically in another way.
4. *The necessary materials and equipment must be available at a reasonable cost.*

CONDUCTING THE PROJECT   Once a project has been selected and approved, the student is ready to proceed with it. As with any other activity, you will find it necessary to help and guide students as they attempt to carry out their plans. However, students can carry a great deal of responsibility for executing these plans. They are also in a particularly good position to evaluate their own progress and its results. Allow your students to accept a good share of this responsibility. Although you should always be ready to help, be careful not to be so solicitous that you stifle the initiative and ingenuity of any student.

RESEARCH PROJECTS   Independent research projects are true inquiry strategies. Students at all levels can profitably conduct independent research activities, but ordinarily the academically talented students are more likely to enjoy and profit from independent study. Students who do not find research activities in keeping with their talents and temperaments should be excused from them. These students, however, may make good contributions to group projects.

Research projects may be done individually or in a group setting. Projects that involve the whole class seem to be very successful at the secondary school level. In either case, the process is the same as that of any other problem-solving activity:

1. Decide exactly what information is to be discovered.
2. Define the problem so that it is manageable in the time available and with the materials and personnel available.
3. Decide what tasks must be done to gather the data necessary and determine who will do each job.
4. Gather the materials and equipment necessary.
5. Perform the data-gathering tasks.
6. Review and analyze the data gathered.
7. Draw conclusions and generalizations from the data gathered.
8. Report the findings and conclusions.

Stop and Reflect

How might you use individual projects in your class? Group projects? Why is it sometimes said that directions for students may be too explicit?

How could you use projects as a means of individualizing classes? How much freedom can you allow talented students in conducting research projects? How would you organize a class to carry out a research project?

Teaching Controversial Issues

Some of the content best-suited for teaching by inquiry and discovery techniques may be controversial. It is not the purpose of classroom instruction to solve controversial issues, but rather to give students an opportunity to become acquainted with the issues, the facts (where they are known), the different positions taken by the various sides, and the arguments supporting the different points of view. Above all, dealing with controversy in the classroom gives the students a chance to learn how to deal with conflict as objectively and wisely as possible. In teaching controversial issues, the emphasis should be not so much on the content as on the process.

According to a policy statement adopted by the New Jersey State Board of Education in December 1949, the following considerations should govern the teaching of controversial issues:

1. Any question that arouses strong reactions in a section of the citizenry is controversial.

2. Controversial questions have a legitimate place in public schools. Students need experience in dealing with such questions. School treatment of such questions should be fair, many-sided, and should help students develop techniques for considering such questions in the future.
3. Indoctrination should not be the goal of the study of controversial questions; rather, it should be learning to see all sides of the questions.
4. Teachers who teach controversial questions must be well-prepared. It would be better that students be uninformed than misinformed.
5. Decisions to teach controversial questions should be based on their timeliness, the maturity of the students, and the purpose of the school.

Selecting the Controversial Issue

Sometimes the study of controversial issues sheds more heat than light. Community feelings run high on many issues. Because some issues can be so touchy, be careful when you select controversial issues for class use. We recommend that before you decide whether or not to include a controversial issue in a course, you should consider such questions as the following:

1. Is the topic pertinent to your teaching goals?
2. Is it worth taking the trouble? Is it important and timely? Is it of concern to all rather than to only a few individuals?
3. Do you know enough about the subject and are you skillful enough to handle the question?
4. Are the students mature enough for rational consideration of the issue? Do they have sufficient background?
5. Can you make enough material available so that students can get a fair picture of the various sides of the issue?
6. Do you have time enough to consider the issue adequately?
7. Is the issue too emotional? Some issues may be too hot to handle. It may be better to omit topics than to disrupt the class and the community.

Once you have decided to tackle a certain controversial issue, you have your work cut out for you. To be sure that all proceeds smoothly and fairly, you must keep on top of the subject with all the teaching skill, tact, sensitivity, and common sense you possess. First, be sure to acquire all the necessary clearances from your supervisors, especially if there seems to be the slightest possibility that the issue will cause an uproar in the community. Then, be sure that all the necessary materials for acquiring the facts and points of view are available. All sides should be fairly represented. If there is to be a classroom discussion of the controversial issue, you must be sure that both you and the students have the background necessary for reasonable discussion. Too often, discussions of controversial issues become an airing of thoughtless prejudices. In the discussion or study, students should have an opportunity to consider all points of view fairly. No student should be cut out simply because of an unpopular point of view; on the other hand, no one should be given more attention than deserved. Neither can you allow errors in fact or logic to go unchallenged.

When pursuing controversial issues, allow students to reach their own conclusions. Avoid influencing them to take one side or another. Be particularly careful not to force your own position on the students, either directly or indirectly. Nevertheless, you do have the right, and perhaps the responsibility, to let students know where you stand so that they will be aware of your biases. You can keep from overinfluencing students by warning them that there are no right answers and by holding back your own position until the end of the discussion.

Sometimes discussions of controversial issues get rather heated. To eliminate this problem, set up guidelines such as the following before the discussion starts:

■ All arguments must be supported by an authority.
■ Everyone must have a chance to be heard.
■ All opinions must be considered respectfully and seriously.
■ No name-calling or "personalities" will be allowed.
■ There will be no direct dyadic argument. (To eliminate arguments, the rules might specify that at least two other students must speak before the same student can speak again, that no one can speak unless recognized by the chairperson, or that no one can make speeches.)

Some Useful Strategies and Tactics

Among the strategies commonly used in the study of controversial issues are the following:

■ Debate
■ Panel discussion
■ Dramatics
■ Role playing
■ Simulation
■ Research techniques (e.g., open-ended problem solving)
■ Interviews
■ Committee work
■ The case-study approach.

Here are some tactics that have proven successful:

■ When an issue is extremely hot locally, study the problem as it has happened at some other time or as it appears in some other place.
■ Use techniques such as clarifying responses, using value sheets, conducting value discussions, using probing questions, applying logical principles to a student's argument, and requesting definitions.
■ Present unpopular positions yourself. Play the devil's advocate when students can see only one side of the question. Introduce different positions

■ FIGURE 9.1
Fact-Opinion Table

Opinion	Fact

that the students have not considered. Student thinking on controversial issues often becomes polarized between two opposite positions when really there are many other positions one might take. When you present a position, say something like "Some people take the position that . . . " or "Some people believe that . . . "

■ Use fact-opinion tables as in Figure 9.1. Have the class recorder fill out the table as the points are discussed. (The recorder can use a chalkboard, an overhead projector, or even a chart for this purpose).

■ Have students argue against their own beliefs. This practice may clarify their thinking and reveal the positions of other people.

■ Insist that students check on the sources of information and the meanings of words. Many arguments have no real factual basis. Try to get students to get at the facts underlying emotional arguments.

■ ■ ■   Role Playing and Simulation Games

Role Playing

Role playing and simulation are both useful for making complicated matters clear to students. By definition, *role playing* (or sociodrama) is an unrehearsed dramatization in which the players try to act out what they would do and how they would feel in a certain situation.* Role playing is particularly useful in clarifying the motivations and feelings of others.

For instance, to teach how prejudice affects both the prejudiced and those prejudiced against, a group in a social studies class attempted to portray the feelings of two boys who were rejected from a fraternity because of their religious beliefs. The players presented two scenes: the discussion of the candidates at the fraternity just prior to the voting; and the scene in which the boys were notified of their rejection. In each of these scenes, the players attempted to show the emotions of the characters they portrayed. They particularly emphasized how the boys felt after the rejection. Three different casts portrayed these scenes. After the presentations, the entire class discussed the justice of the decision and the probable effect of the incident on the persons concerned.

Another example of role playing was an attempt to make the feelings of the American colonists more real to a class of history students. In this class the players represented a group of colonists discussing the news of the stamp tax. The loyalist tried to show the reason for the tax, but the others shouted him down. From role playing of this sort, it is hoped that students will come to understand the tenor of the times being studied.

Use role playing to accomplish the following:

1. Clarify attitudes and concepts.
2. Demonstrate attitudes and concepts.
3. Deepen understanding of social situations.
4. Prepare for a real situation (for example, rehearsing the teaching of a lesson with a group of colleagues or practicing interview techniques before going out to be interviewed).
5. Plan and try out strategies for attacking problems.
6. Test hypothetical solutions to problems.
7. Practice leadership and other social skills.

*The role playing we are describing is the sociodrama. Psychodramas, which are designed to give insight into psychological aspects of human behavior, are beyond the scope of this book.

LIMITATIONS OF ROLE PLAYING   In spite of the many virtues of role playing, be aware of and guard against its dangers and limitations.

1. Students do not always take role playing seriously. They often think of it as entertainment, and as a result, they tend to "ham" up their roles and turn the role playing into a farce instead of a learning experience. Try to avert such behavior by skillful briefing and careful selection of players.

2. Unless students are well-prepared, the role playing may become superficial and result in stereotypical thinking. Role players must know the facts and background of the characters, the situation, and the courses of action open to them. To avoid stereotyping, repeat the role playing with different players and encourage individual interpretations of the roles. If the members of your group do not show signs of creativity and imagination, it may be wise to go easy on role-playing activities until the group's imagination has grown. You can encourage the development of both creativity and imagination by providing a variety of activities in a supportive atmosphere. Dramatic presentations and simulations may prove good avenues to imaginative, creative role playing.

3. Role playing is a time-consuming activity. Be sure to allow enough time for ample briefing, replaying, reinterpreting as needed, as well as a thorough follow-up.

4. Role playing is dependent on an atmosphere supporting free discussion and inquiry. It is a group activity and all should be involved. Therefore you should avoid even the semblance of dictating the conditions and interpretations of the scenes to be portrayed.

5. Unless students know the role players well, they may be inclined to mistake the characteristics the players assume in their roles for real-life qualities. So that no one role will become associated with any particular player, try to have students play a number of different types of roles.

STAGING THE ROLE PLAYING

PREPARING FOR ROLE PLAYING   Although role playing is usually done without scripts or rehearsals, it does require preparation. The students must understand the situation being presented. For this reason, the situation to be role played should be simple. If the situation is too complex, the role playing will probably fail. A situation involving two to four characters is usually most effective. Once a situation that the students can readily comprehend has been selected, you must carefully brief both the players and the rest of the class to be sure that they do understand it. Not only must you see to it that all the players understand the situation, but also that they realize the purpose of the role playing and their parts in it. For this reason, you should spend some time discussing the roles with the players. So that the rest of the class will be prepared to be a receptive audience, you should also brief them on the purpose of the drama and what they should look for as the role playing unfolds. Because of the tendency for students to think of role playing as entertainment, make every effort in your briefing to ensure that they realize that role playing is serious business.

SELECTING THE CAST   As one can readily see, role playing requires serious effort on the part of each player, so the players must be selected carefully—if possible, from volunteers. Selecting the cast is sometimes complicated by the fact that the most eager volunteers sometimes seem quite incapable of carrying out the roles. Consequently, it is not wise to commit yourself to using volunteers only.

At times, you will have to find understudies for the cast. A helpful procedure is to select several casts and have several presentations. This practice may offset poor presentations, give depth to class members' understanding of the situation through the differences in presentation and interpretation of the roles, and offset tendencies toward stereotypical thinking.

PLAYING ROLES   Because quite often the role players become extremely nervous, they may need help and encouragement. Rehearsing the first few lines and preparing a general plan for the development of the role playing may help the participants play their roles more confidently. On the other hand, too much planning may stifle spontaneity and straitjacket the role players' interpretations. Similarly, a warm-up period may be helpful, but when it is overdone, it may take the life out of the actual role playing.

Most role playing is quite loose. Consequently, there is always a danger that inexperienced role players may lose sight of their roles. Carefully selecting the role players and thoroughly explaining their roles to them should minimize this danger. Sometimes, however, these precautions are not sufficient. On such an occasion, if a player does get badly out of character, stop the production and reorient the players. It is better to interrupt the production than to present false information to the class.

FOLLOW-UP   If students are to benefit from role playing, you must follow up on it. A discussion period following the role playing can be the most worthwhile part of the entire lesson. Sometimes role playing a situation up to a critical point and then stopping the role playing to discuss what might or should happen next can be very effective. In any case, the students should discuss and analyze the action and interpret its significance. In the discussion, the participants might explain just what they hoped to do and how they felt during the role playing. Finally, this discussion should end in a summary or perhaps the formulation of some generalization. Do not insist that the students come to a definite conclusion, however. It may be much better to leave the discussion of the role playing open-ended.

It is frequently helpful, after a period of analysis and discussion, for a second group of students to role play the situation so that other interpretations can be seen.

DYADIC ROLE PLAYING   Role playing may be too complex a technique for inexperienced young people to handle effectively and seriously. Zeleny and Gross suggest that teachers use dyadic role playing (i.e., role playing in which only two players participate) to give students experience before they attempt to role play more complex situations.[20] Dyadic role playing, like other role playing, helps students to understand problems and situations better and to develop empathy for people in other situations. Because only two players participate, dyadic role playing is simpler and results in learning that might be difficult to achieve in a more complex situation.

To conduct dyadic role playing, first select two opposing positions or statuses (e.g., management versus labor) and help the students acquire the necessary background so that they understand and identify with the different positions and statuses.

Once the students have been well-briefed, divide the class into pairs (dyads). In each pair, one student represents one position and one the other. Then, all the pairs role play the situation simultaneously. When their role playing is finished, they should reverse their positions and role play the situation again. After each person has played both roles, the pairs evaluate what they have done. In this evaluation, they may discuss how well each side was presented, whether they had all the information they needed, or what the role playing showed them. If it seems that the pairs might have done better with more information, perhaps they should find out the necessary information and replay the roles. Finally, the dyadic role playing can be followed up by a general discussion or some other suitable follow-up. Sometimes, the follow-up might consist of having a dyad that did particularly well role play in front of the entire class. Or perhaps two students whose work seems promising can be formed into a new dyad for a class presentation. In either case, the role playing should be followed up by class discussion.

Stop and Reflect

What should you do if a student seems to be badly misinterpreting the assigned role?
What purposes may a sociodrama serve?
What sort of material is best-suited to a sociodrama?
How would you try to keep students from treating role playing as a joke?

Simulation Games

Simulation games combine role playing and problem solving. In a simulation exercise, students play roles as though they were executing a real-life situation. By acting out roles as though they were real, the students, it is hoped, will learn to understand the important factors in the real situation and learn either how to behave in the real situation or how persons in such situations must behave. Simulations differ from sociodramas and psychodramas in that although the role playing responses are impromptu, the roles of the actors and the scenarios are carefully drafted. This technique is the outgrowth of the war games in which army commandants fought mock battles. It has since been adopted by business, government, and other agencies that prepare people for important situations they must face in the future. Consequently, the actions and scenarios should be as realistic as possible. Essentially simulation entails two things:

1. That students be assigned definite roles requiring certain types of actions that they must perform in a fairly well-defined situation.
2. That the students be confronted with simulations of real-life situations in which they must take necessary action, just as the character whose role they are taking would have to. As a rule, whatever action is taken leads to new incidents that require new action. The actors are not free to act in any way they please, but rather must stay in character and keep their actions within the limits prescribed by the realities of the situation being simulated.

Good simulation games are available through reputable educational publishers and suppliers. At times, you may wish to prepare the simulation scenario yourself. But, unless you build the scenario carefully, it is usually better to use a professionally written one. A slipshod, hastily put together scenario may do more harm than good. However, making up their own simulation scenario can be an excellent exercise for students. Mapping out the scenario and delineating the roles can provide much in-depth learning.

The overall procedure for conducting simulation games is quite simple:

1. Make ready any props, equipment, or other materials that will be needed in the simulation.
2. Introduce the simulation. Explain the reason for it and how it is to be played.
3. Assign students to roles. It is usually best to assign roles in accordance with the students' potential as role players. Calling for volunteers is also a good method, but may result in very poor casting. Sometimes the roles can be described on cards that the students draw; however, if the simulation requires anything but the simplest role playing, drawing cards may be disas-

trous. Giving each player a card bearing a description of the role selected for him or her may be advantageous, however.

4. Once the students understand the simulation and know their roles in it, then conduct the simulation. In doing so follow the scenario to the letter. You may take on the role of umpire, referee, scorekeeper, or consultant yourself or delegate such tasks to designated students if the occasion warrants it.

5. Follow up the simulation with a discussion or similar activities in which the students draw inferences and make generalizations from the simulated activity.

Stop and Reflect

Simulations are among the most powerful of modern teaching strategies. Why?
Why would it be necessary to work out a scenario for use in a driver-training or flight-training simulation? How would simulation be useful in a course you might teach?

Studying the Community

Particularly vivid learning experiences sometimes result from studying the community. There are many ways for students to carry out community studies. One is to read and study. A surprisingly large amount of printed information is available about almost every community. This material may include reports of the federal, state, and local governments; releases by the Chamber of Commerce and similar agencies; stories in the local press; advertising and promotional literature from local concerns; publications of local civic and fraternal organizations; and, sometimes, articles in state and national publications. Unpublished material can sometimes be used to advantage. A student in a New England community was allowed to use old school records to write a historical account of the founding of the local school system in the early nineteenth century.

Community Surveys

One of the most interesting ways to study a community is to do a survey. Well-planned, a survey can bring students face to face with the realities in a community; poorly planned, it can result in erroneous learning and angry parents. Therefore, every community survey should be prepared thoroughly and planned carefully. Take care that the topic is not one to upset the townspeople. There are so many important potential topics that there is little point in selecting one that will cause a furor. Before the students begin, make sure that they are well-versed in the topic to be investigated and the techniques they are to use. A poorly prepared survey is seldom worth the students' effort.

DATA GATHERING Gathering and interpreting the data collected through a survey can be troublesome. The actual gathering of the data may be done in many ways. Among them are interviews, questionnaires, observation, and combinations of these and other techniques. Planning for the use of these techniques should be done carefully so that the time of the respondents is not wasted and the data gathered are really useful. The interpretation of the data should be approached with even more caution. One should set up criteria to differentiate between important and unimportant data and between meaningful and meaningless data. Set up criteria to determine the meaning of the data. This often can be done by inspection, but in some classes you may wish to apply simple statistical procedures that high school students can readily learn to use. Information concerning their use may be found in any textbook on educational measurement or statistics. Many high school mathematics texts discuss these procedures as well.

You and your students may be tempted to make public the results of the survey. In most cases, the temptation should be resisted, and the survey should be reported to the class only. If it seems desirable to make the report public, consult your administrative superior before doing anything. As a rule, make the report public only if it is outstanding and if its public release will enhance the relationship that exists between the school and the community.

Students who plan to use questionnaires or opinionnaires need plenty of help in planning them. The following suggestions may be helpful:

For Questionnaires or Opinion Polls Guidelines

1. Determine *exactly* what you want to know. Include questions pertaining only to those things that you cannot learn from other sources with reasonable ease.
2. Write the questions as clearly as possible. Try them on other students and teachers before you send them to the respondents. Beware of ambiguities. Be sure to explain any terms that may be misinterpreted.
3. Make the questions easy to answer. When possible, use checklists or multiple-choice items. Be sure to leave a place for the respondents to make comments if they want to. At the secondary school level, questionnaire writers should avoid using forced choice items.
4. Set up a system for the respondents' answers that will make your tabulating and interpreting of the data as easy as possible.

INTERVIEW TECHNIQUES   Another common method by which to study a community is to interview its prominent citizens and knowledgeable seniors. This method is not always fruitful because many persons find interview techniques difficult. If students are to apply it in a community study, they should be properly instructed in how to carry out a successful interview. Provide demonstrations of good interview techniques. The students should practice on themselves before practicing on adults. Of course adults, particularly important adults, will make allowances for the errors of students who interview them. Nevertheless, you will want students to make a good impression on the people interviewed. For this reason if no other, the students should be well-rehearsed in their roles before leaving for the interview. So that students actually ask the questions they should ask in the interviews, they should write out their questions beforehand.

In interview surveys it is particularly important that each respondent be asked the same questions in the same way. The use of a form such as the following is recommended:

My name is _____. My class is doing a survey about student participation. I will be speaking to many students in your school and other schools. I would like to ask you a few questions.

    A. Do you often discuss school issues with
       1. Friends?
       2. Class officers?
       3. School officials?
    B. Have you ever attended a meeting (church, school board, union, etc.) in which school policy was discussed?

C. Have you ever taken an active part regarding school issues, such as writing a letter or presenting a petition?(21)

This type of form is advantageous because the interviewer needs only to check off the responses. Train the interviewers to write down the answers to their questions immediately and not to depend on their memories for anything.

OBSERVATION TECHNIQUES   Still another excellent method to use in studying the community is observation. The familiar device of keeping a record of the foods students eat, so often used in health, hygiene, biology, and home economics classes, is an example of this type of study. Counting the number of cars that do not come to a full stop at a stop sign is another. Ordinarily, for observation to be successful, the students need to be well-briefed in what they are looking for. They need to have criteria by which to objectify their observation and some system of recording it. A checklist, rating scale, or similar form is usually helpful to observers both for recording and for objectifying the observations. Since accurate observation is rather difficult, students who engage in such techniques should be instructed in their use. Quite often practice sessions are beneficial.

Community Service and Action Learning

One evening in a suburban city a group of teenagers went from house to house ringing doorbells. They were social studies students conducting a campaign to inform voters of the issues in the coming elections and to persuade them to vote. Such service projects are another effective way to extend the classroom into the community. Quite often, such activities get at objectives that the more usual classroom activities fail to reach. The techniques for preparing students for community study are equally efficacious in preparing them for a service project. Lately, projects in which students go out into the community to learn by actual participation have been called *action learning*, a particularly apt description of what goes on.

Securing Administrative Approval

Community service projects, surveys, and the like can lead to complications if they are not carefully managed. Projects of this sort have been known to upset school-community relations. Always secure the advice and consent of your administrative and supervisory superiors before attempting such activities. In communities where the climate of opinion is not right for them, these activities may have to be foregone. The administration may find it necessary to withhold permission for other reasons also. Perhaps the proposal would interfere with other activities or classes; perhaps the timing would not be propitious; perhaps the community has had a surfeit of school surveys or service projects; perhaps the budget would not stand the expense. The final decision about whether the activity should or should not be attempted is the administrator's responsibility.

Stop and Reflect

What might be a community service project suitable for use in your community? If you were to attempt to use this project, what preparations and precautions would you take?

In your own circle of friends and relatives, how many of them have special skills and knowledge which they might share with secondary school students? How might you use the resources of these people in a secondary school class?

▪ ▪ ▪ **Writing**

Students need much more opportunity to learn to write than they are given in most classrooms. Learning to write well takes practice, and more practice, under guidance. Therefore, teachers of all subjects, not only English, should give students many opportunities to write.

Writing under supervision implies that whatever the student writes will be read and evaluated by you. It does not mean, however, that you must be overcritical. As in oral expression, what is important is the idea being expressed and the mode of expression. Students should learn to express themselves clearly and logically, and good attempts should be rewarded. The red pencil should be used sparingly. At times, grammatical errors may be safely ignored, but good writing should *always* be rewarded—without fail. Reinforce the positive every chance you get.

Good writers revise. Secondary school students and some college students seem never to have heard of the word. Insist that first drafts be reworked into final drafts before papers are ultimately submitted as contributions to the course. And final drafts should always be proofread. When you insist that students take back sloppy work for revision and proofreading, you are doing both yourself and the students a favor.

During the draft stages, much good can come from students' reading and commenting, in pairs or small groups, on one another's papers. The criticism of a friend or colleague can be really helpful, and it has the advantage of being free from the threat of a mark. Therefore, consultation among writers should be welcome. Perhaps students might act as editorial readers such as those used by publishing houses.* They might copyedit one another's drafts. Another technique that may prove helpful is for the students to set up their own guidelines for acceptable themes and other compositions.

One of the major difficulties for students when writing a paper is to find something to write about. In English classes students frequently complain that finding something worthwhile to write about is more difficult than writing. Provide students with as many acceptable suggestions as you can. In English classes, particularly, consider correlating your theme writing with assignments in other classes. Students could then combine their work for two classes. Thus the student who is studying the Reconstruction period for a history class could write an English composition on an aspect of the Reconstruction.

Letter exchanges can be an interesting combination of writing practice and learning about the subject matter of the writer. In a U.S. history class, students from an urban New Jersey "ghetto" wrote letters explaining why they, acting as Separatists living in Holland, thought they ought to emigrate to America. These letters were then exchanged, and some were read to the class by the recipients, who wrote back to tell the writers what they might be getting into in the wilds of North America. Another technique useful in English and social studies, and sometimes in other areas, is for you to read a brief, action-packed account which you have written of some real or imaginary happening and then ask the students to write an ending to fit the circumstances.

Teachers have also had great success with student-written and edited classroom magazines and newspapers. Just to reproduce students' compositions and distribute them to other members of the class can be motivating. Essay test questions and essays that students evaluate themselves have also proved effective. So have

---

*Readers are experts who go over manuscripts before they are published to suggest to the writer ways in which the book might be improved before it goes to press. They point out passages that do not make sense, errors in fact, things that were left out, places that seem illogical, and so on. The writer can accept or reject the readers' suggestions as he or she sees fit.

such games as writing roulette. In this game, at a command, each person starts to write a story. Then on signal, the writing stops, the papers are collected, mixed up, and redistributed at random. At a signal, the students read the stories they have received and add to them until told to stop again. This process is repeated two or three times. Then the final versions are collected and as many as possible are read to the class. Such games are good for students who are having difficulty with their reading and writing skills because they combine practice in reading, writing, and oral reading.

When dealing with students who have academic difficulty, it pays to keep compositions short, but you should require more ambitious essays, compositions, term papers, and imaginative pieces from advanced students. This is the time when, if ever, young people are poetic, imaginative, creative, and eager to express themselves—even though they may be short of academic skill. Give them a chance to be heard and praised.

Stop and Reflect

Prepare a series of topics that your students might write about in one of your courses. Devise a plan or strategy for giving students practice in writing.

SUMMARY

Thinking skills must be taught directly at first. Later they may be used for indirect heuristic high-level cognitive instruction. For such teaching, strive to maintain an open classroom atmosphere congenial to the inquiry process. Inquiry teaching consists of any strategy in which students attempt to seek information and to draw from it their own generalizations and conclusions. Most inquiry strategies involve problem solving. In general, the problem-solving method used in schools follows the steps outlined by Dewey as the act of a complete thought. These steps are selecting and defining a problem, gathering data, making hypotheses, and testing conclusions. Students need help in carrying out each of these steps. It should be noted that this technique is not the only way to solve problems, nor is it always necessary to follow the steps in order. The main objective is for students to seek and discover knowledge for themselves. Among the problem-solving strategies are the case-study method, value sheets, and various kinds of projects. Ideally, a project should consist of a task that the students set for themselves and then carry through to completion under the teacher's guidance. It should have both intrinsic value to the students and be pertinent to the teacher's educational goals. Sometimes projects can be group projects, but whether group or individual, each project should be realistic, lifelike, and of innate value to the students, and each should be conceived, planned, and executed by the students under the teacher's guidance.

Discovery teaching consists of teaching in which students draw their own conclusions from information they have gleaned themselves or that teachers or others have provided. The famous Socratic discussion and its modern counterpart, the controlled discussion, are good examples of discovery teaching. The Socratic method, which is characterized by the logical development of concepts through open-ended, thought-provoking leading questions, is chiefly useful in teaching individuals or small classes. The controlled discussion has been developed for using Socratic techniques with full-size classes. Springboard approaches are especially useful in discovery teaching. They have been used since ancient times in the parable method and in more modern versions such as the value sheet.

Inquiry and discovery teaching sometimes involve controversial issues. Since controversial issues are by definition controversial, teachers should treat them as open-ended and try to see to it that all sides of any issue studied are properly represented.

Field trips, community surveys, and community service projects are time-proven ways to utilize the community for instruction. Community activities should be planned and followed through very carefully to ensure that each activity is worthwhile and to save the school from embarrassment. In activities of this sort, the teacher must always bear in mind their possible effect on school-community relations. Therefore, it is especially important that all such activities be cleared with all the authorities concerned.

One of the most powerful teaching methods, when properly used, is role playing, which basically consists of trying to put oneself in the place of someone else and to act out that person's point of view. In order to be effective, role playing must be an unrehearsed, spontaneous attempt to analyze and understand real problem situations. Simulation games are a type of role playing. The purpose of role playing and simulation is quite different from that of the many other types of dramatic presentations that may be included in the classroom. These other types should be rehearsed as carefully as the time permits to be effective.

Writing can be an important aspect of any academic subject. Students should have plenty of practice in writing in every course. Carefully planned writing assignments can and should be used to build student learning across the curriculum.

ADDITIONAL READING

Alexander, W. M., and P. S. George. *The Exemplary Middle School*. New York: Holt, Rinehart and Winston, 1981.

Baron, J. *Thinking and Deciding*. New York: Cambridge University Press, 1988.

Baron, J. B., and P. J. Sternberg, eds. *Teaching Thinking Skills: Theory and Practice*. New York: W.H. Freeman, 1986.

Barell, J. *Teaching for Thoughtfulness*. White Plains, NY: Longman, 1991.

Bateman, W. L. *Open to Question*. San Francisco: Jossey-Bass, 1990.

Beyer, B. K. *Developing a Thinking Skills Program*. Boston: Allyn and Bacon, 1988.

Beyer, B. K. *Practical Strategies for the Teaching of Thinking*. Boston: Allyn and Bacon, 1987.

Bransford, J. D., and B. S. Stein. *The IDEAL Problem Solver*. New York: W.H. Freeman, 1984.

Bransford, J. D., and N. Vye. "Cognitive Research and Its Implications for Instruction." In *Toward the Thinking Curriculum: Current Cognitive Research*, edited by L. B. Resnick and L. E. Klopfer. Chicago: Association for Supervision and Curriculum Development, 1989.

Caine, R. N., and G. Caine. "Understanding a Brain-Based Approach to Learning and Teaching." *Educational Leadership* 48 (October 1990): 66–70.

Christenbury, L., and P. Kelley. *Questioning: A Path to Critical Thinking*. Urbana, IL: National Council of Teachers of English, 1983.

Chuska, K. R. *Teaching the Process of Thinking, Fastback 244*. Bloomington, IN: Phi Delta Kappa Educational Foundation, 1986.

Costa, A. L. *Developing Minds: A Resource Book for Teaching Thinking*. Alexandria, VA: Association for Supervision and Curriculum Development, 1991, Vols. 1 & 2.

Costa, A. L., and L. F. Flowry. *Techniques for Teaching Thinking*. Pacific Grove, CA: Midwest Publications, 1989.

Friedman, M. I. *Teaching Higher Order Thinking Skills to Gifted Students: A Systematic Approach*. Springfield, IL: Charles C. Thomas, 1984.

Goodman, D. S., and P. F. Goodman. *Teaching Reasoning Skills in Schools and Homes*. Springfield, IL: Charles C. Thomas, 1991.

Grant, G. E. *Teaching Critical Thinking*. New York: Praeger, 1988.

Greenblat, C. S. *Designing Games and Simulations*. Newbury Park, CA: Sage, 1987.

Halpern, D. F. *Thought and Knowledge: An Introduction to Critical Thinking*. Hillsdale, NJ: Erlbaum, 1984.

Harris, T. L., and E. J. Cooper, eds. *Reading, Thinking and Concept Development*. New York: College Board, 1985.

Heiman, M., and J. Slomianka, eds. *Thinking Skills: Instruction Concepts and Techniques*. Washington, DC: National Education Association, 1987.

Hersh, R. H., J. P. Miller, and G. D. Fielding. *Models of Moral Education: An Appraisal*. New York: Longman, 1980.

Jones, K. *Simulations: A Handbook for Teachers and Trainers*, 2nd ed. rev. New York: Nichols, 1987.

Joyce, B., B. Shavers, and M. Weil, eds. *Models of Teaching*. Englewood Cliffs, NJ: Prentice-Hall, 1991.

Keefe, J. W., and H. J. Walberg, eds. *Teaching for Thinking*. Reston, VA: National Association of Secondary School Principals, 1992.

Kourilsky, M., and L. Quaranta. *Effective Teaching: Principles and Practice*. Glenview, IL: Scott Foresman, 1987, Chs. 5–7.

Lohman, D. F. *Teaching Higher Order Thinking Skills*. Elmhurst, IL: North Central Laboratory for Educational Research and Development, 1985.

Marzano, R., and C. Hutchins. *Thinking Skills: A Conceptual Framework*. Aurora, CO: Midcontinent Regional Educational Laboratory, 1985.

McPeck, J. *Critical Thinking and Education*. New York: St. Martin's, 1981.

Meyers, C. *Teaching Students to Think Critically*. San Francisco: Jossey-Bass, 1986.

Moore, W. E., H. McCann, and J. McCann. *Creative and Critical Thinking*. Boston: Houghton Mifflin, 1985.

Nickerson, R. S., D. N. Perkins, and E. E. Smith. *The Teaching of Thinking*. Hillsdale, NJ: Erlbaum, 1985.

Nucci, L. P., ed. *Moral Development and Character Education*. Berkeley, CA: McCutchan, 1989.

Orlich, D. C. et al. *Teaching Strategies: A Guide to Better Instruction*, 2nd ed. Lexington, MA: D. C. Heath, 1985, Parts 8–9.

Ornstein, R., and R. Thompson. *The Amazing Brain*. Boston: Houghton Mifflin, 1984.

Presseisen, B. *Thinking Skills: Research and Practice*. Washington, DC: National Education Association, 1980.

Raths, L., S. Wasserman, A. Jonas, and A. Rothstein. *Teaching for Thinking*, 2nd ed. New York: Teachers College, Columbia University Press, 1986.

Resnick, L. B. *Education and Learning to Think*. Washington, DC: National Academy Press, 1987.

Resnick, L. B., ed. *Knowing Learning and Instruction*. Hillsdale, NJ: Erlbaum, 1989.

Resnick, L. B., and L. E. Klopfer, eds. *Toward the Thinking Curriculum: Current Cognitive Research*. Alexandria, VA: Association for Supervision and Curriculum Development, 1989.

Rogoff, B. *Apprenticeship in Thinking*. New York: Oxford University Press, 1990.

Segal, J. W., S. F. Chipman, and R. Glaser, eds. *Thinking and Learning Skills: Relating Instruction to Research*. Hillsdale, NJ: Erlbaum, 1985, Vol. 1.

Springer, S., and G. Deutsch. *Left Brain, Right Brain*. New York: W. H. Freeman, 1985.

Stiggins, R. J., E. Rubel, and E. Quellmalz. *Measuring Thinking Skills in the Classroom*. Washington, DC: National Education Association, 1988.

Stone, E. *Quality Teaching: A Sample of Cases*. New York: Roultedge, 1982.

Swartz, P., and D. Perkins. *Teaching Thinking: Issues and Approaches*. Pacific Grove, CA: Midwest Publications, 1989.

Whimbey, A., and J. Lockhead. *Problem Solving and Comprehension*, 4th rev. Hillsdale, NJ: Erlbaum, 1984.

Wittrock, M. C. "Students' Thought Processes." In *Handbook of Research on Teaching*, 2nd ed, edited by M. C. Wittrock. New York: Macmillan, 1986.

Woolfolk, A. E. *Educational Psychology*, 5th ed. Boston: Allyn and Bacon, 1992.

NOTES

1. Louis E. Raths, Selma Wasserman, Arthur Jonas, and Arnold Rothstein, *Teaching for Thinking*, 2nd ed. (New York: Teachers College, Columbia University Press, 1986), 1.
2. John Barell, "You Ask the Wrong Questions," *Educational Leadership* 42 (May 1985): 18–23.
3. John Barell, Rosemarie Liebmann, and Irving Sigel, "Fostering Thoughtful Self-Direction in Students," *Educational Leadership* 45 (April 1988): 14–17.
4. Raths et al., *Teaching for Thinking*, 5 ff.
5. Ibid., xxix.
6. Ibid., 24–30.
7. Barry K. Beyer, "Practice Is Not Enough," in Marcia Heiman and Joshua Slomianko, eds., *Thinking Skills Instruction: Concepts and Techniques* (Washington, DC: National Education Association, 1987), 80–81. Reprinted by permission of the author.
8. Raths et al., *Teaching for Thinking*, 14.
9. Based on Raths et al., *Teaching for Thinking*, Part I.
10. James M. Tighe, "Teaching for Thinking, of Thinking, and about Thinking," in Heiman and Slomianko, *Thinking Skills Instruction*, 28.
11. Barak Rosenshine and Carla Meister, "The Use of Scaffolds for Teaching Higher-Level Cognitive Strategies," *Educational Leadership* 49 (April 1992): 26–33.
12. Ibid.
13. Janet Eaton, "There's Hope for General Math," *Educational Leadership* 43 (September 1985): 91–92.
14. Raths et al., *Teaching for Thinking*, xiv.
15. B. O. Smith, "On Teaching Thinking Skills," *Educational Leadership* 45 (October 1987): 35–39.
16. Barell, Liebmann, and Sigel, "Fostering Thoughtful Self-Direction in Students."
17. Lyn Corno and Richard E. Snow, "Adapting Teaching to Individual Differences among Learners," in M. C. Wittrock, ed., *Handbook of Research on Teaching*, 3rd ed. (New York: Macmillan, 1986), 620.
18. Paul D. Eggen and Donald P. Kauchak, *Strategies for Teachers*, 2nd ed. (Englewood Cliffs, NJ: Prentice-Hall), 1988, Chap. 4.
19. Leslie A. Hart, "The Incredible Brain, How Does It Solve Problems? Is Logic a National Problem?" *National Association of Secondary School Principals Bulletin* 67 (January 1983): 36–41.
20. Leslie D. Zeleny and Richard E. Gross, "Dyadic Role Playing of Controversial Issues," *Social Education* 24 (December 1960): 354–358.
21. Thomas S. Popkewitz, "How to Study Political Participation," *How to Do It Series No. 27* (Washington, DC: National Council for the Social Studies, 1974), 5.

Chapter 10

Providing for Individual Differences

Overview

All humans differ; no two people are the same. We differ in a multitude of ways—in physical makeup, in interests, in ability, in aptitude, in home background, in experience, in prior training, in social skill, in ideals, in attitudes, in needs, in vocational goals, and so on *ad infinitum*. This is an inescapable fact of human nature—a fact fraught with profound implications for the teacher. Because of these differences, to treat individuals as though everyone were alike simply does not work. Somehow, some way, we teachers must adapt our teaching to the individual differences in students.

Not only are students different, but they all learn according to their own styles. No two persons ever learn exactly the same concepts from any learning situation, nor do any two persons ever develop exactly the same method and degree of efficiency. Learning is always shaped by individual interests, physical and psychic makeup, past experiences, and goals for the future. As teachers, we should capitalize on these differences and make them a way to further learning.

In other words, insofar as possible, schooling should be individualized. Curricula, courses, and lessons should be built in ways that allow students to adopt different courses; lessons should be built in ways that allow students to adopt different goals, to study different content, to learn by different media and methods, to progress at different rates, and to be judged by different criteria—in accordance with their own specific needs, ambitions, and talents.

In this chapter we describe some of the procedures and devices that educators use in their attempts to cope with the challenges caused by student differences and the need to individualize instruction.

Stop and Reflect

Observe the members of your own class. In what ways do they seem similar? In what ways are they different?

If possible, visit a middle school class or senior high school class. What evidence of individual differences do you find?

Administrative Provisions for Differences in Students

For a long time school administrators have been trying, with rather indifferent success, to find answers for the instructional problems caused by students' individual differences. To this end they have created a variety of curricula designed to meet students' goals, needs, and interests (e.g., college preparatory curricula) and tracks or streams based on students' abilities. They also divided courses into homogeneous groups based primarily on academic ability. Other administrative schemes that allow for individual differences in students include elective course offerings, continuous promotion, non-graded classes, plans involving skipping or repeating grades, and the adoption of flexible school-day plans.

Stop and Reflect

How could you prevent a caste system from developing as a result of homogeneous grouping of class sections throughout the school?

Examine a high school honors class. What range of interests, abilities, life goals, and academic backgrounds do you find?

■ ■ ■   Matching Teaching Styles to Learning Styles

The National Association of Secondary School Principals (NASSP) Learning Styles Task Force has defined *learning style* as "the composite of characteristic cognitive, affective, and physiological factors that serve as relatively stable indicators of how a learner perceives, interacts with, and responds to the learning environment."(1)

As we have mentioned earlier, each student has a learning style of his or her own. These individual learning styles really make a difference in how well students learn. For instance, students who tend to process information with the left hemisphere of their brain are more likely to learn from book-oriented verbal approaches, while students who are oriented to the right hemisphere are likely to learn better through physical, visual, emotional, hands-on instruction.

The differences in orientation that cause students to adopt different learning styles are probably the result of their earlier learning and their emotional and physical development. Learning styles are neither good nor bad; one style may be effective in one type of situation, whereas another may be effective in another. Each learning style has its advantages and its disadvantages as the following comparisons illustrate.

Field-independent persons are relatively independent from external clues. They are more intrinsically oriented, less sensitive in social or interpersonal situations, less influenced by peer pressure, and more likely to favor abstract matter than are field-dependent persons. Researchers tell us that field-independent students do better work in low-structure–inductive-learning situations whereas field-dependent students do better in high-structure–deductive-learning classes.

Analytical persons tend to break ideas down into their component parts, but global thinkers find it difficult to do so. Some students are reflective types; others are impulsive. Impulsive students are more inclined to jump to conclusions, whereas the reflective types are likely to ponder over details. They are more likely than not to be narrow thinkers who are very careful, specific, and analytical, whereas impulsive thinkers think in broad general (global) categories that sometimes may be too broad to be helpful in school learning. Some students sharpen the categories of what they learn, but levelers tend to break down distinctions. Consequently, levelers have trouble keeping track of things.

Similar dichotomies may be seen in the way individuals organize knowledge. Some use simple approaches for organizing information, whereas others' approaches are quite complex. The results of these different approaches may give quite different answers. In like manner, some students are tolerant of new ideas, whereas others resist them. Some are easily distracted, whereas others concentrate. Some students are more inclined to accept conventional viewpoints and practices, whereas others would rather hoe their own rows. Some are divergent thinkers, whereas others are convergent thinkers. Some people's thoughts tend to be creative, original, and far-ranging, whereas others tend to be matter-of-fact, prosaic, and narrow. What is sauce for the goose is not necessarily sauce for the gander; therefore, it pays for the teacher to match a student's instruction to that person's learning style.

Matching instruction styles to learning styles is complicated by the fact that there are many cognitive styles. A number of "inventories" have been published to help determine styles that individual students favor. For instance, Renzulli and Smith's *Learning Style Inventory* describes student attitudes toward the following:

1. Projects
2. Drill and practice
3. Peer teaching
4. Discussion
5. Teaching games
6. Independent study
7. Programmed instruction
8. Lecture
9. Simulation(2)

Other inventories have been provided by Gregorc and by Dunn and Dunn.(3) You can, of course, also learn much about students' learning style preferences by careful systematic observation.

Matching learning styles and instruction is also complicated by the fact that there are so many individuals in each class, each with an individual learning style preference. The answer to this problem, according to the *Learning Styles Network Newsletter*, is to identify a student's learning style by some valid instrument and then attempt to match it with a corresponding teaching style. If that teaching style does not seem to work, then review your decision and try another one. Another approach is to use a variety of teaching styles over a period of time so that in the long run each student will meet a teaching style congruous with his or her learning style at least part of the time.(4) This strategy is probably the best because not only does it allow students opportunities to learn in their preferred learning style, but it also has the added advantage of helping learners become accustomed to a number of teaching styles and helping them gain skill in different learning styles. As a result, your students will learn to use both hemispheres of the brain and become at home in a number of learning styles. Try as best you can to individualize your instruction and match teaching and learning styles systematically.

Stop and Reflect

Examine yourself. What sort of classroom situation do you find most congenial? In what type of class do you do your best work? If your teachers had been more conscious of your learning style, would your classes have been more profitable? Observe your friends. How do their learning styles differ? Under what conditions do they seem to learn best?

■ ■ ■   Differentiating Assignments

The Differentiated Assignment

The first instructional procedure for coping with individual differences that we discuss is the differentiated assignment. A *differentiated assignment* is a class assignment that allows different students to do different things during the time covered by the assignment. Many types of these assignments can be made. Sometimes the differentiated assignment is long, covering several weeks, but it can also be very short.

DIFFERENTIATING THE LENGTH OR DIFFICULTY OF THE ASSIGNMENT   Teachers often arrange their assignments so that at-risk learners will not have to do quite as much as their more gifted colleagues. In the sample assignment shown in Figure 10.1, the teacher attempted to do this by assigning group 3, the gifted group, considerably more work than group 1, the at-risk group. In a mathematics class she might have

---

GROUP 1

Reading Assignment *Your Country and Mine,* pages 36–41:

1. Form into assigned groups.
2. Select one member to serve on each committee:
   a. Bulletin Board
   b. *Who's Who in American History*
3. Choose one of the following assignments:
   a. Write a story about Daniel Boone.
   b. Draw a picture of Boonesborough in its early days.
   c. Draw a map showing how Daniel Boone got to Boonesborough (page 43).

GROUP 2

Reading Assignment *Your Country's Story*, pages 160–163.

1. Form into assigned groups.
2. Select one member for each of the following committees:
   a. Bulletin Board
   b. *Who's Who in American History*
3. Choose one of the following assignments:
   a. Make a report on the nature and characteristics of the Indians as seen by the early settlers in Kentucky and Tennessee.
   b. Make a map showing the different routes to the West.
   c. Write a report telling why the Ohio Valley was so attractive to early settlers.

GROUP 3

Reading Assignment *This is America's Story,* pages 223–231.

1. Form into assigned groups.
2. Select one member to serve on each committee:
   a. Bulletin Board
   b. *Who's Who in American History*
3. Choose one of the following assignments:
   a. Prepare a short report on the history of political parties in the United States.
   b. Make a report on Hamilton's policies in solving this country's financial problems.
   c. Write a short report explaining why Jefferson and Hamilton had different views on many things.
4. Answer completely Check-Up Questions 1–3 (page 227) and 1–4 (page 231).
5. Give a brief account of the Northwest Territory and of its importance in the development of the West.

■ **FIGURE 10.1**
A Short Differentiated Assignment

assigned 5 problems to the below-average students, 8 problems to the average students, and 10 problems to the above-average students. In the sample assignment the work assigned to the groups also varies in difficulty. Group 3 is reading in what the teacher considers a "hard" eighth-grade book; group 2, an "easy" eighth-grade book; and group 1, a sixth-grade book. All are studying about the same thing, but at different levels of difficulty. In a mathematics class the teacher could have assigned more difficult problems to the above-average students.

DIFFERENTIATING THE TYPE OF WORK   Another approach is to differentiate the type of work various students do, thus allowing for their varying interests, abilities, and intelligence. Students who think best with their hands could be allowed to create with them, whereas academically oriented students might be encouraged to undertake minor research problems. Similarly, students who are interested in current affairs might become specialists and keep the class up to date on the stock market or on the situation in the Middle East. Artistically inclined students might form a committee to keep the bulletin board attractive and current. Scientifically minded students might be given reading assignments different from those assignments given to literary types. Give students opportunities to try different types of assignments, however. By skillfully using the students' interests and abilities, you may be able to enlist their enthusiastic cooperation and encourage them to learn more than they would in a dull, humdrum, lockstep class.

ACCEPTING DIFFERENT SIGNS OF ACHIEVEMENT   In order to capitalize on varying abilities and interests, you should not only allow students to engage in various learning activities, but also accept different signs of growth when estimating and evaluating the academic progress of students. For example, writing essays and answering test questions are not the only ways to show one's understanding of the antebellum South. Many other media are available. Artistic youngsters might produce illustrations of life in the South; a young draftsman might draw a layout of a plantation; a beginning gourmet might investigate the menus of the era; a student interested in fashions might design a costume appropriate to the period; a young engineer might construct a cotton gin; a young choreographer might score and dance a ballet in the *Gone with the Wind* motif; a poet might contribute some lyric poetry. Evaluate your students' academic success on the basis of the growth and progress they make toward the prescribed goals through these media. Certainly a student who works toward the learning objectives by performing a well-conceived and well-executed original dance number deserves to be recognized at least as much as a student who writes a sloppy research paper.

Stop and Reflect

Examine the sample differentiated assignment shown in Figure 10.1. How successful do you think this assignment would be?

How would you go about preparing a differentiated assignment for a course in your major field?

It has been said, "We should not have a standard; we should have standards." What do you think this means? Is it advisable to require one student to do more or better work than another? Is it fair? How would you go about implementing this statement?

Grouping Within the Classroom

Teaching is usually easier when the range of differences among students in a group is kept relatively small. Just as school administrators use homogeneous groupings throughout entire schools, teachers can group their students homogeneously within their classes in several ways, such as the following:

1. Placing the low achievers in one group, the average achievers in another, and the high achievers in a third.
2. Placing students into groups according to their interests.
3. Placing students with similar interests and similar goals together in a committee to solve a particular problem or to do some sort of research.
4. Placing students into groups according to special needs.

Certain critics have objected to the use of ability groups within the class for several reasons. One objection is that many experienced high school teachers claim that to teach more than one group in the same room is impossible or too difficult.

Yet anyone who has watched a skillful teacher conduct a one-room school or a primary room knows that this need not be so. Teaching several groups at once is hard work, but then, all good teaching is hard work. Actually, using groups is often easier than attempting to teach the unready something they cannot learn or the uninterested something they will not learn.

As we have already seen, another serious objection is that ability grouping may label some students as inferior. Although the danger does exist, ability grouping within classes is probably not as dangerous as one might expect. The students usually know where the strengths and weaknesses of their classmates lie and recognize which ones are good students, which ones hate to study, which ones are social butterflies, which ones are wallflowers, which ones are sports-oriented, and so on.

Nevertheless, the dangers of grouping by ability are real. We must not allow a caste system to develop in any classroom. The danger may be avoided by seeing to it that the membership of the groups changes frequently, that many types of groups and committees are used so that no student is always in the same group, and that each student has ample opportunities to work both as an individual and as a member of the entire class. To divide a class into three or four ability groups and to keep these groups together constantly for an entire term is malpractice. Instead, center small groups or committees on the changing interests, problems, or needs of the students. Evidently, in reading groups at least, students make better progress in mixed, randomly selected groups than in ability groups.[*]

Stop and Reflect

If you were to divide your class into groups, what basis for grouping would you use? How would you go about grouping the class? How long would you keep the same groups?

Individualizing Instruction

A differentiated assignment does not really individualize instruction; it merely reduces the problem of individual differences somewhat. If instruction is to meet the needs of individual students, ways must be found for individualizing assignments and instruction. At first glance this task may seem to be insuperably difficult, but on closer analysis it is not as overwhelming a task as you might fear.

Acceleration and Enrichment

One way to help gifted students make the most of their talents is to let them proceed through the prescribed course more rapidly than their classmates. In a certain Latin class the teacher arranged the classwork so that the gifted students could do most of the work independently at their own speed without waiting for slower classmates to catch up. One girl completed one year's work early in April and was well into the next year's work by the end of June. The teacher had made this acceleration possible by preparing units for the entire year in advance. When a student had completed one unit, he or she could go right on to the next one.

In such a teaching framework, the accelerated student will finish the regular coursework before the end of the school year, so you will need to provide additional

---

[*]See Chapter 8 for information on teaching by means of committees and small groups.

work for such a student. In the example cited, the student went on to complete units in the next year's work. In other instances, you may prefer that the student study more deeply certain aspects of the present course or aspects of the course ordinarily omitted because of lack of time. This approach we call *enrichment*.

Once your students have started to work individually, you will need to run frequent checks on their progress to make sure that all is going well and to provide help, direction, and redirection as needed. To be sure that the students do have sufficient guidance, it is good to make up a schedule of conferences with them. In addition, you should make yourself available to the students. When a student needs help, be ready to provide it immediately.

Continuous Progress Plans

The Latin teacher's plan for accelerating gifted students is really a form of the continuous progress plan. Continuous progress plans consist of dividing the coursework into short steps, levels, or modules, and allowing the students to advance from step to step as they become ready. Even in schools organized into traditional grades and courses, you can organize your own courses for continuous progress. Briefly, the procedure is as follows:

1. Divide the course into units (commonly called *modules*).
2. Prepare an instructional packet for each unit. (These are also called learning modules, learning activity packets, self-instructional units, or instructional modules.) Each instructional packet should include
   A diagnostic pretest
   Behavioral objectives
   A study guide giving directions and suggestions for study, including required and optional activities—exercises, problems, questions, projects
   Progress tests
   A final mastery test
   Materials for study[*]
3. Give students the pretest of the appropriate unit. Students who do very well may be excused from completing the unit. Use the results of the pretest for diagnosis and guidance. In some courses, this step may be omitted.
4. Let the students work on the unit independently, following the directions included in the study guide in the instructional packet. Students may take progress tests and engage in other activities as they go along.
5. When students seem ready, let them take the final mastery test. Students who meet your criteria are deemed to have met the objective and may go on to another unit. Those who do not pass must do remedial work until they can meet the criteria.

In a true continuous progress course, some students will move through the units easily, whereas others will take longer than the normal time to finish the units. In conducting such courses, it is wise to remember that speed is not always a virtue. The student who proceeds through the units slowly but thoroughly may retain more than the star who flips through them at great speed.

To conduct a course of the continuous progress type requires constant supervision and guidance. You must be constantly available and watchful to prevent students from having to stand around waiting for help or from struggling through work they do not understand. Whenever possible, utilize small-group instruction tech-

[*]See Chapter 6.

niques to help students who are at the same point in the module or who are encountering the same problems. However, the purpose for using learning packets in these courses is to give you a better opportunity for giving students individual attention, as well as to give students a break from the regimentation of the standard recitation.

Other suggestions for teaching continuous progress courses and self-instructional units or modules include the following:

1. Be flexible. Vary the module requirements for various persons as the situation requires.
2. Use bulletin boards, tapes, interviews, guest speakers, simulation games, and the like to add spark to the modules.
3. Be sure to have whole-group activities at least once a week or so. Discussions in which students apply what they have learned are good.
4. Let persons who finish modules become consultants to other students who are finding the work troublesome.
5. Have students rework lessons that they do incorrectly. (This suggestion implies that you must be constantly checking to be sure that students are doing the work correctly.)
6. Use incentives to keep students working.
   a. Check their work frequently. Praise and reward each forward step.
   b. Reward students with free time, quest time, and the like.
   c. Make some units optional, some required.
   d. Utilize the contract procedure in which individuals agree that they will do certain things in exchange for certain rewards.
   e. Have students report to you when they finish a lesson. Make a chart and check off the lessons completed.
   f. Have students report to a "review committee" before reporting that a lesson or unit is completed. This committee should be composed of two or three students who have completed their work. The "review committee" should screen students who need more help before they take the final test for a unit or lesson.
7. Pair students who have reading difficulties with a study partner who is a stronger reader. The stronger reader can help his or her partner with the module.
8. Do not expect everyone to be on the same lesson or module at the same time.

Mastery Learning

In 1962 J.B. Carroll hypothesized that how much students learn depends on the amount of time spent actually engaged in learning in proportion to the amount of time needed to master subject matter perfectly.(5) Consequently, a person who needs a lot of time to learn something but does not take the time necessary will not learn it well. But on the other hand, theoretically if one persists long enough, one can master whatever is to be learned. Carried to the ultimate, this hypothesis implies that one can teach anything to anyone if only one takes the time. This thinking has led to the theory of mastery teaching developed by Bloom and others.(6) Basically the idea behind mastery teaching is to give each person enough engaged time to master the objectives of each unit before moving on to the next one. In general, mastery teaching seems to be successful, although some research does not bear out this generalization.(7)

The essentials in the Bloom "Learning for Mastery" model are as follows:

1. Clearly specified learning objectives
2. Short, highly valid assessment procedures
3. Preset mastery performance standards

4. A sequence of learning units, each comprised of an integral set of facts, contents, principles, and skills
5. Provision of feedback of learning progress to students
6. Provision of additional time and help to correct specified errors and misunderstanding of students who are failing to achieve the preset mastery learning standards.(8)

In theory at least, mastery learning provides not only time for pupils to master the learning but also promotes strong motivation. Because students are given all the time they need, they should expect to succeed. This expectation should strengthen their motivation, for we all tend to do most strongly and willingly those things we expect will lead to success. This motivation should be particularly strong among at-risk students because it might counteract the feeling of "what's the use" that comes from long histories of failure. Another motivating factor is that in the Bloom model pupils have a role in their own evaluation. Also, in this type of teaching, errors are considered to be natural. Everybody makes mistakes, so making mistakes is nothing to be ashamed of.

To conduct mastery learning programs à la Bloom's model, you must first break the course into small units of learning and establish strong specific criterion-referenced instructional objectives for each unit. Then you, as teacher, introduce the unit in your usual manner. Following this presentation, give the students instructional materials with which to practice. Also give them diagnostic tests by which to test their progress toward mastering the unit subject matter. If the students miss points, give them corrective instructional materials for further study. These corrective phases may consist of small-group study sessions, peer tutoring, programmed material, supplementary reading, audiovisual presentations, and so on. Students who finish quickly and do not need corrective work should be given enrichment lessons in which they can go into greater depth on a topic or expand its horizons. Other students keep on with the corrective instructional material until they have mastered the content. Mastery is determined by a summative test. All students who pass the unit summative test are graded "A" for that unit. Units that are not completed are graded "I".(9)

Evidently, these tactics work quite well. However, there is reason to think that in conjunction with such an approach, students of high ability are liable to be neglected because of teacher efforts being concentrated on bringing less able students to mastery. Besides, if everyone who completes the unit gets an "A," gifted students may see little reason to try harder. Evidently some schools have had success in integrating mastery learning schemes with continuous progress schemes.(10)

Completely Differentiating the Work

At times it is desirable to assign to certain students work that is entirely different from that given to the rest of the class. An example of this is the case of Pete, a brilliant tenth-grader who had been doing poor work in his English class. Upon examining the situation, the teacher realized that the boy was finding the assignments too easy. He was bored. To remedy this, the teacher excused the boy from the regular assignment and substituted one she herself had had in college. Rising to this bait, the boy accomplished this assignment in a fashion acceptable for any college introductory literature course. By substituting an entirely different assignment, the teacher was able to inspire this boy to do work well beyond the level of his grade. This is an excellent way to help a gifted youth. If a student is competent in grammar and knows to perfection the parts of speech the class is presently studying, she should be studying something else. Why not put her to work on a problem in literature, or something else worthwhile? It does not matter particularly what the student does as long as it results in the learning desired. Similarly, at-risk students may be favorably motivated by receiving assignments that catch a special personal interest.

Conducting the Class as a Laboratory

A profitable way to provide for individual differences is to conduct the class as a laboratory where the students can work on their various tasks individually or in small groups under your guidance. In such a laboratory, a committee might be working in one corner of the room preparing a dramatization, and in another corner another group might be preparing a report. Individual students might be working at their desks on research projects. Others might be reading required or optional readings. In the rear of the class, a student might be putting the finishing touches on a model to be presented and explained to the class. Around the teacher's desk, another group might be working with the teacher in planning a group project.

As the students work at their tasks, you should help and guide them. Among the many things you can do to help them are the following:

1. Observe students to diagnose poor study habits.
2. Show students where to find information.
3. Show students how to use the tools of learning.
4. Clarify assignments.
5. Show the students how to get the essence out of their studying.
6. Help students form goals for study.
7. Help students summarize.
8. Point out errors and incorrect procedures.
9. Suggest methods for attacking problems.

Laboratory classes of this sort allow the freedom necessary for students to work at a variety of tasks at suitable speeds. To a lesser degree, supervised study periods in which the students work on their assignments under your supervision and guidance can provide the same freedom (see Figure 10.2).

Stop and Reflect

What practical problems arise from allowing a student to go to the next year's work? How might these problems be minimized?

In the example cited, the accelerated students worked individually almost entirely. Is this a good practice? How might one accelerate students in a class without making the work entirely individual?

How would you go about setting up a classroom laboratory in a course you might teach? How could you use a classroom laboratory?

Other Individualized Instruction Schemes

Whatever approach you use, you must find time to work separately with individual students. This does not usually take as much time as you might think. Many students need a minimum of guidance. If you provide them with clear instructions, they can often work alone for considerable periods.

SPECIAL HELP   The most common type of individualized instruction is the special help given to certain students. Teachers have always helped students who were

■ **Figure 10.2**

A Classroom Laboratory

Leonard H. Clark, *Teaching Social Studies in Secondary Schools.* (New York: Macmillan Publishing Company, 1973), p. 126. Used with permission.

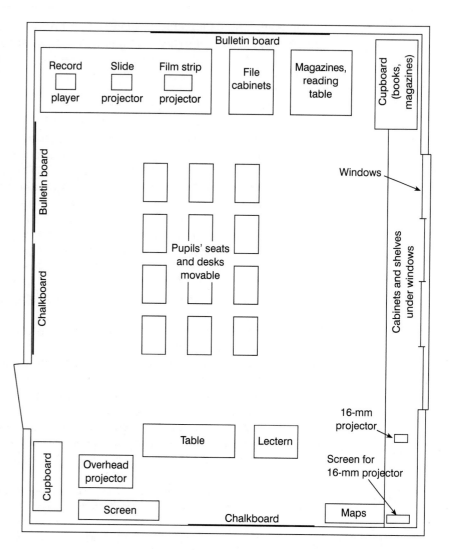

having trouble with their studies through extra help after school, during conferences, in study halls, and in class. No matter what method of teaching you use, you will need to provide special help for some students.

Not only do students having trouble with their studies need special help, so also do students who are doing well. Everyone at times needs encouragement, criticism, discipline, correction, and inspiration. Taking time to look over students' papers, to compliment them on their progress, and to point out possible ways for improvement can be beneficial for both the most successful and the least successful students.

Nevertheless, in spite of the value of special help, it alone cannot meet the demands of individual differences. Stronger measures are needed. Insofar as possible, provide individual instruction designed for individual students. Such provision can usually be made most easily within the framework of the classroom laboratory, the differentiated assignment, the unit approach, or the learning packet. In the following paragraphs, we discuss some techniques that can be used for individual instruction within such plans.

Self-Instructional Devices   The availability of self-instructional devices and materials has made individualizing instruction in ordinary-size classes much easier than in the past. The most spectacular of these devices are the many different sorts of electronic technology now on the market. Among the most versatile of these are the tape or cassette recorder and the video cassette recorder.

For example, in a certain English class one of the major concerns was improving students' oral language skills. Each student was given a blank cassette tape to use during the semester. Every student learned how to run the tape recorder and could use the tape both during and after class hours. Each student was encouraged to record conversations, class discussions, oral reports, and practice material. The recordings were criticized by both the students and the teacher. Students noted their own errors and worked on them individually. They also practiced by themselves on material provided by the instructor until they thought they had improved enough to record their voices again and to listen to the playback. The other work of the class was largely individualized, so that students could use the tape recorder whenever they were ready. They were able to see their errors and, with the teacher's aid, set up a program for improvement. Thus, they were able to see their progress and to judge whether they had improved enough to go on to other work. The teacher felt that the class improved much more than if he had tried to teach these skills directly and had made the criticisms himself.

Tape recorders can also be used to present other types of lessons to individuals or small groups. Before a class, for instance, you might dictate on tape a lesson with instructions for individual self-instruction. Then, during the class, you could give the student the tape recorder and its pretaped lesson for a time. One teacher prepared a tape recording of an account of the religious life of primitive humans. This tape also included a short introduction to tell what the tape was about and to direct the student's attention to important points as well as a short follow-up to reemphasize these points. Individual students or small groups can put on earphones and work on a recorded lesson without bothering anyone else in the class. Whenever they run into difficulty, they simply turn back the tape and replay the bothersome section without disrupting anyone else's progress.

Similar lessons have been worked out for use on eight-millimeter, self-loading, individual-viewing motion picture projectors and videocassette recorders. Sometimes two-by-two slides can be arranged in lessons for individual use by teachers who do not have the desired filmstrips available. Students can follow the slide sequence on photocopied commentary sheets. Such slide sequences should preferably be presented in trays for automatic or semiautomatic projection. If such trays are not available and you must use a single-shot machine, be sure that the slides are numbered in proper order and that the top right-hand corner is marked so that the student can tell which way to insert the slides into the machine. With a little ingenuity, regular 16-millimeter projectors can be used in the same way if you prethread them.

Computer teaching programs and computer-assisted instruction are the most exotic of all the auto-instructional devices. The self-instructional features of the programs and machines make it possible for students to work through programs as rapidly or as slowly as seems most desirable and to pursue different topics or themes at the same time.

Some computer programs can be most useful for individualizing instruction because in effect they make it possible to program a separate course of instruction for every student. In such instruction by computer, each student's performance at any instant determines what the next step in the instructional sequence will be. So because Boy A's responses to the computer's tutoring differ from those of Boy B, the computer can and will give him a different sequence of instructional episodes even if both boys are studying the same topic in the same period. Teaching machines and programmed texts can do the same thing, but without the aid of the computer, they are less proficient.

Other self-instructional materials you can purchase or make include self-administering and self-correcting drill and practice materials. Self-correcting materials can usually be used only for teaching information and skills; the self-correcting format cannot be adapted easily for instruction in the higher mental processes. Even so, such materials can help free you from much busywork so that you can give more time to helping individual students learn at higher levels.

You can also use photocopied study guides, learning activity packets, and contracts to individualize your teaching. Use general guides as a basis for laboratory teaching and special guides for students engaged in different activities. Study guides, learning activity packets, and contracts make it possible for students to proceed at their own pace or to work on different subject matter from that of other students without having to wait for special oral directions from you. Similar study and activity guides can be recorded on tape for students whose reading level is not up to their understanding level.

The use of self-instructional materials does not free you from the necessity of selecting the material, preparing the students and setting for instruction, and guiding or supervising the instruction—including helping students with their difficulties and following up the teaching as well as evaluating the students' progress. The teaching task remains the same, but the use of these techniques and devices does make it possible to spend more time with individuals and to develop the higher goals of instruction that so often are neglected.

INDIVIDUAL AND GROUP PROJECTS   Both individual and group projects as described in Chapter 9 are useful for individualizing instruction. Since the basis of the project is that it be selected, planned, and carried out by the student because of some intrinsic value to him or her, the individual project is one of the techniques best-suited for developing and capitalizing on individual interests and abilities.

INDEPENDENT STUDY   One of the major goals of schooling is to help students to learn to work independently. Independent study is good for motivation. It may lead to better control. It should not, however, be the only method used to teach anyone.

To conduct independent study well requires considerable skill. It is important to give students the right amount of support, help, and leadership without stifling their ideas and initiative. Students must be guided into selecting independent study material appropriate to their individual abilities, experience, interests, and goals. Students tend to bite off more than they can chew. In the beginning of the independent study, try to arrive at a definite understanding with the students about just what is to be accomplished and how. These agreements can be written down. Learning packets and study guides are excellent for this purpose. So are quest proposals in which the students state what they would like to do, how they propose to do it, and what products they will produce as evidence of successful completion of the quest. See Figure 10.3 for a sample quest proposal. As you can see, quest proposals are much like the contracts described in Chapter 6 and are excellent tools for individualizing instruction. In a contract, the student also sets forth what he or she plans to do and what the expected "payment" for the performance is.

INDIVIDUALIZING READING   Individualized reading is based upon the assumption that students can acquire much the same information and concepts even though they may not read the same books or articles. Thus, in the study of ancient man, students with a lower reading ability might read such materials as the Abramowitz pamphlet *World History Study Lessons*, whereas others might read such difficult and esoteric material as the final chapter of Von Koenigswald's *The Evolution of Man*. Others might read such varied works as Chapters 2 and 3 of Van Loon's *The*

■ **Figure 10.3**
A Sample Quest Proposal

Name _____

   I. General statement of what I would like to do:

  II. Things I will need to do to carry out my quest:

 III. At the end of my quest period, I will submit the following as evidence
     of my work:

Approved: _____ _____ _____
                Student   Teacher   Parent

Story of Mankind, Ashley Montagu's *Man: His First Million Years*, a *National Geographic* magazine article, or the Dell Visual paperback *Prehistory*. Or they might read the first unit "Days before History," in Hartman and Saunders' text *Builders of the Old World*, or Chapter 1 of Black's textbook *Our World History*.

In any unit, just what the students read does not matter as long as they achieve the unit objectives; ordinarily there is no need for everyone to read the same selections. When you use the multiple-reading approach in a unit, even though the students are reading different texts, your assignment directs them toward the same instructional objectives. For instance, an assignment might require the readers of Von Koenigswald to find out how early men and women developed their culture and what their first tools were like. Similar questions might be asked of the students reading the Abramowitz material or of those reading Ashley Montagu. You can ask the students reading the *National Geographic* to search for information about life among the ice-age people—their eating habits, hunting techniques, and tools and weapons. You can present the questions to the students orally when giving the assignments or in conferences while they are working. An even better way would be to prepare a photocopied study guide that lists the questions that the students ought to find the answers for and that suggests readings in which the answers might be located. Students could use these guides both to direct their study and as reference lists from which to select their reading.

When conducting individualized reading, guide students to select reading suitable to their reading ability, interests, background, and academic needs. In so far as possible, try to match the reading level of the selection with the reading level of the reader. Do not, however, bar students from reading or attempting selections that they might enjoy and profit from just because the selection seems too hard or too easy. Allow students to try difficult assignments. If they find they have bitten off more than they can chew, let them change to something easier. Encourage good readers to read challenging material, but do not rebuff them if they pick something easy. After all, sometimes the easiest, simplest reading is the best. Common interests and purposes may cause considerable overlap in the reading choices of students, regardless of their ability.

Stop and Reflect

Why do authorities often condemn the use of only one text in the classroom? What is your position on this question?

What advantages does the use of multiple readings have in the subject you wish to teach? What disadvantages? How would you use such a technique in the study of mathematics?

If the students in your class do not all read the same readings, how can you ensure that they all have an opportunity to acquire the important learnings?

BOOK REPORTS AND SUPPLEMENTARY READING   Reading reports can be useful in all courses. They can be especially helpful in multitext courses.

Many teachers use formal book reports for collateral readings. In high school honors sections, students are frequently required to write formal critical essays or book reviews. For gifted, interested students this practice is commendable, but for the average student the accent should be placed on reading rather than reporting. A simple book report form such as the card illustrated in Figure 10.4 or the simple form shown in Figure 10.5 should suffice admirably.

Stop and Reflect

Would you be inclined to use the short, informal book report or the more formal book report approach? Why? Would you use both approaches? If so, for what purposes would you use each type? How would you evaluate them?

How can you find material to suit the varying reading levels of your students on a limited school budget?

How can different types of work areas within a classroom help to provide for individual differences? How can they be used?

How can self-correcting material be used in providing for individual differences?

How can self-evaluation of a student's progress be used to motivate him or her?

How would you organize your class to use self-instructional devices, quest proposals, and individualized units effectively and efficiently?

USING FREE PERIODS   Occasionally, students may be given free periods in which they are permitted to follow their own interests as much as possible. The activities in such free periods should be limited to those that are suitable to the classroom and to the subject. Such periods are usually more appropriate for reading and literature

---

FIGURE 10.4
Book Report Card

Name of student: _____ Date: _____

Name of book: _____

Author: _____

Summary of the book:

Critical comment:

```
┌──────────────────────────────────────────────────────────────┐
│                          HISTORY                               │
│                        BOOK REPORT                             │
│                                                 Hour _____   │
│   Name _____ When book was read _____ │
│   Name of book _____ │
│   Author(s) _____ Type of book _____ │
│                                                                │
│   Setting of story:                                            │
│      Where did it take place? _____ │
│      When did it take place? _____ │
│   Briefly tell what the book is about: _____ │
│   _____ │
│   _____ │
│   _____ │
│   _____ │
│   _____ │
│   _____ │
│   _____ │
│   _____ │
│   _____ │
│   What do you think was the author's aim in writing this book? │
│   _____ │
│   _____ │
│   What about the book was of most interest to you? _____ │
│   _____ │
│   What is your opinion of this book? Where is the book weak? Strong? │
│   _____ │
│   _____ │
│   _____ │
└──────────────────────────────────────────────────────────────┘
```

■ FIGURE 10.5
Book Report
From Lawrence High School, Lawrence, Kansas

than for other subjects, although this does not need to be so. They are often instrumental in forming new tastes in reading, art, music, and other areas, and often open new vistas of appreciation to the student. They also have the additional advantage of giving the teacher opportunities to help students who need individual attention.

Finding Time for Individual Instruction

STUDENT PARTICIPATION IN PLANNING AND EVALUATION   It takes time to provide properly for individual instruction. One of the keys to finding the necessary time is to allow the students to take a greater share in the responsibility for their own studies. Adolescent boys and girls, particularly the gifted ones, are quite capable of planning, directing, and evaluating their own work, particularly if they have study guides to help them. If you allow them to do so, you can not only help them to acquire skill in self-direction, but also free yourself for individual and small-group work. Moreover, using student planning and evaluation makes it possible for students to map out individual plans suitable to their needs.

USING STUDENT HELP   Students often help one another. This help is usually quite effective, since adolescents frequently learn more readily from their peers. Take advantage of this fact by asking students who have mastered a skill or concept to coach other students who are having difficulty. If done carefully this technique, known as peer tutoring, can be quite beneficial. It gives teachers some assistance so that they can find time for more individual teaching; it teaches young people how to share their talents and how to communicate their ideas to others; it helps foster the idea of service; and it helps both the tutor and the tutored learn the subject more thoroughly.

Stop and Reflect

How can students help each other? How can such help be used to provide for individual differences?

How can a teacher of a large class find time to work and confer with individual students?

List occasions when you might consult with pupils informally.

The Need for a Variety of Materials

Providing for individual differences requires a wealth of instructional materials because you cannot expect every member of the class to be interested in the same thing. Materials too easy for high achievers may be so difficult that they frustrate the average or at-risk students. Consequently, provide readings and other materials suitable to the various levels and interests in the class and make sure they are available when individuals need them.

Remedial Teaching

Teaching designed specifically for students who have not achieved desired goals is called *remedial teaching*. Many teachers seem to think there is something esoteric about remedial teaching. There is not. Remedial teaching is merely good teaching concentrated directly on the student and the student's needs. It is usually more effective than ordinary teaching only because it is more thorough and more carefully designed to remedy a specific need.

Some teachers seem to feel that remedial teaching should be reserved for extraordinary students and for remedial classes. Nothing could be further from the truth. Every youth needs remedial teaching at one time or another. To provide remedial teaching in each unit is relatively easy to do if evaluation is continuous and the teacher concentrates on the students rather than on the subject matter.

In the regular class, remedial teaching ordinarily consists of reteaching those things that students have not learned well. For instance, if the students in a class that should already have studied the fulcrum do not seem to understand what it is, a lesson about fulcrums should probably be repeated for all. If only a few persons did not get it, they should be retaught as a special group. If it becomes evident that just one boy missed it, he should be retaught individually. To reteach in this fashion may mean spending several days with the entire class on the missed learning, or revamping the next unit to include this learning again, or it may entail no more than just a few minutes of review and explanation, or perhaps a short conference with one student.

The following illustration serves as an example of remedial teaching in the regular classroom. In going over the test papers from one of her mathematics classes, the teacher noted that one of her students was having considerable difficulty with the problems. An analysis of his papers showed that the student was neglecting to convert all the parts of the problem to the same terms. At the next class meeting, the teacher pointed out to the student the error he was making. She then quizzed him to see that he understood how to convert from one unit to the other and assigned to him several special problems by which to practice the technique directly.

Stop and Reflect

Of what value can self-correcting exercises be in remedial teaching? In what ways is remedial teaching different from regular teaching? How can practice materials be utilized in remedial teaching?

Can you give examples of the need for remedial teaching of gifted youths from your own experience? How should this type of remedial teaching best be handled?

Supposing about one-third of your class missed an essential part of the last unit. You estimate that it would take about two days to reteach it properly. What would you do?

The following is from a junior practicum student's observation report. What would you do as a teacher if you had this boy in class?

Student Report

The student I am reporting on is most unusual. He is in the seventh grade and comes from a bad home environment. His parents are separated. The effect this has on the boy is startling.

He reports to school usually at 7:30 a.m. every morning, although the school requires him to be there at or by 8:30. What does he do? Well, he helps anyone who needs help. If teachers happen to be in at that time or thereafter, he will open the windows and fix the shades.

This is good because it shows a positive attitude. At the same time, however, most teachers think he is a pest. When classes start he tries to quiet the class during homeroom, but this adds to the noise and confusion.

During his classes he is generally quiet, however, seeming to be studious, but actually isn't. He only does "C" work. The guidance officials will not release any information about the student. Most information is from his teachers.

His homeroom teacher explains that the boy complains if the teacher is not in early in the morning or does not stay later after school. This boy is usually one of the last to leave.

He erases the board and straightens chairs; however, all this is not positive. Since he is always demanding attention, he is sometimes very loud and has minor scuffles with the other students, but nothing serious enough to be reported to the office.

I ask him if he wants to go to college, but he doesn't know. He seems only sure about the present. During the first week I was there, he wanted me to sign a petition so he could go on the stage and sing a song. The last week before Easter he wanted to dress up like the Easter bunny.

This student demands attention probably because of his bad home life. The teachers could use this need or his helpfulness for a more positive goal. But most of the teachers feel he is a pest and don't want to be bothered with him.

SUMMARY

Every student is different from every other one, and so each one's education should be different for optimal benefit. These differences cause many pedagogical problems, but they also offer the teachers levers by which to make their teaching more effective.

Insofar as possible, schooling should be individualized. Secondary school administrators have attempted to provide for individual differences through organizational devices. Among these devices have been such things as tracks and streams, homogeneous grouping, electives, minicourses, acceleration of the gifted, and ungraded schools. However, none of these plans has been able to provide the complete answer to the problem. Even when the administrative devices are successful, they can cope with only part of the problem. As in all other instructional matters, the final solution must be worked out by individual teachers.

Luckily, teachers have at their disposal many techniques for coping with individual differences in students. They may differentiate their assignments by varying the difficulty, length, or type of work from student to student. They may find it desirable to group their students within the classes according to needs, interests, or abilities, or to partially differentiate the work through individual or group projects. Sometimes they may find it advantageous to allow some students to move through courses more quickly, or more slowly, than other students, or to encourage some students to enrich their learning by going into topics more deeply than other students do.

Individualizing instruction is not as difficult as teachers fear, and it is necessary. One way to meet this need is by conducting the class as a laboratory. In laboratory periods many students can proceed with a minimum of guidance while the teacher helps students who need assistance. Particularly valuable as a means of freeing the teacher's time for those who need help are the many self-instructional devices that help students teach themselves. Among these devices are computers and teaching programs as well as older devices like self-administering and self-correcting practice material. Photocopied or tape-recorded study and activity guides and learning packets can be extremely helpful and should be used. Combined with the laboratory approach, they are especially effective. The same comment is true of the contract plan, independent study, and continuous progress, all of which require a laboratory atmosphere plus some system of helping and guiding students as they work independently or in groups. Free periods in which students are allowed to follow their own bents are also useful.

Finding time for individual instruction is difficult, but when teachers give students more time to participate in the planning and evaluating of their own studying, they can free a lot of time without slighting any students. Also, teachers can make time by encouraging students to help each other.

If you provide well for individual differences, you must expect to have to evaluate students' learning on new bases because students will not learn the same things in the same way. As a corollary, you must also expect to use a variety of materials. Not only will many readings be required, but also materials for many other kinds of activities.

Remedial instruction is one method of providing for individual differences. It basically consists of finding where a student's learning is weak and then aiming instruction at curing the weakness. It may be in the form of small-group or individual instruction of above-average, average, or below-average students.

ADDITIONAL READING

Charles, C. M. *Individualizing Instruction*, 2nd ed. St. Louis, MO: Mosby, 1980.

Cornett, C. E. *What You Should Know About Teaching and Learning Styles, Fastback 191*. Bloomington, IN: Phi Delta Kappa Educational Foundation, 1983.

Corno, L., and R. E. Snow. "Adapting Teaching to Individual Differences Among Learners" in *Handbook of Research on Teaching*, 3rd ed., edited by M. C. Wittrock. New York: Macmillan, 1986.

Dunn, R., and K. Dunn. *Teaching Students Through Their Learning Styles: A Practical Approach*. Reston, VA: Reston Publishing, 1978.

Fenstermacher, G. D., and J. I. Goodlad. "Individual Differences and the Common Curriculum." *Eighty-second Yearbook of the National Society for the Study of Education, Part I*. Chicago: University of Chicago Press, 1983.

George, P. S. *What is the Truth About Tracking and Ability Grouping Really*. Gainesville, FL: Teacher Education Resource, 1987.

Hardman, M. et al. *Human Exceptionality*, 3rd ed. Needham, MA: Allyn and Bacon, 1990.

Henson, K. T. *Methods and Strategies for Teaching in Secondary and Middle Schools*. New York: Longman, 1988, Chs. 7–9.

Hiemstra, R., and B. Sisco. *Individualizing Instruction*. San Francisco: Jossey-Bass, 1990.

Horton, Lowell. *Mastery Learning, Fastback 154*. Bloomington, IN: Phi Delta Kappa Educational Foundation, 1987.

Hunter, M. *Mastery Teaching*. El Segundo, CA: TIP Publications, 1982.

Keefe, J. W. *Learning Style: Theory and Practice*. Reston, VA: National Association of Secondary School Principals, 1987.

Keefe, J. W., ed. *Profiling and Utilizing Learning Style*. Reston, VA: National Association of Secondary School Principals, 1988.

Knowles, M. S. *Using Learning Contracts*. San Francisco: Jossey-Bass, 1986.

Lazear, D. G. *Teaching for Multiple Intelligences, Fastback 342*. Bloomington, IN: Phi Delta Kappa Educational Foundation, 1992.

Oakes, J. *Keeping Track*. New Haven, CT: Yale, 1985.

Wang, M. C., and H. J. Walberg, eds. *Adapting Instruction to Individual Differences*. Berkeley, CA: McCutchan, 1985.

Waxman, H. C., and H. J. Walberg, eds. *Effective Teaching: Current Research*. Berkeley, CA: McCutchan, 1991.

NOTES

1. James W. Keefe, ed., *Learning Style Theory and Practice* (Reston, VA: National Association of Secondary School Principals, 1987), 36.

2. J.S. Renzulli and L.H. Smith, *The Learning Style Inventory: A Measure of Student Preferences for Instructional Techniques* (Mansfield Center, CT: Creative Learning Press, 1978).

3. A.F. Gregorc, *Gregorc Style Delineators: Development, Technical, and Administrative Manual* (Maynard, MA: Gabriel Systems, 1982); Rita Dunn and Kenneth Dunn, *Teaching Students Through Individual Learning Styles: A Practical Approach* (Reston, VA: Reston, 1978).

4. *Learning Styles Network Newsletter* 3 (Winter 1982): 2.

5. John B. Carroll, "A Model of School Learning," *Teachers' College Record* 64 (1963): 723–732.

6. See for instance Benjamin S. Bloom, "Learning for Mastery," in *Handbook on Formative and Summative Evaluation of Student Learning*, edited by Benjamin S. Bloom, J. Thomas Hastings, and George D. Madaus (New York: McGraw-Hill, 1971), Ch. 3.

7. Theodore A. Chandler, "Mastery Learning: Pros and Cons," *NASSP Bulletin* 66 (May 1982): 9–15; Robert L. Bargert, James A. Kulik, and Chen-Lin C.Kulik, "Individualized Systems of Instruction in Secondary Schools," *Review of Educational Research* 53 (Summer 1983): 143–158.

8. Lorin W. Anderson, "A Retrospective and Prospective View of Bloom's 'Learning for Mastery'" in *Adapting Instruction to Individual Differences*, edited by Margaret C. Wang and Herbert J. Walberg (Berkeley, CA: McCutchan, 1985).

9. Kay Pomerance Torshen, *The Mastery Approach to Competency Based Education* (New York: Academic Press, 1977); Bloom et al., "Learning for Mastery."

10. Jane A. Stalling and Deborah Stipek, "Research on Early Childhood and Elementary School Teaching Programs" in *Handbook of Research on Teaching*, 3rd ed., edited by Merlin C. Wittrock (New York: Macmillan, 1986).

Student Diversity

■■■ Overview

You can expect to have all sorts of students in your classes. One of your most important tasks as you get ready to teach is to consider how you can match your teaching to the different types of students you will find in your classes. For instance, consider to what extent and in what ways you would adapt your teaching strategies for students who have attention-deficit disorder or learning disabilities, or for students who are gifted and talented, or for students with different socioeconomic or ethnic backgrounds. Once you have begun teaching, you may find this task to be one of the most challenging of all your duties. In this chapter we discuss some characteristics common to various types of students; however, you should remember that while individuals are sometimes grouped according to the characteristics they share, their individual differences are also great.

The types of students we consider here include those who are gifted and talented, those who are at-risk because of factors associated with poverty, students of differing cultural backgrounds, students whose performance is below average, and students with disabilities. Each of these student types presents unique challenges to teachers. The first challenge is to spot each student's potential. Giftedness may not be obvious to a casual observer. Poverty may hide a student's intellectual strengths. A student's cultural background may cause him or her to struggle with instruction designed for American school learning. Mild learning disabilities and mental or physical disabilities may impede your best teaching attempts. In short, to teach well the broad range of students you will encounter is difficult and requires special teaching strategies that separate students from the mainstream as little as possible. That is why experts as well as the U.S. government maintain that truly exceptional students need individualized educational plans and that teachers must take special steps to meet the needs of *all* students.

■■■ Teaching Gifted and Talented Learners

One of the more important missions of our schools and of teaching is to provide an education that will help gifted and talented youth make the most of their potentialities. Unfortunately, this is a difficult and demanding task, and one that our schools and teachers have not been able to carry out as effectively as one might desire.

Definitions

The meanings of the words *gifted* and *talented* are rather confusing. According to the *Random House Dictionary of the English Language*, *gifted* means "talented" and *talented* means "gifted."(1) In academic educational circles, however, the word *gifted* refers to a person with intellectual ability well above the average, while *talented* refers to a person having a special ability or aptitude in a particular field or fields, but not necessarily having comparably high general intellectual ability or intelligence. Creative persons, for example, are usually considered members of the talented category. These categories, however, are not mutually exclusive. As used in the profession, an individual may be gifted and talented, gifted but not talented, talented but not gifted, gifted in one area and talented in another, and so on. Therefore, it has become customary to use the term *gifted and talented* as a catchall to describe both categories rather than to differentiate between the gifted and the talented.

As we have said, then, a student who is gifted in one area may or may not be gifted in another. For example, Julian C. Stanley found that the most able of all the students who took the screening test for the talented student program at Johns Hopkins University and who scored highest on the Scholastic Aptitude Test (SAT) turned out to be poor in mechanical comprehension and not very good in mathematics or science.(2) Similarly, a very bright, academically gifted youth may not demonstrate leadership qualities. A student who has never been able to learn to read up to par might excel in playing the saxophone and trumpet, be skilled at music sight-reading, and be a capable leader of the school jazz band. These seemingly diverse behaviors attest to the differing and multiple intelligences of students as identified by Howard Gardner in *Frames of Mind*.(3)

Identifying Students Who Are Gifted and Talented

One way to identify students who are gifted and talented is to take advantage of the aptitude and achievement test scores contained in the students' cumulative records. For example, high IQ scores (115+) and scores in the upper 10th percentile on a verbal achievement test are an indication of potential giftedness in academic subjects. Other talents may be discovered by using such instruments as Renzulli and Smith's *Learning Style Inventory*, and Meeker's *SOI Tests*.(4) However, since tests and inventory scores are not entirely dependable, you should also take advantage of other students' opinions, of anecdotal information, and of autobiographical and biographical information.

Observing the quality of a student's work and of his or her thinking is mandatory. Oftentimes observation will reveal that a student who does not perform exceptionally well in your classes is quite gifted after all. Be especially on the lookout for creative students who are adept at sensing problems or gaps in information, forming ideas or hypotheses, testing and modifying these hypotheses, and communicating their findings. Too often such students go unrecognized in our schools.(5)

Stop and Reflect

Examine instruments such as Renzulli and Smith's Learning Style Inventory and Meeker's SOI Tests. What do they tell you?

Examine some cumulative records of middle and secondary school classes. What do they tell you?

When observing your students at work and at play, look for the following characteristics as indicators of giftedness or talent:

1. Shows verbal facility (e.g., proficiency in verbal reasoning, foreign languages, creative writing, and use of advanced vocabulary).
2. Likes to use his or her talents; maintains an interest in and works hard at academic things; tends to be bored by easy, unchallenging content and assignments.
3. Likes to read and study. Reads fairly sophisticated matter in the discipline.
4. Shows an ability to create and maintain organized approaches to learning.
5. Is persistent in an area of interest.
6. Uses divergent and original thinking.
7. Shows curiosity and inquisitiveness; wants to know why; is intrigued by the abstract.
8. Prefers to work independently without close direction.
9. Is full of ideas.

10. Has a well-developed sense of humor.
11. Tends to be nonconforming; wants to try the new and different.
12. Accepts responsibility.
13. Adapts to the new relatively easily and smoothly.
14. Completes assignments quickly and well (although some bright students are slow, careful, and methodical).
15. Is well-informed about the subject matter at hand.

Teaching Students Who Are Gifted and Talented

You might expect teaching gifted and talented students to be easy, but it is not. Gifted students are likely to find conventional classes boring and without challenge, because many courses move too slowly and are too easy for really bright pupils. Most of these students could do college work easily if given the opportunity. Therefore, their courses need to be enriched or individualized for them. Although this strategy is necessary to challenge the minds and stretch the abilities of gifted and talented students, sometimes special assignments or different coursework can be tantamount to a social kiss of death for students in this age group, who may then shun your help. Even when no such risk exists, building mind-stretching assignments, organizing individual instruction, and providing specialized and supplemental materials, high-level exercises, assessment tests, enrichment problems, and so on can make your preparation, presentation, and follow-up very taxing. Really keeping up with gifted students' minds can be quite a job in itself, because once started, bright youths can be inexorable scholars. Teaching them adequately in special classes or tracks or individually in regular classrooms requires much special effort and care.

SPECIAL TEACHING AND PROGRAMS   Students who are gifted and talented will not develop their potentials adequately unless teachers and other school personnel see to it that these students' learning activities nourish these potentials. A proper teaching environment can build talents, but improper teaching can squelch them. Unfortunately, too many gifted young people do not receive the special teaching and programs they need to develop to their fullest. Probably in every heterogeneously grouped class of 35 students, there are a couple of gifted or talented young people who are not recognized or for whom adequate special education is not provided.

ACCELERATION   A number of solutions have been proposed for meeting the challenges of providing suitable education for the gifted. Among them are acceleration, ability grouping, and individualization. Acceleration is perhaps the oldest of these practices. Really bright students seem to be able to jump forward a year or so in grade level without much academic trouble, although some students have difficulty adjusting to older social groups. Sometimes, however, skipping grades or courses can cause problems, particularly if the skipping results in the student's missing necessary background content. The use of continuous progress techniques is probably more satisfactory, since it does not force a student to spend a whole year in a course he or she could finish in half the time.* Forcing students to spend more time on a subject than is necessary for mastery may lead to problems. For instance, students who are required to take a year of Algebra I and a year of Algebra II when they could easily complete both courses in one year may turn into problem students in one way or another because of boredom.

*See Chapter 10.

ABILITY GROUPING   Ability grouping, in which students are separated into more or less homogeneous groups, was discussed in the previous chapter. While such groupings do not seem helpful for students of average and lower ability, gifted students seem to respond well to them. A special type of ability grouping designed for gifted and talented students is the advanced placement course, a university-level course taught in the high school and for which a student may receive college credit. Some schools offer these or other special classes after school, in the evening, on weekends, or during vacation time on an elective basis. In some instances, these classes are sponsored by universities or colleges. In others, they are sponsored locally. One Pennsylvania school system, for instance, offered a ten-week science seminar for gifted students which met in the field at laboratories, health organizations, and other science centers. Upon satisfactory completion of the seminar, the students were eligible to move on to more advanced study.

Some schools provide special coursework via correspondence courses, video-tapes, or television courses which gifted students can participate in along with or instead of normal courses.*

INDIVIDUALIZATION IN REGULAR CLASSES   When classes are heterogeneously grouped, you can take care of the needs of gifted students by the individualization methods described in Chapter 10. Individualized projects, independent problem solving, laboratory work, self-instructional techniques, computer-assisted instruction, mastery learning, and learning activity packets all can be incorporated into ordinary, heterogeneously grouped classes. If you utilize the special abilities of talented students to lead groups, to tutor less able students, and to investigate and creatively report on the more arcane elements of the subject, the gifted and talented as well as other class members benefit.

Stop and Reflect

Map out strategies you could use to best help gifted and talented students in regular classes of a course you might teach.

INDIVIDUALIZED EDUCATIONAL PROGRAMS   Some authorities recommend and some schools have adopted the use of Individualized Educational Programs (IEPs) for laying out individualized curricula for gifted and talented students. Presumably a plan for a gifted student should be built by a committee of parents, teachers, other school personnel, and the student as is done when mainstreaming a student with disabilities. This procedure is described in the section on mainstreaming found later in this chapter.

Now let us consider some of the strategies and tactics you might use to teach gifted and talented students in either homogeneous or heterogeneous classes.

STRATEGIES AND APPROACHES   Gifted and talented students need chances to fly high. Avoid holding them back. Give them opportunities to stretch their wings by allowing them to attempt high-level assignments, especially those that require productive thought. Let students who are able study complex units and materials,

---

*This is not a new approach. In the first decade of this century a Maine boy, who later became the head of a New England generating plant, prepared for his profession by studying electrical engineering correspondence courses in the back of his high school science and mathematics classes under the guidance of a local teacher while the rest of the class followed the standard curriculum.

engage in action-oriented, thought-provoking learning experiences, and undertake optional activities suited to their individual proclivities. Individual and small-group investigations of real problems may be especially fruitful for students who need challengingly high, but reasonable goals to keep from becoming intellectual drifters. Try to make your courses exciting. Utilize games and simulations to replace drills, quizzes, and reviews. Give students opportunities to debate, to reason logically, to write creatively, to examine the media and media reports, to clarify values, and to engage in community activities as well as opportunities to pursue topics that interest them. Encourage them to use a variety of materials, such as original sources, professional materials, college-level textbooks, and the like. For instance, instead of merely reading about the westward movement in a textbook, the gifted student could be reading Parkman's *The Oregon Trail*. When studying World War II, the gifted student might try to reconcile the accounts given by Sir Winston Churchill, General Eisenhower, and others. In metalworking, the talented youth might, in addition to doing excellent work, study such topics as metallurgy, the metal trades, the economics of metals, and the effect of metals on history.

Specialized projects or activities such as these can be done individually, in small groups, or as reports to the entire class leading to subsequent group discussion. They may often be the heart of learning activity packets. In any case, special projects should not only provide gifted students opportunities to pursue topics that interest them, but also free them to learn through their own activity rather than through lectures.

In addition to attempting assignments of a higher order, talented students should meet high standards of workmanship. They can do excellent work; you must see to it that they do so. Do not accept careless, poorly written, or poorly executed work from talented students. To do so engrains in them laziness and mediocrity.

Along with tackling challenging work, gifted and talented students can accept considerable responsibility for their own direction. They should have experience in planning and evaluating their own work. Many of these students are potential leaders, and as such need opportunities to plan, organize, make decisions, and carry out their plans. Moreover, it is wise to provide opportunities for leadership and service in the classroom. For instance, from time to time, allow students who have mastered a particular concept to act as assistant teachers or mentors to others in the class or to lead certain activities.

Sometimes attempting to hold gifted students to standards higher than those of their classmates may backfire. Some bright students may resent having to do better work than other students; however, by appealing to their pride, by explaining to them why the assignments are really worthwhile, and by making the assignments exciting and challenging rather than drudgery can help to lessen resentment. Some teachers provide opportunities for gifted students to be recognized by adding difficult extra-credit questions to the end of a test to make it possible for students to get more than 100 percent as their final score. This device has been somewhat successful; however, since gifted and talented students often earn good grades with a minimum of effort, the appeal of marks is usually of little value. To get the most from these students, you must call upon more genuine motives. Usually this is not hard to do since most of these young people enjoy challenging tasks. Nevertheless, be sure that the individualized tasks you give them are different, challenging, and valuable to them, not just more of the same.

RESEARCH AND DEPTH STUDY   Not only should the subject matter for gifted and talented students deal with generalizations and abstractions, but also the students themselves should have a chance to develop their own generalizations. Memorizing facts and other information is not enough for these students; they should be encouraged to find things out for themselves. In science their laboratory work could include real problems. In literature, they could write some real criticism. In music, they could compose and perform. Their school projects could be actual scholarly research projects or at least the study of a topic in depth. By studying in this manner, gifted and talented students are not only able to master basic facts and skills, but also are able to move on to the creation of new concepts by making logical inferences from the information available. The topics to be studied might be closely allied with the course syllabus or might range far from it.

In some instances research problems require students to have some knowledge of research techniques and methodology, such as statistics, sampling, polling, and the like. Gifted and talented high school youth are quite up to learning these research skills if given opportunities to do so as well as to use them.

THE SEMINAR APPROACH Small seminar classes made up of gifted students are excellent devices for utilizing the impact of depth study. One type of seminar might consist of a member's presenting a paper on a topic as a basis for group discussion. Another type might involve a general discussion on topics that all have studied in some detail. In either case, the students are encouraged to bring all their knowledge and skill to bear on the problem in a penetrating, logical analysis. In such discussions, the interchange must be free and open. No rules, except those of logical analysis and courtesy, should bar the way. The purpose of the seminar approach is to encourage hard, incisive examination of carefully researched material.

Creative Students

The routine, conformist, unimaginative nature of so many middle and high school classes can be stifling to creative adolescents. In contrast, your classes should provide plenty of opportunities for students to display creative behaviors. They should have lots of inquiry, creative research, and other problem-solving activities. In all classes, these students should be encouraged to venture forth on their intellectual wings without fear of reprisal. Respect their unusual questions, show that you value their ideas, provide them opportunities to learn from themselves, and give them credit for self-initiated learning. Above all, let them figure things out, discover ideas and concepts, and find their own answers to problems without threat of immediate evaluation and correction. In short, plan learning experiences that will stimulate and foster creativity. Not everyone should be forced into the same mold all the time.(6)

Helping Gifted Underachievers

Many gifted adolescents do not live up to their potentials. Their low performance may be the result of physical problems such as poor eyesight, learning disabilities such as dyslexia, social maladjustments, or home influences (or lack thereof). Sometimes they may feel that doing well will cause their classmates to dislike them.

It is extremely easy to mistake gifted underachievers for persons with little potential. To spot them, look for anomalies in their records. For example, their schoolwork may not match their IQs or aptitude test scores, or their present performance may not be in accord with that in lower grades, or their class behavior may fall below their out-of-class behavior.

To catch the attention, interest, and cooperation of these gifted underachievers, it is necessary to use enticing activities that go beyond the activities already recommended for the gifted and talented. Among the learning strategies and tactics that may arouse the enthusiasm of these students are the following:

1. Try to match the learning activities with the students' interests and goals.
2. Introduce real-life problems and learning activities.

3. Use movies, filmstrips, videotapes, and computer programs to attract the students' interest and curiosity.
4. Encourage students to plan learning activities of their own based on what they would be interested in knowing and doing.
5. Provide instruction in learning how to learn, problem-solving techniques, and learning by inquiry and discovery techniques.
6. As far as possible, make your teaching compatible with the social and cultural background of the student.

Stop and Reflect

What can you do to provide gifted students with work that is sufficiently challenging?

A teacher complained that her bright students were not working up to capacity because she could not make them do more work than her average students. What would you suggest that the teacher do to help keep the bright students working up to capacity?

In some schools teachers use the services of gifted students in teaching their less-gifted peers. What is your estimate of this practice?

How would you attempt to catch the interest of a gifted student who was obviously bored in one of your classes?

How would you go about tempting gifted students to do considerably more and harder work than other students?

Managing Cultural Diversity

The United States is a host to many cultures, many of which result from a variety of ethnic heritages—African American, Cuban American, Puerto Rican American, Italian American, Polish American, Native American, Jewish American, and French Canadian American, to mention just a few. There are many more. This diversity is reflected in classrooms across the nation. California students, for example, represent more than 70 language groups and dozens of nations.(7) Some inner-city California school systems are trying to manage school populations made up of students who speak 40 to 50 different languages.

Other cultural groups result from economic differences. For example, the culture of the upper socioeconomic class differs considerably from the culture of the middle class, which in turn differs from that of the urban or rural poor. People within each socioeconomic level tend to develop a culture that influences language use and environment, factors that often create barriers for communication between one socioeconomic level and another.(8) In fact, cultures—by which we mean the customary beliefs, social forms, and material traits of a racial, religious, or social group—are frequently more a product of socioeconomic factors than of ethnic factors.

The Socioeconomically Disadvantaged

Before we begin a discussion of students from low socioeconomic groups, it is imperative that we make an important clarification: All students, regardless of socioeconomic level, are individuals and therefore cannot be lumped together when making teaching decisions. For purposes of discussion, however, it is sometimes necessary to group people according to broad characteristics. In the case of students from socioeconomically disadvantaged backgrounds, one such broad generalization is that children who are poor may come to the classroom with certain problems that can affect their ability to learn. We often think of them as deprived—and of course to be poor is not an advantage. Poverty deprives people of many of life's amenities and opportunities; but not all poor people are deprived. Children from the poorest socioeconomic classes may be the recipients of warm support from parents and grandparents, have a rich cultural heritage, have a sense of pride in their race and ethnicity, and may exhibit skills of independence, caring, and self-reliance. Be careful not to make overquick judgments concerning who is or is not deprived.

Some students from poor neighborhoods are truly deprived, however. Among them are young people

whose homes are hovels, shacks, or run-down tenements;
whose homes are really the streets;
whose home lives are barren and abusive;
who have never lived in homes where reading materials were available or
   where people enjoyed reading;
whose family members are illiterate;
who have had little chance to hear or speak standard English;
who may often be alone or without adult supervision;
who have few adult role models;
whose education has been interrupted by frequent moves; and
whose families cannot supply adequate food and clothing.

A CULTURE OF POVERTY   Just as other socioeconomic groups do, the poor tend to develop a culture of their own. This culture can influence the attitudes and behaviors of poor children when they attend school. To successfully teach all the children in their classes, teachers need to recognize and separate cultural characteristics from behaviors and attitudes that truly interfere with learning.

Generally speaking, a student who comes from a socioeconomically disadvantaged background probably is more likely to appreciate pragmatic and traditional ideas rather than abstract or theoretical ones. A person who sees things this way is more accepting of practices that worked in the past and that are working now, and may be suspicious of new ideas, new ways of doing things, and departures from traditional customs. This point of view tends to espouse the belief that what is right is right now, was always right, and always will be right. A young person who comes from a background of poverty may never have been exposed to new, different opinions, moderate or progressive views, or reforms, so obviously progressive educational teaching strategies are likely to be suspect.

In socioeconomically disadvantaged cultures, people are often family centered. Large, multigenerational, extended families are common. Students from such a culture may belong to families made up of many children and various adults such as parents, grandparents, aunts, and uncles, even in single-parent homes. In large-family homes, the atmosphere tends to become communal; everyone shares, but the adults are still in authority. Often in single-parent families the top authority is a woman—a mother or grandmother who holds the family together. Children who come from large families such as this frequently grow into effective group members who get along well with each other. Consequently, in school situations, they may favor learning in a cooperative environment rather than in an individualistic one.

Perhaps as a result of their experiences and frustration over their inability to control circumstances in other areas, parents from low socioeconomic environments tend to concentrate on controlling their children, who must do as they are told. Discipline may be swift, impressive, and physical. Other interactions within such a family, such as learning methods, means of expression, and ways of showing affection may be physical as well. If a student in your classroom comes from such a background and tends to learn and express himself or herself better through physical means, you may find this student responsive to opportunities to manipulate learning materials, to perform exercises, and in general to work with his or her hands.

TEACHING SOCIOECONOMICALLY DISADVANTAGED CHILDREN   Children who come from socioeconomically disadvantaged backgrounds are frequently lumped together with at-risk learners in teachers' thinking. This is unfortunate because, just as with any other group, the range of native intelligence in students from poor environments is great. Many socioeconomically poor students are truly talented and have much more academic potential than their teachers realize. Still, all too often, the disadvantages of poverty can make it difficult for some students to master school learning. Because of their peculiar problems and because their potentials may be well-hidden, children from economically deprived backgrounds need and deserve special consideration in our classes. Beware of self-fulfilling prophecies: If some students are labeled in your mind as having little potential or as being too difficult to work with, those students will likely be just that. Make an extra effort to discover their individual potentials and to expect them to achieve all that they are capable of.

Children from low-income environments are often wary of school. If their experiences in academic environments have been inadequate up to this point, they may see school as just one more example of the unfairness of society. Because of past failures, these students may see little point in striving to learn what is taught. In addition, the curriculum may seem irrelevant to their lives—past, present, or future. Students who do not see learning as important are not likely to try. It is crucial, then, to show how the subjects they are expected to master are important to their lives. Show them how the "three Rs," science, and even history and literature can help them now and in the future. Otherwise, more often than is necessary, these students will do badly in school and as a result drop out. In Baltimore, for instance, as in many other cities, more than half of the students leave before finishing high school.(9)

Because many students from socioeconomically disadvantaged neighborhoods enter into secondary schools with only meager academic competence and small expectations, to teach them successfully is liable to be difficult—so difficult that many teachers despair and give up, and so compound the students' troubles. However, these youths frequently have much more potential than surface appearances indicate. They deserve more from their schools than faint-hearted teaching. The following suggestions may make the task easier.

1. Often the handicap that is holding back a youth from an impoverished background may be the inability to read well. Sometimes simply adjusting the reading level of the material to be studied may make the difference between student learning and student frustration. Make every effort to bring the students' reading abilities up to par as quickly as possible. Until this objective has been achieved, try to find a variety of easy reading materials suitable for the age and interest levels of secondary school students. For example, use multiple readings in laboratory fashion rather than assigning material from a single textbook. Provide adult materials written at a low reading level. (Certain metropolitan newspapers are written for an adult readership at fairly low reading levels, for instance.) In addition use materials other than reading matter: tape recordings, videotapes, films, and pictures. Where no suitable reading matter is available, prepare your own. Paraphrase difficult reading matter so that students with lower reading abilities can successfully comprehend it. Try to provide materials that are informative, interesting, and adult, yet easy to read and understand. Strive for clarity. Use short, direct sentences and basic everyday words, and keep the text clear, to the point, and sparsely worded. Provide the stu-

[Handwritten margin notes: "Show fairness", "Make curriculum relevant", "Make learning imp.", "Adjust Reading level", "Help students understand content", "Strive for clarity"]

dents with good intellectual food, but do not overload your text with too many ideas.

2. Use simple language in the classroom. Worry less about the words pupils use and the way they express themselves and more about the ideas they are expressing. Let them use their own idioms without worrying too much about grammar, syntax, and the like. However, take care to use proper English yourself; do not conduct classes in dialect.

Use simple language.

3. Be sure the work laid out for all your students is realistic. Forget about covering the subject and concentrate on teaching well. The best procedure seems to be to pick a theme or topic and divide it into short segments. In teaching these segments, seek out feedback from students to be sure that they have learned the essentials of each segment before they move on to the next one. Because the attendance of students from economically disadvantaged backgrounds is likely to be sporadic, try to individualize their assignments so that they can pick up where they left off and move through the course in an orderly fashion, even if they have been absent excessively. Use laboratory techniques, individual instruction, and individual help. Adjust the subject content to the needs of the pupils. For example, provide physically oriented students with concrete projects on which to work, and then move upward toward the more abstract and academic.

Make work realistic
Adjust content to meet students needs.

4. When giving assignments, make directions clear and explicit. You can often help students tremendously if you show them how to study. This is especially true when teaching children from poverty-stricken environments. Be ready to teach any skill that a student might lack but that he or she needs in order to succeed at the secondary school level. For example, make sure students know how to ask questions, how to study, how to take notes, or how to read.

Assignments
ind. - Be clear
The assign.: Show them how to study
- Give them something they can relate to

Assignments should not only be realistic in length and difficulty, but also they should be realistic with respect to the experience, needs, and expectations of your students. Students from low-income areas need a curriculum that seems valuable to them and is close enough to their own lives to have meaning. As with all students, they need to learn about themselves.

5. Try to capitalize on students' interests, experiences, opinions, and values. For example, utilize a student's respect for the fundamentals, the vocational, or the scientific. When encouraging students to read, let them choose what interests them, such as the sports page, a science fiction novel, or anything else that will get them started.

Capitalize on student's interest.

Engaging students in a discussion centered on topics with which the students have some first-hand familiarity can be a lively, informative, thought-provoking learning experience. When, at Jersey City's Snyder High School, one of the "difficult" classes discussed ways to improve the city, the students had an opportunity not only to express themselves in full discussion, but also to think seriously about problems of some importance to themselves personally. All students manufacture their own concepts; they will build on them most effectively when they learn through strategies that emphasize thinking and creativity.

This illustration emphasizes the fact that classes should be interesting, relevant, and active. Role playing and dramatic presentations are often very successful. In Central High School in Newark, New Jersey, for instance, a Black Studies class known for its high rate of absenteeism showed an amazing amount of potential talent when it rehearsed, read, and videotaped a short play. At least one student who was believed to be a nonreader showed that she could not only read, but also read dramatically when the occasion seemed worthwhile.

Other teachers have achieved good results from encouraging students to create a class book made up of their own writing. Another teacher who teaches in an extremely "difficult" school effectively uses student-designed and student-produced bulletin boards and displays. Classes that feature games are usually popular, as well as are classes that make use of various electronic media. Classes that use a variety of materials are always likely to be more interesting than textbook recitations. Books should probably always be thought of as aids to learning, but they should not be the be-all and end-all of instruction.

6. Make sure that each student has real success. Everyone needs the feeling that comes from successfully accomplishing something worthwhile. Adolescents from economically disadvantaged backgrounds do not have such feelings in school often enough. One way to provide them with the opportunity to experience such feelings is to encourage them to help each other with troublesome assignments and to work together in teams. Such arrangements provide students with allies and coworkers with whom they can share both the work and the responsibility. Because they are not alone in the learning endeavor, they can look to other students for support, and so the fear of failure or of appearing foolish is not so pressing. Students frequently learn better from other students, and as a result both the helper and the one being helped are rewarded with a feeling of success and importance.

7. Physical activities are useful in classes of students who are physically oriented. Acting out scenes or role playing can sometimes be very effective, particularly when teaching history or interpreting literature. Students who enjoy working with their hands will take favorably to teaching machines, computers, and other gadgetry. Give them plenty of chances to learn by doing, because such activities will ordinarily be much more successful than lecturing and other primarily verbal techniques.

8. From the preceding paragraphs, you can readily see that students from poverty areas, just like all other students, benefit from taking the responsibility for charting and conducting their own learning activities. Teachers tend to do too much for students when we should be encouraging them to do more for themselves. Since some students tend to be overly dependent on others, be especially careful to encourage independence when teaching them. Try to involve students in the planning and executing of the lessons. If you start with something familiar to them, they are usually able to take a large share in the decision making if they have a little help and guidance.

9. Socioeconomically disadvantaged adolescents need to have opportunities to create and to learn to think. Providing problem-solving activities that are consistent with the ability levels and experiences of these students seems to be an excellent means for attaining this goal.

10. Open-ended questions and discussions can also be used with good results. To make them most effective, you should learn to conduct discussions as conversations. The ordinary teacher-centered discussion is liable to be more like an inquisition than a conversation, which tends to stop students from thinking. Instead, use unstructured discussions of real problems. Unstructured discussions may help you to better understand your pupils as well as to help them learn how to express themselves. In selecting problems to study, (a) be sure the problems seem real to the pupils, and (b) be sure to pick problems the students see as problems. Sometimes situations that adults recognize as problems are not seen in that light by students. Sometimes they do not want to see these circumstances as problems. In such cases, you may get them to see another perspective by challenging their thinking. The Socratic method is useful for this purpose.

11. Respect both the students and their culture. Accept the students as persons, and let them know by your behavior that you are on their side. Because of unfortunate past experiences, some students may need a great deal of convincing. Try to overcome their hostility by deeds, not words. Don't talk down to students by being condescending and patronizing. Tend to your teaching and concentrate on getting

the material across. If your students are convinced that you care about them and their success, you may find their hostility replaced by loyalty and respect.

12. If pupils have not learned basic skills because of failure in the elementary school grades, help them learn those skills. Expect to do a considerable amount of remedial teaching.

13. Be firm, strict, and definite, but not harsh. Harsh measures may seem to work at first, but as a rule, they make it more difficult to carry out any meaningful communication or real learning. Firmness, definiteness, and strong control are absolute necessities, however, especially in the first few weeks of classes when the students will test you to find out what they can get away with.

14. Because disadvantaged youths may be disillusioned and suspicious, you must make an extra effort. Use the same techniques with all your students, but change the tactics to allow for differences in the situation. Avoid watering down courses and course requirements; doing so may lead to further educational deprivation. Do provide intensive remedial techniques wherever needed and make the coursework relevant to the lives of the pupils.

15. Be sure the course content has meaning to the pupils and relates to their lives and interests. Be sure the content helps the pupils to understand themselves and their role in society so that they can see where they fit into the larger picture. Do not present information at a low how-to-do-it level, but provide instruction at a high enough level to help students really understand what is involved. Give them real work; do not feed them drivel. If the pupils cannot do the work required of them, substitute work they can do, but make it something of value.

16. Avoid boring the students; however, use plenty of repetition, review, and drill to develop skills, proper habits, and firm knowledge.

Stop and Reflect

Examine some of the textbooks for middle school courses in your field. Are there any reasons why they would be unsatisfactory for educationally or socioeconomically disadvantaged students?

What could you do to help students from a non-English-speaking background?

Are there any things you could do to combat directly the deterrents to school learning that result from poor living conditions or antiintellectual home environments?

Multicultural Groups

Our school population includes numerous students from racial and ethnic minorities. In recent years, this diversity has been enriched by waves of immigrants, particularly those coming to our country to escape troubles in their own. This influx of immigrants, while enriching life in the United States, also greatly increases the problem of supplying an appropriate education for all our youth.

Every ethnic group has its own culture. Because multicultural groups and lower socioeconomic groups tend to overlap, some of their cultural characteristics may overlap as well. However, all ethnic cultures are rich and different. These differences may be difficult to understand unless you take steps to learn about them and respect them. If you do not do so, you may find teaching your students difficult because cultural differences result in different ways of learning. For example, while some students fall to work immediately upon receiving an assignment, some African American students tend to spend time setting the stage before starting to work on their lessons. Instead of jumping in immediately, these pupils are inclined to take time to look over the assignment, check the lesson material, and ask questions. While this trait tends to reduce the amount of time students spend on task, teachers should be aware that this is not a sign of misbehavior. In some cases, this cultural trait may make the students' studying a better organized procedure.(10)

Similarly, many African American students favor learning styles that may not fare well in rigidly structured classes with fixed time schedules. Students with these types of learning styles do much better in informal, loosely structured class arrangements. Within this context, provide opportunities for students to work together cooperatively at their own pace, preferably having them focus on general principles and ideas rather than on detail. Furthermore, no matter how successful or unsuccessful they have been, students' sincere efforts should be recognized.

Another African American cultural trait you should be aware of is a preference for oral communication over written communication. Students who favor this learning style absorb knowledge best from listening, and perform best when speaking. Sometimes students who especially enjoy oral presentation develop a style of speaking that differs from the styles most often favored in public schools. These differences in communication styles can cause a conflict between school instruction and student learning, which may require you to adjust your teaching style to attain an optimum learning environment.(11)

In addition to becoming aware of the learning styles common to different cultures, you need also to be acquainted with the mores and taboos of the cultures from which your students spring. Things that you do as a matter of course, without thinking, may appear gauche, impolite, or disrespectful to people of other cultures. For instance, most African American students expect to be called by their full names rather than by a nickname. If this is the case with a student in your class, by addressing him as Jim or Jimmy when his name is James, you can appear disrespectful without meaning to be. Similarly, be aware of gestures, signs, and body language that may carry different meanings for different cultures. For example, to cross your fingers to signal good luck is a common gesture in America, but is considered obscene by Southeast Asians. Students from some cultural groups, such as certain Native American tribes, believe that to strive for distinction or praise in class is bad manners. For you to single out a student who feels this way, giving him or her special praise or recognition, could be most embarrassing for that student.

Become familiar with the symbols and superstitions peculiar to some cultures. For a Vietnamese student to dress in white is a sign of mourning, for instance. If you can recognize such factors in your classroom—becoming aware of the signs, symbols, taboos, and customs of other cultures and showing respect for them—your life with students from other cultures can become considerably easier.

As we said before, however, do not assume that the characteristics sometimes attributed to a particular ethnic group are common to all members of that group. Remember that just as in any group of people who share some common characteristics, individuals in every ethnic group differ from one another. Avoid making unwarranted generalizations based on students' race or language. Not all Asian parents, for instance, fit the stereotypes Caucasians often give them (i.e., quiet, submissive, reserved, and cooperative). Everyone has likes and dislikes. Socioeconomic status, place of origin, religion, and so on all have their influence on beliefs, values, and notions about correct behavior. Individual differences are as great in minority ethnic and racial groups as they are in the mainstream society. In a New Jersey suburb, for instance, parents resisted a program set up to introduce youngsters to American schools. The prosperous representatives of Japanese firms who made up a large part of the community did not appreciate what they considered a lesser program for their children; they made their feelings known not only at the school but also in the statehouse.

Remember also that Asia and Latin America comprise many different nationalities, so do not assume that all people from a certain area share the same culture. Again, in a school in metropolitan New Jersey, clashes occurred between Cubans and Puerto Ricans who did not much empathize with one another. Although perhaps all Spanish-speaking, Cubans are not Puerto Ricans, nor are they Mexicans.

Obviously, to make your teaching efficient and effective, your teaching strategies must be as compatible as possible with your students' cultural backgrounds. Therefore, make it a point to learn as much as you can about these cultures. Talk to other more experienced school personnel and to informed lay persons to glean what knowledge you can. They not only can give you tips on what you should know, but also may be able to suggest helpful reading. Take advantage of every opportunity that arises, since studying your students' cultures is worth every effort. For example, Esther Lee Yao suggests that if you are dealing with Asian immigrant youth, you can learn about the local Asian community by visiting local Asian businesses and by attending local Asian festivities. The businessmen and festival attendees will usually be glad to explain the different elements of their world to you if properly approached.(12)

You can also learn much from the parents of your students. However, when speaking to parents, be very polite and tactful. Be careful to use language that could not be interpreted detrimentally. For example, when talking with Asian parents about their children, you would be wise to describe the students' strengths before you bring up any weaknesses or proposals for remediation and requests for support.(13) It is also helpful to become familiar with body language signals so that you will be sensitive to whether parents are receptive to what you are saying or are feeling threatened or defensive.

Along with learning from their parents, you can learn a great deal from your students themselves. Talk with them. Let them present their experiences as topics for themes and discussions. In one class, the students put together a booklet about their experiences. Such experiences can make excellent firsthand resource information for social studies classes, especially if your ethnic students are recent immigrants.

One important step that you can take in your attempts to understand your students and their cultures is to become very familiar with your own ethnic background and the characteristics of your culture. Perhaps, if you become more familiar with the culturally learned opinions, attitudes, and assumptions of your own cultural group, your understanding of and empathy for other cultural beliefs will be enhanced.

Whenever feasible, you should try to incorporate different ethnic materials into your classroom to bolster your teaching, to help students develop a greater awareness of the pluralism of modern American society, and to eliminate racial and ethnic bias. In most school systems, the curriculum builders have provided various curriculum materials for teachers' use. These should be used judiciously so as to eliminate ethnic bias and stereotyping. In every course, students should have opportunities to take pride in their roots and to make the most of their talents.

You will also find it helpful to become familiar with the languages of the different cultures you teach. If many of your students are Spanish-speaking, learn basic Spanish. If "Black English" is a common dialect in your classroom, learn it. When communicating with students, don't worry as much about the words they use and the ways they express themselves as about the ideas they are expressing. Let students use their own idioms without overcorrecting grammar, syntax, and the like. Do, however, try to help them master the skills of standard English. Your own instruction should be in excellent but simple standard English.

Other than these suggestions, your basic strategies for teaching multicultural students should not differ greatly from the teaching strategies you use to teach all students well.

Stop and Reflect

What ethnic cultural group are you from? Does your ethnic background present difficulties in dealing or socializing with students from other groups? What about teaching them?

Find out how many ethnic cultures are represented by the college students in your classes. Try to ascertain their feelings about various aspects of their culture and other cultures.

The text suggests some ways to get to know and understand other cultures. Try them. What have you learned from them?

RECENT IMMIGRANTS   The major problem for recent immigrants and some other ethnic groups is the language barrier. In 1980 more than half of the students in New York City lived with parents whose native tongue was not English; yet standard English is a virtual necessity in most American communities if a person is to become vocationally successful and enjoy a full life. Further, language is the most important medium by which students new to the United States can integrate their former life-style with the new-to-them Americanism they now face. This language problem places a heavy burden on teachers. Learning to communicate reasonably well in English takes an immigrant student at least a year, probably longer; some authorities say three to seven years. Immigrant students' early proficiency in English is seldom good enough for them to cope with school classes, so it becomes necessary for teachers to adjust their teaching considerably to allow for students' lack of facility in English.

Language problems make it quite difficult to know where to place immigrant students in the curriculum. How do you handle a boy who has very little comprehension of English but who is quite gifted in calculus? Intelligence tests are not much help, since they are built on the supposition that the student understands the English language and American ways. Students probably should not be pulled out of the regular program to attend special classes unless absolutely necessary, but they need bilingual support which the school should supply.

In laying out courses for pupils from different cultural groups, take care that the coursework seems relevant to them. However, when dealing with immigrant students from war-torn areas, be cautious. Course content can sometimes be too relevant—too close to home—and concern things that the students would do better to put behind them than to discuss or investigate. Immigrant students who have suffered the traumas of war, revolution, and terrorism should not have to live through it again in your classes. If a situation is not threatening, however, students are usually quite willing to investigate. Your problem is to encourage them, not to discourage them by bringing up their traumatic past or by making them appear foolish as they face your abstraction.

Parents of immigrant children are ordinarily truly concerned about their children, and they are often troubled about the direction in which the American schools seem to be taking their offspring. The value systems, manners, moral standards, traditions, and social behaviors that the children are learning in school often do not conform to those the parents hold dear. Take advantage of parental concern; most parents would be glad to help you and other concerned teachers do well by their children. Sometimes the educational goals of multicultural parents seem to be set extremely high. Unfortunately, these parents often do not know enough about American customs and education to be able to help their children much in reaching these educational goals. However, approach parents; they may do all they can to help, and perhaps you and they can complement each other as you go along.

Stop and Reflect

Suppose you were to teach in a community deluged with new immigrant students. What steps would you take in your teaching? What steps would you expect the school to take? The community?

Eliminating Sexual Bias

Over the years and for various reasons, stereotypes concerning the roles and abilities of men and women have become common. The result has been hardship for both boys and girls. Therefore, take care that neither your teaching techniques nor your teaching materials reflect sexual bias or stereotyping. Your own good judgment should be sufficient to guide you in this aspect of your teaching.

Teaching At-Risk Students

Learners who are at-risk are normal youths who end up ranking at the bottom of their class or are placed in low-ability classes in an ability-grouped system. At-risk students are not grouped with students who have disabilities, because they do not show special signs of disability. Rather, they seem to be plugging along slowly at the rate their test scores and your observations would lead you to expect. At-risk learners are usually deficient in basic skills and have very poor work and study habits, coupled with short attention spans for schoolwork and difficulty in understanding abstract concepts. Being prone to failure, they are liable to develop poor self-concepts, lose interest in their schoolwork, and misbehave.

At-risk learners need careful teaching. Many of them have experienced discouragement and frustration in ordinary middle and secondary school classes. Being lower in ability than most students, they usually have not learned the essentials of one lesson before the class moves on to the next one. Consequently, they keep dropping more and more behind until they are hopelessly buried in the debris of not-yet-learned information, concepts, and skills. Yet, if you will take the time to explain things carefully, to teach unlearned skills and furnish missing background, and to adapt the material to be learned, you may be able to turn at-risk learners around and get them moving forward.

Therefore, take time with them. Present new work slowly in more and shorter steps. Usually, students who are at-risk know quite a bit more than they seem to, but in the process of drawing them out you must avoid shortcuts, teach the details, give plenty of individual attention, and help with study skills. Do not assume that a student already knows something until you have checked it out. Be careful to diagnose the student's strengths and weaknesses so that you can capitalize on the strengths, shore up the weaknesses, and fill in the lacking background information and skills.

When teaching slow learners, keep your emphasis on the developmental rather than the remedial. Remedial work is necessary, but you will be more effective if you focus on teaching your subject. Use remedial strategies as a means to teach the subject rather than as an end unto itself. Do not give a watered-down version of the academic course (watered-down courses are seldom good for anyone), but do keep the course down-to-earth, emphasizing basic principles and specifics. Also, see to it that the students get a chance to practice the skills of clear, critical thinking in practical, realistic situations. *For your learners who are at-risk, try to make the coursework simple, practical, realistic, and meaningful.*

Make judicious use of audiovisual media. Watching demonstrations, observing phenomena, looking at movies and videos, making collections, and building exhibits and models are all examples of concrete, tangible activities that can help at-risk students learn. Be sure, however, that these activities are kept uncomplicated and are clearly explained.

Learners who are at-risk need plenty of instruction. When giving explanations, go into detail. Use plenty of illustrations. Keep your language as plain and direct as possible. Be sure students know the meaning of the words you use; it might be helpful to write them on the chalkboard. Be thorough and avoid shortcuts, since with low-ability students these may turn out to be short circuits. Because at-risk learners may find it difficult to transfer their learning, be careful to point out the implications of each lesson in some detail.

Your teaching strategies and instructional materials for low-ability learners should be easy, but adult. Shorter essays and problems, simplified texts, and simplified readings will make your classes more effective if they do not seem babyish. The importance of making sure that what you are teaching is mature enough for your students cannot be too heavily emphasized. One young teacher of remedial mathematics in a central city high school found that he could not make any headway until he disguised the basic arithmetic he was trying to teach as algebra. When the students worked on the algebra, they began to learn addition and subtraction and also to attend class more regularly (although still continuing to absent themselves from other classes). To walk the tightrope between the too simple and the too complex is often quite difficult.

Realistic activities help motivate at-risk learners and make the transfer of learning relatively easy. For example, sometimes students of lower ability may find it difficult to see the relevance of many mathematics problems, but when the problem has to do with the cost of purchasing, financing, and maintaining a car, the pertinence of the mathematics involved may become both obvious and interesting to a group of 16-year-olds. In English classes, writing letters to real people can make composition more realistic. A class newspaper may help students see the importance of their schoolwork. Similarly, involving students in the presentation of an assembly or the preparation of an exhibit can make the learning process real.

Above all, try to use strategies that build up students' confidence and attract their interest. To catch their interest, try to tie the classwork to their personal lives; give them opportunities to use in your classes what they have learned out of school, as well as pointing out opportunities to apply in the real world things that they learn in your classes. To build up their confidence, teach well-structured lessons and units made up of a variety of relatively short activities, and allow plenty of time for supervised study in which you give help and guidance. Form in-class groups, committees, and other opportunities for students to compare notes and learn from each other; and finally, give frequent summaries and reviews.

While trying to keep things as simple as possible, however, do not teach pap. These students need to be challenged and to achieve success while doing real learning tasks. Recognition of their successes is most important and may lead to real improvement.

Stop and Reflect

If faced with low-ability students in your classes, what steps would you take to help them? Be specific.

Teaching Students With Disabilities

A surprisingly large number of students who are of middle and secondary school age have mental or physical disabilities as a result of birth defects, injury, or illness. These young people include boys and girls who are physically disabled, sensory impaired, emotionally disturbed, autistic, learning disabled, and mentally impaired, as well as students who exhibit more than one disability. It is becoming common practice to enroll such disabled students in "regular" classes. This practice, which should be encouraged, exists in several forms. Among them are

1. *Inclusion*, which means to educate every child to the maximum extent appropriate in the school and classroom he or she would ordinarily attend if not disabled in some way. There are no special education classrooms; instead, the necessary special education is dispensed in regular academic classes serving both disabled and nondisabled students.
2. *Mainstreaming*, in which disabled students are selectively placed in one or more regular classes, but leave these classes to attend special education facilities for remedial instruction.

Programs like these give students with disabilities opportunities to learn how to cope and adjust in ordinary society. Nevertheless, these pupils do need to be treated with special care; just remember to treat them in as ordinary a manner as you reasonably can.

As we just said, while making it a goal to treat pupils with disabilities much like you treat all your pupils, remember that they do have special needs. Physically, they may need therapeutic exercises; they also need opportunities for exercise, play, and games that all pupils require. When pupils cannot join in the sports and games of their peers because of disabilities, some provision should be made to give them compensatory or substitute activities that will give them the exercise, the fun, and the emotional and expressive outlets they need.

You may also have to make intellectual adjustments when teaching pupils with disabilities. Whenever possible, hold them to the same high standards as other pupils of similar intellectual potential. Make sure, however, that pupils do not overcompensate for their disability and so develop lopsided personalities. Pupils with disabilities need much guidance to keep from adopting vocational and life goals that are unrealistically high or low. To help them overcome or compensate for their disabilities, you may need to concentrate early and intensively on skills that will be essential in their adult and vocational life. Guidance is particularly necessary for pupils' emotional and social development. Just as any other students, students with disabilities are subject to feelings of inferiority; they may compensate by aggressive, competitive behavior; they may refuse to recognize their problems and live lives of unreality; they may withdraw and become antisocial; they may become tense, nervous, overanxious, and bad-tempered; they may use their disabilities as a crutch to solicit pity, and to feel sorry for themselves. Socially, pupils with disabilities need to have opportunities to become accepted, valued, successful members of their group.

In summary, the pupil with disabilities should be treated just like anyone else—as a person. The objective in dealing with pupils who have disabilities should be to help them to become independent. They should be given opportunities to participate with other pupils on even terms. Within reason, they should be subject to the same rewards and punishments and held to the same academic standards as other students. To compensate for any feelings of inferiority or self-pity they may have, it is important that pupils with disabilities have real successes in their school life. They should be provided with ample opportunity to make genuine contributions to the school and class, and to become accepted as members of their social group. They may need more help and more guidance than most pupils in both the skill and adjustment phases of education. When you teach pupils with disabilities, you must be prepared to cooperate with parents and agencies in providing them with appropriate learnings. Because of their disabilities, these students may be prone to maladjustment, so be aware of the signs. Care should be taken to ensure that these students do not become the butt of other pupils' jokes. The class that provides special needs students with a healthy, normal atmosphere, and in which they are encouraged to do their best, will provide the most benefit.

Federal Law PL 94–142

Federal Law PL 94–142, which is the basis for mainstream educational programs, guarantees nondiscriminatory assessment, a free and appropriate education in a least restrictive environment, and individual programs for children with disabilities who are ages 3 to 21. According to this law, insofar as it is suitable and possible, youths with disabilities should be included in regular classrooms—the main stream—and in the same manner as other students. You will have to make special provisions for their disabilities and adjust your teaching to their individual educational plans. These plans, which are required by law, have been constructed by teams of specialists, classroom teachers, and parents. You must carry out the portions of the plan that affect your own class to the best of your ability so that youths with disabilities will receive maximum benefit from your teaching and from associating with the other students in your classroom.

When teaching a student with disabilities, an Individualized Educational Program (IEP) is used. This instrument basically consists of

1. an assessment of the student's present level of performance and a diagnosis of his or her particular strengths and weaknesses;
2. a statement of the long-term or annual goals;
3. a statement of the short-term instructional objectives necessary for attaining the stated goals;
4. a description of criteria by which to assess the student's attainment of the goals and objectives;
5. an allocation of the time the student will spend on pull-out special education, relative services, and mainstreamed regular classes;
6. a description of the specific services to be provided for the student;
7. the dates for beginning and ending these services;
8. the person or persons responsible for each service, including the roles of teachers, parents, and specialists; and
9. specific suggestions concerning materials of instruction and teaching strategies.

As a member of the teaching team, you will have the duty to help prepare, execute, and evaluate the student's Individualized Education Program. As a new teacher, you can expect your role to be minor. In high schools, particularly, you may not even be invited to the team meetings at which the IEP goals and objectives are written. Nevertheless, you can provide the committee with information about your content area and related classroom procedures. You can also advise the committee concerning the special services suitable for aiding special students and can help in writing the IEP goals and objectives pertaining to the regular curriculum.(14)

Robinson and VanHuene state that classroom teachers who do their jobs well are the most important resource in meeting the needs of students with disabilities because the teachers help to minimize diagnostic errors, aid in the proper placement of the students, and help to prepare suitable individual student goals and objectives.(15)

You also will be responsible for spotting students in your classroom who may have disabilities but perhaps have been missed. Actual assessment should be done by school specialists, but you can help considerably by suggesting that certain pupils be evaluated. When you do so, pass along relevant data such as reports of your observations of the student, information concerning the student's school history, any special problems of the past and attempts to deal with these problems, any pertinent information passed on by the student's parents, and the signs that have led you to suspect disability and a need for help. Next you should participate in assessing the student's needs and in developing the IEP. At this stage, you should be a key figure in determining proper goals and objectives, teaching strategies, and materials of instruction for the ensuing year. Once the plan is implemented, you will be responsible for providing the student with proper individualized instruction according to the plan. As the year progresses, review the student's IEP from time to time and bring to the team's notice any anomalies. Ask yourself such questions as, "Was the diagnosis of student needs correct? Were the objectives that were set up appropriate?" and "In general, is the plan working?" At the end of the year, you will report your assessment of the plan and the student's response to it.

Actually, when teaching students with disabilities in heterogeneous classes, your strategies will be much the same as those described for individualizing instruction in the preceding chapter. Encourage the students to be self-managers. Show them what to do and how to do it, and then let them go to it. To this end, supply them with study guides, topical outlines, and such student help as glossaries, organizers, overviews, learning activities, computer programs, and teaching programs. Arrange your classroom in an informal, flexible manner such as the laboratory class described earlier. Provide your special needs students with learning centers, classroom libraries, and so on, so that they can progress individually at their own speed and under their own direction.

Use flexible strategies in your heterogeneous classes. Lockstep teaching will not work when there are great differences among students' abilities. Try to develop a congenial, cooperative atmosphere in which students work together and help each other. Utilize peer tutoring and group work to help those with disabilities. For tutors, select pupils who can handle the work, who are compatible with other students, and who are willing and eager to help. Don't forget that sometimes a person with a disability (e.g., a gifted student who has a physical disability) may be able to tutor other students. Also remember that at times someone who is only a little more able than a student in need of tutoring may be a more effective coach than someone who is so outstanding that he or she overshadows the student with disabilities.

Stop and Reflect
Procure an IEP from a special education teacher. Study it. If you were to teach this pupil in one of your regular classes, how could you help in building the plan, in implementing it, and in evaluating it?

Learners With Mild Disabilities

If you have mainstreamed students in your class, most of them will probably be what are called "learners with mild disabilities." These students are "usually able-bodied, normal-appearing children whose learning problems are not compounded by physical disabilities," yet they are "inefficient school learners whose deviations in school achievement, and possibly social adjustment, are so marked as to necessitate specialized intervention."(16) They include learners who are "commonly categorized educable mentally retarded, learning disabled, behavior disordered, mildly emotionally disturbed, or children with minimal brain dysfunction."(17)

Ordinarily one can easily spot these pupils, since their school learning falls considerably below what you would expect of their age and measured intelligence. As Daniel Reschley points out, they differ from other students in that they do not process information well because of an inadequate knowledge base from previous learning and a lack of skill in learning strategies. Also they tend to lack self-confidence, which can lead to crediting successes and failures to outside influences other than their own efforts and abilities, and to a strong dependence on external reinforcement for motivation. He goes on to state that there are enormous differences between students classified as mildly handicapped and students with average levels of performance on measured intelligence, achievement, and social/emotional behavior.

Because of these differences, he recommends that instruction of learners with mild disabilities consist largely of "direct instruction, a focus on learning efficacy to facilitate transfer of information into new domain, and some help with adjustment."(18)

Some experts believe that the curriculum for learners with mild disabilities need not differ greatly from the regular curriculum. It seems to them that if teachers of the mildly disabled use "peer tutoring, cooperative learning, and aides or volunteers in the classroom," learners with mild disabilities do not need to be pulled out for special education classes.(19)

Still, boys and girls who have mild disabilities remain at the bottom of the academic barrel. When they reach the secondary grades, they usually are well below average in mathematics, reading, writing, and general educational know-how. If students with mild disabilities are mainstreamed into your classes, you should take special care to see that you design your teaching strategies and tactics to allow for their differences and to meet their special requirements. If special needs students are assigned to you, the following suggestions should help you:

1. If special needs students have pull-out classes with special education teachers, communicate as soon as possible with these teachers so that you can establish plans for cooperation and special education advice. Mainstreamed classes and special education classes should complement each other.
2. Utilize informed systematic observation and testing techniques to help you understand your students with disabilities and their needs.
3. Arrange your classroom as a classroom laboratory. Place work tables, desks, bookshelves, media aids, and so on to allow a mix of teacher-directed activities, independent work, and special projects. Put materials where they are easily available. Utilize wall space effectively. Be sure that everyone can see and can be seen. The classroom should aid, not hinder, learning.
4. Take time to find out what interests your special needs students; carefully adjust your teaching materials and teaching strategies to accommodate those interests.
5. Select materials and activities at which students with disabilities can succeed, but do not give them anything babyish.
6. Motivate them. Show them how the content will help them later

   To get a job
   To do the job
   To survive as an adult
   To learn other necessary skills
   To go to college or enroll in other training (vocational-technical)
   To graduate
   To have fun
   To function like their "normal" peers

To participate in extracurricular activities

7. Be sure your instruction is clear. Be definite. Repeat key concepts as you move through the lesson. Use graphic organizers so that students can follow your lesson. Point out where you are as the lesson proceeds.
8. Individualize instruction. Use peer tutoring, cooperative learning techniques, and aides and volunteers, if available, to teach learners with mild disabilities. Using these techniques and aides may make it unnecessary to pull out special needs students.
9. Use direct instruction to teach factual information. Teach students actively and supervise them well. Use discussions and oral review. Frequent teacher-student interaction and active instruction seem to work best with special needs students.
10. It is sometimes helpful to use alternative compensating mechanisms; for example, let a student tape record lectures instead of taking notes.
11. Use contingent praise as a reinforcer. Since many students with mild disabilities have histories of failure, their self-esteem may be in short supply. Bolster their confidence levels by using effective praise. To make your praise more productive, always use it contingently; that is, praise only those products and efforts that are truly praiseworthy.
12. Computer-assisted instruction works well with students of low ability. Tutorial and discovery programs are excellent. Drill and practice programs, although not as good, are also useful.
13. Mastery learning strategies are most appropriate for mainstreamed students.
14. Use films, filmstrips, slides, videotapes, audiotapes, and other media, either individually or in groups, to get your points across.
15. As a rule, special needs learners do not require remediation as much as they need new developmental learning that begins at their levels.

Other Learners With Disabilities

Other students that you may have mainstreamed into your classes include sensory impaired, emotionally disturbed, and physically challenged boys and girls.

Sensory impaired students have visual or hearing disabilities. If they are mainstreamed into your class, find out how severe their disabilities are and how long they have had them. Then you can adjust your teaching accordingly. Make special provisions in room arrangement to make sure that students with difficulties can hear and see adequately. Do your best to provide them psychological support in a positive climate, focusing on their abilities and potentials instead of their disabilities. In your instruction, make suitable allowances for their disabilities so that they can see and hear, but do not coddle them.

Characteristically, mainstreamed emotionally disturbed students may be dealing with oversensitivity, social stress, and depression. Students who are oversensitive are liable to have low self-concepts, feel unaccepted, and overreact to criticism. To combat such feelings, arrange for students to have many opportunities for success within a supportive class climate. Avoid placing these students in threatening situations; for example, do not force them to give oral reports in front of the class or to perform other tasks that might cause them anxiety or embarrassment. As much as you can, ensure that they are not ridiculed by other students.

If a physically challenged student is mainstreamed into your class, first consult the counselor and the special education expert to find out the extent of the impairment and its presumed effect on the student's learning and social activities. Each physically challenged student is unique. Some have problems of mobility and control. Some have secondary emotional, social, and mental side effects resulting from their impairment. Others seem to have adjusted well to their disability and proceed through life without discernible difficulty. The better you understand physically chal-lenged students' problems and capabilities, the better you can serve them. Avoid frustrating them by asking them to do tasks that are beyond their powers; on the other hand, persons with physical challenges are often annoyed by other persons who, with the best of motives, assume that these challenged individuals need help when they would much rather be on their own. It is easy to underestimate what the physically challenged can do. If given the chance, they may surprise you.

Stop and Reflect

You have some students with mild disabilities in your classroom. What steps would you take to adapt your teaching to meet their needs?

Visit some middle and high school classes and talk to the teachers. What problems do they have with mainstreaming? What problems do the mainstreamed have with their classes and teachers? What are the teachers doing to solve their difficulties?

SUMMARY

Diverse pupils require exceptional teaching. You must adjust your teaching strate-gies and tactics and your subject content to meet their particular needs.

The key to teaching gifted, talented, and creative students is to urge them for-ward and not to hold them back. Since they generally enjoy the abstract and like to learn, gifted students need plenty of opportunities to exercise their minds. If the teacher gives them adequate guidance, they can accept a great amount of the responsibility for directing and evaluating their own learning.

Youth from low socioeconomic backgrounds often are at-risk because of gaps and differences in their backgrounds. However, there has been a tendency to underestimate the potential of these students. Their academic failures are more often failures of the school and the community then student failures. In dealing with students who are socioeconomically disadvantaged, you must treat them with the respect they deserve. As a rule, they respond best to classes that are task-oriented, practical, and realistic.

Students from different cultures present other challenges for the teacher. Many multicultural students are not proficient in English; learning in American schools is quite impossible for them unless some instruction is given in their native language. This problem is exacerbated in many schools where recent immigration has brought in many non-English-speaking students with whom the teacher cannot communi-cate. Further challenges arise in accommodating the differences among standards, customs, and mores of different cultures. These circumstances require that you as a teacher become as familiar as you can with the cultures and languages of your stu-dents. Also, if you can learn to understand your own cultural biases and differences, it may help you to understand and empathize with your students.

Teaching learners who are at-risk requires much skill and patience. Careful diag-nosis of each student is necessary if all students are to receive the kind of help and attention they need. Diagnostic activity is particularly important since low achieve-ment is often the result of insufficiencies in a student's earlier education. In general, the curriculum for at-risk learners should be simple, practical, realistic, and mean-ingful. Teaching methods should emphasize concrete, simple activities while pro-viding sufficient practice and review to make the learning stick. The materials of instruction used with students of low ability should be less verbal than in other classes. Reading material should be short and easy, but not childish. With these requirements, teachers may find it necessary to develop their own materials.

Mainstreamed students with disabilities require individualized programs. You will have to ensure that the portions of individualized educational programs that concern your classes are carried out fully and that the special needs students feel welcome and comfortable in your class.

To sum up, here are some strategies that you might use to teach students who are culturally diverse, who are at-risk, or who have mild disabilities:

1. Try to find subject matter that relates to the pupils.
2. Use a number of techniques to get the students working.
3. Have students contribute to the planning of their own programs.
4. Teach pupils in heterogeneous groups as much as possible.
5. Try to build up students' self-esteem.
6. Try to use intrinsic rather than extrinsic motivation. Reward improvement.
7. Translate obscure material into clear language that students can understand.
8. Try to treat all students as individuals, and adapt your teaching to their individual needs and characteristics.
9. Try to involve the students' parents.
10. Learn all you can about the students' way of life at home.
11. Use proper standard English, but learn the students' languages and dialects.
12. Allow for cultural differences in attitudes toward learning.
13. Utilize cooperative learning, peer teaching, group activities, and classroom leaders.
14. Treat everyone with respect no matter what their socioeconomic class or ethnic background.
15. Individualize instruction; adjust it to the students' levels.
16. Keep standards high.
17. Utilize programmed material, learning activity packets, computer-assisted instruction, study guides, and the like. Remember that learning guides may be oral-aural as well as written.
18. Use role playing, simulation, and lots of audiovisual media.
19. Help students learn how to study, how to take notes, how to read, and how to listen.
20. Create a wholesome atmosphere. Keep the students in line and on their toes. Make your class lively.

Avoid the following kinds of behavior:

1. Too many workbook and skill sheet assignments.
2. Overemphasizing drill.
3. Speaking in dialect or street English.
4. Stereotyping the students.
5. Focusing on traumatic subjects in class.
6. Coddling, babying, and being too permissive.

ADDITIONAL READING

Banks, J. A., and C. A. M. Banks. *Multicultural Education: Issues and Perspectives*. Needham Heights, MA: Allyn and Bacon, 1989.

Barbe, W. B., and J. S. Renzulli, eds. *Psychology and Education of the Gifted*. New York: Irvington Publishers, 1981.

Brockman, E. M., ed. *Teaching Handicapped Students Mathematics*. Washington, DC: National Educational Association, 1981.

Brophy, J. "Successful Teaching Strategies for the Inner City Child," *Phi Delta Kappan* 63 (April 1982): 527–530.

Clark, B. *Growing Up Gifted*, 3rd ed. Englewood Cliffs, NJ: Merrill/ Prentice Hall, 1988.

Correll, M. M. *Teaching the Gifted and Talented, Fastback 119*. Bloomington, IN: Phi Delta Kappa Educational Foundation, 1978.

Cox, J., N. Daniel, and B. O. Boston. *Educating Able Learners' Programs and Promising Practices*. Austin, TX: University of Texas Press, 1985.

Fox, L. H., and W. G. Durden. *Educating Verbally Gifted Youth, Fastback 176*. Bloomington, IN: Phi Delta Kappa Educational Foundation, 1982.

Friedman, P. G. *Teaching the Gifted and Talented Oral Communication and Leadership*. Washington, DC: National Education Association, 1980.

Gardner, H. *Frames of Mind*. New York: Basic Books, 1983.

Gearhart, B. R., M. W. Weishahn, and C. J. Gearhart. *The Exceptional Student in the Regular Classroom*, 4th ed. Englewood Cliffs, NJ: Merrill/Prentice Hall.

George, W. C., and K. G. Bartkovich. *Teaching the Gifted and Talented in the Mathematics Classroom*. Washington, DC: National Education Association, 1980.

Gollnick, D., and P. C. Chinn. *Multicultural Education in a Pluralistic Society*, 3rd ed. Englewood Cliffs, NJ: Merrill/Prentice Hall.

Good, T., and J. Brophy. *Looking in Classrooms*, 2nd ed. New York: Harper and Row, 1987.

Greenlaw, M. J., and M. E. McIntosh. *Educating the Gifted: A Source Book*. Chicago, IL: American Library Association, 1988.

Hagen, E. *Identification of the Gifted*. New York: Teacher's College Press, 1980.

Hardman, M. et al. *Human Exceptionality*, 3rd ed. Needham Heights, MA: Allyn and Bacon, 1990.

Hargis, C. H. *Teaching Low Achieving and Disadvantaged Students*. Springfield, IL: Charles C. Thomas, 1989.

Heward, W. L., and M. D. Orlansky. *Exceptional Children*, 3rd ed. Englewood Cliffs, NJ: Merrill/Prentice Hall.

Horowitz, F. D., and M. O. Boon, eds. *The Gifted and Talented: Developmental Perspectives*. Washington, DC: American Psychological Association, 1985.

Johnson, S. O., and V. J. Johnson. *Motivating Minority Students: Strategies That Work*. Springfield, IL: Charles C. Thomas, 1988.

Kirk, S. A., and J. J. Gallagher. *Educating Exceptional Children*, 6th ed. New York: Houghton Mifflin, 1989.

Lewis, R. B., and D. A. Doorlag. *Teaching Special Students in the Mainstream*, 3rd ed. Englewood Cliffs, NJ: Merrill/Prentice Hall.

Lonbardi, T. P. *Learning Strategies for Problem Learners, Fastback 345*. Bloomington, IN: Phi Delta Kappa Educational Foundation, 1992.

Oakes, J. *Keeping Track*. New Haven, CT: Yale, 1985.

Ogden, E. *The At-Risk Student*. Lancaster, PA: Technomic Publishing, 1988.

Palomaki, J., ed. *Teaching Handicapped Students Vocational Education*. Washington, DC: National Education Association, 1981.

Parke, B. N. *Gifted Students in Regular Classrooms*. Boston, MA: Allyn and Bacon, 1979.

Passow, A. H., ed. "The Gifted and the Talented: Their Education and Development." *The Seventy-eighth Yearbook of the National Society for the Study of Education,* Part I. Chicago: University of Chicago Press, 1979, Chaps. 1, 2, 11, 18.

Pederson, P. *A Handbook for Developing Multicultural Awareness*. Alexandria, VA: American Association for Counseling and Development, 1988.

Reynolds, M., and J. W. Birch. *Adaptive Mainstreaming*. White Plains, NY: Longman, 1988.

Romey, W. D. *Teaching the Gifted and Talented in the Science Classroom*, 2nd ed. Washington, DC: National Education Association, 1987.

Rose, M. *Lives on the Boundary*. New York: Penguin, 1989.

Shaw, T., ed. *Teaching Handicapped Students Social Studies*. Washington, DC: National Education Association, 1981.

Slavin, R. E., N. L. Karweit, and N. A. Madden. *Effective Programs for Children at Risk*. Boston: Allyn and Bacon, 1989.

Sleeter, C., ed. *Empowerment Through Multicultural Education*. Albany, NY: State University Press, 1990.

Stephens, T. M., A. E. Blackhurst, and L. A. Magliocca. *Teaching Mainstreamed Students*, 2nd ed. New York: Pergamon Press, 1988.

Sternberg, R. J., and J. E. Davidson, eds. *Conceptions of Giftedness*. Cambridge, England: Cambridge University Press, 1986.

Swassing, R. H., ed. *Teaching Gifted Children and Adolescents*. Englewood Cliffs, NJ: Merrill/Prentice Hall.

Swassing, R. H. "Gifted and Talented Students" in *Exceptional Children,* 4th ed., edited by W. L. Heward and M. O. Orlansky. Englewood Cliffs, NJ: Merrill/Prentice Hall.

Tannenbaum, A. J. *Gifted Children: Psychological and Educational Perspectives*. New York: Macmillan, 1983.

Thomas, M. D. *Pluralism Gone Mad, Fastback 160*. Bloomington, IN: Phi Delta Kappa Educational Foundation, 1981.

Tiedt, P. L., and I. M. Tiedt. *Multicultural Teaching*, 3rd ed. Boston, MA: Allyn and Bacon, 1988.

Turner, D. G. *Legal Issues in Education of the Handicapped, Fastback 186*. Bloomington, IN: Phi Delta Kappa Educational Foundation, 1983.

Tuttle, F. B. *Gifted and Talented Students, What Research Says to the Teacher*, rev. ed. Washington, DC: National Education Association, 1983.

Tuttle, F. B., Jr., and L. A. Becker. *Characteristics and Identification of Gifted and Talented Students*. Washington, DC: National Educational Association, 1988.

Tuttle, F. B., Jr., L. A. Becker, and J. A. Sousa. *Program Design and Development for Gifted and Talented Students*, 3rd ed. Washington, DC: National Education Association, 1988.

Van Tassel-Baska, J. et al. *Comprehensive Curriculum for Gifted Learners*. Boston: Allyn and Bacon, 1988.

Wang, M. C., and H. J. Walberg, eds. *Adapting Instruction to Individual Differences*. Berkeley, CA: McCutchan, 1985.

NOTES

1. *Random House Dictionary of the English Language: The Unabridged Edition* (New York: Random House, 1966).
2. Julian C. Stanley, *National Association of Secondary School Principals Bulletin* (March 1976), 32.
3. H. Gardner, *Frames of Mind* (New York: Basic Books, 1983).
4. J. S. Renzulli and L. H. Smith, *The Learning Style Inventory* (Mansfield Center, CT: Creative Learning Press, 1978); M.M. Meeker, *Using SOI Test Results* (El Segundo, CA: SOI Institute, 1979).
5. E. Paul Torrance, *Creativity in the Classroom: What Research Says to the Teacher* (Washington, DC: National Education Association, 1977), 6.
6. Arnold B. Skromme, "Creative Students Are God's Neglected Children," *Education* 108 (Spring 1988): 352–381.
7. Laurie Olsen, "Crossing the Schoolhouse Border: Immigrant Children in California," *Phi Delta Kappan* 70 (November 1988): 211–218.
8. Oscar Lewis, *Current* (December 1966), 28–32.
9. *Sunday Today*, NBC News, November 20, 1988.

10. Shirl E. Gilbert and Geneva Gay, "Improving the Success of Poor Black Children," *Phi Delta Kappan* 133 (October 1988): 137.
11. Ibid.
12. Esther Lee Yao, "Working Effectively with Asian Immigrants' Parents," *Phi Delta Kappan* 70 (November 1988): 223–225.
13. Ibid.
14. Cynthia L. Warger, Loviah E. Aldinger, and Kathy A. Okun, *Mainstreaming in the Secondary School: The Role of the Regular Teacher, Fastback 187* (Bloomington, IN: Phi Delta Kappa Educational Foundation, 1983).
15. Phil C. Robinson and Gail VanHuene, "Meeting Student's Special Needs" in *Helping Teachers Manage Classrooms*, edited by Daniel L. Duke (Alexandria, VA: Association for Supervision and Curriculum Development, 1982), Chap. 4.
16. Donald L. Macmillan, Barbara K. Keogh, and Reginald L. Jones, "Special Educational Research on Mildly Handicapped Learners" in *Handbook of Research on Teaching*, edited by Merlin C. Wittrock (New York: Macmillan, 1986), 786.
17. Ibid.
18. Daniel Reschley, cited in John O'Neil, "How Special Should Special Education Be?" *ASCD Curriculum Update* (September 1988), 3.
19. Ibid., 7.

Reading and Studying

■ ■ ■ Overview

In this chapter we take a brief look at materials used in teaching and the skills students need in order to study them well. We hope that by studying this chapter, you will become familiar with techniques that will help you to

1. Improve students' study techniques.
2. Build up students' skills in taking and using notes.
3. Make your assignments expedite learning.
4. Help with homework problems.
5. Conduct supervised study.

Because one of the most important instructional materials is the textbook, and because many students, even at the college level, do not know how to use their textbooks effectively, it pays to take the time to teach students how to use their textbooks well. However, effective skills in textbook use are not of great value to students unless the textbook they are using serves your teaching objectives, presents the needed content clearly and interestingly, and is in tune with the students' reading level.

Actually, your purposes may be better served by providing multiple readings and taking advantage of community resources. However, if you truly wish students to learn how to study, it is not enough to supply them with an abundance of materials; it is imperative that you teach them specific study skills. This learning is so important that some experts recommend that every student have a short course in study skills in the seventh grade and another in the tenth grade.(1) Among the skills these experts categorize as critical are time management, note taking, listening, proper review techniques, reading comprehension, vocabulary development, following simple and complex written and oral instructions, preparing for tests, and taking tests. In addition they believe that learning how to learn should be part of every course.(2) They assert that students do not need more content to become well-educated, but instead need more skill in learning.(3) Furthermore, these educators are convinced that helping students master learning and study skills will help reduce class absenteeism and the number of school dropouts.(4)

■ ■ ■ Vocabulary Building

One of the most important steps you can take in teaching students how to study in your courses is to familiarize them with the language of the subject. As a rule, content-area textbooks are not easy reading—not even for good readers. They present new concepts in a jargon new to the students; however, both the new ideas and the new language are essential parts of the discipline to be studied. In each discipline, new words are used to express new concepts, and often old concepts have acquired new names and familiar words have taken on new meanings. Note the differences in vocabulary load of five content fields when categorized according to Roget's *Thesaurus*, as reported in the May, 1979 *NASSP Curriculum Report* (Figure 12.1). As can be seen from this chart, evidently history and mathematics use quite different dialects.

Consequently, for your teaching to be successful, you must teach the vocabulary of the field. Unfortunately, to do this job right takes much time and great effort. There just is not time enough to teach all the new words thoroughly. Therefore, you will have to concentrate on teaching the words that seem most important in view of the goals of the unit and the background of the students. Fortunately, your students

	Abstract Relation	Space	Physics	Matter	Sensation	Intellect	Volition	Affections
Biology	15	14	5	52	4	2	8	1
Business	35	5	3	3	0	11	40	4
History	8	8	0	8	0	4	54	18
Math	64	14	0	0	1	14	7	1
Physics	38	22	28	2	4	3	2	0

FIGURE 12.1

Percentages of Textbook Vocabulary by Content Field

NASSP, "Making an Impact by . . . Reading in the Content Fields," *NASSP Curriculum Report* 8 (May 1979): 4.

will not need to master every new word to understand what they hear and read. If they can understand the important words, they can probably figure out other words in context well enough to grasp the gist of their reading. While immersed in the subject, you can explain difficult words or the students can turn to the dictionary. All of this means, of course, that you must be careful that the words you select to teach are truly the key words.

To ensure that your students' vocabularies are adequate for the job at hand, introduce your study of key words early in the course, and then present key technical words in each unit before you get far into the unit. Watch out particularly for "slippery" words, that is, words that mean different things in different contexts. At this point you probably will want to teach the words directly by definition and by drill. Later, as the class moves into the unit, help students use word-analysis skills to figure out any unfamiliar words they encounter in their reading. Following are a number of suggested techniques by which to make your vocabulary teaching effective.

Stop and Reflect

Are there slippery words with double or multiple meanings in the subject which you are preparing to teach? What are they?

1. Preteach difficult words before the beginning of any lesson, unit, or reading assignment. Larry Nook of Wingate High School in New York City did this by listing the words on the chalkboard and then asking the students to
    a. Read each word.
    b. See if they could find another word within each word.
    c. Give the meaning of each word.(5)
In this way, Nook combined elements of word analysis with word definition and created some assurance that students would recognize these words when they came on them during the reading. If the lesson is to be a lecture, however, perhaps it may be more logical to stop during the lecture and explain a new key word when you come to it. In any case, explain the words in context and see to it that they are well understood before the students begin reading them.

2. Sometimes connecting a little history with new words helps. "Who dreamed that up?" "How did they ever come up with a word like that?" The background of some words may be amusing and interest-catching. For instance, the word *ama-*

teur comes from the French word for *lover*; automobile is a combination of *auto* (meaning "self") and *mobile* (meaning "movable"). Sometimes diagramming words' family trees can be both interesting and informative.

3. Show students how to analyze words. [It may be necessary to teach them various roots and affixes, e.g., *bicycle, tricycle, motorcycle*. In the middle school you most probably will have to teach students the prefixes *ab* (from), *ad* (to), *be* (by), *com* (with), *de* (from), *dis* (apart), *en* (in), *ex* (out), *in* (not), *pre* (before), *pro* (in front of), *re* (back), *sub* (under), and *un* (not).](6) Point out blends (e.g., telecast, Texaco) and acronyms (e.g., MASH, UNICEF, NASA). To spice up lessons in word analysis, stage word-building contests in which students race to see who can create the most words by adding prefixes and suffixes to given roots.

4. Use the talk-through process advocated by Dorothy Piercy. In this process, first identify key concept words that students may find troublesome. Then present the words to the students in writing and in context by using the chalkboard, the overhead projector, or a study guide. Ask questions about the topic. Circle the root of each word, thus removing any prefix and suffix. Ask, "What does this word mean? What are other words based on this root?" Finally, show how different prefixes and suffixes change the meaning of the word.(7)

5. Encourage students to use the CSSD system to unlock the meaning of strange new words. *CSSD* stands for context clues, structure, sound, and dictionary, the four steps to use when searching for the meaning of a new word.
   a. *Context clues*   Check for context clues that point out the meaning of the new word.
   b. *Structure*   Examine the word's structure to see if there are roots, prefixes, or suffixes that suggest the word's meaning.
   c. *Sound*   Sound out the word. It may be that the word, while visually unfamiliar, becomes more familiar when sounded out; you may just recognize it by its sound.
   d. *Dictionary*   Finally, if all else fails, go to the dictionary and look up the word's meaning.(8)

6. Teach students how to find and use context clues. Present new words in context, and ask students to figure out the meaning of the word from its setting. Use exercises that force the student to use the word in context and really to learn its meaning.

7. Identify words that have more than one meaning. Note which meaning is apropos in the present context. Explain other possible meaningful uses of the word.

8. Have each student keep a vocabulary notebook in which he or she lists each new term, the context in which it is used, and its meaning. A tabular form with three headings—New Term, Context, Meaning—can be used.

9. Discuss the new words. What exactly do they mean? What connotations do they have? Ask students to define them in their own words. Other pleasant ways to bring out word meanings are to have the students act out the words and to play games in which students try to find the closest synonyms. Also enjoyable are crossword puzzles, bubblegrams, anagrams, acrostics and other puzzles, matching games, and exercises.(9)

10. Review and refresh frequently; do not let the newly learned words slip away.

Stop and Reflect

Make up several exercises that will help students develop skill in the use of prefixes and suffixes. You ought to be able to concoct several varieties of games to spice up such exercises. If you run short of ideas, watch some of the television game shows.

Would your approach to introducing new words to proficient readers be different from that for introducing new words to less able readers? Explain the different strategies you would use, if any. How can a teacher make a vocabulary notebook into a worthwhile learning experience? Note how the context brings out the meaning in each of the following sentences:

1. *Jake is a* pugapoo. *His mother was a cute little black poodle, his father a feisty, sandy-haired pug.*
2. *He was a* rock hound *who loved to wander through the desert hunting for interesting rocks and semiprecious stones.*
3. *The* gemologist, *an expert when it comes to fashioning jewelry out of native gem stones, welcomed us to his shop.*
4. *The* savannah, *a flat grassy plain, stretches from here to there.*
5. *All of a sudden he came to the edge of the hill and saw before him the* savannah *stretching flat and lush all the way from the foot of the hill to the sea.*
6. *They did not* quail *but fought on bravely and staunchly.*
7. *He was a true hero—a* Lochinvar *out of the west.*
8. Orcs *are nasty, despicable, foul-mouthed, foul-breathed, dirty, murderous goblins.*
9. *He drove forward about a* league, *five miles in our reckoning.*
10. *In Europe the most popular game is* association football, *which we call soccer.*
11. *Each element has its own pattern or fingerprint of colors it gives out. We call this fingerprint of colors its* spectrum.
12. *The imprisonment was not* oppressive. *We had airy cells, good food, chances for recreation, but no chance for escape. The guerrillas wanted us to be in good shape when the time came to trade us for their leader.*

In Saturday's newspaper you find an announcement by the Voc-Tech of the courses to be offered in its "winterim" session. What does that mean? How did they ever come up with that word winterim? What does Voc-Tech mean anyway? How does one analyze the words to find their meaning?

Examine a few high school textbooks. What aids do you find for teaching the vocabulary? Do you find many words that seem difficult for average students? For below average students? For you?

Pick a chapter from a high school text. What seem to be the key words? Prepare a plan for making sure that the students understand these words. Would you plan to teach them deductively, by giving the students the definitions before starting the chapter, or by helping them to puzzle out the meanings by word-power techniques as they go along?

Textbooks

Using Textbooks

Textbooks are the most common information source used in our classrooms. As a teaching tool, the ordinary textbook may be flawed. It is often dull; it usually represents only one viewpoint and employs only one style of presentation. Sometimes much of the content of the typical textbook is over the students' heads, because it is likely to leave out basic information necessary to newcomers to the field, since the author often assumes that *everyone* knows *that*. Often the writing in textbooks is bland, noncontroversial, and spineless, carefully avoiding anything and everything that would stimulate young readers to experiment with new ideas and to think for themselves. Worst of all, textbooks are more than likely too difficult for most students to read without great effort.

These faults notwithstanding, the textbook can be a useful tool if you use it well. For example, if it presents only one point of view, find a way to present other viewpoints; if it is dull, liven it up; if the content is obscure, make it plain; if the text omits essential information, supply another source that will furnish the missing data; and if the text is difficult to read, help the students master its language, vocabulary, style, and organization patterns. Finally, if students *will not*—as opposed to *cannot*—read the textbook, you must find some way to entice them.

To get the most out of your textbooks and to avoid their weaknesses, it is recommended that you do the following:

1. Become really familiar with the textbook before you use it.
2. Use the textbook in your planning as a source of structure if it seems desirable to do so, but do not let yourself become chained to the book.
3. Use the text as only one of many materials and activities. Use other readings, simulation, role playing, discussion, films, and pictures.
4. Use problem-solving approaches in which the text is but one source of data.
5. Use only those parts of the book that seem good to you; skip the other parts; rearrange the order of topics if you think it desirable. In other words, adapt the text to your pupils and their needs.
6. Use additional or substitute readings to allow for differences in pupils.
7. Provide help for pupils who do not read well.
8. Teach pupils how to study the text and to use the parts of the text, such as table of contents, index, headings, charts, graphs, and illustrations.
9. Use the illustrations, charts, graphs, and other aids included in the textbook in your teaching. Build lessons around them; study them.
10. Encourage critical reading. Compare the text to source materials and other texts. Test it for logic and bias.
11. Teach vocabulary.
12. Incorporate the textbook into a multiple-text teaching strategy.(10)

Teaching Students to Use the Textbook

Teachers are often surprised because students find reading textbooks to be a difficult task. You should not wonder at this, however; no doubt you find some of your own college texts difficult. Because textbooks are usually written in the jargon of the discipline and present new information and introduce new concepts, it would be strange if they were easy reading. Furthermore, since both skills and the types of reading involved make up and affect students' reading abilities as well as levels of text difficulty, it is only natural that most students will have some trouble with some portions of the text, no matter how well they read. When you consider that many young people have never mastered the skills needed to use a text effectively and efficiently, it is not surprising that so many of them have trouble getting the meat from the textbook's dry bones. Therefore, don't expect what you have no right to expect. Instead of wailing that the kids can't read the text, show them how to do it. After all, that is what teachers are paid to do.(11)

THE AUTHOR'S AIDS TO LEARNING When you distribute a new text, point out the aids to learning that the author has included in the text to help students study it. There are many of them. Check through your college texts to see what aids to learning have been included. Among them you will find tables of contents, prefaces, chapter summaries, chapter introductions, chapter headings and subheadings, problems to be solved, charts, graphs, illustrations, signpost sentences, indexes, glossaries, and notes. Teach your students to use these devices to organize their reading and thinking, to set up goals for studying, to separate the important concepts from the forgettable detail, and to see how the various ideas presented in the text are related.

Matching Reading Levels

THE BOOK'S READING LEVEL   The reading level of the material you use should be compatible with the reading level of the students. Even though strongly motivated readers may manage to cope with reading matter well over their supposed reading level, often too difficult reading assignments lead only to frustration.

To determine the reading level of a text, first check the teacher's manual or teacher's edition. If these do not give the reading levels, then you can turn to a readability formula such as the Fry formula. By analyzing the vocabulary and sentence structure used in a book, this formula estimates the reading difficulty of the book in terms of grade level.

To use the Fry formula:

1. Determine the average number of syllables in three 100-word selections taken one from the beginning, one from the middle, and one from the ending parts of the book.
2. Determine the average number of sentences in the three 100-word selections.
3. Plot the two values on the Fry readability graph (Figure 12.2). Their intersection will give you an estimate of the text's reading level at the 50 to 75 percent comprehension level.(12)

Unfortunately, reading level estimates gained by formulas of this type apply only to the technical difficulty of the reading matter. They do not take into consideration its conceptual difficulty, or such reader characteristics as interest, motivation, purpose, and perseverance.(13) The results may also be misleading. Complex ideas may be stated in simple sentences, and longer, seemingly more complex sentences may make complex ideas easier to understand. Therefore, you must take into account such things as the prior experience of your students with the subject matter, the number of new ideas introduced, the abstraction of the ideas, and the author's use of external and internal clues. These criteria are, of course, all subjective.

In the final analysis, estimating the difficulty of a book is primarily a matter of using your best judgment. We recommend that you first find the technical difficulty of the book by the use of a formula, and raise or lower your estimate in accordance with your judgment of its conceptual difficulty. As you do so, consider also such things as the interest level of the author's style. Some critics claim that authors' attempts to match students' reading levels have deadened the books so much that they have become boring.(14)

THE STUDENTS' READING LEVEL   Just because a formula tells you that a book is at the seventh-grade reading level, it does not mean that the book is suitable for your seventh-graders. Some seventh-graders read much above grade level, and others are almost illiterate. Therefore, first you need to find your students' reading levels.

To find the levels at which your students are reading, you can use the standardized tests given as part of the school testing program. Leave analysis and diagnosis via such instruments to reading and guidance specialists. Do not take reading level scores obtained from the testing program as gospel, however. Your course may require different vocabulary and reading skills from those tested. Short-answer and multiple-choice questions do not call for the same skills as do sustained reading and studying, for instance. Besides, some of your students may have been nervous and consequently scored too low, and others may have been lucky and scored too high.

Test scores or no test scores, you will have to rely on your own resources to tell you whether or not your reading matter is too difficult for your students. Two informal tests that you can use are the silent reading inventory and the oral reading

Average number of syllables per 100 words

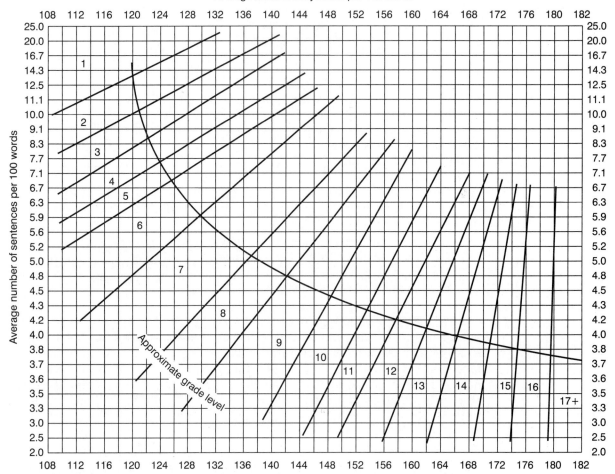

FIGURE 12.2

Fry Readability Graph

Edward Fry, "A Readability Formula That Saves Time," *Journal of Reading* (April, 1968) 11: 587.

inventory. To conduct the silent reading inventory, have your students read silently four or five pages of a book at their supposed grade level and then administer a 10-question test on the information given on those pages. Students who score above 90 percent on the test are presumed to be independent readers at that grade level; those who score between 75 to 89 percent are reading at the instructional grade level; and all who score below 75 percent are reading below grade level. To carry out the oral reading inventory, simply have the students read a 100-word passage from the book orally. All students who can read 95 percent or more of the words are reading at grade level or above; all who cannot read 95 percent of the words are reading below grade level and need help.

The simplest way to find whether a book is too difficult for individual students is to have each student first read it aloud to you and then tell you what he or she has read. If a student can read passages aloud without much stumbling and can explain their gist reasonably well, you can assume that the book is not too difficult for that student.

Another technique that seems to be becoming increasingly popular is the CLOZE procedure. Although authorities seem to differ on the best way to carry out this procedure, we recommend using the following technique. Select from your textbook several typical passages so that you will have a total of 400 to 415 words or so. Delete every eighth word in the passage, except for words in the first and last sentences, proper names, numbers, and initial words in sentences. It will be helpful for scoring if you eliminate 50 words. Duplicate the passages after inserting 10- to 15-space blanks in place of the eliminated words. Pass out these "mutilated" passages to the pupils. Ask them to fill in the blanks with the most appropriate words they can think of. Collect the papers. Score them by counting all the words supplied by the student that are exact words from the original text, and dividing the number of correct responses by the number of possibles.* (Fifty blanks makes the division very easy.)

$$\text{Score} = \frac{\text{Number of correct responses}}{\text{Number of possibles}}$$

You can assume that students who score better than 50 percent can read the book quite well, students who score between 40 and 50 percent can read the book at the instructional level, and students who score below 40 percent will probably find the book frustrating.

Stop and Reflect

Try to apply the Fry formula to a textbook in your field.

Prepare a CLOZE test for the text. If possible, try it on a middle or high school youth.

How can you determine the suitability of a book's reading level for a particular student?

Prepare a list of readings for students of different reading levels for a topic in a course you might teach.

Using the criteria listed in this chapter as a basis, review several textbooks in your field. In what ways are they good? In what ways are they bad? If you had a choice, which would you adopt?

Examine several texts for courses you may teach. What do you like about them? What do you dislike? How do they measure up to the criteria cited here?

Reading and Studying

Not only do various fields of study use different vocabularies, but also they require different reading strategies. After all, reading a page of an algebra text is different from reading a page of a novel! In addition, reading in certain disciplines requires specialized skills. Reading in history or geography requires some fluency with maps; mathematics reading assumes the ability to read equations. As the specialized subject matter teacher concerned, you must be available to teach these special skills to your students.

Therefore, teach your students the special reading and study skills pertinent to your subject courses. Although at times it may be necessary to take time out of your coursework to concentrate on particular reading or study skills, teaching these skills can ordinarily be integrated into your regular subject classwork. Con-

---

*Some persons recommend that only exact words be counted; others allow synonyms. We suggest that you not count synonyms, verbs of differing tense, and so on.

sequently, try to keep special lessons in reading and studying to a minimum, and even then aim the lesson at the content of the unit being studied. Remember, you are a content specialist, not a reading specialist. Although part of your job is to help students read the content of your field well, you are not responsible for determining the causes of reading disabilities, interpreting standardized reading tests, measuring students' reading potential, and the other esoteric business peculiar to the reading field. If you note where students are deficient in reading and take steps to overcome their faults, you will meet most contingencies. When you suspect something to be radically wrong, call for the specialist.

If you teach in a middle school, your job will include teaching both basic reading skills and the study of the discipline. Although some boys and girls may have learned to read quite well in the earlier grades, do not assume that they no longer need instruction in basic reading. Middle schoolers can benefit from instruction in all reading and study skills. They particularly need instruction in the connectives, prefixes, suffixes, and technical vocabulary of the discipline. To prepare your middle school students for their high school courses, carefully read several high school textbooks in your field and use them as a source of vocabulary, connectives, and the like in your own courses.(15)

In the high school, your job will be somewhat different from that in the middle school. In the higher grades, you need to provide students with remedial help, reteaching, and review of the basic reading and study skills taught in the elementary and middle grades.* You should also give your students considerable experience in reading at the higher levels of comprehension. Students should learn to detect an author's mood and purpose, to read independently, to read critically, to adjust their reading speed, and to successfully use the various other techniques of the mature reader and scholar.

Stop and Reflect

In what ways would you expect the teaching of the reading component of your subject in the middle school to differ from that of the senior high school?

What reading skills should you particularly emphasize in teaching your subject?

Can you think of any procedures you might use when teaching your courses to provide for the reading skill differences among your students?

Look through a high school textbook in your field, noting the connective words and technical vocabulary that seem peculiar to the field and essential for middle school students to learn as preparation for high school courses in the field.

Teaching How to Study

Some students seem to think that studying is the same as reading. Not so! Study includes all those activities that have to do with learning through planned effort. It includes such skills as the following:

1. Planning for study
2. Managing time
3. Listening
4. Concentrating

---

*There probably is not a single college student who would not benefit from help in at least one of the reading or study skills.

5. Reading for a purpose
6. Developing an adequate vocabulary
7. Spotting main ideas and supporting details
8. Reading critically, recognizing propaganda, bias, and fact versus opinion and speculation
9. Using charts, graphs, maps, illustrations
10. Taking notes during lectures and readings
11. Reviewing
12. Using reference works
13. Using the library
14. Locating information
15. Analyzing problems
16. Drawing conclusions.

You can expect little success in developing students' study skills unless you teach these skills directly and give students considerable practice with them in your courses. To teach thinking skills, use the model for direct teaching discussed in Chapter 7:

1. Identify the skill.
2. Show how it operates.
3. Provide practice time.
4. Follow up.

As we have already seen, some schools provide courses in how to study. Such courses may be helpful, but they do not relieve you of the responsibility for teaching study skills in your own courses. Why not? For one thing, different subjects require different study techniques if study is to be effective. Consequently, in each of your courses, you should teach study techniques proper to your subject matter to any student who has not mastered them. Furthermore, learning how to study comes only from practicing good techniques, and where else can students practice but in their ordinary courses? Thus, every teacher is responsible for teaching students how to study for each course.

Developing Comprehension Skills

William G. Perry describes how out of 1,500 Harvard and Radcliffe freshmen assigned to read a certain chapter in a history book, only one in 100 was able to glean the sense of the chapter well enough to write a short statement on what the chapter was about.(16) *Ninety-nine percent of these Harvard and Radcliffe freshmen had not learned to read for comprehension well enough in their 12 years of college preparation to complete this simple task.* Evidently teachers in middle and secondary schools need to do a better job of teaching students basic comprehension skills. According to Olive Niles, these skills are (1) "the ability to observe and to use the various and varied relationships of ideas," for example, time, listing, comparison-contrast, cause and effect, (2) "the ability to read with adjustment to conscious purpose, and (3) the ability to make full use of the substantial backlog of real and vicarious experience which almost every reader, even the beginner, possesses."(17) Certainly to become a successful reader one should develop skill in finding the main idea of what one has read. Also it would seem essential to sharpen one's ability to spot details by which the author supports the main idea. Finally, one must work at improving the ability to recognize the patterns in which the ideas and supporting details are organized. Good reading consists of understanding an author's main ideas as well as the supporting details.

Teaching Students to Read with Purpose

Basically, people study to learn something, that is, to find out something. They read or study with purpose. To get students to read with purpose, they must be given a purpose for reading. Therefore, be sure that your assignments point out what the learning goal should be. Advance organizers, study guides, and other scaffolds are very helpful here. Your assignments will be more profitable if they take advantage of students' intrinsic interests while providing them with extrinsic motivation. Assignments, organizers, and intrinsic and extrinsic motivation are discussed more fully in Chapter 3, "Motivation."

One way to stimulate student interest is to show them that they already know quite a bit about the subject under study and that they can use what they already know. Therefore, try to use students' own ideas, experiences, and information as one basis for your lesson. Start a discussion about the topic at hand, see how many words related to the topic students can think of, have students relate experiences pertinent to the lesson, or have students elaborate on something you tell them. The more you encourage them to use their own ideas and the more you use their thoughts and knowledge in your lesson, the more likely they are to read and study your lessons.

You can also use student prediction to arouse interest and persuade students to read. You might, for instance, give the students a list of statements about the topic of the selection to be read and ask them whether they think the selection will agree with these statements. Then have the students read the selection to see whether or not their predictions are correct. Follow up with a discussion during which the students prove that the author's position did or did not agree with their predictions. Note that in such a discussion, nothing is a matter of opinion; it is strictly a matter of what the text says or means.(18)

Not only should your assignments provide students with a sense of purpose and motivation, but also they should help them learn at each of the three comprehension levels: (1) the literal level at which the students understand what the author said; (2) the interpretive level at which the readers understand what the author meant; and (3) the applied level at which the readers can apply the author's meaning to new and different situations. One scheme for helping students reach these comprehension levels is: *first*, ask questions at the literal level; *second*, have the students read the selection; and *third*, have the students answer questions, based on their reading, first at the literal level and then at the higher levels. Figure 12.3 shows a study guide with questions at the three levels.

Locating the Main Idea and Supporting Details

Place considerable stress on teaching students how to locate the main idea of a selection and how to detect the supporting details and their relationship to the main idea. Use questions such as, "What seems to you to be the main idea of this selection? Point out the sentence or sentences that tell you that this is the main idea. What arguments does the author use to justify the main idea?" Use the regular textbook for such practice exercises. As soon as a student has learned to get the meaning out of paragraphs, repeat the procedure with sections and later with chapters. Exercises of this sort can be made more interesting by, among other things, using games in which you attempt to reproduce the author's outline, by dramatizing the main ideas of a selection, and by boiling down a paragraph or section into a telegram or newspaper headline.

Level One

Directions: First read these statements. Then read the selection* that follows. As you read, check the statements that say what the author said.

    1. Robert L. Thorndike believes that reading comprehension is a unitary ability.

    2. Some people believe that reading comprehension is a general skill; others think it is made up of a number of specific skills.

Level Two

Directions: Check the statements that tell what the selection means. Be sure that you can show information in the selection that backs up your choice.

    6. Frederick Daly's theory of reading comprehension is the same as Robert L. Thorndike's.

    7. Thorndike's theory implies that students should think about what they read.

Level Three

Directions: Check the statements that use both your own ideas and ideas in the reading selection. Be able to justify your answer.

    10. We should include reading in the content areas in high schools.

    11. High school teachers in English, history, and mathematics should help students learn how to read in their content courses.

*(In this sample study guide, the selection and items 4, 5, 8, 9, and 12 have been omitted to save space.)

■ **FIGURE 12.3**
A Sample Study Guide

Teaching Organizational Patterns

Textbook authors shape concepts by the way they organize their main ideas and supporting details. Therefore, see to it that the students can detect the pattern of organization in the material they read.

As a rule, paragraphs follow one or another of four types of organizational patterns:

■ Comparison or contrast
■ Cause and effect
■ Time sequence
■ Simple listing(19)

Of course, not all paragraphs fall into any one of these categories.

One approach to teaching organizational patterns is to start by having students run through the selection quickly to identify the pattern the author used. Next have the students read the selection carefully to explore its meaning. Then do exercises in which the students identify the elements of the pattern, that is, the causes and effects, comparisons or contrasts, time order, or items in a simple listing, and finally discuss the exercise.

If, before they read the selection, you give students study guide questions such as the following, it will help them to comprehend the patterns and their significance as they read.

■ The author lists three causes for the beginning of the war. They are

_____

_____

_____

■ The author mentions three events in the paragraph; which occurred first, which second, and which last?

After the reading, the discussion will automatically bring out the pattern and clinch the meaning. Remember, your goal is not for students to identify the pattern as cause and effect; rather it is for them to see what the causes and effects are.

Teaching Students to Utilize What They Know

To motivate students and to give them confidence, try to build on their prior experiences, knowledge, and skills. For this purpose, use discussions in which students draw on their own experiences to set the stage for the reading or to clarify what they have already read. Encourage students to draw upon what they already know to establish the meanings of sentences and unfamiliar words. Certainly the student who works at the checkout counter of a supermarket has some inkling about prices, inflation, and other notions found in economics texts. Capitalize on this knowledge.

One of the most troublesome causes of student inability to comprehend what they read is that they do not see the relationships between what they are reading and what they have read before. Therefore, take time to show how the parts of the course fit together. In your discussions and study guides, point out these relationships. When you start a new unit, review salient points of the old unit and discuss their implications for the new one. Start students thinking along the proper lines by asking, "If that is what happened in that chapter, what might we expect in this one?" Then as the students progress through the new content, force them to think about the relationship between what they are reading and what they have already learned. Presumably as they begin to see the organization of the course and the relationships among the various items of information, concepts, and generalizations, the course content will start to make more sense to them. In addition, it will help them to discover how to develop new learning out of past knowledge.

Stop and Reflect
Practice building study guides for reading selections from textbooks in your field in which you help students to

1. *Read at each of the three levels of comprehension.*
2. *Locate the main ideas and supporting details of the selection.*
3. *Understand the organizational details of the selection.*
4. *Capitalize on what they already know when reading the selection.*
5. *See how the selection fits in with preceding parts of the course.*

Adjusting Reading Speed

In *Of Studies*, Lord Bacon wrote, "Some books are to be tasted, others to be swallowed, and some few to be chewed and digested." Teach students to look for the signposts that indicate the importance and the import of paragraphs, sections, and chapters. Show them how to use both external and internal clues. Let them practice with directional words that tell whether to speed up or slow down their perusal. Have group discussions in which students decide what materials they should examine and what kinds of reading can be treated more lightly. Give your students direct instruction in determining what works should be scanned, skimmed, read, or studied. Point out criteria that indicate the appropriate approach. For instance, it can be said that, in general, reference works are designed to be scanned; fiction and some supplementary reading may deserve only to be skimmed; and most textbooks must be studied. Students can learn how to use such criteria through class discussion and by applying the criteria to various books. They may even develop their own criteria in a group discussion.

To teach students to skim books effectively, first teach directly the techniques involved and then follow up this teaching with practice such as the following:

1. During a class discussion, decide what the class would like to learn from the chapter.
2. Let each student skim the chapter to see what it has to say on these points.
3. Discuss what the class has found in the chapter.

Stop and Reflect

Examine selections having to do with a topic you might teach. Devise specific strategies you might use to stimulate pupils to read these selections with interest.

How does one determine when to skim and when to read carefully?

Can you think of any exercises or games that you might use to teach skimming?

Of what importance is the ability to skim in mathematics, in social studies, in science?

Teaching Students to Read Critically

EVALUATING WHAT ONE READS   "All that glitters is not gold," and all that is printed is neither true nor good. Unfortunately, many young people seem to have considerably more respect for the written word than is warranted. Many high school students might believe something because it is "in the book," and they often become sadly confused when they find that what the book says is not necessarily true. Take it upon yourself to ensure that your students learn to read critically and to evaluate what they read.

How do you teach students to evaluate what they read? One technique is to give them plenty of practice. When they read several texts on a topic, they will soon become aware that differences of opinion exist. So the first step is to give students different readings about various topics, have them consider carefully the differences of opinion, and then discuss why these differences exist.

Another step in evaluating reading material is to try to establish the difference between fact and opinion. Early in life students should learn that some things are fact and some are beliefs. You can teach students how to determine the difference between fact and opinion by asking them such questions as, "Is that so? How do you know? How can you check? Is this true, or does the writer merely think so?"

In their attempts to distinguish fact from opinion, students also should look for signs of bias in the writer. Give assignments asking students to check their reading for such things as sensationalizing, emotionalism, sweeping statements, disregard for facts, and loaded words; this type of exercise will help familiarize students with some of the signs of bias. Another check is to examine the writer's documentation. If a text's references include only out-dated works or works that are in dispute, perhaps the writer has not documented his or her own work carefully. The writer who argues from anecdotes should also be distrusted. Single, isolated cases introduced into the content with the implication that they are typical may be false documentation.

Arguing from anecdote is only one example of writing that violates the rules of logic. When teaching students to evaluate the things that they read, teach them to apply the tests of logic. A technique useful in introducing this application of the rules of logic is to discuss violations of reason in materials they are reading or in television materials. For instance, a television commercial implies that one gasoline is better than another because it is made in a refinery that can make its entire product 100 plus octane gas. Why does this not make good sense? Or again, one reads that a certain athlete smokes Bippos. Is this any reason why anyone else should? What does he know about it? Material of this sort can be used to teach more obvious breaches of logic. As students become familiar with these errors, they can apply these tests to magazine articles and other readings.

Students should also be wary of polemics, propaganda devices, and other attempts to persuade. Newspaper "Letters to the Editor" and editorials often provide excellent examples of political polemics that lend themselves to classroom instruction in critical reading. Examples of such slanted material can be found in almost any newspaper any day. You can utilize them by giving students individual study assignments, by projecting the items via the opaque projector, or, after making a transparency, displaying the items on the overhead projector. Whatever the case, you might ask the students to analyze the selections and to answer such questions as, "Are the arguments logical? Is the presentation just? If not, why not? Can you find instances of loaded words and other propaganda devices?"

Exercises of this sort and others that you may devise should help give students skill in evaluating. Moreover, they will perhaps encourage a questioning attitude in the students. It is hoped that after such teaching the students will not swallow everything they read but will read with an active awareness of the snares of misinformation and poor logic, and that they will also be inclined to test any idea before gulping it down.

STYLISTIC CRITICISM   The process of reading critically also includes being alert to style and skill in writing. Does the style serve the thought? Is it appropriate? Does the writing bring out or obscure the meaning? The feelings? Is the language used symbolic? If so, how is the symbolism used? What does it mean? Are the methods of presentation effective? When students read in such a way as to answer such questions, they are engaging in critical reading.

Reading that results in questioning or actively thinking about the values or implications of what is read is also critical reading. Especially important are reading experiences that help to make students react creatively—by drawing an illustration, by acting out a scene, or by making up an original poem, story, or ballet. Elicit such reactions by giving the students plenty of opportunity to evaluate, question, discuss, and think about what they read; encourage creative responses of all sorts.

Teaching Students to Study Independently

Take special care to make sure that your students learn how to study independently. Use the following technique to help at-risk readers move toward independent reading and studying. Later, when these students have acquired some skill in independent reading, you can move up to directed reading lessons and then, finally, to a more sophisticated system described later.

A General Study Plan for Readers Who Are At-Risk

When teaching at-risk readers beginning study skills, we recommend the following steps:

1. Analyze the content to be read to see what principal ideas and supporting concepts and information it presents. If your objectives in teaching the lesson or unit include principal ideas, concepts, or information not in the reading, then you must change your objectives or provide the knowledge in some other way.

2. Decide just what you expect the students to learn from the reading.

3. Prepare the students for their reading. Try to provide motivation; show through discussion or some other technique how the content relates to previous lessons or students' experiences in and out of school. Go over the vocabulary, making sure that students can match meanings with important key words. Give your students clear directions on how to read the assignment, and try to set up in their minds an anticipation of something desirable to be found in the reading. These directions can be given and the purpose set through discussion and a study guide that shows the students what to do and how to do it. Study guides are probably most effective when they give the students statements or matching exercises that present alternatives from which they can choose correct solutions. (See Figure 12.4 for an example.) In fact, matching/multiple choice study guides are more efficient than are study guides featuring questions, because the former type makes it possible to run through the process of comprehension in a supportive situation when a series of questions would just cause students to founder. In effect the guide puts students in a position where they simulate the skill of comprehension rather than perform it, because it eliminates the need for the students to find the solution to the items completely on their own.

4. Walk the students through the reading in a group situation. It is best to divide the class into random groups that read and discuss the selection together.

5. Follow up with class discussion, questions, and testing as desired. Use this time to clinch the content learning and to clarify the principles, concepts, and information that were to be learned.

You can use this plan for any or all three of the levels of comprehension. All you have to do is set a goal for the lesson and build a study guide and study procedures accordingly. Once the students have mastered the comprehension skills by using the guides, you can gradually remove the guides and allow them to read independently according to the Directed-Reading Activity Plan described in the following section.

Directed-Reading Lesson

For students who do read but have not yet learned to direct themselves, you can use the directed-reading lesson, which is designed to teach students how to study and how to comprehend and retain what they read. Basically, the method consists of five steps:

1. Prepare the students by going over new vocabulary and ideas and reviewing old material and experiences so that they can see the relationships between the new and the old.
2. Have students skim the selection and look at pictures, headings, and so on.
3. Help students formulate questions about the selection to be read, for instance:
   a. What should a student try to find out when studying the selection?
   b. Is this the kind of selection that must be studied carefully?
   c. How does this selection connect with other lessons studied in the past?
   Three or four questions are quite enough. Too many questions may confuse and discourage students. The questions should be student-made rather than teacher-made, if at all possible.

FIGURE 12.4

Example of a Study Guide Suitable for Use with At-Risk Readers

Step 1. Which of the following statements do you believe to be true? Check them in column I.

I   II

Most snakes are dangerous to humans.
Snakes can swallow food bigger than their normal mouth opening.
Snakes smell through their tongues.
Snakes eat live animals.
Usually snakes are full grown by the time they are three years old.

Step 2. Read the selection below. In Column II check the statements that are true according to the selection. How well did your beliefs agree with the facts stated in the selection?

[Selection omitted to save space.]

Step 3. Each of the following items occurs in the selection. Number the items in the order in which they appear in the paragraph.
_____ Snakes are reptiles.
_____ Snakes have large scales on their bellies.
_____ There are 36 kinds of poisonous snakes in the United States.
_____ Snakes' eyelids do not move.
_____ Snakes have small hooked teeth.
_____ There are 250 kinds of snakes in the United States.

4. Let the students read the selection to themselves.
5. Discuss the reading. By using questions, help students see the relationships among the facts presented as well as relationships to what has been learned previously.(20)

READING IN QUESTIONS   All strategies used to teach students how to read for comprehension require students to "read in questions" that set forth what the reader is to find out from the text. The student should ask these questions alone before, during, and after reading a selection. Encourage students to create the questions themselves. At first, however, you may need to ask the questions directly, either orally or by means of a study guide. For instance, if the reading is to be about prehistoric humans, you might ask students to look for answers to such questions as the following:

■ The author implies that prehistoric humans were probably just as intelligent as modern people. What evidence do you find to support that statement?
■ If you were to pick one general idea as the main idea presented in this selection, what would it be?

Another technique that may be useful for developing searching attitudes in students is to have students develop the questions together in a discussion before starting on the readings. Such a discussion might be launched by asking a question such as, "What do you think you want to find out from this reading?" or "What do you think that the reading might tell you?" In the case of the prehistoric humans, students might want to know about such things as the following:

■ What did prehistoric people eat?
■ What did they do for recreation?

As such questions are developed in a class discussion, they could be put on the board by a student recorder. Then, if desired, these questions could be made into a formal list or study guide (Figure 12.5). In some instances at least, it would probably be better to let individual students adapt these questions to their own use, each one taking as many or as few as seems desirable for their own questions, adding other questions if they wish.

Questions for developing students' study skills are only useful when they are asked *before* the student starts reading. Asking questions afterward will merely tell whether the student has understood the reading (which is good to know, of course), but it will not help students develop skill in comprehending. The time for the reader to be active and alert is during the reading.

Learning to Budget Time for Study

Obviously, to study effectively, a student needs to use his or her time effectively. Therefore, in your class selections and your discussions with your students, help them learn how to budget their time. An interesting exercise for students is to have them keep a log of their activities for a day or, better, a week. In this log, they should record the time spent each day in such activities as sleeping, eating, transportation, school class time, other school time, jobs and chores, sports, and any other committed time. By subtracting these hours from the number of hours in the day (24) or

---

Factors in the consideration of Means and Ends.

1. Can necessity create its own law?
2. Can "ends" be judged without previous standards of judgment?
3. Who decides, or how is it decided, that an "end" is good?
4. Are the "means" employed toward making an "end" good?
5. When is necessity "real," when is it "imagined"?
6. Can we separate "means" from "ends"?
7. Are the "means" to be judged before or after the "ends" are achieved?
8. Is the question of the "end justifying the means" equally true for both individuals and states?
9. Do the means determine the ends?
10. Does the pinch of necessity preclude any national consideration of means?
11. How do we consider degrees of "necessity"?
12. How can we determine whether some ends are better than others?
13. Are certain types of "means" and "ends" peculiar to specific aspects of society?
14. Are certain "means" improper, criminal, etc., even when they are not employed?
15. Can means and ends ever be considered amoral?
16. Is law a fact only when it can be enforced?
17. Can evil means ever be employed toward a good end?
18. How can we evaluate abstract ends?
19. How is the concept of what constitutes an end to be reached?
20. Can ends exist independent of the individual?

▦ Figure 12.5
Sample Study Guide
From a 12th-grade philosophy class, Cheltenham, Pennsylvania.

in the week (168), they can find out the amount of time each student had free. On the basis of these time analyses, each student should be able to set up a schedule that will eliminate or reduce wasted time. Within the context of these schedules, each student should indicate the beginning and ending time of each study session planned for every day in the week. When building their plans, students will have to estimate the length of time needed to complete their studying and other assignments for their various courses. To estimate the time necessary for reading assignments, have students test their individual reading speeds by checking to see how many pages of a text they can read in 10 minutes. They can then use this result to plan reading into their time schedule, but they must also allow time for rereading, reviewing, other assignments, as well as some time to think. Also, each student's schedule should allow time for breaks for rest and rehabilitation.

Once the plans have been made, if students use them as a guide, they will undoubtedly arrive in class better prepared. However, students will find it necessary to make adjustments in their plans from time to time.

In addition to helping students develop time schedules, encourage them to arrange for regular places to study. If your discussions with individuals are frank and fruitful, you may find that some students truly have neither the time nor the place for home study. In such cases, you may be able to help the student find time to study in school or in class. Discussions with students should include the importance of learning good study habits and should provide clues by which students may improve their use of time. Do not forget: Efficient learning does not come naturally; it must be learned.

Stop and Reflect

Pick a selection from a textbook that you might use in one of your middle or high school classes. Set up a lesson for teaching this selection by following the general plan for using a study guide to teach at-risk readers. Prepare another plan that follows the directed-reading lesson technique for this or another selection.

In what ways could teachers of various grade levels cooperate in the teaching of study skills in your field?

In what ways is studying algebra different from studying social studies? From home economics? What skills may be used when studying these courses? Do the necessary skills vary from topic to topic within the fields? How?

Multiple Resources

Sometimes instruction can be more profitable if you use several reading resources rather than a single textbook. Students read at different rates, with different abilities and interests, and with different backgrounds. No single text can cope with all these differences. If you adopt a single text, the class is limited to a single point of view, a single reading level, and a single style.

Using several resources has the advantage of making it possible for students to read material suited to their abilities and needs. If a student is attempting to learn the contribution of Samuel Gompers to the labor movement, it matters little whether he searches for his information in the *Encyclopedia Americana*, a biography of Gompers, or a history of the labor movement, as long as he learns the information as efficiently and effectively as he can. Because of this, you can help students pick books to study that are most suitable for their abilities and that may appeal to their individual interests. It is difficult to provide adequately for individual differences if you limit the readings to one text only.

Another important aspect of making many resources available is the opportunity given to students to read original sources. Textbooks often tell about things superficially. In many instances this treatment is justified because of the limitations of time and space, but certainly the students should be allowed to meet some of the originals face to face. Using many resources makes this easily possible, especially now that much first-rate material is available in paperback.

Multiple resources will often serve your purposes better than will a single textbook, since a variety of resources can be more easily matched to the needs, abilities, and inclinations of individual students. Supplemental and alternative reading material can be found not only in various textbooks but also in pamphlets, brochures, magazines, newspapers, and other fiction and nonfiction books. Workbooks and duplicated materials can provide a basis for study and exercise.

You can easily obtain some of these additional instructional materials from government agencies, community service organizations, businesses, and industry by merely asking for them. You can prepare some materials yourself. You must purchase or rent others. No matter where you obtain them, you should gather enough materials to furnish a classroom library that your students can use to bolster their learning. Another resource for teaching is the community. Not only can it serve as a source of reading materials, but also as a reservoir for field trips and resource people.

■ ■ ■   Other Printed and Duplicated Materials

Pamphlets and Brochures

A tremendous amount of reading material suitable for classroom use is available for the asking or for a small fee—one particularly rich source being federal and state government agencies. The Government Printing Office lists thousands of pamphlets and books for sale, and various federal agencies distribute great amounts of interesting, informative material on request. Other sources are large industrial and commercial firms; foreign governments; supragovernmental agencies, such as the United Nations, UNESCO, and NATO; civic organizations, such as the League of Women Voters; and professional organizations, such as the National Education Association.

Workbooks

Many textbook publishers provide workbooks for use by students in secondary and middle school classes. If well-written and well-used, they can be helpful, as is also true of teacher-prepared exercises.

When properly used, workbooks and duplicated exercises make it possible for students to pace themselves and so make allowances for their differences. There is no need for all students to do the same exercise at the same time; indeed, there is no real reason why all students must use the same workbook. Sometimes it may be quite possible to use a workbook that was designed for use with one textbook with other texts as well. However, when so doing take care to see that the selections used are compatible. When differences between the text and a workbook may cause confusion, a little editing and cutting can make the content match well enough to avoid any serious difficulty.

One of the common complaints against workbooks is that they encourage rote learning and discourage creative thought. These criticisms are often justified. To avoid this result, try to select workbooks that present problems and review material, and study guides that elicit high-level thinking.

As with anything else, you must follow up assignments in workbooks and locally produced materials. Reinforcement is usually better if the follow-up is immediate. In some instances, you can achieve good results by providing answer sheets so that students can check their own work. In other cases, it is better to follow up the workbook problems during a classroom discussion or by going over the problem in class. *In no case should you leave the workbook work completely unchecked until you find a propitious moment at some later time to collect and correct it. Do it now!*

Duplicated Material

In many school systems, teachers often provide their students with great amounts of duplicated materials and use them in just the same way as they would printed materials.

Teachers often give such material to students to keep for later use or to use right away. In a good many cases, this practice is desirable, but preparing duplicated material costs time and money. There is no reason duplicated exercises and supplementary reading materials should not be used again and again if you take precautions. For example, you may wish to have students write their answers to exercises and problems in a notebook or on a separate sheet of paper, rather than on the materials directly. If you bind the duplicated, supplementary reading matter in some sort of stiff cover, it will be quite durable. Construction paper or manila file folders are excellent for this purpose. Pamphlets made this way will last longer if the copy is stapled to the cover rather than fastened with paper fasteners.

Some schools provide teachers with enough clerical help to allow all sorts of materials to be duplicated with little time having to be invested by the teacher. More often, however, the job of preparing supplementary materials falls to the teacher. Consequently, as soon as you can, learn how to use the copying and duplicating machines available in your school.

Stop and Reflect

Examine several workbooks. Do they seem to encourage independent learning or rote memorization? Examine teacher-prepared materials in the same way. How can these materials be made to encourage independent thought?

Paperback Books

To provide for the differences in interests, needs, and abilities of young people in your classes and to allow the implementation of laboratory and inquiry teaching, every school and classroom should have a well-stocked library. Paperback books can fill this need at a relatively small cost. By buying paperbacks the school library can acquire a great variety of books of all sorts to augment their more permanent collection and to build classroom libraries.

Paperbacks can supplement or even replace textbook sets. The best thing about paperbacks is that they are inexpensive enough so that students can buy them. In schools that have no classroom libraries, students can pool their resources and start their own classroom libraries with paperbacks. More important, you can encourage students to build their own personal libraries and become really familiar with books of their own.

By providing paperbacks, you can make it possible for students to read primary sources rather than secondary or tertiary ones—whole works rather than snippets—

and to explore them both extensively and intensively rather than being exposed only to a single textbook account. With inexpensive paperbacks, it is much easier to provide students with opportunities to analyze and compare works, a practice that is almost impossible if you use only the ordinary textbook or anthology.

The Classroom Library

To be able to teach in the way you ought to teach, your students must have plenty of material to read. To make this supply of reading material readily available, each classroom should be a library. In the classroom library, all sorts of reading material should be readily accessible to the students—periodicals, pamphlets, brochures, and the like, as well as books. For record keeping, a self-checking system with students acting as librarians from time to time may suffice. Usually, you need worry little about loss of material if such a system is used.

In addition to the classroom library, make good use of the town and school libraries. Although it is true that in some communities these libraries are rather scantily supplied, the librarians are almost invariably eager to cooperate with teachers. They can often obtain additional materials from regional or state libraries. Make the most of this opportunity.

Few young people, or adults for that matter, use libraries well. Although instructing students in the use of the library may ordinarily be the English Department's or the librarian's responsibility, teachers whose students must use the library are also responsible to see that students use the library facilities efficiently. Arranging for students to visit the library early in the year for instruction in its use can well increase the efficient use of its facilities.

Teaching Students to Take Notes

Without any doubt, being able to outline well is one of the most valuable skills a student can have, and teachers in all subjects can help make sure that students master it. To teach students to outline correctly, the National Association of Secondary School Principals has recommended the following techniques, which have been well-proven over the years:

1. Use easy materials and short selections in teaching pupils the mechanics of outlining. The following steps may be followed in teaching pupils to make outlines.
   a. Teacher and pupils working together select the main topics.
   b. Pupils, unaided, select the main topics.
   c. Teacher and pupils select the main topics, leaving space for subheads. Teacher and pupils then fill in these subtopics.
   d. Main topics are selected by the teachers and pupils and are written on the blackboard. Pupils then fill in the subtopics unaided.
   e. Pupils write the main topics and subheads without help.
   f. Pupils organize, in outline form, data gathered from many sources.
2. Train pupils to find the main topics and to place them in outline form. Use books with paragraph headings.
   a. Have pupils read the paragraphs and discuss the headings. Suggest other possible headings and have pupils decide why the author selected the headings he used.
   b. Match a given list of paragraph headings with numbered paragraphs.
   c. Have pupils read a paragraph with this question in mind, "What is the main idea in this paragraph?" Write a number of suggested answers on the blackboard. Choose the best one.

3. Provide practice in filling in subtopics.
   a. The teacher writes the main topics on the board or uses a text that has the main topic headings. Teacher and pupils then fill in the subheads.
   b. Have pupils skim other articles for more information and read carefully when additional material which is suitable for subheads is found. Add these new subheads. Do the same for new main topics.
   c. When pupils have gathered sufficient data, have them reread the complete outline and, if necessary, rearrange the order of the topics.
4. Give instructions in making a standard outline form. Many secondary school pupils do not know how to make an outline. Emphasize the fact that in a correct outline there must always be more than one item in the series under any subdivision. If there is an "a" there must also be a "b"; if there is a "1" there must also be a "2," etc. . . .
5. Have pupils use this outline form in preparing and giving oral reports.
6. To develop ability to draw valid conclusions, have pupils use facts and ideas which have been organized in outline form, not only as a basis for an oral report or as an exercise in outlining a chapter, but also as the basis for drawing conclusions. To check pupils' ability to make outlines, prepare lessons based on the following suggestions.
   a. List main points and subpoints consecutively. Have pupils copy these, indenting to show subordination of subtopics and writing correct numbers and letters in front of each point.
   b. List main topics and subtopics in mixed order and have pupils rearrange and number them.
   c. List main topics with Roman numerals. List subtopics (all one value) with Arabic numerals. Have pupils organize subpoints under correct main points.
   d. Present short paragraphs of well-organized material and have pupils write main topics and the specified number of subtopics.
   e. Present part of a skeleton outline and have students complete it.
   f. Have pupils outline a problem without assistance. Class discussion is valuable in checking a lesson of this type.(21)

■ ■ ■ Sources of Teaching Materials

Occasionally, teachers defend dull, humdrum teaching on the grounds that the school administration will not give them adequate materials. Such complaints are usually merely passing the buck, for with a little ingenuity and initiative, you can find boundless supplies of materials available to schools in even the lowest socioeconomic brackets.

Materials for learning can be found almost everywhere. Curriculum guides, resource units, and references such as those listed at the end of this chapter are all good sources of information telling where to find and how to use instructional materials. You can often pick up samples of materials and leads to locating other sources of inexpensive materials at teachers' conventions and other professional meetings, such as those held by your state teachers' association or the organization of teachers in your field. Teachers' resource centers maintained by college and university schools of education and by the state and county educational departments are also good sources of information about available materials.

Stop and Reflect
Examine a sample resource unit. Note the amount of material it presents. How could you use such a resource unit for your own teaching?

Similarly examine a number of curriculum guides.

Free and Inexpensive Materials

Much teaching material is free or inexpensive. For example, building a file of pictures is easy, inexpensive, and can be considerable fun. Such a file is so useful that the prospective teacher can hardly afford not to build one. You can start by collecting pictures from periodicals. Photographic magazines, such as *National Geographic* or *Smithsonian*, are full of potentially useful pictures. So are special-interest magazines such as those devoted to travel, popular science, and history. You can also obtain pictures from commercial sources such as museums and publishing houses, both by purchase and rental. Many libraries have pictures to lend to teachers.

Not only pictures but other materials, such as slides, specimens, souvenirs, models, and the like, are readily available for the asking. Some museums will lend such material to schools free of charge. In almost every hamlet in the United States, some villager has a collection of interesting materials that could be used with profit in the classroom. Most collectors are pleased to show off their collections. Quite often the most avid collectors are other teachers.

Stores, factories, and commercial concerns of all sorts are willing, and in some instances anxious, to give samples of raw and processed materials to the schools. Many firms offer films, slides, filmstrips, and other similar audiovisual materials free on request. The amount of excellent material available free from local, state, national, and foreign government agencies is almost boundless.

CULLING THE MATERIAL   Although much free material is available, some of it is hardly worth cluttering up your shelves with. Consequently, you should select such materials carefully. Use criteria such as the following:

1. Will the material really further educational objectives?
2. Is it free from objectionable advertising, propaganda, and so on?
3. Is it accurate, honest, free from bias (except when you wish to illustrate dishonesty and bias, of course)?
4. Is it interesting, colorful, exciting?
5. Does it lend itself to school use?
6. Is it well-made?

WRITING FOR FREE MATERIAL   To get free material, usually all you need do is write and ask for it. When writing for free material, use official school stationery. Your letter should state exactly what you want and why you want it. Many firms like to know just how the material will be used and how many persons will see it. Sometimes, teachers ask students to write the letter. Although doing so is excellent practice for the students, some firms will honor only letters from the teacher. You can sidestep this problem by having the students prepare letters for your signature or by countersigning students' letters.

Making Your Own Materials

Teachers frequently need to make their own materials, particularly practice materials and study guides. Modern photocopying methods allow great versatility in copying, arranging, combining, and organizing written, typed, and illustrated materials. With relatively little effort and ingenuity, you can create and duplicate exercises, diagrams, reading materials, assignments, study guides, and a multitude of other things. One advantage of building your own material is that you get what you want—not what some educator or merchandiser thinks you want. Against this advantage you must weigh the cost in time and effort. Teachers often expend great amounts of energy developing materials that are really not worth the effort. On the other hand, once you have prepared useful materials, share them with other teachers. To hoard valuable teaching materials is wasteful.

An interesting technique used by a social studies teacher is to tear chapters out of old books and rebind them into pamphlets by stapling them into folders or notebook binders. From discarded textbooks, *National Geographic* magazines, and other books and periodicals, at practically no expense, she has amassed a considerable library of short articles on many topics pertinent to her social studies courses. Not only is this a cheap method of securing reading matter, but also reducing the books and periodicals to pamphlet form makes a large number of different readings accessible. The scheme has the additional advantage of cleaning out school closets and family attics.

An English teacher collects exercises for punctuation study by having students submit sentences to be punctuated. She collects these sentences until she has a large number of exercises that she reproduces for student use. A science teacher makes a habit of going around to garages and junk shops to pick up old switches and other materials that, with the help of his students, he turns into demonstration equipment for his laboratory. Another science teacher allows gifted students to prepare microscope slides for class use. An art teacher prepares his own clay for ceramics classes by processing, with the help of his students, clay dug from a bank near a river a few miles from the school.

Other materials that you can make for yourself include springboards, study guides, and instructional learning packets.

Stop and Reflect

Look up sources of materials you might use in your teaching. Draft a letter requesting special materials for a course you might teach.

What instructional television is available in your area? What offerings are available that might be useful in your teaching field?

The incidents related in the text illustrate a few examples of the myriad sources of materials available to the ingenious teacher. What materials could you use for a class of your own? Where might you find these materials? How might you use them?

Does your state, county, or university publish a guide to free materials and local resources?

It is none too soon for you to start collecting material for the classes you may someday teach. If you pick up and save all the pertinent material you can find, you will have a start toward becoming a well-equipped teacher.

Examine catalogs to find films and other materials available for use in courses you hope to teach.

Search old magazines and so on to find material suitable for your future classes. It is never too early to start collecting teaching material.

The Community as a Resource

Extending the classroom into the community can make a course exciting and forceful, since every community is a gold mine of resources for teaching. The experiences of the students as they get out into the community are not only a welcome change, but also are potent learning activities. Similar benefits can also come from bringing the community into a classroom. Layspeakers and consultants, for instance, can add practical expertise, specialized knowledge, and reality to your instruction. Every school should have a file of community resources available. Individual teachers sometimes keep such files for use in their own classes, but probably a well-kept central file is more efficient, although you will need to keep your own additional information applicable to your own classes. A 5 × 8 index card file is most satisfactory for this purpose. In it, keep such information as the following:

1. Possible field trips
    a. What is available there to see
    b. Where it is and how to get there
    c. Whom to contact about arrangements
    d. Expense involved
    e. Time required
    f. Other comments
2. Resource people, speakers, and so on
    a. Who they are
    b. How they can help
    c. Addresses
3. Resource material and instructional materials obtainable locally
    a. What material is available
    b. How to procure it
    c. Expense involved
4. Community groups
    a. Names and addresses
    b. Function and purpose
    c. Type of activity they can help with
5. Local businesses, industries, and agencies
    a. Name
    b. Address
    c. Key personnel

FIELD TRIPS   Particularly vivid learning experiences sometimes result from going out into the community. One of the most common devices used for extending the classroom into the community is the field trip, a time-honored method that has been used with great success for centuries. Field trips can take many forms. A nature walk is a field trip. A visit to the museum is a field trip. So is a period spent on the athletic field searching for insect specimens.

Conducting a field trip is much the same as is conducting any other instructional activity. The students must be introduced to it, they must be briefed on what to look for, and the activity should be followed up. However, field trips do present certain special considerations such as scheduling, permissions, transportation, expense, and control.

Before planning the trip, it is a good policy to make the trip yourself, if possible, to see whether it would be worthwhile for your students and how it could be made most productive. Arrange the details at the place to be visited. Many museums, factories, and other places of interest provide their own tour services. If they do, be sure to let the proper persons know the purpose of the visit and what the students should see. Also arrange for the necessary permissions, schedule changes, transportation, and so forth. Students can often help considerably in planning and arranging a field trip. However, be careful to double- and triple-check on the details yourself. Also double-check to be sure that everyone has a mission to perform on the field trip. The trip should not be a joy ride or an outing, but a real learning experience.

Stop and Reflect

What are the advantages of taking students on field trips? What are the disadvantages?

Why must field trips be planned? What particularly must be considered in the planning? To what extent and in what ways can the students participate in planning and carrying out the plans?

Many field trips are not worth the time, trouble, and expense. How can you ensure that your field trips are not merely outings?

RESOURCE PEOPLE   The most important resource of a community is its people. Even in a socioeconomically disadvantaged rural community, there are an amazing number of people who have special knowledge and talent that they can share effectively with a class. These persons can often bring to a class new authority, new interest, new information, and a new point of view. Among the people who can be good resource persons are town, county, state, or federal government employees, hobbyists, travelers, businesspeople, college teachers, specialists, clergy, and people from other lands. Alumni, parents, and relatives of the students are frequently available and usually interested in visiting the schools. A chemistry teacher aroused class interest by featuring a visit from a metallurgist from a local brass mill. Sources sometimes forgotten are the other teachers and school officials in your own or neighboring school systems.

Resource persons can serve many purposes. They can provide students with help in specialized projects. They can also provide information not otherwise readily available. Who would know more about soil conservation in your county than the local Soil Conservation Service agent?

Resource persons are frequently asked to be speakers. Before inviting a layperson to speak to the class, however, check to be sure that there is a reasonable chance for the success of the activity. You can often find out a lot about potential speakers from other teachers and friends. Visit prospective speakers and talk to them about their respective subjects. In your conversation you can probably determine whether a person is the type who understands and can get along with young people. You can also probably determine whether an individual can speak at the young people's level. For example, if a resource person's field is engineering and she discusses jet engines only in the language of the professional engineer, she will not contribute much to the class.

When inviting individuals to speak, brief them carefully on what they are to talk about and the purpose of the talk. Make an agreement about the length of the talk, how questions will be asked, what visual aids will be used, and so forth. It is wise to remind the speaker of these agreements, the time, place, and topic in a letter of confirmation. The letter should be written diplomatically. State the agreements as you understand them, and ask speakers if they concur.

You can also remind speakers of their commitments when you introduce them to the class. The public announcement that your visitor is to speak for 10 minutes and then answer questions often has a desirable effect on long-winded, rambling guests. Such precautions may seem farfetched, but they are sometimes necessary. It is discouraging to have a speaker talk for 40 minutes of a 45-minute period without letting the students ask any of the questions they have prepared.

Prepare students for the meeting. As when dealing with other instructional aids, students should know what to expect and what to look for. Having students make up questions they would like answered is good preparation for listening to the speech and for discussing the topic after the speech. Student questions can also be given to the speaker beforehand as a guide for preparing the speech.

As a rule, speakers cannot be counted on to hold the attention of a class for a whole period. The guest appearance is usually much more successful if the formal speaking is kept quite short and the bulk of the program is devoted to discussion and student questions. It is sometimes more rewarding to bring in resource persons as consultants for pupil discussion groups than it is to arrange a formal lecture.

▪▪▪ Homework

Properly conducted, homework activities can make schooling more effective. For one thing, homework tends to increase time on task.(22) In mathematics, for instance, research studies indicate that young people who are required to do homework do better on tests than those who are not so required. Similar results have been found in studies for eighth-graders in English and social studies. The catch, however, is that the homework should be properly conducted. Otherwise, it can be a waste of time and can actually retard learning.

What Kind of Homework?

In general, homework assignments can be broken into three categories: preparation activities, extension of classroom learning activities, and practice and drill activities.

PREPARATION ACTIVITIES   By far the largest number of homework assignments at present seems to consist of exhortations to read certain pages in the textbook in preparation for the next day's recitation. All too often assignments of this sort fail because the teacher does not give the students proper direction. If, when making homework reading assignments, more care were given to using the procedure outlined in the sections on making assignments, homework results would be more successful. Although reading the text can make an excellent homework assignment, teachers tend to overuse it. The list of other types of activities that could make homework interesting as well as informative is almost endless and includes the following:

- Individualized instruction
- Collateral reading
- Projects
- Committee assignments
- Observation
- Listening to the radio
- Newspaper or magazine study
- Attending meetings, hearings, and so on
- Notebook work
- Problems
- Library work
- Viewing television
- Using community resources
- Preparing oral reports.

There seems to be no excuse for not having a variety of preparatory homework experiences.

EXTENSION ACTIVITIES   In general, however, homework is more suitable for reinforcing or extending previous learning. The homework should consist of activities that students can do on their own. It should be a logical extension of the classroom work that they can do without supervision or assistance. Learning new techniques and new materials is usually best done in class situations where you can guide the students and thus guard them from learning the new techniques or new concepts incorrectly. Moreover, assignments of new materials for study at home usually place too much emphasis on memorizing as opposed to understanding or thinking. *That is why homework assignments that carry on some activity started in class* *often result in better learning*, particularly when the activities are the kinds that require library or laboratory work, such as digging out information from several sources and analyzing and identifying or defining problems. Furthermore, students are less likely to be forgetful when the homework stems out of, or continues, an activity they are already working on and when it is tailored to their interests or needs. Homework never should be just something added on or, even worse, a punishment. It is more likely to be profitable if it extends the learning by applying it to new conditions or situations, requiring students to use their imagination and creative thought, stressing student initiative, individualizing assignments to fit students' talents and interests, and allowing students to plan new projects and to use what they have learned to break new ground. Further investigating a problem that has been launched during class discussion or digging up arguments pro or con for class discussion of controversial issues are examples of the most rewarding type of homework activities. Long-term projects and activities, particularly activities that require independent work, creative or original thought, and individual research and study, can be excellent for extending classroom learning, particularly for gifted, interested students. With proper encouragement and sufficient variety and recognition of student interests, homework can be an avenue for developing permanent interests that carry over into adult life or even become careers.

PRACTICE ACTIVITIES   In some studies, such as mathematics, homework commonly consists of practice activities. However, this approach is not always the most fruitful. To practice activities related to a skill after one has learned the basic technique is an excellent procedure, but not if the practice is merely repetition for repetition's sake. Moreover, gifted students tend to master the learning quickly, then either quit or suffer through the remaining exercises without learning anything more, while other students soon get bored and frustrated and give up. That is one reason why it is better to arrange exercises in order of difficulty. Thus, students who are low achievers, for instance, have success with the easier problems in the beginning of the assignment and then are encouraged to keep on trying.

A JUDICIOUS MIX   It is probably best not to become overcommitted to any one type of homework. A judicious mix of several types is the best approach. In algebra, for instance, "spiral approach" homework assignments that combine some "review exercises, some exploratory exercises designed to set the stage for future work, and the current assignment" seem to work well.(23)

Making Homework Assignments

In general, the rules for making assignments spelled out in Chapter 3 apply to all types of assignments. Perhaps homework assignments require more care than other assignments, for you will not be there to straighten out student misunderstandings and to help them when they get stuck.

First, it is most important that students be well-motivated. Homework that promotes strong student motivation is usually completed satisfactorily. Homework for which students are not well-motivated is better done in school under supervision. Carefully spell out to the students the importance of homework. Make explanations of the role of the homework part of your classroom management techniques. Pass on such explanations to the students' parents by letter or handouts to get good returns on your investment of time and effort.

Second, the homework assignment must be very clear. Ordinary daily homework assignments may not need detailed explanations, but make sure that every student knows the purpose of the assignment, knows how it ties into what has been done before, and knows what will happen later. As with any other assignment, plan with the students how to approach it. Teach whatever skills the students need. This all can be done individually, in small groups, or in large groups as the occasion demands.

Third, the homework should match the abilities, talents, and maturity levels of the students. Since students' abilities differ, these facts imply that homework should be at least somewhat individualized. Students who are having difficulty with a subject, who have schedule problems, who have missed school, who have skipped classwork because of distractions of various kinds, who have special interests or special talents, or who are involved in community and school activities will not all benefit optimally from the same homework assignment. Insofar as possible, adjust students' homework to fit their individual needs, abilities, aptitudes, and interests. Long-term or unit assignments that allow students to select homework activities from a number of options are excellent because they allow for the differences in students.

Homework should not be used as a substitute for independent study, however. Homework can develop independence, but independent study is something else again. Independent study should be done in the classroom, in the resource center, and at home as a total strategy. It is not a tactic to be added on to ordinary teaching as homework.

Fourth, be sure that your homework assignments consist of activities the students can do on their own. If the students cannot complete the assignment without help, do not assign it as homework.

Fifth, when feasible, spread assignments over a period of time. Assignments that distribute the homework over several days seem to result in better learning than do those that mass everything into a single daily assignment. Longer-term assignments can also be used advantageously, as we have seen.

How Much Homework?

How much homework should you assign? The answer depends on your school, your subject, and your students. Perhaps your school administration will have established a policy concerning homework. If so, you must conform. Should the policy be a poor one, you might work for its improvement, but under no circumstances should you flout it.

If your school has no policy concerning homework, you should fall in line with the school tradition, if any. In any case, try to make sure that students are neither overburdened nor underworked. Often a good unit assignment takes care of this problem automatically. At any rate, by giving long-term assignments you give the students an opportunity to adjust their work so that they can avoid being overburdened by simultaneous major assignments in several courses. Therefore, even if you do not use the unit approach, it may be wise to give out homework assignments for a week or more ahead. Almost invariably, it is more satisfactory to give assignments in writing to prevent confusion, misunderstanding, and the need for repeating the assignment. (A homework announcement section on the chalkboard can be a great help.)

In making decisions about how much homework to give, consider the following points:

1. We suggest that the daily homework load (study periods plus home study) of all courses combined should be
   None in grades five and six.
   One to two hours in grades seven and eight.
   Two to three hours in grades nine and ten.
   Three hours in grades eleven and twelve.

In planning homework assignments, do not forget that there may be more important things than homework in adolescent life.

2. A fair estimate of the amount of time available for homework for any one class can be represented by the amount of time available for study during the school day and for a reasonable period after school hours, divided by the number of daily classes the student must prepare for.

3. To avoid excessive homework assignments, it is suggested that teachers in grades seven and eight stagger their assignments (e.g., science and math on Monday and Wednesday, English and social studies on Tuesday and Thursday, and no homework on Friday). The value of giving assignments to be done over the weekend is dubious. In the senior high school grades, homework time can be equally divided among the various courses. At all levels, due allowance should be made for major assignments and tests. (As a rule, college-preparatory classes seem to include more homework than other classes do.)

4. The amount of time it takes a student to do assignments depends upon the student. An assignment that one student can do well in 30 minutes may take another student much more than an hour. For this reason, if no other, individualize homework assignments as much as is feasible.

5. In some classes and schools, students do not do their homework. In such cases, it may be futile to assign it. Instead, use supervised study and laboratory teaching and try to build up the attitudes and ideals that will cause the students to want to study during out-of-class hours. Important ingredients in this process are the introduction of assignments that seem to be worth doing and positive reinforcement when students attempt to do the assignments.

6. From time to time check on the length of time your assignments are taking. In addition to asking students how long an assignment took them, check by giving pupils sample homework assignments to do during class periods so as to see how long it takes pupils to complete them.

At this point a word of warning is in order. Some high school teachers try to illustrate how tough they are and what high standards they hold by piling great amounts of homework on their students. Unreasonably long assignments have no place in the secondary school for several reasons. The first is that *the emphasis should be on quality rather than quantity*. Homework should enrich the classroom study. Avoid homework assignments that are merely more of the same. The more real and significant the homework, the better. At least some of the time students should get out into the community to where the action is. Perhaps they can participate in the action; at least they can witness it. Assignments that are too long often force students to do less than their best, because there is just not enough time for them to do everything well. In addition, overdoses of homework can deprive students of the social and physical activities they need if they are to develop into well-balanced individuals. It is not necessary for a teacher to be an ogre in order to have high standards.

Evaluating Homework

Evaluating written homework presents several peculiar problems. One of them is that the written homework turned in is not always the work of the student alone, but that of his or her friends or relatives. Although teachers may condemn it as cheating, for parents to help their children with homework and for friends to share their work with each other is an accepted part of our American culture which no one else, certainly not the students or their parents, feels to be particularly dishonest. Because of this, assign written homework mainly as practice material from which the students may learn whether someone helps them or not. Homework should not count much in making up a student's grade; rather, marks should be based upon papers and tests done during class. Nevertheless, even though written homework should not carry much weight in your grading, it should always be checked (see Figure 12.6). Unchecked written homework may serve only to grind erroneous techniques and incorrect concepts into students' minds. Recognition of good work serves to stimulate student self-esteem, interest, and effort.

Supervised Study

Many teachers set aside class time for students to study their homework and complete other assignments. This practice has several advantages. It ensures that everyone has time to do some studying. It gives you a chance to guide students toward good study habits. It also gives you a chance to guide students in their studying—to see that they get off on the right foot by using the proper procedures and so on. To be sure that students get a proper start, when giving students difficult assignments in a new subject area, it is wise to start with a supervised study session before sending them to do the assignment on their own. A short period of supervised study may eliminate student mistakes and make it unnecessary for you to reteach while the students unlearn.

To prepare for supervised study periods, establish with the students the purpose of the study assignment and why they should make the effort to study it. This step may not be easy. Students may not see any *real* reason for studying assignments, even when teachers think them essential. Therefore, stretch your talents to make clear to students the relevance and importance of the learning. Also point out or help the students establish what specifically should be learned. Teacher and student questions might include: What important points should we look for? How does the new learning relate to what has gone before? What would you as a student or anyone else want to know about this lesson? The motivation for studying the lesson having been established, you can help students with such details as setting up their own study goals, time schedules, and methods of attacking the subject.

During the supervised study session, be it 10 minutes at the beginning or end of the class period or an entire period, you should supervise the students' studying. During this supervision, you can and should observe individual study habits, keep track of each student's progress, and be alert for misunderstandings, poor techniques, and other difficulties that may arise. Sometimes, it will be evident that the entire class does not understand how to proceed or is on the wrong track. In such instances, you should stop everyone, call attention to the difficulty, and correct misapprehensions. However, occasions of this sort should be rare. The teacher who frequently interrupts students when they are studying does more harm than good.

■ **Figure 12.6**
Homework Checklist

1. Is the assignment clear? Are you sure pupils know how to carry it out? Did you take time to give the assignment properly?
2. Is the assignment really tied to the teaching objectives?
3. Do pupils understand the purpose of the assignment?
4. Does the assignment take a reasonable amount of time?
5. Is the homework assignment individualized? Does it allow for pupil needs and interests?
6. Does the assignment allow for initiative, imagination, and creativity?
7. Is well-done homework recognized?
8. Is there definite follow-up?

As you circulate around the classroom, talk with the students about their progress. Ask them how things are going, but go further than that. Sometimes, students don't know when things are going badly, or they may be unwilling to admit that they are having trouble. A little probing may give you a more realistic picture of their progress.

Insofar as you can, individualize. As you observe, you may find opportunities to differentiate assignments by giving different students work at different levels or by finding things that will appeal to students' peculiar interests or purposes or will help them resolve their difficulties.

Supervised study is such an important technique that you should always include supervised study in your planning. The amount of supervised study will vary according to the lesson or unit, its aims and contents. On some days, no supervised study will be needed. At other times, proper planning requires that an entire period or even longer be given over to supervised study. As we have seen, a supervised study period is an opportunity both for the student to study under guidance and for the teacher to supervise and guide study. Although this can best be done in the regular class, to a lesser extent it can also be done in study halls. Unfortunately, in some schools study halls are looked upon as merely a means for storing students who have no class at the time. This is hardly efficient. Supervised study periods need real supervision. Merely to sit and watch the students should not be the function of the teacher in a supervised study period. If keeping order in the study hall is to be the sole function, the school would do better to hire a police officer for this duty.

Students who attend schools with well-run resource centers (otherwise called learning, or materials, centers) have an advantage over other students. Teachers and aides who work in resource centers usually go out of their way to help students find and use the materials they need to complete their assignments and to become independent learners.

Stop and Reflect

How can you use supervised study periods to develop the study skills essential for success in your subject field?

How would you go about individualizing homework in your classes?

Visit a secondary or middle school departmental resource center if there is one available. How would you try to capitalize on its resources if you were teaching in the school?

Look back at your high school days. Was the homework load reasonable? Did you have too much to do? Too little? Did you always know what to do and how to do it? Did your teachers take time to get you in the proper set? Did they follow up?

A teacher of English says he corrects homework papers carefully about every fifth assignment. The other assignments he merely checks to see if the work has been done. Is this practice proper? Defend your answer.

SUMMARY

Most secondary school students need to be taught how to study. The teachers of the various subjects are responsible for seeing that each student learns how to study each discipline. To this end, each teacher must show students how to perform such scholarly skills as analyzing problems, taking notes, and picking the meat out of lectures. Much of this teaching can be done while giving the assignment.

Young people must be taught how to use books effectively and efficiently. They need to know how and when to skim, how and when to read closely, and how to use the aids provided by the author and publisher. Subject teachers must also help students to develop their vocabularies and to read for comprehension. Part of their job is to point out new words and ideas and to suggest methods by which the students can get the most from their reading. Most important of all is their obligation to teach students to read critically with open minds. For students to learn to evaluate what they read is perhaps just as important as is their learning to read with understanding.

Selecting the proper reading material is essential. Probably no one text can ever be adequate, even though most classroom instruction centers on a textbook. Because of the textbook's importance, do your best to see that the students learn to use their textbooks well and understand how to make the most of the various aids the author has provided. The use of many resources and techniques for individualizing instruction can make classes more effective. For this reason, full use of the library and the development of classroom libraries is essential.

Reading selections should be matched to the reader's skill. To find the reading level of a book, use formulas such as that of Fry. To determine a student's reading skill, use such techniques as the CLOZE procedure or the silent or oral inventory. Do not take the results of these procedures as gospel, however. You must rely to some extent on your own observation and judgment.

If students are ever to become scholars, they must learn to study independently. To develop this skill, it is first necessary to help them develop basic skills and confidence in reading independently, and then move to more sophisticated techniques such as the directed-reading lesson technique. In the initial stages, simple study guides are helpful, but in later stages students should be able to provide their own reading questions.

Students also need to learn how to carry out their learning assignments. For this purpose you will need to provide them with both plenty of freedom to use their own initiative and plenty of guidance. It is helpful if the students can develop these skills in a graded sequence while studying under supervision. In order for students to learn to get the most out of their classes and their reading, teach them how to take careful notes.

Free or inexpensive reading matter on almost any subject is available from government and business agencies. It can be advantageous to make your own duplicated readings, study guides, practice materials, and exercises. When you do, consider methods by which you can save homemade materials for reuse.

Paperback books, newspapers, and periodicals can be sources of up-to-date, interest-catching content in all middle and secondary school courses. They give students opportunities for wide reading and help develop habits and skills in effective critical and pleasurable reading that they may carry into adult life.

Some audiovisual materials are expensive and hard to get, as is true of other materials also, but do not let this fact discourage you. Much material is available for the asking. Much more can be made or improvised. Hints on how to obtain and create such materials can be found in the catalogs, curriculum guides, source units, and periodicals on the subject; many of these materials can be procured by simply asking for them. Today no teacher has an excuse for not having a supply of suitable materials.

The best resource you have is the community itself. It is both a source of subject matter and a source of instructional material and resource persons. Community laypersons can be used as classroom speakers and as consultants and guides.

When assigning homework, consider that the best kind of homework is that which reinforces old learning or which follows up work which has been well started in class. Giving brand new work for homework may result in incorrect learning which must later be untaught in class. This is one reason why supervised study during class time may be more suitable. Because of the tendency of friends and parents to share in the homework process, do not place too much weight on it in evaluating the student. Still, written homework should always be checked.

ADDITIONAL READING

Atwell, N. *In the Middle: Writing, Reading, and Learning with Adolescents*. Portsmouth, NH: Boynton-Cook Publishers, 1987.

Barr, R. et al., eds. *Handbook of Reading Research, Volume II*. White Plains, NY: Longman, 1991.

Cochran, J. A. *Reading in the Content Areas for Junior High and High Schools*. Boston: Allyn and Bacon, 1993.

Cooper, H. M. *Homework*. White Plains, NY: Longman, 1989.

Cunningham, J. W., P. M. Cunningham, and S. V. Arthur. *Middle and Secondary School Reading*. New York: Longman, 1981.

Cushenberg, D. C. *Comprehensive Reading Strategies for All Students*. Springfield, IL: Charles C. Thomas, 1985.

Devine, T. G. *Teaching Study Skills: A Guide for Teachers*, 2nd ed. Boston: Allyn and Bacon, 1987.

Duffy, G., ed. *Reading in the Middle School*, 2nd ed. Newark, DE: International Reading Association, 1990.

Early, M. *Reading to Learn in Grades 5 to 12*. New York: Harcourt, Brace, Jovanovich, 1984.

England, D. A., and J. K. Flately. *Homework—and Why, Fastback 219*. Bloomington, IN: Phi Delta Kappa Educational Foundation, 1985.

Friedman, P. G. *Listening Processes: Attention, Understanding, Evaluation*, 2nd ed. Washington, DC: National Education Association, 1986.

Graham, K. G., and H. A. Robinson. *Study Skills Handbook: A Guide for All Teachers*. Newark, DE: International Reading Association, 1984.

Hennessey, B. A., and T. M. Amabile. *What Research Says to the Teacher: Creativity and Learning*. Washington, DC: National Education Association, 1987.

Hodges, R. E. *Improving Spelling and Vocabulary in the Secondary School*. Urbana, IL: Clearing House on Reading and Communication Skills/National Council of Teachers of English, 1982.

Irving, J. *Reading and the Middle School Student: Strategies to Enhance Literacy*. Boston: Allyn and Bacon, 1990.

Kahn, N. *Learning in Less Time—A Guide to Effective Study*. Montclair, NJ: Boynton-Cook, 1984.

Kornhauser, A. W. *How to Study: Suggestions for High School and College Students*, 3rd ed., rev. by D. M. Enerson. Chicago: University of Chicago Press, 1993.

Krepel, W. J., and C. R. DuVall. *Field Trips: A Guide for Planning and Conducting Educational Experience*. Washington, DC: National Education Association, 1981.

LaConte, R. T., and M. A. Doyle. *Homework As a Learning Experience, What Research Says to the Teacher*, 2nd. ed. Washington, DC: National Education Association, 1986.

Langer, J. A., and A. N. Applebee. *Writing and Learning in the Secondary School*. Stanford, CA: Stanford University School of Education, 1987.

Lock, C. *Study Skills*. West Lafayette, IN: Kappa Delta Pi, 1981.

Lundsteen, S. W. *Listening: Its Impact on Reading and the Other Language Arts*, rev. ed. Urbana, IL: ERIC Clearinghouse on Reading and Communications Skills. National Council of Teachers of English, 1979.

Martin, R. J. *Teaching Through Encouragement. Techniques to Help Students Learn*. Englewood Cliffs, NJ: Prentice-Hall, 1980.

Noddings, N. *Caring: A Feminine Approach to Ethics and Moral Education*. Berkeley, CA: University of California Press, 1984.

Novak, J., and D. Gowen. *Learning How to Learn*. New York: Cambridge University Press, 1984.

Purvis, A. C., and O. Niles, eds. *Becoming Readers in a Complex Society, Eighty-third Yearbook, National Society for the Study of Education, Part I*. Chicago, IL: University of Chicago Press, 1984.

Robinson, H. A. *Teaching Reading and Study Strategies: The Content Areas*, 3rd. ed. Boston: Allyn and Bacon, 1983.

Roe, B., and B. D. Stoodt. *Secondary School Reading Instruction: The Content Areas*, 2nd ed. Boston: Houghton-Mifflin, 1983.

Snider, J. *How to Study in High School*. Providence, RI: Jamestown, 1983.

Thomas, E. L. *Reading Aids for Every Class. 400 Activities for Instruction and Enrichment*. Boston: Allyn and Bacon, 1980.

Thomas, E. L., and H. A. Robinson. *Improving Reading in Every Class*, abridged 3rd. ed. Boston: Allyn and Bacon, 1981.

Tonjes, M. J. *Secondary Reading, Writing and Learning*. Boston: Allyn and Bacon, 1991.

Travers, R. M. W. *Essentials of Learning*, 5th ed. New York: Macmillan, 1982.

Wood, K. et al. *Guiding Reading Through Text: A Review of Study Guides*. Newark, DE: International Reading Association, 1992.

NOTES

1. William L. Christen and Steven M. Brown, "High School Study Skills: Can They Affect Attendance?" *NASSP Bulletin* 66 (October 1982): 123–124.
2. William L. Christen and Thomas J. Murphy, "Learning How to Learn: How Important Are Study Skills?" *NASSP Bulletin* 69 (October 1985): 82–88.
3. Ibid.
4. Christen and Brown, "High School Study Skills."
5. Larry Nook, "Systematic Approach to Vocabulary Building" in *Developing Reading Skills through Subject Areas*, edited by Robert L. Schain, David R. Keefer, and Ethel Howard (Brooklyn, NY: The Wingate High School Press, 1976).
6. Russell G. Stauffer, "A Study of Prefixes in the Thorndike List to Establish a List of Prefixes That Should Be Taught in the Elementary School," *Journal of Educational Research* 35 (February 1942): 453–458.
7. Dorothy Piercy, *Reading Activities in Content Areas: An Idea Book for Middle and Secondary Schools* (Boston: Allyn & Bacon, 1976).
8. Bernice Jensen Bradstad and Sharyn Mueller Stumpf. *Study Skills and Motivation: A Guidebook for Teaching*, 2nd ed. (Boston: Allyn and Bacon, 1987), 66.
9. For examples of games for learning vocabulary, see Carol A. Jenkins and John F. Savage, *Activities for Integrating the Language Arts* (Englewood Cliffs, NJ: Prentice Hall, 1983), and Walter T. Petty, Dorothy C. Petty, and Marjorie Becking, *Experiences in Language Arts* (Newton, MA: Allyn & Bacon, 1985).
10. Joseph F. Callahan and Leonard H. Clark, *Teaching in the Middle and Secondary Schools*, 3rd ed. (New York: Macmillan, 1988), 447–448.
11. Harold L. Herber and John Nelson Herber, *Teaching Reading in Content Areas with Reading, Writing and Reasoning* (Boston: Allyn and Bacon, 1992).
12. Edward Fry, "A Readability Formula That Saves Time," *Journal of Reading* (April, 1968) 11: 587.

13. Bonnie B. Armbruster, Jean H. Osborn, and Alice L. Davison, "Readability Formulas May Be Dangerous to Your Textbooks," *Educational Leadership* 42 (April 1985): 18–20.

14. Gilbert T. Sewall, "American History Textbooks: Where Do We Go from Here?" *Phi Delta Kappan* 69 (April 1988): 552–564.

15. Baird Shuman, *Strategies in Teaching Reading: Secondary* (Washington, DC: National Education Association, 1978), Chapter 10.

16. William G. Perry, Jr., "Students' Use and Misuse of Reading Skills: A Report to the Faculty," *Harvard Educational Review* 29 (Summer 1959): 193–200; cited in Olive S. Niles, *Improvement of Basic Comprehension Skills: An Attainable Goal in Secondary Schools, A Scott Foresman Monograph on Education* (Glenview, IL: Scott, Foresman, 1964), 4.

17. Niles, *Improvement of Basic Comprehension Skills,* 5.

18. Harold L. Herber, *Teaching Reading in Content Areas*, 2nd ed. (Englewood Cliffs, NJ: Prentice Hall, 1978), Chap. 7.

19. Olive Niles, "Organization Perceived," in *Developing Study Skills in Secondary School*, edited by Harold L. Herber (Newark, DE: International Reading Association, 1965), 60.

20. Leonard H. Clark, *Teaching Social Studies in Secondary Schools: A Handbook* (New York: Macmillan, 1973), 122.

21. "Teaching Essential Reading Skills." Reprinted by permission from the Bulletin of the National Association of Secondary School Principals (February, 1950). Copyright: Washington, DC. Based on "How to Teach Pupils to Outline," *Teachers' Guide to Child Development in the Intermediate Grades*. Prepared under the direction of the California State Curriculum Commission. (Sacramento: California State Department of Education, 1936), 294–295.

22. Herbert J. Walberg, Rosanne A. Paschal, and Thomas Weinstein, "Homework's Powerful Effects on Learning," *Educational Leadership* 42 (April 1985): 76–79.

23. Donald J. Dessard, "Algebra," in *Classroom Ideas from Research in Secondary School Mathematics* (Reston, VA: National Council of Teachers of Mathematics, 1983), 9.

Educational Technologies

■■■ Overview

Mark Hopkins, it is said, could conduct a class while sitting on one end of a log. Most teachers need more to work with than that, however. In general, the more resources teachers have available, the better they can teach. This chapter discusses some of the tools available to educators today. Among these are audiovisual media, television, motion pictures and videos, and computers and computer programs. Some of these materials are sophisticated and costly, but most of them are quite easy to use. The important thing is to use them to give clarity and punch to your classes; they can ward off the humdrum and sharpen students' learning of the concepts, skills, and attitudes that are your objectives.

■■■ Audiovisual Media

Uses of Audiovisual Media

Audiovisual media include all sorts of pictorial, graphic, and auditory media such as pictures, movies, audio- or videotapes, slides, charts and graphs, chalkboards, bulletin boards, and so on. These can be teamed up with almost any other instructional technique or strategy. Although no longer fashionable, the term *audiovisual aids* aptly describes these teaching tools. Audiovisual aids are just that: aids to teaching and learning. Their role is to supplement and support, by means of visual and auditory augmentation, other instructional strategies and techniques, although in some lessons audiovisual approaches may be the principal instructional delivery system. If you think of audiovisual media as teaching tools, you are not far wrong. They have many uses by which to make learning more effective. This is true both of simple visual or audiovisual aids as well as the most sophisticated and complex computer-driven instructional media.

Audiovisual media can help make ideas and concepts clear. Although verbalism is one of the banes of the American secondary school, audiovisual media can help raise learning from verbalism to true understanding. For example, while the words *rubber bogey buffer bumper* may mean little to you, if you could see a picture or model of one, or watch one in operation in a movie or video, the words would become meaningful.

Audiovisual instructional media can also make learning interesting and vivid. A Chinese proverb tells us that one picture is worth a thousand words. Whether or not this is true, good audiovisual materials have eye and ear appeal. By snaring students' attention, they make learning more effective. They can be invaluable in promoting motivation and retention.

Making the Most of the Medium

In a suburban school, a beginning student teacher surprised her supervisor by asking, "Is it all right to use filmstrips for my American history class?" "Of course," he replied, "Why not?" "Well," she said, "I tried one last week and the class gave me a lot of trouble. They seemed to think the filmstrip was kid stuff and they really acted up." Yet that same day the supervisor had visited a science class—supposedly a class of difficult youngsters—where another student teacher, who was also using a filmstrip, had elicited excellent interest and attention from the students. The difference seemed to be that one student teacher expected the filmstrip to teach itself; the other was really teaching with the filmstrip as an aid.

As this anecdote demonstrates, the success of audiovisual materials depends on skillful teaching. Just like any other instructional activity, you should select audiovisual aids because they seem best-suited to a certain point in the lesson. And, as with any other activity, you must prepare the class for the audiovisual activity, guide the class through it, and follow up after its completion.

Stop and Reflect

Why is it impossible to substitute audiovisual media for good teaching? Is this statement true of programmed and computer-based teaching? Why, or why not?

In a certain school, the eighth-grade teaching team always shows videos to all the students on Friday afternoon. Criticize this practice.

Selecting the Audiovisual Material

In selecting an audiovisual aid, consider, in addition to its suitability, such things as visibility, clearness, level of understanding, ease of presentation, and availability of material. To be sure that the aid is effective and appropriate, try it yourself before using it with the class. This is particularly important when selecting films, tapes, cassettes, filmstrips, and recordings, and when presenting demonstrations. Films and recordings sometimes seem to bear little resemblance to their descriptions in the catalog, and a demonstration that does not come off well is literally worse than useless.

Planning to Use the Materials

Once you have previewed the audiovisual material, you are in a position to plan how to make the best use of it. In this process, you should

1. spell out the objectives that the material will best serve,
2. note the important terms or ideas presented in the audiovisual material,
3. identify any words or ideas that may cause students difficulty without some preliminary explanation, and then
4. make up your plan for introducing, presenting, and following up on the audiovisual material.

For instance, to introduce and present a film clip, you might plan first to give a short explanation of the source and setting of the film clip; then play the clip through quickly without stopping or commenting; and finally, play the clip again, stopping and analyzing the action in detail. Or you might decide to play the clip through and discuss it. You might also decide, while running through the clip the first time, to stop and analyze the action from time to time. The choice is yours, but you should choose your approach beforehand, instead of spontaneously making decisions as you go.

Preparing for the Audiovisual Activity

To get the most out of any audiovisual activity, you must prepare the students for it by introducing it. Sometimes a short sentence identifying the aid and its purpose will suffice. At other times, it would be better to spend a considerable amount of time discussing the purpose of the activity and suggesting how the students can get the most from it. The introduction to a movie or video, filmstrip, or recording should point out its purpose and suggest points that students should watch for in their viewing or listening.

Not only must you prepare students for the activity, but you must also prepare the activity itself. Nothing can be more embarrassing or more disruptive than movies that do not move, demonstrations that do not demonstrate, and similar audiovisual fiascos. *Competent teachers check the little things.* Do you have chalk? Can everyone see the poster? Will the machine run? Do you have all the transparencies, and are they all in the correct order? Be careful about the details; more than one class has been upset by the lack of a piece of chalk or an extension cord.

Guiding Students Through Audiovisual Activities

Instead of relieving you of your responsibility for guiding students' learning, the use of audiovisual materials gives you an opportunity to make your guidance more fruitful. So that the students get the most from an audiovisual aid, point out what to look for and listen for. It may be necessary to explain to students what they are seeing or hearing. To do this, it is often helpful to provide students with a list of questions or a study guide to direct their attention to salient points (see Figure 13.1). On other occasions you should stop momentarily to discuss vital relationships.

Following Up Audiovisual Activities

In spite of the appeal and vividness of audiovisual media, they cannot prevent some students from misunderstanding or missing part of the instruction. You must follow up the audiovisual activity to bridge gaps and to clear up misunderstandings. Follow-up also renews the learning and thus increases retention. Furthermore, it has motivational aspects. One danger in using films, filmstrips, television, computers, and radio is that students sometimes think of these activities as recreational and so give scant attention to them. If you follow up activities that feature audiovisual aids with discussion, review, practice, and testing, you can usually correct this misapprehension and also point up and drive home the learning desired. Students must realize that a film presentation in your class is not just a movie, but a lesson for which they are responsible.

▨ Figure 13.1

Listening Questions to Accompany The Phoenician Traders

(These questions illustrate the type of questions one might use in a special study guide for use with a recording. They represent different levels and types of questions. In using such study guides, one must guard against merely mechanical exercises.)

1. What seems to be the major business of the Phoenicians?
2. What seems to be the relationship between Tyre and Carthage?
3. What can you learn about the trade routes of the Phoenicians?
4. What was life like on a caravan?
5. What can you note about Phoenician ships and seamanship?
6. What did you learn about Phoenician trade? How did they carry it out? How did they keep accurate accounts and so on? In what way did they trade?
7. How nearly accurate is the reconstruction of Phoenician life? If you do not know, how can you find out?
8. Prepare a list of questions that would emphasize or bring out the important idea expressed in this recording.

Stop and Reflect

Suppose you order a film from an audiovisual center and when it arrives, it turns out not to be what you had expected. What would you do?

If you were to order a film for a class in your field, what criteria would you use in your selection?

Select an audiovisual aid that you might use in one of your courses. What would you have to do to introduce it properly? What would you do to clinch the learning from this audiovisual material?

Kinds of Audiovisual Materials

Probably the most common of all teaching tools are the old-fashioned blackboard and its more modern counterpart, the chalkboard or writing board. These devices are so omnipresent that many of us do not think of them as audiovisual aids at all, yet most teachers would be hard put without them. Other display-type teaching aids include bulletin boards, flannel boards, hook-and-loop boards, magnetic boards, charts, posters, graphs, and overlays. Basic principles to bear in mind when using these display-type teaching tools include:

1. Be sure that all the display material is visible and legible, and while using a display item, make sure to stand out of the students' line of vision.
2. Keep the board neat and orderly. Cluttered boards tend to confuse students.
3. Erase or remove all material you no longer need for the lesson.
4. Keep the board work simple and tasteful. Leave plenty of "white space" so that the material being presented in the display shows clearly.
5. Use color, underlining, diagrams, rough drawings, and the like to emphasize and clarify the message you want to get across.
6. When possible, if you want to use the board work later, cover it until you are ready to use it again.

Stop and Reflect

Observe the board work of your teachers and fellow students. What makes it effective? What keeps it from being more effective?

What advantages can you see in the flannel or hook-and-loop board over an ordinary chalkboard? Why is this type of board often used in television commercials or sales meetings rather than the chalkboard?

Go around the school. Look at bulletin boards and other displays. What techniques have been used to make them effective? What could you do to make them more effective?

PICTURES, MODELS, AND RECORDINGS   Pictures make especially useful teaching aids. So do specimens and other items that relate the subject to real life. When selecting them for classroom use, consider such questions as

1. Do they fit the purpose?
2. Are they relevant and important to the lesson?
3. Are they accurate and authentic?

4. Can their points be easily understood?
5. Are they interesting?
6. Are the size, quality, and color such as to make them easily visible?

No particular technique is necessary to use these materials, but remember to point out whatever the students are to learn from the aid. It is probably more productive to ask questions than to pontificate. Use pictures as springboards for class discussion or for further study and research. Oftentimes an entire lesson can be built around a single picture or specimen.

Avoid passing pictures and other material around the room for pupils to look at while the lecture, recitation, or discussion continues; students cannot examine the aid and concentrate on the lesson at the same time. Instead, display or pass the material around during a laboratory or work session when it is less liable to disrupt the learning process, or, better yet, perhaps use an opaque projector to throw the image of the picture or object on the screen where all can see it.

Not only do models, replicas, and sand tables make excellent aids, but also the students can help in constructing such materials. When using student help to build aids of any sort, be wary of two dangerous faults: one, that students may spend so much time creating the aid that they neglect the things they can learn from it, and two, that inaccurate models may give students erroneous concepts. Be particularly on guard against incorrect proportions, historical anachronisms, and other details that can mislead students. When it is necessary to distort in order to be effective (as is often the case when preparing three-dimensional maps, for instance), be sure to warn the students of the inaccuracies.

TAPES AND COMPACT DISCS   The ability of modern technology to capture outside events and transport them into the classroom is a boon you should exploit to the hilt. Through the use of the tape recorder and compact disc player, you can bring to the class the voice of an eminent mathematician discussing mathematical theory, a famous actor reading an ancient or modern play, a diplomat discussing foreign policy, or a symphony orchestra playing Tchaikovsky. With a videotape you can both see and hear. By using audio and video recording, you can capture class presentations, student speech habits, and the like as a basis for analysis, evaluation, and as an aid to improvement. Prerecorded instructions, lessons, and study guides can be very effective in providing for individual differences.

PROJECTORS   While some of these items are fast being replaced by newer technology, many types of projection equipment are still available: opaque projectors, slide projectors, filmstrip projectors, overhead projectors, microprojectors, as well as the ubiquitous motion picture projectors. These machines can bring to the entire class experiences that would otherwise be impossible, or possible only on an individual basis, or possible only at great cost. For example, if you wish to show English money to a social studies class, you could project the images of various English coins on a screen by means of an opaque projector (if you have some coins). This technique allows everyone to see the coins without interrupting the presentation, which would be impossible if the coins were passed around. If you wish to show students what actually happens during the making of steel, you could show them a video, film, or filmstrip. Sometimes such visual aids can make clear to students things that they could not see even in a real field trip.

THE OPAQUE PROJECTOR   Even though the opaque projector requires almost complete darkness to be effective and even then may be difficult to focus and rather awkward to use, it is a valuable tool. It can project on the screen the image of opaque surfaces that are too small for all students to see readily from their seats and it can do so in color. With it, you can project not only real objects such as the coins mentioned previously, but also pictures and pages from books, pamphlets, and magazines. It can also be used to enlarge maps and the like by projecting them onto a suitable surface for copying; to project students' work for evaluation, correction, or exhibit; and as a basis for student reports.

THE OVERHEAD PROJECTOR   Overhead projectors are also extremely useful and versatile. There should be one in every classroom. They can be used in lighted classrooms without darkening the room, thus allowing students to take notes or do other activities not possible in darkened classrooms. Some teachers use overhead projection to present quiz questions rather than photocopying them or writing them on the chalkboard. Moreover, overhead projectors are so constructed that you can write, draw, and point things out from the front of the room without turning your back on the class and obstructing the students' lines of sight.

The versatility of the overhead projector makes it particularly valuable. Not only are the transparencies easy to make, but also they can be prepared in advance and used over and over, thus avoiding the tedious job of copying material on the chalkboard and tying up the board with "Do Not Erase" signs. In addition, transparencies and overlays can be placed on top of one another so as to present information in almost any combination. The overhead projector can be used effectively for on-the-spot recording and illustrating. Such characteristics are valuable for making teaching more effective and at the same time reducing the amount of tedious busywork that can sometimes interfere with more important teaching tasks.

Stop and Reflect

What advantage does projecting a picture via the opaque projector have over showing the picture itself by passing it around or holding it up in front of the class?

What advantage does the overhead projector have over the chalkboard? The bulletin board?

SLIDE AND FILMSTRIP PROJECTORS   Slide projectors and filmstrip projectors can be discussed simultaneously because the two are often combined into one machine. After all, a filmstrip is little more than a series of slides joined together on a strip of film. The filmstrip has the advantage of having been put together by an expert in a ready-made sequence. Slides are more versatile, but using them requires more careful planning. Just one slide out of order or upside down can throw a well-conceived lesson out of step.

Some filmstrips come with recorded commentary and sound effects. Although these are sometimes quite impressive, you may prefer to provide your own commentary as the filmstrip progresses. If you wish, you can prerecord your own commentary and sound effects and synchronize them to a filmstrip or to a series of slides. Utilizing sound with slides is usually enhanced by the use of an automatic projector. If you can influence the choice of slide projectors, insist on a projector that operates both manually and automatically.

Filmstrip and 2 × 2 slide projectors are small enough and simple enough that small groups or individuals can use them. For individual or small-group viewing, the image can be thrown onto a sheet of cardboard no larger than the projector itself. It is surprising that more teachers do not take advantage of this capability of filmstrip and slide projectors.

MICROPROJECTION   The number of students who never see what it is they are supposed to see through a microscope is probably astronomical. The microprojector can eliminate for practical purposes much of this difficulty by enlarging and projecting the image in the microscope's field onto a screen. This way all students can see the image and the teacher can point out salient features to everyone at once. Another technique that gives much the same result is to take pictures of the slide through the microscope. This technique is not difficult, being merely a matter of screwing a compatible camera to the microscope and taking pictures by means of the optics of the microscope. The resulting 2 × 2 slides can be projected onto a screen. In much the same way, transparencies for overhead projection can be made with a Polaroid™ camera.

Preparing such materials takes time, but almost always the results are worth the effort. In many instances, much of the preparation of such aids can be done by students, thus giving them valuable learning experiences and saving time for the teacher.

FILMS

SELECTING A FILM   Although most school systems now use videocassette recorders and television monitors to provide students with access to many audiovisual materials, some schools still use motion picture films and film projectors. Most of the more valuable classroom films are not lent to the school *gratis* but are rented from film libraries or district, county, or state resource centers. Your school will probably have a clear policy and procedure about renting films. Follow it to the letter. It is critical to order films early, since good films are in demand; a late order may mean that you will have to do without.

Each renting library publishes a catalog of its films. In addition, film companies and other agencies publish catalogs and announcements of films. You can also find hints and reviews pertaining to specific films in textbooks, curriculum guides, and resource units.

PRESENTING THE FILM   Before presenting a film, prepare the setting and the equipment. Check the equipment, since the motion picture projector can be a particularly cranky machine. Run a little of the film before the presentation to be sure all is working well. Repositioning the projector and screen in the room can sometimes make the image on light-struck screens more visible. When the setting and equipment are ready, alert the students to what they are to see and learn. Make sure they realize that viewing the film is a learning experience, not recreation.

Once you have started the film, keep quiet. Do not try to outshout the sound track. Students cannot listen to both you and the film at the same time. If you absolutely must explain something, stop the film before you speak, but you will usually be more effective if you make your comments before or after the viewing. In this respect, the silent film has an advantage over the sound film.

In the past, using motion pictures in the classroom was plagued by two distinct disadvantages. One was that the projection was designed solely for large-group instruction. The other that the films had to be shown in darkened classrooms. Neither condition remains now. Self-threading individual 8-millimeter projection devices make motion picture projection accessible to individuals, and rear projection arrangements allow projection in lighted rooms.

Stop and Reflect

What misconceptions are liable to arise from the use of aids such as the movies and videos? How can these be avoided?

What steps should you as a teacher go through before presenting a film to a class?

MOTION PICTURE PRODUCTION   With modern equipment, production of your own movies has become relatively easy. With help students can carry out the tasks necessary for completing interesting, productive films. If you are interested in producing films, consult your school audiovisual or media center director, as well as such books as Kemp's *Planning, Producing and Using Instructional Media* and technical manuals on the subject.(1) You can use similar techniques with a camcorder to produce videocassette recordings.

Stop and Reflect

What audiovisual aids are available to you personally? What aids can you create? How could you use them? Survey the situation. You will undoubtedly find a wealth of material you had not thought of before. Consider such things as pictures, movies and videos, slides, microprojectors, chalkboards, bulletin boards, charts, graphs, diagrams, demonstrations, schematic representations, opaque projectors, CDs, tapes, models, maps, globes, filmstrips, radio, television, felt boards, overhead projectors, tachistoscopes, displays, exhibits, aquaria, terraria, stereopticon slides, sand tables, and realia.

How can realia be used? Is the real object, if available, always the best aid to learning? Justify your answer.

If you have not done so, videotape yourself as you teach a minilesson.

MULTIMEDIA   Various media can and should be used to reinforce each other. For instance, teachers use mixed media naturally when they use pictures to illustrate a lecture. But teaching can be made more effective by consciously utilizing multimedia presentations to make the learning process more interesting and to promote understanding.

You can mix media by using them sequentially or simultaneously. Thus, in a geography class, you might move through a carefully planned sequence involving the use of several media (e.g., a map, a pictorial representation, a model, and a film). In each step of this sequence, each new medium builds upon the learning brought about by the preceding medium. Or it might be more effective to present the media simultaneously. For example, you might teach the geography lesson by presenting a picture, a model, and a contour map of the terrain simultaneously, moving back and forth from one to another of the media, comparing and analyzing as you build on the concept. Examples of simultaneous presentations suggested by Haney and Ullmer involve the use of two screens. The authors suggest the screens can be used:

1. To hold an overview shot or complete picture on one screen, such as a laboratory experiment arrangement, while moving to a series of detailed close-up pictures on the other.
2. To show two pictures side by side for comparison, such as two works of art, each on a separate slide.
3. To hold a title of a group classification on one screen, with a series of example pictures on the other screen, providing a sort of visual paragraphing.
4. To show a line drawing or labeled schematic diagram of an object or organism next to an actual photograph.
5. To show three to six different photographs to convey a range of examples; any or all can be changed as desired.
6. To display a picture while showing a series of questions or factual notes on a second screen.(2)

In multimedia presentations the media to be used obviously must be compatible and complementary. Unless they work together to bring about your teaching objectives, there is no point in using them. Misused multimedia presentations can confuse rather than clarify.

Stop and Reflect

Think of at least a half dozen ways you could mix media when teaching your classes. Be specific. Find out what is available.

Homemade Visual Aids

Many visual aids can be made easily by you or your students. For example, flannel boards, felt boards, and magnetic boards can all be made, as can 35-millimeter slides and slide shows.

FILMSTRIPS AND SLIDE PROGRAMS   Producing filmstrips is more difficult than is making individual slides. The process involves copying from other slides by means of an adaptation of a 35-millimeter camera. Camera clubs and other local personnel can develop filmstrips and even motion pictures if they wish.

However, the same effect obtained with filmstrips can be achieved with slides. In fact, individual slides, not being locked into a fixed sequence, may sometimes be preferable to filmstrips. Arrange the slides into the order you wish to show them, decide what comments you want to make, and then proceed just as though you were showing your friends the pictures of your latest vacation trip. If you wish, you can write a formal script to be read as the pictures are shown. With surprisingly little extra effort, you can provide synchronized tape recordings for your slide programs. All you need to do is to write a script with clues, noting when the operator should change slides, and then transcribe the script onto a tape. Homemade filmstrips of this sort can be used for large-group instruction in an assembly or lecture hall or for individual instruction in the classroom by using earphones and a miniature screen. If the necessary equipment is available, you can add a signal to the tape that will activate the slide changer on an automatic slide projector. While this is fun to do, it may not be worth the effort since it tends to lock you into a format that you may later wish to change.

TRANSPARENCIES   There are many ways to make transparencies for the overhead projector. A number of photocopying or dry copying office machines will make transparencies of printed, typed, or written material or drawings. Preparing transparencies on some of these machines is something of an art. On others all you need do is push a button and wait a few seconds. You can also make transparencies by using a special carbon paper or by using a China marking pencil or India ink. Some pens can be used to make transparencies in color. With all these sources and acetate sheets being so inexpensive (most clear acetate can be used to make transparencies by hand—the machine-made transparencies require specially treated film), there is no reason you should not have all the transparencies you need. To preserve them and to keep them accessible, we recommend that you frame and file them. Commercial frames are readily available for transparencies.

Flip-ons, which are simply additional sheets that can be placed on top of another transparency to add further detail or information, are made in exactly the same way as other transparencies. If you wish, you can fasten these to the frame of the original transparency with little metallic foil hinges. The use of frames and hinges has the advantage of keeping the transparency and its flip-ons together in proper order.

BUILDING A SIMULATION GAME   Simulation games have become increasingly popular. So many are on the market that it seems hardly necessary for you to build your own. Yet, homemade simulations are often the best. Student-built simulations can also be very effective. To develop a simulation model, follow these steps:

1. Select the process to be simulated.
    a. Determine the specific objectives.
    b. Decide what type of simulation would bring out these objectives.
2. Select a situation.
    a. Historical or current event.
        (1) May give a better understanding of the situation and the problems.
        (2) May be difficult to present because of biases, emotions, or lack of information.
    b. Hypothetical situation.
        (1) Good for demonstrating specific processes, skills, and pressures.
        (2) Likely to involve emotion and bias.
        (3) Easier to control the variables—thus making the simulation simpler and clearer.
3. Research the situation in depth.
4. Develop the essential elements to be replicated.
    a. Try to keep all unessential elements out of the simulation model, for they tend to confuse and obscure the essential elements and complicate the simulation.
    b. Establish the relationships between the various roles (for example, power relationships).
5. Prepare the draft scenario.
    a. Read several other simulations to see how they have been developed. This may give you ideas.
    b. Set up some criteria or media for showing relationships.
    c. Try to keep the simulation from being too simple or too complicated.
    d. Write the draft scenario.
    e. Try out the draft scenario.
    f. Rewrite the draft scenario.
    g. Repeat (e) and (f) until you get a satisfactory draft.
    h. Present it to the class.
    i. Rewrite it (or junk it).(3)

Stop and Reflect
What sources of audiovisual material are available to you in your community?

What materials are available for use in your college classes? What could you do to make more material available if you were one of the teachers?

Pick a course you might teach and see what audiovisual materials you could develop for it.

Television

INSTRUCTIONAL TELEVISION   Commercially produced television and programs that you videotape yourself can supplement and add interest to the class. Telecasts suitable for instructional classes range from video classes taught by master teachers to special programming featuring interesting historical, scientific, geographical, literary, and other topics presented by educational or general television stations. While such programs can bring extraordinarily effective presentations to your classes, they do not relieve you of your responsibility for instruction. Even if a master teacher conducts a television lesson, you still have to go through your standard routine. You must plan, you must select, you must introduce, you must guide, and you must follow up in order to fill in the gaps, correct misunderstandings, and guide students' learning.

Before the television presentation begins, see to it that everything is ready. Students can benefit from television only if they can see and hear clearly.

To ensure good viewing, observe a few rules of thumb for the physical arrangement of the classroom, whether large or small:

1. The television set should have a 21- to 24-inch screen and front directional speakers.
2. The set should be placed so that each student has an unobstructed line of sight.
3. The screen should not be more than 30 feet from any student.
4. The set should be about 5½ feet from the floor.
5. The vertical angle of sight from any pupil to the set should never be more than 30 degrees; the horizontal angle, never more than 45 degrees.
6. The room should be kept lighted so that students can see to take notes.
7. No glare should reflect from the screen. To reduce glare one can
   a. Move the set away from the windows.
   b. Tilt the set downward.
   c. Provide the set with cardboard blinders.
8. The sound should come from front directional speakers; however, if several television sets are in use in one room, it may be better to use the sound from only one set than to have it come from several sources. In large rooms for large-class instruction, it may be more satisfactory to run the sound from one set through a public address system.
9. Students should have adequate surface space for writing.
10. To allow for quick, easy transition from the telecast, television classrooms should be fitted out with adequate audiovisual equipment, display space, and filing and storage space.

Be sure you are familiar with the subject of the telecast and the lesson's plan. If the program is prerecorded, preview it. Well before the lesson, study the study guide and studio script, if they are available. Gather any materials you may need and have them ready and waiting before the telecast. Before the telecast starts, brief the students on the lesson—its purpose, what to look for, and the like. Point out any new vocabulary and fill in any serious voids evident in the presentation.

During a telecast, you must continue your role as a guide to learning. Circulate among the students to determine whether they understand and are proceeding correctly. Sometimes you will have to supplement the television presentation. To do so, make note of student reactions—particularly reactions that show a lack of understanding or evidence of misunderstanding—for use in follow-up activities after the telecast.

The follow-up after the television class is fully as important as is the class itself. Check the students' learning against the objectives of the lesson. If necessary, reteach or provide additional experiences to enrich and carry forward the learning. Center class discussion on such questions as, "What did we learn? Was the learning important? If so, why? If not, why not? What should we do next in view of what we have learned?" Since creative activity is so necessary for effective learning and since television lessons are liable to be largely passive, you should consider the desirability of utilizing many projects, discussions, experiments, investigations, writing, and similar activities that allow students to engage actively in their own learning.

GENERAL TELEVISION PROGRAMS   When matters of great international or national significance are being telecast, it may be wise to stop other class activities and witness the event. Such activities are well worthwhile, particularly when you skillfully introduce and follow up the telecast.

Unfortunately, telecasts usually occur at times that do not allow direct classroom viewing. You can circumvent this difficulty by recording the program and playing significant parts during school hours. Advances in videotape technology have made it possible for schools to do their own video recording relatively cheaply. However, much of the material telecast by commercial and educational television stations is copyrighted. The fair use guidelines for recording copyrighted off-air broadcasts permit the use of the recording by schools for ten days after the broadcast. After 45 days, the tape made from the broadcast must be destroyed. This ruling applies only to programs "recorded simultaneously to the broadcast of the television program," either over the air or from cable systems that are retransmitting a broadcast station. Programs originating on cable, pay cable, pay television, or Instructional Television Fixed Service may not be recorded without express permission of the broadcaster. Purchased or rented videocassette recordings may be used for regular classroom instruction.(4)

Another technique is to assign home viewing of television programs. Because not all students have television sets available to them, it may be necessary to make such assignments selectively, with certain individuals or committees responsible for reporting the results.* At times, in order to get wider experiences to share in class, it may be wise to ask different students to view the coverage of an event on different channels. As with other assignments, television viewing assignments should be clear so that the students know what to look for and what they are trying to do. The use of a bulletin board to list assignments with attendant problems, questions, and projects has proved successful for many teachers.

Determining how best to use educational and cultural television programs can be something of a problem. Television sections of local newspapers and television magazines carry descriptions of featured programs that you can use as a basis for lesson planning and assignments. Professional magazines frequently carry study guides for exceptional programs. You can sometimes secure information about both the proposed scheduling and the content of coming programs in advance by writing to local television stations or to the television networks. When such information is available, classroom activities can be planned around certain television programs, or the planned class sequence can be altered in order to take advantage of exceptional television opportunities.

Selecting Television Programs

Information about television programs suitable for classroom use can be obtained from professional journals such as *Today's Education*, specialized magazines such as *TV Guide*, the television sections of newspapers and magazines, the television stations and networks, and from instructional television (ITV) and school media centers.

Because it is almost impossible for any teacher to keep well-informed about all the television programs that might be potentially useful, it can be helpful to enlist the aid of your students to scout out and report on programs of value. Many teachers regularly post billings of such programs on the chalkboard or bulletin board. These billings may be enhanced by adding commentary and suggested aids for viewing.

---

*When father, mother, brother, and sister want to watch a basketball game on Channel 7, *Romeo and Juliet* on Channel 13 may not be available to a student, even though you have assigned it!

Even television programs that seem to have no direct bearing on the course of study can sometimes be useful. All television dramas have plots, many of them have music, they all take place in time and space, and so almost any one of them can be used for some purpose in English, social studies, art, or music classes. Wild west television dramas, for instance, can be used in a study of the customs and mores of the times, and to bring home the differences between historical fact and fiction, to illustrate plot structure and flat versus round characterization, the use of music in the theater, and so on. Particularly useful are the many documentaries and educational programs that commercial television stations use to fill in blank periods during their less heavily viewed hours and that make up much of public television programs. Instructional television courses telecast for adults are often good sources of enrichment and a means for providing for individual differences. So are similar programs presented by The Learning Channel (TLC) on cable television. The public television stations telecasting such programs usually publish program schedules, reading lists, and study materials that can be purchased for a relatively small fee. Certain states and districts publish curriculum and ITV Match booklets that can be very helpful.

Stop and Reflect

What seem to you to be the arguments for or against the use of instructional television?

What methods could you use as a classroom teacher to keep television instruction on a personal basis? What could you do as a television teacher?

Computers and Teaching Programs

Computers are sweeping the country. In spite of their cost, their use in schools is spreading widely because of their efficiency and effectiveness as teaching tools.(5)

Probably much of the computer's success lies in the fact that students like instruction by computer. The computer does the following for students:

Gives them a sense of control and power.
Allows active learning.
Demands interaction.
Makes them the decision maker.
Allows them to stop and start when ready and motivated.
Doesn't get angry.
Gives immediate feedback.
Provides risk-free simulation.
Provides a sense of mastery.
Is friendly, patient, and never gives detention.(6)

Research seems to indicate that the computer is among the most valuable of teaching tools.(7) It differs from ordinary teaching aids in that it can actually do some teaching. It can, for instance, act as a mechanical tutor that works with students on a one-to-one basis. It can be a drill or practice instructor, an information presenter, a test giver and scorer, and a keeper of records. In carrying out these tasks, the computer presents and follows up on a series of lessons—that is, teaching programs. In reality, of course, it is the teaching program that does the teaching, not the computer. The computer merely acts as a delivery system.

Basically computers are made up of three parts: the central processing unit (CPU) or console, a keyboard, and a monitor. The central processing unit is the engine that runs the computer. It processes data fed it by the keyboard, computer disks, or other computers. The monitor is a television-like screen that shows text, graphics, and other information processed and functions performed by the computer. The keyboard is used like a typewriter to feed the CPU data and directions.

In addition to the CPU, keyboard, and monitor, the computer comes with several attachments or *peripherals*.(8) Among these are printers, modems, CD ROM drives, videodisc players, VCRs (Video Cassette Recorders), mice, and PC viewers. These attachments and the computers themselves are called *hardware*, the programs they use are called *software*, and the supporting exercises, reading materials, and the like are called *courseware*.

In general, software comes in three basic applications—word processing, data base, and spreadsheet. Software programs designed for classroom use usually include elements of each of these three dimensions, plus a fourth category: graphics or illustrations. Word processing applications include typing and editing written materials such as reports, essays, or even books. Data bases are useful for compiling lists such as mailing lists and catalog items. Spreadsheets are used for such mathematical calculations as budgeting, tracking, averaging grades, and the like. Graphics, of course, picture information presented in a program.

When well used, computers can make your teaching more profitable, but they cannot relieve you of your teaching responsibilities. It is you who must decide how best to use computers to accomplish your goals, just as you must decide how to incorporate other media into your instructional strategies. Consequently you should make yourself computer literate not only to use computers skillfully in instruction, but also to select good hardware and software, and to be helpful in the development of useful computer-assisted programs and courseware.

To this end you should know how the computer works, the terms and jargon of "computerese," the history of computers and their use, the uses of computers in education, the nonschool uses of computers, and the relationship between computers and society. In particular, you should be well-versed in the techniques of problem solving and how computers can assist in these problem-solving techniques. In addition, you should know something about computer hardware, its potentials and limitations, and how to evaluate and select software. It is also helpful to know at least one computer language, so as to be able to produce or revise software programs for your classes just as you would make your own exercises and tests.

An interesting, and often exciting to students, feature of PILOT, PASCAL, and some of the other computer languages is that they make it possible to develop tutorial and other programs that can harness such devices as videotape players, videodisc players, and random access slide projectors, giving students greater in-depth experience than would simple graphics.(9)

In sum, you need to be sufficiently computer literate to know "(a) possible applications and how to blend them into your teaching; (b) how to program computers and to modify programs to suit student needs";(10) and most important, (c) how to use the computer as an instructional tool in the subjects you plan to teach. For instance:

- *In social studies* computers can be useful for individualizing instruction, for presenting materials in graphic form, for constructing graphs and maps, for providing drill and practice, and for presenting social or moral problems for solution.
- *In mathematics* computers are excellent for use in problem-solving. You can use them to set up a problem, to develop the steps for solving it, to carry out the steps, and to see why the solution did or did not work.

- ▨ *In science* computers are useful for presenting simulations. With a little coaching students can develop their own simulations.
- ▨ *In business education* computers can be used for such computer-assisted activities as problem solving, drill and practice, simulations, and tutoring. They are excellent for building vocabulary and spelling skills. They are also important for teaching special topics—especially topics having to do with computers in business. In teaching special topics, computers can be used to introduce the topic, to motivate, to conduct drill and practice, to assess progress, and to follow up.
- ▨ *In English* computers are useful for high-level problem solving and drill and practice in grammar, spelling, vocabulary, and the like. Computers can also be used to present literary games and individualized teaching packets.
- ▨ *In any subject area* computers can be helpful in developing thinking skills. Computers require students to describe matters appropriately and to arrange them in proper sequence step by step; they can give students practice in using problem-solving procedures and in modifying them to fit the circumstances; they can help students to develop procedures for attacking and solving new problems.

Actually, writing programs for your computer is probably the best way for you to learn how to use the computer as a teaching tool. Even if you never have to write programs as part of your job, learning to write programs will help you to better understand both computer hardware and software. As a result of interacting with computers in this way, you will come to feel more comfortable with them and will consequently be able to use them more effectively.(11)

Computer Classroom Roles

As the previous section indicates, computers can be used in almost any field to teach subject content and skills; to develop thinking, problem solving, and other intellectual skills (Computer-Assisted Instruction); and as a means for assessing student progress, recording results, and prescribing next steps (Computer-Managed Instruction).

Robert Sherwood, for instance, feels that computers should play the five following roles in classes:

1. Learning about computers
2. Learning from computers
3. Learning with computers
4. Learning about thinking with computers
5. Managing learning with computers.(12)

Let us now look at these five roles in more detail. In this discussion we shall follow Sherwood's lead.

Learning about Computers

The first step in learning about computers is what is sometimes called *computer awareness*. At this stage, learners can get a general idea of what computers can and cannot do and of how to load and run programs. Much of this awareness occurs in the elementary grades. This leads us to the second step: *computer literacy*. This step, which is typical of middle or junior high school students, would ordinarily, according to Kinzer, Sherwood, and Bransford, include such topics as description of computer systems and their components; basic computer language;

introduction to programming; and use of the computer in programs for word processing, data base, spreadsheet, and so on.(13)

At the high school levels, the students should have opportunities to write drills, tutorials, and simulations. The specific computer language they should learn is problematical. BASIC is rather easy to learn, and many seventh and eight graders have learned it successfully. However, some authorities discourage the use of BASIC and encourage the use of PASCAL, LOGO, or one of the other authoring languages mentioned earlier. In any case, from the middle school grades up, students who have become familiar with using computers should be encouraged to improve the programs in use and perhaps to try to write their own programs. Nothing aids learning something better than trying to teach it to someone else. Students who write programs are forced to learn both the use of the computer and programming and also the subject content that they are trying to present.(14)

Learning from Computers

Among the most common educational uses of computers in the past have been conducting drill and practice sessions and tutoring. We call these activities "learning from the computer" because the computer seems to be acting as a drillmaster, coach, or tutor.

DRILL AND PRACTICE   You can use the computer to present practice material to students as individuals or in groups, and to give the students immediate feedback concerning their performance. Drill and practice computer programs can provide an excellent means by which to review, reinforce, and solidify knowledge and skills after initial presentations. Although you can use drill and practice programs for whole-class activities, it probably is better to limit their use to small-group or individual instruction. One technique that seems to work well when you have several computers is to load different computers with different software and then let small groups move from computer to computer. Drill and practice programs are often handled much as a workbook would be, although at times the programs seem more like quizzes. Computers can do more than just present exercises, however. They are patient and allow students to work at their own individual speeds. (In oral drills, too often the questioner so presses for an answer that the student does not have time to think.) To make the drills and practice sessions most effective, the order of the questions should be randomly mixed. Also it is helpful to include questions that call for the students to solve problems rather than just to rehash information. It may also be helpful to provide clues or helps and alternate spellings, and to allow students to drop out when they feel that the program has become a bit much for them. Good programs can provide students with immediate feedback, record the number of questions asked and the number answered correctly, and let the students know how they are progressing from time to time. The feedback should be friendly, however. It should not scold or reprimand students no matter what the errors. In some cases it may, probably should, give the students two or three chances to answer an item correctly before announcing the correct answer. In other cases it may branch so as to reteach the points that the students missed. This process should help the students manage the learning. Programs that present the practice sessions as games usually make them interesting. However, programs that keep close track of mistakes, while motivating the successful, may be discouraging to less successful students.

Drill and practice programs are best for following up on initial instruction in which a student has learned the basics. Sometimes these programs do not move fast enough for gifted students and thus can be frustrating to fast learners. On the other hand, such programs are often good for slow students, since they can be programmed to help the students by giving them prompts. In any case, it is probably better to keep drill and practice sessions short and to space them out. Long drill and practice activities featuring screenfuls of print are seldom motivating or reinforcing. Drill and practice activities are best suited for individualizing learning. When selecting drill and practice materials, you must consider the following:

1. How well does the content fit the curriculum?
2. What is the reading level?
3. How complex are the concepts?

TUTORIALS   Computers can make excellent tutors. They can present new material to students and individuals on a one-to-one basis and then conduct exercises concerning the material presented, correct student responses to the exercises, and then provide follow-up material to strengthen student weaknesses and correct student misunderstandings uncovered by the exercises. Tutorial computer programs are most effective if they are branching—especially if they are constructed so that the program branches as a response to specific types of student errors rather than as generic reteaching. Tutorial programs are effective when they present material in small steps and provide practice with immediate feedback.

Basically, then, tutorial programs are programs that present the students with primary instruction and add practice, exercises, and other aids to learning. You can use tutorial programs for initial instruction, enrichment, or remedial work. Whatever your objective, make sure that students realize what the purpose of the computer exercise is and that the program is compatible with your own teaching strategies. Otherwise, differences between the computer strategy and your strategy may confuse the students. Make sure that the program you are using is neither too hard nor too easy for the students. Programs that are too hard quickly discourage students, while those that are too easy become boring.

For your tutorials to be most effective, they should do the following:

1. State the questions clearly.
2. Permit the learner to respond.
3. Evaluate the learner's response.
4. Provide feedback.

Therefore it is important for a tutorial program to:

1. Respond to all possible student answers.
2. Be user friendly (i.e., easy to use).
3. Provide clear feedback.
4. Be efficient (when practical, it should make use of subroutines).
5. Focus student attention on the screen (put only relevant material on the screen and allow the student to call for more if he needs it).
6. Provide a way for the learner to control the rate of delivery and to erase information that is no longer needed.
7. Make steps logically and pedagogically correct.
8. Provide for review when desirable.

Since programmers find it difficult to meet all these requirements, you may not be able to find as many excellent tutorial programs as you wish.

Learning with Computers

In this section, we describe programs in which the student interacts with the computer or uses it as a tool to shape information he already possesses. The programs we discuss here are simulation and modeling, computer games, and word processing.

SIMULATION AND MODELING   The computer can be used to present simulations to the students and as a medium for students to construct their own simulations or models.

Simulations have been used for years to give students learning experiences that in real life would be too dangerous, too time-consuming, or too expensive. Perhaps the best-known examples are war games, driver training, and pilot training. One of the principal advantages of simulations is that they give the learners opportunities to learn by doing and so allow them to exert some control over their learning, to learn from their mistakes without risk, and to experience in the classroom laboratory experiences that in the real world would be impossible in the time or with the equipment available, or would be dangerous (as in some chemistry experiments, for instance). According to Taber, simulations are useful substitutes for real-life experiences in the following circumstances:

1. When the learning objectives are complex and students are unlikely to be able to develop the needed skills in a real-life environment (e.g., work skills).
2. When the time scale of the real-life event is too long or too short to allow efficient learning (e.g., money management).
3. When the real-life experience involves danger and/or high cost (e.g., driver training).
4. When the real-life event cannot be carried out in a normal teaching environment (e.g., voting).(15)

Simulations can help learners manipulate important principles or variables, obtain immediate feedback from an action, and use the feedback as a basis for the next action—experiences that would probably be too complex or too fleeting to see and understand in real-life situations. Because they lend themselves to definite mathematical formulas, some complex experiences are easy to simulate in such a way that the learner can see what happens, sometimes step by step, in the simulation. When this is impossible, simulations of simplified models of the experience can often present the workings of the experience fairly clearly. These simulations seem to work best in group instruction where groups simulating together can achieve high-level analysis, synthesis, and evaluation of the experience.(16)

Good simulations can stimulate active learning. However, before launching a simulation, make sure that the students are ready for it. Check to see that they have sufficient knowledge to cope with the simulation's concepts. To this end, utilize presimulation discussion, vocabulary, and concept development activities before starting the simulation itself.

In short, as stated by Vockell and Rivers, good simulations include the following elements:

1. A sound mathematical or logical model.
2. A clear mode of presentation that allows the learner to interact with it.
3. A strategy for integrating the simulation with other effective learning activities.(17)

Therefore, they suggest that when you plan to use simulations in your teaching, you should:

1. Write down one's assumptions early and keep them in mind when programming and teaching.
2. Try to develop a user-friendly format with all the necessary information readily available to the learners.
3. Help the students make the connections. Do not assume that they will automatically see them.(18)

COMPUTER GAMES   Computer games can be used to add great interest to a subject and also to clarify understandings. They frequently challenge students to attempt and achieve learning that they might otherwise forgo.

Most students are familiar with the computer games found in video arcades, which differ from simulations in that they do not have to represent reality. The learning in simulation games is often subordinate to the game; any learning that occurs is gained indirectly. Games are valuable and useful learning strategies, however, because they are fun and thus motivating. Still, you must be careful that some students do not get frustrated and discouraged because they lose the game, or that some students do not develop "arcade mentalities" in which trial-and-error thinking and guesswork are substituted for real thought. Therefore, when using computer games, make a special goal of helping your students focus on the thinking and learning objectives rather than on simply winning the game. It is wise to restrict game use to complementary and enrichment activities, and to use games with caution. Although they can be motivating, since they can present skills and knowledge in interesting ways, they may not suit the learning styles of all your students. Some students do not learn well in competitive situations and too much pressure to win games may be discouraging to them. Losing is disheartening. For this reason, it is better to reserve competitive games for group activities when feasible.

WORD PROCESSING   The word processing capabilities of the computer can be used to help students think and express themselves more clearly. One advantage of word processing is that it provides the writer with a clean, revised copy rather than the scratched-out, overwritten copy that so often results from longhand revision. In making these changes, the student writer simply deletes, adds, or rewrites using the capabilities of the computer. In the early stages of revisions, students should stick to large-scale revision and not worry about spelling and grammatical correctness until later, after they have thought through what they want to say. Word processing programs allow students to experiment with sentences and paragraphs. In some cases, the program even will point out to the student stylistic, grammatical, and spelling errors that need fixing.

Learning to Think with Computers

Teaching students how to think, a primary goal of educators, can be aided by the proper use of computers. In fact, some authorities claim that learning to program itself is a very helpful way to develop expertise in thinking, although this may be doubtful. In teaching students to think, you must combine both process and content. Just learning or memorizing content is not enough to encourage thinking, and knowing the thinking processes is not much help either if you have nothing to think about. To be good thinkers, students need to have mastered both the thinking skills and processes, and the appropriate subject content as well. Therefore, when teaching thinking with computers, you must emphasize both content and process. In addition, you should relate the thinking processes exercised during computer usage with those used in ordinary noncomputer thinking. Otherwise, the thinking skills learned with the computer may not transfer to real life. Still, computers can provide help in doing problem-solving tasks. For instance, they can rather easily store, retrieve, and analyze data, and manage tasks that would otherwise be laborious and time-consuming. In the middle school years, you can use games, simulations, creative word processing, collaborative writing projects, peer review, tutoring, and instant publication to enhance thinking and creativity. In the high school, you might provide group projects and activities involving simulations, class writing activities, independent thinking, cooperative educational experiences, and heuristic questioning programs as a basis for both individual and group research projects and writing.

PROBLEM SOLVING   Computers can carry out at least two crucial roles in problem solving: as tools to solve problems, and as a means to learn problem-solving skills.

In its role as a tool for problem solving, the computer is excellent at such tasks as setting forth problems; analyzing data; finding significant facts; presenting information in tabular, graphic, or other easily understood formats; providing trial solutions; and testing those solutions. Exercises for teaching such skills are usually best presented to an entire class or small group, because the complexities of problem-solving content usually require students to support each other rather than going it alone. However, individual problem-solving tasks may be good in enrichment programs, especially for senior high school students. At this level, the use of business software is often advantageous. Also useful for acquiring information are on-line data systems such as *CompuServe*, which are mainframe services available via modems to individuals, schools, and businesses that subscribe to the service.

Many activities can be included in problem-solving programs. In mathematics, for instance, activities may include identifying problems, searching for patterns, writing equations, drawing pictures, comparing equations with simpler or similar problems, guessing and checking, asking questions, gathering data, analyzing problems, testing hypotheses, and estimating and testing possible solutions.

An excellent approach to use in problem-solving situations is to have students work in pairs. As one student works through the problem on the computer, he explains to the other what he is doing and why. They can later switch roles when tackling another problem. Another excellent technique for teaching high-level skills is to have students teach the computer—that is, build programs.

Managing Instruction with Computers

Computer-managed instruction can take several forms:

1. Testing and evaluation
2. Individualizing instruction
3. Diagnosis and record keeping
4. Grading

TESTING AND EVALUATION   You can use computers to give and score tests and to analyze test results. You can also use them to evaluate student performance on exercises and other learning activities.

INDIVIDUALIZING INSTRUCTION   You can use a computer to allow students to progress at their own rates while learning. Programs can present new materials to students when they are ready so that they will not be held up by slower-paced students, and can allow slower students to proceed more slowly without penalty, finishing topics difficult for them as they gain mastery. Computers can permit gifted students to venture onto new ground that other students may not be ready for. They can also let students pursue individual interests without being fettered by the desires and talents of other group members.

DIAGNOSIS AND RECORD KEEPING   Computers can be helpful for diagnostic and record-keeping purposes. In computer-managed instruction, computer programs are used to record each student's progress, to diagnose weaknesses, to recommend remedial work if necessary, to indicate when the student is ready to move on to the next step, and to provide needed additional drill and practice.

For example, in one such program, the course is divided into two-week units, each centered on behavioral objectives and learning activities designed to lead to those objectives. These learning activities use a variety of teaching materials. A computer program is used to diagnose each individual student's progress, to give the student feedback, and to prescribe the next steps. By this means, each student is able to work toward the objectives on a personally prescribed course based on an objective analysis of progress, strengths, and weaknesses.

In such a program, the computer gives an assessment of the student's needs, prescribes an assignment in view of this assessment, gives a follow-up assessment, prescribes an alternate remedial assignment on the basis of this assessment, and finally, certifies the student's mastery of the unit content. Programs of this sort can be used both for individual and small-group instruction.

GRADING   Computers can also be used for computing and recording grades and for various other types of scholastic bookkeeping.

Planning Computer Activities

How you use computers in class depends on the number of computers available. To best utilize drill, practice, tutorial, and some problem-solving activities, you should really have a computer available for every student to enable each learner to control the content and pace the learning.

Computer simulations, games, and some kinds of problem-solving activities are best presented via small-group activities. Activities of these sorts can foster cooperation and interpersonal communication. For this type of teaching to be more effective, you need several computers so that the various groups can each gather around a computer. This will allow the groups to work on the program at the same time, thus permitting them all to discuss the program with each other, to interact, and then to move on to the next step in the sequence. In other situations, you may wish to load different programs into different computers and then have small groups circulate from computer to computer. You must still introduce the program, conduct it, and then follow up with other activities.

If only one computer is available, you must divide the class into groups that take turns at the computer, or you might plan large-group activities. Large-group computer activities can be excellent for introducing or summarizing topics. As with other audiovisual presentations, you must introduce them, follow up on them, and, in general, make them part of your overall strategy.(19)

No matter how you arrange your computer activities, combine computer activities and noncomputer activities into meaningful integrated lessons and units. In order to integrate computer and noncomputer activities, Brumbaugh and Rawitsch recommend that lessons incorporating computer activities be divided into three steps:

First, an activity to stimulate student interest in the topic.
Second, an activity that covers or conveys specific content, skills, and/or activities.
Third, an activity that summarizes learning or has students apply learning to a new situation.(20)

Only one of these three steps should include computer activity. The other two steps should be made up of other activities. Brumbaugh and Rawitsch believe you can encourage well-balanced, well-rounded learning in this way.

SELECTING SOFTWARE   Without appropriate software, computers are fairly useless to students. To select appropriate programs, adopt a procedure such as the following:

1. Decide just what you want the program to do.
2. Set up criteria based on your needs and goals.
3. Find out what software is available. Check catalogs, library directories, and so on.

4. Check the reviews.*
5. Preview the most promising programs.
6. Check on the reliability and supportiveness of the supplier.
7. Determine what supporting courseware is available.
8. Evaluate the supporting courseware for suitability and quality.

In carrying out this procedure, ask yourself questions such as the following:

1. Does the program fit your instructional objectives?
2. Does the program mesh with your content and teaching approaches? Does it aim at important objectives? Are the concepts clearly developed? Are the style, content, and educational philosophy compatible with yours?
3. Is the program motivating? Will it appeal to students? Remember, dull, dry computer programs can be just as boring as any other teaching.
4. Will the program open up students' creativity, imagination, and thinking? Will it encourage logical thought?
5. For whom is the program designed? For individuals? For small groups? For large groups? What ability groups is it aimed at? Can it accommodate a range of ability levels? Is it suitable for the ability levels of your students? Is the reading level suitable? What prerequisites are necessary?
6. For what instructional uses is the program designed? Drill or practice, tutoring, simulation, game-playing, problem solving, exposition, demonstration, testing, analysis, instructional management? Do these uses suit your proposed objectives and teaching style?
7. Is the program usable? Are the instructions easy to follow? Are the responses clear and appropriate? Is the screen formatting well-designed? Does the program have adequate support materials? How long does it take to run?
8. Is the program friendly, supportive, and encouraging, or is it threatening? Does it help students who make errors or does it react harshly? Does it provide for constructed responses? (Some programs provide only "unique responses." These linear programs tell students if they are right or wrong, and then go on to the next question, perhaps after repeating the rule. Programs with constructed responses tell students why they are wrong and may give them clues, or hints, for getting the correct answer. Better programs branch to indicate steps that students should take to get the correct answer. Well-constructed response programs provide for cognitive skills and for effective application of these skills. These intrinsic programs are the kinds of programs educators should buy.)
9. Does the program allow for teacher management? How much teacher supervision is necessary?
10. What does the program cost? Does the program seem durable; that is, will it grow with your students? Will the suppliers give it proper support and backup? Is it worth the expense?

SELECTING A COMPUTER   Chances are that as a beginning teacher, you will not be asked to pick a computer for your own and your students' use. Nevertheless, you should become knowledgeable about computer hardware. In addition, it is crucial that you know something about software, because to meet your needs, the computer must be compatible with the programs selected for instruction. A computer that will not play the software best-suited for your course will not be very serviceable. Therefore, the first things to check are the quality and quantity of the software available for

*Minnesota Educational Computing Consortium, St. Paul, Minnesota, is highly recommended as a source of information about software; also such journals as *The Computing Teacher* and *Classroom Computer News* are helpful.

the computer under consideration. Other points to check are the ease of use, the cost of the computer and supporting hardware and software, the availability and dependability of servicing, what supporting materials and equipment are available, and which of these are necessary or desirable for future expansion of the system.

NETWORKING   Computers lend themselves to laboratory-type classes. In such classes, the computers are joined together in a network. In this network not only are the students' computers connected with each other, but also they are connected with the teacher's computer and with a central computer called a *file server*. This file server stores courseware, administrative tools, and software applications such as word processing and graphics, and provides the teacher with a means to monitor individual students' work. Usually the students work together in small groups called *learning centers,* for whom the teacher provides different learning tasks. As a rule, the use of laboratories of this type results in independent study, cooperative learning, and the development of higher thinking skills.

VIDEODISCS   Traditional classes seem rather dull when compared to the television that pupils watch daily. Ingrid Patton(21) recommends using interactive videodiscs to combat that drabness. Usually videodiscs are used in the same manner as motion picture projectors and videocassettes. However, as new software is developed, the videodisc is becoming a tool of great potential. It can play a program straight through, or play it in slow motion, or stop action to hold a frame. It is also possible to combine videodiscs with computers to produce interactive learning. Twelve-inch interactive discs can store as many as 54,000 images, along with sound effects, on each side.(22) These can be shown on a television monitor or adapted into computer programs. By using a hand-held remote control unit, the teacher easily can present not only illustrations in the lesson, but also illustrate answers to students' questions.

MULTIMEDIA   The computer's many peripherals make it possible to use multimedia in many combinations in computer programs. Elements that may be used in multimedia presentations include

> computers and courseware
> file server
> VCRs and videotapes
> videodisc players
> CD ROM players
> pictures, photographs, graphics
> music
> sound effects and voice.

These elements may be interactive. As the presentation goes on, the user may choose subjects or sequences to view, for example, freezing the motion, playing a segment in slow motion, or switching to another clip.

Stop and Reflect

Look up some computer programs related to your field. How could you use them? Do you think they are worth buying? Why, or why not? What courseware would be needed to support each program?

Look at some classroom computers. What software suitable for courses you might teach is available for these computers?

Ethical Considerations

The educational technology that has resulted in the growth of computer use in our schools has brought with it a number of growing ethical problems. The first of these that we shall consider is the quality of the software. Students should not be subjected to mediocre teaching materials. Because many software programs are not really very good, you should take it upon yourself to be quite choosy about the software that you use in your classes. When choosing software, consider the following:

1. software is expensive
2. it tends to go out of date very quickly
3. you do not want your classes to have less than the best.

In seeking out good software, go to conferences and exhibitions to see what is available. Ask other teachers and students about the software they have used. Study the software manuals carefully. Borrow copies from friends and salespeople and try them out. Develop a comprehensive evaluation form and evaluate the programs; then inform distributors and manufacturers of what you, your colleagues, and your students think of the programs. In short, demand the best!

Since you are demanding high standards from your software distributors, it is only right that you treat them fairly, too. Good software is expensive to produce. A major concern of software producers is the loss of sales that results from unauthorized copying of their programs by school personnel. This practice is piracy and is illegal. Refrain from copying programs unless you are licensed to do so by the copyright owner. What you are licensed to do with a particular software program is usually stated explicitly in the terms of sale when you purchase your software.

Try also to be fair to your students. Be sure that everyone has equal opportunity to learn with the computers. Schedule computer time equally among students. If you do not, you may find that some computer whizzes are monopolizing the computer. Also make sure that both boys and girls have equal opportunities. Much computer programming seems to be oriented toward boys, and studies show that boys are more attracted by the programs being offered than girls are. It follows then that you should make a special effort to pick programs and activities that appeal to girls whenever possible.(23) Also try to ensure that students of low socioeconomic status and the less academically inclined all have opportunities to shine. To make things fair, schedule definite computer time for each and every one of your students.

Finally, take steps to ensure that personal information stored in your computers and programs does not get into unauthorized hands. Talk to your students about the misuses of information. Be sure that they are aware that not only is misusing personal information illegal, so is just looking at private information. Everyone has a right to privacy; neither teacher nor student should be allowed to violate that right. To protect these rights, you and your colleagues should take steps to ensure that records are kept securely under lock and key and that only authorized personnel ever have access to such files and equipment.

S U M M A R Y

Good teachers can be better teachers when they have plenty of materials to work with. Fortunately, teachers in the United States are blessed with materials galore, although some may have to search a little to find them. Prominent on the list are audiovisual aids—films, pictures, maps, globes, charts, models, graphs, mock-ups, simulations, terrain boards, radio, television, chalkboard, and tack boards. All of them are excellent aids to teaching if they are used well, but they are not "miracle drugs." They alone cannot do the job of teaching. The same teaching techniques—

introducing, explaining, problem solving, follow-up, and evaluation—used in other teaching activities—are also needed to get the most from audiovisual aids. These techniques apply particularly to presenting films and filmstrips. When using display devices such as chalkboards, bulletin boards, and the like, it is important to plan and evaluate their impact. These aids should be clearly visible and uncluttered, with a clear center of interest and plenty of white space. Both their content and presentation should be as dramatic as possible. For this reason, and because of their ability to provide better visibility, overhead, opaque, and other projectors are often more effective than are other display methods. For the same reason, flannel boards are often more effective than are chalkboards.

Recent advances in mass media have created many opportunities for teachers to capitalize on the cinema and television. Teachers who do not utilize these commercial media may be missing opportunities to harness their undoubted appeal to youth. The use of media such as television, films, and videotapes has proved valuable as a means of bringing to the classroom outstanding experiences and personalities not otherwise available. Again, do not expect miracles of these items. Television programs, films, and recorded presentations, like anything else, need to be introduced and followed up properly. On their own, they may do nothing; carefully handled, they can work wonders.

Computers can be used as sophisticated teaching machines. They can be used for drill and practice, tutoring, simulating and modeling, data analyses, problem-solving, independent study, individualizing instruction, game playing, and testing and evaluation in all the disciplines. You cannot turn instruction over to the computer, however. You must, after picking your teaching programs and support materials with care, combine computer instruction with other techniques so as to develop well-balanced knowledge and skills in your students.

ADDITIONAL READING

Bitter, G. G., and R. A. Camuse. *Using a Microcomputer in the Classroom*, 2nd ed. Englewood Cliffs, NJ: Prentice-Hall, 1988.

Brown, J. W., R. B. Lewis, and F. F. Harcleroad. *A V Instruction: Technology, Media and Methods*, 6th ed. New York: McGraw-Hill, 1983.

Bullough, R. V. *Creating Instructional Materials*, 3rd ed. Englewood Cliffs, NJ: Merrill/Prentice Hall, 1990.

Callison, W. L. *Using Computers in the Classroom*. Englewood Cliffs, NJ: Prentice-Hall, 1985.

Colburn, P. et al. *Practical Guide to Computers in Education*. Glenview, IL: Scott Foresman, 1985.

Cuban, L. *Teachers and Machines*. New York: Teachers College Press, 1986.

Culbertson, J. A., and L. L. Cunningham, eds. *Microcomputers and Education, Eighty-fifth Yearbook of the National Society for the Study of Education*. Chicago: University of Chicago Press, 1986.

Ellington, H. *Producing Teaching Materials*. London: Kagan Page, 1985.

Gagne, R. M., ed. *Instructional Technology: Foundations*. Hillsdale, NJ: Erlbaum, 1987.

Grady, M. T., and D. D. Gawronski. *Computers in Curriculum and Instruction*. Alexandria, VA: Association for Supervision and Curriculum Development, 1983.

Hanafin, M. J., and K. L. Peck. *The Design, Development, and Evaluation of Instructional Software*. New York: Macmillan, 1988.

Heinich, R., M. Molenda, and J. D. Russell. *Instructional Media*, 3rd ed. New York: Macmillan, 1989.

Hoon, T. V. "Laser Videodiscs in Education: Endless Possibilities," *Phi Delta Kappan* 68 (May 1987): 696–700.

Johnson, J. *Electronic Learning: From Audiotape to Videodiscs*. Hillsdale, NJ: Erlbaum, 1987.

Kampe, J. E., and D. C. Smellie. *Planning, Producing, and Using Instructional Media*, 6th ed. New York: Harper and Row, 1989.

Kepner, H. A., Jr., ed. *Computers in the Classroom*, 2nd ed. Washington, DC: National Education Association, 1986.

Kinzer, C. K., R. D. Sherwood, and J. D. Bransford, eds. *Computer Strategies for Education: Foundations and Content-Area Application*. Englewood Cliffs, NJ: Merrill/Prentice Hall, 1985.

Lillie, D. L., W. H. Hannon, and G. B. Stock. *Computers and Effective Instruction*. White Plains, NY: Longman, 1989.

Locatis, C. N., and F. D. Atkinson. *Media and Technology for Education and Training*. Englewood Cliffs, NJ: Merrill/Prentice Hall.

Potter, R. L. *Using Television in the Curriculum, Fastback 208*. Bloomington, IN: Phi Delta Kappa Educational Foundation, 1984.

Schall, W. E., Jr. et al. *Computer Education, Literacy and Beyond*. Monterey, CA: Brooks/Cole, 1986.

Siegel, M. A., and D. M. Davis. *Understanding Computer-Based Education*. New York: Random House, 1986.

Sloan, D., ed. *The Computer in Education*. New York: Teachers College Press, 1985.

Soltis, J. F. *Computing and Education: The Second Frontier*. New York: Teachers College Press, 1988.

Stakenas, R. G., and R. Kaufman. *Technology in Education. Its Human Potential, Fastback 163*. Bloomington, IN: Phi Delta Kappa Educational Foundation, 1981.

Talab, R. S. *Copyright and Instructional Technologies: A Guide to Fair Use and Permissions*, 2nd ed. Washington, DC: Association for Educational Communications and Technology, 1989.

Tolman, M. N., and R. A. Alfred. *The Computer and Education*. Washington, DC: National Education Association, 1984.

Turner, S., and M. Land. *Tools for Schools: Application Software for the Classroom*. Belmont, CA: Wadsworth, 1988.

Vockell, E. L., and E. Schwartz. *The Computer in the Classroom*, 2nd ed. Santa Cruz, CA: Mitchell/McGraw-Hill, 1992.

White, C. S. *Computers and Education*. New York: Macmillan, 1988.

Williams, C. *The Community as Textbook, Fastback 64*. Bloomington, IN: Phi Delta Kappa Educational Foundation, 1975.

NOTES

1. Jerrold E. Kemp, *Planning, Producing and Using Instructional Media*, 6th ed. (New York: Harper & Row, 1989).
2. John B. Haney and Eldon J. Ullmer, *Educational Media and the Teacher* (Dubuque, IA: Brown, 1970), 102.
3. Leonard H. Clark, *Teaching Social Studies in Secondary Schools: A Handbook* (New York: Macmillan, 1973), 322. Based on Dale M. Garvey and Sancha K. Garvey, "Simulation, Role Playing and Sociodrama in the Social Studies," *The Emporia State Research Studies* 16 (Emporia, KS: Kansas State Teachers College, 1957), 2.
4. Virginia M. Helm, *What Educators Should Know about Copyright, Fastback 233* (Bloomington, IN: Phi Delta Kappa Educational Foundation, 1986).
5. More than 90 percent of schools had videocassette recording equipment, and at least 35 states were using long-distance learning during the 1988–1989 school year. Only a handful of classes had a computer for each

child, however. Most schools do not have enough computers to make them a central tool of instruction. The average in 1988 was one for every 30 students, and the average amount of time students spent with computers was only one hour a week. (Anne C. Lewis, "Washington News," *Education Digest* 54 (November 1988): 69.)

6. Doris A. Mathieson, "Computers: From Confusion to Collaboration," *Educational Leadership* 40 (November 1982): 13–15.

7. Karen Billings, "Research on School Computing," in *Computers in Curriculum and Instruction*, edited by M. Tim Grady and Jane D. Gawronski (Alexandria, VA: Association for Supervision and Curriculum Development, 1983), 13.

8. Faye Goolrick, *Introduction to Technology in the Classroom* (Plymouth, MI: EduQuest, an IBM Company).

9. M. Tim Grady and James L. Poirot, "Teacher Competence: What is Needed," in *Computers in Curriculum and Instruction*, 79.

10. Edward L. Vockell and Robert H. Rivers, *Instructional Computing for Today's Teachers* (New York: Macmillan, 1984), 7.

11. Vockell and Rivers, *Instructional Computing for Today's Teachers.*

12. Robert D. Sherwood, "Models of Computer Use in School Settings," in *Computer Strategies for Education*, edited by Charles K. Kinzer, Robert D. Sherwood, and John D. Bransford (Englewood Cliffs, NJ: Merrill/Prentice Hall, 1986), Chapter 6.

13. Ibid., 107.

14. Vockell and Rivers, *Instructional Computing for Today's Teachers*, 48ff.

15. F. Taber, *Microcomputers in Special Education* (Reston, VA: The Council for Exceptional Children, 1983), cited in Kinzer et al., *Computer Strategies for Education*, 306.

16. Vockell and Rivers, *Instructional Computing for Today's Teachers*, 21–40.

17. Ibid., 41.

18. Ibid., 42–44.

19. Ken Brumbaugh and Don Rawitsch, *Establishing Instructional Computing: The First Step* (St. Paul, MN: Minnesota Educational Computing Consortium, 1982), 34–35.

20. Ibid., 61.

21. Ingrid Patton, "New Jersey Schools Bring Science to Life with Interactive Videodiscs," *Educational Viewpoints* 13 (Spring 1993): 17–18.

22. Ibid.

23. Kate Kroschwitz and Carolyn McClintock Peter, "All Girl Settings for Teaching Math or Science," *Independent School* 55 (Fall 1994): 14–20.

Classroom Evaluation

Overview

Teachers are like the navigators of ships at sea. To know which way to go, they need to know where they are. Therefore, like the navigator who must keep a running record of the ship's approximate position and make frequent checks to fix its exact location, teachers must continually appraise and reappraise their positions. Otherwise, how would teachers know in what direction to aim their course? We call this appraisal and reappraisal of the teaching-learning situation *evaluation*.

Evaluation has many purposes. Teachers use it as a basis for diagnosis, grading, reporting to parents, and promotion. Administrators use it as a basis for categorizing students into groups. Guidance counselors use it as a basis for student advisement. Students use it as a basis for mapping out their own programs. Parents, school officials, and teachers use it as a basis for curriculum revision. But the most important role of evaluation is its use in the teaching-learning process itself. This is because of the following:

1. It gives teachers the feedback they need to discover what the students have learned and what they need to learn next.
2. It gives students the feedback they need to profit from their successes and failures.
3. It helps teachers to understand the students, their abilities, and their needs. It is the essential element in diagnosis.
4. It motivates students.

In this chapter, after a short look at the theoretical aspects of evaluation, we discuss the procedures and techniques by which you can assess your students' progress in units and courses, as well as the selection, construction, and use of measuring devices and techniques. Finally, we discuss standardized tests and their uses, and how to interpret their scores. At the conclusion of the chapter, you should be able to build an evaluation plan for a unit or course, select or construct measuring instruments or procedures appropriate for the learning you wish to evaluate, use these instruments and procedures properly, and evaluate their usefulness and accuracy.

As you read the chapter, note the following:

- *Evaluation is not testing, but instead evaluation is making a judgment.*
- In teaching, evaluation is based on measurements.
- Evaluation must conform to the instructional goals if it is to be valid (curriculum alignment).
- There are many different kinds of measuring devices and procedures.
- You should be careful to pick the devices appropriate to your objectives.
- Whatever measuring instruments you use should be valid, reliable, objective, and usable.
- The evaluation instruments you use must be carefully constructed.
- Finally, all this care may be wasted unless the instruments are carefully administered and scored to provide feedback that both you and the students can use as a basis for the next steps in their learning.

In short, your objectives, subject matter, teaching methods, and evaluation should be aligned.

■ ■ ■ ■   Background

Definitions

The word *evaluation* means to put a value on or assign worth to something. It includes a quantitative and/or qualitative description, plus a value judgment. This is also true of the word *assessment*, which the *Random House Dictionary of the English Language* defines as an estimate or judgment of value, character, etc. The element in evaluation or assessment that makes it different from measurement is judgment. When you measure a situation, you merely describe the situation. When you evaluate or assess the situation, you judge its value.

For example, let us suppose you gave the students a test and found that Susie's score was 70. This information in itself does not tell us much of anything. Is 70 good or bad? It depends. If 70 represents the highest score of all the students in the school, we may decide that it is a very good score. If it represents the lowest score, we may decide that it is a very poor mark. However, if the score is a low one, but reflects the best effort of the student, we may decide that it is not so bad at that. Evaluation, then, is the judgment or interpretation that one draws from the information at hand. Valid evaluations depend on accurate measurement.

Consequently, evaluation of students' progress must be a two-step process. In the first step, you must gather pertinent data to assess the students' status. For this purpose, use the tools and techniques of educational measurement to estimate both the quantity and quality of the students' learning and other pertinent factors. Then, once you have made these estimates, the second step is to use the information to make reasoned judgments about the strengths and weaknesses of your students as well as the merits and inadequacies of your programs in light of your instructional objectives.

A Caveat

Do not expect too much of the evaluation process. All evaluation is subject to some error, although careful design and execution reduce the chance of mistakes. Measurements are only approximations at best. In education, they can never be precise, and sometimes they are wildly inaccurate. No matter what types of instruments you use, they are subject to numerous limitations. For example, there is always some error in sampling; there is always some error inherent in the instrument itself (e.g., true-false tests encourage guessing); there is always some error in the process of administering and scoring (e.g., scoring essay tests is often greatly inconsistent); there is always some error in the interpretation of the results. Therefore, you should never accept an educational measurement or evaluation as conclusive unless it is supported by a sufficient amount of other confirming data. Because of these limitations and the resultant need to support measurement with other data, it has become quite common to speak of and rely on assessment rather than measurement.

Stop and Reflect

In both the popular and professional press, there has been considerable criticism of the use of tests and measurements. Look up some of these articles. How much should we test? Should promotion and graduation depend on test scores? Should high school diplomas be granted only to those who pass a state test? Should test scores be used to evaluate curricula, teaching, and teacher salaries? How can you both gain the benefit that assessment can provide as well as avoid the pitfalls of overdependence on tests and measurements and drawing conclusions from erroneous data? (See later sections of this chapter on interpretation of scores.)

What is the difference between measurement, evaluation, and assessment?

What can test results be used for? What are the most valid uses of test scores?

Evaluation in Units and Courses

Objectives and Evaluation

When assessing student progress in units and courses, the first step is to prepare sound instructional objectives. As stated earlier, evaluation consists of making reasoned judgments in light of the instructional objectives, which implies that you should be certain that the evaluative data you use are pertinent to your objectives. All too many educational decisions are based on data that are irrelevant to the problem at hand. This fault can be avoided by using clear, specific instructional objectives as a basis for both your instruction and your evaluation. In general, specific criterion-referenced behavioral objectives are the most useful types of objectives for the evaluator.[*]

Preparing an Evaluation Plan

The second step in evaluating student progress in the unit or course is to set up a plan for evaluation. To be sure that the evaluation includes all the essential aspects and uses proper measurement techniques, make your plan for evaluating the unit or course *before* you start to teach it. The plan should ensure (1) that the instruments used assess the progress students make toward achieving each objective in proportion to its importance, and (2) that the proper types of instruments are used to assess the progress students are making.

To make an evaluation plan, simply list your objectives and note the procedures you will use to measure the attainment of these objectives, as well as the weight you will give each in the total assessment. This plan is sometimes called a *table of specifications*. A form for planning your evaluation appears in Figure 14.1.

Selecting the *Right* Instrument

The third step is to select or construct the instruments and procedures by which you will carry out your plan. This step is complicated by the fact that there are so many devices and procedures for assessing student progress. The ubiquitous pencil-and-paper tests are the most commonly used. Some teachers use hardly anything else. Such tests are not, however, always the most useful, because they often fail to give the information you most need. By their very nature, paper-and-pencil tests are more likely to test knowing about than knowing, verbalizations rather than the ability to do, or platitudes rather than changes in attitude or behavior. Rating scales, checklists, self-reporting devices, questionnaires, anecdotal reports, behavior logs, and sociometric devices may be more useful for your purposes than tests. Carefully select each measuring device and test item that you need to do a particular job, and match it to the job it can do best.

[*]See Chapter 5 for descriptions and examples of specific objectives.

▦ **Figure 14.1**
Evaluation Plan

Objectives	Type of Items or Devices	Number of Items or Weight

Summative, Formative, or Diagnostic Evaluation

Authorities in the field have divided evaluation into three types: summative evaluation, formative evaluation, and diagnostic evaluation.(1) *Summative evaluation* is that evaluation performed at the end of a course or unit to grade the students and to judge teaching success. *Formative evaluation* is the continuous evaluation performed during the course or unit to decide how well the teacher is doing and what needs to be done next. Formative tests are usually sharper in focus than are summative tests and are less useful for grading students. *Diagnostic evaluation* tends to combine elements of the other two. At the beginning of courses and units, diagnostic evaluation may use the techniques of summative evaluation to determine where students should be placed (e.g., gifted, average, or below-average groups). During the courses and units, diagnostic evaluation uses the techniques of formative evaluation to discover the causes of students' difficulties. In most of your teaching, diagnostic and formative evaluation will converge.

It is most important that you select the proper instruments for making evaluation appropriate to your aim. The instruments in diagnostic and formative evaluation should be criterion-referenced, whereas those used for summative evaluation should be norm-referenced, for instance. Ordinarily, unit assessments should be formative and summative evaluation should be reserved for final examinations and the like.

Criteria for a Good Measuring Device

No matter what type of measuring device you select, you want it to be a good one. Therefore, you should consider four criteria:

1. How valid is it?
2. How reliable is it?
3. How objective it is?
4. How usable is it?

Validity The most important of these criteria is *validity*—that is, the extent to which the device measures what it is supposed to measure. A measuring device that is not valid is worthless. Validity depends on several things. The instrument must be suitable to the nature of what is to be measured. A paper-and-pencil test is hardly a valid measure of a baseball player's ability to bat, for instance. Furthermore, the instrument must measure all the significant aspects of the target in an amount proportional to their importance. If, in testing batting ability, you tested the batter's stance but not his hitting, the test would give a false result because of poor sampling. Moreover, to be valid the test must also discriminate. In testing batting ability, of what use is a test that does not differentiate between good batters and poor batters?[*]

Curriculum validity is a particularly important criterion in establishing the worth of achievement tests. *Curriculum validity* indicates the extent to which a test measures what was supposed to have been taught in the course. Without it, an achievement test cannot be valid. When the items of an achievement test are concerned with learning content that was not part of the course, the test will give incorrect results because of its lack of curriculum validity. Commercial achievement tests sometimes give an inaccurate picture of the achievement of students in a particular school because the curriculum of the school may differ from that for which the commercial test was designed. In the ordinary classroom situation, curriculum validity is determined by examining the instrument to be sure (1) that it does test for the specific goals of the unit or course and (2) that it gives each goal approximately the same weight that the unit or course plan calls for.[**]

RELIABILITY   A second test of the worth of an evaluative device is reliability. An instrument is *reliable* if it can be trusted to give the same results when it is repeated or when different forms of the device are used. In other words, a reliable instrument is consistent and dependable. When a test is reliable, you can be sure that its measurement is fairly accurate because chance errors and other inconsistencies have been largely eliminated. Just as a steel measuring tape is less likely to be stretched out of shape than a cloth tape, or a fine laboratory scale is likely to be more dependable than a bathroom scale, a reliable test is less likely to be affected by irrelevant or chance factors than is an unreliable one.

Statistical methods are used to determine coefficients of reliability for standardized tests, but such techniques are not really suitable for use with teacher-built tests and other classroom instruments. You can make teacher-built tests fairly reliable by (1) making the tests as long as you reasonably can (so that chance errors will tend to cancel out each other), (2) scoring the test as objectively as possible (so that the number of inconsistencies in scoring will be reduced), (3) writing the items and directions as carefully as possible (so that students will not make irrelevant errors because of ambiguities, misunderstood directions, and so on), and (4) administering the test as carefully as possible (so that error will not be introduced by nonstandard conditions such as distracting noise, lack of time, and so on). Careful preparation, administration, and objective scoring help to improve the reliability of other instruments as well.

Validity and reliability are not totally independent. Reliability refers to consistency, and an instrument that is not consistent certainly cannot be counted on to give truthful information. Therefore, to be valid, an instrument must be reliable. But a reliable instrument may not necessarily be valid; it can give wrong information

---

[*]In criterion-referenced testing, a test would discriminate if it ascertained which students met the criterion and which did not.

[**]Perhaps one should make a distinction between content validity and curriculum validity. A standardized test that covers a good sample of the subject matter of a particular discipline, but not the subject matter of the discipline as taught in a particular school, has content validity. A test that reflects the subject matter as taught in a particular school's curriculum has curriculum validity. (A test with content validity may point out where the curriculum in a particular school is lacking.) Sometimes the terms are used interchangeably, as we have done.

consistently. Consequently, to measure progress toward certain high-level objectives, an essay test with fairly low potential reliability, but reasonably high potential validity, may be better than an objective test with much higher potential reliability but lower potential validity.

OBJECTIVITY   Another criterion of a good instrument is objectivity. By *objectivity*, educators mean that the personality of the scorer does not affect the scoring of the test. A truly objective test will be scored in exactly the same way by every scorer. Objectivity in an instrument helps make the scoring fair and the instrument reliable. So long as validity is not sacrificed, the more objective the instrument, the better. However, a valid instrument may be a good instrument even though it is not objective, whereas an objective instrument that is not valid is always worthless.

USABILITY   A fourth criterion of a good evaluative device is its *usability*. Obviously, a 2-hour test is not suitable for a 40-minute class period. Everything else being equal, avoid instruments that are hard to administer, difficult to score, and expensive.

Carrying Out the Plan

The fourth step in evaluating student progress is to teach the unit or course and carry out your evaluation plan. In this step you must pay particular attention to properly using, administering, and scoring the evaluative devices and procedures. We will discuss this more in later sections of the chapter.

Stop and Reflect
What are the most important criteria for judging the worth of a test? Rate these criteria in order of importance. Why did you choose that order? When would you use an objective test? An essay test? Apply these criteria to a test in one of your college courses.

Tools for Assessment

Performance Assessment

At present there is a movement in our schools to make school learning more "authentic." As part of this movement, educators have been replacing traditional test and measurement strategies with "assessments of student performance." The goal of these assessments is to ascertain what the students really understand and how they respond to the knowledge and skills being assessed. To make these instruments really authentic, the assessor must face the students with real-life tasks that require students to use good judgment to determine correct answers, taking into consideration such constraints as time, logistics, etc. In so far as possible, the conditions of the assessment should be the same as those one would face in real life situations.

Tests are liable to be of little help when assessing student performance. Often in an attempt to write an excellent test, the test writer sacrifices validity to make the test reliable and easy to use. In such tests, the writer bases questions on the unthinking use of rules, laws, and algorithms when instead the questions should be assessing students' performance in real situations or simulations. As the Office of Strategic Services stated in its 1948 search for personnel, the best way to judge a candidate's abilities "is to expose the man to a variety of situations of the same sort as those he will find in the field."(2)

OBSERVATION   Observing students and examining samples of their work are the most common bases for judgment of students' behavior and progress. By using these means, an alert teacher can often not only construct authentic assessments of students' schoolwork, but also spot clues to the causes of students' behavior.

Observation, although a technique as old as humankind, has several unfortunate limitations. Observers are notoriously unreliable, and students behave differently when they know they are being observed. However, these limitations can be reduced by careful observation when the observer has determined in advance what to look for and how to look for it, especially if the observer uses a checklist, rating scale, or some other written guide to help objectify the observations.

Observation may be formal or informal. It ranges from formal tests of performance to spontaneous observations of natural classroom activity. Much of it is quite impromptu. Unplanned observation of natural events is particularly useful for spotting clues to students' attitudes, personality traits, and typical performances. Observations of this kind should be recorded in anecdotal reports. Unless recorded immediately, mental notes gleaned from observations such as these are likely to be forgotten or, worse, remembered incorrectly.

Planned observations, both formal and informal, will give you a better sampling of the particular skills and abilities that you wish to assess. They can take the form of a formal performance test in which the students are asked to carry out a planned activity, or careful, planned observation of regular ongoing class activities. Planned observations lend themselves to the following procedures:

1. Decide what you want to assess and why. Will the goal be diagnosis, judging mastery, or grading? These objectives call for somewhat different approaches.
2. Decide how to perform the observations.
   a. Will it be formal, informal, or both? Often a formal performance test would be best, but more often teachers have time only for informal observation.
   b. Which elements will be judged?
   c. What standard will be set?
   d. How will the observation be rated and recorded?
   e. Who will do the observing—teacher, peers, or the individual pupils themselves?
3. Construct any needed checklists or rating scales. Be sure observers are well-briefed.(3)
4. Make sure your observation criteria, standards, and instruments are well-aligned with your teaching objectives and content.
5. Carry out the observation.

WORK SAMPLES   Assessing samples of student work should follow much the same procedure as observation. Determine in advance the factors on which the work will be judged. That these criteria should be passed on to the students before they do the work is axiomatic. Students should always be told the standards by which they are to be evaluated. These criteria should be reflected in the rating scale, checklist, or other written guide used to objectify the evaluator's judgment.

RATING SCALES   Rating scales are especially helpful in judging skills, procedures, and personal social behavior. Rating scales can also be used to help objectify the evaluation of products of the student's work, such as a lampshade made in an industrial arts class or a composition or theme written in an English class. Such devices have the advantage of providing a visual reference for the student as he or she analyzes the rater's evaluation, and also of preventing the rater from being unduly influenced by any one aspect of the work being evaluated.

In using such tools, you can make the final evaluation dependent on a numerical score. However, always remember that often, as in the case of literary and art works and other creative activities, evaluation cannot be safely reduced to numbers. To avoid misinterpretations, allow for the possibility that sometimes a single characteristic may outweigh all others and that some items may be completely inapplicable.

PREPARING A RATING SCALE   Rating scales and checklists are easy to build and to use. To make a rating scale, merely decide which characteristics you wish to rate, then arrange a scale for each of these characteristics. Since a five-point scale is about all a rater can handle, there is little point in making finer distinctions. In any case, do not use more than seven or fewer than three categories. If you label each point of the scale, the rating will be easier.

To illustrate this process, suppose you wish to build a scale to use as a guide for judging the excellence of some posters that students have prepared. First, decide what to consider in judging the posters. Let us say that among other things you wish to include neatness, lettering, eye appeal, and design. Then provide a rating scale similar to the one shown in Figure 14.2. In this rating scale, the gradations are indicated by descriptive words encompassing the gamut from best to worst. These descriptions help make your ratings somewhat more objective than they might be otherwise.

Another type of rating scale is shown in Figure 14.3, where 5 signifies the highest rating and 1 the lowest. "NA" means "not applicable." The scale is used by circling the number desired. Still another plan is simply to list the characteristics you think important and then rate them according to a code, such as * + ✓ - 0, as shown in Figure 14.4.

In preparing the characteristics to be rated in the scale, be sure that each is significant. Sometimes some of the characteristics included in rating scales do not make any real difference. Be sure also that each characteristic is clearly and precisely specified so that the rater knows exactly what to rate. To make the characteristics clear, it may be necessary to break them into components. Characteristics that are too broad are difficult to rate fairly because at one time the rater may emphasize one aspect and another time, another aspect. Be sure also that the characteristics to be rated are readily observable. It is helpful to the rater if the scale allows for ratings between categories. For example, in Figure 14.2 the rater may feel that the lettering should be rated better than average but not quite excel-

Design	Crystalline Beautiful Perfect	Clear Well-balanced Pleasing	Mediocre	Confusing Poorly balanced Crowded	Hodgepodge
Neatness	Meticulous	Excellent	Average	Fair	Sloppy
Lettering	Superior	Excellent	Average	Fair	Poor
Eye Appeal	Overwhelming	Intriguing	Catchy	Dull	Insipid

■ **FIGURE 14.2**
Rating Scale for Posters

■ **Figure 14.3**
Rating Scale for Written Work

Circle number indicating rating.
Code: 5, highest; 1, lowest; NA, not applicable

1. Originality		5	4	3	2	1	NA
2. Clearness		5	4	3	2	1	NA
.							
.							
11. Spelling		5	4	3	2	1	NA
12. Sentence structure		5	4	3	2	1	NA

lent. The rater should also be allowed to skip any of the characteristics that seem not applicable.

Using Rating Scales   Even though using rating scales is relatively easy, there are a few caveats that raters should be aware of. One is the danger of the *halo effect*. Raters frequently rate students of good reputation higher than they rate students of lesser reputation, even when their performances are the same. Similarly, raters tend to rate certain categories higher (or lower) than they should because associated characteristics were rated high (or low). This tendency is called the *logical error*. Another source of error is the common tendency to rate all students in much the same way. Some raters rate everyone high; some raters rate everyone low; and some raters rate everyone average. Yielding to such tendencies reduces the effectiveness of the rating scale and makes it difficult to separate the good performances from the bad performances.

• *Indicate Presence or absence of specific characterstic*

Checklists   Checklists differ from rating scales in that they indicate only the presence or absence of specific characteristics. They are most useful in evaluating products and procedures. You can also use them to gather evidence concerning students' progress toward specific objectives. You cannot use them to measure personal and social growth, however.

When developing checklists, include only characteristics whose presence or absence is significant. Otherwise, prepare checklists in much the same way as rating scales. The same procedures and precautions apply, except that you must provide a place for checking the presence or absence of the characteristic instead of providing a scale.

■ **Figure 14.4**
Simplified Rating Scale for Written Work

Place rating in parenthesis.
Key: * Excellent; + Very Good; ✓ Average; - Less than Average; 0 Poor

1. Original	(	)
2. Clear	(	)
.		
.		
11. Spelling	(	)
12. Sentence structure	(	)

■ **Figure 14.5**
Checklist for Plastic Letter Opener—General Shop I

Check each item if the letter opener complies with that standard.

(   ) 1. The blade is properly shaped.
(   ) 2. All saw marks are removed.
(   ) 3. The plastic is free from warping and pitting.

For instance, in evaluating letter openers that students make in an industrial arts class, you can make up a checklist such as the one in Figure 14.5. Such a list gives you a firm basis for evaluating the product if you check the applicable items only.

In the evaluation device shown in Figure 14.6, which is used for rating the speech of college students preparing for teaching, spaces are left blank so that the rater can either check or make some comment for each of the various items.

THE RANKING METHOD   Another simple procedure for rating students' skills and accomplishments is the rank-order method in which the rater simply ranks the students or products from best to worst, or most to least. For instance, you can rank a set of themes from most original to least original, or a group of posters from most eye-appealing to least eye-appealing.

In using the rank-order method, it is usually best to start at the ends and rank toward the middle. Another procedure is to sort students or products into five groups (e.g., best, better than average, average, less than average, poorest). This procedure is commonly used by teachers grading essays, essay test questions, or projects. On the negative side, this procedure usually involves considerable reshuffling among the groups before it is possible to arrive at the final grouping. Then the students and projects within each group can be rearranged in rank order until you have a ranking from top to bottom of the entire group. As you can see, this last step is time-consuming and cumbersome. In the ordinary classroom, such a system is usually unnecessary; categorizing students or projects into five groups suffices for most classroom purposes.

Rank-order methods have the advantage of ensuring that raters do not rate everyone high or low or average, as they tend to do when using rating scales.

	Explanation	Reading	Questioning
Poised	_____	_____	_____
Direct	_____	_____	_____
Animated	_____	_____	_____
Distinct	_____	_____	_____
Audible	_____	_____	_____
Fluent	_____	_____	_____
Clear (ver)	_____	_____	_____
(vis)	_____	_____	_____
Pronunciation	_____	_____	_____
RECOMMENDATION			

■ **Figure 14.6**
Speech Qualification Rating Sheet

However, rank-order methods do not describe behavior as well as some other measurements and are meaningful only in the group ranked. The student who places lowest in a high-honors group, for example, may be doing very well indeed.

Stop and Reflect

Is it really possible to objectify observations? Explain.

Compare the various types of rating scales and checklists that have been discussed. What are the strong points and weak points of each? Why? What are the strengths and weaknesses of the rank-order method?

Themes, Notebooks, Homework, and Recitation

Themes, homework, papers, and oral recitations can also provide evidence of student progress, and you should check them carefully. A good rule is never to assign anything that is not going to be checked by someone. Practice material, however, need not always be checked by the teacher. Sometimes, students can check their own and each other's work quite effectively.

To provide an objective basis for evaluating written work, you can use rating scales, checklists, and standards. A checklist that might be used to evaluate themes can include such items as the following:

- Does the student develop the thought logically?
- Is the central idea clearly expressed?
- Does the student document the facts?

Sometimes a simple set of standards to use as a guideline is all you need when you correct students' writing. In the case just mentioned, such standards might include items similar to the following:

- The theme clearly expresses a central idea.
- Everything in the theme presented as fact is documented.
- The writer develops his or her thoughts logically.

Obviously, such standards could be used to make up the items in a checklist.

Use both writing exercises and learning devices mainly as aids to instruction. Put the emphasis on diagnosis, practice, and learning rather than on rating.

Portfolios

In the search for authentic learning, a number of school systems have adopted the use of student portfolios as bases for evaluating student progress. A portfolio is a file or folder that contains samples of the student's work, such as themes, homework, papers, teacher ratings of the work performed, descriptions of the student's accomplishments, scores on tests, and other significant materials gathered by the student during the term. The material in the portfolio is intended "to give comprehensive cumulative portraits" that "document a student's experiences and accomplishments."(4)

Although at the present time there is no standard for the use of portfolios, they may be a good way to report progress to parents. A review of the materials contained in a portfolio should give teachers and parents, as well as students, good bases for evaluating the students' progress in the course. Pam Knight, for instance, used portfolios in her algebra class. Although other mathematics teachers limited their portfolios to problem solving, Ms. Knight's student portfolios included long-term projects, daily notes, journal entries, scale drawings, best tests, worst tests, and homework. The standards the students adopted for their portfolios included

- The portfolio should be neat.
- The portfolio should be typed or written in ink.
- The portfolio should include a table of contents.
- The portfolio should include a personal statement explaining why the contents are important.(5)

Stop and Reflect

What would be the best way to test a student's honesty? Ability to swim? Appreciation of a poem? Freedom from prejudices? Understanding that "all men are created equal, with certain inalienable rights"? What do your answers imply as far as a testing program is concerned?

At Metro High School in Cedar Rapids, Iowa, a portfolio is defined as

a record of learning that focuses on the student's work and her/his reflection on that work. Material is collected through a collaborative effort between the student and staff members and is indicative of progress toward the essential outcomes.

It can be used to:

1. assist students and staff members in assessing their progress toward acquiring the essential outcomes;
2. determine personal strengths, weaknesses, and preferences;
3. document the extent of students' willingness to take risks;
4. increase student self-esteem;
5. practice and emphasize reflection;
6. emphasize the importance of both product and process;
7. develop material for a senior seminar/exhibition that might serve as a portfolio for college and/or work;
8. assist with end-of-term evaluations;
9. develop both short- and long-term goals; and
10. provide staff members with information to adjust course content and offerings to meet student needs.(6)

Self-Evaluation Techniques

The most important purpose of evaluation is to help guide students toward educational goals. The person most concerned in any teaching-learning situation is the student. *If evaluation is to be fully effective and the students are to set their goals correctly, they should participate in evaluating their own progress.*

Student self-evaluation can help students by doing the following:

1. Making the instructional objectives clear to them.
2. Showing each student how well he or she has progressed.
3. Showing each student his or her strengths and weaknesses.
4. Developing self-evaluative skills.

5. Creating an attitude toward objective self-evaluation.

For example, an evaluation technique used in an English class is to have the students critique both their own themes and those of other students. Because the primary goal is clarity, the teacher asks the students to read each other's themes and point out ideas that are unclear. Then the teacher, or on occasion another student, tells the writer where to find a discussion of the particular error in the text or the supplementary readings. Sometimes the teacher gives the pupils self-correcting exercises to help remedy their faults. The students work on these exercises independently until they think they have conquered the problem. Because students know these exercises are not to be counted into their marks, they feel no need to cheat. The teacher feels that the students learn much more efficiently than they would have if she corrected each paper herself and doled out marks.

In another school, the members of the class divided into groups, each of which developed a plan for a utopian society. The student teacher conducting this class devised a rating scale (Figure 14.7) by which the class members rated each group's plan of utopia as well as its class presentation.

Students can keep anecdotal reports and behavior logs to measure their own work. For instance, a student working on a project can keep a daily log or diary of progress and a record of his successes and difficulties. While working through a unit, a student can submit short reports on herself at the culmination of different aspects of the work and estimate the worth of her product and the benefits she has gained from the activity. In many cases, students keep records and a report entitled "The Things I Have Done During This Unit." These reports can be free-response papers in which the students simply list what they have accomplished, or more sophisticated papers in which the students evaluate their accomplishments. Some teachers prepare a list of things the students can do and let the students check off what they have done—either as they do them or as they complete the checklist at the end of the unit. Students can also keep profiles of what they have done (see

Category	Excellent	Good	Average	Fair	Poor	Comments
Believability: Might you want to see this place? Does it exist? Can it?						
Appeal: Are you ready to jump up and join this society?						
Justice: Are the laws plausible? Fair?						
Group Participation: Did each member of the panel seem important?						
Preparation: Did they know what they wanted to say?						
Presentation: Could you follow the logic?						

FIGURE 14.7
Creation of a Utopian Society

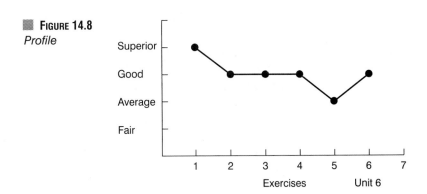

■ FIGURE 14.8
Profile

Figure 14.8). Such records as activity checklists and profiles are especially useful in individualized classes.

The use of cameras, audiotape, and videotape recorders may make it easier for students to judge their own progress. These tools also make it possible for you to analyze your students' actions, to diagnose errors, and to measure progress. You can also use these devices to show students how well they are getting on and what their weaknesses and strengths are. Videos are commonly used by coaches and physical education directors for these purposes. Similarly, tape recorders are often used during speech classes to help in evaluating discussions, panels, and other group activities, and videotape recordings often are used in the evaluation of student teachers.

Students may also participate in self-evaluation through conferences in which they have an opportunity to ask you for help on difficult points and you have an opportunity to evaluate their work, to point out errors, to offer encouragement, and to make diagnoses. These conferences need not be formal; a few words at your desk or at a student's work station may serve just as well as a full-scale interview. In fact, the more informal the conference, the more valuable it is likely to be.

Stop and Reflect

What steps would you take to help ensure that students' self-evaluations are honest and objective?

Of what value would a preassessment, self-evaluative exercise be?

What might you do to eliminate or minimize feelings of embarrassment and resentment when students evaluate one anothers' work?

Tests

Not only are there many types of measuring techniques, there are many types of tests to choose from as well.

INFORMAL AND STANDARDIZED TESTS   Most classroom tests are informal tests of achievement in the cognitive and psychomotor domains. Although there is increased effort by teachers to gather information about the progress of students in the affective domain, most attempts to gain such information must rely on observational and self-report techniques.* As a rule, formal standardized tests are used only on special occasions for special purposes.

---

*These techniques include rating scales, checklists, rankings, anecdotal reports, behavioral logs, guess-who tests, sociometric techniques, and so on.

MASTERY, SURVEY, OR DIAGNOSTIC TESTS Classroom tests may be mastery, survey, or diagnostic in nature.* The *mastery test* is designed to determine whether students have achieved a minimum standard. It does not attempt to compare the worth of various students' performances. The *survey test* is designed to find the difference in students' achievement as an indicator of their general ability in the area being tested. It is used to compare students' scores to give them grades. The *diagnostic test* is used to find where students' abilities and disabilities lie. Although the differences among the different types of tests tend to blur in ordinary classroom testing, if you bear the differences in mind when you are making out your test plans, your testing will be more effective.

CRITERION-REFERENCED VERSUS NORM-REFERENCED TESTS Well-built mastery and diagnostic tests are criterion-referenced. Survey tests are more often norm-referenced. The difference between them is that in criterion-referenced tests, the student's performance on the test is rated against a set standard, whereas in norm-referenced tests the student's performance is rated against the performance of other students (i.e., the norm of the group). Criterion-referenced tests are therefore more likely to be based on the achievement of definite objectives. Because of this fact, they ordinarily do not provide the spread in scores you wish to have when assigning grades. Even so, they are probably of more real value for use in the classroom than are achievement tests of the survey type.

SPEED VERSUS POWER TESTS No matter what the test type, classroom tests should be power tests, not speed tests, except in unusual cases. Therefore, when building and administering a classroom test, try to ensure that all students have plenty of time to do their best on every part of the test. Hurried test situations are grossly unfair to the thorough and methodical student. They also tend to defeat the purpose of testing; you never can be sure whether students did not answer the later portions of the test because of lack of knowledge or lack of time.

OBJECTIVE VERSUS ESSAY TESTS In uninformed circles there is quite a bit of debate about the relative merit of objective and essay tests. Such debate is fruitless. Each type of test has merits and each has limitations. The good test builder does not depend entirely on one or the other, but instead uses each for the purposes for which it is best fitted.

In several ways and for certain purposes, objective tests are better than essay tests. With them it is much easier to provide an adequate sampling. Furthermore, because objective test items limit students' choices, the answers do not wander from the point in the way essay answers sometimes do. Also, they are not as likely to include irrelevant material or to be affected by environmental conditions. For these reasons, objective tests are often more reliable than are essay tests. In addition, they are easier to score. In fact, the scoring is often so easy that it may be delegated to clerks, other nonprofessionals, or even machines. Moreover, the use of keys and automatic scoring devices can make the objective test really objective. It is only when the scorer departs from the key that the test becomes nonobjective. Objective tests have the additional advantage of being less time-consuming than essay tests. Objective tests can often do in a single period more than an essay test can do in a double period.

In spite of their virtues, objective tests have many serious faults. In the first place, good objective test items are difficult to write. Even in carefully built tests, some items are liable to be ambiguous or to contain clues that may give away the answers. Second, to test high-level learning with this type of test is difficult.

*Mastery tests are formative tests; survey tests are summative.

Although objective items can test the ability to organize, the ability to use what has been learned, the ability to show relationships, and the ability to evaluate, such items are extremely difficult to build and frequently even more difficult to key. Consequently, objective tests often test only isolated facts, with a resultant emphasis on verbalism rather than on true understanding.

The essay item has several distinct advantages over the objective item for testing certain types of learning. Because in the essay test each student must create an answer from memory or imagination, essay tests usually elicit a higher level of knowledge than do the run-of-the-mill objective tests. Essay tests can also verify students' abilities to organize, to use materials, to show relationships, to apply knowledge, and to write—abilities that are not easily tested by objective test items. Furthermore, students seem to put more effort into studying for essay tests.

In spite of its virtues, the essay test has innate faults. First, the validity of an essay test is liable to be low because in essay testing, it is very difficult to get an adequate sample of the students' knowledge of what was to be learned. Have you ever taken an essay test in which the questions covered the topics you felt least sure of and never asked a word about the areas in which you felt letter-perfect?

Irrelevancies are likely to enter into the essay item. The validity and reliability of the test are lowered by the tendency of some students to wander off the subject, to shoot the bull, and to speak in vague generalities. The reliability of essay tests is also lowered by the tendency of the scorers to mistake skill in expression, style, glibness, handwriting, neatness, and other irrelevant qualities for knowledge of what was to be learned. Scoring essay test items, when done properly, is a slow, difficult process that greatly reduces the test's usability.

Because essay test items are prone to these faults—low objectivity, low reliability, and low usability—use them with discrimination. They are best-suited for testing a high level of recall or the ability to organize material, for testing students' abilities to apply what has been learned, to evaluate, to show relationships, and to write well. In determining how to evaluate such areas, also consider whether essays instead of essay tests might not be a better measure. When students have time to sit and develop their thoughts in a theme or essay, they usually demonstrate their abilities more accurately than in the rush of an examination. Table 14.1 compares the advantages and limitations of essay and objective tests.

PROBLEM-SITUATION TESTS   Teachers do not always have an opportunity to observe how students act in real situations. To fill this gap, the problem-situation test has been developed. In this device, the examiner confronts the student with a problem situation. The test is to see what the student will do. For example, a common procedure in an auto mechanics course is to give the student a motor that will not run and say, "Find out what the trouble is." Similarly, in a class in which one is attempting to teach students how to conduct a meeting according to Robert's Rules of Order, the teacher may set up a meeting and see how well various members preside.

To set up real-life situations of this type can be quite difficult. It can be very time-consuming to observe every member of a class chairing a meeting, for example. You may do better to devise a paper-and-pencil problem-situation test as a substitute for the real thing. Such a test could consist of questions like this one:

You are senior class president. You have just called to order a special meeting of the class to discuss the class trip, the senior prom, commencement activities, and the class gift. What should the order of business be for this meeting?

In the case of a broken engine, you could devise a problem-situation test with questions like this one:

▓ TABLE 14.1

Comparative Advantages of Objective and Essay Tests
Reprinted with permission of Simon and Schuster, Inc., from Merrill/Prentice Hall text *Measurement and Evaluation in Teaching* by Norman E. Gronlund. © 1985 by Prentice Hall, Inc.

	Objective Test	**Essay Test**
Learning outcomes measured	Is efficient for measuring knowledge of facts. Some types (e.g., multiple-choice) can also measure understanding, thinking skills, and other complex outcomes. Inefficient or inappropriate for measuring ability to select and organize ideas, writing abilities, and some types of problem-solving skills.	Is inefficient for measuring knowledge of facts. Can measure understanding, thinking skills, and other complex learning outcomes (especially useful where originality of response is desired). Appropriate for measuring ability to select and organize ideas, writing abilities, and problem-solving skills requiring originality.
Preparation of questions	A relatively large number of questions is needed for a test. Preparation is difficult and time-consuming.	Only a few questions are needed for a test. Preparation is relatively easy (but more difficult than generally assumed).
Sampling of course content	Provides an extensive sampling of course content because of the large number of questions that can be included in a test.	Sampling of course content is usually limited because of the small number of questions that can be included in a test.
Control of pupil's response	Complete structuring of task limits pupil to type of response called for. Prevents bluffing and avoids influence of writing skill, though selection-type items are subject to guessing.	Freedom to respond in own words enables bluffing and writing skill to influence the score, though guessing is minimized.
Scoring	Objective scoring that is quick, easy, and consistent.	Subjective scoring that is slow, difficult, and inconsistent.
Influence on learning	Usually encourages pupil to develop a comprehensive knowledge of specific facts and the ability to make fine discriminations among them. Can encourage the development of understanding, thinking skills, and other complex outcomes if properly constructed.	Encourages pupils to concentrate on larger units of subject matter, with special emphasis on the ability to organize, integrate, and express ideas effectively. May encourage poor writing habits if time pressure is a factor (it almost always is).
Reliability	High reliability is possible and is typically obtained with well-constructed tests.	Reliability is typically low, primarily because of inconsistent scoring.

A farmer's tractor will not start. What steps would you take to find out what the problem is with the motor?

The items used in a problem-situation test may be either the essay or objective type. Usually, however, some type of free recall item is better than an item that suggests possible solutions to the problem.

Stop and Reflect

What criteria would you use in deciding whether to use an essay or objective test for a specific unit?

What advantages does the use of performance testing have over the ordinary essay or objective test?

Objective tests are not always objective. Why not? Why might a truly objective test in composition be a bad test?

Can you think of any instance in which you should use a speed test in a course you might teach? How can you eliminate the chance for a power test to accidentally become a speed test?

Most of the tests you use in your classes should be mastery or diagnostic. Why? When might you use survey tests?

In another section we spoke of summative and formative evaluations. Into which of these categories would you ordinarily place mastery tests, diagnostic tests, survey tests, and criterion-referenced tests?

Building Classroom Tests

General Procedures for Test Construction

When you build a test, follow these general procedures:

1. Determine what the specific instructional objectives of the unit are going to be. Define these objectives as specific student behaviors.
2. Outline the subject content to be included.
3. Draw up an evaluation plan that shows the objectives and the number or weight of test items (or other measuring devices) to be given to each area (as in Figure 14.1). As you build your evaluation plan, remember that some objectives are best served by performance tests, some by essay tests, some by objective tests, some by observation, and some by samples of work and the like. In your evaluation plan, try to match the objectives with the most suitable types of testing devices. Notice that steps 1, 2, and 3 of this procedure should be completed before you begin teaching the unit. The evaluation plan should influence instruction as well as evaluation.
4. Build the test items in accordance with the table of specifications.
   a. Select the test items.
   b. Arrange the items.
   c. Write the directions.
   d. Publish the test.

SOME RULES FOR TEST BUILDING   As you prepare the test and test items, bear in mind the following rules for test design:

1. Test all teaching objectives in proportion to their importance. If some objectives are overstressed, understressed, or omitted, the test will not be valid.
2. In survey tests, include both items easy enough for the lowest achievers and items difficult enough to challenge the highest achievers. Doing so will give you the needed data to determine which students have done well and which poorly—an aid when it comes to assigning marks. In mastery tests, it is not necessary to include difficult items—include only those items that show

whether the student has reached the standard. In either case, put some easy items at the beginning of the test so that students will not become disheartened and give up.

3. Use only a few types of items. Too many different kinds of items tend to confuse the students and result in accidental errors. Especially do not use both objective and essay items in the same test, which not only confuses students but increases the possibility that students will not do well because of misjudging the time.

4. Place all items of the same type together so as not to confuse the students.

5. Arrange the items from the easiest to the most difficult to encourage low-achieving students to keep on and not become discouraged.

6. Make directions, format, and wording crystal clear. This is no time for trick questions or obscurity. A test should not be a joke or a puzzle. Tricky, obscure questions spoil the test's reliability.

7. To be sure each test item is valid, fit it to the objective it is testing. If it does not call for the type of behavior that the objective calls for, it is not adequate. Because it is easier to write memory questions than to write questions calling for higher mental processes, almost everyone overuses memory questions. Be on your guard. *If your objectives call for students to use higher mental processes, use test items that call for the higher mental processes.*

8. Be sure that the test provides the students with all the information and material they need to complete each item. Every time a person has to ask for information, clarification, or materials, your test becomes less reliable.

9. Be sure to write the items clearly and simply in language the students can read easily. If the reading level is too high, the test results will be worthless.

10. Try to avoid allowing the score to be affected by such irrelevancies as students' writing ability, glibness, reading skill, and quickness. Everyone should have a chance to do well on the test. The only criterion for success on the test should be how well the students have learned the things they were supposed to have learned. Construct the test items so that it is easy for students to demonstrate what they have learned.

11. Aim several test items at each objective; otherwise, a chance error may give you a false assessment of a student's achievement of that objective.

12. Try to make the test a learning exercise. Write the items so that they "contribute to improved teaching-learning practice."(7)

Stop and Reflect

Of what value are the objectives of a lesson or unit when you are devising a test?
Why is it sometimes stated that there is no such thing as an objective test?
In constructing a teacher-built test, what procedure would you follow? Outline what you would do step by step.

Building an Objective Test

The procedures outlined for constructing tests in general also apply specifically to building objective tests. Although further discussion of such matters as arranging items, writing directions for the test, deciding the length of the test, and reproducing the test would be redundant, there are so many kinds of objective test items that it is important to consider the uses, merits, demerits, and writing of each of the various types. Many teachers do not use the most productive types of objective test items. With a little study and practice, you should be able to become familiar with, and relatively expert in, writing the more sophisticated objective test items.

ALTERNATIVE-RESPONSE ITEMS   Perhaps the most familiar type of objective test item is the alternative-response item, in which the student has a choice between two possible responses—for example, true-false or yes-no. Some examples follow:

Circle (or underline) the correct answer.

True-False	1. Milton was a sense realist.
Right-Wrong	2. Reliability is the degree to which the test agrees with itself.
Yes-No	3. Most early scientific discoveries were made by university professors.
Were-Were not	4. Girls _____ allowed to attend school beyond elementary level in Colonial New England.
Forward-Rearward	5. The clutch lever of the Bell and Howell projector must be in the _____ position before it will run.

This type of item can be found in many forms. An interesting variation is the following, in which students must identify synonymous words:

For the following, write *S* in the space provided if the words are essentially the same; write *D* if they are different.

(   )   1. reliability-consistency
(   )   2. scoring-grading
(   )   3. measure-evaluate
(   )   4. norm average

The most common alternative-response item is the true-false item. True-false items have had great popularity. Although they can be useful to find if students can discriminate fact from opinion, cause from effect, valid generalizations from invalid ones, or cases in which there is a clear dichotomy, as a rule multiple-choice items are preferable.

Although true-false items seem to be easy to write, this ease is quite illusory. To make true-false items free from ambiguity or irrelevant clues is really difficult, for most statements are neither true nor false but "iffy." Taking precautions such as the following may help you produce successful true-false tests.

- Avoid broad, general statements. (They are too difficult to key true or false.)
- Avoid trivia. (Trivia obscure the major ideas.)
- Avoid negative statements. (They confuse students.)
- Limit each true-false item to only one central idea. (More than one idea confuses the issue; you cannot tell to which idea a student was responding.)
- Keep each item brief but clear.
- Avoid specific citations.
- Avoid specific determiners.
- Avoid qualifications. (The statement should be true or false without qualification.)
- Make the test reasonably long. (Short true-false tests may be unreliable.)
- Avoid such words as *usual* and *always*. (They give away the answer.)

▓ Try to have about a 50-50, or at least 60-40, percent ratio of true and false statements. A test should never be made up entirely of true or false statements.

▓ Avoid any pattern of true-false responses. Scatter the true and false items haphazardly throughout the test.

CHECKLIST ITEMS   Checklist items are much like alternative-response items. Usually tests that include these items consist of fairly long lists from which the pupil checks the items that apply. In the following example the list includes only 3 items, but it might well consist of 10.

From the following list, check the duties of the local Board of Education:

_____ 1. Hire teachers.
_____ 2. Adopt school budget.
_____ 3. Select superintendent.
_____ 4. (Etc.)

MATCHING ITEMS   Another common type of objective test is the matching test. Again we find several variations of the basic form, which usually consists of two unequal columns of items to be matched, as in the following example:

On the line to the left of each score listed in column I, write the letter from column II of the phrase or statement that accurately describes in whole or in part that type of score. Each statement in column II may be used once, more than once, or not at all.

I	II
_____ 1. z score	a. Has a mean of 50 and a standard deviation of 10.
_____ 2. T score	
_____ 3. Stanine score	b. Its units are equal to one half a standard deviation.
_____ 4. Percentile score	
_____ 5. Deviation IQ score	c. Is computed by a ratio formula.
	d. Gives scores in plus or minus qualities.
	e. Gives scores in fractions.
	f. Has a mean of 100.
	g. Has a median of 50.

Teachers sometimes overuse matching items because they seem to be easy to write, but again, appearances can be deceiving. To make good matching items, be sure that the content of the stimuli (left-hand column) is homogeneous and that there are several plausible responses for each stimulus. Otherwise, students can guess the correct answers by elimination. The column should not be too long, however. Five to eight stimuli and a few more responses are quite sufficient. To cut down on guessing by elimination, always use more responses than stimuli and tell students that they may use each response once, more than once, or not at all. Also clearly state what the basis for matching is to be. It is particularly important that both lists appear on the same page. Students are likely to make accidental errors if they have to turn the page back and forth to search for correct answers.

Matching items have only limited usefulness; they can be used for little more than measuring rote memorization, facts, and simple associations. For most purposes, multiple-choice items are preferable.

MULTIPLE-CHOICE ITEMS   Multiple-choice items have the advantage of being relatively free from guessing if four or more alternative responses are used and if reasonable care is used in picking the incorrect responses. However, if these distractors (i.e., incorrect answers) do not seem reasonable, they can easily give the answer away. Following are two examples of multiple-choice questions.

Select the best answer and write its letter in the space in the margin.

    _____ The U.S. Secretary of Education is
        a. Elected by the people.
        b. Elected by the Senate.
        c. Appointed by the President with the approval of the Senate.
        d. Elected by the House of Representatives.

Underline or circle the correct answer.

    Which was the first college established:
    a. Brown
    b. Columbia
    c. Harvard
    d. Princeton
    e. Yale

The multiple-choice test question is probably the most versatile type of objective test item in your repertoire. You can use it to measure both simple memory as well as many of the complex higher mental processes, although it is difficult to write multiple-choice items that measure problem-solving ability. As a general rule, multiple-choice items that call for best answers are more useful for measuring higher learnings than those that call for correct answers. The latter are most useful for measuring students' knowledge of facts.

Multiple-choice items are relatively easy to write if you keep the following guidelines in mind:

1. Write the stem of the multiple-choice question as a direct question. Then, if there seems to be some reason for doing so, you can change it to an incomplete statement. Most often, however, a direct question plus a list of alternative answers makes the best multiple-choice item. The best way to make up a list of alternatives is to use the stem as a short-answer item and then pick distractors from the incorrect answers.
2. Be sure the items are clearly written. Beware of overly ornate language and heavy vocabulary loads.
3. Be sure that while all the alternatives seem plausible, there is one, and only one, correct response. All responses should be independent and mutually exclusive.
4. Be sure that the stem presents a clear, meaningful central problem. Beware of irrelevancies and window dressing.
5. Include in the stem as much of the item as possible. Insofar as possible the stem should include all words that otherwise would be repeated in the alternatives.
6. Avoid use of the negative except when it is essential. It is seldom important for students to know what was the "least important," the "poorest reason," or the "principle that does not apply." Besides, negatives tend to confuse students. Particularly beware of double negatives.
7. Be sure that the item is grammatically correct and free from rote verbal associations and grammatical inconsistencies. Also be sure that correct responses are not longer (or shorter) than the other alternatives, and beware of other extraneous clues. As far as possible, list alternatives in random, numerical, or alphabetical order.
8. Avoid using "none of the above" or "all of the above" as an alternative (if for no other reason than it seems that you have run out of ideas).

CATEGORY OR IDENTIFICATION ITEMS   A variation of the multiple-choice item that differs in substance as well as form is the category or identification item, which is often used with long lists. For example:

Mark the items that result from the action of the sympathetic nervous system, *S*; those that result from the action of the parasympathetic nervous system, *P*; if neither of these systems controls an item, mark it *X*.

(   ) 1. Increases heartbeat
(   ) 2. Dilates pupils of eyes
(   ) 3. Increases sweating
(   ) 4. Checks flow of saliva
(   ) 5. (Etc.)

ORGANIZATION AND EVALUATION ITEMS   Skillfully made organization and evaluation items can test a high level of learning as well as the ability to use knowledge. Items that require students to organize are especially useful in testing higher learning. The following item, in which the students are asked to place a list of events in chronological sequence, requires more than mere verbalization on the part of the student. In writing such items, beware of making the list too long, because then the item becomes a puzzle rather than a test item and may cause students to make accidental mistakes.

Place the following in chronological order by numbering the first event 1, the second event 2, and so on.

_____ The Declaration of Independence
_____ The Articles of Confederation
_____ The Battle of Lexington
_____ Washington's assumption of command of the Continental Army

Items that ask students to evaluate and rate practices can not only test knowledge, but also can test the ability to draw fine distinctions. Questions of this sort are excellent for getting at the higher mental processes.

Rate the following techniques according to the following scheme: *G*, good; *D*, doubtful; *X*, poor. Place your responses in the parenthesis.

(   ) a. Encouraging students by accepting, at least tentatively, all answers to oral questions that can be used at all.
(   ) b. Scolding students whenever they are unable to answer oral questions. And so on.

PERFORMANCE AND PROBLEM-SITUATION TEST ITEMS   Situation items also demand that students be able to use their knowledge. In the following example, students must know how to do an item analysis in order to answer correctly.

What does the following item analysis tell you about the items in the test? Put your answers in the spaces below.

Students	Items						Total Score
	1	2	3	4	5	6	
John	+	0	0	+	0	+	111
Mary	+	+	0	+	0	+	109
Susan	+	+	0	+	0	0	100
Mike	+	+	0	+	0	+	96
Don	+	0	+	+	0	+	94

Harry	+	0	0	+	0	0	60
George	+	0	+	0	0	+	58
Anne	+	0	+	+	0	0	57
Tom	+	0	+	0	0	0	42
Sally	+	0	+	0	0	0	40

1. Item 1 _____

2. Item 2 _____

3. Item 3 _____

4. Item 4 _____

5. Item 5 _____

6. Item 6 _____

INTERPRETIVE ITEMS Interpretive items consist of an introductory statement and a series of questions that ask the student to interpret the data in the introductory presentation. The introductory material may be presented by a picture, graph, chart, formula, statistical table, film, recording, or an expository statement. The individual test items are ordinarily multiple-choice or alternative-response items. Short-answer items are sometimes used, but they are harder to key and score. The items should require analysis or interpretation of the introductory material. This type of item, like all others that test higher learnings, is difficult to construct. Make the introductory material brief and clear and suitable for interpretation or analysis. You will usually have to revise it several times before it is satisfactory.

The following is an example of a free-response interpretive item.

The two pie graphs presented here show the percentage of the world's gold possessed by various countries in December 1913 and June 1931. Study the graphs and then answer the questions in the places provided.

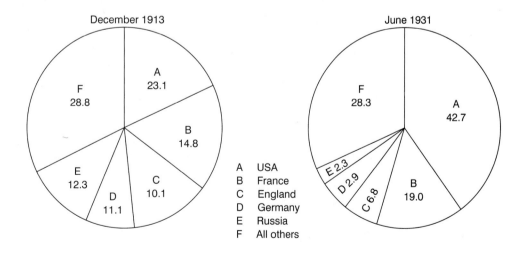

1. Which of the countries possessed the most gold in 1913?

_____

2. Which European country had the biggest increase in gold supply between 1913 and 1931?

_____

3. Which of the countries listed had the smallest supply in 1931?

_____

4. What two countries held 60 percent of the world's gold supply in 1931?

_____

5. In what year was the gold more equally distributed?

_____

The item could be turned into several multiple-choice interpretation items quite easily, as shown in the following examples.

Which of the countries listed possessed the most gold in 1913?
a. England
b. France
c. Germany
d. Russia

Which European country had the largest increase in gold supply between 1913 and 1931?
a. England
b. France
c. Germany
d. Russia

FREE-RESPONSE ITEMS   Free-response items can be either completion items (which call for the completion of an incomplete statement) or short-answer items. Strictly speaking, these items are not objective items. Because they are free-response items, their answers may be open to considerable interpretation and their scoring quite subjective. In fact, short-answer items can be considerably closer to being short-essay items than they are to being objective items. Both completion and short-answer items usually appear in tests that are basically of the objective type. However, because they provide the student with no suggested responses, they can usually test a higher level of learning than truly objective items can.

COMPLETION ITEMS   The most common representative of this type of item in objective tests is the completion item, in which the student merely places the correct answer in the blank provided, as in the following example.

Fill in the blanks:
1. The first permanent secondary school in this country was founded by

_____

2. The Committee of Ten recommended that the elementary schools be limited to grades

_____

To make scoring easier, teachers often require that the answers to the completion question be placed in an answer column.

Place the answers in the blanks provided in the margin.

_____ 1. The student body of the average American high school numbers approximately _____ pupils per school.
_____ 2. A stanine is equal to _____ of a standard deviation.

When using completion items, be wary of ambiguous questions and unexpected correct responses. Good completion items that call for more than isolated, pin-pointed facts are difficult to build. To avoid these faults, try to word the item so that only one answer can be correct and so that the students know just what type of answer is expected. To be sure that the students can decipher the item, never allow more than one or two blanks in any one completion item. Also make sure that blanks represent only key words and that they are placed near the end of the sentence so that the students will not have to waste time figuring out what is being asked. The best procedure for writing completion items is to write the item as a short-answer question and then turn it into a completion item if it seems desirable.

Sometimes teachers are tempted to use phrases and sentences copied from the book as completion items. This practice is undesirable. It encourages rote learning and usually results in items that are hard to key because of unexpected correct answers.

SHORT-ANSWER ITEMS   Short-answer questions are exactly what the name implies—questions that can be answered in a word or phrase. They are extremely useful, but, as with completion questions, it is difficult to write the items so that they rule out undesirable responses. When writing short-answer items, be especially careful that each student knows what is expected. Indicate in the directions, or in the wording of the item, how long and how detailed the answer should be. As in the completion item, the wording should make only one correct answer possible. The following are examples of short-answer test items:

Each of the following can be answered by a single word or phrase. Place the answer to each of the following questions in the space provided.

_____ 1. In an algebra test a boy scored exactly one standard deviation below the mean. What is his T score?
_____ 2. What do Crow and Crow consider to be the best size for a local school board?

Building an Essay Test

Although designing an essay test is much like designing an objective test, because of the time factor the problem of adequate sampling becomes extremely important. As a rule, use many short essay items rather than a few long ones.

Here are some other rules to keep in mind when constructing essay tests:

1. Limit the questions to something the student can answer adequately in the allotted time and be sure each question is worded so that the student real-izes these limits.
2. Be sure the sample is adequate and that the test will actually show how well the students have acquired the learning products that were the goals.
3. Be sure each question tests specific products and that the information nec-essary for the correct answer was included in the course.
4. Be specific. Be sure each question indicates just what the student is to write about. To do this, it may be necessary to write several sentences explaining the question. Avoid questions that ask students to "discuss" something. These kinds of questions are too vague and general.
5. Develop a sample answer for each item before giving the test.
6. Decide what the standards are for scoring the answers before you commit yourself to any question.
7. Be clear.

Stop and Reflect

For what may the various types of objective test items be best used? Critique the items used as illustrations. In what ways might they be improved?

What are the characteristics of a good objective test item? A good essay test item?

Building Criterion-Referenced Tests

The basic difference between criterion-referenced and other tests is that in criterion-referenced tests (e.g., diagnostic and mastery tests), it is most important that the test items clearly measure the degree to which the objectives have been achieved. This requirement means that each objective must be clearly stated, preferably in terms of terminal behavior. It also means that the criterion test must be narrowed in scope so that it can measure the achievement accurately. Survey tests give general information; criterion-referenced tests should be quite specific.

Briefly, the basic procedures for building criterion-referenced tests are as follows:

1. Define the specific objectives in detail as criterion-referenced behavioral objectives. Be sure to include in the objectives the standard that will be considered acceptable.
2. Build test items that will show whether or not these standards have been attained.
   a. Be sure each objective is tested in proportion to its importance. An evaluation plan made in advance will help you give the test the proper balance.
   b. Have several items for each objective.
   c. Use items that show whether the students can actually perform the required behavior.
3. Arrange the items into a test.

Assessing Attitudes, Ideals, and Appreciations

To test attitudes, ideals, and appreciations by means of a paper-and-pencil test is difficult. Students are likely to give the answer you want rather than what they really believe. For instance, one of the attitudes that might be an objective in a unit is: "In international affairs, as well as private affairs, one should deal justly with all." If, to test this attitude, you ask, "Should the United States respect the rights of other nations?", most students would answer "Yes," because they think that is the answer you expect. However, if you pose for discussion a problem in which the United States can gain an advantage by violating the rights of a small nation, you may learn individuals' true attitudes by observing their reactions to the problem. Other methods of getting at attitudes are observation, rating scales, checklists, questionnaires, and analysis of papers.

Administering and Scoring Teacher-Built Tests

Giving the Test

Both essay and objective tests must be administered carefully. Once the test and key have been prepared, the next thing to do is to check the test to be sure it contains no errors. Little slips in typing may cause items to turn out quite differently from what was intended. Also note any directions that may be unclear and any items that need to be explained. A good way to spot unclear items and directions is to ask another teacher to read the test critically.

If possible, correct any errors or obscurities before you take the test to class. Announcing and correcting errors in class take valuable time away from the test itself, and there is often someone who misses the correction and is thus penalized. Because correcting the test before class is not always possible, you may have to explain items and procedures to the class orally. If so, do so before the test begins. In addition, write the explanation or correction on the chalkboard so that students can refer to it as the test progresses and thus will not be penalized if they forget or miss the announcement. Interrupting the test to make announcements is a poor practice, because it breaks up the students' train of thought.

To avoid distracting students once the test has started, be sure that all the students have everything they need before the test begins. It is important for students to check to see that they have a good copy of the complete test. Even the most carefully prepared test may have poorly photocopied, blank, or missing pages. Have extra copies on hand to substitute for defective ones. If this checking is completed before the test starts, it will eliminate confusion and interruptions during the test itself. Confusion and delay may also be minimized by setting up a routine for distributing and collecting the tests.

The physical condition of the classroom makes a difference in the test situation. Comfortable students can do their best work; uncomfortable students often cannot. Pay attention to the light, heat, and ventilation, and if possible, prevent any noises, interruptions, or other distractions. Common practice when giving standardized tests is to post a notice on the door: "Testing; Please do not disturb." There is no reason such a practice should not be used for teacher-built achievement tests as well. Many teachers are guilty of carrying on conversations with students or other teachers during a test. Some leave the classroom doors open while other classes are moving in the corridors. Such disturbances may distract students and reduce the reliability of the test.

Scoring the Essay Test

After you have given the test, it must be scored. Ordinarily, the test should be scored immediately. Otherwise, it becomes difficult to capitalize on the test's motivational and diagnostic aspects.

Essay tests are notoriously hard to score. To score them objectively is almost impossible; however, try to score them as objectively as you can. This is no easy task, but the following procedure can somewhat reduce the difficulty:

1. Before giving the test, answer each question yourself. (*Sometimes you will not want to use the item after you try to answer it!*) Note all the acceptable points and the relative importance of each. If you wish, give each point a numerical value or weight. This trial answer is your scoring key.
2. After you have given the test, read the first essay question in each of the papers and assign scores on the basis of the key. If a student has mentioned an acceptable point not in the key, add the point to the key and reread the papers already scored to be sure that everyone gets credit for the point.
3. After completing the first question in all the papers, repeat the process with the second question. It is much easier to read one question in all the papers at once because you can concentrate on that one question.

Scoring the Objective Test

The objective test is considerably easier to score than is the essay test, because the questions lend themselves to easy automatic scoring. In fact, scoring such questions is often so automatic that they can be scored more profitably by a clerk, student, or machine than by the teacher.

USING A KEY   As in the essay test, the key should be made before the test is given. A good method is to indicate the acceptable answers as the test is being made. Then let the test sit for a day or so, after which you should retest yourself to see whether you still believe that the answers are acceptable. If they are, you are ready to finalize the key. One of the easiest methods of making a key, if the test is arranged so that the responses are in a column, is simply to take an extra copy of the test and fill in all the responses correctly. During the scoring, you can place the key against the test and compare the answers. Often, it is easier to cut off the text of the test so that the key will be a strip that you can lay along either side of the answers on the test you are scoring. This makes it easier to correct answers listed on the left side of the page if you are right-handed. Some teachers find it easier to score by simply checking all correct items, that is, items that agree with the key. Others prefer to mark the wrong answers. If you intend to correct for guessing, you must indicate both right and wrong items. An example follows:

Key	Student Answer	Test
a	a	John Smith was: (a) an explorer, (b) a merchant, (c) an admiral, (d) a general.
c	a	Pocahontas married: (a) John Smith, (b) Myles Standish, (c) John Rolfe, (d) John Winthrop.

USING A MASK   Another common type of key is the mask. Masks are stiff pieces of paper or cardboard that, when placed over the test, cover up all the incorrect responses and allow only the correct responses to appear. You can easily make masks. Just cover the test with a blank paper and then make holes in the mask where the correct answer should appear. With this type of key, all the scorer needs to do is to mark correct all answers that show through the mask. For example:

Test	
1. a b c d	John Smith was (a) an explorer, (b) a merchant, (c) an admiral, (d) a general.
2. a b c d	Pocahontas married (a) John Smith, (b) Myles Standish, (c) John Rolfe, (d) John Winthrop.

Mask
1. ○
2.   ○

CORRECTING FOR GUESSING   The goal of testing is to determine students' progress toward desired learning products, so you should not conduct a guessing contest. When items have fewer than four responses, students can guess the answers relatively easily. Consequently, some teachers correct for guessing when scoring items with fewer than four responses. This correction is easily done. The formula is

$$S = R - \frac{W}{C-1}$$

where S is the corrected score, R is the number of correct responses, W is the number of incorrect responses, and C the number of choices provided for each item. Substituting in the formula, we find that for alternate-answer items the formula becomes Rights minus Wrongs.

$$S = R - \frac{W}{(2-1)} \text{ or } S = R - W$$

For items having three choices, the formula becomes Rights minus ½ Wrongs.

$$S = R - \frac{W}{(3-1)} \text{ or } S = R - \frac{W}{2}$$

These are the only two instances in which the formula is used.

Many teachers and writers in the field of measurement prefer not to use the correction formula at all. They feel that the correction is not worth the trouble because it seldom changes the relative rating of the students. Besides, students do not understand it very well and do not like it. Students' attitudes may also introduce additional errors in measurement.

The best answer to the problem is to use items with at least four choices as much as possible. If it is necessary or advisable to use alternate-answer questions, make the test long enough to accommodate several items directed at each learning product, which will tend to compensate for guessing without you having to use the formula during scoring.

Evaluating Teacher-Built Tests

You can do much of the evaluation of a test before you give it. The most important criterion of a test's worth is its validity. Does it test what it is supposed to test? The easiest and best way to check the validity of a teacher-built achievement test is by inspection. Do the items test the goals of the course? Does the test cover the various goals in proper proportion? Other questions to ask yourself are: Is the test free from catch questions and ambiguous items? Is the physical format correct? Are questions of the same type grouped together? Are the test items arranged from easy to difficult? Is the test free from format blunders such as matching items that run over onto the next page? In other words, is it valid, reliable, objective, and usable?

After you have given the test, you can evaluate it more fully by checking such items as the following:

1. Length
2. Directions
3. Item discrimination
4. Difficulty of items
5. Clearness
6. Balance.

Analyzing Test Items

An analysis of the test items can be helpful in evaluating a test. The procedure for such an analysis is quite simple. On a sheet of graph paper, list the students' names in a column on the left and then list items of the test in the heading. We are interested only in the upper and lower quarters, but it is best to list all the students in rank order because the chart can also be used for diagnosis. By using plus (+) and minus (-) signs, indicate whether each student answered each of the items correctly or incorrectly, as shown in the following chart.

Upper Quarter

	1	2	3	4	5	6	7	and so on
Jerry	+	+	+	-	-	+	-	
John	+	+	+	+	-	+	-	
Sally	-	-	+	+	-	+	-	

Lower Quarter

	1	2	3	4	5	6	7	
Mike	+	-	-	-	-	+	-	
Susy	+	-	+	-	-	-	+	
Tom	-	-	-	+	-	-	+	
George	+	-	-	+	-	-	+	

By studying this chart, you can learn how well the items discriminated and how difficult they were. Such a chart also gives clues to items that are not well-written, are ambiguous, or were not learned.

An achievement test of the survey type should have some items that few students can answer and some that almost everyone can answer. The first are needed to find out who the higher achievers are; the second, to encourage the low achievers. Ordinarily, most items should be answered correctly by about half the students. An item that is answered correctly by fewer than 20 percent of the students may well be a bad item. Examine it to see if it is too difficult, if it tests any of the objectives, if it is pertinent to the course, or if it is poorly written. If the item is answered correctly by more than 80 percent of the students, however, check to see if it is too easy or if the wording gives the answer away. These criteria hold for all tests in which the scores of students are compared with one another, but should not be used for mastery tests and diagnostic tests, as we shall see.

By comparing the answers of students in the upper quarter with those of the students in the lower quarter, you can find other things that help to evaluate the items. If the upper quarter of the students answer an item correctly and the lower quarter of the students answer it incorrectly, the item discriminates between them. If students in the upper quarter and those in the lower quarter answer the question equally well, it does not discriminate. If an item is answered correctly more frequently by the lower-quarter students than the upper-quarter students, something is very wrong indeed. Perhaps the key is wrong, or perhaps the item needs to be rewritten.

Analysis of Criterion-Referenced Tests

Much of what we have just discussed does not really apply to mastery and diagnostic tests. Such tests should be criterion-referenced. If they are, the items will tell whether individual students know or can do what they were supposed to have learned. Therefore, there is no need to spread the scores. If the unit has been well-taught, it is quite possible that 80 percent of the students will get all the items right. Thus, in a criterion-referenced test, an item that 80 percent of the students get right may indicate not that an item is too easy, but that the criterion has been achieved. We thus see that the discrimination and difficulty factors are largely irrelevant for this type of test. The touchstone in these tests is the objective. If the items show whether the objective has been attained, they are good items. For instance, in one college one of the physical education requirements is to demonstrate the ability to swim two lengths of the pool. The test for this requirement is for the students to swim the length of the pool and back. Either they can do it or they cannot. How well they swim, how fast they swim, and how much farther they can swim are all irrelevant.

Some questions to ask yourself when checking on one of your criterion-referenced tests are the following:

1. Are there at least two items aimed at each teaching objective, without exception?
2. Is each item suitable to the objective at which it is pointed—that is, does it require students to meet the action and performance standards called for by the objective?
3. Is every item pointed at an objective?
4. Is the test free from giveaway items, catch questions, poor wording, ambiguity, and similar faults that all types of tests are likely to have?
5. Do students who get one of the items aimed at an objective also get the others? In other words, are the results of the items consistent?
6. Are there any items consistently missed by the better students?
7. Is each item clearly written at a suitable reading level and free from words and expressions students may not understand?
8. Is the test free from scoring difficulties? If several people score the same test, do they all come out with the same score?
9. Do students who do well in class also do well on the test?
10. Is the test usable? Is it relatively easy to administer? To score? To take?

Diagnostic Item Analysis

After you have given and scored the test, what does it tell you? If you have aimed the test items at specific objectives, an analysis of the items can give you the necessary information fairly easily. All you need to do is to see how well each student responded to the items designed to test the various objectives. Table 14.2 is an example of an item analysis of this sort.

A quick look at this table shows us that none of the students seems to have attained the second objective very well. It also seems that although students D and K have mastered the third objective quite well, neither of them has done well with the first or second objective. Pupil H, on the other hand, does not seem to have done well on any of the three objectives. Obviously, you would do well to give addi-

TABLE 14.2
An Item Analysis

Item		A	B	C	D	E	F	G	H	I	J	K
Objective I	1	✓	✓	✓		✓	✓	✓	✓	✓	✓	✓
	2	✓	✓	✓		✓				✓		
	3	✓		✓				✓				
	4	✓	✓	✓		✓	✓	✓			✓	
Objective II	5											
	6	✓			✓							✓
	7											
	8						✓					
Objective III	9	✓	✓	✓	✓		✓	✓		✓	✓	✓
	10	✓		✓	✓	✓		✓		✓	✓	✓
	11		✓	✓	✓			✓				
	12	✓	✓	✓	✓	✓	✓	✓		✓		✓

tional instruction to the entire class on objective 2, and individual or small-group instruction to certain students in the other areas.

▦▦▦ Standardized Tests, Scales, and Inventories

In general, there are three basic types of standardized tests: achievement tests, personality and character tests, and aptitude and intelligence tests. They differ from teacher-built tests in that they are carefully built to provide a common unit of measurement, just as the yardstick provides a common measure for length. The procedures for administering, scoring, and interpreting these tests have been standardized so that the results may be compared all over the country. Standardized scores make these tests especially useful for diagnosis and the evaluation of a particular program, but they are not so useful for judging an individual's progress.

Kinds of Standardized Tests

The standardized *achievement test* comes in two basic types: (1) that which shows strengths and weaknesses of students as a basis for diagnosis, and (2) that which shows the status of individual students as compared with boys and girls throughout the nation. Standardized tests are useful for these purposes, but they are not valuable for determining achievement in any particular course or for evaluating the effectiveness of any particular teacher's teaching. In the first place, they rarely measure exactly what was taught in the course. Moreover, if a course or course sequence differs markedly in content from the courses in the schools that were used for standardizing the test, the test will not measure the true achievement of the students or report accurately how their achievement compares with that of other students. Second, because standardized tests are liable to emphasize facts rather than understandings, abilities, attitudes, and skills, they frequently fail to indicate achievement in the most important aspects of student learning. In spite of these shortcomings, they can be helpful tools for diagnosing academic abilities and the effectiveness of school programs.

Personality and character tests are also important tools for the teacher. They can be a source of vivid insights in the diagnostic process. One of the most effective is the *problem inventory*, which is intended to provide a means for identifying the personal problems of individual students. Similarly, information concerning students' aptitudes, vocational leanings, attitudes, interests and the like may be gleaned from *inventories, scales, and tests* designed for these purposes. Inventories, tests, and scales of these sorts are ordinarily given and interpreted by guidance personnel who make the results available to the teachers. Not only is the administering of such instruments usually a sensitive task, but interpreting their results often requires professional skills that few beginning teachers have mastered. Nevertheless, they can give you considerable guidance as you lay out your strategies for teaching individual students. The data gathered by such instruments are usually included in the students' cumulative records.

Be wary of overenthusiastically accepting information gathered by instruments designed to find students' aptitudes and other potentials. Never take scores of tests and other instruments at face value; too many uncontrolled and uncontrollable variables may have influenced the score. For instance, the IQ test can be a useful tool, but it can also be a delusion; it is not an infallible indicator of an individual's ability to learn. Good intellectual potential may be hidden by low IQ scores. Poor reading ability, lack of motivation, cultural differences, language problems, poor teaching in earlier grades, poor test conditions, and poorly designed intelligence tests are all factors that may result in false IQs. In spite of efforts to avoid injustices, some intelligence tests are notorious in their unfairness to persons whose culture or class is in the minority. In judging the potential of any youngster, never depend on any one criterion—particularly a single test score.

Selecting a Standardized Test

Select standardized tests with care. There are many of them. Some are excellent, others are not. In searching for a suitable test, you can receive considerable help from such sources as curriculum laboratories and test files maintained by local and state departments of education and by colleges and universities. Both the text and appendices of textbooks on tests and measurements often contain lists and critiques of tests. Catalogs of the various test publishing houses tell what they have to offer. Critical analyses may be found in such works as *The Mental Measurement Yearbooks*.(8) New tests are frequently listed in such journals as the *Education Index, Psychological Abstracts, Review of Educational Research,* and *Educational and Psychological Measurement*. Textbooks in specific methods courses often discuss standardized achievement tests in the field with which they are concerned.

These references usually provide information about the test's content, validity, reliability, and usability. Using these references will help you to eliminate the instruments that are patently not appropriate for your purposes and will narrow down the number that you should examine most carefully when making your final selection.

In your final selection, carefully consult sample copies of the test and its manual. (View any test that lacks a manual with particular caution.) The first thing to check for is the validity of the test. Is it designed to do what you wish it to do? If it is an achievement test, does it fit in with the philosophy and objectives of the school and courses concerned? How was the validity established? From what type of population were the norms derived? If the population was greatly different from the type of class you have, the test will not be valid for your group. How were the items selected? Does a careful, logical, and psychological analysis of the test and its manual indicate that the items measure what they purport to measure?

If the test is valid, then go on to check its reliability and usability. Bear in mind that a test with a reliability coefficient of less than 70 is probably a bad risk, and that ease in administering, scoring, and interpreting can lighten what is at best a difficult job.

Administering a Standardized Test

Any standardized test worth its salt gives clear, detailed directions for administering it. Follow these directions exactly. Failure to do so may give false scores. As much as possible, treat standardized tests as routine classroom activities. Making a great to-do about taking a standardized test may cause tension and skew the test results. Particularly reprehensible is coaching students for the test. A standardized test is a sampling. If students are coached on the sample, the test will be much in error and it will be impossible to find out what the test might have told you. The only sure way to give a test a chance to do what you wish it to do is to administer it exactly as the manual prescribes.

Stop and Reflect

If you were to select a standardized test to measure the achievement of students in one of your classes, how would you go about it?

What three qualities would you have to check?

Where does cost appear in your answer?

How would you find out if a standardized achievement test was valid in your situation?
In what ways might poor administering of a standardized test upset the test results?

Traditionally, the standardized test scores reported have been normalized. Such normalized standardized test scores give only a general impression of an individual student's standing in relation to the group. They are not useful for determining to what degree persons have achieved individual goals or attained specific skills or knowledge. For instance, generally a normalized standardized test score may indicate how well a student is progressing in an area, but not indicate what *specific* skills or knowledge the student has or has not learned in that area. Criterion-referenced tests are more useful for determining exactly what a student has or has not learned.

TEST NORMS   Basically, normalized standardized tests provide norms that permit the comparison of one group with another group, and the comparison of individuals with the group as a whole. Norms should not be confused with standards. A *standard* is a level of ability or achievement required for some purpose. A norm is quite a different thing. It is an *average*. A ninth-grade norm, for instance, is the average, or mean, score of the sampling of ninth graders on whom the test was standardized. Similarly, a grade norm of 9.5 is the average score of students halfway through the ninth grade. In short, a grade norm is the point at which the average score of all students at that grade level fall. Likewise, an age norm is the theoretical average score of all the students of that age. Thus, any student who is reading at the tenth-grade level is reading as well as the average tenth-grader. Similarly, a student who scores at the 12-year-old norm is performing as well as the average 12-year-old. Without further information, one cannot tell whether these scores are good or bad.(9)

Norms are useful in that they provide a basis for comparing students from different school systems. They are valuable in evaluating school programs, and they can also tell the approximate standing of students with respect to their peers. Thus, they can be useful in developing individual programs for students and in providing for individual differences. For instance, if you find that an eighth-grade girl seems to have ability at the tenth-grade level, you should investigate the feasibility of giving her work that would be challenging at that level. In doing so, however, remember that this student may not yet have learned specific content that is prerequisite to the tenth-grade work because that content is taught in the ninth grade.

Stop and Reflect

John's score on a standardized test is reported to be at the 8.5 grade level. What does that mean?

One of your ninth-graders is reading exactly at grade level according to the tests. Other tests and your observation of the girl indicate that she is very bright. Is her reading ability good or bad, assuming the test score is accurate?

Age and grade norms are not very useful above the middle school level. Because high school curricula are so fragmented and individual high school courses vary so greatly, grade norms do not provide sufficient common bases to justify using them to compare high school students. Age norms also tend to flatten out at the post middle school levels because the amount of mental growth decreases as one passes through the teens and approaches one's mature limit. At lower levels, the grade norms may be misleading because of the differences in content from grade to grade.

WITHIN-GROUP NORMS   Most standardized tests provide within-group norms with which an individual's score can be evaluated in relationship to the most nearly comparable standardization group (e.g., by showing where an individual's raw score falls in relation to the scores of other students of the age group or grade). These relationships may be expressed as standard scores or percentiles.

STANDARD SCORES   *Standard scores*, sometimes called *z* scores, are often expressed in standard deviations above or below the mean of the normative group. A score falling exactly at the mean is recorded as a standard score, or *z* score, of zero; a score falling one standard deviation below the mean is recorded as a *z* score of -1; and a score falling one standard deviation above the mean is recorded as a *z* score of 1.

To avoid the use of negative numbers and fractions, it has become customary to transform standard scores into positive whole numbers. For instance, in CEEB tests, the mean score is called 500, and each standard deviation is given the value of 100.* Consequently, a math CEEB of 650 indicates that a student's score is 1 and ½ standard deviations above the mean score, and a CEEB score of 450 indicates that the student's score fell one-half deviation below the mean.

Stop and Reflect

Joey's verbal SAT score was 805, John's was 675, and Suzie's was 550. Interpret these scores.

Other kinds of transformed standard scores include converted *z* scores, *T* scores, and stanine scores. In the converted *z* scores, the mean is given the value of 100, and each standard deviation the value of 10. In *T* scores the mean is called 50, and each standard deviation 10. Note that these scores say the same thing but in slightly different dialects: a *z* score of -1 is the same as a converted *z* score of 90, or a *T* score of 40, or a *Z* score of 40. Similarly, a score one-half a standard deviation above the mean could be reported as a *z* score of 0.5, a converted *z* score of 105, a *T* score of 55, or a *Z* score of 55.**

In interpreting standard scores, it may help you to think of a score of from +1 to -1 as falling within the middle two-thirds of the population, and a score of +1 or above as falling in the upper 15 percent, while a score of +2 or above falls in the topmost 3 percent. Similarly, think of a score of below -1 as falling in the lower 15 percent and a score of -2 or below in the lowest 3 percent. (These numbers are approximations. Figure 14.9 indicates the actual percentages of the total these scores represent.)

---

*CEEB stands for College Entrance Examination Board.

**In *T* scores the mean is designated by 50, and the standard deviation has the value of 10. Some writers use the term *T* scores only when dealing with normal distributions. When the distribution is not normal, they call the scores *Z* scores. The *z* score itself has been varied to eliminate signs by taking 5 or 10 or 100 as the mean and expressing the deviation from the mean as a multiple of the standard deviation. Thus, a score of +0.5 may be indicated by 5.5 or 55, or 110, depending on the values used.

■ **Figure 14.9**

Comparison of Various Derived Scores.

Note: Deviation IQs are computed with a standard deviation of 16; stanine scores represent ranges or bands rather than points.

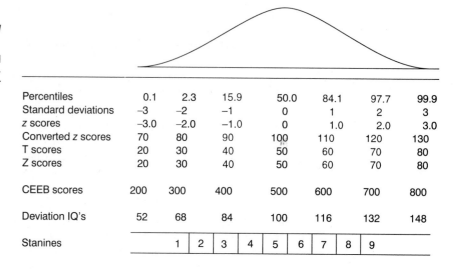

Percentiles	0.1	2.3	15.9	50.0	84.1	97.7	99.9
Standard deviations	–3	–2	–1	0	1	2	3
z scores	–3.0	–2.0	–1.0	0	1.0	2.0	3.0
Converted z scores	70	80	90	100	110	120	130
T scores	20	30	40	50	60	70	80
Z scores	20	30	40	50	60	70	80
CEEB scores	200	300	400	500	600	700	800
Deviation IQ's	52	68	84	100	116	132	148
Stanines		1 2 3	4	5	6	7 8 9	

Stanine Scores   Another useful score based on the normal curve is the *stanine score*. This is a nine-point score in which each unit represents a band equal to one-half a standard deviation; the mean is equal to 5 and the standard deviation, 2. Note that stanines do not indicate specific points on the curve, but instead indicate ranges or bands of raw scores, each one-half deviation wide except for bands 1 and 9, which extend to the tails of the distribution. Stanine 5 includes all the raw scores falling within one-quarter of a deviation on either side of the mean. The remaining stanines are evenly distributed above and below stanine 5.

Comparison of Scores   Figure 14.9 shows the equivalent weight of each of these types of scores. We see that a *T* score of 70 can be interpreted to mean that the student is rated at two standard deviations above the mean or within the top 3 percent of those taking the test, and so would have a *z* score of +2.0 or a *Z* score of 70 and a stanine score of 9. If this were an intelligence test, the student's deviation IQ would be 132. Presumably this is a very good score indeed, but until you know more about the student and the test situation, you cannot be sure. We repeat, to make decisions on the basis of test scores alone can be very dangerous.

Stop and Reflect

In a certain seventh grade, a test indicated that 25 percent of the students were reading below the seventh-grade level. The teacher claimed that there was no cause to worry. Would you agree? Why, or why not? Do you need more information before you can decide?

The parents of a gifted boy have just been informed that their youngster has achieved his grade norm in all areas and is slightly above norm in one area. They are well-pleased. Should they be?

The IQ   Norms of standardized tests are really derived scores provided by the test makers to aid the user in the interpretation of the test. Grade norms and age norms, however, are not the only types of derived scores that may be used. One of the most familiar types of derived scores is the *intelligence quotient* or IQ. Newer tests usually represent the IQ as a standardized score having, for most intelligence tests, a mean of 100 and a standard deviation of 16 (or sometimes 15). In other words, the IQ of a person of average intelligence would be 100, while that of a person whose intelligence was a standard deviation above normal would be 116.

In either case, view these IQ scores with caution. Estimating an individual's intelligence is too complicated a matter to be based on a single test score. Different tests of intelligence do not yield the same scores, and even scores from the same tests can vary considerably. IQs may be accepted as general indexes of giftedness, but they cannot be accepted at their face value.

PERCENTILE SCORES   Another kind of derived score is the centile, or *percentile norm*. The percentile score indicates the percentage of the sample population whose scores fall at or below that score. For example, if a student receives a percentile score of 10, 10 percent of the group did less well than or as well as he, and 90 percent did better. The fiftieth percentile, called the median or midpoint, having as many scores above it as below it, is average. Consequently, percentiles above 50 represent better than average scores; percentiles below 50 are below average. Scores above the seventy-fifth percentile (also known as the third quartile, Q^3) are in the uppermost quarter of the distribution. Scores below the twenty-fifth percentile (also called the first quartile) are in the lowest quartile of the population sampled.

Note particularly that percentile scores are not the same as the percentage grades or marks with which we are all familiar. Those grades represent the percentage of correct items. Percentile scores, on the other hand, are an expression of the percentage of persons who fell below a particular raw score. Although percentile scores have many advantages, they have several disadvantages as well. They cannot be averaged. The differences between raw scores near the center of the distribution (assuming a normal curve) are exaggerated, while the differences in raw scores at the end of the distribution are greatly shrunk (see Figure 14.9). Consequently, although percentile ranks do show the relative positions of students in the normative sample, they do not show the relative differences between scores. However, some builders of standardized tests supply *normal percentile charts* that plot the scores in such a way as to show the correct interscore differences.

SUMMARY

If students are to keep from drifting aimlessly, they need to determine where they are and where they should go scholastically. This process is known as *evaluation*. It differs from measurement in that it involves judgment of worth, whereas measurement merely describes a student's status. Many devices can be used to measure the status of learning. We should use more of these devices than we ordinarily do, but evaluations can be made only by the evaluator. Consequently, goals and standards must be established to give the evaluator touchstones against which to compare the value of what he or she is judging.

The purpose of evaluation is not merely to determine a student's worth, however. Evaluation is the basis for determining what comes next, or where to go from here. Evaluation is also useful as a basis for remedial action or as a basis for deciding whether retention or promotion will be better for a student. Evaluation is a concomitant of good teaching.

Evaluation instruments stand or fall on the basis of their validity. If an instrument is reliable, objective, and usable, so much the better, but one that is not valid is worthless. The key to building a test is to choose items that will ascertain whether the students have attained the teaching objectives. Consequently, aim your test items at specific goals.

Although teachers tend to use test scores as the basis for a large share of their evaluations, many other tools and devices for evaluation are available to them: rating scales, checklists, behavior logs, anecdotal reports, problem-situation tests, themes, notebooks, other written work, homework, class recitation and participation, and various sociometric devices. Students can profitably take on some of the responsibility for their own work. Self-report forms and rating scales make pupil self-evaluation easier and more profitable.

A test is a systematic procedure for measuring behavior. Classroom tests determine how much and how well students have learned. Tests are used as a basis for grading and motivating students and for planning and review. There are many kinds of tests. Most classroom tests are informal tests of cognitive or psychomotor achievement. They may be survey, diagnostic, or mastery in nature. Norm-referenced classroom tests are better as a basis for assigning grades, but criterion-referenced tests are more useful for most classroom purposes.

Both essay test items and objective test items have good and bad points. For many purposes the objective test item, when well-written, is the better of the two. It is the purpose of the test that should determine the type of item used, however, rather than some notion about the innate worth of objective or essay test items.

To build a classroom test, follow these procedures: (1) define the objectives; (2) outline the content to be tested; (3) draw up a table of specifications; and (4) construct test items to meet the specifications. In designing the test itself, make sure that all objectives are tested in proportion to their importance, that at least some relatively easy items are included so that students will not become quickly discouraged, that only a few kinds of items are used in the test, that all items of the same kind are placed together, that the items are arranged from easiest to most difficult, that the items are appropriate for their purpose and for the sophistication of the students, and that the test provides the students with clear directions and the information and materials they need for completing it. Classroom tests should not be designed as jokes or puzzles, but as tools to find out how well the students have learned what it was hoped they would learn.

There are many kinds of objective test items. Each has its merits, and each has its faults. The most useful of them all is the multiple-choice item. However, be careful to use each kind of item to do only the type of thing it is designed to do. Organization and evaluation items, situation items, and interpretation items are excellent for testing higher intellectual learnings and are not used as much as they should be.

Free-response items include completion items, short-answer items, and essay items. They can test a high level of recall but are much more difficult to design than you might expect. Essay tests are also difficult to design, although, again, few people realize it. In designing an essay test, be sure to (1) limit the number and scope of questions to the time allotted for the test; (2) sample the teaching objectives adequately; (3) test specific learning products that were in the course; (4) write items that specify what answers are required; (5) write "correct" answers to the items before you decide whether to use them; and last and most important, (6) be clear.

In designing criterion-referenced tests, there are only two major steps: (1) determine the objectives; and (2) build items that test those objectives adequately. These steps are basically those outlined earlier as the general procedure for test construction.

Tests should be carefully administered, scored, and interpreted. Insofar as possible, scoring should be objective. It is extremely good policy, once a test has been given, to analyze it and save those items that have proven to be good for another time. Item analyses may be useful for this purpose.

Standardized tests can be a source for much useful information about your students. They are not useful for grading, however. Usually standardized test scores are based on normal curves and standard deviations.

ADDITIONAL READING

Archibald, D. A., and F. M. Newman. *Beyond Standardized Testing: Assessing Authentic Academic Achievement in Secondary School*. Reston, VA: National Association of Secondary School Principals, 1988.

Bloom, B. S., G. F. Madaus, and J. T. Hastings. *Evaluation to Improve Learning*. New York: McGraw-Hill, 1981.

Cangelosi, J. S. *Designing Tests for Evaluating Student Achievement*. White Plains, NY: Longman, 1991.

Carey, L. *Measuring and Evaluating School Learning*. Boston: Allyn and Bacon, 1988.

Ebel, R. L. *The Uses of Standardized Testing, Fastback 93*. Bloomington, IN: Phi Delta Kappa Educational Foundation, 1977.

Ebel, R. L., and D. A. Frisbie. *Essentials of Educational Measurement*, 5th ed. Needham Heights, MA: Allyn and Bacon, 1991.

Gay, L. R. *Educational Evaluation and Measurement: Competencies and Application*, 2nd ed. Englewood Cliffs, NJ: Merrill/Prentice Hall, 1985.

Gronlund, N. E. *How to Construct Achievement Tests*. Englewood Cliffs, NJ: Merrill/Prentice-Hall, 1988.

Gronlund, N. E., and R. L. Linn. *Measurement and Evaluation in Education*, 6th ed. New York: Macmillan, 1990.

Henson, K. T. *Methods and Strategies for Teaching in Secondary and Middle Schools*. White Plains, NY: Longman, 1988. Chap. 14.

Hopkins, C. D., and R. L. Antes. *Classroom Measurement and Evaluation*, 2nd ed. Itasca, IL: Peacock, 1984.

Johnson, E. W. *Teaching School*, rev. ed. Boston: National Association of Independent Schools, 1987.

Kubiszyn, T., and G. D. Borich. *Educational Testing and Measurement*, 2nd ed. Glenview, IL: Scott Foresman, 1987.

Linn, R. L., ed. *Educational Measurement*, 3rd ed. New York: Macmillan, 1988.

Lorber, M. A., and W. D. Pierce. *Objectives, Methods, and Evaluation for Secondary Teaching*, 3rd ed. Englewood Cliffs, NJ: Merrill/Prentice-Hall, 1990.

Miller, P. W., and H. E. Erickson. *Teacher-Written Student Tests*. Washington, DC: National Education Association, 1985.

Mitchell, R. *Testing for Learning*. New York: Free Press, 1992.

Perrone, V. *Expanding Student Assessment*. Alexandria, VA: Association for Supervision and Curriculum Development, 1991.

Popham, W. J. *Educational Evaluation*, 2nd ed. Englewood Cliffs, NJ: Merrill/Prentice-Hall, 1988.

Sparzo, F. J. *Preparing Better Teacher-Made Tests, Fastback 311*. Bloomington, IN: Phi Delta Kappa Educational Foundation, 1990.

Weiner, E. A., and B. J. Stewart. *Assessing Individuals: Psychological and Educational Tests and Measurements*. Boston: Little, Brown, 1984.

Wiggins, G. P. *Assessing Student Performance*. San Francisco: Jossey-Bass, 1993.

Wittrock, M. C., and E. L. Baker. *Testing and Cognition*. Englewood Cliffs, NJ: Merrill/Prentice-Hall, 1991.

NOTES

1. For example, Benjamin S. Bloom, J. Thomas Hastings, and George F. Madaus, *Evaluation to Improve Learning* (New York: McGraw-Hill, 1981).
2. Office of Strategic Services, *Assessment of Men: Selection of Personnel for the Office of Strategic Services* (Troy, MO: Holt, Rinehart and Winston, 1948). Quoted by Grant P. Wiggins, *Assessing Student Performance* (San Francisco: Jossey Bass Publishers, 1992), 227.

3. Richard J. Stiggins, *Evaluating Students by Classroom Observation. Watching Students Grow* (Washington, DC: National Educational Association, 1984).

4. Doug A. Archibald and Fred M. Newman, *Beyond Standardized Testing: Assessing Authentic Academic Achievement in the Secondary School* (Reston, VA: National Association of Secondary School Principals, 1988), 29.

5. Pam Knight, "How to Use Portfolios in Mathematics," *Educational Leadership* 49 (May 1992): 71–72.

6. Donald Daws, "Schoolwide Portfolios" in *Student Portfolios*, NEA Teacher-to-Teacher Books. © 1993, Washington, DC, National Education Association. Reprinted by permission of NEA Professional Library. Edited by Mary Dalheim (Washington, DC: National Education Association, 1993), 33ff.

7. Norman E. Gronlund, *Measurement and Evaluation in Teaching*, 5th ed. (New York: Macmillan, 1985), 144.

8. Now published by University of Nebraska Press. Formerly edited by the late O. K. Buros.

9. For a more detailed explanation of norms and the interpretation of standardized test scores, consult such texts as Anne Anatasi, *Psychological Testing*, 6th ed. (New York: Macmillan, 1988), or Carol Schneider Lidz, *Improving Assessment of School Children* (San Francisco: Jossey Bass, 1981). Information about test scores is usually taught in educational psychology courses. We recommend that you take such a course before you begin to teach.

Chapter 15

Marking and Reporting to Parents

Overview

Marks, or grades, are held in high regard in schools.* They are used as a basis for reporting student progress to parents and to other interested persons, as well as a means for determining promotion, graduation, and honors status. Teachers frequently use marks as a means of motivating students to greater effort. Guidance personnel use marks in guiding young people who are considering college entrance or employment. College admission officers and prospective employers use student marks as one basis for their decision making.

Nonetheless, for the past 50 years or so, marks and marking systems have been the target for much criticism. In spite of this dissatisfaction with marks and marking systems, no one has yet come up with an alternative system acceptable to everyone. Therefore, you should become familiar with the marking systems available and know how to use them in ways that are both fair and effective. As you read this chapter, try to develop a personal philosophy concerning marks and marking, their use in reporting student progress to parents, and their use as a basis for determining promotion. Although your philosophy will be a personal matter, it should be based on an understanding of marking systems and their alternatives, as well as on the techniques for determining marks for tests, classwork, papers, units, and courses.

Marks and Marking

To determine marks, most school systems use a plan based on a five-point scale. The most common version is the A B C D F scale. Variations of this scale use the numbers 1 2 3 4 5 or the terms "Superior," "Above Average," "Average," "Below Average," and "Unsatisfactory." Some schools use a scale based on 100 percent, whereas others merely indicate the work to be passing or failing, or in some cases outstanding, passing, or failing.

Criticism of Marking Systems

Unfortunately, the five-point scale has never been completely satisfactory in any of its variations for at least five reasons.

1. Marks seldom give a clear picture of a student's achievement or progress. For example, if someone says that Johnny received an A in ninth-grade social studies, what does that tell you? Does it mean he worked hard, or that he is a gifted loafer? Does it mean that he has mastered some particular bit of subject matter, or does it mean he has a charming personality?

Letter and percentage marks do not provide answers to such questions. They do not show what skills, concepts, attitudes, appreciations, or ideals the students have learned. They do not tell us students' strengths or weaknesses in a subject, nor do they tell how much students have progressed. For instance, because of her excellence in literature, reading, grammar, or written composition, Sally receives an A in English. However, she may be quite poor in conversation skill. The mark of A, therefore, hides the fact that she is deficient in one area of English. Such a marking system is of little value to anyone who really wants to know much about a student's real progress in school. Still, it does predict fairly well students' continued success

---

*In pedagogical literature, the terms *marks* and *grades* are used synonymously. In this book, however, we ordinarily use the word *marks* to denote the results of evaluation, and *grades* to denote class levels (as ninth grade, tenth grade, and so on).

in a subject and gives a rough indication of teachers' estimates of a student's over-all success in a course.

Even as an indication of the teacher's estimate of a student's achievement, how-ever, marks are not always valuable. Teachers' marks are often influenced by extra-neous matters such as gender, effort, extracurricular activities, neatness, school behavior, attitudes, and attendance. Obviously, such factors may result in many inequities; in such cases, marks may give more misinformation than information.

Particularly futile are marking systems that attempt to give precise marks. No human being can make the fine distinctions in the schoolwork of students that the per-centage system requires. Neither have we been able to develop testing instruments capable of such fine distinctions. Because the data on which student marks are based are so rough, computing percentage marks hardly seems worth the trouble.

2. The ordinary school marking system does not adequately allow for individual differences among students. Students have differences in aptitudes, abilities, and backgrounds. All the efforts in the world will not make a true expert out of a student with no aptitude. Not everyone can become president, no matter how much they try.

3. In spite of our high hopes, experience in the adult world does not show a high correlation between school marks and later worldly success.

4. Adult life is competitive, although perhaps not nearly as competitive as some critics claim. Even so, the inherent competition of the school marking system is not a good training ground for the competition in adult life. In the real world of adult-hood, the rules are quite different from those in schools. In schools students must compete with everyone, whereas adults have some choice about their competition. We do not compete with people not in our league.

5. Perhaps the more valid argument for using letter or percentage marks is that they have a certain motivational effect, particularly with high-achieving students. Even this effect, however, may be illusory. If marks really motivated effectively, would not fewer students fail?

Sometimes marks have a poor motivational effect. Altogether too often the mark rather than the learning becomes the major goal. The students concentrate on get-ting marks rather than on learning. The result often is cheating, cramming, electing easy courses, and expending only enough energy to pass. Frequently they cause unsuccessful students to give up trying. Nevertheless, percentage and letter marks and grades are commonly used throughout the United States and other countries. They have the strength of familiarity and tradition behind them. Because parents and other lay people grew up with them and think they understand them, they pre-fer such marking systems.

At present there is a movement toward replacing ordinary tests and measure-ments with "authentic assessments" of students' performance. These assessments would indicate how much the students really understand and respond to the knowledge and skills being tested. To make these tests means for authentic assessment of performance, the tester would have to face the students with real-life tasks. These tests could require students to use their best judgment to respond correctly to simulated tasks, taking into account the constraints of time, logistics, and so forth. In so far as possible, the conditions of the test should be the same as one would face in a real-life situation. The test questions also would be the sort one would face in the real world.

Stop and Reflect

Of what value are marks? Do they serve the purposes to which they aspire? If they do, how do they do it?

What do you think of competitive marking? What values does it have? What weaknesses? For what purposes should marks be used?

Marking Tests

At best, assigning marks is a difficult task. In the following paragraphs, we suggest several ways to do this job. Remember, however, that no procedure can relieve you of the responsibility for making decisions, some of which will be complex.

Teachers may assign marks on the basis of either some set standard or a relative scale. The standard in which students have to have 90 percent or better of the items right to achieve an A, 80 to 90 percent of the test right for a B, 70 to 80 percent for a C, and 60 to 70 percent for a D is one example of the use of an arbitrary standard for marking. Another example is the more modern criterion-referenced, or mastery, test that requires a student to answer correctly 8 problems out of 10 to pass. In relative scales, a student's marks depend on the relationship of his or her scores or performance to the scores or performance of other students in the group. Marking on the curve is an example of the relative scale technique.

MARKING ON THE CURVE   According to the theory of the normal curve, which is based on the laws of chance, any continuous variable will be distributed according to a perfectly smooth bell-shaped curve (Figure 15.1), if no factors are present to throw things off balance. Thus, in a large group, according to the laws of chance, marks should tend to fall according to the normal curve. Letter marks would, according to this theory, be distributed about as follows: A, 7 percent; B, 23 percent; C, 40 percent; D, 23 percent; E (or F), 7 percent. Just what the exact percentages should be is debatable, however.

This theory seldom applies to ordinary classes, since talent in a single class is almost never distributed "normally," especially in the high school. Because of the selection process that occurs when many of the under achieving and less motivated students drop out at age 16 or so, the distribution of marks in high school classes should vary considerably from the normal curve. The marks of twelfth-graders on the whole, for instance, probably should be closer to A, 15 percent; B, 25 percent; C, 40 percent; D, 15 percent; E (or F), 5 percent. When you consider the other factors that may be operating (for instance, ability grouping, selective curriculum tracks, and so on), it seems obvious that the curve in any single class will probably be far from normal. In an honors section the proper distribution of marks might be 40 percent, A; 60 percent, B; in an advanced section, 25 percent, A; 50 percent, B; 25 percent, C; in an at-risk section, 50 percent, C; 30 percent, D; 20 percent, F; and so on.

Furthermore, few classes are large enough to warrant using the normal curve. For the theory of the normal curve to operate, at least several hundred pupils must be marked against the same criteria. To use the normal curve as a basis for marks in a smaller group may lead to errors in marking. Therefore, when marking, teachers must depend largely on their own judgment. Statistical procedures such as using the normal curve are seldom worth the effort.

■ **FIGURE 15.1**
The Normal Curve of Probability

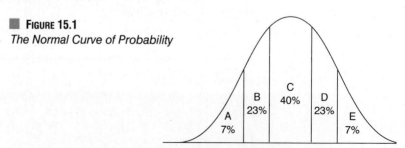

Finally, the ordinary classroom teacher-built test is seldom designed to give a normal distribution. In his investigations, Terwilliger found that classroom tests are usually skewed negatively, that is, the marks tend to fall on the low side.(1) For all these reasons, then, it is most unwise to base A B C D F class marks on the normal curve.

Besides, the practice can lead to behavioral and motivational problems. Marking on a curve almost always dooms some students to failure, and it frequently causes these students to adopt such avoidance techniques as not trying, having low levels of aspiration, giving up, and exhibiting other inappropriate behavior.(2)

RELATIVE-GROWTH GROUPS   Blount and Klausmeier recommend the use of a simple relative growth scale instead of marks or grades. According to this system, instead of reporting marks or grades, the teacher would assign students to the highest, lowest, or middle third (or quarter) of the class. For example, a teacher might report a student's standing in various areas to be

Speaking: In the highest third of the class
Listening: In the middle third of the class
Reading: In the lowest third of the class
Spelling: In the lowest third of the class
Composition: In the lowest third of the class(3)

Comparative groups of this sort can be used for reporting test results or student standings at the end of the marking period.

Although using such relative-growth groups can be quite helpful, students and parents have become so mark-oriented that they do not always willingly accept this practice.

STANDARD SCORES AND STANINES   Some authorities believe that the marks of the future will be either standard scores or stanine scores.

The standard score most useful in marking classroom tests and exercises is the T score, or Z score. To compute a T score or a Z score, use the formula

$$T \text{ score} = 10 \frac{(X - M)}{SD} + 50$$

where

X = any raw score
M = arithmetic mean of raw scores
SD = standard deviation of raw scores.*

*The terms T and Z score both refer to scores derived by the formula

$$T \text{ score} = 50 + 10 \frac{(X - M)}{SD}$$

Some authorities call any set of scores derived from these formulae T scores. Others use the term T score to refer only to normalized scores, and the term Z score to any score derived from the formula

$$Z \text{ score} = 50 + 10 \frac{(X - M)}{SD}$$

To save time and computation, when one has a small distribution and a fairly normal curve, find the approximation of the standard deviation (SD) by dividing the range of the raw scores by 4. If the extremes of the distribution deviate from the normal, divide the range between the 10th and 90th percentile by 4.

Although the statistical procedures suggested here give only approximations, they are quite accurate enough for most class marks. See works on statistics, tests, and measurements for computing by accurate procedures. Shortcut statistics methods can be found in Merle W. Tate and Richard C. Clelland, "Non Parametric and Shortcut Statistics for Teacher-Made Tests," *Evaluation and Advisory Series No. 5* (Princeton, NJ: Educational Testing Service, 1960); and Paul B. Diederich, "Printed Statistics," in *Evaluation as Feedback and Guide*, edited by Fred T. Wilhelms (Washington, DC: Association for Supervision and Curriculum Development, 1967).

To compute approximate stanine scores, use the following procedure:

1. Find the standard deviation of the raw scores.
2. Find the mean of the raw scores.
3. Measure ¼ standard deviation down from the mean and ¼ standard deviation up from the mean to establish the limits of stanine 5.
4. Find the limits of the other stanines by measuring down or up ½ standard deviation for each stanine.

Thus, if the standard deviation of the raw scores is 6 and the mean 40, the stanines will be:

1	0–29	*6*	42–44
2	30–32	*7*	45–47
3	33–35	*8*	48–50
4	36–38	*9*	50+
5	39–41 (38.5–41.5)		

Test results may also be reported as percentiles. There is a danger, however, that students and parents may confuse percentiles with percentages and so misunderstand.

RAW SCORES   Another effective procedure is to give the results of objective tests in raw scores, telling the students the range of the scores and the range of the relative-growth groups. By comparing their scores, high school students soon realize how they stand in comparison with their classmates. If the scores are accompanied by comments such as, "I think you have missed the point of . . . , and should reread it," or "You did not provide enough illustrations," or "You have not differentiated between major and minor points," and so on, students can learn how they stand in relationship to their own potential and the standards of the course. Conferences also help make these points clear. This procedure is probably the fairest of all marking systems. It also has the advantage of being the procedure least likely to be misused by beginners.

Assigning Marks

ASSIGNING MARKS TO TESTS   Both the raw-score plan and the relative-growth plan allow teachers to avoid assigning actual marks to tests. Experts in the field of measurement feel that

Teachers should consider these instruments (e.g., quizzes, tests, homework assignments, term papers, laboratory exercises, etc.) as data-collection devices that yield numerical results which will subsequently provide a basis for value judgments concerning individual students. Scoring procedures, however crude, should be devised so that the results of all classroom measurement can be recorded in quantitative terms. Grades (e.g., A, B, C, D, F) should *not* be assigned every time measurement occurs but, instead, should be withheld until official reports are required.(4)

If you must give marks, the only satisfactory solution seems to be to establish certain criteria for each mark and then mark on the basis of those criteria. Thus, for a 50-item test, you might set up the following criteria: 46–50, A; 41–45, B; 36–40, C; 31–35, D; and 0–30, F.

A less satisfactory approach is to base test marks on a distribution scheme such as the following:

A = 10 percent of pupils tested
B = 25 percent

C = 45 percent
D = 15 percent
F =   5 percent

In this method, you simply find the raw scores of the tests, list them from highest to lowest, and then apportion the letter grades according to the proportions selected—taking advantage of natural breaks wherever possible. Thus, in the example in Figure 15.2 of a class of 25, the teacher assigned 1 A, 9 Bs, 12 Cs, 2 Ds, and 1 F. These marks do not quite correspond to the distribution scheme, but they are close enough given the nature of the distribution of the raw scores. The planned distribution scheme should not be held sacred. When the raw scores cluster together in an obviously skewed distribution, do not hold rigidly to the normal distribution scheme. In marking tests, remember that the purposes of the tests should be primarily to evaluate student progress and to diagnose student learning rather than to give marks. Furthermore, in such schemes the distribution of marks is quite arbitrary and subject to the limitations of any set distribution scheme. Some students, no matter how they try, seem always to get low marks, so they soon learn not to try.(5) Thus, to mark on the basis of set criteria is much more satisfactory.

▓ **FIGURE 15.2**
Distribution of Test Scores and Assigned Letter Grades

1	<u>83</u>	A
	78	
	77	
	76	
	74	
9	73	B
	70	
	68	
	68	
	<u>68</u>	
	65	
	64	
	63	
	62	
	59	
12	58	C
	58	
	57	
	56	
	54	
	53	
	<u>53</u>	
2	50	D
	<u>48</u>	
1	40	F

Stop and Reflect

What procedure would you use to grade an objective test if your school used the five-letter system of marking? Would you use a different procedure for marking an essay test? If so, what?

Why do authorities generally condemn the percentage system of grading tests? What is your own opinion?

What are z scores, T scores, and Z scores? What are the good and bad points of z scores, T scores, and Z scores? How would you use them to mark tests?

In a certain school the school policy holds that students' marks should approximate the normal curve. A teacher of an honors section found that all 15 students did exceptionally well on a test. Would a mark of A for each student be justified?

ASSIGNING MARKS TO COMPOSITIONS AND OTHER CREATIVE WORK   Compositions and other creative work are difficult to mark. Perhaps the following technique used by a veteran teacher of English is as good as any in marking original written work:

First, he selects a comfortable chair with plenty of floor space around him. Then he reads each paper carefully, making notes as he reads them. On the basis of this reading he judges whether the paper is "Superior," "Excellent," "Average," "Fair," or "Poor." Then, without placing any mark on the paper, he places it on a portion of the floor designated for papers of that category. After reading all the papers and placing them into piles according to their categories, he lets them lie fallow for a while. Later, approaching the task with a renewed perspective, he rereads each paper in each group to test his previous judgment, and moves from pile to pile those papers that he believes he has rated too high or too low. He then assigns marks to the papers in the piles. He could have just as easily assigned them to relative-growth groups or even assigned them point scores. Although this technique is not foolproof, with a little ingenuity it can be adapted for marking various types of original work.

Another method is to rate each paper according to each of several qualities such as originality, expression, mechanics, and so on. Rating scales and checklists are particularly useful for this purpose. The ratings produced by these procedures can be converted into point scores if desired.*

Term and Course Marks

THE PURPOSE OF TERM MARKS   As we have already seen, the more one reads about marks and marking, the more one is tempted to believe that there can be no such thing as a fair mark or marking system. Yet marks seem to be necessary for the following reasons:

1. To inform pupils, parents, and other interested persons such as teachers, prospective employers, and college admissions officers of the pupil's achievement in his secondary schoolwork.
2. To motivate pupils by giving them feedback on their progress.
3. To identify the strengths and weaknesses of pupils.
4. To inform those concerned of the progress or achievement of pupils in comparison with other pupils.
5. As a basis for guiding pupils in their choice of courses, activities, curriculum, and career.
6. As a basis for promotion, grouping, graduation, honors, college entrance, and eligibility for certain awards, activities, or programs.
7. To show parents and others the objectives of the school.
8. To indicate pupils' personal social development.(6)

CRITERIA FOR MARKS AND MARKING SYSTEMS   To carry out your purposes, marks and marking systems should meet the following criteria:

---

*See Chapter 14 for information on the use of rating devices.

1. Marks should indicate the attainment of definite worthwhile goals. These goals should be well-defined, or the marks themselves will become the goals.
2. Marks should be easily understood by students and parents.
3. Marks should be as objective as possible.
4. Marks should be free from bias and the influence of other irrelevant considerations.
5. Marks should be based on an abundance of evidence.
6. Students should be informed in advance of what material will be counted in computing the mark.
7. The method used to compute the marks should be objective and statistically valid.
8. Marks for achievement and personal social development should be separated.
9. Marks should be based on positive evidence.
10. Marks should be used as a means to an end; they should not be ends in themselves. Overemphasis on marks distorts the teaching-learning process.

BASES FOR TERM MARKS   Term marks should be based on the teacher's best estimate of a student's achievement in the course. No basis other than achievement is valid for granting subject marks; however, because of the nature of education and educational measurement, no teacher can be completely objective or accurate in determining student achievement. The best you can do is to gather all the evidence you can find and then make a judgment, but do not include effort, attendance, and classroom behavior in the course mark. That you should notice and report such things to school officials, guidance persons, new teachers, and parents is axiomatic, but report them as separate entities, not as part of a course mark. *A coursemark should be an index of achievement in a course, nothing else.* That is why Oliva and Scrafford recommended that teachers should give three types of marks: (a) A subject matter achievement grade determined competitively in relation to the performance of pupils at a particular grade level; (b) a mark that reflects the relationship of the pupils' attainment and ability; and (c) a mark that reflects information concerning personal traits, social skills, and study habits.(7)

Some teachers and theoreticians have proposed that students should be marked on the amount of progress they have made during a year. On the face of it, progress is an admirable criterion for marking. If marks are to be an index of the student's level of achievement, however, then a mark based solely on the amount of progress made during the period may be misleading, as the following case demonstrates.

When they arrived at the first class of their drawing course, Joan already had great—almost professional—skill in drawing, whereas Anne had no skill whatsoever. After a year in class, Joan has progressed comparatively little, although she can still draw much better than anyone else in the class. Anne, however, has become interested in drawing and has made swift progress. She is now slightly better than the average pupil in the class, although still not nearly as good as Joan. How should one mark the two girls? If one bases the marks on progress, then Anne should get the higher mark, but this would lead to the ridiculous situation of giving the higher mark to the less skilled student. To be fair and to give a reasonably accurate picture through the mark assigned to each student, the criterion should be achievement rather than progress.

Other teachers and experts feel that students' marks should be related to their inherent ability. Thus a student who did the very best he could would be marked A, whereas one who did not come up to his potential would be marked less. Again, the system can lead to ridiculous situations in which a low-ability student who does his best, yet his best turns out to be very little, would receive a higher mark than a gifted student who does excellent work without effort.

Stop and Reflect

Suppose you are an eleventh-grade English teacher. What should you wish to know about a boy coming to you from the tenth grade? Would the fact that he got a B help you? If not, what information would be more helpful?

DETERMINING TERM MARKS

COMBINING UNIT MARKS   One way to determine term marks for a course is to give the students marks for each unit. The final mark can then be computed by taking an average of the units, making due allowance for those units that may be more important than others.

Some schools require that marks be recorded and reported as percentages. This presents a problem to the conscientious teacher, because percentage scores often require judgments finer than the human mind can make. However, such scores may be approximated by assigning values to the unit marks. For instance, if the passing grade is 70 percent, then you can assign the following values: A, 95 percent; B, 87 percent; C, 80 percent; D, 73 percent; F, 65 percent or less. To attempt to give finer evaluations for the various units may be merely deceiving yourself and your clientele.

Other methods for determining term marks are discussed in succeeding paragraphs. These methods can also be used to establish unit marks.

TOTAL-PERFORMANCE SCORES   Another highly recommended system of calculating term marks is to rank the students according to their total-performance scores. To use this system, record a point score for each activity to be reflected in the course mark, and then total all the activity scores (test, quizzes, themes, papers, class recitations, and so on). Once you have computed the total scores for every student, assign marks to the individual students using as a basis some such scheme as the following:

Top 15 percent of the pupils	A
Next 20 percent of the pupils	B
Next 45 percent of the pupils	C
Next 15 percent of the pupils	D
Bottom 5 percent of the pupils	F

This technique also can be used to compute unit marks. The percentage of students in each category would be an arbitrary decision based on your estimate of the ability of the class as a whole. It would be patently unfair to use the same percentage breakdown for an honors group as for a class of low achievers, for example. If natural breaks occur, it is usually better to use these breaks as cutoff points rather than to adhere strictly to the percentage scheme.

A METHOD FOR COMPUTING FINAL TERM AND UNIT MARKS   When you give marks to students as the class moves through the course, the following procedure for combining the marks into final marks works quite well.

Decide what weight to give to each mark. (This should have been done in your evaluation plan.) For instance, if you plan to base your marks on daily work, 25 percent; papers and themes, 50 percent; and tests, 25 percent, you could follow the following procedure:

1. Change the letter marks to numerical values: A = 4; B = 3; C = 2, D = 1; F = 0.
2. Combine the daily marks by averaging. For instance, suppose a student had earned the following daily marks: A, B, B, A, C, A, D; we would use the following computation to find her average score:

$$
\begin{array}{rl}
A = & 4 \\
B = & 3 \\
B = & 3 \\
A = & 4 \\
C = & 2 \\
A = & 4 \\
D = & \underline{1} \\
& 21 \div 7 = 3.00
\end{array}
$$

3. Average the marks on the themes and papers. For purposes of illustration, let us assume that there are three themes and one major paper, that the paper is equivalent to three themes, and that the student received a mark of A on one theme and marks of B on the other two themes as well as on the major paper.

First Theme	A	4	4
Second Theme	B	3	3
Third Theme	B	3	3
Major Paper	B	3 x 3	9
			19:6 = 3.17

(Notice that the major paper is counted as three themes, so the divisor is 6.)
4. Combine the test scores; in this case, there is just one test: A = 4.
5. Combine the averages:

Daily work	3.00	3.00
Themes & papers	3.17 x 2	6.34
Test	4	4.00
		13.34:4 = 3.34

(Notice that since our original plan was to weigh the mark on the basis of daily work 25 percent, themes and papers 50 percent, and tests 25 percent, themes and papers are given twice the weight of the other items, and so the divisor is 4.)

The final score is 3.34, or B.

BUILDING MULTICLASS NORMS   When the content for different sections of a course is much the same, it is quite possible that you can combine the score distribution of the sections (or of classes taught in successive years) into performance norms. To make this plan feasible, plan the measurement for the course so that the possible number of points that can be earned is the same in all sections. This usually means that you must use the same or comparable tests and assignments in all sections and score and weigh the tests and assignments in the same way. To make the norms, simply combine the score distribution of the sections into one distribution. You can assign marks from the combined raw scores (e.g., top 10 percent, A; next 25 percent, B; next 45 percent, C; next 15 percent, D; and last 5 percent, F). You can combine standard scores or stanine scores in the same manner.(8)

COMBINING STANDARD SCORES   To combine scores recorded as standard scores is quite easy. If, for instance, the daily marks were to count 50 percent; quizzes, 25 percent; and tests, 25 percent; and the marks were recorded as *T* scores; the computation of a student's mark would follow the pattern:

Daily work	**Quizzes**	**Test**
55	50	$\frac{52}{52}$
71	65	
63	$\underline{65}$	
59	180:3 = 60	
68		
64		
60		
65		
$\underline{60}$		
565:9 = 62.78		

Daily work   62.78 x 2 = 125.56
Quizzes   =   60
Test   = $\underline{52}$
                          237.56

Students' letter marks could then be determined by the position of the total scores in the total distribution. If, for instance, a student's score fell in the middle 45 percent of the total scores, the letter grade should probably be C.

THE TEACHER'S RESPONSIBILITY FOR THE GRADE   You will notice that in each of the previous examples, no matter how much computation the teacher did, in the end the mark was based on the teacher's best judgment. Measuring techniques may make the basis for the judgment more objective, but they cannot make marking a student's progress an automatic process.

MARKS IN ATTITUDE, CITIZENSHIP, BEHAVIOR, EFFORT   Many report cards call for reports of social and personal qualities as well as subject marks. Sometimes these marks are broken into categories as in Figure 15.3, or sometimes all the categories are lumped under the heading *Attitudes* or *Citizenship*, as is done in Figure 15.4 and Figure 15.5. The teacher's basis for making such marks is usually observation, sometimes bolstered with inferences from the student's schoolwork and behavior, or sometimes based on sociometric devices. These marks should be made out more carefully than they usually are. Probably the best method is to rate all students as average at the beginning of the marking period; raise the marks of those students whose attitude, effort, or behavior is excellent; or lower the marks for those students whose behavior, attitude, or effort is poor.

CRITERION-REFERENCED MARKING SYSTEMS   The previously described methods for deriving term marks have all been based on normative or relative marking. Some schools use criterion-referenced marking systems. Such systems base marks on an absolute or arbitrary standard or a set of standards. Students who achieve the standard succeed; those who do not, fail. Those who achieve the standard for C, get C; those who do not, do not. How well others do is irrelevant. For example, let us suppose that you give a 65-item mastery test for which you

FIGURE 15.3

Interim Report in Mathematics, West Hartford, Connecticut

TO PARENTS OF: _____

MATH TEACHER: _____

DECIMAL UNIT

Please call the math teacher if you have any questions or would like a personal conference.	Basic development of decimals	Addition and subtraction	Multiplication	Division	Advanced topics in decimals	Problem solving
Progress						
Test results indicate:						
1. Significant Growth						
2. Reasonable Growth						
3. Little or No Growth						
Progress was hindered by frequent absence from class.						
I believe more growth has taken place than the test data indicate.						
Skill development						
Is at an introductory stage.						
Demonstrates an understanding of the process and is working toward mastery.						
Has demonstrated mastery of the skills involved.						
No work was assigned because:						
1. The pre-test indicated previous mastery.						
2. Work in other topics was deemed more important.						

COMMENTS REGARDING THE STUDENT AS A LEARNER

____ Demonstrates conscientious effort.

____ Demonstrates reasonable effort.

____ Does not seem to be making a reasonable effort.

____ Makes a real attempt to learn from assigned work.

____ Views work as a task to be completed rather than a means of learning.

____ Persists even if understanding does not come immediately.

____ Is willing to settle for incomplete understanding.

____ Tends to seek help prematurely.

____ Seeks help effectively.

____ Seems unwilling to seek help.

____ Uses resources to gain information.

____ Draws conclusions based on well-organized data.

____ Demonstrates a willingness to test conclusions.

____ Effectively seeks alternate or additional assignments.

____ Demonstrates a willingness to evaluate his or her work and set objectives to correct weaknesses.

COMMENTS REGARDING THE STUDENT AS A CLASS MEMBER

____ Generally cooperates with class.

____ Distracts other members of the class.

____ Contributes positively to class welfare.

____ Is easily distracted.

have determined that each student must answer 55 items correctly to pass. Because the criterion set is 55 items, if 28 of the 30 students in the class get from 55 to 65 items correct, they pass; and if the other two students get 54 items correct, they fail. If the situation were reversed and 28 of the 30 students scored in the 50 to 54 range, and two scored in the 55-plus range, then the 28 would fail and the

		1	2	3	4	YEAR M	A	CR.			1	2	3	4	YEAR M	A	CR
ENGLISH	M								COMMERCE	M							
	A									A							
PHYS. ED.	M									M							
	A									A							
HYGIENE	M								ART	M							
	A									A							
LANGUAGE	M								VOCAL MUSIC	M							
	A									A							
	M								INSTR. MUSIC	M							
	A									A							
SOCIAL SC.	M								COOKING	M							
	A									A							
	M								SEWING	M							
	A									A							
SCIENCE	M								WOODSHOP	M							
	A									A							
	M								METAL SHOP	M							
	A									A							
MATH.	M									M							
	A									A							
ABSENT									TARDY								

Fords Junior High School
Woodbridge Township
Grade 7–8   WOODBRIDGE NEW JERSEY   19 ___ 19 ___
JUNIOR HIGH SCHOOL

NAME _____   GRADE _____ HOMEROOM _____

Figure 15.4
Report Card Used in Woodbridge Township Junior High Schools, Woodbridge, New Jersey
Note: M = Academic Mark; A = Attitude Mark; CR = Credit

two would pass.* Similarly, you could set up standards for letter marks—for example, A = 63 and above; B = 60 to 62; C = 55 to 59; D = 51 to 54; F = 50 or below. The percentage correct marking system, so common in the past, is theoretically based on absolute standards (e.g., 90 percent and above, A; 80 to 89 percent, B; 70 to 79 percent, C; 60 to 69 percent, D; 59 percent and below, F). In reality, however, teachers seldom keep to the absolute standards but base the percentage on the students' standing instead of basing the students' standing on the percentage. In fact, criterion-referenced tests or marks based on absolute standards do not work well in most courses as presently organized because there are no real criteria or standards by which to gauge the marking.

Criterion-referenced testing is most useful for mastery situations in which the student proceeds through a sequence of modules or units on a continuous-progress plan. In such a system, the criterion-referenced marking could be based on a go,

---

*Few teachers would have enough courage to let these disastrous results stand, however.

FIGURE 15.5

Reverse Side of Woodbridge Township Junior High School Report Card, Woodbridge, New Jersey

---

WOODBRIDGE TOWNSHIP JUNIOR HIGH SCHOOLS
Woodbridge New Jersey

Grade 7 – 8

REPORT CARD

SIGNIFICANCE OF MARKS

Academic (Designated by M)	Attitude (Designated by A)
A = Superior	O = Outstanding (Above average)
B = Good	
C = Average	
D = Poor	
I = Incomplete	S = Satisfactory
X = Probation (Parental Conference Required)	U = Unsatisfactory
F = Failure Academic marks are based on subject matter achievement only.	Attitude marks are based on behavior, effort, and citizenship.

Two period marks of F in achievement constitute failure in that subject for the year.

Parents should recognize that good attendance has a positive effect on student achievement.

_Patricia Holtz_____ Principal

Parents are requested to study this report carefully, sign, and return it immediately.

1. _____

2. _____

3. _____

4. _____

---

no-go or pass-fail system. To carry out such a system, the following steps are recommended:

1. The teacher, or another authority, sets up a series of behavioral objectives that the student must achieve.
2. The teacher or other authority devises instruments that will measure whether or not the students can perform the behavior required.
3. If the students perform the behavior as required, they pass. If they do not, they do not pass. In a modulated continuous-progress course, students who do not pass should be allowed to go back, restudy, and then try again.

For example, the objective may be for students to type 40 words per minute without making more than one error per minute. If the students meet this standard, they have met the requirement and may go on. Although we have spoken of the criterion-referenced system marking in terms of pass-fail, there is no reason that the same sort of criteria cannot be set up for other letter marks (i.e., for a C the student must be able to type Y words per minute and for a B, Z words per minute). Such standards are easiest to establish in skill subjects, but they can be built for other subjects, too, as the discussion of behavioral objectives in Chapter 5 shows. Creating worthwhile behavioral objectives in some subjects (e.g., literature and most of the social studies areas) may be extremely difficult, however.

In some schools the mark in a criterion-referenced system simply acknowledges that the student has achieved the objective. The student or teacher simply records that a unit has been completed satisfactorily on such and such a day. In some systems the student fills in a square on a bar graph when a unit has been satisfactorily completed (Figure 15.6), or the teacher records and initials the date the student satisfactorily completed the unit. These marks may be turned into letter marks representing student progress or may be combined with other factors to give letter marks, as in the Wilde Lake High School, Howard County, Maryland, Progress Report (Figure 15.7).

In reporting to parents, the criterion-referenced or continuous-progress marking system may simply indicate the units completed, but it usually provides other information concerning student progress, as in the Bishop Carroll High School report shown as Figure 15.8 and the West Hartford report shown as Figure 15.3.

In some schools, a judgment concerning how well the students did the work or to what degree they reached the objective is recorded as the mark. This type of mark can be given in otherwise criterion-referenced programs. In the Plant Junior High School in West Hartford, Connecticut, the student understanding of each social studies unit and tool skill studied was marked on an achievement scale of "Considerable," "Adequate," or "Inadequate" (Figure 15.9).

COMBINATION MARKING SYSTEMS   Perhaps the most satisfactory marking system would be a combination of the normative and criterion-referenced systems.(9) Ter-

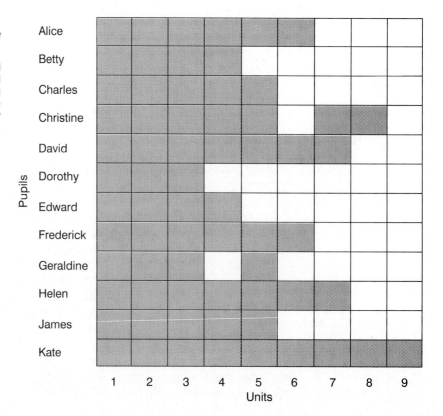

FIGURE 15.6

Bar Graph Recording Pupil Progress

Note: Some pupils have skipped units. Some teachers record progress on such a chart by dating and initialing the proper square when the pupil has satisfactorily completed a unit.

PROGRESS REPORT 19___

WILDE LAKE HIGH SCHOOL   HOWARD COUNTY, MARYLAND   PAGE ____ OF ____

CHRONOLOGICAL   ACADEMIC

GRADE LEVEL _____   GRADE LEVEL _____

STUDENT _____

ADVISOR _____

MARKING   A = EXCELLENCE   Academic Grade Level
OPTIONS   B = GOOD   is determined by num-
          C = SATISFACTORY   ber of credits earned.
          I = INCOMPLETE

Grade Level	Credits Earned
9	0.00–3.75
10	4.00–8.75
11	9.00–13.75
12	14.00–up

THE STUDENT'S MARK IN EACH SEG-
MENT IS DETERMINED BY THE QUAL-
ITY OF HIS WORK.

SEGMENT NUMBERS CORRESPOND
TO THE NUMBERS ON THE COURSE
DESCRIPTION.

STANDARDIZED TEST SCORES WHICH
REFLECT THE STUDENT'S STANDING
IN RELATIONSHIP TO OTHER STU-
DENTS WILL BE REPORTED BY THE
ADVISOR AT APPROPRIATE TIMES
DURING THE SCHOOL YEAR.

ATTENDANCE	1	2	3	4
CUMULATIVE DAYS PRESENT				
CUMULATIVE DAYS ABSENT				
CUMULATIVE DAYS TARDY				

Course _____ Date Ent _____
Evaluating Teacher _____
_____ Segments=_____ Credit   Date Dropped _____
Final Mark _____ Cr Earned _____   Continued Next Year
         Date _____   Yes   No   (Circle)

SEGMENT	1	2	3	4	5	6	7	8	9	10	11	12	13	14	15	16	17	18	19	20
MARK																				

COMMENTS (REPORT 1)	Check PROGRESS	Sat.	Unsat.
COMMENTS (REPORT 2)			
COMMENTS (REPORT 3)			
COMMENTS (REPORT 4)			

Course _____ Date Ent _____
Evaluating Teacher _____
_____ Segments=_____ Credit   Date Dropped _____
Final Mark _____ Cr Earned _____   Continued Next Year
         Date _____   Yes   No   (Circle)

SEGMENT	1	2	3	4	5	6	7	8	9	10	11	12	13	14	15	16	17	18	19	20
MARK																				

COMMENTS (REPORT 1)	Check PROGRESS	Sat.	Unsat.
COMMENTS (REPORT 2)			
COMMENTS (REPORT 3)			
COMMENTS (REPORT 4)			

Course _____ Date Ent _____
Evaluating Teacher _____
_____ Segments=_____ Credit   Date Dropped _____
Final Mark _____ Cr Earned _____   Continued Next Year
         Date _____   Yes   No   (Circle)

SEGMENT	1	2	3	4	5	6	7	8	9	10	11	12	13	14	15	16	17	18	19	20
MARK																				

COMMENTS (REPORT 1)	Check PROGRESS	Sat.	Unsat.
COMMENTS (REPORT 2)			
COMMENTS (REPORT 3)			
COMMENTS (REPORT 4)			

Course _____ Date Ent _____
Evaluating Teacher _____
_____ Segments=_____ Credit   Date Dropped _____
Final Mark _____ Cr Earned _____   Continued Next Year
         Date _____   Yes   No   (Circle)

SEGMENT	1	2	3	4	5	6	7	8	9	10	11	12	13	14	15	16	17	18	19	20
MARK																				

COMMENTS (REPORT 1)	Check PROGRESS	Sat.	Unsat.
COMMENTS (REPORT 2)			
COMMENTS (REPORT 3)			
COMMENTS (REPORT 4)			

Course _____ Date Ent _____
Evaluating Teacher _____
_____ Segments=_____ Credit   Date Dropped _____
Final Mark _____ Cr Earned _____   Continued Next Year
         Date _____   Yes   No   (Circle)

SEGMENT	1	2	3	4	5	6	7	8	9	10	11	12	13	14	15	16	17	18	19	20
MARK																				

COMMENTS (REPORT 1)	Check PROGRESS	Sat.	Unsat.
COMMENTS (REPORT 2)			
COMMENTS (REPORT 3)			
COMMENTS (REPORT 4)			

■ **FIGURE 15.7**

Progress Report from Wilde Lake High School, Howard County, Maryland

Date: October _____

End of October Report

The school year is now well underway. The purpose of this assessment is to ensure that you have made a good start. By now an effort should have been made in all the subjects so that you have a clear idea about difficulty, length, or special features.

	COURSE	CREDIT VALUE	UNITS IN COURSE	UNITS TO DATE	COMPLETED SINCE LAST REPORT			UNITS TO BE COMPLETED BY End of DECEMBER	
					UNITS	CREDITS	FINAL MARK	NEW	TOTAL
1									
2									
3									
4									
5									
6									
7									
8									
9									
10									
11									
12									
	TOTALS								

_____ **instructional days since last report,** _____ **DAYS absent,** _____ **TIMES late**

Student Comments:

PROGRESS ☐ EXCELLENT   ☐ SATISFACTORY   ☐ UNSATISFACTORY   _____
Student signature

T-A Comments:

_____
T-A signature

Parent Comments:

_____
Parent signature

▓ FIGURE 15.8

Excerpt from 1984–1985 Student Progress Report, Bishop Carroll High School, Calgary, Alberta

williger recommends that passing or failing should be determined by the use of absolute criteria. He suggests that every student be required to take a test referenced to minimal instructional objectives. On this test (which could be a performance exercise), the student must achieve the minimum score determined before the administering of the test—usually at least 80 percent of the possible score. Higher marks such as A, B, or C would be figured on the same basis as in any normative marking system.

SOCIAL STUDIES PROGRAM	PUPIL ACHIEVEMENT		
	Considerable	Adequate	Inadequate

TO PARENTS OF _____

SOCIAL STUDIES TEACHER _____

I. Units Taught
Pupil understanding of the unit was judged according to test scores, projects, participation in class activities and teacher observation.

1.			
2.			
3.			

II. Social Studies Tool Skills
Pupil practiced the following skills during the marking period:

III. Pupil As A Learner
This section refers to pupil progress toward becoming an independent and effective learner.[*]

1. Skills			
a. Asks appropriate questions			
b. Finds necessary information			
c. Organizes information logically			
d. Develops answers to questions			
e. Evaluates own work			
2. Attitudes Toward Learning			
a. Seems eager to ask questions			
b. Promptly and freely collects information			
c. Readily organizes data			
d. Enthusiastically develops answers to questions			
e. Willingly evaluates own work			

Topic   IV. Independent Study (where applicable)
Teacher Comments:

V. Teacher Comments (optional)

[*]A more detailed explanation of section III will accompany this form the first time it is distributed during the school year.

■ **FIGURE 15.9**
Social Studies Report from West Hartford, Connecticut, Junior High School

Stop and Reflect

Which of the various marking systems described seems the fairest? Why?
Which marking system would you rather use? Why?
Which is preferable, a criterion-referenced marking system or a normative marking system?

Reporting to Parents

The Right to Know

All parents have the right to know how their children are progressing in school; in fact, they probably are obligated to know, whether they want to or not. The following is a list of what parents should know about the progress of their children in school:

1. How well is the student progressing in each subject?
2. How does the student's progress compare with that of other students of the same age and class?
3. What are the student's potentialities? Is the student developing any particular talents or interests?
4. Is the student's progress up to potential?
5. What specific difficulties does the student have, if any?
6. In what areas has the student done well?
7. How does the student behave in school?
8. How does the student get along with other students? With teachers?
9. Is there any way the parent can help the student?
10. Is there any way the parent can help the teachers?

Such information should be passed on to the parent at regular intervals for many reasons. First, it is through this reporting that the school can fulfill its responsibilities to tell parents about their children's status in school. Second, it gives the school an opportunity to enlist parents' help in educating their child. Third, it gives the school an opportunity to explain its program to the parents and to solicit their understanding and assistance.

Report Cards

By far the most common medium for reporting to parents is the report card. The report card is a vital link in the teacher's relationship with students and parents. Improper marking can upset students' morale and destroy home relationships. If a mark is consistent with what has been going on in class, the students will usually accept it without question, as will most parents if they are forewarned. Therefore, be careful in making out report cards. Quite often the school provides definite instructions for preparing them. When such instructions are provided, follow them exactly. If instructions are not available, be sure to find out from a supervisor or experienced teacher just what the procedures are. It is always better to find out before a disaster than afterward.

Stop and Reflect

Several report cards have been included in this chapter (Figures 15.3 through 15.9). Note the differences in procedure. Note what is included on each card. Critique the cards. Which do you think is most satisfactory? Attempt to fill out the reports for a student. Doing so may point out several things you had not thought of. Which do you prefer? Why?

Look at the report card files in your curriculum library or resource center. Consider the merits of the various student progress cards and marking systems.

Supplementary Reports

Many schools find the report card alone insufficient as a basis for reporting student progress, even when some information over and above marks is supplied to parents. To meet this need to supply more information, several schools issue supplementary progress reports from time to time. Preparing these reports may be the responsibility of the classroom teacher, the homeroom teacher, or guidance personnel. Supplementary reports often take the form of warnings of possible failure or reports of unsatisfactory progress. In a few school systems, such reports are sent on other occasions—for example, to notify the parent that the student is doing well. Progress reports may be in the form of a note to parents, a warning slip, a checklist, a conference, or a letter of commendation.

LETTERS TO PARENTS   Letters to parents usually are of two types: (1) routine letters used as reports to parents in addition to, or in place of, report cards; and (2) letters for special occasions—requests to see the parent, invitations to class functions, letters notifying the parent about the student's work, and letters calling the parent's attention to a concern in the child's behavior.

Letters to parents—no matter what their purpose—should be carefully written. They should always be correct in form and style. Avoid errors in spelling, composition, grammar, and sentence structure. Errors that might never be noticed in the letter of a lawyer, doctor, or dentist may be very embarrassing if made by a teacher, especially in higher socioeconomic neighborhoods. Do not take offense when parents expect high standards in English usage. It is the price of being a teacher. "Teachers *should* know, you know."

Letters used as progress reports should be short and to the point. Unless you are careful, such letters can become stereotyped. If possible, make each letter a personal message to the parents, but even a stereotyped letter is better than an unclear one. In writing to parents, remember that they may not be familiar with the professional jargon of teachers. Consequently, write in clear, idiomatic, everyday English.

In writing such letters, it is usually best to start and end on a pleasant note. Commence by reporting something favorable about the student and ending in an optimistic vein, but do not let your effort to be pleasant outweigh truthfulness. Parents are entitled to an accurate report that reflects your best judgment concerning their child. Sometimes teachers are so careful not to hurt the parents' feelings and so eager to establish amicable relations that they fail to point out the student's weaknesses. This is not fair to the parents. Although you should not be tactless, you should let the parents know the facts about their child. The best rule is to decide what you wish the parent to know and then say it simply and pleasantly.

The body of the report should estimate the progress of the student as accurately as possible. This estimate should indicate the student's progress in relationship to his or her ability and also in relationship to the normal achievement level for students at that grade level. It should point out the student's strong and weak points and show where he or she needs help. The report should not be limited to achievement in subject matter alone, but also should provide information concerning the student's social behavior and other aspects of school life. At times, you will wish to ask the parent for cooperation in some specific way. Always ask the parent for comments.

An example of a homeroom teacher's letter to a ninth-grader's parents follows.

Dear Mr. and Mrs. Smith:

Joan's teachers have reported to me the results of her first quarter's work. They are quite satisfactory except for algebra, in which she is experiencing some difficulty. Her difficulty seems to be caused by a lack of understanding of mathematical principles. Mr. Courtney, her algebra teacher, feels that she should have extra help in his course. In all other respects, Joan seems to be making an excellent start this year.

If you have any suggestions or comments to make about Joan's schoolwork, we would welcome them. Also, we should very much like to have you visit our school whenever it is convenient for you.

Cordially yours,
Jennie Jones

CONFERENCES WITH PARENTS   Parent-teacher conferences are an increasingly popular method of reporting student progress to parents. This procedure has many advantages, such as allowing the teacher and the parent to discuss the student face to face. The conference should serve to create better understanding between parents and teachers and to prevent the parental misunderstandings that sometimes result from teachers' letters and report forms. The conference gives the parent an opportunity to ask questions and to make suggestions. It also gives the teacher an opportunity to solicit additional information about the student and to suggest ways in which the parent can help to improve the child's work.

Conferences can be helpful as supplements to written reports of student progress to parents. It is doubtful whether they should be the sole medium for reporting, although some elementary schools rely almost wholly on them. In secondary schools, conferences are more likely to be arranged to meet certain definite problems.

The following are some suggestions for conducting parent-teacher conferences:

1. Plan what you wish to say and how you wish to conduct the conference. Do not make following your plan an obsession, but do try to keep to the purpose of the conference. If possible, keep the conference moving, but do not rush the parent. Allow enough time to talk things over thoroughly and leisurely.

2. Be pleasant, courteous, tactful, and patient. Remember that the visit to the school may be upsetting to parents. Listen to them and try to understand their point of view. Remember that they have much information that is valuable to you; so let them communicate it to you. When parents are feeling angry and defensive, keep cool and let them talk it out. However, do not be obsequious. You do not need to agree with a parent to be polite. If the parents are severely critical of the school, arrange a conference with the principal or someone else in authority. Remember at all times that a conference is serious business and should be conducted with care and dignity.

3. Be clear and specific. Try to be sure that parents understand you. Use simple English and avoid technical terms. Make specific points and back them up with specific examples. Avoid vague, unsubstantiated generalizations that may lead to misunderstanding. Summarizing at critical points during the conference and at its end may help eliminate confusion and ensure a common understanding of what has transpired.

4. Avoid criticizing other teachers and school officials. First, it is unethical. Second, it will surely hurt your standing with your colleagues. Third, it will probably cause the parent to form a poor impression of you.

5. Solicit the parents' cooperation. The school is as much theirs as it is yours, and they have as much stake in its success as you do. Their interest in their own children is presumably greater than yours. Many parents would be eager to help if

they only knew how. Beware of making suggestions that could be construed as an intrusion on the parents' privacy, home life, or social life, however. If you need to make any suggestions of this sort, be sure that your suggestions are constructive and that the parents are ready to act on them. Frequently, the better part of discretion is to leave such suggestions to guidance personnel, an administrator, or a supervisor.

6. After the conference, write down what has been said, what suggestions have been made, and what conclusions have been reached. Do this as soon as possible so that you do not forget some of the information.

7. Ordinarily there should be some follow-up on every teacher-parent conference.

Stop and Reflect

Marks quite often become a bone of contention between parents and the school. Why? How can this be avoided?

During a conference the parent strongly criticizes the school administration or another teacher. You wholeheartedly agree with the parent. What should you do?

Compare the merits and faults of the following as a means of reporting to parents:

- *letter marks*
- *percentage marks*
- *pass-fail marks*
- *letters to parents*
- *conferences with parents*
- *descriptive marks.*

Which would be the most informative? Which would you rather receive if you were a parent?

Promotion

Continuous Progress

Most logically, promotion should be based on readiness. Students should progress through their coursework in orderly fashion, staying with a particular course or unit only long enough to learn the material well before moving on. The students should be promoted when they are ready. Promotion based on readiness is called *continuous progress*.

Unfortunately, the secondary school is seldom organized in a manner suitable for continuous progress. The difficulty that prevents continuous promotions is that our schools are graded. At the end of a year, the students must go on to the next grade, ready or not, or repeat their present grade, a system that makes little sense. It forces students to repeat material they have already learned, or forces them ahead to more difficult material they are not ready for.[*]

Setting Standards for Promotion

Although most secondary schools are not organized for continuous promotion, its principles do apply to promotion in general. The basic criterion for deciding if students should be promoted is whether they are ready to profit from the next higher

[*]See Chapter 6 for a description of how continuous progress plans are organized and conducted.

course in the subject. Even when the students do not intend to go on to the next course, the principle still holds in general, although perhaps it need not be applied quite so stringently. *In other words, teachers should have standards of minimum achievement for their courses, and these standards should represent what students must know or be able to do before they go on to the next course.* In some states and districts these standards may be mandated by stated promotion policies.

Social Promotion   Although one should ordinarily promote only those students who are ready, on occasion students are promoted whether they are ready or not. This practice is called *social promotion*. Sometimes it is justified. An example of a well-justified social promotion follows.

A junior high school boy was reading well below his grade level. Although evidently of average intelligence, he was quite incapable of doing junior high schoolwork. The boy also suffered from an acute speech defect and certain other emotional problems. The school psychiatrist examined the boy and recommended a social promotion as a means of helping him "find himself."

In this case the promotion was justified, *but automatic promotions are never justified!* Too often young people are promoted to free the classrooms and because of a mistaken attempt to be democratic. Except in cases such as the one just noted, students should be required to meet minimum standards before they move on.

Two Considerations   Although teachers should maintain standards, these standards should be flexible. The fact that a student has not mastered all the material of a course may not be sufficient reason for keeping her back. On the other hand, just because she has spent a year in a classroom is not sufficient reason for promoting her. Some students should repeat courses. Each problem of promotion should be decided on its own merits. In applying promotion standards to a particular case, one should bear in mind two main questions: (1) How will the decision affect the student concerned? and (2) How will the decision affect the other students? The final criterion should be: Which would benefit the student more, repeating the course or moving on?

To Pass or Not to Pass   Deciding if a student should pass or fail often calls for difficult decisions. To illustrate the complexity of the problem, consider the following situation. In your Algebra I class you have a boy who has done poor work. It is your considered opinion that he is just not a mathematician. He is unable to do the work, no matter how hard he tries—and he seems to have tried very hard. He and his family are determined that he go on to college and insist that he continue with mathematics. Presumably, if he passes Algebra I, he will try Algebra II, for which he is definitely not ready. What should you do? What would be best for the boy? To pass him and allow him to attempt Algebra II? To fail him and have him repeat Algebra I? Is there some other way out? What about the effect on the other students? What information do you need and what must you consider to answer this problem intelligently?

As you can see, if you try to think this problem through, it probably has no truly satisfactory answer. Even though we have stated categorically that when students have not been able to achieve the minimum standard they shall not pass, is this perhaps not a case where justice should be tempered with mercy? Fortunately, many schools help the teacher in making similar decisions by establishing quite definite school policies concerning promotion. When they do, you should try to follow the policy. Other schools have no formal policy, although there may be an informal one. Even if there is no policy at all, the principal can advise you on what to do. Even so, the decision of whether or not to promote must be made by you. In spite of statistics and theory, in the end all decisions concerning marks and marking come down to teacher judgment.

An exception to this rule exists when the state or district mandates a specific score on a state- or district-run minimum competency test as a requirement for graduation or promotion. In such cases the state or local law or regulation must prevail.

Stop and Reflect

To what extent can one apply the principle of continuous progress in the ordinary secondary school? To what extent should it be applied?

Do you agree that social promotion was justified in the example given in the preceding section?

Evaluate the following marking system. What seem to be its good points? What are its bad points, if any? Would you be happy to have to use this system?

MARKING SYSTEM
The marking system in this school will be interpreted according to the use of marks, with equivalents in each case.

Grade Books	Report Cards	Percentage Equivalents	Interpretation
4	A	93–100	Excellent
3	B	85–92	Above average
2	C	75–84	Average
1	D	70–74	Passing but unsatisfactory
0	F	0–69	Failing
Inc.	Inc.	Inc.	Work not completed
M	M	—	Medical excuse
W	W	—	Withdrawal

Letter marks are used only on report cards, the final mark on marking sheets, and on permanent records. On tests, quizzes, and in teachers' grade books, numbers (4, 3, 2, etc.) should be used.

The minimum certifying grade for students going to college from this school is 85%, which is the equivalent of a "B" grade.

An incomplete mark (Inc.) at the end of a marking period or semester will deny credit being given for the course. Incompletes will include work not submitted, or examinations not taken, within the prescribed time limits deemed by the administration as excusable.

To arrive at a term average, the four marking period grades and the exam grade are added to determine total points. This total is then divided by 5 to determine the average grade for the term.

Three-fifths or four-fifths of a whole number is treated as the next whole number; one-fifth or two-fifths will not be treated as the next whole number.

CONVERSION TABLE ON TOTALS:
    18–20 points inclusive equals A (4)
    13–17 points inclusive equals B (3)
    8–12 points inclusive equals C (2)
    3–7 points inclusive equals D (1)
    0–2 points inclusive equals F (0)

To arrive at a semester average for one-semester courses, the two marking period grades will be added, and the sum doubled, then the examination grade added to determine total points. The Conversion Table will then give you the proper letter grade.

For example:	1st	2nd	Exam	Average
	A (4)	B (3)	C (2)	B
	$4 + 3 = 7 \times 2 = 14 + 2 = 16$			B (3)

Exception: Teachers of senior students will be required to give a cumulative grade for the first half of full-year courses. This is necessary because class rank must be established for the entire class at the end of the seventh term, since certain colleges request a report on rank and achievement at midyear.

The following table will be used for the purpose of arriving at a midyear average grade, for seniors only, under this requirement:

$$7 - 8 = A$$
$$5 - 6 = B$$
$$3 - 4 = C$$
$$1 - 2 = D$$
$$0 = F$$

For example:	1st Marking Period	2nd Marking Period	Midyear Average
	A (4)	B (3)	A

$$4 + 3 = 7 \text{ (A)}$$

Parents will be notified of the status of pupils who are borderline cases or failing cases by an interim progress report. Interim progress reports will be sent home promptly by teachers, to be signed by the parent and returned, except commendation reports, which may be kept by the parent. When signed reports are not returned from home, the classroom teacher will discipline the pupil. After one day's grace, it is suggested that the teacher refer the student to the assistant principal for discipline. When conferences have been requested, the teacher is expected to follow through.

The original report will be sent to the department chairperson who will deliver all reports of his subject area to the guidance department promptly for counseling purposes. The guidance department will file all reports while they are useful for counseling, and will later file such reports in the individual pupil folders for reference.

Teachers are urgently requested to avoid assigning failure marks without previously having sent a warning or failure notice to the parents and student.

Make-up time after absences from school will be equal to the amount of time that the pupil was absent from school. He will receive an incomplete until all work is satisfactory. Exception: End-of-course average marks may not remain incomplete except in the case of certified illness. In the event a pupil is absent from school during the academic year for personal illness, he may request extra help from his teachers in his make-up assignments. For other absences, termed unexcused, teachers should not be expected or requested to give time for individual help. Such instruction comes under the classification of tutoring and should be arranged privately by the parent with any qualified teacher.

SUMMARY

Parents have the right to know how well their children are doing in school, and teachers have a duty to keep the parents informed. For many years teachers have used marks to meet this obligation. Although many parents, students, and teachers do not realize it, marks, unfortunately, do not tell anyone much of anything. Moreover, present-day marking systems tend to emphasize the mark rather than the learning. About the only value marks have is a certain amount of incentive value, and even that seems to be overrated.

As teachers have come to recognize these facts, they have made numerous attempts to create better methods of evaluating and reporting students' progress. So far none of these attempts has been completely successful. What is needed is a system that explains in writing what students can or cannot do and how well they are doing in relation to the standard for the group and to their own potentialities. In reporting to parents and students, such devices should be supplemented by conferences. Modern systems of reporting to parents seem to be moving in that direction; however, in many cases they still have a long distance to go. In the meantime, we shall have to do the best we can with what we have.

Promotion has always been a problem for the conscientious teacher. Promotion should be based on readiness, but this principle of continuous progress is not readily feasible in the middle and secondary schools as they are now organized.

There is no truly satisfactory answer to the problem of promotion. The final decision, however, should rest with the teacher and should be based on what is best for the student and for the other students in the class and school, and on state or district promotion policy.

ADDITIONAL READING

Anatasi, A. *Psychological Testing*, 6th ed. New York: Macmillan, 1988.

Archibald, D., and F. Newman. *Beyond Standardized Testing: Assessing Authentic Academic Achievement in Secondary School*. Reston, VA: National Association of Secondary School Principals, 1988.

Callahan, J. F., L. H. Clark, and R. D. Kellough. *Teaching in the Middle and Secondary Schools*, 4th ed. New York: Macmillan, 1992.

Cangelosi, J. S. *Evaluating Classroom Instruction*. White Plains, NY: Longman, 1991. Ch. 2.

Carey, L. *Measuring and Evaluating School Learning*. Boston: Allyn and Bacon, 1988.

Ebel, R. L., and D. A. Frisbie. *Essentials of Educational Measurement*, 5th ed. Needham Heights, MA: Allyn and Bacon, 1991.

Finch, F. L., ed. *Educational Performance Assessment*. Chicago, IL: Riverside/Houghton Mifflin, 1991.

Gronlund, N. E. *How to Construct Achievement*, 4th ed. Needham Heights, MA: Allyn and Bacon, 1988.

Gronlund, N. E. *Measurement and Evaluation in Teaching*, 6th ed. New York: Macmillan, 1990.

Hargis, C. H. *Grades and Grading Practices*. Springfield, IL: Charles C. Thomas, 1990.

Johnson, E. W. *Teaching School*, rev. ed. Boston: Association of Independent Schools, 1987.

Kourilsky, M., and L. Quaranta. *Effective Teaching*. Glenview, IL: Scott Foresman, 1987.

Linn, R. *Educational Measurement*, 3rd ed. New York: American Council on Education/Macmillan, 1989.

Lorber, M. A., and W. D. Pierce. *Objectives, Methods, and Evaluation for Secondary Teaching*, 3rd ed. Englewood Cliffs, NJ: Prentice-Hall, 1990.

Mitchell, R. *Testing for Learning*. New York: Free Press/Macmillan, 1992.

Nickse, R. et al. *Competency Based Education*. New York: Teachers College Press, 1981.

Popham, W. J. *Educational Evaluation*, 2nd ed. Englewood Cliffs, NJ: Prentice-Hall, 1988.

Resnick, L. B. *Education and Learning to Think*. Washington, DC: National Academy Press, 1987.

Simon, S. B., and J. A. Bellanca, eds. *Degrading the Grading Myths: A Primer of Alternatives to Grades and Marks*. Washington, DC: Association for Supervision and Curriculum Development, 1976.

Wiggins, G. P. *Assessing Student Performance*. San Francisco, CA: Jossey-Bass, 1993.

Wiggins, G. P. "Assessment Authenticity, Context, and Validity," *Phi Delta Kappan* 75 (November 1993): 200–214.

Wittrock, M. C., and E. L. Baker. *Testing and Cognition*. Englewood Cliffs, NJ: Prentice-Hall, 1991.

NOTES

1. James S. Terwilliger, *Assigning Grades to Students* (Glenview, IL: Scott, Foresman, 1971), 77–78.
2. Robert F. Biehler and Jack Snowman, *Psychology Applied to Teachers*, 4th ed. (Boston: Houghton Mifflin, 1982), 386.
3. Nathan S. Blount and Herbert S. Klausmeier, *Teaching in Secondary School*, 3rd ed. (New York: Harper & Row, 1968), 430–431.
4. Terwilliger, *Assigning Grades to Students*, 23.
5. Biehler and Snowman, *Psychology Applied to Teachers*.
6. Excerpt from *Improving Marking & Reporting Practices In Elementary & Secondary Schools,* copyright 1947 and renewed 1975 by William L. Wrinkle, reprinted by permission of Holt, Rinehart and Winston, Inc., reprinted by permission of the publisher
7. Peter F. Oliva and Ralph A. Scrafford, *Teaching in a Modern Secondary School* (Columbus, OH: Merrill, 1965), 186.
8. See Terwilliger, *Assigning Grades to Students*, Chap. 6, for instructions by which to build norms based on standard scores.
9. Terwilliger, *Assigning Grades to Students*, 97–99.

Chapter 16

The Professional Teacher (Epilogue)

In the first chapter we described in some detail the steps of the model or pattern that we think underlies all good teaching. These steps are as follows:

1. Diagnosing of the situation.
2. Preparing the setting for the learning. This step includes setting up the learning objectives, preparing a plan, and making any necessary logistical arrangements.
3. Guiding the learning activities as the plan is carried out.
4. Evaluating the students' learning and the success of your teaching.
5. Following through by taking whatever next steps seem necessary or advisable in view of your estimate of the situation. You may follow through by redoing any of the earlier steps that need redoing or, if all seems to be going well, by moving on to something new. As you move on, you can repeat the pattern in a new context. However, the evaluation step in one pattern may be used as the diagnostic step in teaching the next topic, unit, or lesson.

These various steps and how to use them have been made clear, we hope, as you have progressed through the text to this point. You probably have realized that the steps apply not only to units and lessons, but also to courses and programs.

The follow-through phase of any teacher education program takes place as you put the methods and knowledge taught in the program to use in your profession and build on them to become a truly professional teacher.

The word *professional* has at least two connotations. One connotation refers to the type of work that is done by professional workers; the other connotation is that which is signified by the common expression "being a real pro," that is to say, a really competent performer.

What makes a competent performance in teaching? In an attempt to answer this question, first semester freshmen English students at Jersey City State College were asked to write anonymous themes in which they described their most effective middle, junior high, or high school teacher. Although the resulting 517 usable essays were interesting and instructive, they contained no real surprises; the characteristics that students noted are just what one would expect. The most commonly remarked qualities of their most effective teachers, in order of their frequency, were as follows:

1. The teacher was helpful and was always ready to take time to help students having problems.
2. The teacher held interesting classes.
3. The teacher explained things clearly—assignments, rules, and expectations, as well as content.
4. The teacher maintained good control and discipline—not necessarily strict, but strong.
5. The teacher maintained a friendly, more or less informal, classroom atmosphere.
6. The teacher held the students to high standards of work, learning, and behavior.
7. The teacher knew and understood the students both in general and as individuals.
8. The teacher treated all the students fairly. There was no favoritism.
9. The teacher treated all the students and their ideas with respect and was willing to listen to student opinions and comments.
10. The teacher knew both the subject and how to teach it.
11. The teacher had a vibrant personality and a good sense of humor.

12. The teacher encouraged students to think.
13. The teacher loved the subject and showed it.
14. The teacher treated the students as individuals and adapted the teaching to their individualities.
15. The teacher introduced variety into the classes.

In some respects, at least, these characteristics are similar to those of successful teachers, and the list outlines the qualities of a real pro.

Although it may be some time before you can become a real pro, try to be a thoroughly professional teacher from the day you start teaching. Truly professional teachers give a full measure of professional service. They do a fine job at the highest possible level; they undertake all professional responsibilities willingly; and they carry out to the best of their abilities whatever task they undertake. In return, they expect to be paid adequately and treated respectfully.

Above all, professional teachers are proud of their profession, although it is arduous and exacting and has not always been rewarded as well as it should be.

It will take you a little while to become a real pro. A retired superintendent of schools says that judging from his 30 years of experience in the superintendency, it takes a beginning teacher at least two years to become "worth his salt." Be that as it may, as you gain experience, you will gain competence. If you are successful, you will become an expert on three essentials—your students, your subject, and how to teach. You will have mastered a large repertoire of techniques and strategies that you can adapt skillfully to whatever type of teaching situation you face, and you will have learned to get the most out of your students and to adapt the curriculum to their needs and abilities.

However, to become a real professional teacher, you should become a reflective teacher who asks such questions as, "What exactly is the teaching situation? Who are the students? What relationship is there between their out-of-school experiences and their course content and school life?" Then try to shape your teaching so it enhances these relationships. If the school does not integrate students' life experiences into the classroom, the schooling is pointless, because students' understanding results from relating new learning to their past experiences and personal goals.(1)

Reflective teaching consists largely of monitoring your teaching and considering its effectiveness and appropriateness for your students. It results in learning what you are doing, why you are doing it, and what results it should bring.(2) Janesick suggests that reflective teaching can be facilitated through self-monitoring by keeping a journal in which you note the thoughts, actions, beliefs, and attitudes that are (1) positive elements in your teaching, and (2) frustrating elements in your classes.(3) Through self-monitoring of this sort, you can draw conclusions by which to guide future teaching.

Actually, reflective teaching is largely a matter of inquiry or problem-solving. It starts when the teacher considers the learning situation. If, from reflecting on the situation, the teacher determines that there is a problem that needs to be solved, he or she attempts to clarify it and to consider solutions. Then one or more of the solutions is tried. If the solutions work, fine. If they do not, then the teacher must search for other possible solutions until he or she finds a good one that works well.

In carrying out educational problem-solving, inquiry teachers follow the ethic of caring.(4) This idea, according to Nel Noddings, is an outlook in which teachers learn as much as possible about their pupils and then try to shape their teaching accordingly. An important strategy in learning about the students is *dialoguing*. Dialogues are conversations with students in which the teacher really listens, and so assists students in finding their individual proclivities and talents and then making the most of them.

As much as possible, then, reflective teachers try to fit the curriculum to the students' backgrounds, interests, and needs. In such teaching the students are not preached at or lectured to. Rather, they are actively involved in the teaching-learning process through teaching methods that build on the students' own judgment, imagination, and originality; the teachers work with the students cooperatively as facilitators of learning, for example, as counselors and advisors in their subject fields, not just as imparters of knowledge.(5)

As we have said, try to be a professional teacher from the day you start teaching. That is a rather high standard. To become a real master of the trade, you must be a special person, for really professional teachers are persons of quality—persons with a sense of high commitment and a great faith in the value of what they are doing; persons with great respect for themselves, their students, and learning; and perhaps most important, persons who care about the students, about themselves, about society, about the content they teach, and about education. They do their best to help young people develop into self-sufficient, knowledgeable adults who will face the future with a repertoire of skills, attitudes, and knowledge that will make them able to cope with the experiences of an unpredictable and perhaps perilous future.

The task may be difficult and arduous, but it is truly rewarding. No professional life can be more exciting, interesting, or important than that of the master teacher. When master teachers work with young minds, there is never a dull moment. The influence of such teachers is great. Through their students they can contribute to the shaping of the community. Teaching is a profession to be proud of. The really professional teacher glories in being able to say, "I am a teacher." There is no greater praise of anyone in any walk of life than for people to say of one, "There goes a master teacher—a real pro." As Cicero tells us, there is no nobler profession than teaching the youth of the Republic.

ADDITIONAL READING

Britt, S., and D. C. Walsh. *The Reality of Teaching*. Dubuque, IA: Kendall-Hunt, 1979.

Cruickshank, D. *Reflective Teaching. The Preparation of Students of Teaching*. Reston, VA: Association of Teacher Educators, 1987.

Dewey, J. *Experience and Education*. New York: Macmillan, 1938.

Dock, L. *Teaching with Charisma*. Boston: Allyn and Bacon, 1981.

Emmens, A. P. *After the Lesson Plan: Realities of High School Teaching*. New York: Teachers College Columbia University Press, 1981.

Gere, A. R. et al. *Language and Reflection*. New York: Macmillan, 1992.

Goddard, R. E. *Teacher Certification Requirements: All Fifty States*, 4th ed. Sarasota, FL: Teacher Certification Publications, 1986.

Good, T. L., and J. Brophy. *Looking in Classrooms*, 4th ed. New York: Harper and Row, 1987.

Gray, J. *Teachers Survival Guide*, 2nd ed. Palo Alto, CA: Fearon, 1976.

Gray, J. *Teaching Without Tears*, 2nd ed. Palo Alto, CA: Fearon, 1976.

Grimmett, R. P., and G. L. Erickson, eds. *Reflection in Teacher Education*. New York: Teachers College Press, 1988.

Highet, G. *The Art of Teaching*. New York: Vintage Books, 1955.

House, E. R., and S. D. Lapan. *Survival in the Classroom*. Urbana, IL: Griffon Press, 1978.

Jackson, P. W. *The Practice of Teaching*. New York: Teachers College Press, 1986.

James, D. *The Taming*. New York: McGraw-Hill, 1969.

Johnson, E. W. *Teaching School*. Boston: National Association of Independent Schools, 1987.

Kelley, J. L. *The Successful Teacher: Essays in Secondary School Instruction*. Ames, IA: Iowa State University Press, 1982.

Moran, S. W. "Schools and the Beginning Teacher," *Phi Delta Kappan* 72 (November 1990): 210–213.

Noddings, N. *Caring: A Feminine Approach to Ethics and Moral Education*. Berkeley, CA: University of California Press, 1984.

Perrone, V. *A Letter to Teachers*. San Francisco, CA: Jossey-Bass, 1991.

Ryan, K., et al. *Biting the Apple: Accounts of First Year Teachers*. New York: Longman, 1980.

Schwarz, C. E., ed. *Chalk Talks*. Springfield, IL: Thomas, 1987.

Strike, K., and J. F. Soltes. *The Ethics of Teaching*. New York: Teachers College Press, 1985.

Stuart, J. *To Teach, To Love*. New York: Penguin, 1973.

Travers, R. M. W., and Jacqueline Dillon. *The Making of a Teacher: A Plan for Professional Self-Development*. New York: Macmillan, 1975.

U.S. Department of Education. *What Works: Research About Teaching and Learning*. Washington, DC: U.S. Department of Education, 1986.

Waxman, H. C., and H. J. Walberg. *Effective Teaching: Current Research*. Berkeley, CA: McCutchan, 1991.

Wragg, E. C., ed. *Classroom Teaching Skills*. New York: Nichols, 1984.

NOTES

1. James G. Henderson, *Reflective Teaching: Becoming an Inquiring Educator* (New York: Macmillan, 1992).
2. D. R. Cruickshank, *Reflective Teaching: The Preparation of Students of Teaching* (Reston, VA: Association of Teacher Educators, 1987).
3. V. Janesick, *Using a Journal to Develop Reflection and Evaluation Options in the Classroom*. Paper presented at the American Educational Research Association meeting, Montreal, April 1983. Cited by Cruickshank, *Reflective Teaching*, 10.
4. Nel Noddings, *Caring: A Feminine Approach to Ethics and Moral Education* (Berkeley: University of California Press, 1984).
5. Nel Noddings, *Caring*, 187.

Student Teaching and Internship

The first major step in moving from an amateur teacher's status toward gaining the competencies that mark the real pro is participating in the student-teaching or internship program. This experience is the neophyte's first real opportunity to put educational theory and methods into practice. Simulations, minilessons, and microteaching are all excellent learning opportunities, but they do not match the reality one finds in internship or student-teaching situations. Even these experiences, however, are not completely real teaching experiences. They are designed to be learning experiences and so are likely to be somewhat artificial.

That student teaching is first and foremost a learning situation cannot be overemphasized.* This is the time for you to master the rudiments of your craft before you have to put your skills on the line in your own classroom. Here is a chance for you to learn from your mistakes without causing harm to the students. Here is your opportunity to try your wings and find out the strategies, tactics, and teaching styles that best suit you. It is a time of trial and error and for growing in confidence and beginning expertise. It is not a time of perfection, but of striving for competence.

Some Facts of Life

The following comments, based on many years of watching student teachers, were written in the hope that they can make your life as a student teacher a little easier and more rewarding. They are not intended to preach; rather, they are intended to point out some pitfalls and some ways to avoid them, as well as to suggest ways to make the most of your student-teaching experience.

BECOMING PREPARED   Student teaching is a difficult experience that requires a lot of hard work. Do not underestimate its demands. Most students find it to be much more time-consuming than any other college work. Students who try to combine full-time student teaching assignments with additional courses or part-time jobs are usually overwhelmed. It is much wiser to concentrate all your time on the student teaching from the very beginning than to have to drop out later on.

Because student teaching is hard work, you need to find out as much as you can about your assignment as soon as you can—long before the student-teaching period begins. If possible, find out what topics you are to teach and prepare yourself for these topics. Most student teachers do not have perfect command of the content that middle and secondary school students study. For instance, mathematics student teachers seldom are at their best in high school geometry; English student teachers cannot possibly be familiar with all the works students may read; and social studies student teachers are not likely to have recently studied all the history, geography, economics, political science, and sociology they may be called upon to teach. *Use the period before student teaching begins to master the content and think about how to teach it!*

The first thing you should do is to procure the curriculum guide, textbook, and other readings used in each of the courses you are to teach, and then master them. In addition, it might be wise to study a review book. Such works may give you a basis for organizing units and lessons as well as ideas for building lessons and tactics. You can also find many ideas in curriculum guides, question banks, and other materials developed by various school systems and on file in the local or university curriculum library or teacher center. If it is feasible, build for yourself a resource unit covering each of the areas you will have to teach. Unless this early preparation is done carefully, you may find yourself having to become an instant expert on something about which you know little or nothing.

---

*From this point on, we use the term *student teaching* to cover both student teaching and internships.

Many student teachers who have not taken time to prepare properly find it necessary to spend so much of their time trying to master the content that they never do learn to teach it well.

A LEARNING EXPERIENCE   As we have said, student teaching is a learning experience. It is not expected that you will be a master teacher from the first day. Few teachers become real masters of the art of teaching even in the first few years. If you find that your lessons do not always go as well as you had hoped, do not be surprised. Every beginner makes mistakes. Learn from them! Teachers who find the first few weeks hard going often develop into the best of teachers if they are sensitive to the situation and learn as they go along. On the other hand, if you find that things at first go very well, do not become overconfident. Many of our poorest teachers are young people who, having had a fair amount of success at first, become overconfident and self-satisfied, and so do not strive to become real pros. As a result, they have remained amateurish ever since.

NO LONGER JUST A STUDENT   Although the student-teaching or internship experience is designed to be a learning experience, remember that student teaching is also a job, and your cooperating teacher and other superiors are the bosses. Student teachers are expected to toe the mark just as other employees are. If they do not, they may be fired! Looseness or slackness that may get by in ordinary college classes has no place in student-teaching situations.

Because the local cooperating teacher and the college supervisor are your immediate supervisors, make it a goal that they be pleased and satisfied with your performance. Therefore, carry out their instructions, directions, and suggestions without "ifs, ands, or buts." Sometimes, however, the instructions, directions, and suggestions of your various supervisors may be incompatible. If this should happen to you, go to the college supervisor for help and advice.

Some student teachers worry about the restraints on their behavior during the student-teaching period. Student teachers are in a peculiarly anomalous situation. They are neophytes learning, and at the same time they are teachers. Therefore, student teaching can be quite trying. Some student teachers rebel against the demands of student teaching, which admittedly are great. Some believe that these demands infringe on their rights. However, it is not wise to press one's rights overmuch during one's student teaching because it is doubtful how many rights the student teacher really has—at least as far as the cooperating school is concerned. Student teachers are guests of the school and their cooperating teacher; they are in the school mostly on sufferance. The teacher-education institution can only try to persuade the local personnel. It cannot dictate or demand. Consequently, both student teachers and college supervisors must do their best to meet the expectations of the school.

RELATIONSHIPS WITH SUPERVISORS   It is extremely important for you to establish and maintain good relationships with your supervisors. If your student-teaching situation is typical, your immediate supervisor will be the cooperating or critic teacher who has lent you the classes you are practicing on. One of the advantages of student teaching, ordinarily, is that the cooperating teacher is there to give you close supervision, help, and support in time of need. Nevertheless, such forced intimacy can be trying. Relationships such as this require tact, patience, understanding, and forbearance on the part of both the individuals concerned.

Most cooperating teachers find the student teaching period a trying interval, because supervision is never an easy assignment. Most cooperating teachers find it more difficult to supervise a student teacher than to teach the classes themselves. Furthermore, many cooperating teachers find student teachers something of a threat to the success of their own teaching. They may fear that the inexperience of a student teacher will cause the progress of their classes to suffer, their discipline to disintegrate, or the class atmosphere to deteriorate. Many a cooperating teacher has had to work extra hard for several weeks in order to reaccustom a class to the rules, regulations, and routines that were ignored by a student teacher. Some cooperating teachers may be insecure as well, so another teacher in the room may seem threatening.

Sometimes student teachers commit tactical errors that cause the relationship with their supervisors to fall apart. Let us consider some of the mistakes that supervisors complain about. Some of these errors are so obvious that it seems ridiculous to mention them, but since they cause so many student teaching failures, perhaps a brief discussion will be helpful.

PREPAREDNESS   Some student teachers do not prepare well enough. Students, of course, become aware that these student teachers do not know what they should be doing. Once this happens, the student teacher is through. To reestablish the confidence of pupils and supervisors in such cases is a monumental task. Student teachers who must continually improvise are a curse to most supervisors.

ATTENTION TO DETAIL   Some student teachers neglect their duties. If unit plans or lesson plans are due on Friday, supervisors expect them on Friday—not Monday. If attendance is to be taken at the beginning of the period, then supervisors expect it to be taken at the beginning of the period. If the student teacher plans to use audiovisual aids, the supervisor expects the student teacher to make all the arrangements beforehand and, insofar as possible, to be sure that all the equipment and materials are ready. Any student teacher who does not attend to details of this sort goes down in the supervisor's book as irresponsible.

RESPONSIBILITY AND DEPENDABILITY   Being responsible and dependable rate very high with most supervisors. They expect student teachers to do what they are supposed to do or at least to try their utmost to do so, and if something does not get done, to admit to it without alibis or excuses. The quickest way to earn the supervisor's disfavor is to try to excuse yourself out of your failure to deliver.

PUNCTUALITY AND ATTENDANCE   Supervisors consider tardiness and unnecessary absences as particularly heinous offenses. As a rule, they consider such irresponsibility to be inexcusable.

COMPLAINING AND CRITICIZING   In no case should a student teacher criticize the school or the cooperating teacher, so be particularly careful about what you say in conversations with other teachers or other student teachers. Also avoid going to the principal or department head with complaints. When you find that you need to complain or criticize, go to your college supervisor. If any action needs to be taken, let the college supervisor be the one to negotiate with the school personnel concerned. If any onus is to fall on anyone because of disagreements over policy or method, it is better that it fall on the college supervisor rather than on you.

CONFORMING TO THE SCHOOL'S EXPECTATIONS   To keep relationships pleasant, try to conform to the standards and customs of the school. Drastic departures from the norm in language, dress, appearance, and so on can be upsetting to principals and cooperating teachers. If you find out early on what is expected of you in these matters and then live up to these expectations, you will find that things will go more smoothly than if you do not.

In this context a word about appearance is in order. How you carry yourself, your expression, your posture, and how you dress make a difference in how your pupils and your colleagues perceive you. Consequently, it will behoove you to be sprightly, attractive, pleasant appearing, and appropriately dressed. Usually it is helpful to conform to the standard and style of dress common to the older teachers. Being a little on the conservative side does not hurt. Some young-looking student teachers find it helpful to dress to look older. The age difference between college seniors and high school seniors is not great. Anything that accentuates your maturity can help you establish yourself, and if nothing more, it may save you from being embarrassingly mistaken for a student.

LISTEN!   One complaint constantly heard is that student teachers do not listen. Cooperating teachers and college supervisors say they have to repeat instructions or advice over and over again before their student teachers take heed. Sometimes this is because the student teachers do not really listen—perhaps because they are too busy worrying about their teaching. Try to listen carefully, ask questions to be sure you understand, and then make a sincere effort to follow the advice or instructions. This will help ensure that your relationships with your supervisors will be easy and cordial.

AVOID COMPETING WITH THE TEACHER   At all costs avoid any appearance of competing with the cooperating teacher. You are there to learn from the cooperating teacher, and there are very few cooperating teachers you cannot learn from. Consult the cooperating teacher before you undertake anything, and then follow the advice given to the best of your ability. Sometimes the students tell student teachers how well they teach and that the students prefer the student teachers to their regular teachers. No matter how flattering this may be, pass off such remarks without comment. Do not allow yourself to get in a position of discussing any other teacher's teaching with a student. To do so can lead only to misunderstanding and unhappiness.

SHOW INITIATIVE   You can raise your stock with your supervisors and cooperating teachers by showing initiative and volunteering to do things before you have to be asked to do them. If you take on arduous tasks willingly and readily, you will endear yourself to your cooperating teacher. Sometimes student teachers feel that they are being used if the cooperating teacher asks them to read papers or to correct tests. You should be glad to do tasks of this sort. Such tasks are an important part of a teacher's job, and you should show your mettle here as well as you do in other tasks. Many cooperating teachers feel that you can learn much about the job and that they can learn much about your capabilities by giving you jobs of this sort. Most cooperating teachers and supervisors expect the student teachers to do their share in cafeteria supervision, extracurricular activities, attendance at PTA meetings, student activities, and all the other additional tasks that make up the teacher's professional life. Principals and department heads find willing participation in these extras by student teachers quite impressive.

Stop and Reflect

How well do you think you measure up to the expectations listed previously? Where do you think you are strong? Where are you least strong? What do you propose to do to make yourself stronger all around?

The Student-Teaching Experience

When you arrive at your student-teaching assignment, it is expected that you will bring with you certain knowledge and competencies, among them the following:

- An understanding of the teacher's role and responsibilities
- A command of the subjects to be taught
- A basic understanding of the nature of the learner and the learning process
- A repertory of teaching skills and some competence in them
- A supply of instructional materials
- Beginning skill in the techniques of evaluation.

If you measure up reasonably well to the standards implied by this list, you can expect your student-teaching experience to be satisfying. If you find yourself deficient in these competencies and understandings, you would be wise not to attempt student teaching until you have brought yourself up to the standard.

OBSERVATION   Student teaching usually starts with a few days of observation. During this period, try to learn as much as you can about the school and how it works—its customs, procedures, requirements, and the like. In particular, become acquainted with the personality and customs of each of the classes you will teach. The more you can learn about the students and the basic situation and routines (e.g., the materials available and the procedures for requisitioning and distributing materials), the better off you will be. It will be especially helpful for you to observe what the students expect from the class and the teacher, what the teacher expects from each student, and how the teacher deals with pupils both as a group and as individuals.

A wise step to take during this period is to learn the names of the students. Sitting down with the seating chart and attempting to match names and faces may pay dividends when you begin to teach the class. If you also learn something about the personalities of the students, it is much easier to create a smooth, personalized atmosphere in the class when you actually begin to teach.

BEGINNING TO TEACH   Most student teachers find their first teaching experience somewhat traumatic. Of course, you will be nervous. Probably anyone who is not nervous is not sensitive enough to be a good teacher. To compensate for this nervousness and to build up your confidence, skill, and understanding, begin your student teaching in small ways—for example, by taking the roll, acting as an assistant teacher, working with a small group, introducing a movie, or attempting similar tasks.

DIFFERENT STYLES AND METHODS   One beauty of a good student-teaching experience is that it gives you an opportunity to try a variety of teaching styles and methods. Seize that opportunity. By trying a variety of methods, you can not only broaden your repertory of teaching skills, but you can also learn which types of approaches are most comfortable to you. The teaching style another teacher finds easy and comfortable may be uncongenial and even disagreeable to you.

Because teaching styles differ, you will find it advantageous to work with two cooperating teachers whose modes of teaching differ. You can observe different teaching styles in action and try them under supervision. Sometimes these differences in styles cause conflicts, however. If such should be the case, consult your college supervisor immediately.

Although you should try various techniques, it is not wise to be too innovative at first. Adolescents, like adults, feel most secure in their established routines. They may not accept new ways of teaching or learning willingly. Furthermore, some cooperating teachers are suspicious of new methods that they fear may upset the even tenor of the class. Cooperating teachers, too, sometimes feel threatened by too much change. Therefore, the best policy is to introduce innovations slowly. As a neophyte, it is best if you master the tried and true methods the class is used to before you branch out; it is necessary to learn to walk before one learns to run.

Do not be too quick, however, to drop an innovative method that does not seem to work. The reason the method did not work may have had nothing to do with the method itself. Perhaps your execution was faulty, or you may have rushed the students into it before they were ready, or the technique was ill-adapted to the class or situation in which you used it. When a technique falls flat, do not conclude that the method is no good. Rather, try to determine why it went wrong. Usually you will find it was because of some ineptness on your part rather than because of a fault in the method itself.

Before you attempt a new approach, talk it over with your cooperating teacher. Sometimes the cooperating teacher may resist your innovation, perhaps because your plan seems flawed, appears to be too great a change from what the class has been doing, requires too much time, does not seem to be suited to the class, or is theoretically uncongenial. Student teachers who are progressively oriented, for instance, may find themselves in very conservative situations where they cannot use the progressive approaches they are so eager to try (or vice versa). In any case, defer to the cooperating teacher's judgment. If the cooperating teacher objects to your plan because of its progressivism or conservatism, do your best to do it well according to the cooperating teacher's orientation. To become a real pro you must learn how to use both conservative and progressive strategies and techniques. Use this teaching experience to become expert in whatever methods are compatible with the orientation of the cooperating teacher and the school. Later, in your own class, you can try other techniques and strategies until you have a complete battery of methods in which you are expert.

PLANNING IN STUDENT TEACHING   Planning is crucial in student teaching. When student teachers fail in their teaching, it is almost always because they have not planned adequately. Every student teacher needs to make specific, detailed plans. Every single day you should know, and should have written down, exactly what you want the students to learn during the lesson, exactly what content will be covered, exactly what methods you plan to use and how you plan to use them, and what materials you need. Try to anticipate every contingency as best you can. Leave little to chance. Work out ahead of time key questions, major points to be covered in the summary, and other details. Once you become experienced, such detailed planning may not be quite so necessary, but you will never outgrow the need to plan thoroughly.

MAKING ASSIGNMENTS   Student teachers frequently find that determining the length and difficulty of assignments is bothersome. Here is an area in which the cooperating teacher can help. The wise student teacher follows the cooperating teacher's lead because any quick change from the accustomed length and difficulty of assignments may upset the class.

SEEKING HELP   Established teachers are usually glad to give beginners the benefit of their experience. Their advice is usually good and their opinions valid, although sometimes their suggestions should be listened to politely and then forgotten as quickly as possible. (The old truism—some teachers have 20 years of experience whereas others have only one year of experience 20 times—still holds.) It is wise to ask for advice and suggestions. It never hurts a beginner to ask an experienced teacher for help—if for no other reason than to show the older teacher that he or she is needed and important.

DEVELOPING A TIME BUDGET   Many student teachers find themselves overwhelmed by the demands on their time during the student-teaching period. This problem can be alleviated somewhat by developing a time budget. By allocating reasonable amounts of time to the tasks that must be performed the day before, during, and after school, you may be able to ensure that all of them get done reasonably well. In making such a time budget, try to be as realistic as you can. If you make your time budget too demanding, trying to follow it may make it worse for you than if you had no budget at all.

Stop and Reflect

Judging from past experience, what types of teaching approaches and methods do you think you would find most congenial?

What in teaching causes you the greatest concern? How do you intend to prepare for it?

If you had your choice, what type of class would you run? Open, closed, or other?

Do you incline to conservative, traditional, or progressive techniques? Why?

Evaluating Your Student Teaching

Your supervisors will evaluate your student teaching from time to time and confer with you on your strengths and weaknesses. In addition, you should evaluate yourself to learn from your successes and your mistakes. Be critical, but not too critical. Sometimes student teachers demand of themselves more than they have a right to expect. Each day set aside some time to think about your lessons, and try to determine what went well, what went poorly, and why.

SELF-ANALYSIS   One of the most satisfactory techniques for self-appraisal is to use a self-analysis form, such as the one shown in Figure A.1, to assess daily the effectiveness of one of your best classes. It is best to do this assessment daily during the first three weeks of your student teaching, and once a week thereafter. If your classroom tests are well-built and criterion-referenced, using the item analysis techniques described in Chapter 14 to analyze the results should be revealing. Vague general test items render such analyses worthless, however.

STUDENT JUDGMENTS   The students' reaction to your teaching is another fairly reliable indicator of its success. The easiest way to find out what students think of your teaching is to observe their reaction to your classes. Apathetic, bored, surly, inattentive, restless students indicate that the instruction is not going very well. Interested, attentive students, on the other hand, indicate that you must be doing at least something right.

Another simple way to determine what students think of your teaching is to ask them. You can use simple questionnaires or rating sheets for this purpose. If the information is to be useful, the ratings should be anonymous. For that reason, forms that call for checking rather than handwritten comments are recommended. Even so, free-response questions that ask students to suggest ways instruction can be made more effective or more interesting may be very useful. Students feel flattered to be asked for their opinions and will not feel too threatened to respond honestly in such a format.

AUDIO AND VIDEO PLAYBACK   Audio and video recordings can be wonderful tools for studying your skill in lecturing, questioning, leading a discussion, and so on. You can greatly improve your teaching skill by reviewing tapes of your lessons and asking yourself such questions as the following:

■ Are my explanations clear?

■ **FIGURE A.1**
Self-Analysis of a Lesson

Use this form to analyze the class you thought went best this day.

1. Do you feel good about this class? Why, or why not?
2. In what way was the lesson most successful?
3. If you were to teach this lesson again, what would you do differently? Why?
4. Was your plan adequate? In what ways would you change it?
5. Did you achieve your major objectives?
6. Was the class atmosphere pleasant, productive, and supportive?
7. Were there signs of strain or misbehavior? If so, what do you think was the cause?
8. How much class participation was there?
9. Which students did extremely well?
10. Were there students who did not learn? How might you help them?
11. Were the provisions for motivation adequate?
12. Was the lesson individualized so that students had opportunities to learn something according to their abilities, interests, and needs?
13. Did the students have any opportunities to think?

■ Do I speak well and clearly?
■ Do I speak in a monotone? Do I slur my words? Do my sentences drop off so that the ends are difficult to hear?
■ Do I involve everyone in the class, or do I direct my teaching only to a few students?
■ Are my questions clear and unambiguous? Do I use broad or narrow questions?
■ Do I dominate class discussion?
■ Do I allow certain students to dominate the class? And so on.

Whatever questions you decide to ask yourself, concentrate on only a few areas when reviewing a tape of your teaching. If you limit yourself to studying your questioning technique in one session and to studying your discussion technique in another, you may find it easier to pinpoint your merits and deficiencies than if you do not concentrate your observation on a particular technique. Nevertheless, generally reviewing the entire lesson can be helpful, particularly if you use a self-analysis form similar to the one described earlier (Figure A.1).

Stop and Reflect
Make a list of check questions that you might use to evaluate your own teaching.

SHARING WITH OTHER STUDENT TEACHERS　When feasible, it can be helpful for student teachers to observe one another. By sharing evaluations of each other's work, you can have added input for your self-evaluation. Student teachers who observe each other would do well to be guided by a checklist or a rating scale similar to that shown in Figure A.1. They can also gather data for interaction analysis. These observations should be followed by free-flowing discussions over lunch or in some other easy social setting. Perhaps the analysis of the characteristics of successful teachers that we have listed earlier will help you and your colleagues to effectively evaluate one another.

Getting Established

The New Job

By the time you begin your student teaching or internship, you should be thinking about finding a job. Actually, early in your college career you should have started planning for securing a job after graduation. By now you should have become quite knowledgeable about the job market and be making plans accordingly.

If you have not already done so, carefully study the certification requirements of the state in which you wish to teach. Do this early. To find, at graduation time, that you are deficient in one of the state requirements can be disconcerting. A small change in your program can sometimes make quite a difference in your certification. For instance, you may have an excellent program mapped out in biology. A glance at the certification requirements may show you that by substituting a course in chemistry for one biology course you can certify for general science as well as biology. Thus, a three-hour course may make a tremendous difference in your worth to a potential employer.

Also bear in mind what courses are offered in typical secondary schools and select college courses that prepare you for them. Although Nordic literature may be an excellent course, it may be that some other course (e.g., a course in writing) would be more helpful to you as a beginning English teacher and make you more employable.

Also bear in mind that teaching positions often call for combinations of subjects. Most secondary school social studies departments, for instance, offer courses in sociology, geography, government, economics, and other social sciences as well as American and European history. Principals and department heads hope to find teachers who can teach several of these areas. A candidate who can teach only sociology may not be of much use to a department, but a sociology major who also has a background in U.S. history and economics may be just what the department needs. Similarly, a school may not need another full-time French teacher, but might have great need for someone who can teach both French and English.

Early in your final college year get in touch with your college placement service to find out what services it can provide. The placement service is usually anxious to coach you on ways to find, apply for, and obtain jobs. It can also tell you how best to prepare yourself for the jobs that are available. Talk over with your education professors such matters as finding job opportunities, writing letters of application, and securing favorable recommendations, job interviews, and the like. The sooner you become knowledgeable in these areas, the better chance you have for securing a satisfactory teaching job.

Stop and Reflect

Where would you like to teach? What courses would you like to teach? What courses will you be able to teach when you finish your college program? For what courses and levels will you be certifiable? What can you do to make yourself most employable?

Applications

Once you have learned of a vacancy, you must apply. The actual application is usually by letter, although sometimes a telephone call may be in order. Writing a letter of application is a serious undertaking. Usually it is your first contact with the prospective employer. Try to put your best foot forward. A surprisingly large number of application letters are sloppily written, replete with errors, and barely legible. Do not let this be said of you. Write your letters with care.

Make the text brief and businesslike. In a few short paragraphs, state your purpose, explain why you are a good prospect, and suggest an interview. Keep your presentation dignified, conservative, and formal, both in style and format. Conservative styles are never incorrect and run no risk of offending the reader. Some administrators resent brash, modern innovations in job application letters. Remember, your purpose is to sell yourself to your prospective employer, so make your letter the acme of clarity, simplicity, brevity, and good taste.

To be sure that the letter of application is free from errors in form, composition, and clarity, have someone you trust read the letter carefully and critically before you mail it. Your advisor or some other professor will be glad to do you this favor.

Send a data sheet with your letter. In the data sheet, state simply in outline form important information about yourself and your qualifications, including the following:

1. Education
2. Current teaching certificate
3. Professional experience (include experiences with teaching in an informal environment, such as camp counselor, Scout troop leader, and playground supervisor)
4. Other work experience
5. Hobbies
6. Extracurricular activities
7. Travel
8. Publications, if any (include theses)
9. Professional organizations
10. Other organizations
11. Honors
12. Names of some persons who will act as references.

The district will probably ask you to fill out an application form anyway, but a good letter of application never hurts one's chance.

Recommendations

Some prospective teachers are careless in selecting persons to recommend them. When you pick people to recommend you, be sure to select persons who know you well and who, you think, have a good opinion of you. A note from a reference that you are unknown to him does not favorably impress a prospective employer. To avoid embarrassment and unpleasantness, always ask permission before submitting anyone's name as a reference.

Most employers consider open letters of recommendation to be worthless. Superintendents pay attention only to confidential letters of recommendation.

The Interview

The most crucial step in securing a position is the interview with the prospective employer. It is here that the principals in the employment drama come face to face, and it is here that the prospective employer makes a decision. Although we have been speaking of "the interview," quite often the interview is really a series of interviews. Not only may you talk with the superintendent or an assistant, you may also be interviewed by the principal, the prospective department head, the director of secondary education, and, in some schools, some classroom teachers.

Because the interview is so important, think through what you wish to say beforehand. Usually your interviewer will not ask you about your academic background, having already found out about that, but will ask questions on a variety of subjects ranging from philosophy of education to why you think you would be an asset to the school system. The interviewer will wish to determine whether you can control your classes, whether you plan to stay in the system a while or whether you are a floater, what extracurricular activities you can handle, and so on. You will be able to answer these questions more successfully if you have thought about them before the interview.

Your interviewer will also expect you to ask some questions. Before going to the interview, decide what you wish to know about the school. Do not be afraid to ask questions. Intelligent questions are welcome; they give the interviewer a chance to get to know you a little better, and they also take some of the burden of the interview off the interviewer.

Be as natural and relaxed as possible during the interview. A calm, collected, easy manner will help make the interview pleasant for both you and the interviewer. If such a manner is more than you can assume, do not be concerned; administrators realize that interviewees are under a strain. There are many other things you can do to make the interview successful.

An important help in any interview is dress. Dress your best in conservative good taste. Not only will your appearance help create a good impression, but the knowledge that you are well and correctly dressed will give you added confidence. Simple clothes are the safest for this type of interview. Remember that you are trying to show the world that you are a cultured young leader of youth. Avoid anything that might make you look bizarre. For this same reason, *never* chew gum. It is also wise not to smoke, since some interviewers react unfavorably to smoking.

Your conduct during the interview should also be determined by good taste. Answer all the questions you can forthrightly. Do not attempt to bluff. If you do not know the answer, say so; it makes a much better impression than attempting to cover up. When the interviewer has finished his or her questions, you may ask the questions you have. Try not to appear too inquisitive, but do find out as much as you can about the position, the school, and the system. Then, when you have finished, thank the interviewer, say your goodbyes, and leave. Usually, the administrator will help you know when he thinks it is time to close the interview. Take the hint and depart gracefully. (More than one person has spoiled a good interview by overstaying the welcome.)

The rules for the interview are very simple. If you just remember your manners, all will go well. As in all other human relations, courtesy and good taste are unbeatable.

Getting Started

Most of what we have said about student teaching and internships applies to the first job as well. As soon as you know what you will be teaching, start preparing for it. Learn as much as you can about the school, community, and students, and work hard to make yourself as expert as you can in the subject field before school starts. On the first day of school, try to get your classes off to a good beginning. If you can, use some sort of interest-catching activity that will launch the course. Remember, this initial activity may set the tone for the whole course.

Your success or failure will mostly be determined by your relationship with the students. Pay particular attention to classroom management, control, and motivation. If you conduct businesslike, no-nonsense classes in a pleasant, workmanlike atmosphere and show that you are interested in and respect your students as people, you will have progressed a long way toward success. Similarly, if you work hard to set up cordial relations with parents, supervisors, and other teachers and carry your share of the workload faithfully, carefully, and ungrudgingly, you will find that your work can be a pleasure. On the whole, school people are pleasant to have for colleagues if you give them a chance.

Growing in the Profession

GROWING PERSONALLY To become a real pro you must combine experience with diligent efforts to learn your business and to keep growing both professionally and personally. Try to avoid the ivory tower and get out into the world to do things. Try to keep your mind sharp by interesting yourself in many things and becoming an expert in some single thing. In short, try to develop an interesting wholesome personality and keep alive your intellectual curiosity.

GROWING PROFESSIONALLY Not only must you grow as a person, you must also develop professionally. The first step in growing professionally is to do a good job of teaching, which means that you must give your heart to your work. Teaching should never be a secondary occupation. You may find it necessary to combine teaching with other work—either part-time work or running a household—but do not let other work detract from teaching. Your first responsibility is to your students.

KEEPING ABREAST WITH YOUR FIELD If you are to teach well, you must keep up with your subject. Without continued study to keep up your competence, your teaching will soon become dry and dusty. Keep abreast of the developments in your field. Occasionally, you may need to take refresher courses at a university or college. You should do advanced work in your field and perhaps some original research. During vacations, you may be able to get work related to your subject and thus acquire additional experience. No matter how you do it, you must move forward with the growth of your field.

KEEPING UP WITH THE PROFESSION You must also become an expert in the study of your profession. Particularly important are changes in methods and curriculum that affect your specialty. Continue to study the nature of learning, the theory and practice of teaching, basic philosophical positions, and current experimentation in education. Reading professional periodicals and books, as well as participating in coursework at colleges and universities, is helpful for this purpose.

To find better ways of teaching, be constantly on the alert for new ideas. Visit other teachers, talk to them, and try to get ideas from them. Try out the material and techniques other teachers have found successful. Visit the teacher conventions and other professional meetings in search of new ideas. A fine source of ideas for teaching is the book exhibit at conventions. Do more than make use of the work of others, however. Share successful experiences of your own. One way is to write about your experiences for publication in a professional journal. Although you may not think that your work is of interest to others, editors are always anxious to obtain articles that tell what teachers are doing. Moreover, setting down your thoughts in writing may help clarify your own professional thinking.

MEMBERSHIP IN PROFESSIONAL ASSOCIATIONS Many teachers get inspiration and help from becoming members of professional organizations. You will find membership in the organizations of teachers in your field rewarding. In almost every instance these organizations publish a professional journal that can help you in keeping abreast of developments in your teaching field and the methods of teaching it. For most teachers, the meetings of these associations are especially valuable. Here you can meet and share experiences with others who face the same problems you do.

In addition to the professional organizations of teachers in your field, become a member of your local teachers' organization and its state and national parent organization. In some communities, you may have a choice between joining the local chapter of the American Federation of Teachers AFL-CIO or the local affiliate of the

National Education Association. The association you join is a choice you must make for yourself. Do not, however, let yourself be rushed into making a decision. Before deciding, look carefully at the goals and programs of both organizations at the local and national levels, then make your decision on the basis of what seems best for the profession and for you.

Stop and Reflect

Think through your philosophy of teaching and working. What sort of relationships do you hope to set up with your students and colleagues? How will you go about doing it?

What practical advantages may be obtained from establishing and maintaining good relationships with the custodial personnel? What would you do to keep up favorable relationships?

How can you keep from becoming a person who merely repeats one year of teaching experience again and again? What do you plan to do to grow on the job?

What type of graduate and in-service work would you be most interested in? What would be most helpful to you in view of your goals? Map out a program of advanced study that you think would be suitable for you after you have started teaching.

Look over the professional journals. Which seem to be most useful for your purposes? Which professional organizations do you think you should join?

Index